CALIFORNIA
GOLF

CALIFORNIA
GOLF

Eleventh Edition

George Fuller

AVALON
TRAVEL

CALIFORNIA GOLF

Eleventh Edition

George Fuller

Text and maps © 2005 by Avalon Travel Publishing.
All rights reserved.

Printing History
1st edition—1989
11th edition—January 2005
5 4 3 2 1

Avalon Travel Publishing
An Imprint of
Avalon Publishing Group, Inc.

AVALON
publishing group incorporated

Some photos and illustrations are used by permission and are the property of the original copyright owners.

ISBN: 1-56691-586-4
ISSN: 1078-9618

Editor: Kathryn Ettinger
Acquisitions Editor: Rebecca K. Browning
Copy Editor: Deana Shields
Proofreader: Donna Leverenz
Graphics Coordinator: Justin Marler, Susan Snyder
Production Coordinator: Darren Alessi
Interior Designer: Darren Alessi
Cover Designer: Justin Marler
Map Editor: Olivia Solís
Cartographers: Mike Morgenfeld, Naomi Adler Dancis, Kat Kalamaras, Suzanne Service
Indexer: Michael Gardner

Front cover photo: Half Moon Bay Golf Links © George Fuller

Printed in the United States of America by Worzalla

Meet Our Expert

Author and photographer George Fuller has been covering golf and travel for more than 15 years. His books and stories have taken him throughout the United States, Asia, Polynesia, Europe, and Mexico.

His journalism career began in California as a sports beat writer for the daily *Santa Cruz Morning Star,* and then as features writer for the daily *Monterey Herald.* He later worked as editor of *Monterey Life,* the lifestyle magazine of Pebble Beach, Carmel, Monterey, and Central California. From 1992 to 1996, he served as editor of *LINKS–The Best of Golf,* a golf lifestyle magazine based in Hilton Head, South Carolina.

Fuller has seven books to his credit, including *Discover Hawaii's Best Golf* (Island Heritage Publishing, 2001) and *Adventures in Nature Hawaii* (Avalon Travel Publishing, 1999). He has contributed to numerous guidebooks, notably Berlitz Travelers Guides, Birnbaum Travel Guides, CitiBank's *Great Resorts of the World,* and *Guest Informant.*

He has also written for many newspapers and magazines, including *The Golfer, Travel + Leisure Golf, New York Times Magazine, Time, San Francisco Chronicle, Golf Magazine,* and *Golf Digest.* He has reported from Hawaii for Reuters and United Press International (UPI), contributed to Copley News Service, and continues to serve as a regular online travel correspondent for the PGA Tour's website. Currently, Fuller is contributing editor for *The Golfer.* His own website is www.golfprose.net.

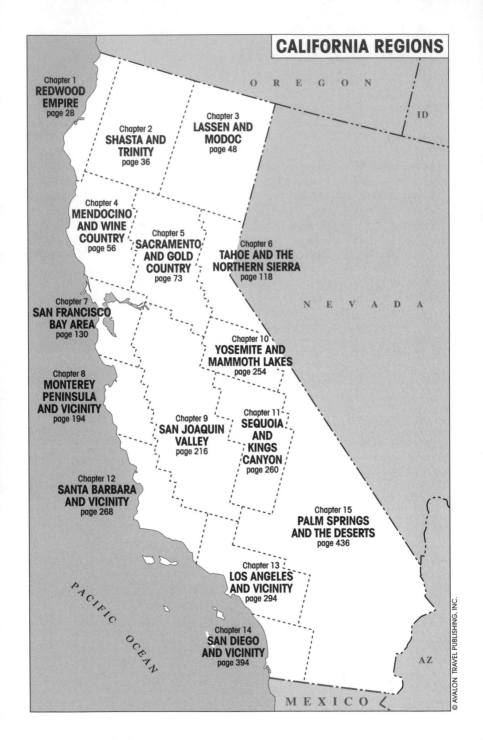

CALIFORNIA REGIONS

Chapter 1
REDWOOD
EMPIRE
page 28

Chapter 2
SHASTA AND
TRINITY
page 36

Chapter 3
LASSEN AND
MODOC
page 48

O R E G O N

ID

Chapter 4
MENDOCINO
AND WINE
COUNTRY
page 56

Chapter 5
SACRAMENTO
AND GOLD
COUNTRY
page 73

Chapter 6
TAHOE AND THE
NORTHERN SIERRA
page 118

Chapter 7
SAN FRANCISCO
BAY AREA
page 130

N E V A D A

Chapter 10
YOSEMITE AND
MAMMOTH LAKES
page 254

Chapter 8
MONTEREY
PENINSULA
AND VICINITY
page 194

Chapter 9
SAN JOAQUIN
VALLEY
page 216

Chapter 11
SEQUOIA
AND
KINGS
CANYON
page 260

Chapter 12
SANTA BARBARA
AND VICINITY
page 268

Chapter 15
PALM SPRINGS
AND THE DESERTS
page 436

Chapter 13
LOS ANGELES
AND VICINITY
page 294

P A C I F I C   O C E A N

Chapter 14
SAN DIEGO
AND VICINITY
page 394

AZ

© AVALON TRAVEL PUBLISHING, INC.

M E X I C O

©GEORGE FULLER

Contents

Our Commitment

We are committed to making *California Golf* the most accurate, thorough, and enjoyable golf guide to the state. With this 11th edition you can rest assured that every course in this book has been carefully reviewed and is accompanied by the most up-to-date information. Be aware that with the passing of time some of the fees listed herein may have changed, and courses may have closed unexpectedly. If you have a specific need or concern, it's best to call the location ahead of time.

If you would like to comment on the book, whether it's to suggest a course we overlooked or to let us know about any noteworthy experience—good or bad—that occurred while using *California Golf* as your guide, we would appreciate hearing from you. Please address correspondence to:

California Golf, 11th edition
Avalon Travel Publishing
1400 65th Street, Suite 250
Emeryville, CA 94608

email: atpfeedback@avalonpub.com
If you send us an email, please put "California Golf" in the subject line.

How to Use This Book

If you've ever waited for a tee time at a popular public course, then you know how many people love this great game. According to the National Golf Foundation, there are now more than 26 million golfers in the United States, and around six million of them are avid golfers—meaning they play at least 25 rounds per year. Yet despite these daunting statistics, numerous courses remain uncrowded and available when you want to play. You just have to know where to find them.

That's where *California Golf* comes in. We have tracked down and mapped close to 1,000 golf courses in the Golden State, organized them into 15 regions, and detailed each one in the corresponding listings. This comprehensive format enables you to explore the great diversity of courses that California has to offer.

In these pages, you'll find courses in every locale that challenge your skill level and fit your budget. Each listing includes contact information, play policy, fees, dress code, tournament information, and driving directions from the nearest major city or highway. In addition, we have provided a narrative description of each course, so you'll know just what to expect when you arrive.

About the Course Types

1. **Public:** Public courses offer the most variety, from short par-3 designs to challenging 18-hole layouts. Generally speaking, they are less expensive than semiprivate or resort courses, and they frequently feature twilight, senior, and junior rates. Municipal courses are also listed in this category.
2. **Semiprivate:** Most semiprivate courses are open for public play, and they may also offer memberships to the public. In some cases, though, memberships are restricted to property owners within the residential community where the course is located.
3. **Resort:** Resort courses are generally open to the public, but offer lower fees to guests staying on property. In many cases, these are among the best courses in the state, and the easiest to access.
4. **Military:** Some military courses allow civilian play, but most limit play to active and retired military personnel and their guests.
5. **Private:** Private courses come in two varieties: those that accept reciprocal play with members of other private clubs, and those that do not. Nonreciprocal clubs are the most exclusive, with only members and their guests permitted to play. Most private clubs, however, do offer reciprocal play privileges. Prior arrangements almost always are required, and most private clubs ask that the pro from your home club make the contact. If you already belong to a club, reciprocal play offers an opportunity to explore the rest of California.

About Price Ranges

Green fees in California vary widely, from less than $10 per round at some public courses to more than $200 per round at the most exclusive resorts. Each listing in this book provides the course's general range of non-discounted fees at the top of the page, while more specific pricing details can be found under the "Play Policy and Fees" heading.

The first dollar amount in the general price range is the lowest regular green fee offered at the course, excluding senior, junior, and residential rates. The second dollar amount is the highest regular fee charged by the course, including weekends and holidays. While we have gathered the most up-to-date prices available, all fees are subject to change, so be sure to call ahead and confirm before heading to the course.

About the Maps

This book is divided into several chapters based on established regions; an overview map of these regions follows the table of contents. At the start of each chapter, you'll find a map of the entire region, and some chapters also include detail maps of specific areas within the region. Courses are plotted on these maps by their course numbers.

About the Golf Course Profiles

Each golf course in this book is listed in a consistent, easy-to-read format to help you choose the ideal course. From a general overview of the setting to detailed driving directions, the profile provides all the information you need. Here is an example:

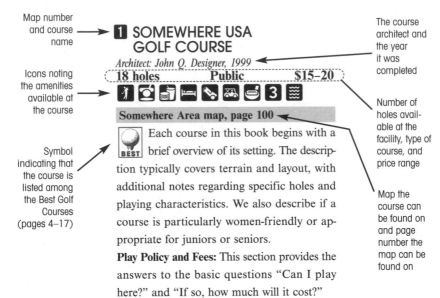

Map number and course name

Icons noting the amenities available at the course

Symbol indicating that the course is listed among the Best Golf Courses (pages 4–17)

1 SOMEWHERE USA GOLF COURSE

Architect: John Q. Designer, 1999

18 holes   Public $15–20

Somewhere Area map, page 100

The course architect and the year it was completed

Number of holes available at the facility, type of course, and price range

Map the course can be found on and page number the map can be found on

Each course in this book begins with a **BEST** brief overview of its setting. The description typically covers terrain and layout, with additional notes regarding specific holes and playing characteristics. We also describe if a course is particularly women-friendly or appropriate for juniors or seniors.

Play Policy and Fees: This section provides the answers to the basic questions "Can I play here?" and "If so, how much will it cost?"

Tees and Yardage: Every tee box available is listed, along with its yardage, par, USGA rating, and slope rating.

Tee Times: This section provides information regarding how to reserve a tee time.

Dress Code: This section notes dress requirements, if any.

Tournaments: Most courses welcome tournaments, including private courses. This section gives details on how many players, what days of the week, and so forth.

Directions: This section provides driving directions to the course from the nearest major city or town.

Contact: This section provides an address, phone number, and Internet address, if available, for each course.

About the Icons

Listings in this book feature symbols that represent the amenities available at each facility.

ⅈ — A driving range is available.

◯ — A practice green is available.

⊟ — Food and beverages are available.

🛏 — On-site accommodations are available.

◥ — Pull carts are available.

⛟ — Power carts are available.

🏌 — Club rental is available.

3 — The course is a par-3 course, meaning that it consists entirely of par-3 holes.

≋ — The course offers ocean views.

Preface

Welcome to the 11th edition of *California Golf*. The newest thing longtime readers will notice about this book, along with information about California's bevy of more than 30 new courses and roughly the same number of major renovations to existing layouts since our last edition, is that we've had an extensive renovation ourselves! After 15 years of publication and 10 successful editions, like every golf course we cover, we felt it was about time to improve and upgrade the product.

Our new layout, as you can see by thumbing through the pages of this book, is very easy to read, while still providing all the information you need about golf in California. Significantly, we have eliminated scorecards from the pages, allowing more room for course descriptions and a smaller page count. The previous edition was more than 1000 pages long, and many of you felt it was getting a tad heavy for the golf bag!

Now it's smaller. But with more than 800 courses covered in the Golden State, it is no less comprehensive.

Other new additions to this edition are a Top 10 California Bargains list, which highlights some of the best green fee values in the state, and a Top 20 California Golf Resorts list, which acknowledges the best golf vacation destinations. If you're like most of the other 26 million golfers in the United States, you want to know the best places to play, and a great course at a reasonable rate is always a welcome tip.

Finally, I would herewith like to acknowledge my regional representatives, without whose help the work on this book would be infinitely more difficult: Dave and Edie Barkin, Leonard Finkel, Barry Lotz, and Robert Arrata. It's tough work, I know, but they played many courses to make this book better. Thanks also to Melissa Bix and Rachel Kaufman, whose hours of telephone calling ensured the accuracy of the information—invaluable! And thanks especially to my wife, Landry, who not only puts up with me obsessing about golf so much, but who actually plays a darn good game herself. Thanks to all!

—George Fuller
Marina del Rey, California

FOUR SEASONS RESORT AVIARA GOLF CLUB © GEORGE FULLER

Introduction

Introduction

This is a very good time to be a golfer, particularly in California. Because of a boom in new course construction over the past decade, and the level demand, green fees at some California courses have actually dropped, while others have held steady and the majority have imposed a very small increase.

Most new course construction is real estate–oriented. The demand for homes in master-planned communities continues to rise, and often these developments build golf courses as the recreational centerpiece. This is true with the new private courses (The Hideaway Club, Santaluz, Shady Canyon, and others), as well as the new public-access courses (Moorpark Country Club, Trilogy at La Quinta, Empire Ranch).

From California's "Ring of Fire," the Palm Springs area, all the way up the "Lost Coast" around Eureka, we have endeavored to cover every course in the state, existing and new.

If you want mountains, consider Tahoe or Shasta. If you want ocean, well, there are some classic designs, with Pebble Beach being at the head of the class. But don't forget about Half Moon Bay, Pelican Hill, or the newly renovated Torrey Pines. And have you had a chance to play the full 18 at Trump National Golf Club Los Angeles (formerly Ocean Trails), now open after several years playing as a 15-hole course, following the devastating landslide that closed three holes in 1999? It is one heck of a golf course.

Much of the new construction in the state has been taking place in the desert. La Quinta, once a dusty roadside stop below Palm Springs, now offers some of the best golf in the United States. Most golfers already know about PGA West and La Quinta Resort, but new courses in the area such as The Hideaway Club, Mountain View, and Trilogy at La Quinta are excellent additions. If you were to draw a circle around the region, new courses have sprung up all over the Coachella Valley, from Cathedral City to Hemet, with more on the drawing boards.

Another area priming for expansion is the Truckee region, near Lake Tahoe. One course, the Nicklaus design at Old Greenwood, celebrated a 2004 opening, with quite a few others projecting 2005 and 2006 as their opening dates.

We're lucky to have some of the best course designers in the business call California home. Ted Robinson Sr. and Jr., Robert Trent Jones II, Algie Pulley, Casey O'Callaghan, Cary Bickler, Tom Johnson, Ron Fream, Kyle Phillips, Cal Olson, Brad Benz, JMP Golf Design Group, Don Knott, and Damian Pascuzzo are among those who live and design in the Golden State. Robin Nelson, the talented architect whose work is well known throughout Asia, recently relocated his home and offices to Mill Valley. And PGA Tour professional Fred Couples is designing more and more courses (often with the Arizona firm of Schmidt Curley Golf Design) from his home in Santa Barbara.

Of the design trends emerging over the past several years on California courses, perhaps the one I find most interesting is the move toward making some of the toughest as well as some of the most forgiving courses in many years. Among the most difficult of the new courses is Morgan Creek in Roseville, a 2003 Kyle Phillips design that measures more than 7300 yards from the back tees and carries a rating of 75.6/143; the Nicklaus design at Old Greenwood that measures more than 7500 yards (granted it's at high elevation, but still . . .); Maderas Golf Club, more than 7100 yards, rated 75.6/145 from the tips; and the TPC at Valencia, more than 7220 yards with a rating of 75.8/140.

But on the other end of the spectrum is Gary Panks' Trilogy at La Quinta design, where a stated philosophy of "having fun on the golf course" led to a 6883-yard design with a 72.7/127 rating; Empire Ranch, a 6668-yard design rated 70.9/125; and Los Lagos, a short city course for San Jose that measures only 5393 yards (par 68), with a rating of 65.4/112.

Those readers who may be looking for a club membership will be happy to know we have seen the opening of some very, very good new private facilities in the past few years, including Santaluz (San Diego), The Bridges at Rancho Santa Fe, The Crosby at Rancho Santa Fe, The Golf Club of California (Fallbrook), Shady Canyon (Irvine), and two courses at The Hideaway Club (La Quinta).

One of the most interesting new courses is Dublin Ranch Golf Club, an 18-hole Robert Trent Jones Jr. design in the San Francisco Bay Area that measures but 4820 yards, par 63, but is a delight to play. Not a par-3 or executive course, the concept here is to have the opportunity to play a first-rate design in very pleasant surroundings in less than four hours. Or maybe a quick nine-hole walk before work a couple times a week. Beats the gym!

Each of these design concepts will find its audience; hence the phrase, "There are horses for all courses, and courses for all horses."

For those of us who love the game—who can't wait to get out to play next—it is indeed, a very good time to be a golfer, especially in California.

 # Best Golf Courses

George Fuller's Top 50 Courses Open to the Public

This top 50 list is different from the previous edition of *California Golf*, in which we selected the top 50 overall, including private facilities. This change allows golfers to pick from those courses at which they know they can get tee times, as opposed to being turned away as nonmembers.

This also allows us to expand the list to incorporate some of the new and exciting public-access courses in California, such as TPC at Valencia, DarkHorse in Auburn, and CrossCreek in Temecula. The criteria were straightforward: Courses were evaluated on how enjoyable they are to play, site aesthetics, strategic shot values, maintenance, service, and amenities.

The list is in alphabetical order, thus it is not a "ranking." Rankings can be found in many national publications. Instead, we have endeavored to acknowledge that there are many excellent designs and layouts in the Golden State.

A second list spotlights the top 30 courses overall in California. This is where we pay homage to the state's "best of the best," including the private clubs.

Certainly every reader has his or her own list of favorites. We'd love to see your list and hear your thoughts on ours, so please send your comments and suggestions to atpfeedback@avalon pub.com.

Alisal Guest Ranch and Resort, Ranch Course
(Santa Barbara and Vicinity, pages 278–279)
A beauty in the serene Santa Ynez Valley, the Ranch Course at Alisal combines ambience with some strategic golf holes to make for a wonderful experience.

Bailey Creek Golf Course
(Lassen and Modoc, page 51)
Designed by Homer Flint and completed in 2001, this course boasts great views of Mount Lassen, while providing golfers a fun and memorable round.

Barona Creek Golf Club
(San Diego and Vicinity, page 422)
Gary Roger Baird's design gem in San Diego County, Barona Creek plays across a serene valley and into some gentle foothills next to a gaming casino. The course is one of California's newest and best.

Bayonet Golf Course
(Monterey Peninsula and Vicinity, page 203)
Overlooking Monterey Bay, this is quietly one of the best tests of golf in California and has often hosted Regional PGA Qualifying. Another interesting 18 holes called Black Horse adjoin.

The Course at Wente Vineyards
(San Francisco Bay Area, pages 175–176)
This upscale Greg Norman–designed course features spectacular terrain, making the holes the most exciting in Livermore Valley.

Coyote Moon Golf Course
(Tahoe and the Northern Sierra, page 122)
A scenic course at the 6300-foot level of the Sierra Nevada, Coyote Moon plays among granite bluffs and trout streams. Wonderful views, well-maintained course.

CrossCreek Golf Club
(San Diego and Vicinity, pages 397–398)
This tight course in Temecula features an abundance of sharply elevated and "inverted saucer"–shaped greens. Keep the driver in the bag, especially on the front side.

DarkHorse Golf Club
(Sacramento and Gold Country, pages 83–84)
A fun and rugged design in the Sierra foothills, this course is a pleasure to play. The views of the surrounding mountains are great, and the hole variations keep things lively.

Desert Willow Golf Resort, Firecliff Course
(Palm Springs and the Deserts, page 462)
This upscale Palm Desert municipal facility is generously sprinkled with bunkers that define the challenge and make a most dramatic impression.

The Dragon at Gold Mountain
(Tahoe and the Northern Sierra, page 121)
This course is one of a handful admitted into the Audubon International Signature Program for its preservation of wildlife habitat and conservation programs. The Dragon uses its magnificent natural surroundings to create a challenging layout. Dramatic setting, Frank Lloyd Wright clubhouse.

Four Seasons Resort Aviara Golf Club
(San Diego and Vicinity, page 407)
Unsurpassed in greater San Diego for public-access golf, Aviara has an interesting layout that features remarkable waterscaping. Bordered by a wildlife preserve.

The Golf Resort at Indian Wells, East Course
(Palm Springs and the Deserts, page 473)
With the 17th hole being one of the most beautiful par-3s in California, this parkland-in-the-desert course brings together everything we love about Palm Springs: mountain views, great weather, fun golf.

Griffith Park Golf Course, Wilson Course
(Los Angeles and Vicinity, page 316)
This historic parkland course in Los Angeles is the hub of one of the country's busiest golf complexes.

Half Moon Bay Golf Links, Ocean Course
(San Francisco Bay Area, pages 147–148)
This sometimes windy, always spectacular test boasts ocean views from nearly every hole. Good luck trying to par 18!

Harding Park Golf Course
(San Francisco Bay Area, pages 141–142)
Recently renovated, this historic San Francisco layout is back to its full glory. Many consider the back nine of this course, with holes playing around Lake Merced, one of the best in the area.

La Costa Resort & Spa, Composite Course
(San Diego and Vicinity, pages 409–410)
Located in Carlsbad, this course is well bunkered. The original 18, built by Dick Wilson, annually hosts the PGA Tour's Tournament of Champions.

La Purisima Golf Course
(Santa Barbara and Vicinity, pages 277–278)
Nearby ocean winds and rolling terrain make this inland course one of the state's most formidable rounds of golf.

La Quinta Resort & Club, Mountain Course
(Palm Springs and the Deserts, page 479)
A Pete Dye sparkler in the desert. With its greens snuggled into the surrounding mountains, this course is both beautiful and challenging. It's not overly long, but accuracy is the key.

The Links at Bodega Harbour
(Mendocino and Wine Country, pages 66–67)
Boasting rugged ocean views, this Sonoma Coast course is one of the most challenging, yard for yard, that you will ever encounter. Golfers will play two different styles of nines built at different times.

The Links at Spanish Bay
(Monterey Peninsula and Vicnity, page 204)
This Pebble Beach course represents one of golf's outstanding examples of restoring and enhancing the environment. It is the closest thing to a Scottish-style course that you can play in California.

Lost Canyons Golf Club, Sky Course
(Los Angeles and Vicinity, pages 303–304)
Set in the hills of Simi Valley, this Pete Dye design boasts an outstanding setting and a tough layout. Golfers will find it a fair but stern test of their skills, with elevated greens, sharp falloffs, and some deep bunkers.

Maderas Golf Club
(San Diego and Vicinity, page 409)
This new course in the northern San Diego area is a gem. Wonderful playing characteristics combine with a great setting in the area's rolling hills.

Marriott's Shadow Ridge Resort Golf Club
(Palm Springs and the Deserts, page 463)
Nick Faldo's first U.S. design, this Palm Desert course will remind you of Australian sand-belt courses, with wide fairways and fescue grasses adorning many holes.

Moorpark Country Club
(Los Angeles and Vicinity, page 302)
The 27 holes of Moorpark Country Club meander through canyons, arroyos, along creeks and ridgelines. With nice views of the surrounding valleys, the Pacific Ocean and the Channel Islands are seen in the background on very clear days.

Oak Quarry Golf Club
(Los Angeles and Vicinity, pages 339–340)
One of the more spectacular courses you'll ever play, this Schmidt Curley design in Riverside plays through an old limestone quarry. It is a great test of your game, and a very scenic layout, with holes above, on the rim of, and embraced by the towering walls of the quarry.

Ojai Valley Inn & Spa
(Santa Barbara and Vicinity, pages 284–285)
This beautiful, playable old classic is in idyllic surroundings with excellent resort hospitality.

Pacific Grove Golf Course
(Monterey Peninsula and Vicinity, pages 203–204)
A bargain and a semihidden gem on Monterey Peninsula, this locals' favorite is worth the cash for holes 11 through 17 alone. Great ocean views, solid golf.

Pasatiempo Golf Course
(Monterey Peninsula and Vicinity, page 196)
Regularly regarded among the best 100 courses in the nation, this tree-lined Alister Mackenzie beauty in Santa Cruz offers some of the most interesting greens in golf. Ocean views from many holes.

Pebble Beach Golf Links
(Monterey Peninsula and Vicinity, page 207)
Pebble Beach is one of the best and most famous golf courses open for public play in the world. Terrific ocean and forest scenery combines with history and challenge to make this course the experience of a lifetime.

Pelican Hill Golf Club, Ocean South Course
(Los Angeles and Vicinity, pages 382–383)
A Tom Fazio design, the Ocean South Course along the Newport Coast features spectacular ocean and canyon views. The greens can be tricky to putt, but the overall design is top-notch.

PGA of Southern California Golf Club at Oak Valley
(Los Angeles and Vicinity, pages 364–365)
This facility features two very well-serviced, well-maintained courses, the Legends and the Champions. Both are distinguished by some exciting holes, strong par-3s, and nice mountain vistas.

PGA West: Nicklaus Tournament Course
(Palm Springs and the Deserts, page 486)
A Jack Nicklaus classic in the desert, PGA West Nicklaus Tournament will keep you on your toes. Forced carries over water, huge multitiered greens, and some tough angles make this design a challenge.

PGA West: Stadium Course
(Palm Springs and the Deserts, page 487)
Famous or infamous for its difficulty, this Pete Dye design is actually very fair, and is perhaps the best example in California of the architect's genius.

Poppy Hills Golf Course
(Monterey Peninsula and Vicinity, page 205)
Home of the Northern California Golf Association and a PGA Tour stop, this is a demanding thinker's course that takes full advantage of the Del Monte Forest at Pebble Beach.

Poppy Ridge Golf Course
(San Francisco Bay Area, page 176)
Featuring terrific, bold bunkering, these 27 Northern California Golf Association holes at Livermore exude an inland links feel.

Presidio Golf Course
(San Francisco Bay Area, page 140)
Formerly private, this venerable old San Francisco course is an exceptional, undulating, wooded layout. Some nice city views.

Quail Lodge
(Monterey Peninsula and Vicinity, pages 210–211)
Renovations at Quail Lodge have brought this Carmel Valley favorite new life. Nestled on the valley floor, the course is dotted with weeping willow trees, scenic plantings, and some solid golf holes.

Resort at Squaw Creek
(Tahoe and the Northern Sierra, page 124)
This challenging mountain layout meanders through pine trees and parallels the granite peaks of the famed Squaw Valley ski area before making a transition into a scenic meadowland.

Riverbend Golf Club
(San Joaquin Valley, pages 232–233)
An elegant course in Fresno that doesn't get much notice, Riverbend is a solid design with some memorable holes. It hosted a 1999 NCAA Regional Qualifying Tournament, if that says anything about the respect it gets from the golf industry. It is also one of the better bargains in the state.

Robinson Ranch, Mountain Course
(Los Angeles and Vicinity, page 301)
There are two 18-hole layouts here. The Mountain Course, while shorter than its sister Valley Course, has many more elevation changes and tight driving holes. Be cautious with the driver.

Rustic Canyon Golf Club
(Los Angeles and Vicinity, pages 302–303)
Built on a former sheep ranch in Moorpark, this Gil Hanse design is one of the better bargains in California. Generous greens and wild bunkers reflect a Scottish style.

San Juan Oaks Golf Club
(Monterey Peninsula and Vicinity, pages 200–201)
Attractively bunkered, playable yet testy, this course is a must-play when you are near Monterey. A Fred Couples design.

The Sea Ranch Golf Links
(Mendocino and Wine Country, page 60)
Formerly one of the country's best nine-hole courses, Sea Ranch now boasts 18 oceanside holes.

Silverado Country Club & Resort, North Course
(Mendocino and Wine Country, page 68)
Redesigned by Robert Trent Jones Jr., this course plays host to a Champions Tour event each year. It features a sprawling layout with large, undulating greens and a back nine with demanding par-4s.

Spyglass Hill Golf Course
(Monterey Peninsula and Vicinity, pages 205–206)
Used annually in the AT&T Pebble Beach National Pro-Am, this long course is unforgiving. Fairways are bordered by thick stands of Monterey pine. The opening holes play through sand dunes with magnificent ocean views.

Stevinson Ranch Golf Club
(San Joaquin Valley, pages 228–229)
This tough course is tucked away in a small San Joaquin Valley town, so it gets less play than many of its higher-profile equals. But it is a strong design that demands accuracy, touch around the greens, and solid putting.

StoneTree Golf Club
(San Francisco Bay Area, pages 137–138)
Just north of the Golden Gate Bridge is StoneTree, a course with excellent conditioning, an eye toward service, and some fun golf. Strong par-3 holes.

Torrey Pines Golf Course, South Course
(San Diego and Vicinity, page 420)
When Rees Jones remodeled this course prior to the 2002 Buick Invitational, he made a great design even better, boosting it into the national rankings. Great views, challenging holes. A must-play in California.

The Tournament Players Club (TPC) at Valencia
(Los Angeles and Vicinity, page 299)
The only TPC course in California, this layout is one of the best-run, best-maintained facilities in the state. Straightforward in that you know where you are supposed to hit the ball, but it's a real test to find birdies.

Trump National Golf Club Los Angeles
(Los Angeles and Vicinity, page 352)
Formerly known as Ocean Trails, this is the course that lost its 18th hole in a landslide in 1999. Now open as an 18-hole layout, the mastery of the tough Pete Dye design comes fully to life.

George Fuller's Top 30 Courses Overall

Below we name the top 30 courses overall in California in all categories: public, private, resort, semiprivate, and military. This list is really the best of the best, and includes some of the most respected courses in the world.

Bel-Air Country Club
(Los Angeles and Vicinity, page 324)
This much-revised but sporty and enjoyable Los Angeles club with celebrity members has one of golf's most unusual routings.

Bighorn Golf Club, Mountains Course
(Palm Springs and the Deserts, pages 465–466)
Carved into the Santa Rosa Mountains, this dramatic desert course provides spectacular views of the hilly terrain and the Coachella Valley.

The Bridges at Rancho Santa Fe
(San Diego and Vicinity, pages 410–411)
Set amidst a private, upscale residential development, this Robert Trent Jones Jr. design is one of his finest. The layout winds around deep canyons, naturally flowing creeks, citrus orchards, olive groves, and cypress and eucalyptus trees.

CordeValle
(Monterey Peninsula and Vicinity, page 198)
This facility south of San Jose features an inspired routing, dramatic bunkering, and a vineyard. The serene setting alone is worth the visit.

Cypress Point Club
(Monterey Peninsula and Vicinity, pages 206–207)
Simply stated, this is one of the most beautiful courses in the world. It features oceanside, forest, and meadow holes. A must-play, if you can.

Dove Canyon Country Club
(Los Angeles and Vicinity, page 381)
This rolling course features beautiful old oaks and plenty of wildlife. It is among Nicklaus's more user-friendly courses, although from the championship tees, it can pose a definite challenge.

Lahontan Golf Club
(Tahoe and the Northern Sierra, page 123)
Tom Weiskopf's Sierra/Tahoe gem combines wonderful ambience with solid golf. The course takes full advantage of its natural surroundings, which include mature trees, constant elevation changes, water features, and mountain vistas.

The Los Angeles Country Club, North Course
(Los Angeles and Vicinity, page 324)
This rolling, tight George C. Thomas Jr. masterpiece is always considered among America's best courses.

Mission Hills Country Club, Dinah Shore Tournament Course
(Palm Springs and the Deserts, pages 456–457)
An LPGA Tour stop designed by Desmond Muirhead, Mission Hills has evolved into a desert classic in Rancho Mirage.

Monterey Peninsula Country Club, Dunes Course
(Monterey Peninsula and Vicinity, pages 204–205)
One of the most underrated courses in the country, this layout combines forest and coastal beauty. Remodeled and reopened in 1999, the Dunes Course was used for the Bing Crosby National Pro-Am for nearly two decades.

Olympic Club, Lakeside Course
(San Francisco Bay Area, page 143)
This U.S. Open course in San Francisco is one of America's most punishing, with avenues of trees and small, treacherous greens guarding par.

Olympic Club, Ocean Course
(San Francisco Bay Area, page 143)
Though shorter and tighter than the neighboring Lakeside Course, these 18 holes are equally challenging. Wind and fog often come into play.

Pasatiempo Golf Course
(Monterey Peninsula and Vicinity, page 196)
Regularly regarded among the best 100 courses in the nation, this Alister Mackenzie gem in Santa Cruz offers exquisite Pacific views and some challenging driving holes.

Pauma Valley Country Club
(San Diego and Vicinity, pages 400–401)
This long, Robert Trent Jones Sr. design is hidden away in north San Diego County, and so not as well known as some of the state's other gems. But it is very good, and its 75.5 USGA rating is well deserved.

Pebble Beach Golf Links
(Monterey Peninsula and Vicinity, page 207)
Pebble Beach is among the best and most famous golf courses available for public play in the world. Terrific ocean and forest scenery combined with history and challenge make playing here one of the "must" experiences in golf.

Pelican Hill Golf Club, Ocean South Course
(Los Angeles and Vicinity, pages 382–383)
This original oceanside course along the Newport coast features spectacular ocean and canyon views, although many feel the newer North Course is the more difficult test of golf.

PGA West: Jack Nicklaus Private Course
(Palm Springs and the Deserts, pages 485–486)
This desert layout in La Quinta is one of the toughest, most exacting Nicklaus courses you will ever encounter—but it is also pleasing to the eye.

PGA West: Stadium Course
(Palm Springs and the Deserts, page 487)
Famous or infamous for its difficulty, this Pete Dye design is actually very fair, and is perhaps the best of all the California courses to showcase the architect's genius.

The Preserve
(Monterey Peninsula and Vicinity, page 211)
Set in the coastal foothills of the Santa Lucia Mountains, this course is distinguished by old oak trees, rolling hills, and a picturesque design by Tom Fazio and Sandy Tatum.

The Quarry at La Quinta
(Palm Springs and the Deserts, page 487)
A stellar Tom Fazio design, this course is nestled in dramatic foothills near Palm Springs. Its routing leads through an abandoned rock quarry and covers 375 acres.

Riviera Country Club
(Los Angeles and Vicinity, pages 322–323)
An historic, straightforward George C. Thomas Jr. design in Pacific Palisades that emphasizes strategy and shot-making, Riviera Country Club ranks with America's best championship layouts.

San Francisco Golf Club
(San Francisco Bay Area, page 142)
This exclusive golf club is considered among architect A. W. Tillinghast's finest, with raised, flashed bunkering that has been imitated but never surpassed. A rebuild of the greens, under the supervision of golf historian/architect Tom Doak, has made this venerable course even better.

Shady Canyon Golf Club
(Los Angeles and Vicinity, page 379)
A Fazio masterpiece that forms the centerpiece of an exclusive real estate community, Shady feels like you're playing Central California: rolling hills, mature oak and pepper trees, a quiet wind. But you're just over the hill from Newport Beach.

Sherwood Country Club
(Los Angeles and Vicinity, pages 311–312)
This rolling, oak-studded Nicklaus design in Thousand Oaks features some wonderful holes and is the epitome of upscale country club courses.

Spyglass Hill Golf Course
(Monterey Peninsula and Vicinity, pages 205–206)
Used annually for the AT&T Pebble Beach National Pro-Am, this course is long, unforgiving, and irresistibly beautiful. Its fairways are flanked by Monterey pines, and the first five holes wind through sand dunes and offer magnificent ocean views.

Stanford University Golf Course
(San Francisco Bay Area, page 150)
This 1930 William P. Bell/George C. Thomas Jr. classic is tough, but a real pleasure to play. The

design doesn't let up. Between the mature trees and the demand for accuracy, players will find a real test of golf.

Torrey Pines Golf Course, South Course
(San Diego and Vicinity, page 420)
When Rees Jones remodeled this course prior to the 2002 Buick Invitational, he made this great design even better, boosting it into the national rankings. Great views, challenging holes. A must-play in California.

Tradition Golf Club
(Palm Springs and the Deserts, page 481)
Set in the Santa Rosa Mountains, this traditional course features an unusual twist: It has five par-5s and five par-3s. In general, it offers generous fairways but punishes those players who miss the greens.

The Valley Club of Montecito
(Santa Barbara and Vicinity, page 284)
This exclusive course, located at a publicity-shy Santa Barbara club, is widely considered one of the country's very best, with wonderful Mackenzie-designed greens.

The Vintage Club, Mountain Course
(Palm Springs and the Deserts, page 472)
One of Tom Fazio's earlier works, this spectacular desert garden–style course enjoys beautiful scenery at its Indian Wells mountainside location.

Top 10 California Bargains
This list names the top 10 bargains in California in the public-access category. At these courses you get top quality at surprisingly low rates.

Bidwell Park Golf Course
(Sacramento and Gold Country, page 75)
A lovely, tree-lined layout in Chico's upper Bidwell Park, this course is teeming with wildlife. It is always in great condition, too.

Fall River Valley Golf & Country Club
(Lassen and Modoc, page 50)
Set between the Shasta and Lassen National Forests near the Oregon border in the far northeast corner of California, this Clark Glasson design is truly a hidden gem. One of the state's longest and toughest layouts.

Griffith Park Golf Course, Wilson Course
(Los Angeles and Vicinity, page 316)
This historic, George C. Thomas Jr.–designed parkland course in Los Angeles is the hub of one of the country's busiest golf complexes.

La Purisima Golf Course
(Santa Barbara and Vicinity, pages 277–278)
In Lompoc, this is one of the top-ranked public courses in the state. Nearby ocean winds and rolling terrain also make this inland course one of the state's most formidable rounds of golf.

Los Verdes Golf Club
(Los Angeles and Vicinity, pages 351–352)
Set above the Pacific in Rancho Palos Verdes, this course offers ocean views on several holes. The design by the ubiquitous William F. Bell is strong, and at the price, you can't beat it!

Pacific Grove Golf Course
(Monterey Peninsula and Vicinity, pages 203–204)
A bargain and a semihidden gem on Monterey Peninsula, this locals' favorite is worth the cash for holes 11 through 17 alone. Great ocean views, solid golf.

Peter Hay Golf Course
(Monterey Peninsula and Vicinity, page 206)
There's not much you can do in golf for less than $25, particularly not at Pebble Beach. But the nine-hole Peter Hay course, with its longest hole but 118 yards, is a ball to play for the whole family.

Riverbend Golf Club
(San Joaquin Valley, pages 232–233)
This elegant course in Fresno doesn't get much notice, but it is a solid design with some memorable holes. It hosted a 1999 NCAA Regional Qualifying Tournament.

Sherwood Forest Golf Club
(Sequoia and Kings Canyon, pages 261–262)
This scenic and well-run golf facility in Sanger runs along the Kings River. Its many trees give credence to its name. This is a solid test of the game in a very picturesque setting.

Wawona Hotel Golf Course
(Yosemite and Mammoth Lakes, page 255)
It's not often that you get to play an Alister Mackenzie design for less than $25, but here it is. Granted, it's only nine holes, but look at the bright side: You're in Yosemite National Park playing a Mackenzie classic!

Top 20 California Golf Resorts
There are many wonderful places to stay and play in the Golden State. Below is our list of the 20 best full-service golf resorts, alphabetically. Criteria included quality of accommodations and golf offerings.

Alisal Guest Ranch and Resort
(Santa Barbara and Vicinity, pages 278–279)
This hideaway resort above Santa Barbara boasts comfortable cowboy elegance and two excellent golf courses in the rolling hills of Santa Ynez Valley.

Barona Valley Ranch
(San Diego and Vicinity, page 422)
Gary Roger Baird designed a rolling, ranch-style gem at this popular San Diego County casino resort. The accommodations and dining are top-notch, too.

Carmel Valley Ranch
(Monterey Peninsula and Vicinity, page 212)
Boasting spacious, well-appointed rooms, many with fireplaces and outdoor hot tubs, this ranch includes a Pete Dye golf course in peaceful Carmel Valley. Great food is part of the package.

Fairmont Sonoma Mission Inn & Spa
(San Francisco Bay Area, page 136)
This historic hotel is now the only avenue to get tee times on the Sonoma Golf Club, home of the Charles Schwab Cup of the Champions Tour. Between the golf and the spa (and the wine), everyone is happy here.

Four Seasons Resort Aviara
(San Diego and Vicinity, page 407)
In Carlsbad, where the weather is predictably great, expect the excellence of the Four Seasons brand, along with one of Arnold Palmer and Ed Seay's best golf designs in a scenic setting.

The Inn at Rancho Santa Fe
(San Diego and Vicinity, page 418)
Guests at this classic California-style inn have playing privileges at Rancho Santa Fe Golf Club (1929)—home of the original Bing Crosby National Pro-Am—which is worth a visit in itself. Excellent dining and a relaxed setting make this resort a charmer.

La Costa Resort & Spa
(San Diego and Vicinity, pages 409–410)
Located in Carlsbad, this resort has long been a California favorite. The original 18-hole course, built by Dick Wilson, annually hosts the PGA Tour's Tournament of Champions.

La Quinta Resort & Club
(Palm Springs and the Deserts, pages 478–480, 485, 486)
The best golf and accommodations package the Southern California desert has to offer—take your pick of five excellent golf courses and some luxurious, mission-style accommodations.

The Lodge at CordeValle
(Monterey Peninsula and Vicinity, page 198)
This exclusive lodge south of San Jose provides all the exclusivity of a private club, along with the service quality of Auberge Resorts. Robert Trent Jones Jr. created the excellent golf course here.

Lodge at Torrey Pines
(San Diego and Vicinity, page 420)
When the Lodge at Torrey Pines opened, it offered an avenue for tee times on the two courses, including the South, where the PGA Tour's Buick Invitational is played.

Meadowood Napa Valley
(Mendocino and Wine Country, page 66)
Though only a nine-hole course is available at this St. Helena resort, the combination of Napa Valley charm, low-key elegance, and a gorgeous setting in a redwood forest is enough for repeat visits here.

Nakoma Resort & Spa
(Tahoe and the Northern Sierra, page 121)
If you are looking for a fabulous high Sierra getaway, this is it, with an extremely good and scenic Robin Nelson golf course called The Dragon, and elegant, lodge-style accommodations.

Ojai Valley Inn & Spa
(Santa Barbara and Vicinity, pages 284–285)
This beautiful, playable old classic is in idyllic Southern California surroundings with old-school resort hospitality.

Pebble Beach
(Monterey Peninsula and Vicinity, pages 204–207)
This is the best California golf resort in part because of its variety of excellent choices. Accommodations include The Lodge, the Inn at Spanish Bay, and Casa Palmero. Golf choices include Pebble, Spyglass, Poppy Hills, and Spanish Bay.

Quail Lodge
(Monterey Peninsula and Vicinity, pages 210–211)
Renovations have brought this resort, a longtime favorite in Carmel Valley, new life. The course is dotted with weeping willow trees and scenic plantings; it possesses a wonderful serenity.

Resort at Squaw Creek
(Tahoe and the Northern Sierra, page 124)
This challenging mountain layout near Lake Tahoe meanders through pine trees and parallels the granite peaks of the famed Squaw Valley ski area before making a transition into a scenic meadowland.

Ritz-Carlton Half Moon Bay
(San Francisco Bay Area, page 148)
Combine the two Half Moon Bay course designs with a cozy Ritz-Carlton hotel and the mix is marvelous, as fine a setting for golf as any in the state.

Sea Ranch Lodge
(Mendocino and Wine Country, page 60)
Subdued elegance describes Sea Ranch Lodge, which now boasts 18 oceanside holes of wonderful golf. On Highway 1 along the Mendocino coast, few settings can rival this.

Silverado Resort
(Mendocino and Wine Country, page 68)
If you ever get tired of these two classic, well-maintained, and serene courses, well . . . go wine-tasting, sightsee in Napa Valley, or, better yet, spend an afternoon in the resort's relaxing spa.

St. Regis Monarch Beach
(San Diego and Vicinity, page 395)

Ocean views abound from both the golf course and the luxurious hotel. One hole plays down to the sea spray. This is a very women-friendly design. All the attractions of artsy Laguna Beach are nearby.

What's New in California

New Courses

These courses, listed by region, have opened since the last edition of this book:

Sacramento and the Gold Country

Empire Ranch Golf Club • public (page 97)
The Golf Course at Lava Creek • public (page 76)
Morgan Creek Golf & Country Club • private (pages 92–93)
Quail Valley Golf Course • public (pages 80–81)

Tahoe and the Northern Sierra

Old Greenwood • public (page 122)

San Francisco Bay Area

Deer Ridge Country Club • semiprivate (page 168)
Dublin Ranch Golf Club • public (page 172)
Eagle Vines Golf Club • public (page 151)
Fremont Park Golf Course • public (pages 176–177)
Los Lagos Golf Course • public (page 183)
Metropolitan Golf Links • public (pages 161–162)
The Ranch Golf Club at Silver Creek • public (pages 185–186)

San Joaquin Valley

Lakeview Golf Club • public (page 239)

Sequoia and Kings Canyon

Woodlake Ranch Golf Course • public (page 262)

Los Angeles and Vicinity

Arroyo Trabuco Golf Club • public (page 387)
Black Gold Golf Club • public (pages 368–369)
Moorpark Country Club • public (page 302)
Rustic Canyon Golf Club • public (pages 302–303)
Shady Canyon Golf Club • private (page 379)
TPC at Valencia • public (page 299)
Trilogy Golf Club at Glen Ivy • public (page 372)

San Diego and Vicinity

The Bridges at Rancho Santa Fe • private (pages 410–411)
The Crosby at Rancho Santa Fe • private (page 411)
CrossCreek Golf Club • public (pages 397–398)
The Golf Club of California • private (page 399)
Maderas Golf Club • semiprivate (page 409)

Reidy Creek Golf Course • public (page 408)
The Santaluz Club • private (pages 411–412)

Palm Springs and the Deserts
Cimarron Golf Resort • public (page 453)
The Hideaway Club • private (pages 482–483)
Landmark at Hemet Golf Club • public (page 449)
Mountain View Country Club at La Quinta • private (page 483)
Trilogy Golf Club at La Quinta • public (pages 483–484)
The Vineyards Golf Club • semiprivate (page 482)

Renovations and Additions
Alhambra Golf Course
(Los Angeles and Vicinity, page 322)
Designer Tom Johnson completed extensive bunker and tee renovations, some cart-path improvements, and some drainage work at this popular Los Angeles area course in late 2004.

Borrego Springs Resort & Country Club
(Palm Springs and the Deserts, page 489)
Architect Cary Bickler added a new nine holes to his existing design here in 2002. The new holes, called the Palms, bring the total number of holes at this resort to 27.

Chardonnay Golf Club
(San Francisco Bay Area, pages 151–152)
This facility combined nine holes from the old Club Shakespeare course with the 18 existing holes of The Vineyards course to create a 27-hole design. At the same time, Johnny Miller designed nine new holes, which, combined with the remaining nine of Club Shakespeare, became Eagle Vines Golf Club. The project was completed in 2004.

Diamond Mountain Golf Club (formerly Emerson Lake Golf Course)
(Lassen and Modoc, pages 50–51)
Nine holes were added to this pleasant, scenic course in 2004.

Eldorado Country Club
(Palm Springs and the Deserts, pages 473–474)
Tom Fazio was brought in to renovate the entire 18 holes at this 1957 Indian Wells club. The work, completed in late 2003, included new grasses on fairways, tees, and greens, giving new life to this classic design.

Foxtail Golf Club
(Mendocino and Wine Country, page 67)
In May 2003, a $5 million remodel was completed on this 36-hole facility (originally called Mountain Shadows). The renovations of the South Course included irrigation and drainage improvements. Work on the North Course involved remodeling the tees, greens, bunkers, and cart paths.

Harding Park Golf Course
(San Francisco Bay Area, pages 141–142)
A multimillion-dollar renovation to this 1925 Willie Watson San Francisco classic was completed in 2003. The work extended the length of the course to more than 7200 yards and brought the facility back to its glory days, when it was respected as one of the region's best. A new clubhouse also opened, as well as a PGA Tour First Tee facility for city youngsters.

Indian Canyons Golf Course (formerly Canyon South Golf Course)
(Palm Springs and the Deserts, page 457)
It is hard to consider Indian Canyons a remodel, since the work done created practically an entirely new course. Architect Casey O'Callaghan did the design, and LPGA professional Amy Alcott consulted on this course, which reopened in late 2004. The work done included a rerouting of the holes, creating five new lakes, and extensive earth-moving and -shaping to create mounding. The result is a fun, resort-style layout with many lovely mature palm trees that were saved from the previous course.

Jess Ranch Golf Club
(Palm Springs and the Deserts, page 445)
This course in Apple Valley, currently only 4800 yards in length, is planning expansion of its existing layout to regulation length, plus the addition of nine new holes. All this is slated for completion in 2005.

Monterey Peninsula Country Club
(Monterey Peninsula and Vicinity, pages 204–205)
The Shore Course at this venerable 36-hole club in Pebble Beach was completely redesigned by Mike Strantz in 2004. Look for this design to make some headlines in the golf media.

Monterey Pines Golf Course
(Monterey Peninsula and Vicinity, pages 209–210)
In spring 2003, work was completed on an upgrade and remodel of this course, also on the Monterey Peninsula. It is owned by the U.S. Navy but is now open to the public. The upgrades included new tee boxes, ponds, bunkers, a practice area, and an expanded pro shop and clubhouse.

Morro Bay Golf Course
(Santa Barbara and Vicinity, pages 271–272)
A long-range renovation project, including a new driving range, is slated at this facility for 2005.

Ojai Valley Inn & Spa
(Santa Barbara and Vicinity, pages 284–285)
This venerable property completed a $70 million facelift in 2004, which included the introduction of 305 new guest rooms. At that time, the nines were reversed on the golf course. In 1999, two "missing" holes of the original George C. Thomas Jr. design were replaced.

Old River Golf Course
(San Joaquin Valley, page 222)
A second set of nine holes was added to this Tracy course in summer 2004. In addition, a new clubhouse is planned that will contain meeting and banquet space.

Olivas Park Golf Course/Buenaventura Golf Course
(Santa Barbara and Vicinity, pages 287–288)

These neighbor courses in Ventura are both being upgraded. Buenaventura, the 1932 William P. Bell design, is being shortened by almost 300 yards, and par will move from 72 to 70. At the same time, irrigation, greens, and tees will be improved. This work is slated to be finished by early 2005. When Buenaventura reopens, Olivas Park will close for roughly 16 months as it is being completely redesigned. When it reopens in 2006 it will be a links-style layout with no trees, subject to the ocean breezes from the nearby Pacific.

Quail Lodge
(Monterey Peninsula and Vicinity, pages 210–211)

In July 2003, work was completed on a $25 million remodel of the clubhouse at this popular Carmel Valley resort. Both the interior and exterior were renovated, along with landscaping enhancements.

The Quarry at La Quinta
(Palm Springs and the Deserts, page 487)

A 70-acre, 10-hole par-3 course designed by Fazio Designers opened at this exclusive club in early 2004. The layout is unique in that it has 10 greens and 10 tees that can be played in any order. A putting course was also added.

Richmond Country Club
(San Francisco Bay Area, page 156)

This course was renovated in 2003 with a complete rebuild of all greens and surrounds, and most bunkers. A classic design that was built in the 1920s, it hosted touring professionals in the 1940s but had seen much better days by the year 2000. Thus, when the wrong chemicals were applied to the greens in late 2002, killing the grass, it was a perfect time to bring in architect Neal Meagher to get the course back to its best.

San Francisco Golf Club
(San Francisco Bay Area, page 142)

Respected architect Tom Doak was asked to oversee renovation work to this classic San Francisco club course, including restoring all 18 greens, which were damaged by nematodes. Work was completed in 2002.

San Juan Hills Golf Club
(San Diego and Vicinity, page 395)

A renovation project rebuilt the tees and bunkers on this San Juan Capistrano course. Additional plans call for a new clubhouse, parking lot, and maintenance facility, which if approved would alter several holes, including the current 10th, 11th, and 1st. The work is scheduled for 2004 and 2005.

Skylinks Golf Course
(Los Angeles and Vicinity, pages 347–348)

New elevated tees, enlarged greens, rerouted fairways, new grass, 475 yards of additional length, four new lakes, upgrades to the bunkers and drainage, new cart paths, 660 new trees, 1000 new shrubs, renovations to the clubhouse, and a new name (possibly Long Beach Legends Golf

Course) are all part of a year-long renovation at this Long Beach facility. It is scheduled to reopen in late 2004 or early 2005.

Sonoma County Fairgrounds Golf Center
(Mendocino and Wine Country, page 65)
The nine-hole course at Sonoma County Fairgrounds will reopen in spring 2005 after a renovation due to a new racetrack surface being installed.

Torrey Pines Golf Course, South Course
(San Diego and Vicinity, page 420)
Extensive work was done on this course, site of the Buick Invitational, prior to the 2002 tournament. Rees Jones and company completed a major renovation, including the rebuilding of all tees, greens, and fairway features. Since the renovations, it has been selected to host the United States Open Championship in 2008.

Trump National Golf Club Los Angeles
(Los Angeles and Vicinity, page 352)
Purchased by Donald Trump in November 2002, this oceanfront course formerly known as Ocean Trails has been the best 15-hole course in the world for the past several years. Its 18th hole fell into the ocean in 1999, and it has taken the ensuing couple of years to get it back on line. By fall 2004 the full 18 holes were scheduled to open under the Trump name. A long-needed driving range was planned for an early 2005 opening.

Virginia Country Club
(Los Angeles and Vicinity, page 348)
Renovations to the greens and bunkers of this traditional William P. Bell design were completed in 2002 by architect John Harbottle.

Future Courses
There are many projects large and small that are on the drawing boards and in front of planning commissions around the state. To list them all would take many additional pages. The courses listed below are those that are either already under construction or seem likely to be approved and developed. However, there being many hurdles to cross with any golf course development project, changes are inevitable, and some will never be built. So while the following courses are planned and in many cases likely, the editors wish you to know there are no guarantees that the timelines will be adhered to or that the courses will ever open.

• An eco-friendly 18-hole golf course in San Martin, now called Bear Ranch, is planned as part of a Santa Clara County Parks Department project. Projected open date is 2005.

• A real estate development between Auburn and Lincoln called Bickford Ranch is planning an 18-hole Arthur Hills course for sometime in late 2005 or 2006. It is part of a 55-plus community.

• A new 27-hole golf course called Coda Resort and Golf Community is being planned for Palm Springs. Mid-2006 is the projected open date.

• The first Rees Jones design in the La Quinta area is on track for an early 2005 opening. The project is called Coral Mountain at La Quinta, and 36 holes are planned around an upscale residential community. The site is next to PGA West.

- A Del Webb Sun City–like project in Galt (formerly known as Delta Greens) is shaping up for 2005 or 2006. It includes 18 holes of golf.
- A Schmidt Curley design in Cathedral City, called Desert Cove, is slated to open in 2005. This project includes a hotel.
- An Algie Pulley design in Woodland called Dunnigan Hills Ranch is projected for a 2005 opening. Plans are for 18 holes, a clubhouse, vineyard, and equestrian center.
- Redevelopment of the old El Toro Air Station in Irvine is moving ahead. Possible plans call for 45 holes of golf by 2006. This massive, 3700-acre project will also include residential communities, commercial space, various recreational facilities, schools, and so forth.
- In Indio, a project of the Cabazon Band of Mission Indians called Fantasy Springs Casino Golf Project is projected for development by 2006. The $200 million project includes a casino, hotel, and 18-hole golf course.
- In Crescent City, Arnold Palmer is on board to design an 18-hole public facility called The Grove. Possible completion by 2006.
- Hasley Canyon is a golf and residential development in Castaic projected for a spring 2005 debut. The site contains the old Del Valle Golf Course, which was abandoned 25 years ago.
- In mid-March 2003, the Lewiston Community Services District began looking for someone to build a nine-hole course on 28 acres in Lewiston. They are hoping to have a course by 2005.
- A golf course project near Rolling Hills Estates, at the closed Palos Verdes Landfill, is projected involving 18 holes of public Fred Bliss/Johnny Miller designed golf.
- The long-awaited eighth course at Pebble Beach, which Tom Fazio designed long ago, is still in the planning stages. When and if developed, it will likely include some golf cottages, some single-family homes, and some new rooms at the Lodge. Also discussed is the relocation of the existing equestrian facility.
- The PGA of Southern California Golf Club at Oak Valley in Calimesa is in discussions to add a third golf course to its current 36-hole facility. This may be on the boards for 2005 or 2006.
- Rancho Royale Golf & Country Club is a planned 36-hole facility in Desert Hot Springs. The first course should be open in 2005, while the entire development, including homes, may take until 2007 to complete.
- A course in Merced at Red Rock Winery is being discussed by some former employees of the defunct Merced Hills Golf Course. This may be on the books for 2005.
- River Ridge Golf Club in Oxnard is expanding to 36 holes. Nine of the new holes opened in 2004, and the balance are scheduled to debut in summer 2005.
- In Indio, a project by Del Webb called Sun City Shadow Hills is slated for a spring 2005 opening. This Schmidt Curley design is for 18 holes.
- Toscana Country Club in Indian Wells is a private 36-hole facility, with the first 18 holes opening late 2004. The courses have been designed by Jack Nicklaus. The second course is under construction and should open in 2005.
- The Truckee area is very actively developing, with one project having opened in 2004 (Old Greenwood) and others in various stages of development. Siller Ranch, Gray's Crossing, Hopkins Ranch, Eaglewood, and a project by Sierra Pacific Industries are all on the drawing boards. Plans call for several new courses, residential and resort development, and other recreational amenities. Projected opening dates vary, but look for a couple to open as early as 2005 and 2006.
- Grant Haserot of Schmidt Curley Golf Design is the architect of a golf course at the West Covina Landfill. The project, slated for a 2005 opening, also includes ballfields and retail.

- West Hills Golf & Country Club near Palm Springs plans 18 holes of semiprivate golf. The course is part of a residential development and is projected for 2005.
- A gated community in Woodland has plans for Wild Wings Golf Course, a nine-hole facility with clubhouse planned for 2005.
- The Woodlands in Nipomo has plans for 45 holes of golf, a 500-room hotel, commercial center, and research park. Projected completion is 2007.

Name Changes

Old Name	New Name
Bodega Harbour Golf Links (Bodega Bay)	The Links at Bodega Harbour
Canyon South Golf Course (Palm Springs)	Indian Canyons Golf Course
Emerson Lake Golf Course (Susanville)	Diamond Mountain Golf Club
Fountaingrove Resort & Country Club (Santa Rosa)	Fountaingrove Golf & Athletic Club
Green Valley Oaks Golf Course (Rescue)	Bass Lake Golf Course
Harvest Valley Golf and Country Club (Lemoore)	Farmers Golf Course & Paintball
Hoberg's Forest Lake Golf Club (Cobb)	Cobb Meadows Golf Club
Landmark Golf Club at Oak Quarry (Riverside)	Oak Quarry Golf Club
Meadows Del Mar (Del Mar)	Del Mar National Golf Club
Mountain Shadows Golf Course (Rohnert Park)	Foxtail Golf Club
PineRidge Golf (Truckee)	Coyote Moon Golf Course
Polvadero Golf Course (Coalinga)	Lonesome Dove Golf Course
Recce Point Golf Course (Beale AFB)	Coyote Run Golf Course
River Creek Golf Course (Ahwahnee)	Sierra Meadows at River Creek
River Ridge Golf Course (Pico Rivera)	Pico Rivera Golf Course
Sonoma Mission Inn Golf Course (Sonoma)	Sonoma Golf Club
South Gate Municipal Golf Course (South Gate)	South Gate Par-3 Golf Course
Twelve Bridges (Lincoln)	Catta Verdera Country Club
Yountville Golf Club (Yountville)	Vintner's Golf Club

Chapter 1

© GETTY IMAGES/PHOTODISC BLUE

Redwood Empire

Redwood Empire

There are only a few golf courses in this northwestern section of the state, which has also been called California's "Lost Coast." Of course, residents in this region like it that way. Most would prefer it stay "lost."

The region is known for its rugged beauty, both on the Pacific Coast and inland in the Siskiyou Mountains, Klamath National Forest, Six Rivers National Forest, and Redwood National Park. The crashing waves of the rocky coast are matched in drama by the tall and stately redwood trees that are so common here.

Visitors come for all the same reasons residents have been drawn to live here: for the secluded natural beauty, the get-away-from-it-all feeling, and the many recreational opportunities. Hiking, biking, camping, fishing—all are readily at hand.

The coastal communities of Humboldt, Eureka, Arcata, and McKinleyville are the main population centers. Here, golfers will find a string of designs to play, including Eureka Golf Course, a 1960 Bob Baldock public design. A bit farther south in the remote village of Shelter Cove, which requires a trek from the main highway, Shelter Cove Golf Course boasts nine holes with tremendous ocean views from every hole. Like Oregon, this region gets more rain than much of California, so golfers, be prepared with your rain gear.

As you continue north toward Redwood National Park, Crescent City, and the Oregon border, fewer and fewer towns dot the landscape. It is a region of quiet beauty and rugged wonder, where relatively few tourists venture. Those who do are rewarded with solitude and unpopulated vistas.

Father inland, there are plenty of great trails to hike, particularly in the Klamath Mountains and Trinity National Forest, but no golf.

Overall, golfers, it is a wonderful region to visit with your clubs in your trunk—packed behind your hiking boots and fishing pole.

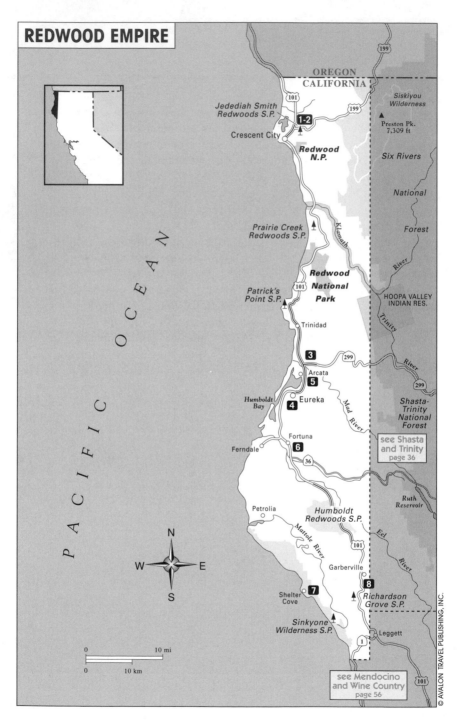

REDWOOD EMPIRE

OREGON
CALIFORNIA

[199]

Siskiyou
Wilderness

Jedediah Smith
Redwoods S.P.

[101]

[199]

1-2

Preston Pk.
7,309 ft

Crescent City

**Redwood
N.P.**

Six Rivers

National

Prairie Creek
Redwoods S.P.

Forest

Klamath River

**Redwood
National
Park**

Patrick's
Point S.P.

[101]

HOOPA VALLEY
INDIAN RES.

Trinidad

Trinity River

3

[299]

River

Arcata

5

[299]

Humboldt
Bay

4

Eureka

Mad River

*Shasta-
Trinity
National
Forest*

Fortuna

6

see Shasta
and Trinity
page 36

Ferndale

[36]

P A C I F I C   O C E A N

Petrolia

*Humboldt
Redwoods S.P.*

Ruth
Reservoir

Mattole River

Eel River

[101]

Garberville

N

W   E

S

7

8

*Richardson
Grove S.P.*

Shelter
Cove

*Sinkyone
Wilderness S.P.*

Leggett

0   10 mi

[1]

0   10 km

© AVALON TRAVEL PUBLISHING, INC.

see Mendocino
and Wine Country
page 56

[101]

1 KINGS VALLEY GOLF COURSE

Architect: Course designed, 1965

9 holes   **Public**   **$8–12**

🏌 📷 🍴 🏌 🚗 🍺 3

Redwood Empire map, page 28

Located in a remote country setting, this is a flat par-3 course with one par-4. It's a fun course for players of all abilities. Redwoods abound, and the course is walkable.

Play Policy and Fees: Green fees are $8 for nine holes and $12 for 18 holes.

Tees and Yardage: *Men and Women:* Regular: yardage 1259, par 56, rating 55.8, slope 85; Forward: yardage 1197, par 56, rating 55.8, slope 85.

Tee Times: Reservations are not accepted. All play is on a first-come, first-served basis.

Dress Code: Anything goes.

Tournaments: This course is available for outside tournaments.

Directions: From U.S. 101 in Crescent City, drive north to Grants Pass/Exit 199. Turn left on Elk Valley Road, then turn right on Lesina Road. The course is just down the road on the left.

Contact: 3030 Lesina Road, Crescent City, CA 95531, pro shop 707/464-2886.

2 DEL NORTE GOLF COURSE

Architect: Course designed, 1953

9 holes   **Public**   **$12–20**

🏌 📷 🍴 🏌 🚗 🍺

Redwood Empire map, page 28

Del Norte is in a beautiful setting, with redwoods lining each fairway and two creeks winding back and forth across the course. The par-4 fourth, the number-one handicap hole, is known as the Bell Hole since golfers up ahead must ring a bell to inform those on the tee that they are out of the way. The course features a nice mix of holes, with some traditional par-4s as well as some shorter par-4s with hazards. An enjoyable round in a great setting. Note: Plans are on the boards to expand this course to 18 holes.

Play Policy and Fees: Green fees are $12 for nine holes and $20 for 18 holes every day. Carts are additional. Twilight rates offered.

Tees and Yardage: *Men (18 holes):* Blue/White: yardage 6117, par 71, rating 67.3, slope 116; *Women (18 holes):* Red: yardage 5454, par 72, rating 71.8, slope 122.

Tee Times: Reservations can be booked 30 days in advance.

Dress Code: Shirts and shoes are necessary.

Tournaments: This course is available for outside tournaments. One month notice is appreciated.

Directions: From U.S. 101 in Crescent City, drive north to Highway 197; turn right and then left on Club Drive. Drive north to the course.

Contact: 130 Club Drive, Crescent City, CA 95531, pro shop 707/458-3214.

3 BEAU PRE GOLF COURSE

Architect: Opened 1967; expanded Don Harling, 1975

18 holes   **Semiprivate**   **$20–25**

🏌 📷 🍴 🏌 🚗 🍺 〰

Redwood Empire map, page 28

This scenic course one-half mile from the Pacific has lush fairways and some ocean views. Pine and spruce trees line both sides of the fairways, sometimes interrupting a pleasant round of golf. Water comes into play on nine holes, and the bunkers are strategically placed. The par-5 seventh hole offers an excellent view of the Pacific Ocean. Don Harling, who took the original 1967 nine-hole course and expanded it to 18, will be happy to spend some time giving the ins and outs of the course he has nurtured for so many years.

Play Policy and Fees: Outside play is welcome. Green fees are $20 Monday–Thursday and $25 Friday–Sunday. Twilight and high school rates are available. Power carts are $20 for 18 holes.

Tees and Yardage: *Men:* Blue: yardage 5748, par 71, rating 68.3, slope 121; White: yardage 5417, par 71, rating 66.9, slope 119; *Women:* Red: yardage 5056, par 72, rating 68.4, slope 124.

Tee Times: Reservations can be booked seven days in advance.

Dress Code: Shirts and shoes are necessary.

Tournaments: This course is available for

outside tournaments. A 24-player minimum is needed to book a tournament. Events must be booked at least one month in advance. The banquet facility can accommodate up to 50 people inside and 100 people outside. **Directions:** From U.S. 101 in McKinleyville, take the Murray Road exit to Central Avenue. Turn north on Central Avenue to Norton Road and drive to the course.

Contact: 1777 Norton Road, McKinleyville, CA 95519, pro shop 707/839-2342, clubhouse 800/931-6690, fax 707/839-5037, www.beaupregc.com.

4 EUREKA GOLF COURSE

Architect: Bob Baldock, 1958

18 holes   Public $17–22

Redwood Empire map, page 28

An interesting layout with a creek that meanders throughout, Eureka Golf Course plays longer than its yardage indicates due to climatic conditions. If you want to score well, give your ego a break and club up. With pretty wide fairways, this is a great place to give your driver another chance. The par-4 10th hole doglegs 90 degrees and measures 400 yards from the regular tees. The course is surrounded by beautiful California redwoods.

Play Policy and Fees: Green fees are $17 on weekdays and $22 on weekends. Twilight, senior, and junior rates are available.

Tees and Yardage: *Men:* White: yardage 5713, par 71, rating 68.0, slope 117; *Women:* Red: yardage 5296, par 71, rating 69.8, slope 117.

Tee Times: Reservations are recommended but not required.

Dress Code: Appropriate attire and soft spikes are required.

Tournaments: This course is available for outside tournaments. Events should be booked at least two weeks in advance.

Directions: From U.S. 101 in Eureka, take the Herrick exit east. Drive one-quarter mile to the golf course.

Contact: 4750 Fairway Drive, Eureka, CA 95503, pro shop 707/443-4808.

5 BAYWOOD GOLF & COUNTRY CLUB

Architect: Bob Baldock, 1956

18 holes   Private $60

Redwood Empire map, page 28

In the midst of towering redwoods, this scenic course offers a challenging, tree-guarded layout. It's often foggy or misty. The downhill 11th hole is a 443-yard par-4, featuring a green surrounded by bunkers. The back nine is much tighter than the front.

Play Policy and Fees: Reciprocal play is accepted with members of other private clubs at a rate of $60. Carts are $20.

Tees and Yardage: *Men:* Blue: yardage 6427, par 72, rating 71.2, slope 132; White: yardage 6149, par 72, rating 70.1, slope 127; *Women:* Red: yardage 5757, par 74, rating 73.3, slope 127.

Tee Times: Tee times can be made seven days in advance for reciprocal play.

Dress Code: Golf attire is a must. No blue jeans, tee shirts, or short shorts may be worn. Nonmetal spikes are required during dry conditions, which typically last April–November.

Tournaments: Outside tournaments are allowed on a limited basis. Events must have a member sponsor and a 50-player minimum. Events should be booked at least four months in advance. The banquet facility can accommodate 200 people.

Directions: From U.S. 101 in Arcata, take the Sunny Brae exit east, past the California Highway Patrol station. Turn left on Buttermilk Lane and drive to the course.

Contact: 3600 Buttermilk Lane, Arcata, CA 95521, pro shop 707/822-3688, clubhouse 707/822-3686, fax 707/822-8680.

6 REDWOOD EMPIRE GOLF & COUNTRY CLUB

Architect: Course designed, 1955

9 holes   Private $30

Redwood Empire map, page 28

Situated on a ridge, this course is tight and hilly with lots of trees, sidehill lies, prevailing winds, and little roll. It's a great test of your short game. The greens are fast, but they hold well. A new set of gold tees has been added for senior golfers and those who wish to play a shorter course.

Play Policy and Fees: Reciprocal play is accepted with members of other private clubs. Green fees are $30 for reciprocal players. Otherwise, guests must be accompanied by a member.

Tees and Yardage: *Men (18 holes):* Black: yardage 6214, par 72, rating 69.2, slope 125; White: yardage 5896, par 72, rating 67.9, slope 122; Gold: yardage 5344, par 72, rating n/a, slope n/a; *Women (18 holes):* Red: yardage 5070, par 72, rating 68.5, slope 115.

Tee Times: Reservations may be made at any time.

Dress Code: Appropriate golf attire is required.

Tournaments: This course is available for outside tournaments.

Directions: From U.S. 101 in Fortuna, take the Kenmar Road exit to Fortuna Boulevard. Drive east past Rhonerville Road to Mill Street and turn right. Turn right on Country Club Drive.

Contact: 352 Country Club Drive, Fortuna, CA 95540, pro shop 707/725-5194, fax 707/725-1640.

7 SHELTER COVE GOLF COURSE
Architect: Course designed, 1960
9 holes   Public $16–20

🔥 🏌 🛒 🍽 🏌 📷

Redwood Empire map, page 28

This links course, with one par-5 and four par-3s, has spectacular ocean views from every hole. This course borders a daytime airstrip. One of the local rules is that if your ball lands near the airstrip it must be moved at least 10 yards away; no penalty. Camping, lodging, and dining are all within walking distance. The pro shop and lounge opened in 1999, practice greens in 2000.

Play Policy and Fees: Green fees are $16 for nine holes, $20 for unlimited play. Carts are $18.

Tees and Yardage: *Men (18 holes):* Regular: yardage 4759, par 66, rating n/a, slope n/a; *Women (18 holes):* Forward: yardage 4363, par 66, rating n/a, slope n/a.

Tee Times: Reservations can be made seven days in advance and are recommended for holidays and weekends.

Dress Code: Reasonable attire is expected.

Tournaments: A 12-player minimum is needed to book an event. Two months advance notice is required.

Directions: From Garberville on U.S. 101, go west 22 miles to Shelter Cove. Turn right onto Upper Pacific Drive, then left onto Lower Pacific Drive.

Contact: 1555 Upper Pacific Drive, Shelter Cove, CA 95589, pro shop 707/986-1464, fax 707/986-7435.

8 BENBOW VALLEY RV RESORT & GOLF COURSE
Architect: Course designed, 1927
9 holes   Public $14–18

🏌 📷 🍺 🍽 🗡 🚗 🍴

Redwood Empire map, page 28

This course in a redwood forest provides views of both the Eel River and Benbow Lake. It's called the "Bowling Alley" for its tree-lined fairways, and it features several severe slopes, making it extremely difficult to keep the ball in play. Though it has its share of hills, the course is walkable. Within the regular course is a junior golf course designed for beginning golfers ages 6–12.

The Benbow Inn is within walking distance of the course. Call 707/923-2124 for reservations.

Play Policy and Fees: For those staying in the adjacent RV park, weekday green fees are $14 for unlimited play. For outside guests, green fees are $16 on weekdays. In summer, rates go to $16 unlimited play on weekdays for RV park guests and $18 on weekends. Power carts are $11 for nine holes; $22 for 18 holes.

Tees and Yardage: *Men (18 holes):* Blue: yardage 5276, par 70, rating 67.2, slope 113; *Women (18 holes):* Forward: yardage 5084, par 70, rating 69.8, slope 115.

Tee Times: Reservations are not required, but they are accepted up to 30 days in advance.

Dress Code: Shirts must be worn and soft spikes are preferred.

Tournaments: Outside tournaments are welcome, and they may be booked a month in advance. The banquet facility can accommodate 140 people.

Directions: From U.S. 101 two miles south of Garberville, take the Benbow exit directly to the course.

Contact: 7000 Benbow Drive, Garberville, CA 95542, pro shop 707/923-2777, fax 707/923-2821, www.benbowrv.com.

Chapter 2

Shasta and Trinity

Shasta and Trinity

-5 cuts straight up this region, from Red Bluff to the Oregon border. As heavily traveled as that freeway is, it's often quite amazing how little traveled are some of region's back roads.

To the west of I-5 are the Trinity Mountains, and to the east lie the Cascade Range, Shasta Lake, and Mount Shasta. These areas are alive with outdoor opportunities, including hiking, camping, and water sports.

If you veer off on Highway 97 northeast from Weed, you will encounter some magnificent scenery, towering mountains—topped with snow in winter—and wild areas undamaged by encroaching civilization. There are wide meadows where deer, hawks, and other wildlife live uninterrupted. Though the area is cold and often snowy in winter, many people find Weed and environs to be an adventure-filled summer getaway.

This is also where two of the region's few golf courses can be found:

Weed Golf Course, a nine-holer, and Lake Shastina Resort, a fun 27-hole design set in a meadow with the north face of Mount Shasta towering beyond. A little farther south, Mount Shasta Resort features an 18-hole track, also within the shadow of the 14,000-foot mountain. These courses are subject to cold or closing in winter due to weather.

In the region's lowlands, around Redding and Red Bluff, there is a cluster of courses from which to choose. This part of the region is less mountainous, therefore less dramatic, and the courses are flatter, relying on water and trees to beautify the fairways and provide challenge to golfers. On the other hand, these courses are open year-round.

The Shasta and Trinity region is a good place to take your golf clubs because there are some nice options. But the relatively few golf courses may not be your primary motivation for visiting this lovely segment of California, thanks to the abundance of other recreational activities.

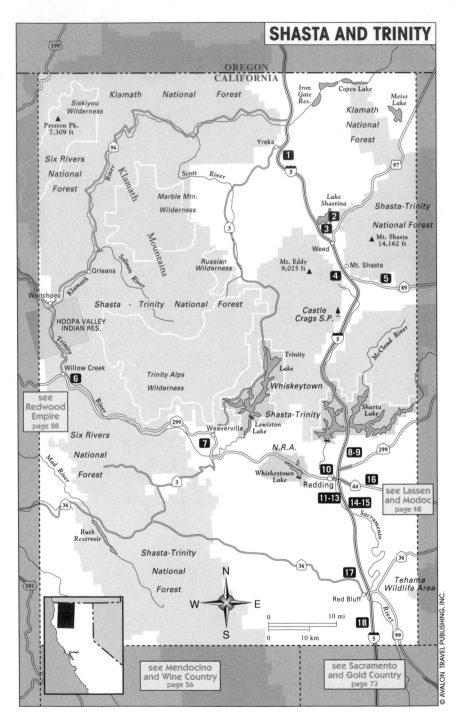

SHASTA AND TRINITY

OREGON
CALIFORNIA

Klamath National Forest

Siskiyou Wilderness

Preston Pk. 7,309 ft

Six Rivers National Forest

Iron Gate Res.

Copco Lake

Meiss Lake

Klamath National Forest

Yreka

1

Scott River

Klamath River

Marble Mtn. Wilderness

Russian Wilderness

Lake Shastina

2

3

Shasta-Trinity National Forest

Mt. Shasta 14,162 ft

Weed

Mt. Eddy 9,025 ft

4

Mt. Shasta

5

Orleans

Salmon River

Mountains

Shasta - Trinity National Forest

Castle Crags S.P.

McCloud River

Weitchpec

Klamath River

HOOPA VALLEY INDIAN RES.

Trinity River

Trinity Alps Wilderness

Trinity Lake

Willow Creek

6

see Redwood Empire page 28

Six Rivers National Forest

Weaverville

7

Lewiston Lake

Whiskeytown

Shasta-Trinity

N.R.A.

Shasta Lake

8-9

Mad River

Whiskeytown Lake

10

Redding

11-13

14-15

16

see Lassen and Modoc page 48

Ruth Reservoir

Shasta-Trinity National Forest

Sacramento River

17

Tehama Wildlife Area

N
W — E
S

Red Bluff

18

0   10 mi
0   10 km

see Mendocino and Wine Country page 56

see Sacramento and Gold Country page 73

© AVALON TRAVEL PUBLISHING, INC.

1 SHASTA VALLEY GOLF COURSE

Architect: Clark Glasson, 1968

9 holes   **Public**   **$13–18**

Shasta and Trinity map, page 36

There is a lot of water to contend with on this short course, so the premium is on accuracy. In addition, many sand bunkers and other hazards have been built into this fun and walkable layout.

Play Policy and Fees: Green fees are $13 for nine holes and $17 for 18 holes weekdays, and $14 for nine holes and $18 for 18 holes weekends. Carts are $9 for nine holes and $16 for 18 holes.

Tees and Yardage: *Men and Women (18 holes):* yardage 6280, par 72, rating 68.0, slope 114.

Tee Times: Reservations are not necessary.

Dress Code: Appropriate attire is requested.

Tournaments: A 72-player minimum is needed for a shotgun tournament.

Directions: From I-5 in Yreka, drive east on Highway 3 to Montague. Exit south onto Golf Course Road.

Contact: 500 Golf Course Road, Montague, CA 96064, pro shop 530/842-2302.

2 LAKE SHASTINA GOLF RESORT

Architect: Robert Trent Jones Jr., 1973

27 holes   **Resort**   **$30–50**

Shasta and Trinity map, page 36

One of Robert Trent Jones Jr.'s earliest designs, this large, scenic course is long and sprawling, with five lakes. The 16th hole is one of the toughest par-3s in Northern California. There is also a nine-hole Scottish links layout, par 35. Both courses offer spectacular views of Mount Shasta. PGA Tour pro Peter Jacobsen earned his first professional win here at the 1976 Northern California Open.

There are condominiums and houses available for rent on the course. Play-and-stay packages are available at the resort. Call 800/358-4653 for information.

Play Policy and Fees: Green fees vary depending on season. The 18-hole course fee is $30 October–May; $50 through summer. Nine-hole rates are available. The nine-hole Scottish course rates are $15 year-round. Twilight rates are available on both courses. Check the website for specials. Carts additional.

Tees and Yardage: *Men:* Blue: yardage 6933, par 72, rating 72.6, slope 132; Gold: yardage 6536, par 72, rating 70.6, slope 130; White: yardage 6268, par 72, rating 69.4, slope 127; *Women:* Red: yardage 5530, par 72, rating 70.0, slope 121.

Tee Times: Reservations are accepted up to a month in advance.

Dress Code: Collared shirts and nonmetal spikes are required.

Tournaments: Events may be booked a year in advance. The banquet facility accommodates 135 people.

Directions: Lake Shastina Golf Resort is seven miles north of Weed on U.S. 97. Turn right at Big Springs Road.

Contact: 5925 Country Club Drive, Lake Shastina, CA 96094, pro shop 530/938-3205, fax 530/938-4653, www.shastinagolf.com.

3 WEED GOLF COURSE

Architect: Course designed, 1927

9 holes   **Semiprivate**   **$15–20**

Shasta and Trinity map, page 36

This rolling course, bordered by trees and a creek, has magnificent views of Mount Shasta and Eddy Mountain. The greens are fast, and water comes into play on four holes. Watch out for the first hole, a tricky 327-yard par-4 with a dogleg left. Have you ever wanted to own part of a golf course? Here is your chance. Weed Golf Club is a membership-owned-and-operated corporation. The corporation is authorized to sell 200 shares of stock. Golf club members are eligible to purchase one share. All dividends go to improve the golf course.

Play Policy and Fees: Green fees are $15 for nine holes and $20 for 18 holes every day.

Twilight rates are available. Carts are $12 for nine holes and $20 for 18 holes.

Tees and Yardage: *Men (18 holes):* Back: yardage 5469, par 70, rating 65.1, slope 112; *Women (18 holes):* Forward: yardage 4819, par 70, rating 67.3, slope 116.

Tee Times: Reservations are not needed, but call ahead to make sure there are no tournaments in progress.

Dress Code: Shirts and shoes are necessary.

Tournaments: Outside tournaments are accepted with board of directors' approval.

Directions: From Weed, drive one-half mile north on I-5. Take the north Weed exit to the golf course.

Contact: 27730 Old Edgewood Road, Weed, CA 96094, pro shop 530/938-9971.

❹ MOUNT SHASTA RESORT

Architect: Jim Summers, Sandy Tatum, 1993

18 holes   **Resort**   **$35–50**

🏌️ 📷 🍴 🛒 🛍️ 🚜 🍺

Shasta and Trinity map, page 36

Set above the 3500-foot level, this lovely course features contoured fairways, with stands of trees and water in play on several holes. The signature hole is the par-3 seventh, which features an elevated tee and great views over water. The course sits below snowcapped Mount Shasta and provides spectacular scenery and shot-making. It is open year-round, weather permitting.

For reservations at the resort, call 800/958-3363.

Play Policy and Fees: Rates for 18 holes are seasonal: $35 spring and fall, $50 summer. Fees for nine holes are $15 in spring and fall, $25 in summer. Twilight, junior, and guest rates are available.

Tees and Yardage: *Men:* Blue: yardage 6035, par 70, rating 68.1, slope 129; White: yardage 5673, par 70, rating 66.0, slope 126; *Women:* Gold: yardage 5092, par 71, rating 66.6, slope 118.

Tee Times: Reservations may be made seven days in advance for the public, and at any time for lodge guests.

Dress Code: No sleeveless shirts are allowed.

Tournaments: The course is available for outside events. Contact the pro shop for tournament information.

Directions: From I-5 in Mount Shasta, take the Central Mount Shasta exit. Follow signs for the Mount Shasta Resort.

Contact: 1000 Siskiyou Lake Boulevard, Mount Shasta, CA 96067, pro shop 530/926-3052, fax 530/926-0333, www.mountshastaresort.com.

❺ MCCLOUD GOLF CLUB

Architect: Course designed, 1927

9 holes   **Public**   **$12–20**

🏌️ 📷 🍴 🛒 🚜 🍺

Shasta and Trinity map, page 36

On a clear day, McCloud offers one of the most beautiful sights in California golf: a majestic, bird's-eye view of Mount Shasta. The course features native pine and quaking aspen, with Squaw Creek meandering through. Water comes into play on six of the nine holes. The par-3 seventh hole has a fountain offering cold, pure water that is piped onto the course from Mount Shasta.

Play Policy and Fees: Green fees are $12 for nine holes and $18 for 18 holes. Carts are $10 for nine holes and $20 for 18 holes. The course is open April–November. On Monday, senior citizens get a $2 discount on 18 holes.

Tees and Yardage: *Men (18 holes):* Regular: yardage 6060, par 72, rating 68.2, slope 114; *Women (18 holes):* Forward: yardage 5262, par 74, rating 69.4, slope 112.

Tee Times: Reservations are not accepted. All play is on a first-come, first-served basis.

Dress Code: Appropriate attire and soft spikes are required.

Tournaments: This course is available for outside tournaments. A 72-player minimum is needed. Events should be booked nine months in advance.

Directions: From I-5 north of Redding and Dunsmuir, take the Highway 89 exit. Drive east to McCloud. In McCloud, turn right on Squaw Valley Road and follow it south to the course.

Contact: 1001 Squaw Valley Road (P.O. Box 728), McCloud, CA 96057, pro shop 530/964-2535.

6 BIGFOOT GOLF & COUNTRY CLUB

Architect: Course designed, 1964

9 holes **Semiprivate** **$12–25**

Shasta and Trinity map, page 36

Although short from a yardage standpoint, Bigfoot requires accuracy on its small greens. It has water on five of nine holes. The par-4 seventh hole, for instance, is reachable for big hitters at 267 yards, but out-of-bounds lurks behind and to the left of the green. The par-5 fourth hole, at 487 yards, features a green that is just 15 yards deep from front to back, and water encircles two-thirds of the putting surface.

Play Policy and Fees: Outside play is accepted. Weekday green fees are $12 for nine holes and $17 for 18 holes. Weekend rates are $15 for nine holes and $25 for 18 holes. Carts are additional.

Tees and Yardage: *Men (18 holes):* White/Blue: yardage 4949, par 70, rating 64.4, slope 121; *Women:* White/Blue: yardage 4949, par 70, rating 68.5, slope 118.

Tee Times: Starting times are preferred. Call 800/788-9548.

Dress Code: Shirts must be worn at all times. Shorts and tee shirts are acceptable.

Tournaments: This course is available for outside tournaments. Events should be booked two months in advance. The banquet facility can accommodate 100 people.

Directions: From U.S. 101 in Arcata, take Highway 299 east to Willow Creek. Turn left on Country Club Road and cross the Trinity River. Turn left on Patterson, then right on Bigfoot Avenue. Take the first left into the course.

Contact: 333 Bigfoot Avenue, Willow Creek, CA 95573, pro shop 530/629-2977, fax 530/629-1969.

7 TRINITY ALPS GOLF & COUNTRY CLUB

Architect: Course designed, 1973

9 holes **Semiprivate** **$10–15**

Shasta and Trinity map, page 36

There are two water hazards on this rolling, short and walkable course. It is pretty, with lots of trees and views of the Trinity Alps. Water comes into play on four of the nine holes.

Play Policy and Fees: Public play is accepted. Green fees are $10 for nine holes and $15 for 18 holes.

Tees and Yardage: *Men (18 holes):* Blue/Red: yardage 3456, par 62, rating 58.6, slope 108; *Women:* Red: yardage 3456, par 62, rating 59.2, slope 110.

Tee Times: Not required.

Dress Code: Shirts must be worn at all times.

Tournaments: This course is available for outside tournaments. The banquet facility can accommodate 140 people.

Directions: From Redding, drive 49 miles west on Highway 299 to Weaverville. Exit south on Glen Road and continue to Fairway Drive and the course.

Contact: 111 Golf Course Road, Weaverville, CA 96093, pro shop 530/623-2205.

8 GOLD HILLS GOLF CLUB

Architect: Phil Holcomb, 1978

18 holes **Public** **$30–40**

Shasta and Trinity map, page 36

This course is a challenging test in a beautiful setting. Golfers have views of Mount Lassen and Mount Shasta on clear days. The opening hole is formidable—405 yards with out-of-bounds left, Churn Creek right. Carts are recommended due to the hilly terrain.

Play Policy and Fees: Green fees are seasonal, but typically $30 any day and $40 holidays. Carts are $15 per person.

Tees and Yardage: *Men:* Blue: yardage 6562, par 72, rating 72.2, slope 135; White: yardage 6164, par 72, rating 70.3, slope 132; Gold:

yardage 5556, par 72, rating 67.5, slope 122; *Women:* Red: yardage 4836, par 72, rating 68.8, slope 120.

Tee Times: Reservations may be booked seven days in advance.

Dress Code: Collared shirts are required.

Tournaments: A 20-player minimum is needed to book a tournament. Large tournaments should be booked six months in advance. The banquet facility will hold up to 200 people.

Directions: From I-5 just north of Redding, take the Oasis Road exit east and drive one-half mile. Turn right on Gold Hills Drive and follow it to the course.

Contact: 1950 Gold Hills Drive, Redding, CA 96003, pro shop 530/246-7867, fax 530/246-4607, www.goldhillsgolf.com.

9 THE GOLF CLUB OF TIERRA OAKS

Architect: Sandy Tatum, Jim Summers, 1993
18 holes   Private $75

Shasta and Trinity map, page 36

Built in the rolling hills of north Redding, this course features oak- and pine-lined fairways, which give it a mature feel. The signature hole is the par-4 12th, a sharp double-dogleg right, with a creek guarding the left side of the fairway. Those who decide to play it safe will face a demanding second shot to an elevated green. A popular clubhouse discussion is whether the 12th should be a par-5!

Play Policy and Fees: Reciprocal play is accepted from other private clubs at a rate of $75 for reciprocal guests. Carts are $12 per person.

Tees and Yardage: *Men:* Black: yardage 6830, par 72, rating 73.3, slope 138; White: yardage 6375, par 72, rating 71.4, slope 135; Blue: yardage 5721, par 72, rating 69.5, slope 123; *Women:* Gold: yardage 5110, par 73, rating 71.2, slope 125.

Tee Times: Tee times may be booked two days in advance for reciprocal play. Call the head professional to make reservations.

Dress Code: Appropriate golf attire is required.

Tournaments: A limited number of outside events are allowed each year. Events may be booked 2–3 months in advance.

Directions: From I-5 in Redding, drive north to the Oasis Road exit. Drive east for 3.2 miles to the club entrance on the left.

Contact: 19700 La Crescenta Drive, Redding, CA 96003, pro shop 530/275-0887, fax 530/275-0895.

10 LAKE REDDING GOLF COURSE

Architect: Course designed, 1959
9 holes   Public $10–16

Shasta and Trinity map, page 36

This short executive course is known for requiring accuracy, because its narrow fairways are lined with trees. Four lakes come into play. Lake Redding is popular with seniors and beginners.

Play Policy and Fees: Green fees are $10 for nine holes and $16 for 18 holes. Senior rates are available Monday–Friday. Carts are $10 for nine holes and $17 for 18 holes. Pull carts are $3 all day.

Tees and Yardage: *Men (18 holes):* yardage 3685, par 62, rating 57.8, slope 87; *Women (18 holes):* yardage 3685, par 62, rating 60.1, slope 88.

Tee Times: Tee times generally are not needed, but they may be reserved a few days in advance.

Dress Code: Shirts are required. No tank tops are allowed.

Tournaments: This course is available for outside tournaments.

Directions: Heading north on I-5 in Redding, take the Highway 299 East exit. Turn left, drive to the second stoplight, and turn left again. At the bottom of the hill, take the first right, which is Benton Drive. Take Benton Drive to the course.

Contact: 1795 Benton Drive, Redding, CA 96003, pro shop 530/243-5531.

11 ALLEN'S GOLF COURSE

Architect: Course designed, 1961

9 holes   **Public**   **$6–14**

Shasta and Trinity map, page 36

This short course is in a parklike setting with many trees and a creek coming into play on five holes. The ninth hole has everything—a pond, trees, and a blind shot to an elevated green. Most of the fairways are narrow, and every hole has out-of-bounds areas. Hone up your short game skills here.

Play Policy and Fees: Weekday green fees are $6 for nine holes and $14 for 18 holes. Twilight, senior, and junior rates are available.

Tees and Yardage: *Men and Women:* Back: yardage 3412, par 62, rating 57.0, slope 92; Forward: yardage 3324, par 62, rating 58.2, slope 89.

Tee Times: Reservations are on a first-come, first-served basis.

Dress Code: Shirts and shoes are required.

Tournaments: This course is available for outside events and offers a nice barbecue area for banquets.

Directions: From Redding on I-5, take the Bechelli Lane exit and head west. After you cross the Sacramento River, take your second left on East Side Road. Follow East Side Road until you reach Start Road; turn left. The course is on the left.

Contact: 2780 Sacramento Drive, Redding, CA 96001, pro shop 530/241-5055.

12 RIVERVIEW GOLF & COUNTRY CLUB

Architect: Course designed, 1947

18 holes   **Private**   **$60**

Shasta and Trinity map, page 36

The first hole, a par-5 of 580 yards, has been called "the most scenic in California." The Sacramento River borders the left side with a spectacular view of the mountains in the background. The traditional-style course is narrow with countless trees, and the greens are mostly small. The par-3s measure 208, 183, 193, and 138 yards. There is not much elevation change here, making this a fine walking course. Members have been known to sacrifice a ball into the Sacramento River as an act of resignation.

Play Policy and Fees: Reciprocal play is accepted with members of other private clubs. Reciprocal fees are $60. Carts are $11.

Tees and Yardage: *Men:* Back: yardage 6617, par 72, rating 70.8, slope 129; Middle: yardage 6406, par 72, rating 69.8, slope 127; *Women:* Forward: yardage 5819, par 72, rating 67.3, slope 121.

Tee Times: Tee times may be booked one week in advance.

Dress Code: Collared shirts and nonmetal spikes are required. Denim is not permitted.

Tournaments: Board approval is a must for outside events.

Directions: From I-5 in Redding, take the Bonneyview Road/Churn Creek exit. Cross the overpass and turn right on Bechelli Lane. Follow it to the course on the left.

Contact: 4200 Bechelli Lane, Redding, CA 96002, pro shop 530/224-2250, fax 530/224-2246.

13 RIVER BEND GOLF & COUNTRY CLUB

Architect: Bill Ralston, 1990

9 holes   **Private**   **$12–25**

Shasta and Trinity map, page 36

This course was designed and built by Bill Ralston with the assistance of retired pro Eric Batten. With its tight layout, two ponds, and the Sacramento River Slough coming into play on five holes, this is a target course of the most demanding dimensions. The course is generally in outstanding condition. The eighth hole, a short par-4, is deceptively difficult, with out-of-bounds right, water left, and a green that slopes heavily left.

Play Policy and Fees: Members and restricted guest play allowed. Limited reciprocal play is accepted. Only players with NCGA, SCGA, or out-of-state golf association handicaps, or guests of members are allowed to play the course. Guest fees are $12 for nine holes with a member and range to $25 for 18 holes without a member. Carts are $8 for nine holes, $16 for 18 holes.

Tees and Yardage: *Men (18 holes):* Blue/White combo yardage 4104, par 64, rating 61.5, slope 97; *Women (18 holes):* White/Red combo yardage 3712, par 64, rating 62.4, slope 103.

Tee Times: Reservations are accepted two days in advance for reciprocal play.

Dress Code: Nonmetal spikes and shirts with sleeves are required.

Tournaments: Tournaments are accepted and should be booked six months in advance. The banquet facility holds 175 people.

Directions: From I-5 in Redding, take the Churn Creek/Bechelli exit and turn west. Cross over the Sacramento River and turn right on Indianwood Drive, which leads to the River Bend Estate. Drive through the subdivision. The course is at the rear of the residential area.

Contact: 5369 Indianwood Drive, Redding, CA 96001, pro shop 530/246-9077, fax 530/246-9995.

14 ANDERSON TUCKER OAKS GOLF COURSE

Architect: William Tucker Jr., 1964

9 holes   **Public**   **$10–20**

Shasta and Trinity map, page 36

Like most Redding-area courses, Tucker Oaks is distinguished by numerous trees. There are bunkers on every hole, and two lakes come into play. The best hole is the third, a 434-yard par-4 that doglegs left. Out-of-bounds come into play on the first three holes.

Play Policy and Fees: Green fees are $10 for nine holes and $20 for 18 holes.

Tees and Yardage: *Men (18 holes):* Back: yardage 6371, par 72, rating 68.5, slope 111; *Women (18 holes):* Forward: yardage 5896, par 74, rating 72.2, slope 115.

Tee Times: Reservations are not accepted. All play is on a first-come, first-served basis.

Dress Code: Appropriate golf attire is preferred.

Tournaments: This course is available for outside tournaments. An 80-player minimum is required for shotgun tournaments, which should be booked six months in advance.

Directions: From I-5 in Anderson, take the Riverside exit to Airport Road north. Drive across the Sacramento River and turn left on Churn Creek Road. Continue to the course.

Contact: 6241 Churn Creek Road, Anderson, CA 96007 (P.O. Box 678, Redding, CA 96002), pro shop 530/365-3350, fax 530/365-9398.

15 CHURN CREEK GOLF COURSE

Architect: D. A. Divine, 1976

9 holes   **Public**   **$10–20**

Shasta and Trinity map, page 36

The course is primarily flat, but numerous trees separate adjoining fairways, and there are out-of-bounds on all but two holes. The course is a good test of moderate length, with trees and small greens giving it a distinctive flavor.

Play Policy and Fees: Green fees are $10 for nine holes and $20 for 18 holes. Carts are $10 for nine holes and $20 for 18 holes.

Tees and Yardage: *Men (18 holes):* Back: yardage 6299, par 72, rating 70.9, slope 118; *Women (18 holes):* Forward: yardage 6264, par 72, rating 70.1, slope 118.

Tee Times: Reservations can be made seven days in advance.

Dress Code: Appropriate sports attire is requested.

Tournaments: This course is available for outside events. A 72-player minimum is needed to book a shotgun tournament. Events should be booked 12 months in advance. The banquet facility holds 90 people.

Directions: From I-5 in Redding, take the Knighton Road exit east. Knighton Road turns into Churn Creek Road, which leads to the course.

Contact: 7335 Churn Creek Road, Redding, CA 96002, pro shop 530/222-6353.

16 PALO CEDRO GOLF CLUB

Architect: Bert Stamps, 1992

9 holes   **Semiprivate**   **$10–20**

🚶 📷 🍴 🏌 🚠 🍺

Shasta and Trinity map, page 36

There are lots of water hazards and many maturing trees on this slightly hilly layout. The par-5 ninth hole is 481 yards and doglegs left over a stream. The green is guarded on both sides by bunkers that will catch any errant shots. The signature hole is the 165-yard, par-3 sixth. It is flanked on the left by pine and oak trees and a creek, and on the right by two huge oak trees. Playing from the elevated tee, you have to channel your ball through the narrow fairway to reach the green.

Play Policy and Fees: Green fees are $10 for nine holes and $20 for 18 holes. Carts are $7 for nine holes and $12 for 18 holes.

Tees and Yardage: *Men (18 holes):* Back: yardage 6114, par 72, rating 69.4, slope 123; Middle: yardage 5940, par 72, rating 68.6, slope 121; *Women (18 holes):* Forward: yardage 5432, par 72, rating 70.2, slope 113.

Tee Times: Reservations may be booked seven days in advance.

Dress Code: All shirts must have sleeves, and nonmetal spikes are required.

Tournaments: Outside events are accepted.

Directions: From Redding, take I-5 north to Highway 44. Drive east on Highway 44 for eight miles to Silver Bridge Road and turn left. The course is on the left.

Contact: 22499 Golf Time Drive, Palo Cedro, CA 96073, pro shop 530/547-3012, fax 530/547-2889.

17 WILCOX OAKS GOLF CLUB

Architect: Ben Harmon, 1976

18 holes   **Private**   **$55**

Shasta and Trinity map, page 36

Wilcox Oaks has been called "the toughest 6100-yard course in Northern California." The back nine is appreciably more difficult than the front side, starting with the 311-yard 10th

hole that doglegs up a steep hill. Wild turkeys frequent this course.

Play Policy and Fees: Reciprocal play is accepted with members of other private clubs. Fee is $55.

Tees and Yardage: *Men:* Blue: yardage 6329, par 72, rating 69.7, slope 120; White: yardage 6144, par 72, rating 68.9, slope 118; *Women:* Red: yardage 5811, par 72, rating 74.3, slope 127; *Senior:* Gold: yardage 4999, par 72, rating 63.3, slope 104.

Tee Times: Reservations may be made seven days in advance for reciprocal play.

Dress Code: Nonmetal spikes are required. Shirts for men and boys must have sleeves and collars. Tee shirts and tank tops are not acceptable. Tops for women and girls should be appropriate for golf—no halter tops, tank tops, spaghetti straps, or bare midriffs. Shorts should be no less than five inches above the back of the knee or at least a six-inch inseam. Sweats and spandex pants are not acceptable. Men and boys must remove their hats in the dining room. If you ever wondered about the definition of appropriate golf attire, wonder no more.

Tournaments: A 100-player minimum is needed to book a tournament. A banquet facility is available that can accommodate up to 120 people.

Directions: From I-5 just north of Red Bluff, take the Wilcox Golf Road exit. The course is on the west side of I-5.

Contact: 2 Wilcox Golf Road (P.O. Box 127), Red Bluff, CA 96080, pro shop 530/527-7087, fax 530/527-4667.

18 OAK CREEK GOLF COURSE

Architect: Course designed, 1978

9 holes   **Public**   **$10–18**

🚶 📷 🍴 🏌 🚠 🍺

Shasta and Trinity map, page 36

Mount Shasta and Mount Lassen are visible from this flat course. The course is usually in fine shape. The seventh hole is only 321 yards but requires a carry of 200 yards. The Red Bluff Junior Golf Championship is held here the second Saturday in August.

Play Policy and Fees: Green fees are $10 for nine holes and $18 for 18 holes. Senior rates are $9 for nine holes and $16 for 18 holes. Twilight rates available. Carts are $10 for nine holes, $18 for 18 holes.

Tees and Yardage: *Men (18 holes):* Blue: yardage 5276, par 70, rating 64.5, slope 107; *Women (18 holes):* White & Red: yardage 5125, par 70, rating 68.1, slope 115.

Tee Times: Reservations can be booked seven days in advance.

Dress Code: Golf attire is encouraged. Soft spikes are required.

Tournaments: This course is available for outside tournaments. A 20-player minimum is needed to book an event. Tournaments can be scheduled 12 months in advance.

Directions: From I-5 in Red Bluff traveling north, take the Main Street exit. Turn north onto Main Street. Turn left on Montgomery Road and follow it to the course.

Contact: 2620 Montgomery Road, Red Bluff, CA 96080, pro shop 530/529-0674, fax 530/529-4834.

Chapter 3

Lassen and Modoc

Lassen and Modoc

This is among the loveliest regions in California, known more for its national parks than its golf courses. Incorporating Lassen National Forest, Modoc National Forest, and parts of Shasta National Forest and Plumas National Forest, the region boasts excellent sightseeing, hiking, and camping opportunities, as well as many mountains, lakes, and streams for fishing and recreational pursuits.

What better location could there be for golf? Expansive views, lush, tree-lined fairways, natural elevation changes, water everywhere: It's a perfect setting to play.

Of course, due to the sensitive nature of the environment, golf course construction is limited and there are few layouts from which to select in this region. But golfers will find each one of those that do exist charming and beautiful. Keeping in mind that some are closed in winter due to their elevation and proximity to mountain ranges, a golfing visit to this region is just right in late spring and summer months.

Perhaps the most active region for golf is around Lake Almanor. A new course opened here in 2001, Bailey Creek, adding to a roster that already included Lake Almanor Country Club and Lake Almanor West Golf Course. These picturesque mountain layouts feature towering pine trees, lake and mountain views, and a very relaxed ambience.

Just to the east is Susanville, where Diamond Mountain Golf Club has expanded from nine to 18 holes. Formerly known as Emerson Lake Golf Course, this course features evergreens flanking the fairways and a couple of lakes in play.

Farther north, this region includes the northernmost course in the state, Indian Camp Golf Course. It's a nine-hole layout in a very scenic area just 300 yards from the Oregon border, or about the length of a John Daly 3-wood.

All outdoor enthusiasts enjoy this most treasured region of California, and golfers will too.

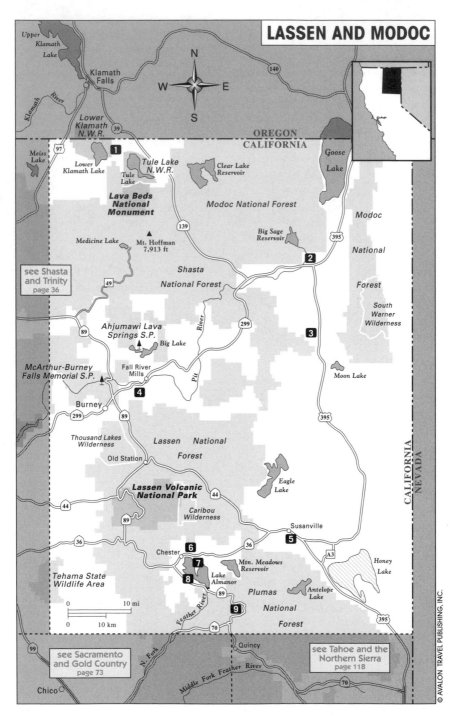

N
W E
S

140

OREGON
CALIFORNIA

Upper
Klamath
Lake

Klamath
Falls

Klamath River

Lower
Klamath
N.W.R.

39

97

Meiss
Lake

Lower
Klamath Lake

1

Tule
Lake

Tule Lake
N.W.R.

Clear Lake
Reservoir

Goose
Lake

**Lava Beds
National
Monument**

Medicine Lake

▲ Mt. Hoffman
7,913 ft

139

Modoc National Forest

Big Sage
Reservoir

395

2

Modoc

National

see Shasta
and Trinity
page 36

49

Shasta

National Forest

River

299

3

Forest

South
Warner
Wilderness

89

*Ahjumawi Lava
Springs S.P.*

▲ Big Lake

Moon Lake

**McArthur-Burney
Falls Memorial S.P.**

Fall River
Mills

Pit

395

Burney

299

89

4

*Thousand Lakes
Wilderness*

Lassen   National

Old Station

Forest

Eagle
Lake

44

**Lassen Volcanic
National Park**

44

89

*Caribou
Wilderness*

Susanville

36

89

36

5

A3

36

Chester

6

Mtn. Meadows
Reservoir

Honey
Lake

*Tehama State
Wildlife Area*

7

8

Lake
Almanor

Antelope
Lake

89

Plumas

0   10 mi

0   10 km

Feather River

9

National

70

Forest

395

99

see Sacramento
and Gold Country
page 73

N. Fork

Quincy

see Tahoe and the
Northern Sierra
page 118

Chico

Middle Fork Feather River

70

CALIFORNIA
NEVADA

© AVALON TRAVEL PUBLISHING, INC.

1 INDIAN CAMP GOLF COURSE

Architect: Malcolm Crawford, 1982

9 holes   Public $10–16

🏃 📷 💰 🔧 🚙 🍽️

Lassen and Modoc map, page 48

Indian Camp is the northernmost golf course in California. In fact, it's less than 300 yards from the Oregon border, less than a Tiger Woods tee shot. There are some lovely mountain views from this course, which is on the site of a historic Native American hunting and fishing camp. Indian Camp closes in winter months because there is snow on the ground.

Play Policy and Fees: Green fees are $10 for nine holes and $16 for 18 holes. Senior rates available.

Tees and Yardage: *Men:* Back: yardage 1512, par 28, rating n/a, slope n/a; *Women:* Forward: yardage 1421, par 28, rating n/a, slope n/a.

Tee Times: All play is on a first-come, first-served basis.

Dress Code: Soft spikes are preferred.

Tournaments: This course is available for tournaments.

Directions: The course is 25 miles southeast of Klamath Falls, Oregon. From Highway 39, turn right on Malone Road. Drive south two miles to Stateline Road and follow the signs to the course.

Contact: 17334 Stateline Road, Tulelake, CA 96134, phone 530/667-2922.

2 ARROWHEAD GOLF COURSE

Architect: John Briggs, 1969

9 holes   Public $11–19

🏃 📷 💰 🔧 🚙 🍽️

Lassen and Modoc map, page 48

This course has wide fairways and elevated greens. Irrigation ditches come into play on every hole, but there are no bunkers. The toughest hole is the par-5 eighth, which measures 505 yards from the regular tees. Because this course is in a remote area of the northeastern part of the state, Arrowhead is one of those rare spots where you can almost always drive up and tee off within minutes.

Play Policy and Fees: Green fees are $11 for nine holes and $19 for 18 holes. Senior rates available.

Tees and Yardage: *Men (18 holes):* Red/White: yardage 6247, par 72, rating 68.3, slope 115; *Women (18 holes):* Blue/Yellow: yardage 5450, par 72, rating 70.6, slope 120.

Tee Times: Reservations are accepted.

Dress Code: Appropriate attire and soft spikes are required.

Tournaments: This course is available for tournaments. The banquet facility can accommodate 100 people.

Directions: From I-5 in Redding, drive east on Highway 299 to Alturas. Take the Warner Street exit and drive north to the course.

Contact: 1901 North Warner Street, Alturas, CA 96101, pro shop 530/233-3404, fax 541/947-2653.

3 LIKELY LINKS GOLF CLUB

Architect: Rich Hamel, 1999

9 holes   Resort $12–19

🏃 📷 💰 🔧 🚙 🍽️

Lassen and Modoc map, page 48

You can grip it and rip it; the average fairway on this course, which is affiliated with Likely Place RV Resort, is 50 yards wide. Likely Links offers subtle elevation changes and large greens. Outside the fairways the rough is extremely rough, and if you can find your ball, it will be among the sagebrush and rocks. The signature hole is the slightly downhill 630-yard par-5 sixth hole from the championship tees. An afternoon breeze can be a factor. At 4500 feet near both the Oregon and Nevada borders, you will find an abundance of wildlife and fresh air. Yes, that's right—fresh air and California in the same sentence. RV sites are available.

Play Policy and Fees: Green fees are $12 for nine holes weekdays and $14 on weekends, $17 for 18 holes on weekdays and $19 on weekends. Carts are $10 for nine holes and $15 for 18 holes.

Tees and Yardage: *Men (18 holes):* Blue: yardage

6702, par 72, rating 69.8, slope 119; White: yardage 6380, par 72, rating 68.4, slope 116; *Women (18 holes):* Red: yardage 6046, par 72, rating 67.4, slope 112.

Tee Times: The course closes for the winter, opening mid-April. Reservations are not required but are recommended during July and August. Call one day in advance.

Dress Code: Casual, but shirts and shoes are required.

Tournaments: Outside events are allowed with two weeks advance notice.

Directions: From Alturas, take U.S. 395 south for 20 miles to Jess Valley Road. Take a right to the course.

Contact: Jess Valley Road, Likely, CA 96116, pro shop 530/233-6676, fax 530/233-4466, www.likelyplace.com.

4 FALL RIVER VALLEY GOLF & COUNTRY CLUB

Architect: Clark Glasson, 1978

18 holes   **Public**   **$26–31**

Lassen and Modoc map, page 48

One of California's longest and toughest courses, for men and women, Fall River is located in a mountain valley best known for its first-rate fishing. But the golf course is a jewel, winding its way through the trees with a wide variety of holes. Its length is subdued somewhat by the elevation, and golfers can expect extra carry and roll here. The eighth hole, a par-3 over a lake, is named "Bing's Bluff" in honor of the old crooner. Clark Glasson was building the course when he noticed Bing Crosby watching from a distance. Crosby owned the nearby Rising River Ranch. The course is closed mid-November–April. For the price, it is quite a bargain.

Play Policy and Fees: Green fees are $26 weekdays and $31 weekends. Senior rates are available Monday. Twilight rates also available. Carts are $30.

Tees and Yardage: *Men:* Black: yardage 7402, par 72, rating 74.7, slope 134; Blue: yardage 6997,

par 72, rating 72.7, slope 132; White: yardage 6557, par 72, rating 70.9, slope 122; *Women:* Red: yardage 5876, par 72, rating 72.6, slope 124.

Tee Times: Reservations can be booked 14 days in advance.

Dress Code: Golf attire is encouraged.

Tournaments: The banquet facility can accommodate up to 120 people.

Directions: From I-5 in Redding, drive east on Highway 299 to Fall River Mills. The course is on the right.

Contact: 42889 Highway 299 East (P.O. Box 827), Fall River Mills, CA 96028, pro shop 530/336-5555.

5 DIAMOND MOUNTAIN GOLF CLUB

Architect: Front nine designed, 1967; back nine Dave Tanner, 2004

18 holes   **Public**   **$20–30**

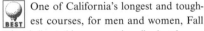

Lassen and Modoc map, page 48

This rolling course is well maintained, and, even though there is some elevation change, it is very walkable. With the 2004 expansion from nine to 18 holes, this course changed its name from Emerson Lake Golf Club to Diamond Mountain. It has two creeks, two lakes, and some hills. Evergreens flank the entire course. The greens are excellent, and there is a beautiful view of Diamond Mountain. Along with the new nine holes, a new clubhouse with pro shop, restaurant, and driving range has been completed, giving Susanville its first full 18-hole facility.

Play Policy and Fees: Green fees range $20–30 for 18 holes. Carts are additional.

Tees and Yardage: *Men:* Blue: yardage 6417, par 72, rating 70.4, slope 124; White: yardage 5914, par 72, rating 68.1, slope 121; *Women:* Red: yardage 5118, par 72, rating n/a, slope n/a.

Tee Times: Reservations can be booked 14 days in advance.

Dress Code: Shirts must be worn.

Tournaments: A 40-player minimum is needed to book an event. Tournaments should be scheduled at least four months in advance.

Directions: From I-5 in Red Bluff, take Highway 36 to Susanville. Turn right on Weatherlow, which turns into Richmond Road. Make a right turn on Wingfield Road. From Reno, take U.S. 395 to Susanville. Turn left on Richmond Road and drive about three miles. Turn left on Wingfield Road and drive one-quarter mile to the clubhouse.

Contact: 470-835 Wingfield Road, Susanville, CA 96130, pro shop 530/257-6303, fax 530/257-6849.

6 BAILEY CREEK GOLF COURSE

Architect: Homer Flint, 2001

18 holes   **Public**   **$55–75**

Lassen and Modoc map, page 48

 Just next to scenic Lake Almanor, this course features rolling hills, waterfalls, fountains, three lakes, and pine trees aplenty. The fairways are wide and accommodating, and there are plenty of beautiful views of Mount Lassen. The 17th is a strong par-5, while the 18th is a fun finishing hole that gives golfers the opportunity to bite off as much of the sharp, left-turning dogleg as they can chew. Of course, trouble awaits the errant shot. A very strong design.

Play Policy and Fees: Green fees are seasonal, beginning at $55 for 18 holes and ranging to $75 for 18 holes. Carts are included. This course closes for the winter and reopens mid-May.

Tees and Yardage: *Men:* Black: yardage 7040, par 72, rating 72.8, slope 129; Blue: yardage 6485, par 72, rating 70.1, slope 121; White: yardage 5883, par 72, rating 67.4, slope 119; *Women:* Red: yardage 5381, par 72, rating 68.7, slope 121.

Tee Times: Reservations are accepted for the season.

Dress Code: Appropriate golf attire is required.

Tournaments: This course is available for outside events.

Directions: From Chico, take Highway 32 east 55 miles to Highway 36. Take a right at the four-way stop and follow Highway 36 through Chester. Make a right turn on County Road

A13 and then another right on Clifford Drive. The course is on the right.

Contact: 433 Durkin Drive, Lake Almanor, CA 96137, pro shop 530/259-4653, www.baileycreek.com.

7 LAKE ALMANOR COUNTRY CLUB

Architect: Ed Clifford, 1958

9 holes   **Semiprivate**   **$18–40**

Lassen and Modoc map, page 48

This rolling, scenic mountain course is tight and has big trees and undulating greens. The par-4 second hole provides a breathtaking view of Mount Lassen, and the seventh hole offers a view of Lake Almanor. Osprey and deer are frequent visitors.

Play Policy and Fees: Members only until 3 P.M. Green fees are $18 for nine holes and $40 for 18 holes.

Tees and Yardage: *Men (18 holes):* White/Blue: yardage 5873, par 71, rating 67.5, slope 115; *Women (18 holes):* Red/Yellow: yardage 5630, par 72, rating 71.0, slope 126.

Tee Times: Members and their guests may book tee times one week in advance. Nonmembers may reserve only on the day of play.

Dress Code: The dress code is casual.

Tournaments: This course is not available for outside events.

Directions: From I-5 in Red Bluff, take Highway 36 through Chester. Turn right on County Road A13 and drive about one mile. Turn right on Walker Road and drive to the gate.

Contact: 951 Clifford Drive, Lake Almanor, CA 96137, pro shop 530/259-2868.

8 LAKE ALMANOR WEST GOLF COURSE

Architect: Homer Flint, 1976

9 holes   **Public**   **$21–31**

Lassen and Modoc map, page 48

This picturesque mountain layout offers dramatic views of Mount Lassen. It has towering pines and large, undulating greens. Most fairways are spacious. The third hole—a par-3 of 176 yards from the regular tees and 131 yards from the forward tees—requires a firm shot over water. Deer abound on this fun, interesting layout.

Play Policy and Fees: Green fees are $21 for nine holes and $31 for 18 holes. Shoulder season rates, annual play, early bird, and other special rates are available. The course closes in winter and opens again in mid-April. Call ahead.

Tees and Yardage: *Men (18 holes):* White/Blue: yardage 6318, par 72, rating 69.3, slope 122; *Women (18 holes):* Red/Yellow: yardage 5347, par 72, rating 69.6, slope 124.

Tee Times: Reservations can be booked seven days in advance.

Dress Code: Shirts must be worn at all times. Cutoffs are not allowed.

Tournaments: Tournaments should be booked at least one month in advance. A banquet facility is available that can accommodate 75 people.

Directions: From I-5 in Red Bluff, take Highway 36 to Highway 89. Drive south on Highway 89 to Lake Almanor West. Turn left on Slim Drive to the course. The course is 65 miles from Chico. Take Highway 99 north.

Contact: 111 Slim Drive (P.O. Box 1040), Chester, CA 96020, pro shop 530/259-4555, fax 530/259-4556.

in 1981. Many seniors enjoy this course because it isn't too hilly. However, flat doesn't mean easy. The par-3s are long, although the best might be the fourth hole, which measures just 135 yards but plays much tougher because of water.

Play Policy and Fees: Green fees are $10 for nine holes and $17 for 18 holes weekdays, $12 and $19 weekends and holidays. Carts are $9 for nine holes and $16 for 18 holes.

Tees and Yardage: *Men (18 holes):* Blue: yardage 4602, par 66, rating 60.8, slope 95; White: yardage 4276, par 66, rating 60.8, slope 95; *Women:* Red: yardage 3832, par 66, rating 61.1, slope 93.

Tee Times: Reservations can be booked seven days in advance.

Dress Code: Nonmetal spikes are preferred.

Tournaments: Tournaments should be booked three months in advance.

Directions: From I-5 in Red Bluff, take Highway 36 to Highway 89. Follow Highway 89 to Crescent Mills (between Greenville and Quincy). The course is on Highway 89 at the Taylorsville junction. From Oroville, take Highway 70 east to Highway 89. Turn left on Highway 89 and drive six miles to the course.

Contact: Highway 89 at Taylorsville "T," Greenville, CA 95947 (P.O. Box 569, Crescent Mills, CA 95934), pro shop 530/284-6204.

9 MOUNT HUFF GOLF COURSE
Architect: Course designed, 1974

9 holes   **Public**   **$10–17**

Lassen and Modoc map, page 48

The course originated as a six-hole layout about 25 years ago and was expanded into nine holes

Chapter 4

SILVERADO COUNTRY CLUB AND RESORT © GEORGE FULLER

Mendocino and Wine Country

Mendocino and Wine Country

Napa, Sonoma, and the Wine Country of California—it seems like the world already knows what a fun region this is to explore.

There are so many enticements for the visitor. Choices in Napa Valley include wine-tasting at some of the world's best and most respected wineries; dining at the region's celebrated restaurants, including French Laundry—often voted the best restaurant in the United States in reader and expert polls; sightseeing; shopping; and playing golf on some very good golf courses. From the mud baths of Calistoga to the shopping malls of Napa, there is always something to do.

But that covers just one part of this diverse region. One should not overlook Bodega Bay, Sea Ranch, Little River, Mendocino, or Fort Bragg, clinging to the Pacific Coast along Highway 1. These scenic coastal towns offer visitors much in the way of ocean vistas, antiquing, craft galleries, dining, and relaxation—and just enough golf courses to keep the golfer coming back for more. It can get chilly here in winter months, so take a sweater for those late afternoon rounds.

Both The Links at Bodega Harbour and Sea Ranch Golf Links— two 18-hole beauties with ocean views—rank among our top public-access courses in California. And the hidden gem Northwood Golf Course, a 1928 Alister Mackenzie design, is nearby in Monte Rio, not too far from Bohemian Grove. Another coastal village worth exploration, although there are no golf courses, is Fort Bragg, one of the cutest little towns in the state, with antique and craft shops in which to wander about all day long.

But really, the best collection of golf courses is found over in the Wine Country. The 36 holes at Silverado Country Club & Resort in Napa have been used for many professional tournaments over the years, and Sonoma Golf Club (technically in the San Francisco Bay Area but very near Napa) currently hosts a popular PGA Champions Tour event.

Four nine-hole facilities are available for play in this area: Meadowood Napa Valley in St. Helena, which is attached to a very luxurious resort of the same name; Tayman Park Golf Course in Healdsburg, a delightful nine-hole design; another hidden gem called Aetna Springs in Pope Valley; and one of the newest designs in the valley, Vintner's Golf Club. All will provide a relaxing day of golf for avid golfers or the whole family.

With its varied topography, and a landscape that stretches from the Pacific Coast to the grape fields of Napa Valley, this region offers golfers what it offers all visitors: very scenic surroundings, excellent off-course activities, the best in dining, shopping, and accommodations, and proximity to San Francisco.

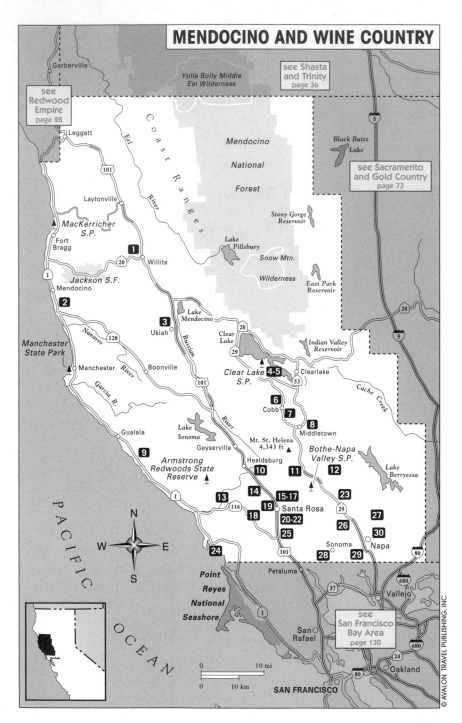

MENDOCINO AND WINE COUNTRY

Garberville

Yolla Bolly Middle
Eel Wilderness

see Shasta
and Trinity
page 36

5

see
Redwood
Empire
page 28

Leggett

Mendocino

National

Forest

Black Butte
Lake

see Sacramento
and Gold Country
page 73

101

Laytonville

Stony Gorge
Reservoir

MacKerricher
S.P.

Fort
Bragg

Lake
Pillsbury

Snow Mtn.

20

1

Willits

Wilderness

East Park
Reservoir

20

1

Jackson S.F.

Mendocino

2

Lake
Mendocino

3

Ukiah

Indian Valley
Reservoir

20

5

Manchester
State Park

128

Clear
Lake

20

29

4-5

Clearlake

Cache Creek

Manchester

Navarro
River

Boonville

Clear Lake
S.P.

53

6

Cobb

7

Gualala

Garcia R.

Lake
Sonoma

River

8

Middletown

Mt. St. Helena
4,343 ft

Bothe-Napa
Valley S.P.

Lake
Berryessa

9

Armstrong
Redwoods State
Reserve

Geyserville

Healdsburg

10

11

12

1

13

14

116

18

19

15-17

Santa Rosa

20-22

25

23

29

26

27

30

N

W   E

S

24

28

Sonoma

29

Napa

80

Point
Reyes
National
Seashore

Petaluma

101

37

Vallejo

680

1

San
Rafael

see
San Francisco
Bay Area
page 130

680

24

P A C I F I C

80

Oakland

O C E A N

0   10 mi

0   10 km

SAN FRANCISCO

© AVALON TRAVEL PUBLISHING, INC.

◼1 BROOKTRAILS GOLF COURSE

Architect: Robert Muir Graves, 1961

9 holes   **Public**   **$11–17**

Mendocino and Wine Country map, page 56

A wonderfully scenic course set in the redwoods, Brooktrails is short but tricky, with a creek winding across seven fairways. The greens are small but quick. An addition of yardage on several holes stretched this course out a couple hundred yards. Now, five holes measure greater than 200 yards. A fun round in a pleasant setting.

Play Policy and Fees: Green fees are $11 for nine holes and $15 for 18 holes weekdays, $12 for nine and $17 for 18 weekends. Senior rates are available. Pull carts are $3.

Tees and Yardage: *Men and Women (18 holes):* yardage 3015, par 56. Rating 57.4, slope 98.

Tee Times: Reservations may be made 14 days in advance.

Dress Code: Appropriate attire is requested.

Tournaments: A 20-player minimum is required to book a tournament.

Directions: Drive north on U.S. 101 through Willits, then take the Sherwood exit northwest 2.5 miles to Brooktrails. Take a left on Brooktrails. Brooktrails meets Birch Street.

Contact: 24860 Birch Street, Willits, CA 95490, pro shop 707/459-6761.

◼2 LITTLE RIVER INN

Architect: Course designed, 1957

9 holes   **Resort**   **$20–35**

Mendocino and Wine Country map, page 56

This favorite of Mendocino County tourists is tight and hilly with lots of sidehill, uphill, and downhill lies. The best hole is the 510-yard, par-5 fourth, a sharp dogleg left. Ocean views, deer, and other wildlife abound. Accommodations at Little River Inn are rustic and offer great ocean views. Many have fireplaces. Try Ole's Famous Swedish hotcakes for breakfast!

Play Policy and Fees: Public play is accepted. Green fees are $20 for nine holes and $30 for 18 holes weekdays, $25 for nine holes and $35 for 18 holes weekends and holidays.

Tees and Yardage: *Men (18 holes):* Back: yardage 5458, par 71, rating 67.8, slope 121; *Women (18 holes):* Front: yardage 5000, par 70, rating 68.6, slope 121.

Tee Times: Reservations may be made one year in advance.

Dress Code: Sleeveless shirts are not allowed. Golf or tennis shoes are required.

Tournaments: Shotgun tournaments are allowed, and the banquet facility holds up to 85 people. Carts are not mandatory.

Directions: The course is on Highway 1 south of Mendocino in the town of Little River.

Contact: 7751 North Highway 1, Little River, CA 95456, pro shop 707/937-5667, fax 707/937-3944, www.littleriverinn.com.

◼3 UKIAH MUNICIPAL GOLF COURSE

Architect: Paul Underwood, 1931

18 holes   **Public**   **$22–26**

Mendocino and Wine Country map, page 56

Ukiah means "deep valley," and this municipal course does nothing to refute that definition. This short course with elevated greens has plenty of hills, oak trees, and other obstacles to keep you entertained, challenged, or frustrated. The first hole is the most picturesque, a par-4 of 275 yards heading straight uphill to an elevated green.

Play Policy and Fees: Green fees are $22 for 18 holes weekdays and $26 for 18 holes weekends. Twilight, senior, and nine-hole rates are available. Carts are $21.

Tees and Yardage: *Men:* Blue: yardage 5850, par 70, rating 68.2, slope 117; White: yardage 5657, par 70, rating 67.5, slope 116; *Women:* Red: yardage 5312, par 70, rating 71.1, slope 117.

Tee Times: Reservations can be made seven days in advance.

Dress Code: Shoes and shirts are required.

Tournaments: A 100-player minimum is required for a shotgun tournament, and 28 carts are required. The banquet facility holds 200 people.

Directions: From U.S. 101 in Ukiah, take the Perkins Street exit west to North State Street. Turn left on Scott Street and follow it two blocks to Walnut Street. Walnut Street turns into Park Boulevard.

Contact: 599 Park Boulevard, Ukiah, CA 95482, pro shop 707/467-2832.

4 BUCKINGHAM GOLF & COUNTRY CLUB

Architect: James Young, 1960

9 holes   Semiprivate $25-29

🚶 📷 🍴 🛏 🗝 🛺 🧹

Mendocino and Wine Country map, page 56

This scenic, challenging course circles a 25-acre lake called Little Borax. Pine and oak trees come into play, and large boulders dot the fairways. The par-5 fourth features a sand trap around an oak tree 50 yards short of the green. It is a layout that requires accuracy.

Play Policy and Fees: This course is available for public play. Weekday green fees for 18 holes are $25 and weekends $29. Nine-hole rates are offered. Power carts are $14/person for 18 holes. Pull carts available.

Tees and Yardage: *Men (18 holes):* Back: yardage 6327, par 72, rating 69.2, slope 121; *Women (18 holes):* Forward: yardage 5662, par 73, rating 71.9, slope 119.

Tee Times: Reservations are usually required and may be booked up to six months in advance.

Dress Code: No tank tops, cutoffs, or gym shorts are allowed. Nonmetal spikes are required.

Tournaments: Outside events are welcome. Three to six months advance notice is preferred. The banquet facility can accommodate up to 200 people.

Directions: From U.S. 101 north of Ukiah, exit on Highway 20 and drive to Highway 29. Bear south on Highway 29 through Lakeport to Highway 281. Turn left (it becomes Soda Bay Road) and proceed six miles to Crystal Drive.

Turn right. Crystal Drive runs into Eastlake Drive.

Contact: 2855 Eastlake Drive, Kelseyville, CA 95451, pro shop 707/279-4863, fax 707/229-2949.

5 CLEAR LAKE RIVIERA YACHT & GOLF CLUB

Architect: Ed DeFelice, 1965

9 holes   Semiprivate $18-30

📷 🍴 🗝 🛺 🧹

Mendocino and Wine Country map, page 56

With different tees to allow for variety on an 18-hole round, this hilly, picturesque course offers views of Clear Lake. It has sidehill lies, big greens, and elevated tees. There is some dramatic elevation change that offers breathtaking panoramic views. There are no adjacent fairways. There is also a six-hole pitch-and-putt course, which is run by volunteers.

Play Policy and Fees: Outside play is accepted. Memberships are available. Green fees are $18 for nine holes and $25 for 18 holes on weekdays, $20 for nine holes and $30 for 18 holes on weekends. Carts included in fee.

Tees and Yardage: *Men (18 holes):* yardage 5608, par 72, rating 67.3, slope 122; *Women (18 holes):* yardage 5132, par 72, rating 69.9, slope 125.

Tee Times: Reservations can be made at any time.

Dress Code: No tank tops or jeans are allowed on the golf course. All spikes accepted.

Tournaments: This course is available for outside tournaments. A 20-player minimum is required to book a tournament. The banquet facility can accommodate up to 80 people.

Directions: From Napa on Highway 29, drive to Lower Lake, turn left, and drive to Soda Bay Road. Turn right and drive to Fairway Drive. From Ukiah, take Highway 20 to Lakeport and Kelseyville. Turn left on Soda Bay Road and travel to Fairway Drive.

Contact: 10200 Fairway Drive, Kelseyville, CA 95451, pro shop 707/277-7129, fax 707/277-9458.

6 ADAMS SPRINGS GOLF COURSE

Architect: Jack Fleming, 1962

9 holes   **Public**   **$10–20**

Mendocino and Wine Country map, page 56

This walkable mountain course has rolling terrain with generous fairways. Three lakes come into play on five holes. The par-3 fourth hole, 181 yards long, has a great view. You'll see lots of wildlife.

Play Policy and Fees: Green fees are $10 for nine holes and $16 for 18 holes weekdays, $14 for nine holes and $20 for 18 holes weekends. Carts additional. Thursday is "Seniors Day," with green fees at $7.

Tees and Yardage: *Men:* yardage 2640, par 34, rating 64.6, slope 111; *Women:* yardage 2499, par 34, rating 69.1, slope 119.

Tee Times: Reservations can be booked 30 days in advance.

Dress Code: No tank tops are allowed on the course.

Tournaments: This course is available for outside tournaments.

Directions: From Highway 29 in Middletown, take Highway 175 west. Drive 11 miles to the course (one mile past Hoberg and one mile south of Loch Lomond). There are signs on the road to direct you.

Contact: 14347 Snead Court, Loch Lomond, CA 95426, pro shop 707/928-9992, fax 707/928-4131.

7 COBB MEADOWS GOLF CLUB

Architect: Norman S. Wren, 1954

9 holes   **Public**   **$10–12**

Mendocino and Wine Country map, page 56

A creek meanders through this pretty mountain course, formerly Hoberg's Forest Lake Golf Club, located 3600 feet above sea level. There are bunkers on every hole, and many pine trees come into play. This course is open for play year-round, weather permitting. There

are six par-4s and three par-3s. The pride of the course is the 398-yard, par-4 eighth.

Play Policy and Fees: Green fees are $10 weekdays and $12 weekends. Yearly passes are available.

Tees and Yardage: *Men (18 holes):* yardage 4581, par 66, rating 61.8, slope 109; *Women (18 holes):* yardage 4581, par 69, rating 64.7, slope 114.

Tee Times: Reservations can be booked seven days in advance.

Dress Code: Nonmetal spikes are required in summer.

Tournaments: This course is available for outside tournaments. Tournaments should be booked six months in advance.

Directions: Drive north on Highway 29 to Highway 175. Take Highway 175 north to the town of Cobb. The course is at Highway 175 and Golf Road.

Contact: 10200 Golf Road (P.O. Box 350), Cobb, CA 95426, pro shop 707/928-5276.

8 HIDDEN VALLEY LAKE GOLF & COUNTRY CLUB

Architect: William F. Bell, 1970

18 holes   **Semiprivate**   **$40–50**

Mendocino and Wine Country map, page 56

This sprawling course is scenic and hilly. The front nine is long and flat. The back nine is shorter with elevated tees. Water comes into play on 10 holes, mostly during the winter months. The most dramatic hole is the 389-yard, par-4 15th. The tee is 200 feet above the fairway. It's a spectacular shot, with Sutter Home vineyards on the left and Mount St. Helena in the background. It looks like you have to hit it a country mile, but you don't. Try aiming for the swimming pool and you're safe.

Play Policy and Fees: Green fees are $40 Monday–Friday, $50 weekends and holidays. Senior, twilight, nine-hole, and resident rates are available. Carts are included in the fees.

Tees and Yardage: *Men:* Blue: yardage 6700, par 72, rating 73.0, slope 128; White: yardage

6200, rating 70.9, slope 125; *Women:* Red: yardage 5300, par 74, rating 70.6, slope 124.
Tee Times: Reservations can be booked seven days in advance.
Dress Code: Shirts with collars must be worn. Nonmetal spikes are required.
Tournaments: Tournaments are accepted. Carts are required. The banquet facility holds 100 people.
Directions: From Middletown, drive five miles north on Highway 29. The course is on the right.
Contact: 19210 Hartman Road, Middletown, CA 95461, pro shop 707/987-3035, fax 707/987-4903.

9 THE SEA RANCH GOLF LINKS

Architect: Robert Muir Graves, 1973;
course redesigned, 1996

18 holes   **Public**   **$50–70**

🏌️ 📷 🍴 🛍️ 🛒 🏧 🚡

BEST One of the top courses in the state, Sea Ranch Golf Links is a seaside Scottish-style design. Although the layout is not long in distance, the prevailing northwest winds add a significant challenge to golfers. There is a view of the ocean from every hole. To score well here, you not only have to hit the ball well, but you also need to be creative. A premium is placed on shot-making.

The Sea Ranch Lodge (707/785-2371) and Sea Ranch Escapes (888/SEA-RANCH) both offer play-and-stay packages. Call for details.
Play Policy and Fees: Green fees Monday–Friday are $50. Green fees for Saturday, Sunday, and holidays are $70. Carts are $12.50 per person every day. Twilight and nine-hole rates are available, as are 10-play cards.
Tees and Yardage: *Men:* Black: yardage 6604, par 72, rating 70.3, slope 134; Blue: yardage 6217, par 72, rating 70.9, slope 125; White: yardage 5423, par 72, rating 67.1, slope 118; *Women:* Red: yardage 4802, par 72, rating 70.2, slope 120.
Tee Times: Reservations can be booked up to one month in advance.

Dress Code: Appropriate golf attire is required.
Tournaments: A 16-player minimum is needed to book a tournament. Tournaments should be booked three months in advance.
Directions: From the south, drive 40 miles northwest from Jenner on Highway 1 to the course, located in the Sea Ranch development. From the north, the course is one mile south of Gualala.
Contact: 42000 Highway 1 (P.O. Box 10), Sea Ranch, CA 95497, pro shop 707/785-2468, fax 707/785-3042, www.searanchvillage.com.

10 TAYMAN PARK GOLF COURSE

Architect: W. H. Tayman, 1922;
Ron Fream/Golf Plan 2004

9 holes   **Public**   **$12–15**

🏌️ 📷 🍴 🛍️ 🏧 🚡

This hilly, tree-lined course on top of a mountain in the middle of wine country has been undergoing some big changes in a slow fashion. Roughly 30 percent of the holes were redesigned in 2004, the balance in 2005. Because of the methodical nature of the changes, no interruption in play will occur. When finished, this picturesque, historic layout will be a very exciting addition to the public golf offerings in the area, with some of the best views anywhere. A new, all-weather driving range was added in 2002. Note: Because of the remodeling, yardage and ratings will be changing from what is listed below.
Play Policy and Fees: Green fees are $12 for nine holes weekdays, $15 for nine holes weekends and holidays. Replays are an additional $6. Carts are additional. Twilight, senior, and junior rates are offered.
Tees and Yardage: *Men (18 holes):* Back: yardage 5090, par 70, rating 63.8, slope 109; Middle: yardage 4850, par 70, rating 63.8, slope 109; *Women:* Forward: yardage 4474, par 70, rating 67.7, slope 117.
Tee Times: Reservations can be booked seven days in advance.

Dress Code: Soft spikes required.

Tournaments: A 16-player minimum is needed to book a tournament. Carts are required. The banquet facility can accommodate 75 people.

Directions: Driving north on U.S. 101 into Healdsburg, take the Central Healdsburg exit onto Healdsburg Avenue. Drive on Healdsburg Avenue through two lights before turning right on Matheson Street (Matheson turns into Fitch Mountain Road). The course is on the left.

Contact: 927 South Fitch Mountain Road, Healdsburg, CA 95448, pro shop 707/433-4275, fax 707/433-7846, www.taymanparkgolf.com.

11 MOUNT SAINT HELENA GOLF COURSE

Architect: Jack Fleming, 1952

9 holes   **Public**   **$18–24**

Mendocino and Wine Country map, page 56

This course is in the middle of the Napa County Fairgrounds. It's short and flat, with narrow fairways. Accuracy is important. There are no par-5s from the white tees, two from the forward. Water comes into play on two holes. A new pro shop was completed in 2003.

Play Policy and Fees: Green fees are $18 on weekdays and $24 on weekends. Twilight, junior, and senior rates are available. The course is closed during the Napa County Fair over the Fourth of July weekend.

Tees and Yardage: *Men (18 holes):* White: yardage 5518, par 68, rating 66.4, slope 102; *Women:* Red: yardage 5300, par 70, rating 68.1, slope 111.

Tee Times: Reservations are not accepted. All play is on a first-come, first-served basis.

Dress Code: Shirts must be worn at all times. No short shorts are allowed. Soft spikes only.

Tournaments: A 60-player minimum is needed to book a tournament. Events should be scheduled four months in advance.

Directions: Driving north into Calistoga off Highway 29, turn left on Stephenson Street and take it to Grant Street. Turn left and fol-

low the road to the course at the fairgrounds on the left.

Contact: 2025 Grant Street (P.O. Box 344), Calistoga, CA 94515, pro shop 707/942-9966, fax 707/942-5125.

12 AETNA SPRINGS GOLF COURSE

Architect: E. F. Mutton, 1891

9 holes   **Public**   **$16–22**

Mendocino and Wine Country map, page 56

Built in 1891 as part of the Aetna Springs Resort, this is one of the oldest courses in California. It is nestled in the mountains, with gentle hills and two creeks running through it. Excellent drainage makes it a great course for winter play. Quiet and peaceful, the course is marked by towering oak trees, meandering creeks, and excellent greens. Bring the family—picnic tables border the course. There is also a barbecue area. Walk the resort grounds and relive Napa history. The course will cater for small groups.

Play Policy and Fees: Green fees are $16 weekdays and $22 weekends for 18 holes. For nine holes, fees are $10 weekdays and $16 weekends. Senior, student, and twilight rates are available. Carts are $10 for nine holes and $18 for 18 holes.

Tees and Yardage: *Men (18 holes):* White: yardage 5381, par 70, rating 66.4, slope 115; *Women (18 holes):* Red: yardage 4856, par 70, rating 68.0, slope 107.

Tee Times: Reservations are not necessary but can be booked 30 days in advance.

Dress Code: Nonmetal spikes are required.

Tournaments: A 32-player minimum is needed to book an event, and tournaments should be scheduled 4–6 months in advance. A banquet facility is available that holds up to 100 people.

Directions: From Napa on Highway 29 heading north toward Calistoga, drive one mile past Saint Helena. Turn right on Deer Park Road. Stay on this road and drive through Angwin. The road turns into Howell Mountain Road.

Once in Pope Valley, veer to the left where the road branches at the service station. Drive four miles to Aetna Springs Road (just past Hub Cap Ranch). Turn onto Aetna Springs Road and drive one mile to the course.

Contact: 1600 Aetna Springs Road, Pope Valley, CA 94567, pro shop 707/965-2115, www.aetnasprings.com.

13 NORTHWOOD GOLF COURSE

Architect: Alister Mackenzie, 1928

9 holes   **Public**   **$15–32**

Mendocino and Wine Country map, page 56

This course is situated in the Russian River resort area near the Bohemian Grove. The huge redwoods and firs give Northwood a quiet, peaceful feeling even before you tee off. After you tee off, the huge redwoods and firs can become quite disturbing for the golfer who can't hit it straight. As if that weren't enough, the greens are small and guarded by mounds and a few bunkers. The tee shot on the third hole, a par-3 of 145 yards, must navigate a narrow gap between tall, overhanging redwood branches. If you successfully make the green, a birdie is possible. The course condition has improved dramatically over the last few years, and playing a round here is a must for golfers with a sense of history—it is, after all, an Alister Mackenzie design.

Golf packages are available at nearby Rio Villa or the Applewood Inn.

Play Policy and Fees: Weekday green fees are $15 for nine holes and $22 for 18 holes. Weekend rates are $22 for nine holes and $32 for 18 holes. Carts are $5 per nine holes. Twilight, junior, senior, and yearly rates are available.

Tees and Yardage: *Men:* White: yardage 2858, par 36, rating n/a, slope n/a; *Women:* Front: yardage 2780, par 36, rating n/a, slope n/a.

Tee Times: Reservations are accepted two weeks in advance.

Dress Code: Appropriate golf attire is required, and nonmetal spikes are preferred.

Tournaments: This course is available for outside tournaments of at least 16 players. Events should be booked a year in advance.

Directions: From Guerneville, drive three miles west on Highway 116. The course is on the left.

Contact: 19400 Highway 116 (P.O. Box 930), Monte Rio, CA 95462, pro shop 707/865-1116, fax 707/865-1290, www.northwoodgolf.com.

14 WINDSOR GOLF CLUB

Architect: Golf Plan, Fred Bliss, 1989

18 holes   **Public**   **$32–51**

Mendocino and Wine Country map, page 56

This course boasts a winding creek, four lakes, and many mature oaks. The pride of the course is the par-3 13th, a 194-yarder to a rock-banked green. The par-4 second at 432 yards and the 217-yard par-3 seventh were among the toughest holes on the Nike Tour from 1990 to 1995. The course is driver-friendly, but don't miss the small greens if you want to score well. A nice practice area is next to the clubhouse.

Play Policy and Fees: Green fees are $32 Monday–Thursday, $38 Friday, and $51 on weekends. Carts cost $12 per rider. Twilight, senior, and junior rates are available.

Tees and Yardage: *Men:* Tournament: yardage 6650, par 72, rating 71.7, slope 127; Championship: yardage 6169, par 72, rating 69.4, slope 122; Regular: yardage 5628, par 72, rating 66.6, slope 122; *Women:* Forward: yardage 5116, par 72, rating 69.3, slope 125.

Tee Times: Reservations can be booked seven days in advance.

Dress Code: Nonmetal spikes are required.

Tournaments: A 12-player minimum is needed for tournament play. Carts are required. Events should be booked 24 months in advance. The banquet facility can accommodate 300 people.

Directions: From U.S. 101 in Santa Rosa, take the Shiloh Road exit. Drive one-half mile west of the freeway. Turn right on Golf Course Drive and left on 19th Hole Drive.

Contact: 1340 19th Hole Drive, Windsor, CA 95492, pro shop 707/838-7888, fax 707/838-7940, www.windsorgolf.com.

15 MAYACAMA

Architect: Jack Nicklaus, 2001
18 holes   **Private**

Mendocino and Wine Country map, page 56

Opened in 2001, this ultra-private Jack Nicklaus signature course is set on 675 acres of rolling hillsides, majestic live oaks, and sweeping meadows of native grasses. This is a gem of a course, and not easy, as the slope rating of 150 from the back indicates.

Play Policy and Fees: Members and guests only. No reciprocal play is accepted.

Tees and Yardage: *Men:* Back: yardage 6787, par 72, rating 74.3, slope 150; Middle: yardage 6159, par 72, rating 71.3, slope 144; *Women:* Forward: yardage 4795, par 72, rating 70.0, slope 120.

Tee Times: Not applicable.

Dress Code: Traditional golf attire is requested. Soft spikes only.

Tournaments: Outside events cannot be booked at this course.

Directions: From Highway 101 north of San Francisco, take the Shiloah Road exit and turn west toward the course.

Contact: 500 Shiloah Road, Santa Rosa, CA 95403, pro shop 707/543-8040, fax 707/543-8094, www.mayacama.com.

16 WIKIUP GOLF COURSE

Architect: Clark Glasson, 1963
9 holes   **Public**   **$11–21**

Mendocino and Wine Country map, page 56

This is a challenging, short course with no adjacent holes. It is scenic and well bunkered, with two par-4s. The short 264-yard, par-4 second hole is a temptation. It makes players choose between laying up or carrying a water hazard. The gentle slopes make the course easily walkable. Power carts are available for seniors over 60 only. Two sets of tees on each hole make for some variation on a replay.

Play Policy and Fees: Green fees are $11 for nine holes and $16 for 18 holes on weekdays,

$14 for nine holes and $21 for 18 holes on weekends. Junior and senior rates are available.

Tees and Yardage: *Men and Women (18 holes):* yardage 3223, par 58 (men)/59 (women), rating 57.7, slope 91.

Tee Times: Reservations are not accepted. All play is on a first-come, first-served basis.

Dress Code: Shirts are required.

Tournaments: This course is available for outside tournaments.

Directions: From Santa Rosa, drive four miles north on U.S. 101 to River Road. Turn east on River Road. Turn north on Old Redwood Highway and drive one-half mile. Turn east on Wikiup Drive and turn right on Carriage Lane.

Contact: 5001 Carriage Lane, Santa Rosa, CA 95403, pro shop 707/546-8787.

17 FOUNTAINGROVE GOLF & ATHLETIC CLUB

Architect: Ted Robinson Sr., 1998
18 holes   **Private**   **$75–95**

Mendocino and Wine Country map, page 56

"Demanding off the tee" is an understatement. This is a tight, hilly layout with lots of trees and excellent greens. The picturesque 17th hole is a par-3 that requires a 215-yard shot downhill over water. The very pretty course is in north Santa Rosa. This club has gone fully private.

Play Policy and Fees: Reciprocal play is accepted at a rate of $75 weekdays and $95 weekends. Carts and range balls are included.

Tees and Yardage: *Men:* Black: yardage 6940, par 72, rating 73.5, slope 137; Green: yardage 6439, par 72, rating 71.5, slope 132; White: yardage 5951, par 72, rating 69.1, slope 128; *Women:* Gold: yardage 5419, par 73, rating 71.8, slope 127.

Tee Times: Reservations may be booked 48 hours in advance.

Dress Code: Collared shirts and nonmetal spikes are required. No denim is allowed.

Tournaments: This course is available for outside tournaments on weekdays, and also on weekends after 1 P.M. The banquet facility can accommodate up to 250 people.

Directions: In Santa Rosa on U.S. 101, take the Mendocino Avenue/Old Redwood Highway exit. Drive east and turn left on Fountaingrove Parkway. Continue up the hill to the course, which is on the left.

Contact: 1525 Fountaingrove Parkway, Santa Rosa, CA 95403, pro shop 707/579-4653, fax 707/544-3109, www.fountaingrovegolf.com.

18 SEBASTOPOL GOLF COURSE

Architect: Course designed, 1958
9 holes　　　**Public**　　　**$12-14**

Mendocino and Wine Country map, page 56
This short course is all par-3s and par-4s. The most notable is the par-3 second hole, which requires an uphill shot to a two-tiered green. Water comes into play on the 195-yard, par-4 eighth hole.

Play Policy and Fees: Green fees are $12 for nine holes and $5 for each replay weekdays, $14 for nine holes and $6 for each replay on weekends. Senior and junior rates on weekdays only. Carts are $10 for nine holes and $15 for 18 holes.

Tees and Yardage: *Men:* yardage 2992, par 62, rating 57.8, slope 84; *Women:* yardage 2992, par 66, rating 57.8, slope 84.

Tee Times: Reservations are not accepted. All play is on a first-come, first-served basis.

Dress Code: Soft spikes only.

Tournaments: A 54-player minimum is needed to book a private event.

Directions: From Sebastopol, drive three miles north on Highway 116 to Scotts Right-of-Way. Turn right and drive to the course.

Contact: 2881 Scotts Right-of-Way, Sebastopol, CA 95472, pro shop 707/823-9852.

19 SANTA ROSA GOLF & COUNTRY CLUB

Architect: Ben Harmon, 1958
18 holes　　　**Private**　　　**$128-138**

Mendocino and Wine Country map, page 56
This sprawling course is lined with beautiful oak trees and is tougher than it looks. Out-of-bounds areas come into play on six holes, so accurate tee shots are essential for good play. On the par-4 eighth, the tee shot must carry over a lake, and an oak tree comes into play on the approach. The course has small greens and many false fronts, so good touch is essential. The 17th hole includes a lake guarding the left front portion of the green.

Play Policy and Fees: Reciprocal play is accepted with members of other private clubs; otherwise, members and guests only. Reciprocal green fees are $128 on weekdays and $138 on weekends.

Tees and Yardage: *Men:* Black: yardage 6688, par 72, rating 71.8, slope 124; Silver: yardage 6301, par 72, rating 70.0, slope 121; Gold: yardage 5152, par 72, rating n/a, slope n/a; *Women:* Green: yardage 5806, par 73, rating 72.1, slope 122.

Tee Times: Can be made seven days in advance.

Dress Code: Shirts must have a collar, and shorts must have a six-inch inseam. No blue jeans, halter tops, or tank tops may be worn. Nonmetal spikes are required.

Tournaments: Only six outside events are allowed here each year.

Directions: From U.S. 101, take Highway 12 west toward Sebastopol. Turn right on Fulton Road and left on Hall Road. Turn left on Country Club Road and drive to the parking lot.

Contact: 5110 Oak Meadow Drive, Santa Rosa, CA 95401, pro shop 707/546-6617, fax 707/546-9525, www.santarosagolf.com.

20 SONOMA COUNTY FAIR-GROUNDS GOLF CENTER

Architect: Redesign, 2005
9 holes **Public**

🏌 📷 🍺 🛍 🛺 🍽

Mendocino and Wine Country map, page 56

Situated in the center of the Santa Rosa Fairgrounds racetrack, at press time this course was being remodeled due to a surface change on the racetrack. Among other changes, it is being shortened somewhat. It is due to reopen sometime in 2005. Please call ahead.

Play Policy and Fees: Not available at press time.

Tees and Yardage: Not available at press time.

Tee Times: Not available at press time.

Dress Code: No metal spikes are allowed on the course.

Tournaments: Not available at press time.

Directions: In Santa Rosa on U.S. 101 north, take the Highway 12 exit east, then take the first off-ramp (the Downtown exit), which leads straight to the fairgrounds and the course on the right.

Contact: 1350 Bennett Valley Road, Santa Rosa, CA 95405, information 707/545-4200, ext. 208, www.sonomacountyfair.com.

21 BENNETT VALLEY GOLF COURSE

Architect: Ben Harmon, 1969
18 holes **Public** **$22–30**

🏌 📷 🍺 🛍 🛺 🍽

Mendocino and Wine Country map, page 56

This is a level, well-conditioned course with lots of trees. The greens are fast and the course is walkable. A creek wanders through the course, providing some water hazard encounters. In the summer the course averages 350–400 players a day. The 433-yard 17th hole is the toughest on the course. Overall, this course is a good test for all golfers.

Play Policy and Fees: Green fees are $22 weekdays and $30 weekends for nonresidents. Senior, junior, and resident rates are available. Carts are $24 for 18 holes.

Tees and Yardage: *Men:* Blue: yardage 6548, par 72, rating 71.0, slope 121; White: yardage 6207, par 72, rating 69.4, slope 118; *Women:* Red: yardage 5788, par 75, rating 71.7, slope 121.

Tee Times: Reservations are issued eight days in advance for Sunday tee times and a week in advance for all other days.

Dress Code: All spikes accepted.

Tournaments: Please inquire.

Directions: In Santa Rosa, take Highway 12 east toward Sonoma/Napa. At the first stoplight (Farmers Lane), take a right. Farmers Lane dead-ends at Bennett Valley Road. Turn left at the stoplight. Bennett Valley Road leads to the course.

Contact: 3330 Yulupa Avenue, Santa Rosa, CA 95405, pro shop 707/528-3673.

22 OAKMONT GOLF COURSE

Architect: Ted Robinson Sr., 1963
36 holes **Semiprivate** **$20–50**

🏌 📷 🍺 🛍 🛺 🍽

Mendocino and Wine Country map, page 56

The West Course is the championship course here, with lots of trees. The nines were reversed and a new clubhouse was built in 2000. There is water on 14 holes. The pride of the West Course is the 399-yard, par-4 17th hole, which boasts two lakes and out-of-bounds on both sides. The East Course is a challenging executive course with some tough par-3s. The 171-yard, par-3 14th hole, for example, requires a longish carry over a creek to a green surrounded by trees. It has its own small clubhouse. Both courses are busy and in excellent shape.

Play Policy and Fees: Public play is accepted. West Course green fees are $32 Monday–Thursday, $37 Friday, and $50 on weekends. East Course green fees are $20 on weekdays and $22 on weekends. Twilight rates are available. Memberships are available.

Tees and Yardage: West Course—*Men:* Blue: yardage 6377, par 72, rating 70.8, slope 128; White: yardage 6059, par 72, rating 69.5, slope 124; *Women:* Red: yardage 5573, par 72, rating 71.8, slope 125. East Course—*Men:* yardage

4293, par 63, rating 61.2, slope 100; *Women:* yardage 4067, par 63, rating 62.8, slope 102.

Tee Times: Reservations are recommended and may be booked one week in advance.

Dress Code: Shirts must have collars. No tank tops may be worn. Soft spikes are recommended.

Tournaments: Tournaments welcome.

Directions: From Santa Rosa, take Highway 12 east toward Sonoma. Turn right on Oakmont Drive into the community of Oakmont. The course is on the right, eight miles east of U.S. 101.

Contact: 7025 Oakmont Drive, Santa Rosa, CA 95409, pro shop 707/539-0415, fax 707/539-0453.

23 MEADOWOOD NAPA VALLEY

Architect: Jack Fleming, 1964

9 holes   Private/Resort $45

Mendocino and Wine Country map, page 56

 This is a short, tight, and tricky course with lots of trees bordering fairways. There are some hills and undulating greens. It's an excellent course for beginners and intermediates. The 334-yard third hole is a par-4 that doglegs to the right. Although Meadowood is short, the setting with the beautiful resort nearby is pretty and peaceful. A world-class croquet pitch is next to the golf course.

Play Policy and Fees: Reciprocal play is accepted with members of other private clubs. Hotel guests are welcome. Green fees are $45.

Tees and Yardage: *Men (18 holes):* Back: yardage 3858, par 62, rating 60.2, slope 106; *Women (18 holes):* Forward: yardage 3714, par 62, rating 60.5, slope 93.

Tee Times: Guests can make tee times up to six months in advance.

Dress Code: Shirts with collars must be worn. No jeans are allowed on the course.

Tournaments: No outside tournaments.

Directions: From Napa, drive north on Highway 29. Turn right on Pope Street and take Pope Street to Silverado Trail. Take a left on Silverado Trail, then make a quick right onto Howell Mountain Road. Follow Howell Mountain Road to Meadowood Lane and the course.

Contact: 900 Meadowood Lane, Saint Helena, CA 94574, pro shop 707/963-3646, fax 707/963-3532, www.meadowood.com.

24 THE LINKS AT BODEGA HARBOUR

Architect: Robert Trent Jones Jr., 1977

18 holes   Resort $45–75

Mendocino and Wine Country map, page 56

 The Links at Bodega Harbour (formerly Bodega Harbour Golf Links) is two courses in one. On the front side, you will play a hilly, links-style course with few level lies and narrow fairways. On the back side (the original nine), you will play a meadow course that is slightly more open off the tee. Although completely different designs, the two nines have several things in common: They are well maintained, with fast tricky greens and beautiful ocean views. A steady ocean breeze is common, and when it blows this challenging course can be downright difficult. We can't guarantee even the best golfers a good score, but we can promise that the three finishing holes will give you something to talk about on your ride home.

Play Policy and Fees: Outside play is accepted. Green fees are $45 Monday–Thursday and $55 Friday. Weekend and holiday green fees are $75. Carts additional. Twilight rates are available.

Tees and Yardage: *Men:* Blue: yardage 6253, par 70, rating 71.4, slope 127; White: yardage 5711, par 70, rating 68.9, slope 121; *Women:* Gold: yardage 5075, par 69, rating 71.8, slope 126; Red: yardage 4751, par 69, rating 69.7, slope 120.

Tee Times: Reservations may be booked up to 90 days in advance. Changes must be made at least 24 hours in advance.

Dress Code: Proper golf attire is required, including collared shirts for men. Metal spikes are permitted.

Tournaments: Outside events may be scheduled up to two years in advance. The banquet facility can accommodate up to 150 people.

Directions: From Bodega Bay, drive south on Highway 1. Take the South Harbour Way exit to the right and travel 150 yards to Heron Drive. Turn right on Heron Drive and drive one-half mile to the course.

Contact: 21301 Heron Drive (P.O. Box 368), Bodega Bay, CA 94923, pro shop 707/875-3538, fax 707/875-3256, www.bodegaharborgolf.com.

25 FOXTAIL GOLF CLUB

Architect: Bob Baldock, 1963; Gary Roger Baird, 1978
36 holes   **Public**   **$28–48**

🏃 📷 🍴 ⛏ 🛺 ☕

Mendocino and Wine Country map, page 56

Formerly called Mountain Shadows Golf Course, these 36 holes are quite tight, with rolling terrain and large, undulating greens. Notable is the seventh hole on the North Course. It's long, and every shot is tough to negotiate. Off the tee you face out-of-bounds to the left and a lake running down the entire right side. If you hit it down the middle, you're faced with a green that sits on a well-bunkered peninsula. The South Course is a bit shorter, but still a very solid test of your game. Renovation of the South Course, including irrigation and drainage, was completed in 2002. Renovation of the North Course, improving tees, greens, bunkers, and cart paths, was completed in 2003.

Play Policy and Fees: The green fees are $32 Monday–Friday and $48 on weekends and holidays on the North Course. South Course fees are $28 Monday–Friday and $36 weekends and holidays. Twilight and other special rates are available.

Tees and Yardage: North Course—*Men:* Black: yardage 6851, par 72, rating 73.0, slope 126; Blue: yardage 6394, par 72, rating 70.3, slope 121; White: yardage 5846, par 72, rating 67.9, slope 115; *Women:* Gold: yardage 5261, par 72, rating 69.7, slope 114. South Course—*Men:* Gold: yardage 6492, par 71, rating 71.0, slope 124; Blue: yardage

6224, par 71, rating 69.8, slope 121; White: yardage 5830, par 71, rating 67.7, slope 120; *Women:* Red: yardage 5343, par 71, rating 70.7, slope 120.

Tee Times: Reservations can be booked 14 days in advance.

Dress Code: Soft spikes required.

Tournaments: Tournaments welcome. The banquet facility can accommodate 250 people.

Directions: From Santa Rosa, drive seven miles south on U.S. 101. Take the Wilfred exit east to Golf Course Drive.

Contact: 100 Golf Course Drive, Rohnert Park, CA 94928, pro shop 707/584-7766, fax 707/584-8469, www.playfoxtail.com.

26 VINTNER'S GOLF CLUB

Architect: Casey O'Callaghan, 1999
9 holes   **Public**   **$18–38**

🏃 📷 🍴 ⛏ 🛺 ☕

Mendocino and Wine Country map, page 56

Vintner's is an upscale nine-hole course and practice center. Next to the Domaine Chandon Winery in Yountville, it's a perfect place to play for golfers who need a fix while touring the wine country. For the serious golfer the course is challenging enough to have fun, while for the recreational golfer the course is fun but not overly demanding. The course offers spacious greens and holes ranging 85–501 yards. The driving range is covered. Mats and grass areas available.

Play Policy and Fees: Green fees for nine holes are $18 Monday–Thursday, $28 Friday–Sunday and holidays. Green fees for 18 holes are $24 Monday–Thursday, $38 Friday–Sunday and holidays. Junior, Napa County resident, and senior rates are available. Carts are additional.

Tees and Yardage: *Men (18 holes):* Black: yardage 5638, par 68, rating 66.3, slope 121; White: yardage 5035, par 68, rating 65.0, slope 118; *Women:* Gold: yardage 4292, par 68, rating 64.8, slope 108.

Tee Times: Reservations can be made 14 days in advance. If possible let the pro shop know whether you plan to play nine or 18.

Dress Code: Appropriate golf attire is required. Metal spikes are not allowed.

Tournaments: Tournaments accepted; please inquire.

Directions: From Highway 29 in Napa, head north toward St. Helena. Take the Yountville exit, head west, and make a left on Solano Avenue to the clubhouse.

Contact: 7901 Solano Avenue, Yountville, CA 94599, pro shop 707/944-1992, fax 707/944-1993, www.vintnersgolfclub.com.

27 SILVERADO COUNTRY CLUB & RESORT

Architect: Robert Trent Jones, 1953
36 holes   Private/Resort $70–175

Mendocino and Wine Country map, page 56

 Water and oak trees are everywhere in this serene setting. Although the North Course is longer, the South Course requires more finesse shots. Both are big, sprawling layouts with large, undulating greens. The back nine on the North Course sports demanding par-4s. The South Course is not as long, but it's equally challenging. There are three par-5s on the back nine—holes 11, 13, and 18—and two are guarded by water. Redesigned by Robert Trent Jones Jr., the South Course is the former site of the Senior PGA Tour's Transamerica Open. A new clubhouse is on the drawing boards for spring 2005.

The Silverado Resort is one of the finest golf resorts in Northern California. The resort now offers a full-service spa, salon, and fitness facility. Call 707/257-0200 for information and reservations.

Play Policy and Fees: Reciprocal play with other private clubs is accepted. Hotel guests are welcome. Green fees are seasonal, $155 March 16–November 30 on both courses, $175 for reciprocal players. Green fees December 1–March 15 are $70 Monday–Thursday, $85 Friday, weekends, and holidays. Carts are mandatory and included in the green fees.

Tees and Yardage: North Course—*Men:* Blue: yardage 6900, par 72, rating 73.1, slope 134; White: yardage 6347, par 72, rating 69.9, slope 130; *Women:* Red: yardage 5857, par 72, rating 73.3, slope 128. South Course—*Men:* Blue: yardage 6685, par 72, rating 72.1, slope 131; White: yardage 6247, par 72, rating 70.1, slope 126; *Women:* Red: yardage 5642, par 72, rating 72.7, slope 127.

Tee Times: Tee times can be made up to one year in advance for resort guests, 60 days for reciprocators.

Dress Code: Appropriate golf attire is required, including collared shirts. No denim is allowed.

Tournaments: Shotgun tournaments are available Monday, Wednesday, and Friday, and carts are required. The banquet facility holds up to 250 people.

Directions: From Highway 29 in Napa, take a right on Trancas Street. Take a left on Atlas Peak and drive less than a mile to the course.

Contact: 1600 Atlas Peak Road, Napa, CA 94558, pro shop 707/257-5460, fax 707/226-6829, www.silveradoresort.com.

28 LOS ARROYOS GOLF CLUB

Architect: Course designed, 1968
9 holes   Public $12–14

Mendocino and Wine Country map, page 56

This narrow, tree-lined executive course is level, and ideal for sharpening iron play. A creek winds through the layout, adding some fun to some shots. A second set of tees to differentiate a second round was added in 2004. Los Arroyos also features a nine-hole course for chipping and putting. Some of the best Sonoma Valley wineries are within minutes of Los Arroyos.

Play Policy and Fees: Green fees for nine holes are $12 weekdays and $14 weekends. Replay, senior, and junior rates are available. No power carts. Pull carts are $2.

Tees and Yardage: *Men and Women (18 holes):* yardage 1725, par 60, rating n/a, slope n/a.

Tee Times: All play is on a first-come, first-served basis.

Dress Code: Appropriate attire and soft spikes are required.

Tournaments: Small tournaments (up to 20 players) are allowed.

Directions: From San Francisco heading north on U.S. 101, take the Highway 116 exit east to Sonoma. The course is at the intersection of Highway 116 and Highway 121.

Contact: 5000 Stage Gulch Road, Sonoma, CA 95476, pro shop 707/938-8835.

29 NAPA GOLF COURSE

Architect: Jack Fleming, 1967

18 holes   Public $21–41

Mendocino and Wine Country map, page 56

This underrated course is long, tough, and tight. It has many trees, and water comes into play on 14 holes. Nicknamed Kennedy Park because it is in Napa's John F. Kennedy Park, this course was used for U.S. Open qualifying in 1972 and for several PGA Tour events at the Silverado Country Club.

Play Policy and Fees: Green fees for nonresidents are $31 weekdays and $41 weekends and holidays. Resident green fees are $21 weekdays and $28 weekends and holidays. Twilight and senior rates are available.

Tees and Yardage: *Men:* Black: yardage 6704, par 72, rating 72.7, slope 131; Blue: yardage 6478, par 72, rating 71.8, slope 130; White: yardage 6266, par 72, rating 70.8, slope 128; *Women:* Gold: yardage 5690, par 73, rating 72.8, slope 126.

Tee Times: Reservations are recommended seven days in advance.

Dress Code: Soft spikes recommended.

Tournaments: A 16-player minimum is needed to book a tournament. A banquet facility can accommodate 130 people.

Directions: From Highway 12 in Napa, take Highway 29 north. Take the Lake Berryessa exit at the fork. Drive two miles to Streblow Drive and turn left to get to the course.

Contact: 2295 Streblow Drive, Napa, CA 94558, pro shop 707/255-4333, fax 707/255-4009, www.playnapa.com.

30 NAPA VALLEY COUNTRY CLUB

Architect: Course designed, 1914 (front); Ron Fream, 1990

18 holes   Private $125

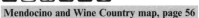

Mendocino and Wine Country map, page 56

This scenic course has tight fairways and small, undulating greens. There are many oak trees. The course was expanded in 1990 to 18 holes, and additional work was completed in 2004, including a new clubhouse and a lengthened first hole. Many holes offer views of the Bay Area and Napa Valley. From the 11th tee, the Golden Gate Bridge is visible. When you're not looking at the view, check out this par-3; it's 140 yards to an island green. If you miss the green, you're not in water, but in a mean barranca. The course has small greens on the front and bigger greens on the back. It's a member's course, where local knowledge prevails over talent.

Play Policy and Fees: Reciprocal play is accepted with members of other private clubs. Green fees for reciprocators are $125, including cart.

Tees and Yardage: *Men:* Blue: yardage 6169, par 72, rating 70.4, slope 131; White: yardage 5711, par 72, rating 68.5, slope 124; *Women:* Red: yardage 5319, par 72, rating 70.8, slope 123.

Tee Times: Can be made seven days in advance.

Dress Code: Collared shirts are required. No denim, tank tops, or short shorts are allowed. Soft spikes only.

Tournaments: Outside events must receive board approval and are usually limited to Monday. A 72-player minimum is needed to book a tournament. Events can be booked 2–4 months in advance. The banquet facility can accommodate 130 people.

Directions: From Highway 121 in Napa, drive 1.5 miles on Hagen Road to the course.

Contact: 3385 Hagen Road, Napa, CA 94558, pro shop 707/252-1114, fax 707/252-1188, www.napavalleycc.com.

Chapter 5

DARKHORSE GOLF CLUB © GEORGE FULLER

Sacramento and
Gold Country

Sacramento and Gold Country

The state capital anchors this fast-growing region, but there are many smaller towns in the area with lots to do and some very good golf courses to play. The Sacramento and Gold Country area extends from Plumas National Forest in the north to the fertile fields of the Central Valley in the south, and from the Sierra foothills in the east to the easternmost San Francisco Bay communities in the west. With so great a reach of geography and history, it is no surprise that visitors find activities of almost every kind—from exploring historic gold mines to strolling quaint downtown Chico—not the least of which is golf.

Even Sacramento, which, like all major California cities, has too little land to develop new courses, boasts the Alister Mackenzie Course at Haggin Oaks. Built in 1932, this tree-lined classic underwent extensive remodeling in 2002 but still features Mackenzie's trademark bunkering.

Leading out of downtown Sacramento and up to the Sierra foothills on I-80, the towns of Roseville, Rocklin, Lincoln, and others have experienced a building boom over the past 10 years, and with this expansion came some very good golf courses, such as Granite Bay, Turkey Creek, Lincoln Hills, and Sun City Roseville. In addition, anyone who loves the outdoors already knows the extreme beauty of the Sierra foothills. Not as climatically extreme as Tahoe, the foothills also offer hiking, river rafting, and camping.

Around the historic gold-mining areas near Auburn is another cluster of good courses. DarkHorse opened in 2002 and has since been earning well-deserved praise from golfers and the media. One of the best new private clubs in the region, Winchester Country Club in Auburn, opened in 1999. To the south, the rolling, oak-studded terrain along Highway 50 offers up several courses, including El Dorado Hills, Serrano Country Club, and Empire Ranch.

West of Sacramento, in flatter terrain, is Teal Bend Golf Club, Wildhorse, and the ever-popular Davis Golf Course. North of the city is Rio La Paz (a 2000 design by Peter Jacobsen), Tuscan Ridge, and the charming Bidwell Park in Chico.

Whether you're in the Sacramento region on business or pleasure, or have the pleasure of living here, make sure your golf clubs are ready to go—there are so many places to play.

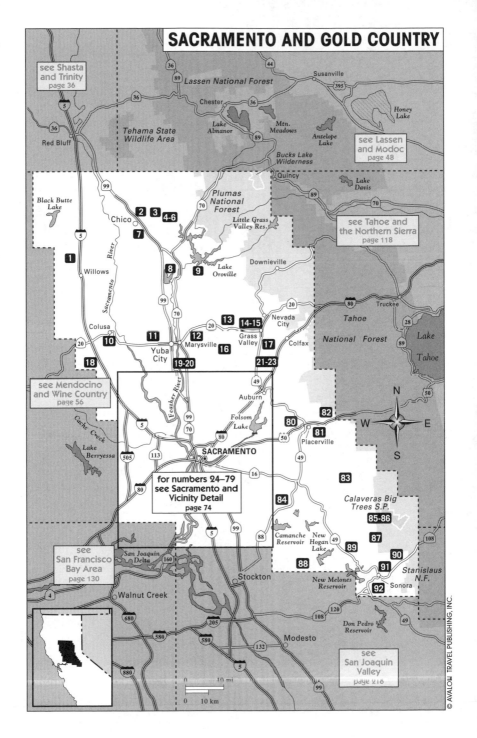

SACRAMENTO AND GOLD COUNTRY

see Shasta
and Trinity
page 36

Lassen National Forest

Susanville

Chester

Red Bluff

Tehama State
Wildlife Area

Lake
Almanor

Mtn.
Meadows

Honey
Lake

Antelope
Lake

Bucks Lake
Wilderness

see Lassen
and Modoc
page 48

Black Butte
Lake

Plumas
National
Forest

Quincy

Lake
Davis

see Tahoe and
the Northern Sierra
page 118

Chico

Willows

Sacramento River

Little Grass
Valley Res.

Downieville

Lake
Oroville

Colusa

Nevada
City

Truckee

Grass
Valley

Tahoe

National Forest

Lake
Tahoe

Marysville

Colfax

Yuba
City

see Mendocino
and Wine Country
page 56

Cache Creek

Lake
Berryessa

Auburn

Folsom
Lake

Feather River

SACRAMENTO

Placerville

for numbers 24–79
see Sacramento and
Vicinity Detail
page 74

Calaveras Big
Trees S.P.

see
San Francisco
Bay Area
page 130

San Joaquin
Delta

Camanche
Reservoir

New
Hogan
Lake

Stanislaus
N.F.

Sonora

Stockton

New Melones
Reservoir

Walnut Creek

Don Pedro
Reservoir

Modesto

see
San Joaquin
Valley
page 218

© AVALON TRAVEL PUBLISHING, INC.

Sacramento and Vicinity Detail

Courses 24–79

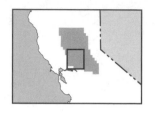

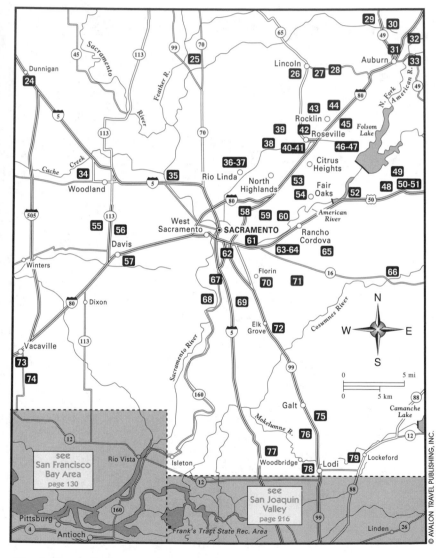

Dunnigan
24

Sacramento River

Feather R.

45

113

99

70

25

65

Lincoln
26   27   28

Auburn

29   30
31   32
33

49

N. Fork American R.

49

80

43   44

Rocklin

39   42   45

Roseville

38   40-41

46-47

Folsom Lake

5

113

70

Cache Creek

34

Woodland

35

Rio Linda

36-37

North Highlands

Citrus Heights

49

50-51

48   52

50

53

Fair Oaks

54

American River

505

113

55   56

Davis

West Sacramento

58   59   60

SACRAMENTO

61

Rancho Cordova

63-64   65

Winters

57

Florin

70   71

16

66

80   Dixon

113

67

68   69

Vacaville

73

74

Elk Grove

72

Cosumnes River

N
W   E
S

0   5 mi
0   5 km

88

Camanche Lake

160

Galt

75

76

12

Mokelumne R.

see
San Francisco
Bay Area
page 130

12

Rio Vista

Isleton

77

Woodbridge

78

Lodi

79   Lockeford

see
San Joaquin
Valley
page 216

88

Pittsburg

160

4   Antioch

Frank's Tract State Rec. Area

12

99

Linden   26

© AVALON TRAVEL PUBLISHING, INC.

1 GLENN GOLF & COUNTRY CLUB

Architect: Ben Harmon, 1960
9 holes   Public $12-20

Sacramento and Gold Country map, page 73
This long course is lined with weeping willows and eucalyptus. It has outstanding greens and a great view of the Sierras. There are four par-5 holes. The number-one handicap hole is the fourth, a par-3 of 215 yards. There are out-of-bounds to the left and in the back of the green, which is guarded by bunkers in the front. A different set of tees is offered for those who wish to play 18 holes.

Play Policy and Fees: Green fees are $12 on weekdays and $20 on weekends. Twilight and senior rates are $9 on weekdays and $12 on weekends.

Tees and Yardage: *Men (18 holes):* yardage 6544, par 72, rating 70.2, slope 118; *Women (18 holes):* yardage 5970, par 72, rating 72.7, slope 118.

Tee Times: Reservations not required.

Dress Code: Nonmetal spikes are required.

Tournaments: Tournaments are available week-days only and should be scheduled at least a month in advance. The banquet facility can accommodate up to 200 people.

Directions: From I-5 in Willows, drive five miles north and take the Bayliss Blue Gum Road exit west to the course.

Contact: 6226 Country Road 39, Willows, CA 95988, pro shop 530/934-9918, fax 530/934-2211.

2 BIDWELL PARK GOLF COURSE

Architect: Course designed, 1948
18 holes   Public $22-29

Sacramento and Gold Country map, page 73
Situated in a beautiful part of upper Bidwell Park, this course is flanked by trees and water. Lots of wildlife species call this course home. The front nine is set in the foothills, and the back nine is longer and flat. Accuracy is important. The 12th and 13th holes

offer an excellent tandem of par-4s. The 12th is 365 yards and a slight dogleg left over water, while the 13th is 403 yards with a blind, down-hill fairway shot into the green. With excellent drainage, this course is often playable when others in the region are not.

Play Policy and Fees: Green fees are $22 week-days and $29 weekends. These are all-day rates. Carts are $11/person.

Tees and Yardage: *Men:* Blue: yardage 6363, par 72, rating 70.4, slope 127; White: yardage 5991, par 71, rating 68.8, slope 121; *Women:* Yellow: yardage 5540, par 73, rating 70.8, slope 120.

Tee Times: Reservations can be made one week in advance for weekends and holidays and two days in advance for weekdays.

Dress Code: Soft spikes are preferred.

Tournaments: Tournaments welcome.

Directions: From Highway 99 in Chico, take the East Avenue exit and drive east. Turn left and head two miles to Wildwood Avenue. Turn right on Golf Course Road and continue a short distance to the course.

Contact: 3199 Golf Course Road, Chico, CA 95973, pro shop 530/891-8417, fax 530/891-5623.

3 CANYON OAKS COUNTRY CLUB

Architect: Jim Summers, 1985
18 holes   Private $75

Sacramento and Gold Country map, page 73
Located at the mouth of Dead Horse Slough Canyon, this hilly course has narrow fairways and greens of varying size and contour. The course is tree-lined, and a creek bed runs throughout. Water is everywhere but only comes into play on three holes. The sixth hole is a par-3 of 170 yards over water, and the 18th, a par-4, measures 486 yards from the back tees. Many consider the large greens some of the finest in Northern California.

Play Policy and Fees: Reciprocal play accepted with other private clubs. Otherwise, members and guests only. Reciprocators' fee is $75 including cart.

Tees and Yardage: *Men:* Professional: yardage 6804, par 72, rating 73.9, slope 142; Championship: yardage 6376, par 72, rating 71.7, slope 132; Back: yardage 6038, par 72, rating 70.3, slope 131; Middle: yardage 5531, par 72, rating 68.0, slope 123; *Women:* Forward: yardage 5030, par 72, rating 70.8, slope 125.

Tee Times: Reciprocal players can reserve times one week out.

Dress Code: Collared shirts are required.

Tournaments: This course is available for outside tournaments. The banquet facility can accommodate 200 people. Events should be booked 12 months in advance.

Directions: From Highway 99 in Chico, take Highway 32 east. Turn left on Bruce Road and then right on California Park Drive. Then turn right again on Yosemite Drive.

Contact: 999 Yosemite Drive, Chico, CA 95928, pro shop 530/343-1116, fax 530/343-1865.

4 PARADISE PINES GOLF COURSE

Architect: Bob Baldock, 1972

9 holes   **Public**   **$16–20**

🏌️ 📷 🍴 🏌️ 🚗 🍺

Sacramento and Gold Country map, page 73

This short course has tight, tree-lined fairways and offers diversity from hole to hole. Holes five through seven are the course's best. The fifth is a par-3 of 188 yards; the sixth is a narrow, dogleg par-4 measuring 360 yards; and the seventh is a dogleg par-5 of 463 yards. This is an interesting course with plenty of undulating lies and small greens.

Play Policy and Fees: Green fees are $16 for nine holes and $19 for 18 holes on weekdays, and $17 for nine holes and $20 for 18 holes weekends and holidays. Carts are $13 for nine holes and $18 for 18 holes. Junior and regular memberships available.

Tees and Yardage: *Men (18 holes):* White/Blue: yardage 4988, par 68, rating 63.8, slope 101; *Women (18 holes):* Red/White: yardage 4804, par 68, rating 67.3, slope 120.

Tee Times: Reservations can be booked seven days in advance.

Dress Code: Shirts are required.

Tournaments: This course is available for outside tournaments, and the banquet facility can accommodate up to 98 people.

Directions: From Highway 99 in Chico, take the Skyway exit and drive to Magalia. In Magalia, turn left on South Park Drive.

Contact: 13917 South Park Drive, Magalia, CA 95954, pro shop 530/873-1111.

5 THE GOLF COURSE AT LAVA CREEK

Architect: Joe Balch, 1962/2002

9 holes   **Public**   **$10–12**

🏌️ 📷 🍴 🏌️ 🍺

Sacramento and Gold Country map, page 73

Formerly Tall Pine Golf Course, this layout first opened in 1962. It closed for almost five years in the 1990s until it was purchased and restored by some new owners in 2002. It is a slightly hilly course with tree-lined fairways and lots of huge oak and pine trees. From a maintenance and playability standpoint, it plays better in fall, winter, and spring.

Play Policy and Fees: Green fees are $10 Tuesday–Thursday for nine holes, $12 Friday, weekends, and holidays. Carts are additional. Junior rates are available.

Tees and Yardage: *Men (18 holes):* Blue/White: yardage 4195, par 68, rating 61.6, slope 107; *Women (18 holes):* Red/White: yardage 3991, par 68, rating 63.1, slope 104.

Tee Times: Reservations can be made anytime in advance, but they are not generally needed.

Dress Code: No dress requirements. Any spikes okay.

Tournaments: Tournaments welcome.

Directions: From Highway 99/149 (north of Yuba City), get onto Highway 191 north/Clark Road. The course is at the intersection of Clark Road and Roe Road.

Contact: 5325 Clark Road, Paradise, CA 95969, golf shop 530/872-4653.

6 TUSCAN RIDGE GOLF CLUB

Architect: Algie M. Pulley Jr., 2001

18 holes   **Semiprivate**   **$20–25**

🧍 📷 🍴 🛺 ⛳

Sacramento and Gold Country map, page 73

Featuring bent-grass tees and greens and rye-grass fairways, Tuscan Ridge boasts a panoramic view of the Sacramento Valley from every hole. When all 18 of its holes are complete, the course will play 5000–7200 yards, giving all skill levels an appropriate tee. Nine holes and the Learning Center have been open since 2001. The yardage listed includes only the holes open for play as of press time.

Play Policy and Fees: This is a public facility, but memberships are available. Green fees are $20 for 18 holes weekdays, $25 weekends. Golf carts are additional. Junior, senior, and nine-hole rates are available. Note: Fees were expected to increase somewhat, as the full 18 holes opened. Exact amounts were not available at press time.

Tees and Yardage: *Men:* Back: yardage 3730, par 37, rating n/a, slope n/a; Middle: yardage 3380, par 37, rating n/a, slope n/a; *Women:* Forward: yardage 2960, par 37, rating n/a, slope n/a.

Tee Times: Reservations may be made up to one week in advance.

Dress Code: Collared golf shirts are required for men. Women's shirts must have a collar if they do not have sleeves, and halter tops are not permitted. Nonmetal spikes are required.

Tournaments: Outside events are welcome.

Directions: From Highway 99 south of Chico, exit at Skyway/Park Avenue and travel east on Skyway. Halfway up Skyway toward Paradise, you will see the course on your left.

Contact: P.O. Box 1668, Chico, CA 95927, pro shop 530/343-3862, fax 530/343-3853, www.tuscanridge.com.

7 BUTTE CREEK COUNTRY CLUB

Architect: Bob Baldock, 1965

18 holes   **Private**   **$75**

🧍 📷 🍴 🛺

Sacramento and Gold Country map, page 73

Butte Creek is arguably one of the top courses in the Sacramento Valley. The creek for which the course is named comes into play on five holes. Relatively open, this course has enough old oak trees to cause trouble, and the greens are large and undulating. The par-3 17th is a beauty, set over water, with flowers and railroad ties surrounding the green. Butte Creek played host to the U.S. Open local qualifying round in 1992.

Play Policy and Fees: Reciprocal play is accepted with private clubs that allow reciprocal play; otherwise, members and guests only. Reciprocal fees are $75.

Tees and Yardage: *Men:* Gold: yardage 6977, par 72, rating 73.4, slope 132; Black: yardage 6581, par 72, rating 71.6, slope 128; Blue: yardage 6206, par 72, rating 69.8, slope 123; White: yardage 5517, par 72, rating 66.6, slope 110; *Women:* Green: yardage 4948, par 72, rating 68.1, slope 110.

Tee Times: Reservations can be booked 30 days in advance.

Dress Code: Appropriate golf attire is required. No denim pants or denim shorts are allowed. Tucked-in collared shirts and nonmetal spikes are required.

Tournaments: This course is available for outside tournaments Monday only, and the banquet facility holds 300 people.

Directions: From Highway 99 in Chico, take the Estates Drive exit. Drive one mile west to the course.

Contact: 175 Estates Drive, Chico, CA 95928, pro shop 530/343-8292, fax 530/343-2406, www.buttecreekcountryclub.com.

8 TABLE MOUNTAIN GOLF CLUB

Architect: Bob Baldock, 1956

18 holes   **Public**   **$18–23**

Sacramento and Gold Country map, page 73

Table Mountain is a wide-open course with firm fairways, considerable hard pan, and quick greens. Forty bunkers and nine ponds make things difficult. The signature hole is the 18th, a par-5 covering 474 yards. This course is a challenging test in a scenic setting.

Play Policy and Fees: Green fees are $18 Monday–Thursday. Friday–Sunday and holidays the fees are $23. Nine-hole rates also available.

Tees and Yardage: *Men:* Black: yardage 6690, par 72, rating 71.2, slope 118; Blue: yardage 6254, par 72, rating 69.0, slope 114; White: yardage 5739, par 72, rating 66.3, slope 109; *Women:* Gold: yardage 5068, par 72, rating 67.7, slope 108.

Tee Times: Reservations can be booked seven days in advance.

Dress Code: Shirts must have either sleeves or a collar.

Tournaments: A 100-player minimum is needed to book a shotgun tournament, and events should be booked six months in advance. The banquet facility can accommodate 144 people.

Directions: From Sacramento, take Highway 99 North to Highway 162 and head east. This course is in Oroville on Highway 162 (Oro Dam Boulevard) between Highway 99 and Highway 70.

Contact: 2700 West Oro Dam Boulevard (P.O. Box 2769), Oroville, CA 95965, pro shop 530/533-3922, fax 530/533-0550.

9 KELLY RIDGE GOLF & COUNTRY CLUB

Architect: Homer Flint, 1974

9 holes   **Semiprivate**   **$13–21**

Sacramento and Gold Country map, page 73

Situated in the Sierra Alton foothills near the Oroville Dam, this short course is hilly and tight, with narrow fairways and well-bunkered greens. Balls tend to kick right. Many players are intimidated by the 135-yard, par-3 third hole, which requires a carry over a deep ravine. There are six par-4s and three par-3 holes.

Play Policy and Fees: Green fees are $13 for nine holes and $19 for 18 holes weekdays, $15 and $21 weekends and holidays. Carts are additional.

Tees and Yardage: *Men:* Blue/Black: yardage 2111, par 33, rating n/a, slope n/a; White/Blue: yardage 1993, par 33, rating n/a, slope n/a; *Women:* Red/White: yardage 1818, par 33, rating n/a, slope n/a.

Tee Times: Reservations can be made 1–2 weeks in advance.

Dress Code: Shirts and nonmetal spikes are required.

Tournaments: This course is available for outside tournaments. The banquet facility can accommodate 250 people.

Directions: From Highway 70 in Oroville, take the Oroville Dam Boulevard exit east for 1.5 miles to Olive Highway (Highway 162) and turn right. Drive 5.5 miles to Kelly Ridge Road and turn left. Turn left at Royal Oaks Drive and drive to the course.

Contact: 5131 Royal Oaks Drive, Oroville, CA 95966, pro shop 530/589-0777, fax 530/589-3572.

10 COLUSA COUNTRY CLUB

Architect: Course designed, 1956

9 holes   **Semiprivate**   **$12–23**

Sacramento and Gold Country map, page 73

This flat, tree-lined course is tight and walkable. It's more challenging than meets the eye. A new sprinkler system has improved fairway conditions. The par-5 sixth hole (503 yards) is a challenge, requiring a difficult second shot to avoid trees in the fairway.

Play Policy and Fees: Outside play is accepted. Green fees are $12 for nine holes and $15 for 18 holes weekdays, $23 for 18 holes weekends and holidays. Twilight, senior, and junior rates are available. Closed Monday.

Tees and Yardage: *Men (18 holes):* Blue/White: yardage 6523, par 72, rating 70.9, slope 120; *Women (18 holes):* Red/Yellow: yardage 5813, par 74, rating 73.0, slope 121.

Tee Times: Reservations can be made on Tuesday prior to the weekend. Otherwise they are not necessary.

Dress Code: Shirts with sleeves or collars and nonmetal spikes are required.

Tournaments: This course is available for outside tournaments.

Directions: From I-5 in Williams, drive east on Highway 20 to Colusa. The course is on Highway 20.

Contact: 2224 Highway 20 (P.O. Box 827), Colusa, CA 95932, pro shop 530/458-5577, fax 530/458-7331.

11 SOUTHRIDGE GOLF CLUB

Architect: Cal Olson, 1991

18 holes   Semiprivate $30–40

🏌️ 🛖 🍴 🚜 🍽️

Sacramento and Gold Country map, page 73

A most interesting layout, Southridge features a back nine that would fatigue a mountain goat, and a links-style front nine. The Sutter Buttes (back) nine is picturesque and features one of the most challenging (and exasperating) holes in Northern California, a 619-yard par-5 that requires a radar-straight drive and a well-placed second shot, among other skills. Love it or loathe it, you'll remember it. The links side is easier, though not by much, with water coming into play on seven holes. If you want diversity, this is the course.

Play Policy and Fees: Weekday green fees are $30, including cart. Weekend rates are $40, including cart. Carts are a necessity due to the severe terrain on the back nine. Senior, junior, noon, and twilight rates are available.

Tees and Yardage: *Men:* Gold: yardage 7047, par 72, rating 72.7, slope 130; Blue: yardage 6611, par 72, rating 71.2, slope 123; White: yardage 6105, par 72, rating 68.9, slope 118; *Women:* Red: yardage 5541, par 72, rating 69.8, slope 123.

Tee Times: Reservations may be booked 14 days in advance.

Dress Code: Collared shirts are required, and cutoffs are not permitted.

Tournaments: This course is available for tournaments. The banquet facility can accommodate up to 250 people.

Directions: From Yuba City, drive west on Highway 20. The course is seven miles west of Yuba City and can be seen from the highway on the north.

Contact: 9413 South Butte Road, Sutter, CA 95982, pro shop 530/755-4653, clubhouse 530/755-4653, fax 530/755-1404, www.southridge.com.

12 PEACH TREE GOLF & COUNTRY CLUB

Architect: Bob Baldock, 1960

18 holes   Private $50–75

🏌️ 🛖 🍴 🚜 🍽️

Sacramento and Gold Country map, page 73

This course is characterized by its mature trees: walnut and cypress, but only one peach tree. The fairways are Bermuda grass, and the greens are bent grass. Peach Tree is a very tight course with fairway bunkers strategically placed. The greens are fast and bowl-shaped. The seventh, a par-3 of 218 yards from the back tees, is the signature hole. It requires a carry over water that fronts about half the green, and there's a bunker on the left side.

Play Policy and Fees: Reciprocal play is accepted with members of other private clubs at a rate of $50 weekdays and $75 weekends. Carts are $20. The course is closed on Monday.

Tees and Yardage: *Men:* Blue: yardage 6817, par 72, rating 72.6, slope 127; White: yardage 6506, par 72, rating 71.0, slope 124; Red: yardage 6203, par 72, rating 69.6, slope 120; Gold: yardage 5824, par 72, rating 67.9, slope 115; *Women:* Silver: yardage 5045, par 73, rating 68.8, slope 117.

Tee Times: Reservations can be booked seven days in advance.

Dress Code: Appropriate golf attire and nonmetal spikes are required.

Tournaments: A 100-player minimum is needed to book a tournament, and carts are mandatory.

Directions: From Sacramento, take Highway 70 through Marysville to Highway 20. Turn right on Ramirez Road and drive to Simpson-Dantoni Road. Turn left and drive to the course.

Contact: 2043 Simpson-Dantoni Road (P.O. Box 231), Marysville, CA 95901, pro shop 530/743-2039, www.peachtreecountryclub.com.

13 LAKE WILDWOOD COUNTRY CLUB

Architect: William F. Bell, 1971;
Robert Muir Graves, 1977

18 holes **Private** **$55**

Sacramento and Gold Country map, page 73

This rolling course is lined with mature oaks. Water comes into play on five holes, and the back nine is hilly. The most memorable hole is the par-4 12th. It requires a difficult carry over water on the second shot. Appropriately, there is an old "hanging" tree behind the green. Three of the course's par-5s are reachable in two by good players.

Play Policy and Fees: Reciprocal play is accepted with members of other private clubs. Reciprocal fees are $55. Carts are an additional $22. Nine-hole rates offered.

Tees and Yardage: *Men:* Blue: yardage 6492, par 72, rating 71.2, slope 126; White: yardage 6230, par 72, rating 69.8, slope 123; Red: yardage 5749, par 72, rating 67.5, slope 118; *Women:* Gold: yardage 5230, par 72, rating 69.7, slope 124.

Tee Times: Reciprocators should have their club pro call to make arrangements.

Dress Code: Appropriate golf attire and nonmetal spikes are required.

Tournaments: This course is available for a limited number of outside events.

Directions: From Marysville, drive 30 miles east on Highway 20 to Pleasant Valley Road. Turn left and drive one mile to the four-way stop. Turn right onto Cottontail Way.

Contact: 11255 Cottontail Way, Penn Valley, CA 95946, pro shop 530/432-1163, fax 530/432-2951, www.lakewildwood.com.

14 NEVADA COUNTY COUNTRY CLUB

Architect: Sam Whiting, 1925

9 holes **Semiprivate** **$12–20**

Sacramento and Gold Country map, page 73

This course is relatively wide open except for the fifth and sixth holes. The greens are small and tricky, invariably breaking toward the nearby (but unseen) hospital. The par-5 eighth is the toughest, a 400-yard hole with a tiny green. Some of the older members caddied here in the 1920s, and many of them were miners in the nearby gold country.

Play Policy and Fees: Green fees are $12 for nine holes and $20 for 18 holes Monday–Thursday, $15 for nine and $25 for 18 holes weekends and holidays. Junior rates offered. Carts are additional.

Tees and Yardage: *Men (18 holes):* Blue/White: yardage 5475, par 68, rating 65.4, slope 114; *Women:* Red: yardage 5158, par 70, rating 68.5, slope 119.

Tee Times: Reservations are not accepted. All play is on a first-come, first-served basis.

Dress Code: No tank tops are allowed on the course. Nonmetal spikes are required.

Tournaments: Limited. Please inquire.

Directions: From Highway 49 in Grass Valley, take the Idaho Maryland exit. At the end of the ramp, turn left and drive to East Main Street. Turn right and drive to the course on the left.

Contact: 1040 East Main Street, Grass Valley, CA 95945, pro shop 530/273-6436.

15 QUAIL VALLEY GOLF COURSE

Architect: Tom Conway, 2001

9 holes **Public** **$8**

Sacramento and Gold Country map, page 73

This short but fun course has seven par-3 holes and two par-4s, the longest being 378 yards.

Perhaps the most interesting hole is the ninth, a par-3 where you hit your tee shot over a barn. It's a good course for practicing your iron game.
Play Policy and Fees: Green fees are $8. Carts are additional.
Tees and Yardage: *Men:* White: yardage 1607, par 29, rating 57.0, slope 76; *Women:* Red: yardage 1460, par 30, rating n/a, slope n/a.
Tee Times: No tee times needed; first-come, first-served.
Dress Code: No metal spikes are allowed on the course.
Tournaments: Small tournaments welcome.
Directions: From Highway 20, turn south on McCourtney Road, then left on Auburn Road. The course will be on your right in 1.5 miles.
Contact: 12594 Auburn Road, Grass Valley, CA 95945, golf shop 530/274-1340.

16 COYOTE RUN GOLF COURSE

Architect: Course designed, 1968; Golf Plan, 1998

18 holes **Military** **$27**

Formerly known as Recce Point, this is a flat course on Beale AFB with some elevated greens. There are enough trees to make things challenging, and the fifth hole is distinguished by a large lake, one of three on the course. In 1998, Golf Plan finished a complete remodel that included additional yardage, new lakes, creeks, 10 new greens, and four sets of tee boxes.

Base lodging is available for military personnel. Call 530/634-2953.
Play Policy and Fees: Public play is accepted with prior arrangement. Guest fees are $27.
Tees and Yardage: *Men:* Gold: yardage 6824, par 72, rating 72.6, slope 130; Blue: yardage 6353, par 72, rating 70.4, slope 125; White: yardage 5578, par 72, rating 66.6, slope 116; *Women:* Red: yardage 4600, par 72, rating 66.8, slope 112.
Tee Times: Reservations can be made seven days in advance on weekends for military personnel. Civilians can make tee times one day in advance on weekends.

Dress Code: Appropriate golf attire and non-metal spikes are required.
Tournaments: A 20-player minimum is needed to book a regular tournament. The banquet facility holds up to 250 people. Events should be booked 12 months in advance.
Directions: From Highway 70 in Marysville, take the North Beale Road exit east. Drive to the main gate of Beale Air Force Base.
Contact: 17440 Warren Shingle Boulevard, Beale AFB, CA 95903, pro shop 530/788-0192, fax 530/788-0191, www.bealeservices.com.

17 ALTA SIERRA COUNTRY CLUB

Architect: Bob Baldock, 1965

18 holes **Semiprivate** **$22.50–50**

This hilly, scenic course has a links-style layout with big greens. There are no parallel fairways. Deer and other wildlife are plentiful. The 18th hole is a challenging par-5 that doglegs right with water on the right and a hazard that interferes with the second shot. Alta Sierra is a well-conditioned course that is particularly challenging from the forward tees, since there's little difference in yardage from the regular tees on several tough holes.

For information on the Alta Sierra Village Inn (across the street), call 530/273-9102.
Play Policy and Fees: Public play is accepted after 2 P.M. Green fees range $22.50–50, and carts are $24.
Tees and Yardage: *Men:* Blue: yardage 6537, par 72, rating 70.9, slope 127; White: yardage 6344, par 72, rating 70.1, slope 125; *Women:* Red: yardage 5912, par 73, rating 74.6, slope 134.
Tee Times: Reservations may be booked up to one month in advance.
Dress Code: Traditional golf attire is required.
Tournaments: This course is available for a limited number of outside tournaments per year.
Directions: From Highway 49 between Grass Valley and Auburn, take the Alta Sierra Drive

East exit. Travel two miles to the course on Tammy Way.

Contact: 11897 Tammy Way, Grass Valley, CA 95949, pro shop 530/273-2010, fax 530/273-2207, www.altasierracc.com.

18 ARBUCKLE GOLF CLUB

Architect: Course designed, 1925

9 holes   Semiprivate $15–25

Sacramento and Gold Country map, page 73

This challenging course has rolling hills, tight fairways, and some of the fastest greens in the Sacramento Valley. The par-4, 416-yard third hole presents a postcard setting with a view of the Sacramento Valley and Sutter Buttes. Arbuckle is one of the finest nine-hole courses in the state—challenging and exceptionally well conditioned. This course was built in 1925 by the residents of the town. Arbuckle was voted the best nine-hole course in Northern California by the *Lake County Record-Bee*.

Play Policy and Fees: Outside play is accepted. Green fees are $15 Tuesday–Friday and $25 weekends and holidays. Carts are $22. Junior and twilight rates offered. Closed Monday except for holidays.

Tees and Yardage: *Men (18 holes):* White/Blue: yardage 6460, par 72, rating 69.8, slope 119; *Women (18 holes):* Yellow/Red: yardage 5912, par 72, rating 73.8, slope 123.

Tee Times: Reservations can be booked seven days in advance.

Dress Code: Appropriate golf attire is required. Nonmetal spikes are preferred.

Tournaments: Carts are required for tournament play. A banquet facility is available that can accommodate 120 people.

Directions: From Sacramento, travel 35 minutes north on I-5. Take the Arbuckle/College City exit. Head west on Hillgate Road for 4.6 miles, and the course will be on the left.

Contact: 5918 Hillgate Road (P.O. Box 1009), Arbuckle, CA 95912, pro shop 530/476-2470, fax 530/476-3044.

19 MALLARD LAKE GOLF COURSE

Architect: Course designed, 1980

9 holes   Public $10–16

Sacramento and Gold Country map, page 73

This mostly flat course has water on all nine holes. It's short and tough with small, well-maintained greens. The toughest hole is the fourth (357 yards), with out-of-bounds on both sides of the fairway and a pond situated right where the average hitter usually drives. Great for tune-up rounds and beginning golfers.

Play Policy and Fees: Green fees are $10 for nine holes and $14 for 18 holes weekdays, $12 for nine holes and $16 for 18 holes on weekends. Carts additional. Twilight rates are available. Memberships are offered.

Tees and Yardage: *Men (18 holes):* Blue: yardage 5388, par 68, rating 65.8, slope 119; White: yardage 5200, par 68, rating 65.4, slope 117; *Women (18 holes):* Red: yardage 4804, par 68, rating 68.6, slope 118.

Tee Times: Reservations can be booked seven days in advance.

Dress Code: Tank tops and coolers are not allowed. Nonmetal spikes are required.

Tournaments: This course is available for outside tournaments.

Directions: From Yuba City, drive south approximately four miles on Highway 99. The course is one-quarter mile south of Oswald Road on Highway 99.

Contact: 4238 South Highway 99, Yuba City, CA 95991, pro shop 530/674-0475, fax 530/674-1337.

20 PLUMAS LAKE GOLF & COUNTRY CLUB

Architect: Jack Beasley, 1926; Bob Baldock, 1960

18 holes   Semiprivate $21–26

Sacramento and Gold Country map, page 73

Plumas Lake is a well-known jewel among golf insiders throughout Northern California. It is mostly flat and not exceedingly tight, but there are a number of monster holes, starting with the eighth, a 399-yarder with a giant oak blocking the entrance to the green. Holes 12 (423 yards), 13 (208 yards), and 14 (414 yards) are Plumas Lake's answer to Amen Corner. This course is also known for its excellent greens. A new clubhouse and banquet facility was completed in 2002, after flooding had damaged the old one.

Play Policy and Fees: Green fees are $21 Monday–Thursday and $26 Friday–Sunday. Carts are an additional $11 per person. Junior rates are offered; senior rates are available Monday–Friday.

Tees and Yardage: *Men:* Blue: yardage 6437, par 71, rating 71.3, slope 130; White: yardage 6153, par 71, rating 70.3, slope 128; *Women:* Red: yardage 5753, par 72, rating 73.4, slope 127.

Tee Times: Reservations can be booked seven days in advance.

Dress Code: No tank tops or short shorts are allowed on the course. Soft spikes required.

Tournaments: Tournaments are accepted. Banquet facilities are available.

Directions: From Marysville, drive south on Highway 70. Take the Feather River Boulevard exit and drive about 6.5 miles. Turn left on Country Club Road.

Contact: 1551 Country Club Road, Marysville, CA 95901, pro shop 530/742-3201, fax 530/742-1469, www.plumaslake.com.

21 LAKE OF THE PINES COUNTRY CLUB

Architect: Course designed, 1969
18 holes   Private $37

🏌 📷 🍴 🛒

Sacramento and Gold Country map, page 73

This hilly course is nearly 25 years old. It's narrow, with lots of out-of-bounds. Water comes into play on seven holes. The eighth hole can be a headache. At 505 yards, it's a tough par-5 with hazards everywhere. Your drive must clear a creek, then the fairway doglegs to the left, and there are out-of-bounds stakes on both sides. The green is small but holds well.

Play Policy and Fees: Reciprocal play is accepted with members of other private clubs; otherwise, members and guests only. Reciprocal fees are $37.

Tees and Yardage: *Men:* Back: yardage 6140, par 71, rating 69.3, slope 119; Middle: yardage 5897, par 71, rating 68.2, slope 117; *Women:* Forward: yardage 5371, par 71, rating 71.5, slope 129.

Tee Times: Reciprocators should have their club pro call to make arrangements.

Dress Code: Appropriate golf attire is required. Nonmetal spikes are encouraged.

Tournaments: A 40-player minimum is needed to book an event. Carts are mandatory.

Directions: In Auburn, drive north on Highway 49 to Combie Road East. Turn right and drive to Lakeshore North. Turn right and drive to the course.

Contact: 11665 Lakeshore North, Auburn, CA 95602, pro shop 530/268-0572.

22 DARKHORSE GOLF CLUB

Architect: Keith Foster, 2002
18 holes   Public $39–69

🏌 📷 🍴 🛒 ⛳

Sacramento and Gold Country map, page 73

🏌 Located in the Sierra foothills, this scenic and challenging layout features mature oaks, rolling meadows, and hardy hillsides. Streambeds, grass hollows, and natural wetlands surround the greens. The design requires strategic thinking, risk-taking, and shot-making skills. The par-3 holes are particularly fun and memorable. Because of its elevation, Dark-Horse is able to sustain bent-grass greens. Home sites are being sold around the course.

Play Policy and Fees: Green fees vary $39–69, depending on time of day and day of week. Junior and senior rates are available. Cart fees are included.

Tees and Yardage: *Men:* Black: yardage 7203, par 72, rating 75.0, slope 140; Copper: yardage 6826, par 72, rating 72.4, slope 135; Blue: yardage 6425, par 72, rating 71.0, slope 130; White: yardage 5984, par 72, rating 68.7, slope

127; *Women:* Jade: yardage 5058, par 72, rating 68.3, slope 122.

Tee Times: Reservations can be made 30 days in advance.

Dress Code: Golf shirts required; no denim; no metal spikes allowed.

Tournaments: A full menu of tournament options is offered. The course will customize your event for you.

Directions: Heading east from Sacramento on I-80, exit onto Highway 49 toward Grass Valley (north). In approximately 10 miles, Combie Road will be on your right. Turn right and follow Combie to the course.

Contact: 13450 Combie Road, Auburn, CA 95602, pro shop 530/269-7900, fax 530/269-7903, www.darkhorsegolf.com.

23 WINCHESTER COUNTRY CLUB

Architect: Robert Trent Jones Sr. and Jr., 1999

18 holes   **Private**   **$200**

🏌 📷 🍺 🚜 🍽

Sacramento and Gold Country map, page 73

Set in the foothills, this course offers spectacular views of both the Sierra Nevada range and the Sacramento Valley. It is one of very few design collaborations between the late golf course architect Robert Trent Jones Sr. and his son Robert Trent Jones Jr. and is generally thought of as one of the best courses in Northern California. The layout features two distinct nines, with the front more tree-lined and rolling, the back set around some wetlands. The landing areas are fairly generous, but touch and accuracy are rewarded around the greens.

Play Policy and Fees: Play is restricted to members and their guests; limited reciprocal play is accepted. Reciprocal fees are $200 including cart and range balls.

Tees and Yardage: *Men:* Gold: yardage 7144, par 72, rating 74.7, slope 141; Black: yardage 6819, par 72, rating 73.0, slope 139; Blue: yardage 6363, par 72, rating 70.8, slope 136; White: yardage 5856, par 72, rating 68.4, slope

125; *Women:* Green: yardage 5289, par 72, rating 70.8, slope 129.

Tee Times: Reciprocal players' club pro should call five days in advance to arrange for reservations.

Dress Code: Appropriate golf attire is required. Soft spikes only.

Tournaments: Tournaments must be proposed to the board of directors.

Directions: The course is five miles east of Auburn. From I-80, take the Meadow Vista exit; go north one mile. Turn west on Sugar Pine Road to the course.

Contact: P.O. Box 125, Auburn, CA 95604, pro shop 530/878-9585, fax 530/878-2119, www.winchestercountryclub.com.

24 CAMPERS INN RV PARK & GOLF COURSE

Architect: Course designed, 1989

9 holes   **Public**   **$5.50–18**

📷 🍺 🏌 🍽 3

Sacramento and Vicinity Detail map, page 74

This short par-3 course is excellent for beginners and seniors. The course features ponds, sand traps, and mature trees, and is often windy. This is a good test for the short game. RV and tent sites are available. Facilities include showers and a pool.

Play Policy and Fees: Green fees are $5.50 for nine holes, $10.50 for 18 holes, and $15.50 all day on weekdays. Green fees are $6.50 for nine holes, $12 for 18 holes, and $18 all day on weekends.

Tees and Yardage: *Men and Women:* yardage 1134, par 27, rating n/a, slope n/a.

Tee Times: Reservations can be booked seven days in advance.

Dress Code: Nonmetal spikes are required.

Tournaments: This course is available for outside tournaments. The banquet facility can accommodate 100 people.

Directions: From Sacramento, take I-5 north to the Dunnigan exit. Turn left over the freeway and drive one mile. Turn right on Road 88 and drive 1.6 miles to course.

Contact: 2501 Road 88 (P.O. Box 71), Dunnigan, CA 95937, pro shop 530/724-3350, fax 530/724-3110.

25 RIO LA PAZ GOLF CLUB

Architect: Peter Jacobsen, 2000

18 holes   Semiprivate $20–42

Sacramento and Vicinity Detail map, page 74

Built among stately old oak trees, this course sits on fairly flat terrain. There is plenty of water in play, and it can present some challenges from all the way back. Overall, though, the course layout is user-friendly and the ambience is serene.

Play Policy and Fees: This is a public facility that also offers memberships. Monday–Friday, green fees are $20 walking and $32 with a cart; twilight rates available. On weekends and holidays, green fees are $26 walking and $42 with a cart.

Tees and Yardage: *Men:* Black: yardage 6505, par 71, rating 71.3, slope 126; Green: yardage 6037, par 71, rating 69.3, slope 125; Gold: yardage 5401, par 71, rating 66.5, slope 115; *Women:* Red: yardage 4740, par 71, rating 67.5, slope 117.

Tee Times: Reservations may be made up to one week in advance.

Dress Code: No blue jeans or tank tops are permitted. Collared shirts and traditional golf attire are encouraged. Spikeless shoes only.

Tournaments: Tournaments are welcome and may be booked two years in advance.

Directions: From Highway 99 above Sacramento, take the Nicolaus exit. Turn west and drive for roughly 1.5 miles. The course is on the left and is visible from the road.

Contact: 201 Lee Road, Nicolaus, CA 95659, pro shop 530/656-2182, fax 530/656-2185, www.riolapazgolf.com.

26 LINCOLN HILLS GOLF CLUB

Architect: Billy Casper and Greg Nash, 1999

18 holes   Public $50–60

Sacramento and Vicinity Detail map, page 74

This course features young greens that require accurate approach shots. Picturesque water features, broad fairways, interesting elevation changes, and views of the distant hills will add to the enjoyment of your round. Pockets of pine, oak, and redwood help define the course, while four lakes, five waterfalls, and more than 50 bunkers make par a respectable score. The back nine meanders around a native wetland preserve.

Play Policy and Fees: Lincoln Hills is a daily fee golf course open to the public and residents of Del Webb's Sun City Lincoln Hills. Green fees, including cart and range balls, are $50 Monday–Friday, $60 Saturday and Sunday. Resident, twilight, and nine-hole rates are offered.

Tees and Yardage: *Men:* Black: yardage 6985, par 72, rating 73.2, slope 127; Blue: yardage 6466, par 72, rating 70.8, slope 120; White: yardage 6001, par 72, rating 69.2, slope 118; *Women:* Red: yardage 5411, par 72, rating 70.8, slope 117.

Tee Times: Can be made 10 days in advance.

Dress Code: Proper golf attire and nonmetal spikes are required.

Tournaments: A 20-player minimum is required to book an event. A banquet facility is available that can accommodate up to 250 people.

Directions: From Sacramento, take I-80 toward Reno. Exit at Highway 65 heading north torward Lincoln. The entrance to the course is one-half mile before the town of Lincoln.

Contact: 1005 Sun City Lane, Lincoln, CA 95648, pro shop 916/434-3366, 24-hour reservations 916/434-7454, fax 916/434-3371, www .lincolnhillsclubgolf.com.

27 CATTA VERDERA COUNTRY CLUB

Architect: Richard Phelps, 1996
18 holes   Semiprivate $50-80

Sacramento and Vicinity Detail map, page 74

This course, formerly known as Twelve Bridges, is situated in a bowl surrounded by oak trees. The challenging and beautiful layout has no parallel fairways, and 10-minute tee times are designed to give golfers a feeling of solitude. The pride of the course is the 218-yard, par-3 17th hole, fronted by water and flanked by traps on the right side. Considerable work was done on this layout in 2003, including an expansion of the pond on 17 and the addition of a pond and waterfall on the 18th. Many new tee boxes were added for playability.

Play Policy and Fees: Public green fees Monday–Thursday are $50 to walk, $65 to ride. Friday–Sunday and holidays fees are $65 to walk, $80 to ride. Junior rates available. The course plans to go private in 2005, at which point public play will be limited to Monday.

Tees and Yardage: *Men:* Black: yardage 7019, par 72, rating 74.9, slope 145; Orange: yardage 6628, par 72, rating 72.9, slope 137; Purple: yardage 6017, par 72, rating 70.4, slope 129; *Women:* Yellow: yardage 5028, par 72, rating 69.8, slope 121.

Tee Times: Reservations may be booked seven days in advance.

Dress Code: Collared shirts and nonmetal spikes are required. No denim is allowed.

Tournaments: This course is available for tournaments. Please inquire.

Directions: From Roseville, take I-80 east to the Sierra College Boulevard exit. Follow Sierra College Boulevard 5.3 miles north to Twelve Bridges Drive and the course entrance.

Contact: 1111 Catta Verdera, Lincoln, CA 95648, pro shop 916/645-7200, fax 916/645-6729, www.cattaverdera.com.

28 TURKEY CREEK GOLF CLUB

Architect: Brad Bell, 1999
18 holes   Public $45-65

Sacramento and Vicinity Detail map, page 74

Turkey Creek is set on rolling foothills, featuring tree-lined fairways and a natural quarry. The course offers generous landing areas, but for those golfers who like to use more room than the fairways have to offer, trouble awaits in the form of trees—many trees. With yardages ranging 4800–7000 yards, this is truly a course for all skill levels.

Play Policy and Fees: Green fees are $45 Monday–Thursday, $55 Friday, and $65 weekends and holidays. Twilight, senior (Monday–Friday), and junior rates are available. Carts included in fees. Golfers can repeat their round for $20.

Tees and Yardage: *Men:* Black: yardage 7012, par 72, rating 73.4, slope 138; Blue: yardage 6617, par 72, rating 71.3, slope 135; White: yardage 6003, par 72, rating 68.5, slope 125; *Women:* Gold: yardage 4887, par 72, rating 67.3, slope 121.

Tee Times: Reservations can be made seven days in advance.

Dress Code: Proper golf attire and nonmetal spikes are required.

Tournaments: Tournaments welcome. An outdoor facility can accommodate up to 152 people.

Directions: From the Sacramento area, take I-80 east to Highway 65, head north to Highway 193, and turn right (east). This course is a couple of miles along on the left.

Contact: 1525 Highway 193, Lincoln, CA 95648, pro shop 916/434-9100, fax 916/434-9477, www.turkeycreekgc.com.

29 AUBURN VALLEY COUNTRY CLUB

Architect: Bob Bissett, 1959
18 holes   Private $70

Sacramento and Vicinity Detail map,
page 74

This is a long, hilly, and challenging course with fast greens and 11 lakes that come into play. It is a beautiful course, set in the foothills, with numerous elevated tees that afford excellent views. The fairways are generally narrow and the greens fast. Auburn Valley has one of the most difficult starting holes around, measuring 423 yards onto an elevated green. This course is one of Northern California's hidden jewels.

Play Policy and Fees: Reciprocal play is accepted. Reciprocator fees are $70, including cart. Otherwise, guests must be accompanied by a member.

Tees and Yardage: *Men:* Blue: yardage 6846, par 72, rating 72.8, slope 129; White: yardage 6487, par 72, rating 71.0, slope 127; Gold: yardage 5735, par 72, rating 67.4, slope 119; *Women.* Red: yardage 5605, par 73, rating 72.4, slope 128.

Tee Times: Reservations may be booked seven days in advance. Reciprocators should have their club pro call to make arrangements.

Dress Code: Collared shirts and nonmetal spikes are required. No denim or tank tops are allowed on the course.

Tournaments: The event schedule fills up quickly, so tournaments should be reserved early. Bookings are accepted a year in advance. The banquet facility can accommodate 200 people.

Directions: From Auburn, drive eight miles north on Highway 49. Take the Lone Star Road exit west to Auburn Valley Road.

Contact: 8800 Auburn Valley Road, Auburn, CA 95602, pro shop 530/269-1837, fax 530/269-1725, www.auburnvalley.com.

30 BLACK OAK GOLF COURSE

Architect: John Walker, 1984
9 holes   Public $12–20

Sacramento and Vicinity Detail map,
page 74

This challenging, nine-hole course is one of the toughest of its kind in Northern California. It has an up-and-down, wide-open terrain with mature oaks, water, and sand. The greens are fast and undulating. Every hole is a killer, but a standout is the par-4, 376-yard second. It plays uphill and is longer than it looks. The green is guarded by a bunker on the right, and everything slopes to the left. You can three- or four-putt this hole easily if you're careless.

Play Policy and Fees: Green fees are $12 for nine holes and $17 for 18 holes on weekdays, $13 for nine holes and $20 for 18 holes on weekends. Senior and junior rates are available Monday–Friday.

Tees and Yardage: *Men (18 holes):* Blue: yardage 6326, par 72, rating n/a, slope 129; White: yardage 5966, par 72, rating n/a, slope 125; Yellow: yardage 5690, par 72, rating n/a, slope 121; *Women (18 holes):* Red: yardage 5568, par 72, rating n/a, slope 118.

Tee Times: Reservations can be booked seven days in advance.

Dress Code: Nonmetal spikes are encouraged. Tank tops and sleeveless shirts are forbidden.

Tournaments: Events may be booked 12 months in advance.

Directions: From I-80, take the Dry Creek Road exit west and drive two miles. Turn right on Black Oak Road and follow it to the course.

Contact: 2455 Black Oak Road, Auburn, CA 95602, pro shop 530/878-1900, fax 530/878-7652.

31 THE RIDGE GOLF COURSE

Architect: Robert Trent Jones Jr., 1998
18 holes   **Public**   **$55-70**

Sacramento and Vicinity Detail map,
page 74

Using the environment's natural rock out-croppings, rambling creeks, and plenty of mature oaks, Robert Trent Jones Jr. created a new course with a traditional, refined feel. The 13th hole is a long par-4 that requires an uphill drive to an elevated and visually deceptive green.

Play Policy and Fees: Green fees are $55 Monday–Friday, $70 weekends and holidays. Prices include a cart and range balls. Nine-hole, junior, and twilight rates are available.

Tees and Yardage: *Men:* Gold: yardage 6734, par 71, rating 72.2, slope 137; Blue: yardage 6345, par 71, rating 70.8, slope 132; White: yardage 5855, par 71, rating 67.7, slope 126; *Women:* Red: yardage 5354, par 71, rating 70.7, slope 128.

Tee Times: Tee times may be booked seven days in advance.

Dress Code: Proper golf attire and nonmetal spikes are mandatory. No denim is permitted.

Tournaments: Tournaments are welcome but subject to availability. Events may be booked 18 months in advance.

Directions: From Sacramento, take I-80 east to the Bell Road exit in Auburn. Head north on Bell Road for 1.8 miles. Make a right on Airport Road and then turn right on Golf Course Road.

Contact: 2020 Golf Course Road, Auburn, CA 95602, pro shop 530/888-7888, fax 530/888-8870, www.ridgegc.com.

32 RASPBERRY HILL GOLF COURSE

Architect: Fred Strong, 1982; Randall Dawson, 1996
9 holes   **Public**   **$9-11.50**

Sacramento and Vicinity Detail map,
page 74

This short course has several water hazards and is tougher than it looks. Raspberry Hill has small greens that require accurate approaches. There is a moderate amount of water. The toughest hole is the second, a par-3 with a new tee box location, which demands a long iron or wood downhill to a small target.

Play Policy and Fees: Green fees are $9 weekdays and $11.50 weekends for nine holes. Special rate all day Tuesday.

Tees and Yardage: *Men and Women:* yardage 1533, par 29, rating n/a, slope n/a.

Tee Times: Not necessary.

Dress Code: Appropriate attire and soft spikes are required.

Tournaments: This course is available for outside tournaments. Tournaments should be scheduled at least two weeks in advance. The banquet facility accommodates 350 people.

Directions: From I-80 east in Auburn, take the Belle Road exit. Take a right on Belle and a left onto Musso Road. The course can be seen from Musso Road.

Contact: 14500 Musso Road, Auburn, CA 95603, pro shop 530/878-7818, fax 530/878-0526.

33 AUBURN LAKE TRAILS GOLF COURSE

Architect: Course designed, 1970
9 holes   **Private**   **$10-15**

Sacramento and Vicinity Detail map,
page 74

This is an executive-type course that is maintained for and by the local property owners. The course is short and hilly with lots of out-of-bounds. There are two par-4s, one of which, the ninth, is the most compelling hole. It measures 296 yards with a slight bend to the right around oak trees, with the green guarded on the left and right by a lake.

Play Policy and Fees: Members and guests only. Guest fees are $10 weekdays and $15 weekends when authorized by a property owner.

Tees and Yardage: *Men and Women (18 holes):* Red/White: yardage 2745, par 58, rating 27.4 (M)/27.8 (W), slope 77 (M)/80 (W).

Tee Times: Not required.

Dress Code: Appropriate golf attire and non-metal spikes are required.

Tournaments: No outside events.

Directions: From Auburn, drive six miles south on Highway 49. Turn left onto Highway 193 and drive three-quarters of a mile to the course.

Contact: 1400 American River Trail (P.O. Box 728), Cool, CA 95614, pro shop 530/885-6526.

34 YOLO FLIERS CLUB

Architect: Designed 1922; Bob Baldock, 1950; Michael J. McDonagh, 1955

18 holes   Private $55

Sacramento and Vicinity Detail map, page 74

This historic California course began with 18 sand greens in 1922 and has been remodeled and expanded many times over the years. Its initial membership consisted of World War I flying aces, and it carries on a proud heritage of fliers today. Yolo Fliers has the feel of an old course, with mature trees and well-maintained greens. The number-one handicap hole is the 14th, a par-4 measuring 445 yards. There is a fair amount of out-of-bounds. If you are a member of a reciprocal club, this is a course well worth checking out.

Play Policy and Fees: Reciprocal play is accepted with members of other private clubs. Reciprocal fees are $55.

Tees and Yardage: *Men:* Blue: yardage 6823, par 72, rating 72.6, slope 124; White: yardage 6474, par 72, rating 71.0, slope 123; *Women:* Red: yardage 5892, par 72, rating 73.5, slope 124.

Tee Times: Reciprocators should have their club pro call to make arrangements.

Dress Code: Appropriate golf attire and non-metal spikes are required.

Tournaments: Shotgun tournaments are available weekdays only.

Directions: From I-505 in Woodland, take Highway 16 east. Drive four miles and turn north on Road 94-B. The course is next to Watts Municipal Airport.

Contact: 17980 Country Road, Woodland, CA 95695, pro shop 530/662-8050, www.yolofliers.org.

35 TEAL BEND GOLF CLUB

Architect: Brad Bell, 1997

18 holes   Public $42-62

Sacramento and Vicinity Detail map, page 74

Built on 250 acres, this course features gently rolling hills and natural wetlands. The greens are undulating and true. Open in the front, they lend themselves to a variety of shots, including bump and run. With four sets of tees, this is a great course for players of all abilities.

Play Policy and Fees: Green fees are $42 Monday–Thursday, $55 Friday, and $62 weekends and holidays. Twilight rates are available. All fees include cart and use of the range.

Tees and Yardage: *Men:* Black: yardage 7061, par 72, rating 73.9, slope 134; Blue: yardage 6588, par 72, rating 71.7, slope 129; White: yardage 6022, par 72, rating 69.3, slope 120; *Women:* Gold: yardage 5077, par 72, rating 68.8, slope 112.

Tee Times: Reservations can be booked seven days in advance.

Dress Code: Nonmetal spikes are required.

Tournaments: Tournaments welcome. A 16-player minimum is needed.

Directions: From Sacramento, take I-5 north to Highway 99 North. Exit at Elverta Road and take a left. Follow Elverta Road and make a left on Garden Highway to the course.

Contact: 7200 Garden Highway, Sacramento, CA 95837, pro shop 916/922-5209, fax 916/646-8716, www.tealbendgolf.com.

36 CHERRY ISLAND GOLF COURSE

Architect: Robert Muir Graves, 1990

18 holes   Public $21-26

Sacramento and Vicinity Detail map, page 74

Cherry Island is an unusual course in that it forces a golfer with average or above-average length to leave the driver in the bag on several holes. Water comes into play on 10 holes, requiring numerous layup shots off the tee. The front nine has two in-course out-of-bounds areas. The third hole (par-5, 543 yards) wraps around a large lake and forces a difficult decision on the second shot. The par-3s are excellent, including the 158-yard 13th hole, over a creek onto a green framed by trees. The 15th hole, a par-5 of 544 yards, is a tough nut. There are out-of-bounds areas left, water on the right, and an elevated green surrounded by bunkers.

Play Policy and Fees: Green fees are $21 Monday–Thursday, $24 Friday, and $26 weekends and holidays. Carts are an additional $13. Twilight, junior, and senior rates are available.

Tees and Yardage: *Men:* Blue: yardage 6562, par 72, rating 71.9, slope 129; White: yardage 6207, par 72, rating 70.8, slope 124; *Women:* Gold: yardage 5556, par 72, rating 71.8, slope 121; Red: yardage 5163, par 72, rating 70.0, slope 117.

Tee Times: Reservations can be booked 7.5 days in advance.

Dress Code: Appropriate attire and soft spikes are required.

Tournaments: Shotgun tournaments are available weekdays only. A 20-player minimum is needed to book a tournament.

Directions: From I-80 in Sacramento, take the Watt Avenue exit north. Drive five miles to Elverta Road and turn left. Drive one mile to the course on the left.

Contact: 2360 Elverta Road, Elverta, CA 95626, pro shop 916/991-6875, fax 916/991-6512, www.empiregolf.com.

37 ANTELOPE GREENS GOLF COURSE

Architect: Don Reiners, 1994

18 holes **Public** **$16–20**

Sacramento and Vicinity Detail map, page 74

This short course features four par-4s, and water comes into play on five holes. The sig-

nature hole is the par-3 seventh, which features a three-tiered island green. Tune up your short game here.

Play Policy and Fees: Green fees are $16 weekdays and $20 weekends. Twilight, nine-hole, junior, and senior rates available. Carts additional.

Tees and Yardage: *Men (18 holes):* Blue: yardage 3195, par 58, rating 57.6, slope 81; White: yardage 3007, par 58, rating 57.0, slope 80; *Women (18 holes):* Red: yardage 2546, par 58, rating 55.4, slope 79.

Tee Times: Reservations can be booked seven days in advance.

Dress Code: Appropriate attire and soft spikes are required.

Tournaments: This course is available for outside tournaments. Events should be booked two months in advance.

Directions: From I-80 north of Sacramento, turn north onto Watt Avenue. Drive six miles to Elverta Road. Turn left onto Elverta and drive one-half mile. The course will be on your right.

Contact: 2721 Elverta Road, Antelope, CA 95843, pro shop 916/334-5764, fax 916/334-9074.

38 WOODCREEK GOLF CLUB

Architect: Robert Muir Graves, 1995

18 holes **Public** **$30–44**

Sacramento and Vicinity Detail map, page 74

Woodcreek is spread out over 210 acres of gently rolling terrain. More than 1000 mature oaks are scattered throughout and give the course an older feel. Natural wetlands, lakes, streams, and 80 bunkers give golfers plenty to think about, along with the large greens. This course has great finishing holes.

Play Policy and Fees: Green fees are $30 weekdays and $44 weekends. Carts are $14. Junior, senior, and twilight rates are available.

Tees and Yardage: *Men:* Gold: yardage 6518, par 72, rating 71.8, slope 132; Blue: yardage 6041, par 72, rating 70.2, slope 123; White:

yardage 5483, par 72, rating 67.8, slope 118; *Women:* Red: yardage 4739, par 70, rating 66.2, slope 112.

Tee Times: Reservations can be booked seven days in advance.

Dress Code: No tank tops are allowed on the course.

Tournaments: Please inquire.

Directions: From Sacramento, take I-80 north to the Riverside exit in Roseville. Turn left on Cirby Way. Take Cirby Way to Foothills and turn right. Take Foothills to Pleasant Grove Road and turn left. Take Pleasant Grove Road to Woodcreek Oaks Boulevard and turn right. Continue one-quarter mile to the course.

Contact: 5880 Woodcreek Oaks Boulevard, Roseville, CA 95747, pro shop 916/771-4653, fax 916/771-4651, www.golfroseville.com.

39 SUN CITY ROSEVILLE GOLF COURSE

Architect: Billy Casper, 1996

27 holes   **Semiprivate**   **$48-53**

Sacramento and Vicinity Detail map, page 74

This 27-hole facility offers an 18-hole loop combining the Lakes and Oaks nines, and a nine-hole loop called Sierra Pines. The terrain features native California oak trees and some nice mountain views. Large, undulating greens make play somewhat friendly. Water comes into play on six of the nine holes on the front side of Lakes/Oaks. The signature hole is the 516-yard, par-5 18th, where water on the left and bunkers on the right face you off the tee. The second shot offers a risk/reward option: Go for it over a creek to a narrow green, or play it safe.

Play Policy and Fees: Public play is accepted. Green fees are $48 weekdays and $53 weekends. Twilight rates are also available. Carts are included.

Tees and Yardage: Lakes/Oaks—*Men:* Casper: yardage 6500, par 72, rating 70.5, slope 123; Blue: yardage 6040, par 72, rating 68.7, slope 118; Gold: yardage 5627, par 72, rating 67.3,

slope 114; *Women:* Red: yardage 5176, par 72, rating 70.4, slope 119. Sierra Pines—*Men:* Casper: yardage 3175, par 36, rating 35.2, slope 113; Blue: yardage 3010, par 36, rating 34.6, slope 108; Gold: yardage 2825, par 36, rating 33.8, slope 102; *Women:* Red: yardage 2525, par 36, rating 32.3, slope 99.

Tee Times: Reservations can be booked seven days in advance.

Dress Code: Collared shirts and nonmetal spikes are required, and no denim is allowed.

Tournaments: This course is available for tournaments, which can be booked up to one year in advance. Call the pro shop for more information.

Directions: From I-80 heading toward Reno, take Highway 65 toward Yuba City. Exit on Blue Oaks. Follow Blue Oaks all the way to the golf course.

Contact: 7050 Del Webb Boulevard, Roseville, CA 95747, pro shop 916/774-3850, fax 916/774-3889, www.suncityroseville.org.

40 DIAMOND OAKS GOLF COURSE

Architect: Ted Robinson Sr., 1963

18 holes   **Public**   **$15-32**

Sacramento and Vicinity Detail map, page 74

Mature oaks line the fairways of this rolling course. Diamond Oaks is fairly forgiving for the most part, and the greens are in excellent shape for a municipal course that hosts 90,000 rounds per year. The ninth hole (par-4 and 443 yards) has oak trees right and left. The 18th is a superb finishing hole, measuring 392 yards uphill with a large oak tree dominating the right side of the fairway.

Play Policy and Fees: Green fees are $15 for nine holes and $25 for 18 holes on weekdays. Fees are $19 for nine holes and $32 for 18 holes on weekends. Carts are $7.50 for nine holes and $13 for 18 holes. Twilight, junior, and senior rates are available.

Tees and Yardage: *Men:* Blue: yardage 6179, par

72, rating 69.1, slope 118; White: yardage 5885, par 72, rating 67.8, slope 115; *Women:* Red: yardage 5481, par 73, rating 71.5, slope 119.
Tee Times: Reservations can be booked seven days in advance.
Dress Code: Shirts and shoes are necessary. No tank tops are allowed on the course.
Tournaments: A 24-player minimum is required to book a tournament. Tournaments must be booked at least two weeks in advance. No shotgun tournaments are allowed.
Directions: From I-80 in Roseville, take the Atlantic Street exit to Yosemite Street. Turn right and drive to Diamond Oaks Road. Turn left and drive 400 yards to the course.
Contact: 349 Diamond Oaks Road, Roseville, CA 95678, pro shop 916/783-4947, fax 916/783-3442, www.golfroseville.com.

41 SIERRA VIEW COUNTRY CLUB

Architect: Jack Fleming, 1956
18 holes   **Private**   **$45**

Sacramento and Vicinity Detail map, page 74

Sierra View, a rolling course with mature trees and exceptional greens, is at the base of the Sierra foothills. Designed by Jack Fleming, the right-hand man of famed architect Alister Mackenzie, it offers a wide variety of short and long par-4s. The toughest is the third hole, a 459-yarder, which plays like a par-5 for all but the biggest hitters. The par-5 18th hole (554 yards) is an outstanding test, tightening as it goes along. Sierra View has served as a qualifying site for the U.S. Senior Open and the U.S. Women's Amateur.
Play Policy and Fees: Reciprocal play is accepted, with fees based on reciprocating club's fees, starting at $45. Otherwise, guests must be accompanied by a member.
Tees and Yardage: *Men:* Black: yardage 6481, par 72, rating 71.1, slope 126; Middle: yardage 5936, par 72, rating 64.6, slope 106; *Women:* Forward: yardage 5197, par 73, rating 70.2, slope 123.

Tee Times: Reciprocators should have their club pro call to make arrangements.
Dress Code: Collared shirts and nonmetal spikes are required. Shorts may not be more than three inches above the knee.
Tournaments: This course is available for outside tournaments.
Directions: From I-80 in Roseville, exit at Atlantic Street and take the second right onto Yosemite Street. Drive a few blocks until the road bends. Look for Alta Vista and turn left to the course.
Contact: 105 Alta Vista, Roseville, CA 95678, pro shop 916/783-4600, www.sierraviewcc.com.

42 MORGAN CREEK GOLF & COUNTRY CLUB

Architect: Kyle Phillips, 2003
18 holes   **Private**   **$75**

Sacramento and Vicinity Detail map, page 74

The centerpiece of a family-oriented, 546-acre master-planned community, the golf course occupies a relatively flat piece of land, graced by hundreds of mature oaks and native grasses. Designer Phillips did a wonderful job of keeping the layout simple and in keeping with the serenity of the land. Strategic bunkering requires some shot-making skills, but the greens are not too severe, so recovery is often possible if you're out of position. In this sense, the course is suited to all members of the family, regardless of skill level.
Play Policy and Fees: Public play accepted on Monday only at $75. Otherwise, this private course accepts members by invitation only. Membership invitations can be obtained on the course's website or by calling.
Tees and Yardage: *Men:* Black: yardage 7303, par 72, rating 75.6, slope 143; Gold: yardage 6929, par 72, rating 73.7, slope 137; Blue: yardage 6585, par 72, rating 72.4, slope 133; White: yardage 6186, par 72, rating 70.5, slope 131; *Women:* Green: yardage 5431, par 72, rating 72.3, slope 125.

Tee Times: Reservations for Monday play can be made seven days in advance.

Dress Code: Appropriate golf attire is required. No metal spikes are allowed on the course.

Tournaments: Tournaments and group events accepted on any day.

Directions: From Sacramento, take I-80 east to Riverside Avenue and loop over the freeway. Turn left on Cirby Way, then right on Foothills Boulevard. A left onto Vineyard Road will lead to Morgan Creek Lane. Turn left on Morgan Creek and you'll see the course.

Contact: 8787 Morgan Creek Lane, Roseville, CA 95747, golf shop 916/786-4653, fax 916/780-4623, www.morgancreekclub.com.

43 SUNSET WHITNEY COUNTRY CLUB

Architect: William F. Bell, 1962

18 holes   **Private**   **$60–70**

Sacramento and Vicinity Detail map, page 74

Situated in the Sierra Nevada foothills, this tight, twisting course has water, bunkers, and undulating greens. It plays longer than the scorecard since fairways allow minimal roll. Sunset has one of Northern California's best short par-3s in the ninth, a 113-yarder. From the elevated tee, it seems as though the golfer can almost reach across the small pond and touch the green. But the two-tiered green is wide and shallow. The tee shot had better bite or it's sand city. Then there is the par-4 12th, a 439-yarder requiring a tee shot to carry over a large pond.

Play Policy and Fees: Reciprocal play is accepted with members of other private clubs. Green fees for reciprocal players are $60 weekdays and $70 weekends, carts included. The course is closed on Monday.

Tees and Yardage: *Men:* Blue: yardage 6607, par 72, rating 72.4, slope 134; White: yardage 6218, par 72, rating 70.5, slope 130; *Women:* Red: yardage 5507, par 72, rating 72.8, slope 128.

Tee Times: Reservations are recommended and can be booked seven days in advance.

Dress Code: Soft spikes are preferred.

Tournaments: Shotgun tournaments are available Monday, Thursday, and Friday. Carts are required, and a 50-player minimum is needed. Events should be scheduled at least two months in advance. The banquet facility can accommodate 300 people.

Directions: From I-80 in Rocklin, take the Taylor Road exit north. Turn left on Midas Avenue and drive to the course.

Contact: 4201 Midas Avenue (P.O. Box 788), Rocklin, CA 95677, pro shop 916/624-2610, clubhouse 916/624-2402, fax 916/624-9360, www.sunsetwhitney.com.

44 WHITNEY OAKS GOLF CLUB

Architect: Johnny Miller & Fred Bliss, 1997

18 holes   **Public**   **$49–69**

Sacramento and Vicinity Detail map, page 74

Whitney Oaks has it all—wetlands, meadows, ancient oak trees, granite outcroppings, picturesque hills, and views of the Sacramento skyline. The par-4 fifth hole forces you to lay up off the tee to avoid a ravine. This leaves a long second shot into a narrow and sloping green. The green is guarded by bunkers on the left and a hazard on the right. Whitney Oaks is on a portion of the J. Parker Whitney Ranch, site of what is believed to be the first golf course in Northern California. Expertly run by Troon Golf.

Play Policy and Fees: Green fees are $49 Monday–Thursday, $59 Friday, and $69 weekends and holidays. Twilight, junior, and senior rates available. All green fees include cart, yardage book, and range balls.

Tees and Yardage: *Men:* Black: yardage 6794, par 71, rating 74.2, slope 138; Grey: yardage 6322, par 71, rating 72.2, slope 134; Tan: yardage 5881, par 71, rating 70.3, slope 126; Gold: yardage 5469, par 71, rating 67.9, slope 121; *Women:* Jade: yardage 4980, par 71, rating 70.0, slope 125.

Tee Times: Reservations can be made seven days in advance.

Dress Code: Collared shirts and nonmetal spikes are required. No denim is allowed on the course.
Tournaments: A 16-player minimum is required to book an event. Tournaments should be scheduled 30 days in advance. The banquet facility can accommodate 175 people.
Directions: From I-80 east of Roseville, take Highway 65 north to Stanford Ranch Road exit. Follow Stanford Ranch Road three miles to Park Drive. Turn right on Park Drive and go to Whitney Oaks Drive. Turn left and continue to Clubhouse Drive.
Contact: 2305 Clubhouse Drive, Rocklin, CA 95765, pro shop 916/632-8333, fax 916/630-0972, www.whitneyoaksgolf.com.

45 INDIAN CREEK COUNTRY CLUB

Architect: Course designed, 1966
9 holes   **Public**   **$11–20**

Sacramento and Vicinity Detail map, page 74

A short course, Indian Creek is a natural layout in the rolling hills of Placer County. Low-handicappers are often surprised at the difficulty of these holes. The second hole is a downhill dogleg over water, with the second shot played to an elevated green. A good course for practice rounds and beginning golfers.
Play Policy and Fees: Green fees are $11 for nine holes and $18 for 18 holes weekdays, $12 for nine holes and $20 for 18 holes weekends. Senior, junior, and twilight rates are available. A special Tuesday rate offers "two-for-the-price-of-one" green fees.
Tees and Yardage: *Men:* Blue: yardage 2215, par 32, rating n/a, slope n/a; White: yardage 2170, par 32, rating n/a, slope n/a; *Women:* Red: yardage 1996, par 32, rating n/a, slope n/a.
Tee Times: Reservations can be made at any time.
Dress Code: Appropriate attire and soft spikes are required.
Tournaments: This course is available for outside tournaments. A private room with patio is available.
Directions: From I-80 east in Rocklin, take the Rocklin Road exit (not the exit for the town of Rocklin). Turn right on Rocklin Road and drive about two miles to the end. Turn left on Barton Road and drive one mile to the course.
Contact: 4487 Barton Road, Loomis, CA 95650, pro shop 916/652-5546, fax 916/652-8933.

46 GRANITE BAY GOLF CLUB

Architect: Robert Trent Jones Jr., 1994
18 holes   **Private**

Sacramento and Vicinity Detail map, page 74

Architect Robert Trent Jones Jr. combined the influence of the old-style designers with a modern-day touch to create one of the best new courses in the state. This sprawling, oak-lined layout was set into the existing topography and has a natural look and feel. Granite outcroppings abound, Linda Creek meanders through the course, and most holes provide scenic vistas. The par-4 16th and 18th holes are already among the most talked-about holes in the Sacramento area. This one is a real gem.
Play Policy and Fees: Members and guests only. Guests must be accompanied by a member. Closed Monday.
Tees and Yardage: *Men:* Tournament: yardage 6909, par 71, rating 73.3, slope 137; Granite: yardage 6520, par 71, rating 71.5, slope 134; Club: yardage 6100, par 71, rating 69.7, slope 126; *Women:* Cobble: yardage 5750, par 71, rating 74.1, slope 135; Pebble: yardage 5046, par 71, rating 70.3, slope 127.
Tee Times: Reservations may be booked one week in advance.
Dress Code: Tucked-in collared shirts are required, as are soft spikes. No denim, jogging suits, or gym clothes are permitted. Shorts with at least a six-inch inseam are preferred.
Tournaments: This course is open to outside tournaments on Monday only. Tournaments

may be booked up to a year in advance. The banquet facility can accommodate 250 people.

Directions: From Sacramento, take I-80 east. Exit at Douglas Boulevard in Roseville. Proceed two miles to Roseville Parkway. Turn right on Roseville Parkway and drive three miles to the course entry gate on the right.

Contact: 9600 Golf Club Drive, Granite Bay, CA 95746, pro shop 916/791-5379, fax 916/791-3214, www.granitebayclub.com.

47 ROLLING GREENS GOLF COURSE

Architect: Course designed, 1951

9 holes   Public $10–17

Sacramento and Vicinity Detail map, page 74

This short, par-3 course has rolling terrain and can be tough, especially the 223-yard, par-3 sixth, which has only been aced once. Good for honing up your iron play.

Play Policy and Fees: Green fees are $10 for nine holes and $17 for 18 holes.

Tees and Yardage: *Men and Women:* yardage 1500, par 27, rating n/a, slope n/a.

Tee Times: Reservations are not accepted. All play is on a first-come, first-served basis.

Dress Code: Shirts must be worn.

Tournaments: This course is available for outside tournaments.

Directions: From I-80 in Roseville, take the Douglas Street exit east. Turn right on Sierra College Boulevard and left on Eureka Road.

Contact: 5572 Eureka Road, Roseville, CA 95746, pro shop 916/797-9986.

48 EL DORADO HILLS GOLF CLUB

Architect: Robert Trent Jones Sr., 1963

18 holes   Public $20–25

Sacramento and Vicinity Detail map, page 74

Although primarily a test for irons, this course does have several par-4s and one par-5. The front nine is hilly. The course is well maintained and has lots of trees and water. The par-3 14th is one of the Sacramento area's finest short holes, a challenging shot onto a green fronted by a bunker with water on the left.

Play Policy and Fees: Green fees are $16 weekdays before 9 A.M., $20 after 9 A.M., and $20 weekends before 9 A.M., $25 after 9 A.M. Twilight rates are also available.

Tees and Yardage: *Men:* Back: yardage 3860, par 62, rating 60.7, slope 103; *Women:* Front: yardage 3530, par 62, rating 59.2, slope 91.

Tee Times: Reservations can be booked 14 days in advance for weekdays and seven days in advance for weekends.

Dress Code: Golf attire is encouraged.

Tournaments: This course is available for outside tournaments.

Directions: From Sacramento, drive 25 miles east on U.S. 50. Take the El Dorado Hills Boulevard exit north and drive to the course, which is on the right.

Contact: 3775 El Dorado Hills Boulevard, El Dorado Hills, CA 95762, pro shop 916/933-6552, fax 916/933-5090.

49 BASS LAKE GOLF COURSE

Architect: Gene Thorne, 1996

18 holes   Public $20–25

Sacramento and Vicinity Detail map, page 74

This well-maintained course has plenty of pine and oak trees and an eight-acre pond loaded with bass. One of the more unusual holes has you teeing off from an elevated deck over the water. Those less daring can hit from the tees in front of the pond. New cart paths, a remodel of the clubhouse, and other improvements were completed here in 2004.

Play Policy and Fees: Green fees weekdays are $20, $25 weekends. Carts are $10. Junior, senior, and twilight rates are available.

Tees and Yardage: *Men:* Blue: yardage 6028, par 72, rating 69.5, slope 126; White: yardage 5564, par 72, rating 66.7, slope 118; Yellow:

yardage 5141, par 72, rating n/a, slope n/a; *Women:* Red: yardage 4638, par 72, rating 68.0, slope 118.

Tee Times: Reservations can be booked seven days in advance.

Dress Code: No tank tops are allowed on the course. Soft spikes only.

Tournaments: This course is available for outside tournaments.

Directions: From U.S. 50 near Cameron Park, take the Bass Lake Road exit. Head north on Bass Lake Road for three miles to the golf course.

Contact: 3000 Alexandrite Drive, Rescue, CA 95672, pro shop 530/677-4653, fax 530/677-5216.

50 CAMERON PARK COUNTRY CLUB

Architect: Bert Stamps, 1960
18 holes   **Private**   **$65**

Sacramento and Vicinity Detail map, page 74

At a 1300-foot elevation, Cameron Park would be a tough course due to its tightness alone, but the real trick to scoring well is in mastering the greens. They are fast—so fast that some putts simply won't stop short of the hole. Holes of particular note are the 14th and 17th. The 17th is a par-3 of 204 yards over water, and the 14th is a par-4 measuring 389 yards with out-of-bounds to the right. The layout is particularly demanding from the women's tees.

Play Policy and Fees: Reciprocal play is accepted with members of other private clubs. Green fees for reciprocal players are $65. Closed Monday.

Tees and Yardage: *Men:* Blue: yardage 6531, par 72, rating 71.6, slope 125; White: yardage 6303, par 72, rating 70.7, slope 123; *Women:* Red: yardage 5894, par 73, rating 74.4, slope 136.

Tee Times: Reservations can be booked seven days in advance. You must have your club professional call to book a time.

Dress Code: Appropriate golf attire is required. No denim is allowed.

Tournaments: Outside events must be approved by the tournament committee.

Directions: From Sacramento, drive 30 miles east on U.S. 50. Take the Cameron Park Drive exit. Turn left and drive under the overpass. Make the first left (don't get back on the freeway) onto Country Club Drive. Drive one-half mile to just past the driving range. Make the first right past the driving range (Royal Drive) and drive to the course entrance.

Contact: 3201 Royal Drive, Cameron Park, CA 95682, pro shop 530/672-9840, www.cameronparkcc.com.

51 SERRANO COUNTRY CLUB

Architect: Robert Trent Jones Jr., 1996
18 holes   **Private**   **$60–125**

Sacramento and Vicinity Detail map, page 74

This sprawling course is packed with mature oak trees that come into play on 10 holes. The rolling terrain is mostly forgiving, and the majority of greens are open in front. Water comes into play on six holes, and wind is often a factor. Set in the Sierra foothills, this course offers spectacular views of Folsom Lake and the snowcapped Sierras to the east. Serrano played host to the Gold Rush Classic, a Senior PGA Tour event, 1996–2001. The course is patterned after Shinnecock Hills Golf Club in New York.

Play Policy and Fees: Reciprocal play is accepted with members of other private clubs on a limited basis. The reciprocal fee is $125, including cart. Guest fees are $60 Tuesday–Thursday and $80 Friday–Sunday. Guests may play unaccompanied by a member.

Tees and Yardage: *Men:* Copper: yardage 6975, par 72, rating 74.2, slope 134; Black: yardage 6525, par 72, rating 71.6, slope 132; White: yardage 6189, par 72, rating 69.7, slope 127; *Women:* Gold: yardage 5720, par 72, rating 72.6, slope 130; Green: yardage 5232, par 72, rating 69.9, slope 124.

Tee Times: Reciprocators should have their home pro call in advance to arrange tee times.
Dress Code: Appropriate golf attire and non-metal spikes are required. No cellular phones are allowed on the course.
Tournaments: Outside events are allowed on an extremely limited basis. Shotgun tournaments are available Monday only. Carts are required.
Directions: From downtown Sacramento, drive 25 miles east on U.S. 50. Take El Dorado Hills Boulevard exit. Drive one-quarter mile north on El Dorado Hills Boulevard to Serrano Parkway and turn right. Drive east to the course.
Contact: 5005 Serrano Parkway, El Dorado Hills, CA 95762, pro shop 916/933-5716, www.serranocountryclub.com.

52 EMPIRE RANCH GOLF CLUB

Architect: Brad Bell, 2002
18 holes   Public $42–62

Sacramento and Vicinity Detail map, page 74

At the base of the Sierra Nevada foothills east of Sacramento, this links-style golf course is set amidst an ambitious residential development. The scenic layout includes an interesting variety of holes that will test your game with marsh carries, strategic bunkering, and undulating greens. The signature hole is the par-3 18th, a 211-yard shot over water, very difficult when the wind is working against you.
Play Policy and Fees: Green fees are $42 weekdays, $52 Friday, and $62 weekends and holidays, including cart. Twilight (begins at noon), super twilight, junior, and senior rates are available.
Tees and Yardage: *Men:* Blue: yardage 6668, par 71, rating 70.9, slope 125; White: yardage 6056, par 71, rating 68.3, slope 120; *Women:* Red: yardage 5036, par 71, rating 68.0, slope 110.
Tee Times: Reservations can be made seven days in advance.
Dress Code: No metal spikes are allowed on the course. Collared golf shirts are required.

Tournaments: Tournaments welcome.
Directions: Take U.S. 50 east from Sacramento to East Bidwell exit in Folsom. Turn left on East Bidwell (back over the freeway), then turn right on Broadstone (third signal light). Turn left on Golf Links Drive then left on East Natoma Street. Empire Ranch Golf Club is on the right.
Contact: 1620 East Natoma Street, Folsom, CA 95630, golf shop 916/817-8100, fax 916/817-8110, www.empireranchgolfclub.com.

53 SUNRISE GOLF COURSE

Architect: Course designed, 1981
9 holes   Private $7–15

Sacramento and Vicinity Detail map, page 74

This executive-style course has rolling hills, tree-lined fairways, and small greens. The par-5 ninth hole has a creek running through the fairway and is very tight—a demanding finish. While the course is private, the adjacent driving range is open to the public until 10 P.M. nightly.
Play Policy and Fees: Reciprocal play is accepted with members of other private clubs. Guest and reciprocal fees are $7 for nine holes and $11 for 18 holes on weekdays, $8 and $15 weekends.
Tees and Yardage: *Men and Women (18 holes):* yardage 4090, par 62, rating 60.8 (M)/62.3 (W), slope 108 (M)/105 (W).
Tee Times: Reservations not necessary for weekdays. Weekend and holiday reservations taken beginning Monday for the current week.
Dress Code: Appropriate golf attire and non-metal spikes are required.
Tournaments: This course is available for outside tournaments. A 20-player minimum is needed. Events should be booked three months in advance.
Directions: From I-80 in Citrus Heights (northeast of Sacramento), take the Greenback Lane exit east. Drive four miles to Sunrise Boulevard and turn left. The course is on the right.
Contact: 6412 Sunrise Boulevard, Citrus Heights, CA 95610, pro shop 916/723-0481.

54 NORTH RIDGE COUNTRY CLUB

Architect: William F. Bell, 1952

18 holes　　　**Private**　　　**$81**

Sacramento and Vicinity Detail map, page 74

This tree-lined course has Bermuda grass fairways and long par-4s. It tends to play longer than the yardage because of the number of uphill holes. North Ridge features a classic par-5, the 15th hole. It narrows each step of the way and demands a precise second shot to the left of the tree line. The small green caps things off.

Play Policy and Fees: Reciprocal play is accepted with members of other private clubs for $81, including cart. The course is closed on Monday.

Tees and Yardage: *Men:* Blue: yardage 6553, par 72, rating 71.5, slope 130; White: yardage 6251, par 72, rating 70.1, slope 127; *Women:* Red: yardage 5835, par 72, rating 74.6, slope 136.

Tee Times: Reciprocators should have their club pro call to make arrangements.

Dress Code: Appropriate golf attire and non-metal spikes are required; shirts must be collared and tucked in. No jeans are allowed on the course, and hats must be removed in the clubhouse.

Tournaments: Outside tournaments accepted.

Directions: From Sacramento, drive east on I-80. Take the Madison Avenue exit east. Follow Madison Avenue for five miles and make a right into the club at Mariposa Avenue.

Contact: 7600 Madison Avenue, Fair Oaks, CA 95628, pro shop 916/967-5716, www.north ridgegolf.com.

55 DAVIS GOLF COURSE

Architect: Bob Baldock, 1964

18 holes　　　**Public**　　　**$14–18**

Sacramento and Vicinity Detail map, page 74

This short, level course has strategically placed trees and six lakes that come into play on 12

holes. The seventh hole may be short, but that doesn't make it easy. The green is surrounded by water. The course is extremely popular with seniors and women.

Play Policy and Fees: Green fees are $14 weekdays and $18 weekends. Senior, twilight, and junior rates are available during the week.

Tees and Yardage: *Men:* Blue: yardage 4953, par 67, rating 63.1, slope 107; White: yardage 4472, par 67, rating 60.9, slope 100; *Women:* Red: yardage 4428, par 67, rating 64.9, slope 105.

Tee Times: Reservations can be booked seven days in advance.

Dress Code: Appropriate attire and soft spikes are required.

Tournaments: A 24-player minimum is needed to book a tournament. The banquet facility can accommodate up to 60 people. Events should be scheduled at least two months in advance.

Directions: From I-80 in Davis, take the Highway 113 exit. Drive five miles north to County Road 29. The course is on the left.

Contact: 24439 Fairway Drive, Davis, CA 95617 (P.O. Box 928, Davis, CA 95616), pro shop 530/756-4010, fax 530/756-0647.

56 WILDHORSE GOLF CLUB

Architect: Jeff Brauer, 1999

18 holes　　　**Public**　　　**$26–41**

Sacramento and Vicinity Detail map, page 74

This is a links-style course with five lakes, 64 traps, and an environmentally sensitive area running throughout. The greens are good sized, true, firm, fast, and well protected by bunkers. Although the course only plays 6700 yards from the back tees, the slope rating is 135. The back tees present a great challenge for even experienced golfers; however, the forward tees make the course playable for anyone.

Play Policy and Fees: Green fees are $26 Monday–Friday and $41 on weekends and holidays. Carts are $11 per player.

Tees and Yardage: *Men:* Black: yardage 6733,

par 72, rating 72.7, slope 134; Blue: yardage 6406, par 72, rating 71.0, slope 129; White: yardage 6002, par 72, rating 69.0, slope 124; *Women:* Gold: yardage 5324, par 71, rating 69.0, slope 126.

Tee Times: Reservations can be made seven days in advance.

Dress Code: Collared shirts and soft spikes are required.

Tournaments: A 16-player minimum is required to book an event. Tournaments should be scheduled 12–24 months in advance.

Directions: From I-80, take the Mace exit and head north to Covel, take a right on Wright Boulevard, and turn left on Moore Street until you get to Rockwell. Take a right on Rockwell to the course.

Contact: 2323 Rockwell Drive, Davis, CA 95616, pro shop 530/753-4900, fax 530/753-9879, www.wildhorsegolfclub.com.

57 EL MACERO COUNTRY CLUB

Architect: Bob Baldock, 1961

18 holes   Private $60

Sacramento and Vicinity Detail map, page 74

This long, narrow course has lots of out-of-bounds areas, challenging fairway bunkers, excellent greens, and three lakes. The talk of this course is the 516-yard, par-5 15th hole. There are two fairway bunkers in the right landing zone, and the undulating green is surrounded by more bunkers. Trees are everywhere. Out-of-bounds areas mark both sides of the wide fairway. If shots stray, the player is hitting out of the trees.

Play Policy and Fees: Reciprocal play is accepted with members of other private clubs at a rate of $60.

Tees and Yardage: *Men:* Championship: yardage 6853, par 72, rating 72.9, slope 131; Back: yardage 6499, par 72, rating 71.4, slope 126; *Women:* Middle: yardage 5893, par 72, rating 74.9, slope 129; Forward: yardage 5284, par 72, rating 70.8, slope 122.

Tee Times: Reciprocators should have their club pro call to make arrangements.

Dress Code: Appropriate golf attire and non-metal spikes are required.

Tournaments: Outside tournaments Monday only. A 100-player minimum is needed to book a shotgun tournament.

Directions: From Davis, drive two miles east on I-80. Take the Mace Boulevard exit south in El Macero to Clubhouse Drive.

Contact: 44571 Clubhouse Drive, El Macero, CA 95618, pro shop 530/753-5621, fax 530/753-4832.

58 HAGGIN OAKS GOLF COURSE

Architect: Alister Mackenzie, 1932 (Alister Mackenzie Course); Michael J. McDonagh, 1958 (Arcade Creek Course)

36 holes   Public $25–55

Sacramento and Vicinity Detail map, page 74

These two layouts are among the most popular in the Sacramento area and get heavy play. The Alister Mackenzie Course, named after its famous Scottish-born designer, was extensively remodeled in 2002, including some rerouting and a new lake. It is now in the best shape it has been in many years. A tree-lined course, Mackenzie features large greens and extensive trademark Mackenzie bunkering. The Arcade Creek Course is more wide open.

Play Policy and Fees: Green fees for the Alister Mackenzie Course are $45 Monday–Thursday and $55 Friday, weekends, and holidays. Carts included. Green fees for the Arcade Creek Course are $25 Monday–Thursday and $29 Friday, weekends, and holidays. Carts extra on Arcade Creek. Haggin Oaks offers off-peak rates as well as senior and junior rates.

Tees and Yardage: Alister Mackenzie—*Men:* Black: yardage 6691, par 72, rating 72.7, slope 125; Burgundy: yardage 6542, par 72, rating 70.7, slope 123; Cream: yardage 6057, par 72, rating 68.3, slope 118; *Women:* Green: yardage

5452, par 72, rating 70.5, slope 117. Arcade Creek—*Men:* Blue: yardage 6889, par 72, rating 71.2, slope 114; White: yardage 6552, par 72, rating 69.9, slope 110; *Women:* Red: yardage 5786, par 72, rating 71.7, slope 111.

Tee Times: Reservations can be booked seven days in advance for weekdays. Weekend and holiday reservations are taken on the Tuesday prior starting at 6 A.M., by calling the Sacramento City Tee Time Hotline at 916/665-1202. The phone number for the Arcade Creek Course is 916/481-4508.

Dress Code: Soft spikes are required.

Tournaments: Tournaments welcome. Please inquire.

Directions: Take the Fulton Road exit north off Business 80 in Sacramento and follow it to the course.

Contact: 3645 Fulton Avenue, Sacramento, CA 95821, pro shop 916/481-4653, fax 916/575-2523, www.hagginoaks.com.

59 DEL PASO COUNTRY CLUB
Architect: Herbert Fowler, 1916
18 holes   **Private**   **$85**

🏌 📷 🍴 ⛳ 🚙 🍺

Sacramento and Vicinity Detail map, page 74

This rolling, tree-lined layout is narrow with small, undulating greens. The fairways and greens are well bunkered. The most distinct holes are the second, a par-5 of 488 yards that horseshoes around a creek and trees; the 16th, a 200-yard par-3; the 17th, a par-4 of 403 yards into a well-bunkered green; and the 18th, a 396-yarder with the stately clubhouse serving as a backdrop. The men's course record is 63, set by Lee Elder and Bob E. Smith during the old "Swing at Cancer" benefits. Del Paso has hosted several USGA events: the 1957 and 1976 U.S. Women's Amateur and the 1964 Senior Women's Amateur. The 1982 U.S. Women's Open was held here.

Play Policy and Fees: Reciprocal play is accepted. Fees are $85 and carts are $15 per player.

Tees and Yardage: *Men:* yardage 6300, par 72,

rating 70.6, slope 122; *Women:* yardage 5816, par 74, rating 73.8, slope 129.

Tee Times: Reservations can be booked seven days in advance. Reciprocal players' club pro must call to arrange tee times.

Dress Code: Appropriate golf attire is required. A seven-inch inseam is required for all shorts.

Tournaments: This course is available for outside tournaments. Call the pro shop for more information.

Directions: From Business 80 in Sacramento, take the Marconi Avenue exit east. Drive one-half mile to the course on the left. From I-80, take the Watt Avenue exit. Travel on Watt Avenue to Marconi Avenue and turn right on Marconi. Follow it to the course.

Contact: 3333 Marconi Avenue, Sacramento, CA 95821, pro shop 916/483-0401, fax 916/489-4011, www.delpasocountryclub.com.

60 ANCIL HOFFMAN GOLF COURSE
Architect: William F. Bell, 1965
18 holes   **Public**   **$25–42**

🏌 📷 🍴 ⛳ 🚙 🍺

Sacramento and Vicinity Detail map, page 74

Situated in Ancil Hoffman Park on the American River, this course has oak and pine trees coming into play on nearly every hole. The fairways are tight, and the greens are contoured. Although it shows the wear of a high number of rounds each year, Hoffman is one of the premier public courses in Northern California. The seventh hole, a par-5 of 542 yards, is outstanding, requiring a pinpoint drive down a tree-lined fairway. The second shot is almost as difficult to place, and the green is large. This course is consistently ranked among the top public courses in the country.

Play Policy and Fees: Green fees are $25 Monday–Thursday to walk, $38 to ride, and $29 Friday–Sunday to walk, $42 to ride. Twilight, senior, junior, and nine-hole rates are available.

Tees and Yardage: *Men:* Blue: yardage 6794, par 72, rating 72.6, slope 129; White: yardage 6434,

par 72, rating 70.9, slope 128; *Women:* Red: yardage 5954, par 73, rating 74.2, slope 123.

Tee Times: Reservations can be booked seven days in advance for weekdays. For weekend reservations, call on the Monday prior starting at 6:30 A.M.

Dress Code: Shirts must be worn.

Tournaments: Shotgun tournaments are limited and must have a full field of 144. Carts are required.

Directions: From Business 80 in Sacramento, take the Marconi Avenue exit east. Drive five miles to Fair Oaks Boulevard and turn right. Turn left on Kenneth Avenue. Turn right on California Avenue and left on Ancil Hoffman Park Road (Tarshes Drive) and follow it to the course.

Contact: 6700 Tarshes Drive, Carmichael, CA 95608, pro shop 916/575-4653, fax 916/482-3089.

61 CAMPUS COMMONS GOLF COURSE

Architect: Bill McDowell, 1973
9 holes   **Public**   **$10–18**

Sacramento and Vicinity Detail map, page 74

This rolling executive course is bordered by the American River. The greens are elevated, and there is a lot of roll to the fairways. The river comes into play on the fifth, seventh, and eighth holes. The fifth plays 187 yards, with the river an intimidating presence on the right.

Play Policy and Fees: Green fees are $10 for nine holes and $17 for 18 holes weekdays, $11 for nine holes and $18 for 18 holes weekends. Carts are $10 per nine holes.

Tees and Yardage: *Men:* yardage 1673, par 58, rating 54.0, slope 84; *Women:* yardage 1508, par 60, rating 56.0, slope n/a.

Tee Times: Reservations can be booked seven days in advance.

Dress Code: Appropriate attire and soft spikes are required.

Tournaments: This course is available for events.

Directions: From U.S. 50 in Sacramento, take the Howe Avenue North exit. Take a left on Fair Oaks Boulevard and a right on Cadillac Drive. Follow Cadillac Drive to the course.

Contact: 2 Cadillac Drive, Sacramento, CA 95825, pro shop 916/922-5861.

62 WILLIAM LAND GOLF COURSE

Architect: Course designed, 1927
9 holes   **Public**   **$12.50–13.50**

Sacramento and Vicinity Detail map, page 74

Set in beautiful William Land Park, this course is a favorite of women, seniors, and locals interested in a peaceful round of golf. The par-3 third hole (153 yards) has long been considered one of the area's best, with its two huge cottonwoods guarding the green. Former U.S. Women's Amateur champion Barbara Romack learned how to play here, as did "Mr. 59," Al Geiberger. When the city threatened to close the golf course in the early 1950s, one of its staunchest defenders was Sis Kennedy, mother of Supreme Court Justice Anthony Kennedy.

Play Policy and Fees: Weekday green fees are $12.50. Weekend green fees are $13.50. Senior, junior, early bird, afternoon, and twilight rates are available. Capitol City card rates available.

Tees and Yardage: *Men and Women:* yardage 2612, par 34, rating n/a, slope n/a.

Tee Times: Weekday reservations can be booked seven days in advance. Weekend and holiday reservations are taken on the Tuesday prior, starting at 6 A.M., by calling the Sacramento City Tee Time Hotline at 916/665-1202.

Dress Code: Nonmetal spikes are required.

Tournaments: This course is available for outside tournaments.

Directions: From I-5 heading north to Sacramento, take the Sutterville exit and head east to Land Park. The course is on the left.

Contact: 1701 Sutterville Road, Sacramento, CA 95822, pro shop 916/277-1207, fax 916/277-1216.

63 BRADSHAW RANCH GOLF COURSE

Architect: Steve Legarra, 1989
9 holes   **Public**   **$6.50–18.50**

Sacramento and Vicinity Detail map,
page 74

Particularly popular with seniors and women, this short par-3 course is well maintained, with good greens. The 111-yard fourth hole has a lake and features the only real sloping green on the course. This is a good place to sharpen your iron play. No observers are allowed on the golf course.

Play Policy and Fees: Green fees are $6.50 weekdays for nine holes, $11 for 18 holes, $15 all day. On weekends and holidays fees are $8 for nine holes, $13.50 for 18 holes, $18.50 all day. Pull carts are $1. Club rentals are $5. Senior rates are available.

Tees and Yardage: *Men and Women:* yardage 1096, par 27, rating n/a, slope n/a.

Tee Times: Reservations can be booked seven days in advance.

Dress Code: Nonmetal spikes are preferred.

Tournaments: This course is available for outside tournaments. A 20-player minimum is needed to book an event. Tournaments should be scheduled two months in advance.

Directions: Take the Bradshaw exit south off U.S. 50 or Florin Road east off Highway 99 and drive several miles to Bradshaw Road. Turn left on Bradshaw.

Contact: 7350 Bradshaw Road, Sacramento, CA 95829, pro shop 916/363-6549.

64 CORDOVA GOLF COURSE

Architect: Course designed, 1956
18 holes   **Public**   **$10–15**

Sacramento and Vicinity Detail map,
page 74

Cordova is a flat, walkable course with small greens and tough par-3s. The third hole, for instance, is 201 yards in length, and the 18th is 191 yards. The only par-5 is the sixth hole.

This is among the busiest courses in the Sacramento area, because of its low rates and short yardage. It is an excellent choice for honing your iron play.

Play Policy and Fees: Green fees are $10 weekdays and $15 weekends. Carts $20.

Tees and Yardage: *Men:* yardage 4787, par 63, rating 61.9, slope 92; *Women:* yardage 4728, par 66, rating 64.9, slope 96.

Tee Times: Weekend tee times are made after 10 A.M. on Monday. Weekday tee times are made after 10 A.M. on Friday.

Dress Code: Appropriate attire and soft spikes are required.

Tournaments: No shotgun starts are allowed. A 24-player minimum is needed to book a tournament. Arrangements must be made through the Cordova Park District. Events should be booked six months in advance.

Directions: From U.S. 50 in Sacramento, take the Bradshaw exit south to Jackson Road. The course is between Bradshaw Road and south Watt Avenue.

Contact: 9425 Jackson Road, Sacramento, CA 95826, pro shop 916/362-1196, www.crpd.com.

65 MATHER GOLF COURSE

Architect: Jack Fleming, 1958
18 holes   **Public**   **$24–30**

Sacramento and Vicinity Detail map,
page 74

This long course is lined with mature trees. It demands length off the tee. There are five par-4s that are 420 yards or longer. The final two holes are a tough finish. The 17th is 463 yards and par-4. It is straight away and long with trees left and right. The front of the large green is open, but there is a bunker to the left. The 18th hole is a 420-yard, par-4 dogleg left with trees down both sides.

Play Policy and Fees: Green fees are $24 Monday–Thursday, $26 Friday, and $30 weekends. Carts are $13.

Tees and Yardage: *Men:* Blue: yardage 6734, par 72, rating 71.8, slope 125; White: yardage 6436,

par 72, rating 70.3, slope 123; *Women:* Red: yardage 5751, par 74, rating 71.1, slope 123.

Tee Times: Reservations may be booked eight days in advance starting at noon.

Dress Code: Nonmetal spikes are encouraged.

Tournaments: Tournaments welcome. Please inquire.

Directions: From U.S. 50 south, take the Sunrise exit east and travel 3.5 miles. Take a right on Douglas Avenue and a left onto Eagles Nest.

Contact: 4103 Eagles Nest Road, Mather, CA 95655, pro shop 916/364-4354, fax 916/364-4360, www.mathergc.com.

66 RANCHO MURIETA COUNTRY CLUB

Architect: Ted Robinson Sr., 1980 (North Course); Bert Stamps, 1971 (South Course)

36 holes   **Private**   **$75–85**

Sacramento and Vicinity Detail map, page 74

The North Course at Rancho Murieta is generally considered to be the Sacramento area's top layout. It features out-of-bounds areas on virtually every hole, and gigantic, undulating greens. The fourth, 10th, and 18th holes are outstanding par-4s. The third and 15th holes are rugged par-5s. On the South Course, water comes into play on 10 of 18 holes, and scoring is almost as difficult as on the North Course. The North Course was home to the Senior PGA Tour's Raley's Senior Gold Rush for several years. A clubhouse renovation was completed in 2003.

Play Policy and Fees: Reciprocal play is accepted with members of other private clubs. Reciprocal fees are $75–85.

Tees and Yardage: North Course—*Men:* Blue: yardage 6839, par 72, rating 73.5, slope 141; White: yardage 6335, par 72, rating 71.2, slope 132; *Women:* Red: yardage 5608, par 73, rating 73.8, slope 135. South Course—*Men:* Blue: yardage 6894, par 72, rating 73.4, slope 132; White: yardage 6307, par 72, rating 70.7, slope 130; *Women:* Red: yardage 5583, par 72, rating 72.1, slope 125.

Tee Times: Reciprocal guests should have their golf pro call three days in advance.

Dress Code: Appropriate golf attire and non-metal spikes are required.

Tournaments: A 120-player minimum is needed to book a shotgun tournament.

Directions: From Sacramento, drive east on U.S. 50. Take the Bradshaw Road exit south. Turn left on Highway 16/Jackson Road to Rancho Murieta. The club entrance is on the left.

Contact: 7000 Alameda Drive, Rancho Murieta, CA 95683, pro shop 916/354-2400, www.ranchomurieta.com.

67 BARTLEY CAVANAUGH GOLF COURSE

Architect: Perry Dye, 1995

18 holes   **Public**   **$28–45**

Sacramento and Vicinity Detail map, page 74

This Perry Dye design has a links feel because of extensive mounding and frequency of wind. The course is adjacent to the Sacramento River and is built on 91 acres, so accuracy is important. The signature hole is the par-3 17th, which is played to an island green.

Play Policy and Fees: Monday–Thursday green fees are $28 to walk, $41 to ride. Friday, weekend, and holiday green fees are $32 to walk, $45 to ride. Twilight, junior, Capitol City card, and senior rates are available.

Tees and Yardage: *Men:* Gold: yardage 6158, par 71, rating 69.0, slope 116; Blue: yardage 5788, par 71, rating 67.3, slope 113; White: yardage 5393, par 71, rating 65.4, slope 110; *Women:* Black: yardage 4714, par 71, rating 66.3, slope 107.

Tee Times: Weekday reservations can be booked seven days in advance. Weekend and holiday reservations are taken on the prior Tuesday, starting at 6 A.M., by calling the Sacramento City Tee Time Hotline at 916/665-1202.

Dress Code: Shirts and shoes are necessary. Nonmetal spikes are required.

Tournaments: A 24-player minimum is needed to book a tournament.

Directions: From Sacramento, take I-5 south to the Pocket Road exit. Turn left over the freeway to Freeport Boulevard. Turn right on Freeport Boulevard. Drive 1.5 miles to the course on the left.

Contact: 8301 Freeport Boulevard, Sacramento, CA 95832, pro shop 916/665-2020.

68 BING MALONEY GOLF COURSE

Architect: Mac MacDonald, 1952
18 holes   Public $26–30

Sacramento and Vicinity Detail map, page 74

A flat course, Bing Maloney requires accurate tee shots because large trees border each fairway. Site of the Sacramento Regional Four-Ball Championship each year, this heavily used course has large greens surrounded by bunkers. The most difficult hole, without question, is the 12th, a par-4 measuring 440 yards. A huge cottonwood tree stands out like a sore thumb directly in front of the tee, forcing the golfer to A) bail out right; B) hook it around the tree and risk going out-of-bounds; or C) hit a sharp cut shot. Good luck! Bing Maloney is a shot-maker's course. Bing Maloney also has a short executive course that is around 1300 yards from the back tees. Call 916/433-2284 to reach the executive course.

Play Policy and Fees: Green fees are $26 Monday–Thursday and $30 Friday, weekends, and holidays. Rates are seasonal. Carts are additional. Cardholder, twilight, and other rates are offered.

Tees and Yardage: *Men:* Championship: yardage 6588, par 72, rating 70.7, slope 120; White: yardage 6548, par 72, rating 70.0, slope 119; *Women:* Red: yardage 5912, par 72, rating 72.2, slope 120.

Tee Times: Reservations may be booked one week in advance.

Dress Code: Nonmetal spikes are required.

Tournaments: Groups larger than eight players are considered a tournament. Please inquire.

Directions: From Sacramento, drive six miles south on I-5. Take the Florin Road exit east. Turn left on Freeport Road and drive toward the Sacramento Executive Airport. The course is on the right.

Contact: 6801 Freeport Boulevard, Sacramento, CA 95822, pro shop 916/433-2283, fax 916/433-6386.

69 VALLEY HI COUNTRY CLUB

Architect: William F. Bell, 1959; Martin Miller, 2001
18 holes   Private $75

Sacramento and Vicinity Detail map, page 74

Valley Hi's reputation grows with each year as the trees and the course mature. It has three large lakes that seem to crop up everywhere. The toughest holes are the second (434 yards), the 11th (409 yards), and the 15th (412 yards). Those three par-4s invariably play into the wind. The greens are bent grass, without much undulation, but they are fairly fast and difficult to read. Valley Hi holds numerous amateur tournaments for men and women. A redesign of holes 16 and 17 was completed in 2001.

Play Policy and Fees: Reciprocal play is accepted with members of other private clubs. Reciprocal fees are $75 or the rate of the reciprocating club.

Tees and Yardage: *Men:* Black: yardage 7009, par 72, rating 72.9, slope 131; White: yardage 6432, par 72, rating 70.8, slope 125; *Women:* Red: yardage 5888, par 73, rating 68.0, slope 118; Gold: yardage 5345, par 72, rating 70.8, slope 124.

Tee Times: Reciprocators should have their club pro call to make arrangements.

Dress Code: Appropriate golf attire and nonmetal spikes are required.

Tournaments: This course is available for outside tournaments. Weekend shotgun tournaments are reserved for member play.

Directions: From Sacramento, drive south on Highway 99. Take the Elk Grove Boulevard exit west. Drive 3.5 miles to Franklin Boulevard. Turn right. The course is on the right.

Contact: 9595 Franklin Boulevard, Elk Grove,

CA 95759 (P.O. Box 850, Elk Grove, CA 95624), pro shop 916/423-2170, fax 916/684-2121.

70 CHAMPIONS GOLF LINKS
Architect: Richard Bigler, 1996

9 holes   **Public**   **$10.50–15**

Sacramento and Vicinity Detail map, page 74

This links-style executive course features one par-4. Most greens have at least two tiers. Three lakes come into play, notably on the ninth, the signature hole.

Play Policy and Fees: Green fees are $10.50 weekdays for nine holes and $15 weekends. Senior, junior, and twilight rates are available. Carts are $10 for nine holes. Champions Club cardholders receive additional discounts.

Tees and Yardage: *Men:* Blue: yardage 1813, par 30, rating 58.6, slope n/a; White: yardage 1660, par 30, rating 57.8, slope n/a; *Women:* Gold: yardage 1352, par 30, rating n/a, slope n/a.

Tee Times: Reservations can be booked seven days in advance.

Dress Code: Shirts and shoes are necessary.

Tournaments: This course is available for outside tournaments. A banquet facility is available.

Directions: From Sacramento, take Highway 99 south to Florin Road exit. Go east on Florin Road to Elk Grove/Florin Road. Turn right on Elk Grove/Florin Road. Drive about one mile to Gerber Road and the course.

Contact: 8915 Gerber Road, Sacramento, CA 95828, pro shop 916/688-9120, fax 916/688-3530, www.championsgolf.com.

71 WILDHAWK GOLF CLUB
Architect: J. Michael Poellot, 1997

18 holes   **Public**   **$31–41**

Sacramento and Vicinity Detail map, page 74

J. Michael Poellot created an intriguing course out of what was once a flat and featureless piece of land. By adding extensive mounding, well-placed bunkers, and contoured greens, the architect designed a challenging course where wind is a factor. There are two lakes, and a creek runs throughout.

Play Policy and Fees: Green fees are $31 weekdays and $41 weekends. Senior, junior, nine-hole, and twilight rates are available. Carts additional.

Tees and Yardage: *Men:* Gold: yardage 6718, par 72, rating 71.4, slope 126; Blue: yardage 6260, par 72, rating 69.9, slope 121; White: yardage 5840, par 72, rating 67.9, slope 116; *Women:* Green: yardage 4847, par 72, rating 67.2, slope 109.

Tee Times: Reservations can be made seven days in advance starting at 7 A.M. Advance reservations can be made for a $10 fee per player.

Dress Code: Appropriate golf attire and non-metal spikes are required. No denim is allowed.

Tournaments: A 12-player minimum is required to book an event. Events should be scheduled 12 months in advance. The banquet facility can accommodate up to 200 people.

Directions: From U.S. 50, take the Bradshaw Road exit. Take Bradshaw south to Gerbar Road. Take Gerbar east one mile. Make a right on Vineyard; the course is on the left.

Contact: 7713 Vineyard Road, Sacramento, CA 95829, pro shop 916/688-4653, fax 916/688-9489, www.wildhawkgolf.com.

72 EMERALD LAKES GOLF CENTER
Architect: Rick Yount, 1991

9 holes   **Public**   **$11–13**

Sacramento and Vicinity Detail map, page 74

The layout consists of one par-5, four par-4s, and four par-3s. The fairways are relatively narrow. Three lakes come into play on six holes. The greens, which are the best part of this young course, are undulating and fast. Two of the greens are two-tiered. The signature hole is the par-3 fifth, a 111-yarder to an island green. The lighted driving range is open in summer months until 10 P.M. and in the winter until 7 P.M.

Play Policy and Fees: On weekdays, green fees are $11 for the first nine holes and $6 for an additional nine. On weekends, fees are $13 for nine holes and $7 for an additional nine. Twilight and senior rates are offered. Carts are additional.

Tees and Yardage: *Men (18 holes):* yardage 4614, par 66, rating 62.0, slope 106; *Women (18 holes):* yardage 3904, par 66, rating 61.4, slope 97.

Tee Times: Reservations may be booked seven days in advance.

Dress Code: Appropriate golf attire is required.

Tournaments: This course is available for outside tournaments.

Directions: From Highway 99 in Elk Grove, take the Grant Line Road exit east. Drive south on East Stockton Boulevard (frontage road). East Stockton Boulevard dead-ends in the parking lot of the course.

Contact: 10651 E. Stockton Boulevard, Elk Grove, CA 95624, pro shop 916/685-4653.

73 GREEN TREE GOLF CLUB
Architect: William F. Bell, 1963

27 holes   **Public**   **$22–32**

Sacramento and Vicinity Detail map, page 74

The course is well maintained. The length is not too demanding, but the greens have subtle breaks that make local knowledge a big advantage. The course underwent extensive renovations several years ago, and many of the hundreds of trees that were planted have grown in. The two-tiered 18th green caps a par-5, double-dogleg finish over water. You will find Green Tree easy to walk. The executive course has been known for its good greens.

Play Policy and Fees: On the 18-hole course, Monday–Friday, green fees are $22. Weekends and holidays, green fees are $32. Carts are $12. On the executive course, rates are $10 weekdays, $11 weekends. Junior, twilight, and senior rates are available.

Tees and Yardage: 18-hole course—*Men:* Blue: yardage 6261, par 71, rating 69.3, slope 117; White: yardage 5881, par 71, rating 68.5, slope 114;

Women: Red: yardage 5184, par 71, rating 69.9, slope 118. Executive course—*Men and Women:* yardage 1530, par 29, rating n/a, slope n/a.

Tee Times: Reservations can be booked seven days in advance.

Dress Code: Appropriate golf attire and nonmetal spikes are required.

Tournaments: Events are welcome. The banquet facility can accommodate up to 150 people.

Directions: The course is one-quarter mile south of I-80 on Leisure Town Road at the east end of Vacaville.

Contact: 999 Leisure Town Road, Vacaville, CA 95696 (P.O. Box 1056, Vacaville, CA 95687), pro shop 707/448-1420, fax 707/446-0810.

74 CYPRESS LAKES GOLF COURSE
Architect: Joseph Finger, 1960

18 holes   **Military**   **$27–32**

Sacramento and Vicinity Detail map, page 74

This course boasts big greens, seven lakes, and lots of trees. It's flat and easily walkable. Plan to play into the wind. The greens are usually in great condition, and the course can become a challenge from the blue tees. The last three holes are the best: the par-4 16th, which doglegs right over a lake; the par-5 17th, which doglegs left over a lake; and the par-4 18th, which requires an approach shot over a lake.

Play Policy and Fees: Military and guests only. Guest green fees are $27 weekdays, $32 weekends. Carts additional. Twilight rates available.

Tees and Yardage: *Men:* Championship: yardage 6873, par 72, rating 72.7, slope 125; Regular: yardage 6505, par 72, rating 70.9, slope 121; *Women:* Forward: yardage 5785, par 73, rating 73.0, slope 120.

Tee Times: Reservations can be made seven days in advance.

Dress Code: Collared shirts and nonmetal spikes are required.

Tournaments: Available for tournaments.

Directions: From Vallejo, drive east on I-80.

Take the Elmira exit east. Turn right on Meridian and continue to the course.

Contact: 5601 Meridian Road/Building 2012, Vacaville, CA 95687, pro shop 707/448-7186, fax 707/452-9961.

75 DRY CREEK RANCH GOLF COURSE
Architect: Jack Fleming, 1962
18 holes   **Public**   **$22–34**

🚶 📷 🍴 🏌 🚙 🍺

Sacramento and Vicinity Detail map, page 74

This testy, tree-lined course has a difficult combination of first and last holes. The first hole tees off into a narrow chute with a grove of oaks as out-of-bounds. The 18th hole doglegs to the left with oak trees and a creek bed that provide headaches. Rounds are made or ruined on either hole. Other outstanding holes include the par-4 sixth, a monster of 442 yards from the back tees; and the 13th, a par-4 of moderate length that, due to placement of the trees, leaves little room for error on either the drive or the approach. Dry Creek has been highly ranked by several publications over the years.

Play Policy and Fees: Green fees are $22 weekdays and $34 weekends and holidays. Carts are $20. Nine-hole and twilight rates offered.

Tees and Yardage: *Men:* Black: yardage 6752, par 72, rating 72.5, slope 131; Blue: yardage 6508, par 72, rating 71.3, slope 129; White: yardage 6094, par 72, rating 69.5, slope 125; *Women:* Red: yardage 5647, par 74, rating 72.1, slope 128.

Tee Times: Reservations may be booked 14 days in advance.

Dress Code: Standard golf dress is required.

Tournaments: Tournaments welcome. The banquet facility can accommodate up to 120 people. Call for details.

Directions: From Sacramento, drive 24 miles south on Highway 99 to Galt. Take the Central Galt exit onto C Street and drive east. Turn right on Crystal Way and drive to the course. From Stockton, take Highway 99 north and exit at Crystal Way.

Contact: 809 Crystal Way, Galt, CA 95632, pro shop 209/745-4653, fax 209/745-2230.

76 FOREST LAKE GOLF CLUB
Architect: Course designed, 1941
18 holes   **Public**   **$14–17**

🚶 📷 🍴 🏌 🚙 🍺

Sacramento and Vicinity Detail map, page 74

This short course offers tight fairways with mature trees and some water. It is fairly flat, so can be walked easily.

Play Policy and Fees: Green fees are $14 weekdays and $17 weekends and holidays. Carts are $9 per rider. Twilight rates are offered.

Tees and Yardage: Blue Course—*Men:* yardage 4925, par 66, rating n/a, slope n/a; *Women:* yardage 4925, par 72, rating n/a, slope n/a. Red Course—*Men:* yardage 3700, par 60, rating n/a, slope n/a; *Women:* yardage 3700, par 64, rating n/a, slope n/a.

Tee Times: Reservations can be booked seven days in advance.

Dress Code: Nonmetal spikes are preferred.

Tournaments: Shotgun tournaments are available weekdays only, and a 150-player minimum is required.

Directions: From Highway 99 in Acampo (just north of Lodi), take the Jahant Road exit west, which turns into Woodson Road. Take Woodson Road one mile to the course on the left.

Contact: 2450 East Woodson Road, Acampo, CA 95220, pro shop 209/369-5451, www.forestlakegolfclub.com.

77 WOODBRIDGE GOLF & COUNTRY CLUB
Architect: Harold Sampson, 1923; Robert Muir Graves, 1985
27 holes   **Private**

🚶 📷 🍴 🏌 🚙 🍺

Sacramento and Vicinity Detail map, page 74

Built in 1923, the greens are small and traditional. Of the three nines at Woodbridge, the River Course is the oldest. The Middle Course has rolling terrain, and the Lake Course is the youngest and boasts lots of water. All three reward accuracy over distance.

Play Policy and Fees: Reciprocal play is accepted on a limited basis with members of other private clubs; otherwise, members and guests only. The fee for reciprocators is based on what Woodbridge members would be charged at the reciprocating course. The course is closed on Monday.

Tees and Yardage: Lake/Middle Course—*Men:* Blue: yardage 6611, par 73, rating 72.4, slope 130; White: yardage 6401, par 73, rating 71.5, slope 128; *Women:* Red: yardage 6066, par 74, rating 75.6, slope 134. River/Lake Course—*Men:* Blue: yardage 6445, par 72, rating 71.5, slope 129; White: yardage 6246, par 72, rating 70.5, slope 127; *Women:* Red: yardage 4946, par 74, rating 74.4, slope 131. Middle/River Course—*Men:* Blue: yardage 6438, par 71, rating 70.9, slope 129; White: yardage 6217, par 71, rating 70.0, slope 127; *Women:* Red: yardage 5832, par 72, rating 74.2, slope 131.

Tee Times: Reciprocator's home professional should call.

Dress Code: Appropriate golf attire and non-metal spikes are required.

Tournaments: Tournaments must have board approval.

Directions: The course is between I-5 and Highway 99 in Woodbridge on Woodbridge Road.

Contact: 800 E. Woodbridge Road (P.O. Box 806), Woodbridge, CA 95258, pro shop 209/369-2371.

78 MICKE GROVE GOLF LINKS

Architect: Bob Dorham, 1990

18 holes   Public $22–32

Sacramento and Vicinity Detail map, page 74

This highly acclaimed links-style course is set among the vineyards. The greens are large, and there is plenty of water. The signature hole is the 14th, a par-3 of 179 yards over water. Beware of the strong winds that often blow. This is a well-maintained course that stays lush and green in the hot summer months.

Play Policy and Fees: Green fees are $22 weekdays and $32 weekends. Carts are additional. Afternoon, twilight, senior (weekdays only), and junior rates are available.

Tees and Yardage: *Men:* Blue: yardage 6565, par 72, rating 71.0, slope 118; White: yardage 6026, par 72, rating 68.0, slope 115; *Women:* Red: yardage 5286, par 72, rating 65.6, slope 102.

Tee Times: Reservations can be booked 30 days in advance for a $2 fee per person.

Dress Code: Hemmed shorts and sleeved shirts are a must. Soft spikes are preferred.

Tournaments: Tournaments accepted. An outdoor banquet facility can accommodate up to 144 people.

Directions: Take Highway 99 south from Sacramento and north from Modesto to Armstrong Road. Take Armstrong about one-half mile west, then turn left on Micke Grove Road. The course is on the right.

Contact: 11401 North Micke Grove Road, Lodi, CA 95240, pro shop 209/369-4410, fax 209/369-8635, www.americangolf.com.

79 LOCKEFORD SPRINGS GOLF COURSE

Architect: Jim Summers and Sandy Tatum, 1995

18 holes   Public $25–40

Sacramento and Vicinity Detail map, page 74

This traditional, flat valley course in the middle of Lodi wine country features lots of mounding and contours, large, undulating greens, and mature trees. Fourteen holes wander through an old walnut grove. The 514-yard, par-5 18th hole is one of the best on the course. It's a dogleg left around a lake and includes an eye-catching waterfall.

Play Policy and Fees: Green fees are $25 weekdays and $40 weekends. Carts are $15 per rider. Twilight and senior rates offered.

Tees and Yardage: *Men:* Blue: yardage 6861, par 72, rating 73.8, slope 130; White: yardage 6483,

par 72, rating 71.4, slope 125; *Women:* Red: yardage 5951, par 72, rating 74.0, slope 123.

Tee Times: Reservations can be booked seven days in advance.

Dress Code: No swimwear or tank tops are allowed on the course. Nonmetal spikes required.

Tournaments: A 16-player minimum is needed to book a tournament. Carts are required. Tournaments can be booked 6–12 months in advance.

Directions: From Sacramento, take Highway 99 south to the Highway 12 exit. Drive east approximately six miles to Highway 88 and turn right. The course is approximately one mile up on the left.

Contact: 16360 North Highway 88, Lockeford, CA 95237 (P.O. Box 1315, Lodi, CA 95240), pro shop 209/333-6275, www.lockeford springs.com.

80 COLD SPRINGS GOLF & COUNTRY CLUB

Architect: Bert Stamps, 1960
18 holes   **Private**   **$50**

Sacramento and Gold Country map, page 73
Weber Creek winds through this course, which is very tight with a preponderance of short, dogleg par-4s. Cold Springs is moderately hilly and has plenty of oaks and pines. The fourth hole (par-4, 402 yards) is a handful. It doglegs right with out-of-bounds right and hard pan left for those driving through the fairway. There is a huge oak on the right side of the green, which slopes severely.

Play Policy and Fees: Reciprocal play is accepted with members of other private clubs; otherwise, members and guests only. The green fee for reciprocal players is $50.

Tees and Yardage: *Men:* White: yardage 6155, par 72, rating 69.7, slope 123; Gold: yardage 5638, par 72, rating 67.6, slope 118; *Women:* Red: yardage 5597, par 72, rating 73.7, slope 128.

Tee Times: Reciprocators should have their club pro call to make arrangements.

Dress Code: Collared shirts and nonmetal

spikes are required. Shorts must have a four-inch inseam.

Tournaments: This course is available for outside tournaments, but they must be board approved. The banquet facility can accommodate at least 200 people.

Directions: From U.S. 50 in Placerville, take the Placerville Drive/Forni Road exit. Drive over the overpass to the second stop sign. Turn left on Cold Springs Road. Drive three miles and turn left on Richard Avenue, which turns into Clubhouse Drive.

Contact: 6500 Clubhouse Drive, Placerville, CA 95667, pro shop 530/622-4567, fax 530/626-6942, www.clubconnectweb.com/coldsprings golfcc.

81 SIERRA GOLF COURSE

Architect: Course designed, 1959
9 holes   **Public**   **$9–14**

Sacramento and Gold Country map, page 73
This short course is flat, with sloping greens. Oak, pine, and cedar trees line the fairways, but there is no water. The eighth hole features a challenging green.

Play Policy and Fees: Green fees are $9 for nine holes and $12 for 18 holes weekdays, $10 for nine holes and $14 for 18 holes weekends. Junior and twilight rates are available.

Tees and Yardage: *Men:* yardage 1674, par 31, rating n/a, slope n/a; *Women:* yardage 1528, par 31, rating n/a, slope n/a.

Tee Times: Reservations are not accepted. All play is on a first-come, first-served basis.

Dress Code: Shirts and shoes are required.

Tournaments: This course is available for outside tournaments.

Directions: From U.S. 50 in Placerville, take the Main Street exit. Take Cedar Ravine to Country Club Drive and the course. Watch for the airport sign and you'll find the course.

Contact: 1822 Country Club Drive, Placerville, CA 95667, pro shop 530/622-0760.

82 APPLE MOUNTAIN GOLF RESORT

Architect: Algie M. Pulley Jr., 1997
18 holes   **Resort**   **$45–75**

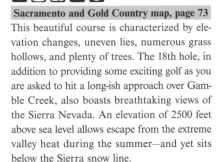

Sacramento and Gold Country map, page 73

This beautiful course is characterized by elevation changes, uneven lies, numerous grass hollows, and plenty of trees. The 18th hole, in addition to providing some exciting golf as you are asked to hit a long-ish approach over Gamble Creek, also boasts breathtaking views of the Sierra Nevada. An elevation of 2500 feet above sea level allows escape from the extreme valley heat during the summer—and yet sits below the Sierra snow line.

Play Policy and Fees: Summer green fees are $45 Monday–Thursday, $60 Friday, and $75 weekends and holidays. Winter rates are less. Twilight, senior, firefighter, and law enforcement rates are also available.

Tees and Yardage: *Men:* Blue: yardage 6176, par 70, rating 69.5, slope 130; White: yardage 5569, par 70, rating 67.2, slope 121; *Women:* Gold: yardage 4507, par 70, rating 70.4, slope 122.

Tee Times: Reservations may be booked seven days in advance. For a $5-per-person fee on weekdays and a $10-per-person fee on weekends, tee times may be reserved up to a year in advance.

Dress Code: Collared shirts are required, and jeans are acceptable. Soft spikes only.

Tournaments: Tournaments welcome. The banquet facility can accommodate up to 180 people.

Directions: From Sacramento, take U.S. 50 east toward South Lake Tahoe. Five miles east of Placerville, take the Carson Road exit. At the intersection, turn right and proceed one-quarter mile to the entrance.

Contact: 3455 Carson Road, Camino, CA 95709, pro shop 530/647-7400, fax 530/647-7404, www.applemountaingolfresort.net.

83 MACE MEADOW GOLF & COUNTRY CLUB

Architect: Jack Fleming, 1972; expanded, 1988
18 holes   **Public**   **$23–33**

Sacramento and Gold Country map, page 73

The most picturesque hole on this scenic course is the first, a par-5 with a red barn and a noisy rooster behind the green. Originally a nine-hole course designed by Jack Fleming, Mace Meadow was expanded into 18 holes in 1988 by the club membership. The old and new nines were mixed together.

Play Policy and Fees: Green fees are $23 weekdays and $33 weekends. Carts $12. Twilight and junior rates are available.

Tees and Yardage: *Men:* Blue: yardage 6310, par 72, rating 69.9, slope 128; White: yardage 6010, par 72, rating 68.5, slope 124; *Women:* Red: yardage 5387, par 72, rating 70.7, slope 120.

Tee Times: Reservations can be booked up to 14 days in advance.

Dress Code: Appropriate golf attire is required.

Tournaments: This course is available for outside tournaments.

Directions: The course is 18 miles east of Jackson on Highway 88 and five miles east of Pioneer in Buckhorn. In Buckhorn, look for Meadow Drive and the parking lot. Fairway Drive is right there.

Contact: 26570 Fairway Drive, Pioneer, CA 95666, pro shop 209/295-7020, fax 209/295-7272, www.macemeadow.com.

84 CASTLE OAKS GOLF CLUB

Architect: Bradford Benz, 1994
18 holes   **Public**   **$42–58**

Sacramento and Gold Country map, page 73

Rolling hills, water, and strategically placed oak trees characterize this course. There are few flat lies and several elevated greens. The premium is on accuracy, not length. The par-4 finishing hole, measuring 438 yards from the back tees, is one of the best in Northern California. The dogleg left features a split fairway—the safe right side or the shorter left side, an island fairway surrounded by water. The left side shortens the hole, but it requires a 200-yard carry. A new clubhouse was completed in 2003.

Play Policy and Fees: Green fees are $42 Monday–Thursday, $44 on Friday, and $58 on Saturday and Sunday, carts included. Twilight, junior, and senior rates are available.

Tees and Yardage: *Men:* Black: yardage 6739, par 71, rating 72.2, slope 131; Blue: yardage 6356, par 71, rating 70.3, slope 126; White: yardage 5948, par 71, rating 68.4, slope 124; *Women:* Gold: yardage 5447, par 71, rating 71.6, slope 119; Red: yardage 4953, par 71, rating 69.3, slope 114.

Tee Times: Reservations can be booked seven days in advance.

Dress Code: Collared shirts are required. Soft spikes only.

Tournaments: Shotgun tournaments are available weekdays only. A 16-player minimum is needed for a regular tournament. Tournaments can be booked up to 12 months in advance.

Directions: From Sacramento, take Highway 16 to Ione Road. Turn right on Ione Road and go to Highway 104. Turn left at Highway 104 and continue 2.2 miles to the course entrance.

Contact: 1000 Castle Oaks Drive (P.O. Box 1368), Ione, CA 95640, pro shop 209/274-0167.

85 MEADOWMONT GOLF COURSE

Architect: Dick Fry, 1962
9 holes   Public $15–27

🏌️ icons

Sacramento and Gold Country map, page 73
On land that was once used as an apple orchard, this flat course is narrow, thanks to the forest of pine trees lining each fairway. The greens are small, and Rae's Creek—no relation to the more famous Rae's Creek of Augusta National fame—runs through the entire course. The fifth hole (354 yards) is an absolute beauty, with out-of-bounds left and a lake right. The green is tucked into the pines. Gary Plato holds the course record of 64.

Play Policy and Fees: Weekday green fees are $15 for nine holes and $22 for 18 holes. Weekend green fees are $18 for nine holes and $27 for 18 holes. Twilight, senior, and junior rates and annual memberships are available.

Tees and Yardage: *Men (18 holes):* Back: yardage 5824, par 72, rating n/a, slope n/a; *Women (18 holes):* Forward: yardage 5565, par 72, rating n/a, slope n/a.

Tee Times: Reservations may be booked 14 days in advance.

Dress Code: Soft spikes are preferred.

Tournaments: Outside events may be booked up to a year in advance.

Directions: From Highway 99, drive 70 miles east on Highway 4 past Murphys to Arnold. The course is on the left.

Contact: Highway 4 and Country Club Drive (P.O. Box 586), Arnold, CA 95223, pro shop 209/795-1313, fax 209/795-1313, www.meadowmontgolf.com.

86 SEQUOIA WOODS COUNTRY CLUB

Architect: Bob Baldock, 1970
18 holes   Private $55–65

🏌️ icons

Sacramento and Gold Country map, page 73
This sprawling, mountain course is tougher than the ratings indicate. The front nine is situated in a spacious meadow and is long and open. Trade the woods for irons on the back nine, because it gets narrow and steep. Out-of-bounds run along both sides of the fairways. Par is 38 on the front side, with the par-5 sixth hole measuring 527 yards uphill. The sixth hole doglegs right around a creek and offers no room for error off the tee.

Play Policy and Fees: Reciprocal play is accepted with members of other private clubs. Reciprocal fees are $55 weekdays, $65 weekends.

Tees and Yardage: *Men:* Blue: yardage 5600, par 70, rating 66.1, slope 120; White: yardage 5261, par 70, rating 64.9, slope 116; *Women:* Red: yardage 4881, par 70, rating 68.0, slope 122.

Tee Times: Reservations can be made two weeks

in advance. Reciprocal players should have their head pro call to make a tee time.
Dress Code: Appropriate golf attire is required. Nonmetal spikes are encouraged.
Tournaments: This course is available for outside tournaments only when sponsored by a member. A 24-player minimum is needed. Events can be booked one month in advance. The banquet facility can accommodate 120 people, and the outdoor deck area accommodates 200 people.
Directions: From Highway 99, drive east on Highway 4 to Arnold. Exit right on Blue Lake Springs and follow the signs to the club. The course is a 90-minute drive from Stockton.
Contact: 1000 Cypress Point Drive (P.O. Box 930), Arnold, CA 95223, pro shop 209/795-2141, clubhouse 209/795-1000, fax 209/795-5981, www.sequoiawoods.com.

87 FOREST MEADOWS GOLF COURSE

Architect: Robert Trent Jones Jr., 1971
18 holes   Public $20–25

Sacramento and Gold Country map, page 73
This beautiful Sierra Nevada executive course is traversed by the Stanislaus River canyon. Situated at 3500 feet, its panoramic layout mixes aesthetics and serious play, offering a challenge to low and high handicappers alike. Known for its excellent, fast greens, the course places a premium on putting.
Play Policy and Fees: Green fees are $20 weekdays, $25 weekends. Carts are $22 for 18 holes. Winter play is subject to weather conditions. Twilight, senior, and annual rates are offered.
Tees and Yardage: *Men:* White: yardage 3886, par 60, rating 60.3, slope 110; *Women:* Forward: yardage 3221, par 60, rating 58.8, slope 99.
Tee Times: Reservations can be booked 14 days in advance.
Dress Code: Shirts and shoes are required. No short shorts may be worn. Nonmetal spikes are preferred.
Tournaments: A 72-player minimum is required

for shotgun tournaments, and a 20-player minimum is necessary for regular tournaments. Carts are required.
Directions: From Highway 99, drive east on Highway 4 to Murphys. The course is about 3.5 miles east of Murphys on Highway 4.
Contact: 633 Forest Meadows Drive, Murphys, CA 95247, pro shop 209/728-3439, clubhouse 209/728-3440, www.forestmeadows.com.

88 LA CONTENTA GOLF CLUB

Architect: Richard Bigler, 1973
18 holes   Semiprivate $21–46

Sacramento and Gold Country map, page 73
Set in the rolling foothills 35 miles east of Stockton, this tight, hilly course challenges players with out-of-bounds areas on 14 holes and water on nine. The trademark hole is the 13th, a par-3 that drops 100 feet from the tee to an L-shaped green almost completely surrounded by water. Be ready to hit plenty of blind shots, as well as approaches from sidehill lies. La Contenta is in excellent shape and affords outstanding vistas on virtually every hole.

Play-and-stay packages are available at the 10th Green Inn. Call 209/772-1084 for information and reservations.
Play Policy and Fees: Monday–Thursday, green fees are $21 to walk and $34 to ride. Friday, fees are $26 to walk and $39 to ride. Weekends and holidays, fees are $33 to walk and $46 to ride. Senior rates are available Tuesday–Thursday.
Tees and Yardage: *Men:* Black: yardage 6425, par 71, rating 70.1, slope 133; White: yardage 5895, par 71, rating 68.5, slope 130; *Women:* Red: yardage 5150, par 72, rating 69.5, slope 127.
Tee Times: Reservations may be booked two weeks in advance.
Dress Code: Collared shirts are required.
Tournaments: Events may be scheduled up to 12 months in advance. The banquet facility can accommodate up to 200 people.
Directions: From Highway 99 in Stockton, take

the Fremont (Highway 26) exit east. Drive 28 miles on Highway 26 to the course on the right. **Contact:** 1653 Highway 26 (P.O. Box 249), Valley Springs, CA 95252, pro shop 209/772-1081, fax 209/772-1082, www.empiregolf.com.

89 GREENHORN CREEK

Architect: Don Boos, 1996; Robert Trent Jones Jr., 2000
18 holes   Semiprivate $70–85

Sacramento and Gold Country map, page 73

Greenhorn Creek is a hidden gem in a serene setting, with gently rolling fairways surrounded by oaks, pines, ponds, creeks, and excellent greens. Do not let the surroundings fool you— this course is no walk in the park. Although several tee boxes accommodate players of all skill levels, better golfers will find this a course that is taxing on the brain and scorecard for those who can't manage their game. A driver on many holes is not a good option, as oak trees, ponds, creeks, and out-of bounds come into play. Historical landmarks from the Gold Rush are incorporated into the course. A new two-sided driving range designed for instruction was completed in 2004.

Elegant on-site cottages are available.

Play Policy and Fees: Green fees are seasonal. In high season (April–October), fees are $70 Monday–Friday, $85 weekends and holidays. Twilight rates are available. Carts included. November–March rates decrease. Please inquire.

Tees and Yardage: *Men:* Gold: yardage 6749, par 72, rating 72.8, slope 132; Blue: yardage 6214, par 72, rating 70.1, slope 128; White: yardage 5708, par 72, rating 68.0, slope 121; *Women:* Red: yardage 5162, par 72, rating 71.3, slope 126; Forward: yardage 4887, par 72, rating 69.5, slope 122.

Tee Times: Reservations can be booked seven days in advance.

Dress Code: Collared shirts and nonmetal spikes are mandatory. No denim is allowed on the course.

Tournaments: A 20-player minimum is needed to book a tournament. Carts are required. Tournaments can be booked 12 months in advance.

Directions: From Highway 99 between Modesto

and Stockton, take Highway 4 east. The course is on the corner of Highway 4 and Highway 49. **Contact:** 676 McCauley Ranch Road (P.O. Box 1419), Angels Camp, CA 95222, pro shop 209/736-8110, fax 209/736-8119, www.greenhorncreek.com.

90 TWAIN HARTE GOLF & COUNTRY CLUB

Architect: Clark Glasson, 1961
9 holes   Semiprivate $13–20

Sacramento and Gold Country map, page 73

Plenty of trees make this executive course a challenge. There are two ponds. The best hole is the seventh, a par-3 where the player is hitting to an elevated green with a large bunker in front. This is an excellent course for beginners in a setting all players can enjoy.

Play Policy and Fees: Green fees are $13 for nine holes and $17 for 18 holes weekdays, $15 for nine holes and $20 for 18 holes weekends. Senior and junior rates are available.

Tees and Yardage: *Men (18 holes):* yardage 3353, par 58, rating n/a, slope n/a; *Women (18 holes):* yardage 3330, par 64, rating n/a, slope n/a.

Tee Times: Reservations can be booked seven days in advance.

Dress Code: Casual dress is acceptable. Soft spikes only.

Tournaments: This course is available for outside tournaments.

Directions: From Highway 108 in Twain Harte (10 miles east of Sonora), turn left on Meadow Lane and follow it to the course.

Contact: 22909 Meadow Lane, Twain Harte, CA 95383, pro shop 209/586-3131.

91 PHOENIX LAKE GOLF COURSE

Architect: Bert Stamps, 1968
9 holes   Public $13–30

Sacramento and Gold Country map, page 73

The relatively short yardage of this course is deceptive, because Phoenix Lake Golf Course is extremely narrow, with pines and oaks lining the fairways. Only two holes run parallel to one another. Sullivan's Creek comes into play on five holes. The second hole (par-4, 361 yards) requires a tee shot that carries 180 yards over the creek down a narrow fairway. The par-3 sixth hole is a bear, measuring 231 yards downhill.

Play Policy and Fees: Green fees are $13 for nine holes and $18 for 18 holes weekdays, $25 all day. On weekends and holidays, fees are $15 for nine holes and $20 for 18 holes, $30 all day. Carts are $12 for nine holes and $20 for 18 holes. Senior and junior discounts are available on weekdays.

Tees and Yardage: *Men (18 holes):* White/Black: yardage 5322, par 70, rating 65.2, slope 118; *Women (18 holes):* Red/Blue: yardage 4677, par 70, rating 62.8, slope 112.

Tee Times: Reservations can be booked 60 days in advance.

Dress Code: Proper golf attire is required.

Tournaments: Tournaments are welcome. Bookings can be made one year in advance.

Directions: From Highway 108 in Sonora, take the Phoenix Lake Road exit left. The course is on the left on Paseo de Los Portales, about three miles from Highway 108.

Contact: 21448 Paseo de Los Portales, Sonora, CA 95370, pro shop 209/532-0111, fax 209/532-0583.

92 MOUNTAIN SPRINGS GOLF COURSE

Architect: Robert Muir Graves, 1990
18 holes   Semiprivate $25–36

Sacramento and Gold Country map, page 73

This hilly, target-oriented layout plays longer than the yardage indicates. It is in the heart of the Gold Country and offers sweeping vistas. Six lakes and 70 bunkers come into play. Scenic views are offered on the first, fifth, 10th, 15th, and 17th holes. The pride of the course is the 200-yard, par-3 17th hole across water.

Play-and-stay packages at the historic Gunn House in Sonora are available. Call the course for more information.

Play Policy and Fees: Public play is accepted. Green fees are $25 Monday–Thursday, $30 Friday, and $36 on weekends and holidays. Twilight rates (hours vary depending on season) are $15 Monday–Thursday, $18 Friday, and $21 on weekends and holidays. Senior (Monday and Tuesday only) and junior rates are available.

Tees and Yardage: *Men:* Black: yardage 6529, par 72, rating 71.9, slope 128; White: yardage 6149, par 72, rating 70.0, slope 125; Gold: yardage 5592, par 72, rating 67.5, slope 117; *Women:* Red: yardage 5084, par 71, rating 70.2, slope 120.

Tee Times: Reservations may be booked 14 days in advance.

Dress Code: Collared shirts are required.

Tournaments: Tournaments should be booked 12 months in advance. The banquet facility can hold 140 people.

Directions: Driving east on Highway 108 in Sonora, turn right on Lime Kiln Road. Drive 2.5 miles to the course entrance on the right.

Contact: 17566 Lime Kiln Road, Sonora, CA 95370, pro shop 209/532-1000, fax 209/532-0203, www.mountainspringsgolf.com.

Chapter 6

COURTESY OF THE DRAGON AT GOLD MOUNTAIN

Tahoe and the Northern Sierra

Tahoe and the Northern Sierra

T he Sierra Nevada is a world-class playground any season of the year. In winter, skiing is king, with the slopes in and around Lake Tahoe providing some of the best downhill skiing and snowboarding in the country. But in summer, those same slopes are alive with wildlife, hikers, mountain bikers, anglers, kayakers, rafters, and just about everyone else who loves the outdoors.

There's nightlife on both the Nevada side of the border, in South Shore Tahoe where gaming casinos are popular, and on the California side, where families relax lakeside in restaurants, at campsites, and on patios enjoying the starry skies.

For golfers there are several courses from which to choose around Lake Tahoe and more clustered around the town of Truckee on I-80. Another 50 miles north on Highway 89 around Graeagle, there are also some excellent choices.

Starting at the top of the region, Graeagle, Clio, and Blairsden are the towns to discover. Among the best golf courses in this area are Graeagle Meadows, a scenic design with the Feather River running through it, and the nine-hole course at Feather River Inn, which opened in 1915. One of the best courses in the state is The Dragon at Gold Mountain in nearby Clio, a 1997 Robin Nelson design.

Right on I-80, as it goes over the summit from Sacramento to Reno, the little town of Truckee, with its historic town center, is an attractive stop. The Truckee area is primed for growth, with some new residential projects that include golf courses slated to open over the next couple of years; several others are in planning stages. Old Greenwood is one of these new developments, and attached to it is a wonderful Jack Nicklaus golf course. But don't pass up an opportunity to play Coyote Moon Golf Course, a lovely 2000 Brad Bell design that features exciting mountain views, loaded trout streams, and granite bluffs, typical of what you can expect on the region's golf courses.

The Resort at Squaw Creek is among the top designs in the state, just off Highway 89 on the way to Lake Tahoe. And once you get to the lake, several courses are sprinkled around the shoreline, including Lake Tahoe Golf Course, Tahoe City Golf Course, and Tahoe Paradise Golf Course.

Definitely put your clubs in the trunk when you visit this activity-filled, scenic region. And don't forget your warmest jacket—late afternoons can get chilly at this altitude.

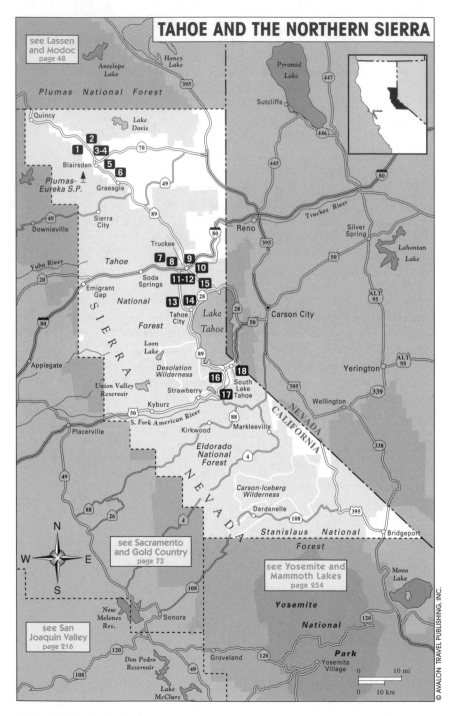

TAHOE AND THE NORTHERN SIERRA

see Lassen and Modoc page 48

see Sacramento and Gold Country page 73

see Yosemite and Mammoth Lakes page 254

see San Joaquin Valley page 216

© AVALON TRAVEL PUBLISHING, INC.

1 GRAEAGLE MEADOWS GOLF COURSE

Architect: Ellis Van Gorder, 1968
18 holes   Semiprivate $45–70

Tahoe and the Northern Sierra map, page 118

This popular mountain course is set in a picturesque valley with the Feather River running through it. Though pine trees abound, most holes are fairly wide open off the tee. Graeagle's signature hole is the sixth, a 386-yard par-4 with a bunker across the fairway and a stunning view of Eureka Peak.

Play Policy and Fees: Green fees range $45–60 weekdays, $55–70 weekends. Carts are additional. The course is open April–mid-November.

Tees and Yardage: *Men:* Blue: yardage 6725, par 72, rating 72.1, slope 129; White: yardage 6345, par 72, rating 70.1, slope 128; *Women:* Red: yardage 5589, par 72, rating 71.0, slope 127.

Tee Times: Reservations can be made one year in advance.

Dress Code: Appropriate attire and soft spikes are required.

Tournaments: A 144-player minimum is needed to book a shotgun tournament.

Directions: From Truckee, drive 50 miles north on Highway 89. The course is on Highway 89 in Graeagle, three miles south of Highway 70.

Contact: Highway 89 (P.O. Box 310), Graeagle, CA 96103, pro shop 530/836-2323, fax 530/836-2024.

2 PLUMAS PINES GOLF RESORT

Architect: Homer Flint, 1980
18 holes   Resort $70–85

Tahoe and the Northern Sierra map, page 118

This scenic, hilly course is in the midst of Plumas National Forest and is bordered by the Middle Fork of the Feather River. The fairways are tight, with lots of trees. One notable hole is the second, a 419-yard par-4, with the river to the left and trees to the right. Another tough hole is the 201-yard, par-3 third over water. Accuracy is more important than

length here, so smart players use irons off many tees.

Play Policy and Fees: Green fees are $70 Monday–Thursday and $85 Friday–Sunday. Carts included. Twilight, nine-hole, and other rates are offered. The course is open April–November.

Tees and Yardage: *Men:* Blue: yardage 6524, par 72, rating 71.3, slope 132; White: yardage 5942, par 72, rating 68.5, slope 123; *Women:* Red: yardage 5240, par 72, rating 70.5, slope 125.

Tee Times: Reservations are not required but are strongly recommended. Tee times for the season are available starting March 1.

Dress Code: Collared shirts are required.

Tournaments: A 12-player minimum is needed to book an event. Tournaments should be booked 12 months in advance. The banquet facility can accommodate up to 250 people.

Directions: From Truckee, take Highway 89 north toward Graeagle. Just before Graeagle, turn left on County Road A14 and follow the signs (about two miles) to the course.

Contact: 402 Poplar Valley Road (P.O. Box 1210), Graeagle, CA 96103, pro shop 530/836-1420, fax 530/836-0801, www.plumaspines golf.com.

3 FEATHER RIVER INN GOLF COURSE

Architect: Harold Sampson, 1915
9 holes   Resort $14–20

Tahoe and the Northern Sierra map, page 118

This scenic course is tight, with lots of trees and small, elevated greens. It opened in 1915, making it the oldest course in the Mohawk Valley and one of the oldest in the state. The ninth hole has strong character. It measures 272 yards but plays longer to an elevated green. It is said that Dwight D. Eisenhower played here during his many travels.

For reservations at the Feather River Inn, call 530/836-2623.

Play Policy and Fees: Green fees are $14 for nine holes and $20 for 18 holes every day. Carts are additional. Senior, junior, and twilight rates are available.

Tees and Yardage: *Men (18 holes):* Back: yardage 5657, par 69, rating 66.0, slope 105; *Women (18 holes):* Forward: yardage 5605, par 72, rating 70.4, slope 122.

Tee Times: Reservations are required on holidays. At all other times, reservations are not necessary, but they can be made.

Dress Code: Appropriate golf attire and soft spikes are required.

Tournaments: A 16-player minimum is needed to book a tournament. Events may be booked up to a year in advance. The banquet facility can accommodate up to 200 people.

Directions: The course is 49 miles north of Truckee and 60 miles northwest of Reno. From Highway 70, the course is just one-eighth mile west of the intersection of Highway 70 and Highway 89 in Graeagle.

Contact: 65899 Highway 70 (P.O. Box 67), Blairsden, CA 96103, pro shop 530/836-2722, fax 530/836-0927.

❹ WHITEHAWK RANCH GOLF CLUB
Architect: Dick Bailey, 1995
18 holes   Semiprivate $115–140

Tahoe and the Northern Sierra map, page 118

This scenic mountain course is bordered by five lakes and numerous streams. Five holes are situated in a meadow, while the rest of the course meanders through trees. There is lots of mounding, but only 30 bunkers. Greens are medium-sized, and several have tiers. The course also features a complete practice facility.

One- and two-bedroom cabins are available, including some meals and golf privileges. Please call 530/836-4985 for reservations and information.

Play Policy and Fees: Fees during prime season are $115 Monday–Thursday and $140 Friday, weekends, and holidays. Price includes cart and use of the practice facility. Lodge guests are given a discount, and shoulder season rates

are offered, as well as junior and replay rates. The course is open May–late October.

Tees and Yardage: *Men:* 4 Hawk: yardage 6927, par 71, rating 72.6, slope 133; 3 Hawk: yardage 6457, par 71, rating 70.3, slope 123; 2 Hawk: yardage 5673, par 68, rating 66.5, slope 115; *Women:* 1 Hawk: yardage 4816, par 71, rating 65.4, slope 122.

Tee Times: Reservations can be booked six months in advance. Group reservations (12 players or more) are booked beginning January 1 each year. Regular tee times may be made March 1.

Dress Code: Collared shirts are required and denim is allowed. Metal spikes are prohibited.

Tournaments: A minimum of 12 players is needed to book an event, and tournaments should be scheduled six months in advance.

Directions: From Truckee, drive 38 miles north on Highway 89 to the course.

Contact: 1137 Highway 89 (P.O. Box 170), Clio, CA 96106, pro shop 800/332-HAWK, fax 530/836-4504, www.golfwhitehawk.com.

❺ FEATHER RIVER PARK RESORT
Architect: Bert Stamps, 1922
9 holes   Public $16–18

Tahoe and the Northern Sierra map, page 118

This scenic course is level, open, and walkable. There are two par-5s, both reachable in two, and three par-3s, the 179-yard third being the longest one. This course is popular with women, seniors, and particularly juniors, who can learn to play in a low-pressure environment.

Play Policy and Fees: Green fees are $16 for 18 holes on weekdays and $18 on weekends. Carts additional. The course is open late April–mid-October.

Tees and Yardage: *Men and Women:* yardage 2633, par 35, rating n/a, slope n/a.

Tee Times: Reservations are not accepted. All play is on a first-come, first-served basis.

Dress Code: Casual dress is acceptable.

Tournaments: This course is available for outside events.

Directions: From Truckee, drive about 50 miles north on Highway 89. The course is on Highway 89 just past the town of Graeagle.
Contact: 8339 Highway 89 (P.O. Box 37), Blairsden, CA 96103, pro shop 530/836-2328, fax 530/836-2707.

6 THE DRAGON AT GOLD MOUNTAIN

Architect: Robin Nelson, 1997
18 holes   Resort $129–139

Tahoe and the Northern Sierra map, page 118

The Dragon at Gold Mountain is an unusual name for a course, which is fitting, because nothing about Gold Mountain is ordinary. The Dragon is one of the few courses admitted into the Audubon International Signature Program for the preservation of animal wildlife and conservation. This inspired design by Robin Nelson uses the natural surroundings to create a challenging layout instead of forcing itself upon the land. The course plays from 7000 yards from the back tees, but with six sets of tees available, the course is enjoyable for all skill levels. There are also some outstanding views of the Sierras and the Feather River. The clubhouse is a Frank Lloyd Wright design that will inspire as much conversation as the golf course itself.

Accommodations are available at the on-site Nakoma Resort & Spa. Please call 800/368-7786 for information and reservations.

Play Policy and Fees: Prime season green fees are $129 Monday–Thursday, $139 Friday–Sunday and holidays. Fee includes cart and range balls. Shoulder season rates are offered, as are twilight and junior rates.

Tees and Yardage: *Men:* 6 Dragons: yardage 7077, par 72, rating 74.2, slope 147; 5 Dragons: yardage 6749, par 72, rating 72.5, slope 142; 4 Dragons: yardage 6380, par 72, rating 70.6, slope 136; 3 Dragons: yardage 5945, par 72, rating 69.0, slope 132; *Women:* 2 Dragons: yardage 5289, par 72, rating 70.9, slope 136; 1 Dragon: yardage 4611, par 72, rating 66.6, slope 128.

Tee Times: Reservations are accepted up to one year in advance.
Dress Code: Appropriate golf attire and non-metal spikes are required. No denim is allowed.
Tournaments: Tournament play is accepted. Call the pro shop for more information.
Directions: From Sacramento, take I-80 north to Highway 89. North of Truckee 35 miles, you will come to County Road A-15. Make a right and follow County Road A-15 for five more miles to the course.
Contact: 3887 CR A-15, Clio, CA 96106 (P.O. Box 880, Graeagle, CA 96103), pro shop 800/368-7786, fax 530/832-0884, www.dragongolf.com.

7 TAHOE DONNER GOLF & COUNTRY CLUB

Architect: Joseph B. Williams, 1976; remodel 2003/2005
18 holes   Semiprivate $110

Tahoe and the Northern Sierra map, page 118

A golfer must search high and low to find a tighter golf course than Tahoe Donner. Pines line both sides of all 18 fairways. There are no out-of-bounds, and the course is walkable despite its 6600-foot altitude. Four holes were remodeled in 2003, and four others are being remodeled each year until the course is completely renovated. Members joke about having to walk single file down the fairways of this spectacular, but extremely tight, course.

Play Policy and Fees: During prime season, public green fees are $110 every day, including cart. Shoulder season, local resident, nine-hole, and twilight rates are available, as are memberships. Please call for details.

Tees and Yardage: *Men:* Blue: yardage 6931, par 72, rating 73.5, slope 132; White: yardage 6598, par 72, rating 72.3, slope 129; *Women:* Red: yardage 5848, par 73, rating 72.7, slope 137. (Note: At press time, post-remodel yardage was not available.)

Tee Times: Reservations can be made 10 days in advance on weekdays. For weekend play, reservations can be made the Friday before the weekend you want to play.

Dress Code: Collared shirts and golf shoes are required. Shorts must be mid-thigh length.

Tournaments: This course is available for outside tournaments. A 13-player minimum is needed to book a tournament. Events should be booked 12 months in advance. The banquet facility can hold 120 people.

Directions: From I-80 east, take the first Truckee exit (Donner Pass Road). Turn left on Donner Pass Road and drive to the blinking red light. Turn left on Northwoods Boulevard. The course is three miles from I-80.

Contact: 11509 Northwoods Boulevard, Truckee, CA 96161, pro shop 530/587-9443, fax 530/587-9496, www.tahoedonner.com.

8 COYOTE MOON GOLF COURSE

Architect: Brad Bell, 2000

18 holes   Public $140–150

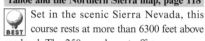

Tahoe and the Northern Sierra map, page 118

 Set in the scenic Sierra Nevada, this course rests at more than 6300 feet above sea level. The 250-acre layout offers panoramic views as it plays among granite bluffs and trout streams. Water comes into play on seven holes. Coyote Moon is one of the better courses in the Tahoe region.

Play Policy and Fees: Green fees are $140 if reservations are made within 14 days of play, $150 if made 15–30 days from play. Twilight rates are offered.

Tees and Yardage: *Men:* Black: yardage 7177, par 72, rating 74.1, slope 138; Blue: yardage 6704, par 72, rating 71.1, slope 134; White: yardage 6211, par 72, rating 69.1, slope 130; *Women:* Gold: yardage 5022, par 72, rating 73.1, slope 138.

Tee Times: Reservations may be made up to two weeks in advance.

Dress Code: Men must wear collared shirts. Soft spikes are recommended.

Tournaments: Events are welcome and may be booked up to one year in advance.

Directions: From I-80, take the Donner Pass Road exit. Turn left on Donner Pass Road and travel half a mile to the first light. Turn left on Northwoods Boulevard. The course is half a mile up Northwoods on the right.

Contact: 10685 Northwoods Boulevard, Truckee, CA 96161, pro shop 530/587-0886, fax 530/550-2211, www.coyotemoongolf.com.

9 OLD GREENWOOD

Architect: Jack Nicklaus, 2004

18 holes   Public $160–170

Tahoe and the Northern Sierra map, page 118

This course is the centerpiece of an upscale residential community. Though it measures more than 7500 yards from the back tees, the design is at an elevation of 6000 feet above sea level, where tee shots can travel 10–15 percent farther than at sea level. The setting is alpine magnificent, playing through towering pine trees and open fields of sage, and past four lakes connected by a series of meandering trout streams that not only require accuracy from the golfer, but also offer abundant trout fishing after a round.

Play Policy and Fees: Green fees are $160 if made within seven days of tee time, $170 if made 8–30 days in advance.

Tees and Yardage: *Men:* 4 Trees: yardage 7518, par 72, rating 75.6, slope 146; 3 Trees: yardage 6944, par 72, rating 72.9, slope 138; 2 Trees: yardage 6457, par 72, rating 71.1, slope 129; *Women:* 1 Tree: yardage 5419, par 72, rating n/a, slope n/a.

Tee Times: Tee times may be reserved 30 days in advance.

Dress Code: Appropriate golf attire is required. Soft spikes only.

Tournaments: Tournaments are accepted. Please call.

Directions: From San Francisco, travel east on I-80 toward Truckee. Approximately two miles east of central Truckee, take the Prosser Village Road exit. Turn right and follow the signs to the Old Greenwood Welcome Center.

Contact: 12915 Fairway Drive, Truckee, CA 96161, phone 530/550-7010, fax 530/550-2020, www.oldgreenwood.com.

PONDEROSA GOLF CLUB

Architect: Bob Baldock, 1961
9 holes   **Public**   **$32–52**

Tahoe and the Northern Sierra map, page 118

The first three holes at Ponderosa are heavily wooded, after which things open up a bit. The ninth hole, a par-5 covering 507 yards from the back tee, doglegs right. Ponderosa is popular with golfers of all ages and abilities.

Play Policy and Fees: Green fees are $32 for nine holes and $52 for 18 holes. Carts are additional. Twilight rates are offered. Season passes offered.

Tees and Yardage: *Men (18 holes):* Blue: yardage 6044, par 70, rating 67.7, slope 118; White: yardage 5800, par 70, rating 67.2, slope 117; *Women (18 holes):* Red: yardage 5112, par 70, rating 68.2, slope 108.

Tee Times: Reservations may be booked 10 days in advance.

Dress Code: Shirts must be worn at all times on the course.

Tournaments: This course is available for outside events.

Directions: From I-80 in Truckee, take the Northshore Boulevard (Highway 267) exit south and drive to the course. The course is a 12-minute drive from Lake Tahoe.

Contact: 10040 Reynold Way (P.O. Box 729), Truckee, CA 96160, pro shop 530/587-3501, fax 530/587-8463, www.ponderosagolfclub.com.

LAHONTAN GOLF CLUB

Architect: Tom Weiskopf, 1998
18 holes   **Private**

Tahoe and the Northern Sierra map, page 118

 This high Sierra course takes full advantage of the natural surroundings, which include mature trees, constant elevation changes, water features, and mountain vistas. It is not a target golf course, nor does it have a lot of long forced carries. The generous fairways and large greens will allow golfers to keep their ball in play. There is also a nine-hole par-3 course available.

Play Policy and Fees: This course is for members and accompanied guests only. Caddies are available.

Tees and Yardage: *Men:* Green: yardage 7316, par 72, rating 74.8, slope 142; Black: yardage 6753, par 72, rating 72.1, slope 137; Blue: yardage 6100, par 72, rating 68.8, slope 128; *Women:* Red: yardage 5158, par 72, rating 76.7, slope 124.

Tee Times: Not applicable.

Dress Code: Appropriate golf attire is required.

Tournaments: This course is not available for outside events.

Directions: From Highway 267 in Truckee heading toward Northstar, take the Schaffer Mill exit. Turn right onto Schaffer Mill Road. The golf course is on the left.

Contact: 12000 Lodgetrail Road, Truckee, CA 96161, pro shop 530/550-2424.

 NORTHSTAR-AT-TAHOE GOLF COURSE

Architect: Robert Muir Graves, 1975
18 holes   **Resort**   **$95–105**

Tahoe and the Northern Sierra map, page 118

The two nines contrast sharply. There are either wide-open tee shots or tight, tree-lined fairways. The front side is set in a meadow, while the back nine is set in a forest. Water comes into play on 14 holes. The 15th hole (par-3, 180 yards from the back tees) features a 120-foot drop to a postage-stamp green. Former U.S. Women's Open champ Susie Berning once lost eight balls on the back nine. In winter, Northstar is a popular ski resort.

For information about the Northstar Resort, call 800/GO-NORTH (800/466-6784).

Play Policy and Fees: Green fees are $95 weekdays, $105 weekends. Guests of the lodge receive a discount. Afternoon, twilight, and nine-hole rates are also available. All fees include carts. This course is open May–October.

Tees and Yardage: *Men:* Gold: yardage 6692, par 72, rating 72.5, slope 140; Blue: yardage 6246, par 72, rating 70.3, slope 133; White: yardage 5892, par 72, rating 68.7, slope 127;

Women: Red: yardage 5470, par 72, rating 70.8, slope 136.

Tee Times: Reservations can be booked 21 days in advance.

Dress Code: Golf attire is encouraged; men must have collared shirts. Soft spikes only.

Tournaments: This course is available for outside tournaments.

Directions: In Truckee, drive six miles south on Highway 267. Exit at Northstar Drive. Turn right on Basque Drive and follow it to the clubhouse.

Contact: 168 Basque Drive, Truckee, CA 96160 (P.O. Box 129, Truckee, CA 96161), pro shop 530/562-2490, fax 530/562-2035, www.ski northstar.com.

13 RESORT AT SQUAW CREEK

Architect: Robert Trent Jones Jr., 1991

18 holes   Resort $85–115

🏌 📷 ⛳ 🏨 🚗 🍴

Tahoe and the Northern Sierra map, page 118

🏆 **BEST** This is a challenging target golf course with four sets of tee boxes to accommodate most skill levels. The mountain layout meanders through pine trees and parallels the granite peaks of the famed Squaw Valley ski area before making a transition into a scenic meadowland. The par-4 17th requires a long drive over wetlands, followed by an equally difficult second shot to a green bordered by Squaw Creek. In the winter, Squaw Creek doubles as a first-class ski resort.

The resort has rooms available for a range of prices. For reservations call 800/327-3353.

Play Policy and Fees: Summer green fees are $115, and fall green fees are $85. Twilight and junior rates are available. Carts are included in prices, but walking is permitted. Squaw Creek is generally open May 15–October 28, depending on the weather.

Tees and Yardage: *Men:* Gold: yardage 6931, par 71, rating 72.9, slope 143; Blue: yardage 6453, par 71, rating 70.8, slope 139; White: yardage 6010, par 71, rating 69.3, slope 125; *Women:* Red: yardage 5097, par 71, rating 69.0, slope 132.

Tee Times: Resort guests may book tee times 90 days in advance, and day golfers may book times 30 days in advance.

Dress Code: Collared shirts are required. No blue jeans are allowed on the course. Soft spikes only.

Tournaments: This course is available for outside tournaments. Carts are required. The banquet facility can accommodate up to 600 people. Events can be booked 12 months in advance.

Directions: Take Highway 89 from Truckee south toward Squaw Valley. Turn right on Squaw Valley Road, then left on Squaw Creek Road.

Contact: 400 Squaw Creek Road (P.O. Box 3333), Olympic Valley, CA 96146, pro shop 530/581-6637, fax 530/581-5407, www.squaw creek.com.

14 TAHOE CITY GOLF COURSE

Architect: May Dunn, 1917

9 holes   Public $30–50

🏌 📷 ⛳ 🛒 🚗 🍴

Tahoe and the Northern Sierra map, page 118

This is the oldest course on Lake Tahoe, but remodeling is planned for 2004–2005. Offering great views of the lake, Tahoe City Golf Course is lined with pine, fir, and cedar trees. The greens are nicely maintained, and the fairways are tight. This layout has the rare distinction of being designed by a woman. A course with a lot of history, Tahoe City Golf Course was host to big money games in the 1950s involving, among others, Bing Crosby, Bob Hope, the Mills Brothers, Ken Venturi, Harvey Ward, Frank Sinatra, Dean Martin, Sammy Davis Jr., and Andy Williams.

Play Policy and Fees: Green fees are $30 for nine holes and $50 for 18 holes. Carts are additional. Twilight, junior, and senior rates are available.

Tees and Yardage: *Men (18 holes):* Blue: yardage 5261, par 66, rating 65.2, slope 117; *Women (18 holes):* Red: yardage 4806, par 68, rating 65.7, slope 105.

Tee Times: Reservations can be booked 14 days in advance.

Dress Code: Soft spikes are preferred.
Tournaments: Events are welcome. The banquet facility can accommodate up to 100 people.
Directions: This course is near the intersection of Highway 89 and Highway 28 in Tahoe City. At the junction, turn onto Highway 28 (North Lake Boulevard) and follow it to the course.
Contact: 251 North Lake Boulevard (P.O. Box 226), Tahoe City, CA 95730, pro shop 530/583-1516, fax 530/583-8163, www.tcgc.com.

15 OLD BROCKWAY GOLF COURSE

Architect: John Duncan Dunn, 1924
9 holes   **Public**   **$38–65**

🏌️ 📷 🍴 🛍️ 🛺 🍺

Tahoe and the Northern Sierra map, page 118

Highly regarded among nine-hole courses, this scenic mountain course is tight, with narrow, tree-flanked fairways and small greens. The most notable hole is the seventh, a par-5 of 553 yards. Old Brockway has a new log cabin–style clubhouse. A full renovation brought the course back to its original 1924 layout. History buffs will like this course.
Play Policy and Fees: Green fees are $38 for nine holes and $65 for 18 holes. Weather permitting, the course is open April 15–November 15. Twilight rates are offered.
Tees and Yardage: *Men (18 holes):* Black: yardage 6724, par 72, rating 71.6, slope 132; Blue: yardage 6562, par 72, rating 70.6, slope 131; White: yardage 5940, par 72, rating 68.0, slope 122; *Women:* Red: yardage 4922, par 72, rating 66.9, slope 113.
Tee Times: Reservations can be booked 30 days in advance.
Dress Code: Appropriate attire and soft spikes are required.
Tournaments: This course is available for outside tournaments.
Directions: This course is on the north shore of Lake Tahoe where Highway 28 (North Lake Boulevard) and Highway 267 intersect.
Contact: 7900 North Lake Boulevard (P.O. Box 1368), Kings Beach, CA 96143, pro shop

530/546-9909, fax 530/546-7476, www.oldbrockway.com.

16 LAKE TAHOE GOLF COURSE

Architect: William F. Bell, 1960
18 holes   **Resort**   **$49–71**

🏌️ 📷 🍴 🛍️ 🛺 🍺

Tahoe and the Northern Sierra map, page 118

The Truckee River runs through this scenic course, which also features five ponds. Water comes into play on 14 holes. The greens are smooth and true, particularly in late summer and early fall. The front nine is relatively wide open, though water comes into play on six holes. The back nine is the strength of the course, beginning with a tee shot against the mountain backdrop on the 10th. The 14th, 15th, 16th, and 17th are wonderful tight, scenic holes alongside the river.
Play Policy and Fees: Green fees to walk are $49 weekdays; on weekends the fee is $71 including mandatory cart. Twilight rates are also available. Seasonal rates may be available; call for details. The course is open mid-April–October.
Tees and Yardage: *Men:* Gold: yardage 6741, par 71, rating 70.6, slope 127; Black: yardage 6327, par 71, rating 68.7, slope 119; *Women:* Silver: yardage 5703, par 71, rating 71.2, slope 117.
Tee Times: Reservations can be booked 8–60 days in advance with a major credit card, plus a $7-per-player nonrefundable fee. Reservations made seven days or fewer in advance require a credit card, but there is no reservation fee.
Dress Code: No tank tops or short shorts are allowed.
Tournaments: A 16-player minimum is required to book a tournament. Events can be scheduled up to one year in advance. The banquet facility can accommodate 200 people.
Directions: This course is on U.S. 50 between South Lake Tahoe and Meyers.
Contact: 2500 Emerald Bay Road, South Lake Tahoe, CA 96150, pro shop 530/577-0788, fax 530/577-4469.

17 TAHOE PARADISE GOLF COURSE

Architect: Bruce Beeman, 1959

18 holes   **Public** $36–52

Tahoe and the Northern Sierra map, page 118

This valley course has hilly, rolling terrain with narrow, tree-lined fairways. The greens are small, and there are very few bunkers. The longest hole (the number-one handicap hole) is the 18th—a tough 372-yard par-4 for men, 326-yard par-4 for women. This is a seasonal golf course.

Play Policy and Fees: Green fees are $36 to walk, $52 to ride any day of the week. Twilight, super twilight, and senior rates are also available.

Tees and Yardage: *Men:* Back: yardage 4034, par 66, rating 59.9, slope 94; *Women:* Forward: yardage 3572, par 69, rating 61.7, slope 96.

Tee Times: Reservations are not required but can be booked seven days in advance.

Dress Code: Appropriate attire and soft spikes are required.

Tournaments: Shotgun tournaments are available weekdays only. No shotgun tournaments are held in July or August.

Directions: This course is in Meyers on U.S. 50, three miles south of the Lake Tahoe Airport.

Contact: 3021 Highway 50, Meyers, CA 96150, pro shop 530/577-2121, fax 530/577-1813, www.tahoeparadisegc.com.

18 BIJOU MUNICIPAL GOLF COURSE

Architect: Course designed, 1920

9 holes   **Public** $18

Tahoe and the Northern Sierra map, page 118

This executive mountain course is in a pleasant meadow and offers spectacular views. The course is mostly flat and walkable and is bordered by trees. No water comes into play. There are five par-4s and four par-3s. It is a good course for beginning golfers and those looking for a low-key game.

Play Policy and Fees: Green fees are $18 for nine holes. Resident, senior, and twilight rates are available.

Tees and Yardage: *Men:* Back: 2002, par 32, rating n/a, slope n/a; *Women:* Forward: yardage 1733, par 32, rating n/a, slope n/a.

Tee Times: Reservations are not accepted. All play is on a first-come, first-served basis.

Dress Code: Shirts, shoes, and pants are necessary.

Tournaments: This course is available for tournaments with the advance approval of the manager.

Directions: From Sacramento, take U.S. 50 through South Lake Tahoe. Turn right at the Johnson Boulevard Safeway. Turn left on Fairway and proceed to the course driveway.

Contact: 1180 Rufus Allen Boulevard, South Lake Tahoe, CA 96150, pro shop 530/542-6097, fax 530/542-2981.

Chapter 7

HALF MOON BAY GOLF LINKS © GEORGE FULLER

San Francisco Bay Area

San Francisco Bay Area

It is always tempting to think of only the classic courses when discussing golf in San Francisco, and why not? Between the Olympic Club, San Francisco Golf Club, Harding Park, and Presidio, we have a roster of some of the best courses in the state, all designed before 1930.

Better yet, of those above-mentioned designs, two are open for public play: Harding Park and Presidio. Although both should be on your play list in the area, Harding Park should top the list. It recently received a multimillion dollar facelift, with investment from the PGA Tour, which brought this 1925 Willie Watson design back to the shape of its glory days. Expect some of golf's biggest tournaments to be held here in coming years.

There are also delightful classic designs across the San Francisco Bay, in Oakland (Lake Chabot Golf Course, 1917) and Berkeley (Tilden Park, 1938). The same is true in the South Bay, with both San Mateo (The Peninsula Golf & Country Club, 1922) and Hillsborough (Burlingame Country Club, 1893) being home to classic-age designs.

But farther east where the population continues to swell, it's newer courses that have been opening at a steady rate for the past decade and more. Similarly, as the region extends south to San Jose and environs, new courses, often affiliated with residential developments, are more the norm.

The three major population centers are San Francisco, Oakland, and San Jose, and as with every other large metropolitan zone in the state, most new growth is at the edges. Thus, cities like Brentwood and Antioch in the East Bay have seen new residential communities spring up in recent years, and with them golf courses and other recreational opportunities. The courses include The Golf Club at Roddy Ranch in Antioch (2000), Dublin Ranch in Dublin (2004), and Deer Ridge Country Club in Brentwood (2004), three designs distinguished by rolling land and views of Mount Diablo. Fremont and Oakland also have new courses to brag about, and both are within their city limits, quite rare feats with suitable tracts of available land being so scarce.

In the San Jose area, the push is to the south, with The Ranch Golf Club at Silver Creek (2004) and the 36 holes at Coyote Creek Golf Club (1999–2000) being among the best new designs.

The San Francisco region has always been strong on private clubs, and it still provides some of the best membership opportunities in the Golden State. We've already mentioned Olympic Club and San Francisco Golf Club, but from one end of the region to the other, there are fine private clubs from which to choose or be chosen. They include Sonoma Golf Club (Sonoma), Orinda Country Club (Orinda), Claremont Country Club (Oakland), Menlo Country Club (Redwood City), and many others.

And it would be remiss not to recommend the luxurious new Ritz-Carlton Half Moon Bay and the two excellent oceanfront courses there called Half Moon Bay Golf Links.

Rule of thumb is, the closer you are to the coast, the more likely you are to be playing in fog or chill. But as you move inland toward San Jose, Brentwood, and the East Bay, the more likely you'll find warmer weather. Residents and visitors alike love San Francisco and the whole Bay Area for all its charm, beauty, lifestyle, and, luckily for golfers, for its collection of top-notch courses.

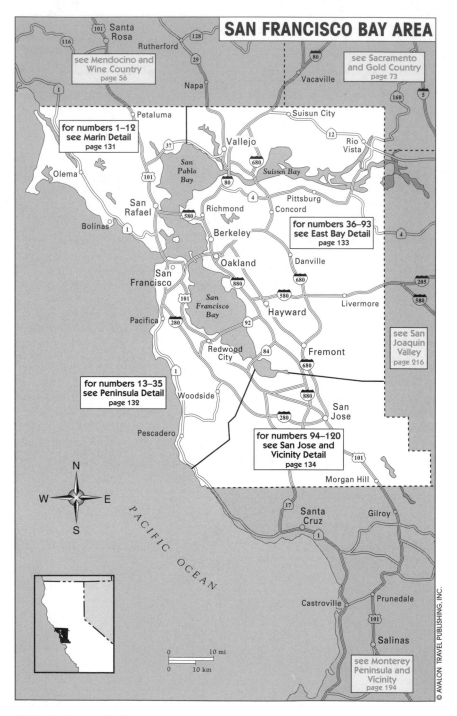

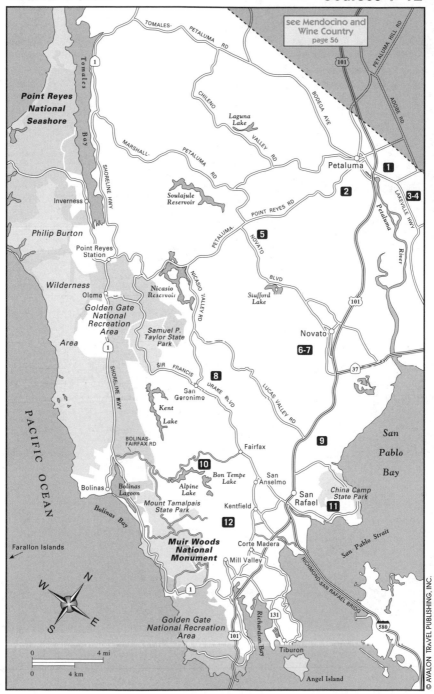

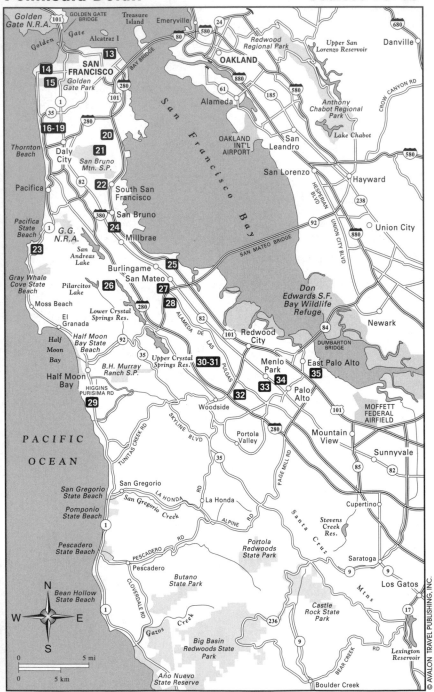

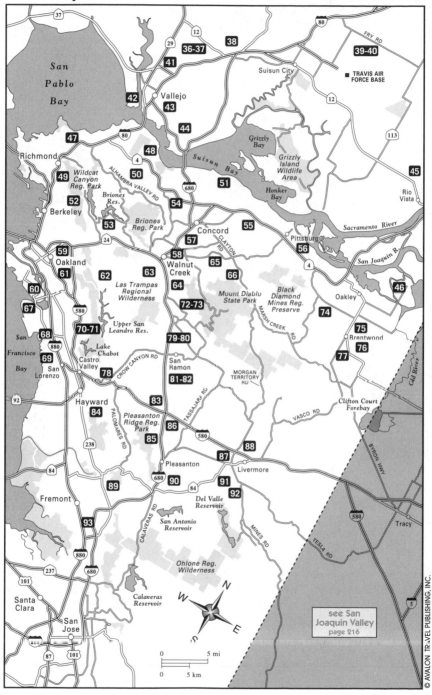

San Jose and Vicinity Detail

Courses 94–120

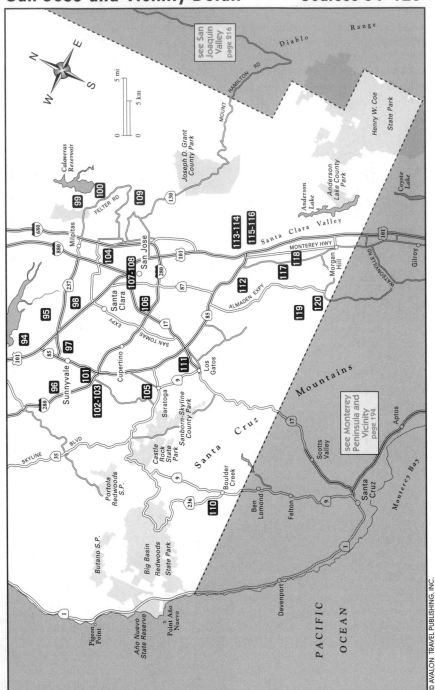

© AVALON TRAVEL PUBLISHING, INC.

1 ADOBE CREEK GOLF CLUB

Architect: Robert Trent Jones Jr., 1990

18 holes   **Public**   **$32–75**

Marin Detail map, page 131

This sprawling, links-style course is situated in the Sonoma County countryside. Five lakes, a stream, and 70 bunkers make accuracy a must. Beware of the seventh hole: It's a par-4, 388-yard challenge with a creek on the right and another creek fronting the large green. The ninth, 16th, 17th, and 18th holes will test golfers of every ability. Adobe Creek is a great place to play in the rainy winter months. Built on adobe, this course is blessed with exceptional natural drainage. An extensive practice area is popular, as are the golf schools held throughout the year.

Play Policy and Fees: Monday–Thursday green fees are $32 to walk and $45 to ride, Friday $35 to walk, $48 to ride. Weekend and holiday fees are $62 to walk and $75 to ride. Senior, junior, resident, early bird, and twilight rates are available.

Tees and Yardage: *Men:* Gold: yardage 6886, par 72, rating 73.5, slope 132; Blue: yardage 6290, par 72, rating 70.8, slope 124; White: yardage 5743, par 72, rating 68.1, slope 117; *Women:* Red: yardage 5085, par 72, rating 69.4, slope 120.

Tee Times: Reservations may be booked seven days in advance.

Dress Code: Collared shirts and nonmetal spikes are required.

Tournaments: Events are welcome and may be booked up to a year in advance.

Directions: From U.S. 101 in Petaluma, take the Highway 116 exit east and drive 1.25 miles. Turn left on Frates Road and drive three-quarters of a mile to the course on the left.

Contact: 1901 Frates Road, Petaluma, CA 94954, pro shop 707/765-3000, ext. 0, fax 707/765-3022, www.adobecreek.com.

2 PETALUMA GOLF & COUNTRY CLUB

Architect: Opened 1922;
redesign Gary Roger Baird, 1983

9 holes   **Private**   **$20–35**

Marin Detail map, page 131

This short course is known as "Goat Hill." It has plenty of well-positioned bunkers, good putting surfaces, and many rolling hills. The sixth hole is a 136-yard par-3, guarded on the right by a huge oak tree.

Play Policy and Fees: Reciprocal play is accepted with members of other private clubs. Fees are $20 for nine holes, $35 for 18 holes. Carts are $7 for nine holes, $10 for 18 holes.

Tees and Yardage: *Men (18 holes):* yardage 5651, par 70, rating 67.9, slope 113; *Women (18 holes):* yardage 5410, par 70, rating 70.0, slope 120.

Tee Times: Reciprocators should have their club pro call to make arrangements.

Dress Code: Collared shirts are required.

Tournaments: This course is available for outside tournaments.

Directions: Heading north on U.S. 101 toward Petaluma, take the Petaluma Boulevard South exit into town. Take McNear Avenue south to Country Club Drive and the course.

Contact: 1500 Country Club Drive (P.O. Box 26), Petaluma, CA 94953, pro shop 707/762-7041, fax 707/762-0314.

3 ROOSTER RUN GOLF CLUB

Architect: Fred Bliss, 1998

18 holes   **Public**   **$33–53**

Marin Detail map, page 131

This course epitomizes the saying, "Drive for show, and putt for dough." The majority of the fairways on this level course are driver-friendly, but the greens are sloping, undulating, and quick. Aiming straight at the cup on even the shortest putts can make for a three-putt day. Water comes into play on 15 holes, and wind can be a factor. With four sets of tee boxes, Rooster Run is accommodating and challenging for all skill levels. From the back tees, the 18th hole is a 606-yard par-5 into the wind—hitting your driver off the tee is mandatory, not for show but for survival. A bonus for those who like to pilot small planes: The golf course is next to Petaluma Airport.

Play Policy and Fees: Green fees are $33 Monday–Thursday, $38 Friday, and $53 weekends and holidays. Senior green fees and seasonal twilight rates are available. Discounts are available for juniors and residents of Petaluma. Carts are $13 per rider.

Tees and Yardage: *Men:* Tournament: yardage 7001, par 72, rating 73.9, slope 128; Championship: yardage 6464, par 72, rating 71.2, slope 124; Regular: yardage 5889, par 72, rating 68.5, slope 116; *Women:* Forward: yardage 5139, par 72, rating 69.1, slope 117.

Tee Times: Reservations can be booked seven days in advance.

Dress Code: Appropriate golf attire and nonmetal spikes are required.

Tournaments: This course is available for outside tournaments. Tournaments should be booked 6–12 months in advance.

Directions: On U.S. 101 in Petaluma, take the East Washington exit. Head east on East Washington one mile to the course.

Contact: 2301 East Washington Street, Petaluma, CA 94954, pro shop 707/778-1211, clubhouse 707/778-1232, fax 707/778-8072, www.roost errun.com.

4 SONOMA GOLF CLUB

Architect: Sam Whiting and Willie Watson, 1926; Robert Muir Graves, 1991

18 holes   **Private/Resort**   **$160**

Marin Detail map, page 131

This is one of the top resort courses in the state and host to the Charles Schwab Cup of the PGA Champions Tour. The course features plenty of mounding and subtle elevation changes. The greens are also very subtle, and they maintain a traditional flavor. Lots of oaks and redwoods guard several tight doglegs.

If you love a classic, straightforward golfing experience, then this is the course for you. Sonoma plays host to U.S. Open sectional and U.S. amateur qualifying.

The historic Fairmont Sonoma Mission Inn & Spa owns the golf course. The inn is five minutes from the course. For reservations, call 707/938-9000.

Play Policy and Fees: Green fees are $160. Members and Fairmont Sonoma Mission Inn & Spa hotel guests only. No nonresort or reciprocal play.

Tees and Yardage: *Men:* Black: yardage 7081, par 72, rating 74.1, slope 132; Blue: yardage 6670, par 72, rating 71.7, slope 130; White: yardage 6123, par 72, rating 69.4, slope 125; *Women:* Red: yardage 5511, par 72, rating 71.8, slope 125.

Tee Times: Hotel guests should book through the concierge.

Dress Code: Nonmetal spikes and collared shirts are required, and denim is not allowed.

Tournaments: Monday only; must buy out the course. Please inquire.

Directions: From San Francisco, drive north on U.S. 101. Take Highway 37 east to Highway 121 north. Follow Highway 121 to Highway 116. Continue north on Highway 116 for two miles. Take the Arnold Drive exit and drive about four miles to the club.

Contact: 17700 Arnold Drive, Sonoma, CA 95476, pro shop 707/996-0300, clubhouse 707/996-4852, fax 707/996-8464, www.sono magolfclub.com.

5 INDIAN VALLEY GOLF CLUB

Architect: Robert Nyberg, 1957

18 holes   **Public**   **$33–55**

Marin Detail map, page 131

This scenic course is challenging and diverse. There are rolling hills and many trees. Water comes into play on 10 holes. A premium is placed on chipping and putting. One of the best holes is the 16th, a par-5 that drops 250 feet from the tee. There is an elevator from the 13th to the 14th hole.

Play Policy and Fees: Green fees are $33 Monday–Thursday, $41 Friday, and $55 weekends. Carts are $26. Senior and twilight rates are available.

Tees and Yardage: *Men:* Blue: yardage 6143, par 72, rating 68.3, slope 118; White: yardage 5730, par 72, rating 67.4, slope 116; *Women:* Red: yardage 5128, par 72, rating 70.4, slope 124.

Tee Times: Reservations can be booked seven days in advance.

Dress Code: No tank tops or cutoff shorts are allowed.

Tournaments: Shotgun tournaments are available weekdays only. There is a 24-player minimum for tournament play, and carts are required. Events should be booked 12 months in advance. The banquet facility can accommodate up to 120 people.

Directions: From U.S. 101 in Novato, take the San Marin Drive exit west to Novato Boulevard. Turn right on Novato Boulevard to the course.

Contact: 3035 Novato Boulevard, Novato, CA 94948 (P.O. Box 351, Novato, CA 94947), pro shop 415/897-1118, fax 415/892-9719, www.ivgc.com.

⑥ MARIN COUNTRY CLUB

Architect: Lawrence Hughes, 1959;
Robert Muir Graves, 1986

18 holes   **Private**

🏌️ 📷 🍴 🛍️ 🚌 🍺

Marin Detail map, page 131

This sprawling course winds through a posh suburban neighborhood, offering tight fairways, fast and undulating greens, and sidehill lies. Lovely, mature trees line many fairways. Wind can become a factor, but club selection is the key here on any day. The 411-yard fifth hole is a dogleg right, with water on the right and out-of-bounds on the left. All the par-3s are demanding, and the greens are typically fast, placing a premium on the short game. The well-respected course was used as a qualifying site for the 1993 U.S. Open.

Play Policy and Fees: Reciprocal play is accepted with members of other private clubs.

Tees and Yardage: *Men:* Back: yardage 6428, par 72, rating 71.6, slope 130; Regular: yardage 6188, par 72, rating 70.5, slope 127; *Women:* Forward: yardage 5804, par 72, rating 74.8, slope 133.

Tee Times: Reservations can be booked seven days in advance.

Dress Code: Appropriate golf attire and non-metal spikes are required.

Tournaments: This course is available for outside tournaments. Please inquire.

Directions: From U.S. 101 in Novato, take the Ignacio Boulevard exit west. Drive 1.5 miles. Turn left on Country Club Drive to the course.

Contact: 500 Country Club Drive, Novato, CA 94949, pro shop 415/382-6707, fax 415/382-6703, www.marincountryclub.com.

⑦ STONETREE GOLF CLUB

Architect: Sandy Tatum and Jim Summers, 1999

18 holes   **Public**   **$85–115**

🏌️ 📷 🍴 🚌 🍺

Marin Detail map, page 131

StoneTree features well-maintained playing surfaces, including greens that can get rolling quite quickly; a wood-and-stone clubhouse; and close attention to customer service. Most of the course is built on a relatively flat piece of land, with six or seven holes playing across a hilly area. Strong par-3 holes front and back, along with some tricky pin placements, add to the challenge. This course was designed with counsel from Napa Valley's Johnny Miller and Fred Bliss.

Play Policy and Fees: Green fees are $85 Monday–Thursday, $115 Friday–Sunday and on holidays. Twilight rates available.

Tees and Yardage: *Men:* Championship: yardage 6810, par 72, rating 73.3, slope 143; Black: yardage 6295, par 72, rating 70.2, slope 137; *Women:* White: yardage 5232, par 72, rating 66.4, slope 127.

Tee Times: Reservations may be made up to 30 days in advance.

Dress Code: No denim jeans are allowed. Non-metal spikes are mandatory, and men must wear collared shirts.

Tournaments: Tournaments are welcome any day of the week, but there is a lower per-player charge Monday–Thursday.

Directions: From Highway 101 above San Francisco, take Highway 37 east toward Napa/Sonoma. The course is 2.5 miles east of Highway 101 on Highway 37 between Novato and Sonoma.

Contact: 9 StoneTree Lane, Novato, CA 94945, pro shop 415/209-6090, fax 415/209-6925, www.stonetreegolf.com.

8 SAN GERONIMO GOLF COURSE

Architect: Robert Muir Graves, 1967; renovated 1985

18 holes   **Public**   **$36–76**

⬛🏌️🪧⛳🏌️

Marin Detail map, page 131

Straight driving and accuracy to the small greens is required on this layout. The greens are tough, and there are a few blind holes at San Geronimo. Playing into a prevailing wind, the 394-yard sixth requires a 210-yard carry off the tee. Trees and a creek guard the right side. The 11th hole is one of the toughest holes in the area. It's 421 yards, and the tee shot has to be left-center to open up an approach shot to the green, which is guarded on the right and front by a creek and trees. There are nice views of the surrounding hills, and some redwoods on the layout.

Play Policy and Fees: Green fees are $36 to walk, $50 to ride weekdays, and $62 to walk, $76 to ride weekends. Twilight rates are available.

Tees and Yardage: *Men:* Black: yardage 6801, par 72, rating 73.5, slope 138; Gold: yardage 6442, par 72, rating 71.6, slope 137; White: yardage 6003, par 72, rating 69.1, slope 132; *Women:* Red: yardage 5140, par 72, rating 69.9, slope 125.

Tee Times: Reservations can be booked 14 days in advance.

Dress Code: No tank tops are allowed on the course. Nonmetal spikes are required.

Tournaments: This course is available for morning shotguns. Carts are required. A 20-player minimum is required to book a tournament. Tournaments can be booked one month in advance. The banquet facility holds 150 people.

Directions: Driving on U.S. 101 south of San Rafael, take the San Anselmo exit to Sir Francis Drake Boulevard and drive 12 miles west to the course.

Contact: 5800 Sir Francis Drake Boulevard (P.O. Box 130), San Geronimo, CA 94963, pro shop 415/488-4030, fax 415/488-4385, www.sangeronimogolf.com.

9 PEACOCK GAP GOLF & COUNTRY CLUB

Architect: William F. Bell, 1957

18 holes   **Semiprivate**   **$34–62**

🏌️⬛🏌️🪧⛳🏌️

Marin Detail map, page 131

This sprawling, tree-lined course is mostly flat and features water on 12 holes. A creek meanders through the course. On the 16th hole, there's a 155-yard shot over an inlet of San Pablo Bay. The sixth, a dogleg left of 305 yards, demands a mid-iron off the tee and an approach over a lagoon—a fun hole. PGA Tour legend Raymond Floyd holds the course record of 63.

Play Policy and Fees: Green fees are $34 Monday–Thursday, $38 on Friday, and $62 (includes cart) on weekends and holidays. Twilight rates are available. Carts are mandatory on weekends.

Tees and Yardage: *Men:* Championship: yardage 6359, par 71, rating 70.0, slope 118; White: yardage 6001, par 71, rating 68.3, slope 116; *Women:* Red: yardage 5596, par 73, rating 71.9, slope 126.

Tee Times: Reservations are recommended seven days in advance for weekdays. Call Tuesday at noon for the following weekend.

Dress Code: No tank tops, jeans, or cutoffs may be worn. Nonmetal spikes are required.

Tournaments: This course is available for tournaments. Contact the pro shop for more information.

Directions: From U.S. 101 in San Rafael, take the Central San Rafael exit. Turn east onto Second Street and drive five miles. Turn left on Biscayne Drive.

Contact: 333 Biscayne Drive, San Rafael, CA 94901, pro shop 415/453-4940, www.peacock gapgolf.com.

10 MEADOW CLUB

Architect: Alister Mackenzie, 1926
18 holes   Private $175

Marin Detail map, page 131

This is a tight course nestled in the foothills of Mount Tamalpais; it's built on light, rolling terrain that used to be Marin County Water District property. Many of the fairway bunkers and greens are being restored to Mackenzie's original specifications. This is a tough little course.

Play Policy and Fees: Limited reciprocal play is accepted with members of other private clubs at a rate of $175, cart included.

Tees and Yardage: *Men:* Blue: yardage 6583, par 71, rating 72.3, slope 134; White: yardage 6306, par 71, rating 70.9, slope 132; Gold: yardage 6116, par 71, rating 70.1, slope 131; *Women:* Red: yardage 5897, par 73, rating 75.2, slope 135.

Tee Times: Pro from reciprocating course should make arrangements.

Dress Code: Appropriate golf attire and non-metal spikes are required.

Tournaments: This course is available for outside tournaments on Monday only.

Directions: From U.S. 101, take the Sir Francis Drake Boulevard exit west (toward Fairfax). Turn left on Bolinas Road and follow it to the course.

Contact: 1001 Bolinas Road, Fairfax, CA 94930, pro shop 415/456-9393.

11 McINNIS PARK GOLF CENTER

Architect: Fred Bliss, 1994
9 holes   Public $15-18

Marin Detail map, page 131

This well-maintained executive course has four par-4s and five par-3s, with water coming into play on four holes. The hardest hole on the course is the fourth hole, a dogleg right to a green guarded by water. McInnis Park features a double-decker driving range, a putting and chipping practice area, miniature golf, batting cages, and a four-star restaurant (reservations are a must). The driving range is open until 9:45 P.M., and in the spring and summer, range players can hit off grass tees 7-10 A.M. Monday–Thursday.

Play Policy and Fees: Green fees are $15 for nine holes Monday–Friday, $10 replay, and $18 weekends and holidays, $12 replay. Senior rates available. Carts available for handicapped only.

Tees and Yardage: *Men:* Blue: yardage 1842, par 31, rating 61.0, slope 96; White: yardage 1695, par 31, rating 60.2, slope 94; *Women:* Red: yardage 1458, par 31, rating 60.6, slope 92.

Tee Times: Reservations can be booked seven days in advance.

Dress Code: Appropriate golf attire is required.

Tournaments: This course is available for outside tournaments. A 16-player minimum is required to book a tournament. Events should be booked at least one week in advance. The banquet facility can accommodate 200 people.

Directions: From U.S. 101 in San Rafael, take the Smith Ranch Road exit. Go east on Smith Ranch Road to the golf course.

Contact: 350 Smith Ranch Road, San Rafael, CA 94903, pro shop 415/492-1800, www.mcinnisparkgolfacademy.com.

12 MILL VALLEY MUNICIPAL GOLF COURSE

Architect: "Dad" Clark, 1919
9 holes   Public $15-27

Marin Detail map, page 131

Originally built as a private club in 1919, this course was a victim of the Great Depression, when it was sold by the 38 remaining members to the city of Mill Valley. Today it is a popular nine-hole public facility, with a creek in play on half the holes. It is a short, hilly course, but still walkable. The par-4 fourth is tight, so most players hit long irons off the tee.

It's a dogleg uphill. The redwood groves make this a very scenic course.

Play Policy and Fees: Green fees are $15 for nine holes and $24 for 18 holes on weekdays, $18 for nine holes and $27 for 18 holes on weekends. Senior and junior rates are available. Power carts are additional.

Tees and Yardage: *Men:* Back: yardage 2082, par 33, rating n/a, slope n/a; *Women:* Forward: yardage 2041, par 32, rating n/a, slope n/a.

Tee Times: Reservations can be booked seven days in advance.

Dress Code: Golf spikes are mandatory October–April.

Tournaments: A 60-player minimum is needed to book a tournament. Events should be scheduled at least three months in advance.

Directions: From U.S. 101 in Mill Valley, take the East Blithedale Avenue exit west. Turn right on Carmelita Avenue and then right again on Buena Vista Avenue to the course.

Contact: 280 Buena Vista Avenue, Mill Valley, CA 94941, pro shop 415/388-9982, www.mv golf.com.

13 PRESIDIO GOLF COURSE
Architect: Robert Johnstone, 1895
18 holes   Public $58–93

🏌 📷 🍴 🛒 🥤

Peninsula Detail map, page 132

This is a must play for golf enthusiasts. **BEST** The course originated as a member-built, nine-hole layout in 1895 and expanded to 18 holes in 1910. Operated by the military since the 1950s, the course opened for public play in late 1995. Arnold Palmer Golf Company has done an excellent job of restoring and improving the club. This hilly course meanders through the San Francisco Presidio and offers spectacular views of the city. It is challenging, steep, and heavily wooded with cypress and eucalyptus. Beware of the 526-yard, par-5 second hole—it has a blind elevated green that is guarded by bunkers. The course record of 64, probably dating back to the late 1920s, is held by the late Lawson Little.

Play Policy and Fees: Green fees are $58 Monday–Thursday, $81 Friday, and $93 weekends and holidays. Fee includes cart. Twilight and super twilight rates are available. Call 415/561-4653 to reserve tee times.

Tees and Yardage: *Men:* Back: yardage 6477, par 72, rating 72.3, slope 136; Middle: yardage 6141, par 72, rating 70.8, slope 132; *Women:* Forward: yardage 5785, par 72, rating 73.2, slope 127.

Tee Times: Reservations are accepted 30 days in advance. There is no cost to make reservations for play within seven days, but otherwise there's an $8-per-golfer fee Monday–Thursday and a $12-per-golfer fee Friday, weekends, and holidays.

Dress Code: Collared shirts must be worn. No jeans are allowed, but long shorts are permitted. Soft spikes are preferred.

Tournaments: Tournaments and group events for 9–144 players may be booked up to one year in advance.

Directions: Driving into San Francisco over the Golden Gate Bridge on U.S. 101, take the 19th Avenue exit south. At the first light after passing through the tunnel (Lake Street), turn right. Make a U-turn and head east on Lake to Arguello Boulevard and turn left. The course is at the top of the hill.

Contact: 300 Finley Road (P.O. Box 29063), San Francisco, CA 94129, pro shop 415/561-4661, fax 415/561-4667, www.presidiogolf.com.

14 LINCOLN PARK GOLF COURSE
Architect: Tom Bendelow, 1910;
remodel Herbert Fowler and Jack Fleming, 1922
18 holes   Public $31–35

📷 🍴 🔧 🛒 🥤

Peninsula Detail map, page 132

Situated around the Palace of the Legion of Honor with views of San Francisco below, this extremely scenic course is short, but tight and twisty. Part of the course runs along steep cliffs above the ocean. The 240-yard 17th hole is a tough but spectacular par-3 with a stunning view of the Golden Gate Bridge (and often lots of tourists wandering across the hole).

There are lots of trees, and good placement shots are vital. Lincoln Park is hilly but walkable. Pro golfers Johnny Miller and George Archer grew up playing here. This is a very busy course. Architects Herbert Fowler and Jack Fleming remodeled the original design.

Play Policy and Fees: Green fees are $31 Monday–Thursday and $35 Friday, weekends, and holidays. Senior and junior rates are available. Cash only.

Tees and Yardage: *Men:* Blue: yardage 5416, par 68, rating 66.0, slope 109; White: yardage 4948, par 68, rating 65.1, slope 107; *Women:* Red: yardage 4732, par 70, rating 66.0, slope 105.

Tee Times: San Francisco residents with a reservation card (obtained from San Francisco City Hall) can make tee times seven days in advance.

Dress Code: Appropriate attire and soft spikes are required.

Tournaments: Shotgun tournaments are available weekdays only. Carts are required. A 24-player minimum is needed to book a tournament.

Directions: Crossing over the Golden Gate Bridge on U.S. 101 into San Francisco, take the 19th Avenue exit south, follow it through the tunnel, and then turn right onto Clement Street. Follow Clement a few miles to the entrance of the course on the right.

Contact: 34th Avenue and Clement Street, San Francisco, CA 94121, pro shop 415/221-9911, www.playlincoln.com.

15 GOLDEN GATE PARK GOLF COURSE

Architect: Jack Fleming, 1950

9 holes   Public $10–18

🏌 📷 🍴 🏌 🚙 ⛳ 🅱

Peninsula Detail map, page 132

Situated at the end of Golden Gate Park near the ocean, this short, fun course is tight and curvy with lots of trees. The longest hole is the 193-yard fifth, and the shortest is the 109-yard eighth. The course offers good practice for your iron game and hosts the annual San Francisco Family Championship.

Play Policy and Fees: Green fees are $13 weekdays and $18 weekends and holidays; San Francisco residents pay $8 weekdays, $10 weekends. Senior and junior rates are available.

Tees and Yardage: *Men and Women:* yardage 1359, par 27, rating n/a, slope n/a.

Tee Times: Reservations are not accepted. All play is on a first-come, first-served basis.

Dress Code: Appropriate attire and soft spikes are required.

Tournaments: This course is available for outside tournaments.

Directions: This course is at the far west end of Golden Gate Park, on Fulton Street off 47th Avenue. Take the 19th Avenue exit off U.S. 101 into San Francisco. Follow 19th Avenue (Park Presidio) until you reach Fulton Street. Turn right and follow it along the park to 47th Avenue. Turn into the park and the course.

Contact: 47th Avenue and Fulton Street, San Francisco, CA 94117, pro shop 415/751-8987, www.goldengateparkgolf.com.

16 HARDING PARK GOLF COURSE

Architect: Willie Watson, 1925; renovated Sandy Tatum, 2003

27 holes   Public $33–88

🏌 📷 🍴 🏌 🚙 ⛳ 🅱

Peninsula Detail map, page 132

This sprawling, tree-lined course surrounded by Lake Merced was completely remodeled in 2003 and is once again the pride of San Francisco. Sandy Tatum, working with the PGA Tour, preserved much of the character and routing of the original design. But some new bunkers and recontoured greens have enhanced play on a course that had admittedly become somewhat tired. Also, 400 yards were added to the length to challenge the PGA Tour players, who are scheduled to compete here in 2005 and beyond. The course is home to the San Francisco City Championship. The Fleming Course, a nine-hole, par-3 beginner layout, is 2700 yards, and par is 32.

Play Policy and Fees: Green fees are $76 Monday–Thursday and $88 Friday, weekends, and holidays at the Harding Course. Golfers with a resident card pay $33 Monday–Thursday and $45 Friday, weekends, and holidays. The Fleming Course fees are $18 Monday–Thursday and $22 Friday, weekends, and holidays. Golfers with a resident card pay $16 Monday–Thursday and $18 Friday, weekends, and holidays. Senior, junior, and twilight rates are also available. Carts additional.

Tees and Yardage: *Men:* Blue: yardage 6845, par 72, rating 72.8, slope 126; White: yardage 6370, par 72, rating 70.6, slope 123; *Women:* Red: yardage 5865, par 73, rating 73.2, slope 123; Gold: yardage 5370, par 73, rating 70.4, slope 116.

Tee Times: Reservations can be booked six days in advance for the general public by calling the automated reservations line at 415/750-GOLF (4653). A $1 charge will be added to your green fee at the time of play for using this system. Players with a resident card can make tee times seven days in advance.

Dress Code: Appropriate attire and soft spikes are required.

Tournaments: A 12-player minimum is required to book a tournament.

Directions: Heading north into San Francisco on I-280, take 19th Avenue and make a left on Skyline Boulevard. Follow Skyline to Morton Drive and turn left to the course.

Contact: Harding Park/Skyline Boulevard, San Francisco, CA 94132, pro shop 415/661-1865, www.harding-park.com.

17 SAN FRANCISCO GOLF CLUB

Architect: A. W. Tillinghast, 1915; remodel Tom Doak, 2002

18 holes   **Private**

Peninsula Detail map, page 132

 This serene, immaculate course is rated among the best in the country. It's a medium-length, sprawling course with fast, undulating greens and lots of bunkers. Every hole is a treat, and the course has strategically placed bunkers and pine trees that make accuracy essential. Tom Doak completed renovation work on the greens and greenside bunkers in 2002, the first time the greens had been rebuilt since the course opened in 1915. Despite its length, it is tough to score out here. This historic layout played host to the 1974 Curtis Cup Match and has been used for U.S. Open sectional qualifying. Adjacent to the seventh tee are monuments commemorating the last dueling spot in California.

Play Policy and Fees: Members and guests only. No reciprocal play is accepted.

Tees and Yardage: *Men:* Championship: yardage 6754, par 71, rating 73.3, slope 130; Regular: yardage 6434, par 71, rating 71.7, slope 128; *Women:* Red: yardage 6015, par 73, rating 75.8, slope 137.

Tee Times: Not applicable.

Dress Code: Appropriate golf attire is mandatory and enforced. No shorts are allowed on the golf course. Nonmetal spikes are required.

Tournaments: This course is not available for outside events.

Directions: Heading into San Francisco on U.S. 101, take the 19th Avenue exit through town until it turns into Junipero Serra Boulevard (past San Francisco State University). Turn right on Brotherhood Way and take the first left onto Saint Thomas More Way to the course on the left.

Contact: Junipero Serra Boulevard and Brotherhood Way, San Francisco, CA 94132, pro shop 415/469-4122.

18 LAKE MERCED GOLF & COUNTRY CLUB

Architect: William Lock, 1922; Alister Mackenzie, 1927; Rees Jones, 1997

18 holes   **Private**   **$200**

Peninsula Detail map, page 132

This is a long, challenging course with big, undulating greens, huge pines, and San Francisco weather. There are some difficult par-3s, especially the 15th hole. This course is well maintained and walkable. The uphill, dogleg-right fourth hole and dogleg-left seventh are among the toughest holes in the area.

Play Policy and Fees: Reciprocal play is accepted with members of other private clubs at a rate of $200, including cart.

Tees and Yardage: *Men:* Black: yardage 6863, par 72, rating 74.1, slope 136; Blue: yardage 6503, par 72, rating 72.5, slope 133; White: yardage 6236, par 72, rating 71.2, slope 130; *Women:* Red: yardage 5823, par 72, rating 73.8, slope 132.

Tee Times: Reciprocal players should have their home professional make arrangements.

Dress Code: Appropriate golf attire and non-metal spikes are required.

Tournaments: This course is available for limited outside events with board approval.

Directions: On 19th Avenue in San Francisco or Highway 1, merge onto Junipero Serra Boulevard toward Daly City and follow it to the course.

Contact: 2300 Junipero Serra Boulevard, Daly City, CA 94015, pro shop 650/755-2239, fax 650/755-4569.

19 OLYMPIC CLUB
Architect: Willie Watson, 1924;
Jay Morrish and Tom Weiskopf, 1994
45 holes   Private

Peninsula Detail map, page 132

The Lakeside Course, perennially among the top 10 in the country, has been the site of four U.S. Opens (1955, 1966, 1987, 1998). It is long and tight, with lots of trees and small, undulating greens. Long par-4s dominate the Lakeside Course, making it seem like the longest 6800 yards in golf. The Ocean Course is shorter and tighter, but equally challenging. Wind and fog often come into play. The Cliffs Course, a scenic nine-hole, par-3 course overlooking the ocean and designed by Jay Morrish and Tom Weiskopf, opened in October 1994. The nine-hole Cliffs Course is 1506

yards from the long tees and 780 yards from the short tees. Par is 27. The course is not rated.

Play Policy and Fees: Members and guests only. All guests must be accompanied by a member.

Tees and Yardage: Lakeside Course—*Men:* Black: yardage 6830, par 71, rating 73.9, slope 138; Blue: yardage 6523, par 71, rating 72.3, slope 132; White: yardage 6229, par 71, rating 70.9, slope 129; *Women:* Green: yardage 5593, par 72, rating 73.8, slope 131. Ocean Course—*Men:* Black: yardage 6862, par 72, rating 73.5, slope 133; Blue: yardage 6429, par 72, rating 71.1, slope 129; White: yardage 5881, par 72, rating 68.8, slope 121; *Women:* Green: yardage 5568, par 71, rating 71.2, slope 125.

Tee Times: Not applicable.

Dress Code: Appropriate golf attire is required.

Tournaments: This course is not available for outside events.

Directions: Driving south on 19th Avenue through San Francisco, turn right on Sloat Boulevard. Follow it until it splits into a Y (before the San Francisco Zoo). Turn left onto Skyline Boulevard. The course is at the top of the hill on the left.

Contact: Mailing address: 524 Post Street, San Francisco, CA 94102, pro shop 415/587-8338, clubhouse 415/587-4800, www.olyclub.com.

20 GLENEAGLES INTER-NATIONAL GOLF COURSE
Architect: Jack Fleming, 1963
9 holes   Public $13–16

Peninsula Detail map, page 132

This sleeper course is patterned after a Scottish links–type course with a rolling terrain. You'll find tight, tree-lined fairways and tricky greens. Good target shots are required. The course is well maintained and often foggy and windy. The greens and tee boxes are usually in great shape. Lee Trevino played this course. According to legend, he shot 71 on his first try and 72 on his second try. There is another local legend, however: No one has ever broken par the first time out.

Play Policy and Fees: Green fees are $13 for nine holes Monday–Thursday, $14 Friday, and $16 weekends. Carts are $7 per rider. Call for special rates.

Tees and Yardage: *Men (18 holes):* Back: yardage 6390, par 72, rating 72.6, slope 138; *Women (18 holes):* Forward: yardage 5860, par 72, rating 75.6, slope 136.

Tee Times: Reservations can be booked seven days in advance for weekends and holidays. Reservations for weekdays are on a first-come, first-served basis.

Dress Code: No tank tops are allowed. Golf spikes are mandatory.

Tournaments: This course is not available for outside events.

Directions: Driving north on U.S. 101 into San Francisco, take the Cow Palace/Brisbane exit to Old Bayshore and go left at Geneva Street. In 1.5 miles, turn right on Moscow and then right again on Persia. It's three blocks to Sunnydale Avenue.

Contact: 2100 Sunnydale Avenue, San Francisco, CA 94134, pro shop 415/587-2425, fax 415/587-8434.

21 CYPRESS GOLF COURSE

Architect: Jack Fleming, 1958
9 holes   Public $14–18

🏌️ 📷 🏌️ 🚗 🏌️

Peninsula Detail map, page 132

This executive course is tight and well-guarded by trees. It features flat, relatively fast *Poa annua* grass greens and winter ryegrass fairways. Some water comes into play. There has been talk of adding nine new holes to this layout, but they were not complete as of press time.

Play Policy and Fees: Green fees for nine holes are $14 weekdays and $18 weekends and holidays. Senior rates are available before 10 A.M., and junior rates are available on weekdays only.

Tees and Yardage: *Men and Women:* yardage 1705, par 29, rating 29.6, slope 97.

Tee Times: Reservations are recommended for weekend play.

Dress Code: Collared shirts and soft spikes are required. No tank tops are allowed.

Tournaments: This course is available for tournaments.

Directions: Take I-280 north to Hickey Boulevard and turn right. Take Hickey Boulevard to El Camino Real and turn left. Take El Camino Real one mile to Serramonte Boulevard, turn right, and take Serramonte Boulevard to Hillside Boulevard. Turn right onto Hillside Boulevard to the course. From the north, take I-280 south to Serramonte. Follow Serramonte to Hillside. The course is 800 yards south on the left.

Contact: 2001 Hillside Boulevard, Colma, CA 94014, pro shop 650/992-5155, fax 650/992-5160, www.cypressgc.com.

22 CALIFORNIA GOLF CLUB

Architect: A. Vernon Macaan, 1918
18 holes   Private

🏌️ 📷 🏌️ 🚗 🏌️

Peninsula Detail map, page 132

This rolling, challenging course is situated above San Francisco International Airport. It's hilly, windy, and loaded with 185 bunkers. The par-5s and par-3s are especially challenging. Lakes have been added, one on the right side of the 11th and another on the left of the 18th green. This is a real sleeper course, giving the best golfers everything they want. The par-5 fourth is a double dogleg, with heavy trees on the right—a true three-shot hole, with six bunkers guarding the approach. The 14th, a dogleg left through a chute, is 442 yards. At one point some trees were removed to let in air and light. The open space did not make the hole any easier.

Play Policy and Fees: Members and guests only.

Tees and Yardage: *Men:* Blue: yardage 6735, par 72, rating 74.0, slope 136; White: yardage 6477, par 72, rating 72.8, slope 133; Gold: yardage 6013, par 72, rating 70.0, slope 130; *Women:* Red: yardage 5948, par 72, rating 74.9, slope 132.

Tee Times: Not applicable.

Dress Code: Appropriate golf attire is required.

Tournaments: This course is not available for outside events.

Directions: From San Francisco, take I-280 south to the Westborough Avenue exit east. At the bottom of the hill, turn right on West Orange Avenue and follow it to the course.

Contact: 844 West Orange Avenue, South San Francisco, CA 94080, pro shop 650/589-0144.

23 SHARP PARK GOLF COURSE

Architect: Alister Mackenzie, 1929

18 holes   **Public**   **$31–35**

Peninsula Detail map, page 132

This is a flat, tree-lined course at sea level. It is an Alister Mackenzie design, but not in the same league as Cypress Point Club or Pasatiempo. Nevertheless, it's a fun course to play. The front nine is inland, and the back nine runs along the ocean. The fairways are tight, with medium-sized greens. You'll find sand, water, views, and challenging golf. The 13th hole is a par-5, 525-yard dogleg left over water, and it's a doozy. The par-3 15th, at 135 yards over water, is also a tester.

Play Policy and Fees: Green fees are $31 weekdays and $35 weekends and holidays. Twilight rates are available.

Tees and Yardage: *Men:* White: yardage 6299, par 72, rating 70.3, slope 117; *Women:* Red: yardage 6093, par 74, rating 73.0, slope 120.

Tee Times: Reservations can be booked six days in advance for the general public starting at 7 P.M. by calling 415/750-GOLF (4653). A $1 charge will be added to your green fee at the time of play for using this system. San Francisco residents with a reservation card can make tee times seven days in advance.

Dress Code: Casual dress and metal spikes are allowed.

Tournaments: A 32-player minimum is needed to book a tournament. Carts are mandatory. Events should be scheduled at least eight months in advance. The banquet facility can accommodate 150 people.

Directions: From Highway 280, take Skyline Boulevard. Follow Skyline Boulevard to Sharp Park Road. Take a left on Sharp Park Road to the golf course.

Contact: Sharp Park Road and Highway 1 (P.O. Box 1275), Pacifica, CA 94044, pro shop 650/359-3380.

24 GREEN HILLS COUNTRY CLUB

Architect: Alister Mackenzie, 1930

18 holes   **Private**   **$80–100**

Peninsula Detail map, page 132

This short, tricky Alister Mackenzie course is situated in the foothills among eucalyptus, pine, and cypress trees. It has small, undulating greens and is well bunkered, typical of a Mackenzie design. The pride of the course is the uphill, 180-yard, par-3 15th hole, which crosses a ravine. You must hit to a two-level green with severe undulation between the levels. Count on the back level to be the toughest. When you play here, bring your nerves—it's the longest 6300 yards you may ever encounter.

Play Policy and Fees: Limited reciprocal play is accepted; otherwise, members and guests only. Reciprocal fees are $80 weekdays and $100 weekends. Carts are additional.

Tees and Yardage: *Men:* Blue: yardage 6300, par 71, rating 71.8, slope 140; White: yardage 6033, par 71, rating 70.6, slope 137; *Women:* Red: yardage 5724, par 72, rating 74.5, slope 136.

Tee Times: Reciprocal players must have their club professional call to make arrangements at least two days in advance.

Dress Code: Appropriate golf attire is required, and shorts to the knee are acceptable.

Tournaments: This course is available for outside tournaments. Please inquire.

Directions: This course is between I-280 and U.S. 101 in Millbrae. Exit on Millbrae Avenue off Highway 101 and drive north on El Camino Real. Turn left on Ludeman Lane and drive up the hill to the course.

Contact: End of Ludeman Lane, Millbrae, CA 94030, pro shop 650/583-0882, fax 650/588-0338, www.greenhillscc.com.

25 POPLAR CREEK GOLF COURSE

Architect: Course designed, 1934
18 holes   **Public**   **$35–43**

Peninsula Detail map, page 132

This course is short and flat, with tight, eucalyptus-lined fairways. The greens are in the traditional style: very small, elevated, well bunkered, and well contoured. Because of this, there is a premium on approach shots and putting. This walkable course is usually windy because of its proximity to San Francisco Bay. There are also several water hazards. It is a friendly course for all skill levels.

Play Policy and Fees: Green fees are $35 weekdays, $43 weekends. Resident, senior, junior, twilight, early bird, and super twilight rates available. Carts are $12 per rider.

Tees and Yardage: *Men:* Black: yardage 6042, par 70, rating 69.0, slope 113; Gold: yardage 5645, par 70, rating 67.3, slope 111; Silver: yardage 5220, par 70, rating 65.2, slope 107; *Women:* Yellow: yardage 4768, par 71, rating 67.6, slope 113.

Tee Times: Reservations can be booked seven days in advance.

Dress Code: Golf attire is encouraged.

Tournaments: No shotgun tournaments are allowed. A 12-player minimum is needed to book a tournament.

Directions: This course is on the east side of U.S. 101 in San Mateo and visible from the freeway. From the north, take the Poplar Avenue exit. From the south, take the Dore exit. Follow the signs marked Coyote Point Drive from both exits to the course.

Contact: 1700 Coyote Point Drive (P.O. Box 634), San Mateo, CA 94401, pro shop 650/522-4653, www.poplarcreekgolf.com.

26 CRYSTAL SPRINGS GOLF COURSE

Architect: Herbert Fowler, 1924
18 holes   **Public**   **$42–80**

Peninsula Detail map, page 132

This hilly, meandering course will give you plenty of sidehill lies and requires good placement shots. Situated in the midst of a California State game preserve, the course enjoys an abundance of wildlife. It has some steep holes, but it is walkable. The view from the sixth tee opens up on the game preserve. Deer regularly come onto the course. The first hole is a hard dogleg left, 397 yards, requiring a long, accurate tee shot, and the green is severely sloped. Weather ranges from San Francisco fog to peninsula sun. It is a fun and popular course.

Play Policy and Fees: Green fees are $42 to walk Monday–Thursday, $56 to ride, and $80 Friday–Sunday, including mandatory cart. Twilight rates are available.

Tees and Yardage: *Men:* Blue: yardage 6557, par 72, rating 72.0, slope 123; White: yardage 6207, par 72, rating 70.4, slope 121; Gold: yardage 5786, par 72, rating 69.4, slope 119; *Women:* Red: yardage 5710, par 72, rating 72.5, slope 126.

Tee Times: Reservations can be booked seven days in advance.

Dress Code: Collared shirts required. No tank tops or denim are allowed on the course.

Tournaments: A 16-player minimum is required to book a tournament. Carts are required. Events should be booked 12 months in advance. The banquet facility can accommodate 200 people.

Directions: On I-280 heading north or south in Burlingame, take the Hayne and Black Mountain Road exit. Head west and follow the road until it dead-ends at Golf Course Drive. Turn right onto Golf Course Drive. The course is visible from the highway.

Contact: 6650 Golf Course Drive, Burlingame, CA 94010, pro shop 650/342-0603, www.play crystalsprings.com.

27 BURLINGAME COUNTRY CLUB

Architect: Herbert Fowler, 1893;
Harold Sampson, 1906; Robert Trent Jones Sr., 1954
18 holes   Private

🧍 📷 💰 🔧 🛻 🍴

Peninsula Detail map, page 132

Significant changes to the course have been made by various architects, most notably Robert Trent Jones Sr. in 1954. Today it has a sprawling, tree-lined layout and narrow fairways that require precise shots off the tee. It's fairly flat and walkable. This course has been used for U.S. Open sectional qualifying. This course is the oldest west of the Mississippi, dating back to 1893. It premiered as a three-hole course, then expanded to nine in 1899. Bing Crosby was one of the many prominent members of this highly exclusive club.

Play Policy and Fees: Members and guests only.
Tees and Yardage: *Men:* Blue: yardage 6394, par 70, rating 70.9, slope 128; White: yardage 6182, par 70, rating 70.9, slope 127; *Women:* Red: yardage 5728, par 72, rating 72.3, slope 125.
Tee Times: Not applicable.
Dress Code: Collared shirts are required.
Tournaments: This course is not available for outside events.
Directions: Driving on U.S. 101 in Burlingame, take the Broadway exit southwest to El Camino Real. Go left on El Camino Real and turn right on Floribunda Avenue. When it dead-ends, turn left on Eucalyptus Avenue. Turn right on New Place Road. The course is on the right.
Contact: 80 New Place Road, Hillsborough, CA 94010, pro shop 650/342-0750.

28 THE PENINSULA GOLF & COUNTRY CLUB

Architect: Donald Ross, 1922
18 holes   Private $150

🧍 📷 💰 🔧 🛻 🍴

Peninsula Detail map, page 132

This mature Donald Ross design offers undulating greens and tight fairways lined with redwood, Monterey pine, stone pine, and eucalyptus trees. It was completely remodeled in 2003. From a few of the tee boxes you can see a full view of Mount Diablo in the East Bay. This is the only Donald Ross–designed golf course on the West Coast.

Play Policy and Fees: Reciprocal play is accepted with members of other private clubs. The green fee for reciprocators is $150. The course is closed on Monday.
Tees and Yardage: *Men:* Black: yardage 6538, par 71, rating 71.7, slope 127; Blue: yardage 6230, par 71, rating 70.3, slope 124; White: yardage 5827, par 71, rating 68.4, slope 119; *Women:* Red: yardage 5370, par 72, rating 70.3, slope 121.
Tee Times: Reciprocal players should have their home professional call to make arrangements.
Dress Code: Appropriate golf attire is required.
Tournaments: This course is available for outside events on Monday.
Directions: The course is between U.S. 101 and I-280. Take Highway 92 to Alameda de Las Pulgas and bear south. Turn right on Madera Drive.
Contact: 701 Madera Drive, San Mateo, CA 94403, pro shop 650/638-2239.

29 HALF MOON BAY GOLF LINKS

Architect: Arnold Palmer and Francis Duane, 1973;
Arthur Hills, 1997
36 holes   Public $125–145

📷 💰 🛻 🍴 〰️

Peninsula Detail map, page 132

 These are two excellent courses. This Old Course is long and demanding. The 18th hole spans 428 yards along an ocean cliff and has been rated one of the top 100 holes in the country. Be wary of the back pin placement on this hole. Fog and wind often come into play. Big, undulating greens and long par-3s add to the challenge. The links-style Ocean Course offers ocean views from every hole, and the three finishing holes sit directly on the Pacific Ocean. It is a demanding course, and weather can be a factor, but you'll

love every minute of it, just like in Ireland or Scotland.

The elegant Ritz-Carlton Half Moon Bay is adjacent to these courses. For information or reservations, call 650/712-7000.

Play Policy and Fees: Green fees on both courses are $125 Monday–Thursday and $145 Friday, weekends, and holidays. Twilight rates are available. Carts are included in fees and are mandatory.

Tees and Yardage: Old Course—*Men:* Blue: yardage 7090, par 72, rating 75.3, slope 135; White: yardage 6410, par 72, rating 72.1, slope 130; *Women:* Red: yardage 5305, par 72, rating 73.1, slope 126. Ocean Course—*Men:* Blue: yardage 6712, par 72, rating 72.5, slope 128; White: yardage 6319, par 72, rating 70.4, slope 123; *Women:* Red: yardage 5089, par 72, rating 68.5, slope 112.

Tee Times: Reservations can be booked three weeks in advance.

Dress Code: Appropriate golf attire and non-metal spikes are required.

Tournaments: Carts are required. Shotgun tournaments can be held Monday–Thursday. A 72-player minimum is needed for a semishotgun start, and 120 players are needed for a full shotgun start. A 24-player minimum is needed for a regular tournament. Events should be booked 12 months in advance. The banquet facility can accommodate 144 people.

Directions: Head toward Half Moon Bay via Highway 1 or Highway 92. The course is three miles south of the junction of Highway 1 and 92, south of Half Moon Bay on the ocean side.

Contact: 2000 Fairway Drive, Half Moon Bay, CA 94019, pro shop 650/726-4438, fax 650/726-5831, www.halfmoonbaygolf.com.

30 MENLO COUNTRY CLUB

Architect: Tom Nicoll, 1900; Robert Trent Jones Jr., 1970
18 holes **Private**

Peninsula Detail map, page 132

This is a short but sneaky course. Overhanging old oaks add character and line the fair-ways. Beware of the 16th hole, where there's a massive oak in the middle of the fairway. Located at a very exclusive club, this course is known for its pristine condition and traditional presence. It's mostly flat and walkable.

Play Policy and Fees: Guests must be accompanied by a member. No reciprocal play is accepted.

Tees and Yardage: *Men:* Blue: yardage 6315, par 70, rating 70.5, slope 126; White: yardage 6034, par 70, rating 69.3, slope 124; *Women:* Red: yardage 5641, par 72, rating 72.5, slope 123.

Tee Times: Not applicable.

Dress Code: Appropriate golf attire is required.

Tournaments: This course is not available for outside events.

Directions: Take I-280 to Redwood City. Exit on Woodside Road. The course is on the north side of the street, three-quarters of a mile from I-280.

Contact: 2300 Woodside Road, Redwood City, CA 94064 (P.O. Box 729, Woodside, CA 94062), pro shop 650/366-9910, fax 650/367-6195.

31 EMERALD HILLS GOLF CLUB

Architect: Course designed, 1956
9 holes **Public** **$11–15**

Peninsula Detail map, page 132

This is a short starter course composed of par-3s. It's hilly but walkable and is a perfect layout for juniors, seniors, and beginners. This is a good course for advanced golfers to sharpen their short game. With a driving range and putting green, it's a good place to learn the game. The course is owned by the Redwood City Elks Lodge.

Play Policy and Fees: Green fees are $11 for nine holes weekdays and $15 for nine holes weekends and holidays. Senior and junior rates are available.

Tees and Yardage: *Men:* yardage 1156, par 27, rating n/a, slope n/a; *Women:* yardage 1003, par 27, rating n/a, slope n/a.

Tee Times: Reservations can be made 14 days in advance.

Dress Code: Shoes and shirts are required.
Tournaments: A 40-player minimum is required to book an event. A banquet facility is available that can accommodate 300 people. Events should be booked three months in advance.
Directions: From I-280 in Redwood City, exit on Edgewood Road southwest and turn left on Cañada Road. Drive 1.5 miles to Jefferson Avenue and turn left again, following the road to Wilmington Way. Turn right to the course.
Contact: 938 Wilmington Way, Redwood City, CA 94062, pro shop 650/368-7820, fax 650/366-4760, www.emeraldhillsgolf.com.

32 SHARON HEIGHTS GOLF & COUNTRY CLUB

Architect: Jack Fleming, 1962
18 holes   **Private**

Peninsula Detail map, page 132

This course is long and challenging. Redwoods ranging in height 40–80 feet often come into play. The course boasts some of the best greens between San Francisco and Monterey. They're large, smooth, and fast. The course is hilly but walkable. A new club house opened in 2003.
Play Policy and Fees: Reciprocal play is accepted with members of other private clubs upon approval of the head pro; otherwise, members and guests only. Please inquire.
Tees and Yardage: *Men:* Gold: yardage 6837, par 72, rating 73.4, slope 138; Blue: yardage 6476, par 72, rating 71.7, slope 134; White: yardage 6085, par 72, rating 69.8, slope 132; *Women:* Red: yardage 5734, par 72, rating 73.7, slope 132.
Tee Times: Reciprocal players should have their home professional call to inquire.
Dress Code: Appropriate golf attire and nonmetal spikes are required.
Tournaments: Outside events are allowed on an extremely limited basis.
Directions: From I-280 in Menlo Park, take the Sand Hill Road exit toward Stanford Uni-

versity. The course is on the left, less than one-quarter mile off Sand Hill Road.
Contact: 2900 Sand Hill Road, Menlo Park, CA 94025, pro shop 650/854-6429, fax 650/854-5630, www.shgcc.com.

33 PALO ALTO HILLS GOLF & COUNTRY CLUB

Architect: Clark Glasson, 1960; Neal Meagher, 1998
18 holes   **Private**   **$70–85**

Peninsula Detail map, page 132

Although this tight, hilly course is short, it plays considerably longer than the yardage indicates. It's a defensive course, with undulating fairways and elevated fast greens. Water comes into play on five holes. Watch out for the par-4 third hole, a nasty, downhill tester. The par-5 18th hole is the signature hole, with a lake and waterfall fronting the green, resulting in a risky approach shot. Situated in the hills, the course offers picturesque views of San Francisco Bay, so don't forget to look up. The first head professional was Ken Venturi in 1960.
Play Policy and Fees: Reciprocal play is accepted with members of other private clubs; otherwise, members and guests only. The green fee for reciprocators is $70 weekdays, $85 weekends. Optional carts are $13.50 per rider. The course is closed on Monday.
Tees and Yardage: *Men:* Four Trees: yardage 6269, par 71, rating 71.7, slope 133; Three Trees: yardage 6005, par 71, rating 70.5, slope 131; Two Trees: yardage 5605, par 71, rating 68.6, slope 125; *Women:* One Tree: yardage 5032, par 72, rating 70.7, slope 128.
Tee Times: Reciprocal players should have their home professional call to make arrangements one week in advance.
Dress Code: Appropriate golf attire is required.
Tournaments: Outside tournaments are available on Monday only. A 100-player minimum is required to book an event. Tournaments should be scheduled 12 months in advance. The banquet facility can accommodate 400 people.
Directions: From I-280 west, take the Page Mill

exit. Drive one mile to Alexis Drive and continue one-half mile to the course. From U.S. 101, take the Oregon Expressway. Cross El Camino Real and the road turns into Page Mill. Continue to the course.

Contact: 3000 Alexis Drive, Palo Alto, CA 94304, pro shop 650/948-2320, www.pahgcc.com.

34 STANFORD UNIVERSITY GOLF COURSE

Architect: William P. Bell and
George C. Thomas Jr., 1930

18 holes   Private $75–150

Peninsula Detail map, page 132

This sprawling layout is dotted with eucalyptus and oak trees. It has large, contoured greens and many bunkers. There are no breathers, especially on the infamous, nerve-racking par-4 12th hole. It's extremely long, with two oak trees in the middle of the fairway. The second and the 10th holes are cast-iron tests. This course can get very crowded, but it's worth the wait. Stanford has played host to several NCAA Men's Championships, NCAA Women's Championships, the USGA Junior Championship, and the Western Amateur. It was, of course, Tiger Woods's home course as a collegian. Note: There has been discussion over the years about modifying the layout to widen adjacent Sand Hill Road and alleviate traffic congestion, but no plans had been finalized at press time.

Play Policy and Fees: Stanford students, alumni, faculty, staff, and guests only. Guests must be accompanied by a constituent. Guest fees are $75 weekdays and $150 weekends and holidays. Current students receive a discounted rate. The course is closed on Monday except on university holidays.

Tees and Yardage: *Men:* Red: yardage 6785, par 71, rating 73.3, slope 141; Black: yardage 6390, par 71, rating 71.3, slope 135; White: yardage 5997, par 72, rating 71.3, slope 128; *Women:* Blue: yardage 5576, par 72, rating 72.4, slope 129.

Tee Times: Stanford students, alumni, faculty, and staff can make reservations one day in advance.

Dress Code: Nonmetal spikes are required.

Tournaments: Outside events are limited to Monday. Carts are required. A 120-player minimum is required. Tournaments should be booked 12 months in advance. The banquet facilities can accommodate up to 150 people.

Directions: From I-280, take the Sand Hill Road exit in Menlo Park. Drive east toward Stanford University. Turn right on Junipero Serra Boulevard and proceed one-half mile to West Campus Drive. Turn right and proceed to the course. From U.S. 101, take the University Avenue exit, which turns into Palm Drive. Turn right on West Campus Drive and continue to the course.

Contact: 198 Junipero Serra Boulevard, Stanford, CA 94305, pro shop 650/323-0944, fax 650/323-0995, www.stanfordgolfcourse.com.

35 PALO ALTO GOLF COURSE

Architect: William F. Bell, 1956

18 holes   Public $32–43

Peninsula Detail map, page 132

Palo Alto has a links feel, with wide-open, driver-friendly fairways and large greens. Although wind is a factor, the greens allow players several approach options, including bump and run. Annual tournaments played at the Palo Alto Golf Course include the Palo Alto City Women's Amateur (April), the Santa Clara Valley Best-Ball (May), and the Palo Alto City Seniors Amateur (October). It is a popular course. A new restaurant opened in 2003.

Play Policy and Fees: Green fees are $32 weekdays and $43 weekends. Carts are additional. Resident, twilight, super twilight, nine-hole, and seasonal rates are available. Please inquire.

Tees and Yardage: *Men:* Black: yardage 6833, par 72, rating 72.4, slope 118; Blue: yardage 6580, par 72, rating 71.1, slope 117; White: yardage 6227, par 72, rating 69.5, slope 115; *Women:* Red: yardage 5679, par 72, rating 66.6, slope 109.

Tee Times: Reservations can be booked seven days in advance.

Dress Code: Appropriate attire and soft spikes are required.

Tournaments: This course is available for outside tournaments.

Directions: From U.S. 101 in Palo Alto, take the Embarcadero Road exit east. The course is on the left about one-half mile from the highway. It's just before the airport.

Contact: 1875 Embarcadero Road, Palo Alto, CA 94303, pro shop 650/856-0881, clubhouse 650/856-0133, www.city.palo-alto.ca.us/golf.

36 EAGLE VINES GOLF CLUB

Architect: Jack Barry and Johnny Miller, 2004

18 holes   Public $95–110

East Bay Detail map, page 133

Eight new holes, combined with 10 existing holes from the old Club Shakespeare layout, created the Eagle Vines course, next to the Chardonnay Golf Club. For those who remember Club Shakespeare, the terrain is similar: gently rolling, with some nice mountain and valley views. From the back tees, this course will be a challenge to better golfers, typical of Johnny Miller–influenced designs. A new clubhouse will serve this course. Ladies, the course plays long from the red tees.

Play Policy and Fees: Green fees are $95 Monday–Friday, $110 weekends and holidays. Carts included in fee. Twilight and senior rates are available.

Tees and Yardage: *Men:* Black: yardage 7251, par 72, rating 74.8, slope 134; Blue: yardage 6761, par 72, rating 72.9, slope 130; White: yardage 6311, par 72, rating 70.5, slope 122; *Women:* Red: yardage 5652, par 72, rating 73.2, slope 128.

Tee Times: Reservations can be made 30 days in advance.

Dress Code: Appropriate golf attire is required. Soft spikes only.

Tournaments: Please inquire.

Directions: From Highway 29 south of Napa, take Highway 12 east. The entrance to the course is roughly 1.3 miles from the intersection.

Contact: 620 South Kelly Road, Napa, CA 94558, phone 707/257-4470.

37 CHARDONNAY GOLF CLUB

Architect: Algie M. Pulley Jr., 1987

27 holes   Public $80–95

East Bay Detail map, page 133

Formerly there were two courses here, The Vineyards and Club Shakespeare. In 2004, nine holes from the Shakespeare course were added to The Vineyards to form a 27-hole facility. The remaining nine holes of Shakespeare were combined with nine new holes designed by Johnny Miller to form Eagle Vines Golf Club, also on the same site (see preceding listing). The courses are surrounded by 150 acres of working grapevines, set in a lovely valley. Note: At press time, the reconfiguring of the courses was not complete, so no yardages or ratings were available.

Play Policy and Fees: Green fees are $80 on weekdays and $95 on weekends. Twilight rates are available after 2 P.M.

Tees and Yardage: Lakes/Meadows—*Men:* Black: yardage 6751, par 72, rating 73.8, slope 141; Blue: yardage 6492, par 72, rating 72.7, slope 136; White: yardage 6015, par 72, rating 70.3, slope 127; *Women:* Red: yardage 5361, par 72, rating 71.8, slope 126. Meadows/Vineyards—*Men:* Black: yardage 6740, par 72, rating 73.2, slope 137; Blue: yardage 6415, par 72, rating 71.7, slope 133; White: yardage 6008, par 72, rating 69.7, slope 128; *Women:* Red: yardage 5147, par 72, rating 70.1, slope 118. Vineyards/Lakes—*Men:* Black: yardage 6821, par 72, rating 74.0, slope 136; Blue: yardage 6519, par 72, rating 72.6, slope 133; White: yardage 6083, par 72, rating 70.4, slope 127; *Women:* Red: yardage 5286, par 72, rating 71.1, slope 124.

Tee Times: Reservations may be made up to 30 days in advance.

Dress Code: Collared shirts are required, and no denim or cutoffs are allowed. Shorts must be at least mid-thigh in length.

Tournaments: Tournaments are welcome.

Directions: From Highway 29 south of Napa,

take Highway 12 east. The entrance to the course is 1.3 miles from the intersection. **Contact:** 2555 Jamieson Canyon Road (P.O. Box 3779), Napa, CA 94558, pro shop 707/257-1900, fax 707/257-0613, www.chardonnaygolf club.com.

38 GREEN VALLEY COUNTRY CLUB

Architect: Elmer G. Borders, 1950; Robert Muir Graves, 1965

18 holes   **Private**   **$55–65**

East Bay Detail map, page 133

This is a rolling, tree-lined layout with good, fast greens. The front nine is flat, while the back winds through the hills. The 12th hole requires a long-iron off the tee, then a mid- to short-iron to a green that is severely contoured. It's a good example of Green Valley's charm, which includes a creek running through four holes. The wind can become a factor.

Play Policy and Fees: Reciprocal play is accepted with members of other private clubs. Reciprocal fees are based on referring club fees. Guest fees are $55 with a member weekdays and $65 weekends.

Tees and Yardage: *Men:* Blue: yardage 6497, par 72, rating 71.6, slope 129; White: yardage 6280, par 72, rating 70.4, slope 128; *Women:* Red: yardage 5866, par 72, rating 73.4, slope 130.

Tee Times: Reciprocators should have their club pro call to make arrangements.

Dress Code: No jeans are allowed on the course. Appropriate golf attire is required. Soft spikes only.

Tournaments: Outside events are held on Monday only. A 100-player minimum is needed, and events should be scheduled 12 months in advance. A banquet facility accommodates 200 people.

Directions: From Vallejo, take I-80 to Green Valley Road. Head north to Country Club Drive and turn left to the course.

Contact: 35 Country Club Drive, Suisun City, CA 94585, pro shop 707/864-0473, fax 707/864-3501, www.greenvalleycc.com.

39 RANCHO SOLANO GOLF COURSE

Architect: Gary Roger Baird, 1990

18 holes   **Public**   **$33–60**

East Bay Detail map, page 133

Rancho Solano has some of the largest greens in California. The green on the ninth hole measures 150 feet front to back. The course is situated in rolling hills dotted with oak trees. There are five lakes and 87 bunkers. Practicing long putts on the putting green is a must at Rancho Solano. The enormous greens demand a good putting touch; it's one of the few places where pros have been known to four-putt. The course record is 64, held by Jeff Wilson from the blue tees and Charles Millard from the white tees.

Play Policy and Fees: Green fees are $33 to walk and $48 to ride Monday–Thursday, $37 to walk and $52 to ride Friday, and $45 to walk and $60 to ride on Saturday, Sunday, and holidays. Resident, senior, junior, and twilight rates are offered.

Tees and Yardage: *Men:* Blue: yardage 6616, par 72, rating 71.2, slope 127; White: yardage 6129, par 72, rating 69.2, slope 125; *Women:* Red: yardage 5201, par 72, rating 69.6, slope 117.

Tee Times: Reservations can be booked seven days in advance without fee. A small fee is charged if you wish to make a reservation up to 30 days out.

Dress Code: No tank tops are allowed. Soft spikes only.

Tournaments: A 16-player minimum is required for tournament play. Events should be booked 12 months in advance. The banquet facility can accommodate 300 people.

Directions: From I-80 in Fairfield, take Waterman Boulevard west and follow it two miles. Go right on Rancho Solano Parkway and continue to the course.

Contact: 3250 Rancho Solano Parkway, Fairfield, CA 94533, pro shop 707/429-4653, fax 707/427-8944, www.fairfield-golf.com.

40 PARADISE VALLEY GOLF COURSE

Architect: Robert Muir Graves, 1993

18 holes   **Public**   **$35–45**

East Bay Detail map, page 133

This is a mostly flat, challenging course where wind plays a major role. When it's calm, the course lets down its guard. Most days, however, wind influences almost every shot. Water comes into play on nine holes, and accurate driving is a must. One of the signature holes is the 433-yard, par-4 18th, a dogleg right guarded by a lake on the right. Don't get too greedy on your tee shot. This is one of the best-draining courses in Northern California. All golf carts are equipped with ProShot Electronic Caddy. What's that? From anywhere on the course, your cart can tell you the exact yardage to the middle of the green.

Play Policy and Fees: Green fees are $35 Monday–Thursday, $39 Friday, and $45 weekends. Senior, resident, and twilight rates are available. Carts are $15.

Tees and Yardage: *Men:* Black: yardage 6993, par 72, rating 73.9, slope 129; Blue: yardage 6704, par 72, rating 72.7, slope 124; White: yardage 6128, par 72, rating 70.6, slope 122; *Women:* Red: yardage 5413, par 72, rating 71.7, slope 119.

Tee Times: Reservations can be booked seven days in advance.

Dress Code: There are no tank tops, bare midriffs, or short shorts allowed on the golf course. Soft spikes only.

Tournaments: A 20-player minimum is needed for tournament play, and carts are required. Tournaments should be booked 12 months in advance. A banquet facility is available and can accommodate 200 people.

Directions: From San Francisco, take I-80 east to the North Texas Street exit. Turn right on North Texas Street to Dixon Hill and turn left. Follow Dixon Hill to Dover Street and turn left. Follow Dover Street one-half mile to the club.

Contact: 3950 Paradise Valley Drive, Fairfield, CA 94533, pro shop 707/426-1600, fax 707/426-1745, www.fairfield-golf.com.

41 HIDDENBROOKE GOLF CLUB

Architect: Arnold Palmer, 1995

18 holes   **Public**   **$65–95**

East Bay Detail map, page 133

Gorgeous views are afforded from many elevated tees at this Arnold Palmer–designed course. It is well bunkered, with rolling hills and large greens. Water comes into play on eight holes. One of the most spectacular holes is the 560-yard, par-5 18th. This course hosted the LPGA Samsung World Championship from 2000 to 2002.

Play Policy and Fees: Green fees are $65 Monday–Thursday, $75 Friday, $95 Saturday and holidays, and $85 Sunday. Prices include a cart. Limited junior and senior rates available. Memberships available.

Tees and Yardage: *Men:* Palmer: yardage 6782, par 72, rating 73.4, slope 143; Championship: yardage 6241, par 72, rating 71.1, slope 136; White: yardage 5769, par 72, rating 69.1, slope 126; *Women:* Executive: yardage 5199, par 72, rating 71.1, slope 128; Red: yardage 4647, par 72, rating 67.6, slope 121.

Tee Times: Reservations can be booked up to two weeks in advance.

Dress Code: Golfers must wear appropriate golf attire, including collared shirts. Bermuda shorts are permitted. Nonmetal spikes are required.

Tournaments: This course is available for tournaments.

Directions: From Vallejo, take I-80 north to the American Canyon exit. Turn right and proceed to the golf course.

Contact: 1095 Hiddenbrooke Parkway, Vallejo, CA 94591, pro shop 707/558-1140, clubhouse 707/558-0330, fax 707/558-1144, www.hiddenbrookegolf.com.

42 MARE ISLAND GOLF CLUB

Architect: Course designed, 1898; Robin Nelson, 2000
18 holes　　**Public**　　**$30–45**

East Bay Detail map, page 133

Water comes into play on several holes, and the course is very hilly. The course forces players to be accurate with the irons. Locals like to think of it as a small version of the Olympic Club. The clubhouse and restaurant were upgraded in 1999. A new nine holes designed by Robin Nelson and a driving range were completed in 2000, which greatly upgraded this facility.

Play Policy and Fees: Formerly a military course, this course is now open to the public. Green fees are $30 Monday–Friday, $40 weekends and holidays. Twilight and senior rates (55-plus) are available.

Tees and Yardage: *Men:* Blue: yardage 6150, par 70, rating 69.8, slope 124; White: yardage 5788, par 70, rating 68.0, slope 121; *Women:* Red: yardage 4832, par 70, rating 71.4, slope 112.

Tee Times: Reservations can be booked seven days in advance.

Dress Code: Collared shirts and soft-spiked shoes are required.

Tournaments: This course is available for outside tournaments. Call the pro shop for more information.

Directions: From Vallejo, take I-80 to Highway 37. Take Highway 37 to the Mare Island exit. Follow Walnut Street to the north gate. Enter the gate and drive two miles to the course.

Contact: 1800 Club Drive/Mare Island Naval Station, Vallejo, CA 94590, pro shop 707/562-4653, fax 707/562-8891, www.mareislandgolf club.com.

43 JOE MORTARA GOLF COURSE

Architect: Joe Mortara Sr. and Jack Fleming, 1981
9 holes　　**Public**　　**$11–12**

East Bay Detail map, page 133

This short course is flat and a good test for beginners or for brushing up on the irons.

There is only one par-4, the 320-yard seventh. The course is situated in the middle of the track of the Solano County Fairgrounds.

Play Policy and Fees: Green fees are $11 for nine holes weekdays with $7 for each additional nine holes, and $12 for nine holes weekends with $8 for each additional nine holes. Junior and senior rates are available. The course is closed two weeks in July for the fair.

Tees and Yardage: *Men and Women:* yardage 1592, par 28, rating n/a, slope n/a.

Tee Times: Reservations are not accepted. All play is on a first-come, first-served basis.

Dress Code: Appropriate attire and soft spikes are required.

Tournaments: This course is not available for outside events.

Directions: From I-80 at the north end of Vallejo, take the Redwood exit. Turn right on Fairgrounds Drive. The course is at the Solano County Fairgrounds.

Contact: 900 Fairgrounds Drive, Vallejo, CA 94590, pro shop 707/642-5146.

44 BLUE ROCK SPRINGS GOLF COURSE

Architect: Joe Mortara Sr., 1941;
Robert Muir Graves, 1994
36 holes　　**Public**　　**$28–32**

East Bay Detail map, page 133

The new East Course at Blue Rock Springs, designed by Robert Muir Graves, is a sprawling, hilly layout with sidehill lies and large, undulating greens. Wind is usually a factor. The signature holes are the uphill, par-4 15th hole, measuring 413 yards, and the 159-yard, par-3 16th, featuring a plateau green surrounded by rocks. The West Course is flanked by trees and is flatter than the East Course. The par-4 14th hole, a severe dogleg over a deep ravine, and the par-3 15th are especially challenging.

Play Policy and Fees: Green fees for both courses are $28 on weekdays and $32 on weekends. Carts are additional. Resident, twilight, and junior rates available.

Tees and Yardage: West Course—*Men:* Blue: yardage 5948, par 71, rating 67.9, slope 121; White: yardage 5701, par 71, rating 66.9, slope 119; Gold: yardage 5400, par 71, rating 65.4, slope 115; *Women:* Red: yardage 5161, par 72, rating 69.1, slope 114. East Course—*Men:* Blue: yardage 6133, par 70, rating 69.4, slope 128; White: yardage 5776, par 70, rating 67.8, slope 123; Gold: yardage 5332, par 70, rating 65.6, slope 117; *Women:* Red: yardage 4869, par 70, rating 68.2, slope 117.

Tee Times: Reservations can be made the Tuesday before for weekend play, one week in advance for weekday play.

Dress Code: Appropriate golf attire is required, and nonmetal spikes are encouraged.

Tournaments: Shotgun tournaments are available weekdays only. A 24-player minimum is needed to book an event. Tournaments should be scheduled 12 months in advance. A banquet facility is available that can accommodate up to 100 people.

Directions: From I-80 in Vallejo, take the Columbus Parkway exit and drive three miles east to the course on the right.

Contact: 655 Columbus Parkway, Vallejo, CA 94591, pro shop 707/643-8476, fax 707/642-1065, www.bluerockspringsgolf.com.

45 RIO VISTA GOLF CLUB

Architect: Ted Robinson Sr., 1996

18 holes   **Public**   **$26-65**

This course is based on the philosophy of risk and reward, giving the golfer plenty of options. The signature hole is the 18th, a par-4 dogleg left that plays into a prevailing wind. A bunker is strategically placed at the corner of the dogleg. Once around the corner, you are faced with a lake guarding the majority of the green, with waterfalls on both sides.

Play Policy and Fees: Green fees are $26 for nine holes and $50 for 18 holes Monday–Thursday, $30 for nine holes and $55 for 18 holes Friday, and $33 for nine and $65 for 18 on weekends and holidays. Carts are included. Twilight rates and annual passes are offered.

Tees and Yardage: *Men:* Championship: yardage 6800, par 72, rating 73.9, slope 131; White: yardage 6393, par 72, rating 71.9, slope 126; *Women:* Red: yardage 5330, par 72, rating 72.4, slope 124.

Tee Times: Reservations can be booked seven days in advance by calling the pro shop.

Dress Code: Collared shirts are preferred, and nonmetal spikes are required.

Tournaments: A 16-player minimum is needed to book a tournament. Carts are required. Tournaments should be scheduled 12 months in advance.

Directions: Travel two miles west of Rio Vista on Highway 12 and exit on Summerset Drive.

Contact: 1000 Summerset Drive, Rio Vista, CA 94571, pro shop 707/374-2900, fax 707/374-4405, www.riovistagolf.com.

46 BETHEL ISLAND GOLF COURSE

Architect: Bob Baldock, 1966

18 holes   **Public**   **$21-31**

East Bay Detail map, page 133

This links-style layout is flat and windy, with lots of trees, water, and bunkers. It's a challenging but fair test. The parking lot and cart paths have been repaved, and the clubhouse and restrooms have been remodeled.

Play Policy and Fees: Green fees are $21 for 18 holes Monday–Friday, $31 weekends and holidays. Carts are $12 per person. Twilight rates are offered.

Tees and Yardage: *Men:* Blue: yardage 6592, par 72, rating 71.4, slope 122; White: yardage 6292, par 72, rating 70.0, slope 120; *Women:* Red: yardage 5839, par 72, rating 72.2, slope 117.

Tee Times: Reservations can be booked seven days in advance.

Dress Code: Collared shirts with sleeves are required.

Tournaments: This course is available for outside events. Tournaments should be booked one month in advance.

Directions: Take Highway 4 through Oakley to Brentwood and exit at Cypress Road east. Turn left at Bethel Island Road and then right at Gateway Road to the course.

Contact: 3303 Gateway Road, Bethel Island, CA 94511, pro shop 925/684-2654, fax 925/684-0720.

47 RICHMOND COUNTRY CLUB

Architect: Ed Sawyer, 1924; Pat Markovich, 1939; renovated Neal Meagher, 2003

18 holes   **Private**   **$85–100**

East Bay Detail map, page 133

This mature course is short and very secluded. The fairways are tight and tree-lined. The terrain is gentle and rolling, with very tall and broad pine and eucalyptus trees. This is the norm among old East Bay courses: short holes with slanted greens—very tricky. The 16th, 17th, and 18th holes offer views of the bay through the trees. On the third tee you can catch a glimpse of the Golden Gate Bridge, fog permitting. But you have to play some good golf on this severely uphill par-3, as it is affectionately known as "the shortest par-5 on the course."

In the late 1940s and '50s, men's and women's professional tournaments were held here, featuring such players as Patty Berg, Babe Zaharias, Ben Hogan, and Sam Snead. The men's course record is 63, set by George Archer; the women's course record is 64, set by Patty Berg.

Play Policy and Fees: Reciprocal play is accepted with members of other private clubs. Green fees for reciprocal guests are $85 on weekdays and $100 on weekends and holidays. Carts are not required and cost an additional $10. The course is closed on Monday.

Tees and Yardage: *Men:* Blue: yardage 6571, par 72, rating 72.0, slope 127; White: yardage 6313, par 72, rating 70.9, slope 125; *Women:* Red: yardage 5723, par 73, rating 72.7, slope 124; Gold: yardage 5214, par 73, rating 69.1, slope 116.

Tee Times: Make reservations one week in advance.

Dress Code: Wear suitable golf attire. No tank tops, blue jeans, or shorts of inappropriate length may be worn.

Tournaments: Outside events are held Monday only with board approval.

Directions: From I-80, take the Richmond Parkway to the Giant Highway and follow it to Markovich Lane, which leads to the golf course.

Contact: 1 Markovich Lane, Richmond, CA 94806, pro shop 510/232-7815, fax 510/232-0846, www.richmondcc.com.

48 FRANKLIN CANYON GOLF COURSE

Architect: Robert Muir Graves, 1969

18 holes   **Public**   **$25–52**

East Bay Detail map, page 133

This hilly, sprawling course has two ponds that come into play on four holes. Several tight doglegs require accurate positioning. The wind often affects play, and the large, undulating greens are difficult to read. Locals seem to prefer the front nine, including the par-3 second and the par-4 third, a dogleg right over a barranca. The fifth hole, downhill with pine trees on the right side, seems easy, but bunkers and a tricky green can wreck a scorecard. The lateral hazards make this course. Junior golf programs are held for children ages 6–17 June–September.

Play Policy and Fees: Green fees are $25 to walk and $37 to ride Monday–Thursday, $30 to walk and $42 to ride Friday, and $40 to walk and $52 to ride on weekends and holidays. Call for early bird and twilight rates.

Tees and Yardage: *Men:* Back: yardage 6761, par 72, rating 70.9, slope 118; Middle: yardage 6201, par 72, rating 68.9, slope 114; *Women:* Forward: yardage 5516, par 72, rating 71.2, slope 123.

Tee Times: Reservations can be booked seven days in advance.

Dress Code: Golf attire is encouraged, and nonmetal spikes are recommended but not mandatory.

Tournaments: This course is available for outside tournaments and has a complete banquet facility.

Directions: Follow Highway 4 in Rodeo. The course is three miles east of the junction with I-80.

Contact: Highway 4, Rodeo, CA 94572, pro shop 510/799-6191, fax 510/799-3807.

49 MIRA VISTA COUNTRY CLUB
Architect: Willie Watson, 1924
18 holes   **Private**   **$125**

East Bay Detail map, page 133

This classic, sprawling Willie Watson–designed course (who also designed the Lake and Ocean Courses at Olympic Country Club and Harding Park) features small, severe greens. Several holes offer great views of the San Francisco Bay, such as from the 18th green, where golfers get an awesome view of the Golden Gate Bridge. Because of its location so close to the water, it often gets windy. The course is undulating, with lots of trees. Water comes into play on one hole. All greens are elevated and require precise shot-making. Stay below the pin whenever possible.

Play Policy and Fees: Reciprocal play is accepted with members of other private clubs. Green fee is $125. Carts optional for additional fee.

Tees and Yardage: *Men:* Blue: yardage 6527, par 71, rating 72.9, slope 131; White: yardage 6148, par 71, rating 71.1, slope 127; *Women:* Red: yardage 5755, par 75, rating 74.4, slope 131; Gold: yardage 5053, par 72, rating 70.3, slope 123.

Tee Times: Have the golf pro from your club call in advance to arrange tee times.

Dress Code: Appropriate golf attire is required.

Tournaments: Outside events are limited, and board approval is necessary.

Directions: From I-80 in Oakland, take the Potrero exit straight across San Pablo Avenue, go up Hill Street, and turn left on Elm. Elm flows into Cutting Boulevard. Follow Cutting to the end and the course.

Contact: 7901 Cutting Boulevard, El Cerrito, CA 94530, pro shop 510/237-7045, www.miravistacc.com.

50 PINE MEADOW GOLF COURSE
Architect: Jim Coward, 1966
9 holes   **Public**   **$11–13**

East Bay Detail map, page 133

This course has rolling hills and lots of trees. The longest hole is the 215-yard seventh. Although short in length, this course is no cakewalk.

Play Policy and Fees: Green fees are $11 for nine holes Monday–Thursday and $13 Friday, weekends, and holidays. Senior rates are available weekdays.

Tees and Yardage: *Men and Women:* yardage 1663, par 29, rating n/a, slope n/a.

Tee Times: Reservations can be booked seven days in advance.

Dress Code: Shirts must be worn.

Tournaments: This course is available for outside tournaments.

Directions: From I-80, take Highway 4 to the Morrelo exit in Martinez. Drive past two stop signs and turn left on Center. Turn left again at Vine Hill Way. The course is on the left.

Contact: 451 Vine Hill Way, Martinez, CA 94553, pro shop 925/228-2881.

51 DIABLO CREEK GOLF COURSE
Architect: Bob Baldock, 1963; Robert Muir Graves, 1966
18 holes   **Public**   **$18–32**

East Bay Detail map, page 133

This is one of the best-kept municipal courses in Northern California. The course has its own water, so it's always in good shape. There are five lakes on the front nine, and the back nine is tight and narrow. The third hole requires a shot into the wind around two ponds. The course is flat, but wind can be a factor. The driving range is open and lighted until 10 P.M. Diablo Creek features a teaching center.

Play Policy and Fees: Monday–Thursday, green fees are $18 for nine holes and $24 for 18. Friday–Sunday and holidays, green fees are $20 for nine holes and $32 for 18. Concord resident, senior, junior, winter, and twilight rates offered.

Tees and Yardage: *Men:* Blue: yardage 6830, par 71, rating 72.1, slope 123; White: yardage 6509, par 71, rating 70.4, slope 117; *Women:* Red: yardage 5717, par 71, rating 72.2, slope 120.

Tee Times: Reservations may be made one week in advance.

Dress Code: No tank tops are allowed on the course.

Tournaments: Tournaments may be scheduled up to a year in advance.

Directions: From Highway 4 in Concord, exit on Port Chicago Highway and travel north to the course.

Contact: 4050 Port Chicago Highway, Concord, CA 94520, pro shop 925/686-6262, fax 925/681-1536, www.diablocreekgc.com.

52 TILDEN PARK GOLF COURSE
Architect: William P. Bell, 1938
18 holes   Public $32–55

East Bay Detail map, page 133

Situated in the Berkeley hills, this course has squirrels, raccoons, and deer. Overall, it allows little margin for error, with lots of trees and tricky greens. This course has a lot of fun holes, with the 10th through the 12th particularly interesting. The 411-yard, par-4 first hole is straight uphill and plays like a par-5. The first is the toughest, but the 400-yard 18th is no bargain. Extensive work has been done on the entire course, including remodeled greens, practice greens, and new cart paths. The course now offers a three-tiered lighted and heated driving range and a Nike Golf Learning Center.

Play Policy and Fees: Green fees are $32 Monday–Thursday, $47 Friday, and $55 on weekends. Junior, twilight, early-bird, and nine-hole rates are available. Tilden also offers seniors' and women's discount passes.

Tees and Yardage: *Men:* Back: yardage 6294,

par 70, rating 69.9, slope 120; Middle: yardage 5823, par 70, rating 67.8, slope116; *Women:* Forward: yardage 5399, par 71, rating 69.8, slope 116.

Tee Times: Reservations can be booked seven days in advance.

Dress Code: Appropriate attire and soft spikes are required.

Tournaments: Shotgun tournaments are available weekdays only. Carts are required. A 16-player minimum is required to book a tournament.

Directions: From Highway 24 in Berkeley, take the Fish Ranch Road exit (on the east side of the Caldecott Tunnel) and drive one mile north. Turn right on Grizzly Peak Boulevard and follow it to the course.

Contact: Grizzly Peak and Shasta Road, Berkeley, CA 94708, pro shop 510/848-7373, www.ebparks.org.

53 ORINDA COUNTRY CLUB
Architect: Willie Watson, 1925
18 holes   Private $150

East Bay Detail map, page 133

This tight, rolling course has traditional small greens. A creek winds through it. Two long par-4s, the ninth and 11th holes, create the most trouble. The ninth is a rolling 428-yard demon. You can see the green from the tee box, but you're driving over two mounds to a blind fairway. Long hitters can fly both hills on the fairway, but most will land in the second bank, requiring a long iron or wood for the second shot. It's considered the best hole on the course. The 11th hole, called "Graveyard," is 434 yards from the back and doglegs 220 yards out to the left. There is a creek 75 yards short of the green that you must carry if you're going for it. Beware: The green has very interesting natural mounds all around it and out-of-bounds to the left.

Play Policy and Fees: Reciprocal play is accepted with members of other private clubs. Guest fees are $150. No reciprocal play is allowed on weekends.

Tees and Yardage: *Men:* Blue: yardage 6352, par 72, rating 71.3, slope 136; White: yardage 6127, par 72, rating 70.3, slope 133; Gold: yardage 5846, par 72, rating 69.0, slope 131; *Women:* Red: yardage 5723, par 74, rating 73.4, slope 134.

Tee Times: Reciprocators should have their club pro call to make arrangements.

Dress Code: Appropriate golf attire is required.

Tournaments: Outside events are limited to Monday only and must be member-sponsored.

Directions: From Highway 24, take the Orinda-Moraga exit. Turn left on San Pablo Dam Road. Turn right at the second stoplight at Camino Sobrante. Follow Camino Sobrante and take a left at the stop sign in front of the lake. The course is on the left.

Contact: 315 Camino Sobrante, Orinda, CA 94563, pro shop 925/254-0811, fax 925/254-0406, www.orindacc.org.

54 CONTRA COSTA COUNTRY CLUB

Architect: Course designed, 1920's; Robert Muir Graves, 1992

18 holes   Private $85

East Bay Detail map, page 133

Redesigned greens and new tees and bunkers, coupled with a beautiful setting, make this one of the better courses in Northern California. Designer Robert Muir Graves was in charge of the project. Originally, this course dates back to the 1920s and was designed and built by members. It offers scenic views of Mount Diablo. The greens are large, with lots of undulation. Almost every green is bunkered, and there are barrancas on the 13th and 17th holes.

Play Policy and Fees: Reciprocal play is accepted with members of other private clubs. Fees are $85.

Tees and Yardage: *Men:* Blue: yardage 6550, par 72, rating 71.6, slope 132; White: yardage 6230, par 72, rating 70.2, slope 127; *Women:* Red: yardage 5820, par 72, rating 74.2, slope 131; Gold: yardage 5300, par 72, rating 71.3, slope 125.

Tee Times: Have your club pro call for arrangements.

Dress Code: Appropriate golf attire and non-metal spikes are required.

Tournaments: This course is available for outside events.

Directions: From I-680 in Pleasant Hill, take either the Willow Pass or Concord Avenue exit, turning onto Contra Costa Boulevard and then onto Golf Club Road.

Contact: 801 Golf Club Road, Pleasant Hill, CA 94523, pro shop 925/685-8288, contracostacc.org.

55 PITTSBURG'S DELTA VIEW GOLF COURSE

Architect: Alister Mackenzie, 1947; Robert Muir Graves, 1991

18 holes   Public $20–30

East Bay Detail map, page 133

This course gets windy, but it rewards the accurate driver. Hills abound, as do several varieties of trees. The course plays harder than the yardage would indicate. It's murder for the slicer, particularly on the newer nine. Pittsburg's Delta View has an extensive junior program.

Play Policy and Fees: Green fees are $20 for 18 holes Monday–Friday and $30 for 18 holes weekends and holidays. Senior and junior rates are available. Pittsburg residents receive a discount.

Tees and Yardage: *Men:* Blue: yardage 6373, par 71, rating 70.7, slope 127; White: yardage 5784, par 71, rating 68.1, slope 122; *Women:* Red: yardage 5288, par 71, rating 71.4, slope 125.

Tee Times: Reservations can be booked seven days in advance.

Dress Code: Shirts and shoes must be worn at all times. Soft spikes are preferred.

Tournaments: This course is available for outside tournaments. Carts are required.

Directions: From Concord, drive east on Highway 4. Take the Bailey Road exit south. Turn left on West Leland Road to Golf Club Road.

Contact: 2242 Golf Club Road, Pittsburg, CA

94565, pro shop 925/439-4040, fax 925/439-8287, www.deltaviewgolf.com.

56 THE GOLF CLUB AT RODDY RANCH

Architect: JMP Designs and Bob Moore, 2000

18 holes   **Public**   **$45–75**

East Bay Detail map, page 133

In the golden hills east of Mount Diablo, built over 235 acres of highland ridges and gently rolling foothills, this course is a strong design and in good shape. It features strong par-3 holes, and the farther back you play, the tougher the angles. Homes are eventually planned around some of the fairways.

Play Policy and Fees: Regular green fees are $45 Monday–Friday and $75 weekends and holidays. Carts included. Twilight, junior, and senior rates are offered.

Tees and Yardage: *Men:* Black: yardage 7024, par 72, rating 74.5, slope 136; Gold: yardage 6529, par 72, rating 72.6, slope 134; Silver: yardage 6043, par 72, rating 70.4, slope 130; *Women:* Rust: yardage 5390, par 72, rating 71.7, slope 120.

Tee Times: Reservations are available 30 days in advance.

Dress Code: Collared shirts and spikeless shoes are required.

Tournaments: Events of 16 or more may book up to a year in advance.

Directions: Take Highway 4 east and exit at Lone Tree Way. Head south from the freeway, then turn right on Deer Valley Road. The course is 2.8 miles south of Lone Tree Way on Deer Valley.

Contact: 1 Tour Way, Antioch, CA 94509, pro shop 925/978-4653, fax 925/706-0222, www.roddyranch.com.

57 BUCHANAN FIELDS GOLF COURSE

Architect: Robert Muir Graves, 1960

9 holes   **Public**   **$11–12.50**

East Bay Detail map, page 133

This course is relatively short and flat, with a creek and a large lake. The greens are undulating. This is a great practice course for any golfer and an excellent test for juniors and seniors. Buchanan Fields provides lessons for all ages and has a strong youth program.

Play Policy and Fees: Green fees are $11 for nine holes Monday–Thursday, $6.50 for repeat rounds, and $12.50 for nine holes, $7.50 for repeat rounds on Friday, weekends, and holidays. Senior and junior rates are available Monday–Thursday.

Tees and Yardage: *Men:* Blue: yardage 1982, par 31, rating n/a, slope n/a; White: yardage 1811, par 31, rating n/a, slope n/a; *Women:* Red: yardage 1545, par 31, rating n/a, slope n/a.

Tee Times: Reservations can be booked seven days in advance.

Dress Code: Shirts and shoes must be worn on the golf course at all times. Soft spikes are preferred.

Tournaments: This course is available for outside tournaments.

Directions: From I-680 in Concord, take the Concord Avenue exit. Take a left on Diamond Avenue. Take a right on Concord Avenue to the course.

Contact: 1091 Concord Avenue, Concord, CA 94520, pro shop 925/682-1846, fax 925/689-6113.

58 DIABLO HILLS GOLF COURSE

Architect: Robert Muir Graves, 1975

9 holes   **Public**   **$15–20**

East Bay Detail map, page 133

This course winds through condominiums, but it is wide open. There are slightly rolling yet walkable hills with many sand traps. This is an ideal course for beginning and junior golfers. **Play Policy and Fees:** Green fees are $15 Monday–Thursday and $20 Friday, weekends, and holidays. Senior rates are available Monday–Thursday. **Tees and Yardage:** *Men:* yardage 2302, par 34, rating 61.6, slope 106; *Women:* yardage 2173, par 34, rating 65.4, slope 106. **Tee Times:** Reservations can be booked seven days in advance. **Dress Code:** Shirts with collars must be worn. Soft spikes only. **Tournaments:** This course is available for outside tournaments. A 16-player minimum is needed to book a tournament. The banquet facility can hold 150 people. **Directions:** From I-680 in Walnut Creek, take the Ygnacio Valley Road exit to Marchbanks Drive. Drive approximately one-half mile to the course. **Contact:** 1551 Marchbanks Drive, Walnut Creek, CA 94598, pro shop 925/939-7372, fax 925/939-7532.

59 CLAREMONT COUNTRY CLUB

Architect: Jim Smith, 1904; remodel Alister Mackenzie, 1929; remodel Tom Doak, 2003

18 holes   Private

East Bay Detail map, page 133

Alister Mackenzie expert Tom Doak rebuilt four greens and some bunkering on this historic, rolling course in the Oakland hills in 2003. Built in 1904, Claremont is one of the oldest courses in Northern California. Its original design is credited to Jim Smith, but it has all the earmarks of its 1929 Alister Mackenzie redesign. The long par-3 13th requires a tee shot through a narrow opening. Sam Snead is credited with saying it's the only fairway that requires players to walk single file. The course looks easy on the card, but the par-3s and contoured greens make this a tough test. It's also one of the few courses that still has caddies. Sam Snead won the Oakland Open here in 1937.

Play Policy and Fees: Members and guests only. No reciprocal play is accepted. Guests must be accompanied by a member. **Tees and Yardage:** *Men:* Blue: yardage 5495, par 68, rating 67.4, slope 121; *Women:* White: yardage 5284, par 71, rating 70.9, slope 125. **Tee Times:** Not applicable. **Dress Code:** Appropriate golf attire is required. **Tournaments:** This course is available for member cosponsored outside events. Please inquire. **Directions:** From Highway 24 in Oakland, exit onto Broadway southwest. Turn left on Broadway Terrace. The course is one-half mile on the right. Another route is to take Highway 13 and exit on Broadway Terrace west. **Contact:** 5295 Broadway Terrace, Oakland, CA 94618, pro shop 510/655-2431.

60 METROPOLITAN GOLF LINKS

Architect: Fred Bliss and Johnny Miller, 2003

18 holes   Public $38–60

East Bay Detail map, page 133

A nice course in a city setting, Metropolitan Golf Links fills a niche in the Oakland area. Not that far from the Oakland Airport, there are some strong holes here and some nice views of the Oakland and San Francisco skylines, as well as the Bay Bridge. There are few trees on this layout, and occasional winds off San Francisco Bay will be a factor. With weekday walking prices less than $40, the course presents a good option for the regular golfer. **Play Policy and Fees:** Green fees are $38 Monday–Thursday, $50 Friday, $60 weekends and holidays. Carts are an additional $14. Twilight, junior, and senior rates are available. **Tees and Yardage:** *Men:* Black: yardage 7015, par 72, rating 73.4, slope 125; Blue: yardage 6600, par 72, rating 71.3, slope 120; White: yardage 6135, par 72, rating 69.3, slope 116; *Women:* Red: yardage 5665, par 72, rating 71.0, slope 118; Gold: yardage 5099, par 72, rating 68.5, slope 114.

Tee Times: Reservations can be made 60 days in advance.

Dress Code: Appropriate golf attire is required. No metal spikes are allowed on the course.

Tournaments: Tournaments welcome.

Directions: Take the Hegenberger Road exit off I-880 next to the Oakland Airport. Turn left onto Doolittle Drive to the course.

Contact: 10505 Doolittle Dr., Oakland, CA 94603-1025, golf shop 510/569-5555, fax 510/562-6129, www.playmetro.com.

61 MONTCLAIR GOLF COURSE

Architect: Course designed, 1973

9 holes   **Public**   **$5–6**

 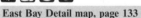

East Bay Detail map, page 133

This mostly flat, short, par-3 course is in the Oakland Hills. It's a good beginner's course. The 85-yard first hole is the longest. Montclair has redesigned and lengthened the second hole. Nice little pitch-and-putt for family fun.

Play Policy and Fees: Green fees are $5 Monday–Thursday and $6 Friday, weekends, and holidays.

Tees and Yardage: *Men and Women:* yardage 605, par 27, rating n/a, slope n/a.

Tee Times: Reservations are not accepted. All play is on a first-come, first-served basis.

Dress Code: Appropriate attire and soft spikes are required.

Tournaments: This course is available for outside tournaments.

Directions: From Highway 13 in Oakland, take the Park Boulevard exit west. Follow it to Monterey Boulevard and drive one-quarter mile to the course.

Contact: 2477 Monterey Boulevard, Oakland, CA 94611, pro shop 510/482-0422.

62 MORAGA COUNTRY CLUB

Architect: Robert Muir Graves, 1974

18 holes   **Private**   **$107**

East Bay Detail map, page 133

This course demands a good short game. It's tight and hilly, with bunkers and slick greens. The course expanded to 18 holes in the fall of 1992 under the design expertise of Algie Pulley. The new ninth, a 499-yard par-5, has water on the right, includes big mounds on the left, and plays into a breeze. The green is long and narrow. The 10th, a par-3 over a creek, is a beauty. From there the course goes uphill. Some deceptive par-4s with mounds in the greens make this course memorable and exasperating. The 14th, for example, has a five-tiered green. Take advantage of the course's public-access policy when you can!

Play Policy and Fees: Reciprocal play is accepted with members of other private clubs in the area at a rate of $107, including a mandatory cart. Public play is accepted at the reciprocal rate on the first Tuesday of even months: February, April, June, August, October, and December.

Tees and Yardage: *Men:* Blue: yardage 6105, par 71, rating 71.2, slope 125; White: yardage 5696, par 71, rating 69.4, slope 123; Gold: yardage 5292, par 71, rating 66.5, slope 120; *Women:* Red: yardage 5112, par 71, rating 71.1, slope 132.

Tee Times: Reservations are required and can be booked one day in advance.

Dress Code: Appropriate golf attire is required. Nonmetal spikes are encouraged. No jeans are allowed.

Tournaments: Shotgun tournaments are available Monday only. Carts are required. An 80-player minimum is needed to book a tournament. The banquet facility can accommodate 100 people.

Directions: From Highway 24 in Moraga, take the Moraga Way exit south four miles to Saint Andrews Drive.

Contact: 1600 Saint Andrews Drive, Moraga, CA 94556, pro shop 925/376-2253, fax 925/376-7835.

63 ROSSMOOR GOLF COURSE
Architect: Robert Muir Graves, 1965
27 holes   **Private**

🏌 📷 🏌 🚙 🍽

East Bay Detail map, page 133

These are retirement community courses that are mostly flat and walkable, although the 18-hole Dollar Ranch course has some hills. The 372-yard second hole on Dollar Ranch requires an uphill approach. The par-5 10th hole doglegs left, with two big oak trees at the turn. Both layouts feature tricky greens and are a good test of irons and short-game strategy. This course is the home of the Rossmoor Pro-Am, which benefits Children's Hospital of Oakland. The Creekside Course is a nine-hole layout.

Play Policy and Fees: Members and guests only.

Tees and Yardage: Dollar Ranch—*Men:* Blue: yardage 6162, par 72, rating 69.5, slope 125; White: yardage 5830, par 72, rating 68.2, slope 120; *Women:* Red: yardage 5396, par 72, rating 70.3, slope 122. Creekside—*Men:* Blue: yardage 3067, par 36, rating 69.0, slope 124; White: yardage 2968, par 36, rating 68.0, slope 123; *Women:* Red: yardage 2814, par 36, rating 71.4, slope 125.

Tee Times: Not applicable.

Dress Code: Golf attire is encouraged. Soft spikes only.

Tournaments: Limited outside events are allowed with approval of the board of directors. A 50-player minimum is needed. Events should be booked six months in advance. The banquet facility can hold 200 people.

Directions: From Highway 24 east of Lafayette, take the Pleasant Hill Road exit south to Olympic Boulevard east. Then turn right on Tice Valley Boulevard and right again on Rossmoor Parkway. From there turn right on Stanley Dollar Drive.

Contact: 1010 Stanley Dollar Drive, Walnut Creek, CA 94595, pro shop 925/933-2607.

64 ROUND HILL COUNTRY CLUB
Architect: Lawrence Hughes, 1960
18 holes   **Private**   **$125**

🏌 📷 🍽 🚙 🍽

East Bay Detail map, page 133

This tight, rolling course is in the San Ramon Valley. It has undulating greens, many trees, lots of sidehill lies, and narrow approach shots. LPGA events have been held here. The course was closed for several months in summer 2004, as some major remodeling was being done. It was completed in late 2004 with new tees and greens and some new water features. Note: The remodeling work will cause the course ratings and yardage listed here to change.

Play Policy and Fees: Reciprocal play is accepted with members of other private clubs at a rate of $125, including mandatory cart.

Tees and Yardage: *Men:* Blue: yardage 6422, par 72, rating 72.2, slope 136; White: yardage 6149, par 72, rating 71.1, slope 134; *Women:* Red: yardage 5937, par 74, rating 74.9, slope 134; Gold: yardage 5328, par 72, rating 73.2, slope 130.

Tee Times: Have your head professional call for a tee time.

Dress Code: Appropriate golf attire and non-metal spikes are required.

Tournaments: This course is available for outside tournaments on Monday only. The banquet facility can accommodate 300 people.

Directions: From I-680 in Alamo, take the Stone Valley Road east to Round Hill Road north. The course is one mile from I-680.

Contact: 3169 Round Hill Road, Alamo, CA 94507, pro shop 925/837-7424, clubhouse 925/934-8211, fax 925/831-8291.

65 BOUNDARY OAK GOLF COURSE
Architect: Robert Muir Graves, 1969
18 holes   **Public**   **$13–30**

🏌 📷 🍽 🏌 🚙 🍽

East Bay Detail map, page 133

This is a large, demanding layout with both trees and water coming into play. It's a good driving course. The 11th hole requires a big drive to reach the green in two. The second shot is over a lake. When the greens are in good condition, this is a fun, challenging course. **Play Policy and Fees:** Green fees for residents of Walnut Creek are $13 for nine holes and $18 for 18 on weekdays, $17 for nine holes and $24 for 18 holes on weekends. Nonresident fees are $17 for nine holes and $24 for 18 on weekdays, $20 for nine holes and $30 for 18 on weekends. Senior, twilight, under-18, and early bird rates are available. Carts are $14–27. **Tees and Yardage:** *Men:* Black: yardage 7063, par 72, rating 73.8, slope 132; Blue: yardage 6739, par 72, rating 72.2, slope 128; White: yardage 6372, par 72, rating 70.7, slope 122; *Women:* Red: yardage 5699, par 72, rating 72.1, slope 120.

Tee Times: Reservations are usually required, but walk-ons can be accommodated. All tee times must be reserved through the course's automated system at 925/934-6211.

Dress Code: Tank tops are not permitted. Soft spikes are preferred.

Tournaments: Tournaments and special events are welcome. To arrange an event, contact the tournament director at 925/934-4775, ext. 13.

Directions: From I-680, take the Ygnacio Valley Road exit east. Drive three miles into Walnut Creek. Turn right on Oak Grove Road, then left on Valley Vista Road.

Contact: 3800 Valley Vista Road, Walnut Creek, CA 94598, pro shop 925/934-4775, fax 925/932-9128, www.boundaryoak.com.

66 OAKHURST COUNTRY CLUB

Architect: Ron Fream, 1990

18 holes   **Private**   **$50–75**

🏌 📷 🍴 🛒 🍽

East Bay Detail map, page 133

This course, which went private in 2002, is a solid test of any player's game. It's a highly rated layout with lots of lateral hazards and out-of-bounds. The fairways are undulating, with few even lies. The large greens are quick and true. The 535-yard 12th hole plays along

a barranca on the right, and the next two par-4s require precision tee shots. The 18th hole, which plays over a huge barranca, can be misleading, if not downright deceptive. You have to play the tee shot just left of the right fairway bunkers.

Play Policy and Fees: Some reciprocal play is accepted at a rate of $50 weekdays and $75 weekends; otherwise, members and guests only. Carts are mandatory and included in fee.

Tees and Yardage: *Men:* Black: yardage 6747, par 72, rating 73.4, slope 142; Gold: yardage 6283, par 72, rating 71.1, slope 135; White: yardage 5839, par 72, rating 68.8, slope 127; *Women:* Red: yardage 5316, par 72, rating 70.7, slope 127.

Tee Times: Reservations can be booked seven days in advance by calling 877/625-4877.

Dress Code: Collared shirts and nonmetal spikes are required. No blue jeans are allowed on the course.

Tournaments: This course is available for outside tournaments on Monday.

Directions: From I-680, take the Ygnacio Valley exit east to Clayton Road. Turn right on Clayton Road and drive two miles. Turn left on Peacock Creek Drive.

Contact: 1001 Peacock Creek Drive, Clayton, CA 94517, pro shop 925/672-9737.

67 CHUCK CORICA GOLF COMPLEX

Architect: William F. Bell, 1957 (Jack Clark Course), remodeled Robert Muir Graves, 1978; William P. Bell, 1927 (Earl Fry Course)

45 holes   **Public**   **$29–33**

🏌 📷 🍴 🛒 🛺 🍽 3

East Bay Detail map, page 133

These are flat, challenging courses. The Jack Clark Course, designed by William Francis Bell and remodeled by Robert Muir Graves in 1978, is longer and more difficult. It is the more popular course, with the par-3 15th—bunkers left and right and a water hazard behind the green—serving as the signature hole. The Earl Fry Course was designed by William Park Bell.

Both are well-maintained and walkable courses with lots of trees and some water. The complex features a lighted driving range, teaching academy, and nine-hole executive course.

Play Policy and Fees: Green fees are $29 Monday–Thursday and $33 Friday–Sunday. Alameda residents receive a discount. Carts are $14 per rider.

Tees and Yardage: Earl Fry—*Men:* Black: yardage 6307, par 70, rating 70.9, slope 123; Blue: yardage 5985, par 70, rating 69.2, slope 120; White: yardage 5651, par 69, rating 67.7, slope 116; *Women:* Red: yardage 5202, par 72, rating 69.6, slope 113. Jack Clark—*Men:* Black: yardage 6560, par 71, rating 71.8, slope 119; Blue: yardage 6271, par 71, rating 70.5, slope 116; White: yardage 5718, par 69, rating 67.7, slope 114; *Women:* Red: yardage 5310, par 70, rating 70.0, slope 113.

Tee Times: Reservations may be made seven days in advance.

Dress Code: Standard golf attire is encouraged, and no tank tops are allowed. Soft spikes are preferred but not required.

Tournaments: Tournaments should be scheduled a year in advance. A banquet facility is available and can accommodate 100 people.

Directions: From I-880 south of the Oakland Coliseum, take the Hegenberger Road exit west one mile. Turn right on Doolittle Road to Island Drive and turn left. Turn left again on Memorial Drive to the course.

Contact: 1 Clubhouse Memorial Road, Alameda, CA 94501, pro shop 510/522-4321, fax 510/522-0848.

68 MONARCH BAY GOLF CLUB

Architect: William F. Bell, 1982; John Harbottle, 2001
27 holes   **Public**   **$10–65**

East Bay Detail map, page 133

Home of San Leandro Golf Club, this facility has large greens and is easy to walk. The newly redesigned Tony Lema Course features 14 holes with a view of the San Francisco Bay. It is a flat course built much like a Scottish links, very open with few trees. Four sets of tees make Monarch Bay suited for all levels of accomplishment. The Marina Course is a short course that offers family fun and great practice rounds. A Nike Learning Center is on the property.

Play Policy and Fees: Monday–Thursday, green fees for the Tony Lema Course are $40 including cart. Friday–Sunday, fees are $65. Optional carts are $13 per rider. For the Marina Course, fees range $10–18.

Tees and Yardage: Tony Lema Course—*Men:* Championship: yardage 6567, par 71, rating 71.1, slope 117; Member: yardage 6060, par 71, rating 68.8, slope 115; Resort: yardage 5502, par 68, rating 66.3, slope 109; *Women:* Forward: yardage 5140, par 71, rating 69.8, slope 117. Marina Course—*Men:* yardage 1734, par 30, rating n/a, slope n/a; *Women:* yardage 1484, par 30, rating n/a, slope n/a.

Tee Times: Reservations are accepted up to 30 days in advance.

Dress Code: Collared shirts are required, and no blue jeans are allowed.

Tournaments: Events are welcome and may be booked one year in advance.

Directions: From I-880 in San Leandro, take the Marina Boulevard exit west, then follow Marina to Neptune Drive. Turn left and drive up Neptune to the third stop sign. The course is on the left.

Contact: 13800 Neptune Drive, San Leandro, CA 94577, pro shop 510/895-2162, fax 510/895-0221, www.americangolf.com.

69 SKYWEST GOLF COURSE

Architect: Bob Baldock, 1964
18 holes   **Public**   **$27–36**

East Bay Detail map, page 133

This flat course has lush, well-maintained, wide fairways and lots of trees. It tests every club in the bag. The nines were flopped in 2003, so don't be surprised if you haven't played here in a while. This course holds many tournaments.

Play Policy and Fees: Green fees are $27 weekdays and $36 weekends. Resident, midday, junior, and senior rates are available. Carts are

$14 per rider but are included in some specials. Please inquire.

Tees and Yardage: *Men:* Blue: yardage 6789, par 72, rating 72.9, slope 123; White: yardage 6513, par 72, rating 71.6, slope 121; *Women:* Red: yardage 6212, par 73, rating 74.6, slope 127.

Tee Times: Reservations can be booked eight days in advance. To make your reservations, call 510/888-0106.

Dress Code: Collared shirts are required.

Tournaments: A 20-player minimum is required to book a tournament. Carts are required.

Directions: From I-880 in Hayward, take the A Street exit west to Hesperian and turn right on Hesperian. Take the first left at Golf Course Road. The course is next to Hayward Air Terminal.

Contact: 1401 Golf Course Road, Hayward, CA 94541, pro shop 510/317-2300.

70 SEQUOYAH COUNTRY CLUB

Architect: Course designed, 1913
18 holes   **Private**   **$119**

🏌 📷 🍴 ⛳ 🚙 🏌

East Bay Detail map, page 133

This mature course is short, hilly, and tight. The elevated tees and fast greens make for exciting par-3s. Member Dr. Wayne Wright has scored a hole-in-one on all of the five par-3s. This exclusive course is very tough, and local knowledge of the greens is the only way to survive. The 445-yard 11th, with a panoramic view of the bay, is a great challenge. This course was the site of the PGA Tour's Oakland Open in the 1930s, featuring players such as Ben Hogan and Sam Snead.

Play Policy and Fees: Reciprocal play is accepted with members of other private clubs at a rate of $119, including mandatory cart. Otherwise, members and guests only.

Tees and Yardage: *Men:* Championship: yardage 6085, par 70, rating 70.4, slope 134; Regular: yardage 5827, par 70, rating 69.3, slope 132; *Women:* Red: yardage 5559, par 72, rating 72.6, slope 131.

Tee Times: Reciprocators should have their club pro call to make arrangements.

Dress Code: Appropriate golf attire and nonmetal spikes are required.

Tournaments: Events should be scheduled 12 months in advance. The banquet facility can accommodate 250 people.

Directions: From I-580 in Oakland, take the 98th Avenue exit off the left side of the freeway. Turn left onto Mountain Boulevard. Turn right on Sequoyah Road and travel three-quarters of a mile. Turn right at the stop sign onto Heafey Road and drive to the course.

Contact: 4550 Heafey Road, Oakland, CA 94605, pro shop 510/632-4069, clubhouse 510/632-2900, fax 510/638-2670, www.sequoyahcc.com.

71 LAKE CHABOT GOLF COURSE

Architect: William Lock, 1917; Robert Muir Graves, 1989
18 holes   **Public**   **$22–37**

🏌 📷 🍴 🚙 🏌

East Bay Detail map, page 133

This course is hilly but walkable. The 18th hole is a unique 677-yard par-6, which starts off level and slopes down, then up. Out-of-bounds is to the left, and trees are on the right. Take your complaints to course manager Raymond Chester, former All-Pro tight end with the Oakland Raiders. Tony Lema, 1964 British Open champion, grew up near Lake Chabot. The course is one of the oldest in Northern California.

Play Policy and Fees: Green fees are $22 for Oakland residents and $26 for nonresidents Monday–Thursday, $30 for residents and $37 for nonresidents Friday, weekends, and holidays. Carts additional. Senior and twilight rates are available.

Tees and Yardage: *Men:* Blue: yardage 5976, par 72, rating 69.4, slope 123; White: yardage 5681, par 72, rating 68.1, slope 119; *Women:* Red: yardage 5228, par 71, rating 68.5, slope 116.

Tee Times: Reservations may be made up to six days in advance.

Dress Code: Appropriate golf attire is encouraged. Short shorts and tank tops are not permitted. Soft spikes only.

Tournaments: This course is available for outside tournaments booked 30 days in advance.

Directions: From I-580 in Oakland, take the Golf Links Road exit and follow the road to the end.

Contact: 11450 Golf Links Road, Oakland, CA 94605, pro shop 510/351-5812, fax 510/358-4812.

72 DIABLO COUNTRY CLUB

Architect: Jack Neville, 1914
18 holes   Private $135

East Bay Detail map, page 133

This beautiful, traditional, tree-lined layout has small, demanding greens and tough par-3s. Holes 9–13 could be the best string of holes in Northern California. Huge oak trees come into play often. The 17th and 18th play through oaks that are 300 years old.

Play Policy and Fees: Reciprocal play is accepted with members of other private clubs. Reciprocal fees are $135, including cart. The course is closed on Monday.

Tees and Yardage: *Men:* Blue: yardage 6563, par 72, rating 72.1, slope 130; White: yardage 6249, par 72, rating 70.5, slope 126; *Women:* Red: yardage 5758, par 72, rating 73.9, slope 131; Gold: yardage 5635, par 72, rating 73.3, slope 129.

Tee Times: Reciprocal players should have their home professional call to make arrangements.

Dress Code: Appropriate golf attire is required. Nonmetal spikes are encouraged.

Tournaments: Call the head professional for tournament information.

Directions: From I-680 in Danville, take the Diablo Road exit into the Village of Diablo development. Go one-quarter mile, veering left at the fork in the road, then turn left on Clubhouse Road.

Contact: 1700 Clubhouse Road, Diablo, CA 94528, pro shop 925/837-9233, fax 925/837-4711.

73 BLACKHAWK COUNTRY CLUB

Architect: Robert Von Hagge, 1981; Bruce Devlin, 1981 (Lakeside); Ted Robinson Sr., 1988 (Falls)
36 holes   Private $132

East Bay Detail map, page 133

The Lakeside Course is rolling and imaginative. It has large, undulating greens, lots of water, and tight fairways. Many up-and-down holes thread through oak trees. The course requires precise shot-making. The 404-yard eighth has a creek all the way down the right side. The Falls Course is a shorter version with emphasis on placement. It is rolling and hilly between holes. The first hole is a straight drop, but then it flattens out. The Falls' 14th, a 384-yard dogleg, has a barranca on the right side. A moon crater in the green puts precision on the approach. Each course has a clubhouse and pro shop.

Play Policy and Fees: Reciprocal play is allowed at a rate of $132. Otherwise, guests must be accompanied by a member at time of play. Carts are additional.

Tees and Yardage: Falls Course—*Men:* Back: yardage 6738, par 72, rating 73.3, slope 136; Middle: yardage 6262, par 72, rating 70.9, slope 134; Intermediate: yardage 5805, par 72, rating 69.3, slope 130; *Women:* Forward: yardage 5367, par 72, rating 71.0, slope 131. Lakeside Course—*Men:* Back: yardage 6836, par 72, rating 74.1, slope 141; Middle: yardage 6390, par 72, rating 71.7, slope 137; Intermediate: yardage 5883, par 72, rating 69.1, slope 135; *Women:* Forward: yardage 5434, par 72, rating 72.3, slope 134.

Tee Times: Reciprocal players should have their home professional call to make arrangements.

Dress Code: No denim is allowed on the golf course or in the clubhouse. Nonmetal spikes are required.

Tournaments: Tournaments are available Monday and Tuesday only. Carts are required.

Directions: From I-680, take the Crow Canyon exit, head east, and take a right on Blackhawk Club Drive.

Contact: 599 Blackhawk Club Drive, Danville, CA 94506, pro shop 925/736-6565, fax 925/736-2746, www.blackhawkcc.com.

74 LONE TREE GOLF COURSE

Architect: Bob Baldock, 1957;
renovated John Harbottle, 2002

18 holes	Public	$18–33

East Bay Detail map, page 133

This hilly yet open course has been improved and rerouted, including the building of a new clubhouse and expanded banquet facilities in 2004. At the same time the routing was reversed, including changing the 10th hole to a tough 434-yard par-4. It is a popular course for local tournaments.

Play Policy and Fees: Green fees for residents of the city of Antioch are $18 weekdays and $26 weekends. Nonresident green fees are $23 Monday–Thursday and $33 Friday–Sunday. Many special rates are available.

Tees and Yardage: *Men:* Blue: yardage 6437, par 72, rating 71.2, slope 125; White: yardage 6117, par 72, rating 69.6, slope 123; Gold: yardage 5811, par 72, rating 68.2, slope 121; *Women:* Red: yardage 5596, par 72, rating 71.9, slope 121.

Tee Times: Reservations can be booked seven days in advance. Players should check in 30 minutes prior to teeing off.

Dress Code: Shirts must be worn, and non-metal spikes are required.

Tournaments: This course is available for outside tournaments.

Directions: From Highway 4 in Antioch, take the Lone Tree Way exit south. Veer to the right and continue through six lights. Turn right onto Golf Course Road.

Contact: 4800 Golf Course Road, Antioch, CA 94509, pro shop 925/706-4220, fax 925/706-7709, www.lonetreegolfcourse.com.

75 DEER RIDGE COUNTRY CLUB

Architect: Andy Raugust, 2004

18 holes	Semiprivate	$40–43

East Bay Detail map, page 133

Set amongst rolling foothills dotted with massive oak trees, which is typical of inland California, this layout features many land contours and moguls, so placement of the ball is critical to scoring well. A seasonal stream cuts across several holes. The green complexes feature some false fronts, strategic bunkering, and tiered pin positions. For the thinking man, this is a fun round of golf. Note: The course had not yet been rated at press time.

Play Policy and Fees: Green fees are $40 weekdays, $43 weekends. Cart fees additional. Memberships are offered.

Tees and Yardage: *Men:* Black: yardage 6304, par 71, rating n/a, slope n/a; Gold: yardage 5797, par 71, rating n/a, slope n/a; Blue: yardage 5317, par 71, rating n/a, slope n/a; *Women:* Green: yardage 4755, par 71, rating n/a, slope n/a.

Tee Times: Reservations can be made nine days in advance.

Dress Code: Appropriate golf attire is required. No metal spikes are allowed on the course.

Tournaments: Tournaments welcome. Call for details.

Directions: From Highway 580, exit onto Highway 4/Brentwood Boulevard. Turn left on Balfour Road, then left on Foothill Drive/East Country Club, which leads to the entrance.

Contact: 801 Foothill Drive, Brentwood, CA 94513, 925/516-6600, fax 925/516-6677, www.deerridgecc.com.

76 SHADOW LAKES GOLF CLUB

Architect: Gary Roger Baird, 2001

18 holes	Public	$50–75

East Bay Detail map, page 133

Shadow Lakes features dramatic changes in elevation, sharply sculpted bunkering, and native grasses outlining each hole. Architect Baird blended traditional design with modern playing characteristics in a pleasing way. Strong par-3s and a good finishing hole highlight your round. Water comes into play on a couple of holes, and there are some very nice views.

Play Policy and Fees: Fees are $50 Monday–Friday, $75 weekends and holidays. Cart and range balls included.

Tees and Yardage: *Men:* Black: yardage 6710, par 71, rating 72.2, slope 130; Gold: yardage 6327, par 71, rating 70.5, slope 128; Silver: yardage 5962, par 71, rating 68.5, slope 125; *Women:* Jade: yardage 5402, par 71, rating 71.4, slope 123.

Tee Times: Reservations may be booked up to 30 days in advance.

Dress Code: Collared shirts and Bermuda-length shorts are required. No denim or metal spikes are permitted.

Tournaments: Groups of 16 or more may book tournaments up to a year in advance. Shotgun starts may be accommodated for groups of 40 or more.

Directions: From Highway 80, take Route 4 east to Brentwood. Exit at Hillcrest Avenue and proceed south. Hillcrest becomes Lone Tree Boulevard. Follow Lone Tree approximately seven miles to Balfour Road. Go east on Balfour for 1.5 miles to West Country Club Drive. The golf course is on the northeast corner of Balfour and West Country Club.

Contact: 401 West Country Club Drive, Brentwood, CA 94513, pro shop 925/516-2837, www.shadowlakesgolf.com.

77 BRENTWOOD GOLF CLUB

Architect: Ted Robinson Sr., 1994
36 holes **Public** **$12–65**

🏃 📷 🍴 🚗 🍺

East Bay Detail map, page 133

There are three nine-hole layouts: Hillside, Creekside, and Diablo. There is also a nine-hole executive course. The three championship nines are mostly level, except for Hillside, and all have water features. The greens are large and challenging. The newest of the three is

Creekside, which opened in 2000. It is the most difficult of the three nines, with the par-3 sixth hole being a standout. A beautiful lake and waterfall await stray tee shots on the shortest yet most challenging of all the par-3s. Waterfalls and lakes, designer Ted Robinson's signature on a golf course, are in abundance on all three layouts.

Play Policy and Fees: Green fees for 18 holes are $50 Monday–Thursday and $65 Friday–Sunday and holidays, including cart. Carts are mandatory. Green fees for the executive course are $12 Monday–Thursday, $14 Friday–Sunday and holidays. Carts are not mandatory on the executive course.

Tees and Yardage: Hillside/Diablo—*Men:* Black: yardage 6456, par 72, rating 71.9, slope 131; Blue: yardage 6241, par 72, rating 71.9, slope 130; White: yardage 5837, par 72, rating 69.4, slope 124; *Women:* Red: yardage 5234, par 72, rating 71.2, slope 125. Creekside/Hillside—*Men:* Black: yardage 6824, par 72, rating 73.6, slope 132; Blue: yardage 6413, par 72, rating 71.7, slope 130; White: yardage 5992, par 72, rating 69.8, slope 126; *Women:* Red: yardage 5357, par 72, rating 71.9, slope 130. Creekside/Diablo—*Men:* Black: yardage 6570, par 72, rating 72.1, slope 129; Blue: yardage 6374, par 72, rating 71.2, slope 127; White: yardage 5961, par 72, rating 69.6, slope 121; *Women:* Red: yardage 5353, par 72, rating 71.3, slope 124.

Tee Times: Tee times can be booked three days in advance.

Dress Code: Appropriate golf attire and non-metal spikes are required.

Tournaments: This course is available for outside tournaments.

Directions: From Livermore, take I-580 to the Vasco Road exit. Take Vasco Road to Balfour Road. Turn left on Balfour and drive to the course clubhouse on the left.

Contact: 1740 Balfour Road, Brentwood, CA 94513, pro shop 925/516-3400, fax 925/516-3405, www.brentwoodgolf.com.

78 WILLOW PARK GOLF COURSE

Architect: Bob Baldock, 1967
18 holes   **Public**   **$23–32**

East Bay Detail map, page 133

This course is mostly flat with narrow fairways. A creek borders the front nine holes. There are often deer in the outlying areas. The driving range has an unusual feature: You hit into a lake about 175 yards out. Floating balls are provided. It's a fun, low-key course.

Play Policy and Fees: Green fees are $23 Monday–Thursday, $25 Friday, and $32 weekends. Carts are $12 per rider.

Tees and Yardage: *Men:* Blue: yardage 5846, par 71, rating 68.0, slope 120; White: yardage 5516, par 71, rating 66.6, slope 118; *Women:* Red: yardage 5227, par 71, rating 69.6, slope 121.

Tee Times: Can be made seven days in advance.

Dress Code: Shirts must be worn.

Tournaments: Shotgun tournaments are not allowed. Events should be booked 12 months in advance.

Directions: The course is in Castro Valley, two miles north of I-580 on Redwood Road.

Contact: 17007 Redwood Road (P.O. Box 2407), Castro Valley, CA 94546, pro shop 510/537-8989, fax 510/537-6775.

79 CROW CANYON COUNTRY CLUB

Architect: Ted Robinson Sr., 1977
18 holes   **Private**

East Bay Detail map, page 133

This is a hilly, tight, rolling course. The sixth hole is a notable par-3. It's 190 yards against the wind to an elevated green. The par-4 third can get you into trouble. The fairway is only 15 yards from out-of-bounds on the right. And watch out for the 400-yard, par-4 18th hole with an elevated tee and water along the left side. This course is known for being very well manicured, with great drainage during the rainy season. The course is well bunkered, with water

coming into play on nine holes. There are very nice views of Mount Diablo from many holes.

Play Policy and Fees: Reciprocal play is accepted with members of other private clubs, fees not published.

Tees and Yardage: *Men:* Blue: yardage 5908, par 69, rating 69.5, slope 128; White: yardage 5584, par 69, rating 68.0, slope 124; *Women:* Red: yardage 5436, par 70, rating 72.9, slope 127.

Tee Times: Reciprocal players should have their home professional call to make arrangements.

Dress Code: Shirts with collars are required. No jeans, tank tops, tee shirts, short shorts, gym shorts, or tennis shorts may be worn. Nonmetal spikes are mandatory.

Tournaments: Tournaments are allowed on Monday only. Carts are required. A 72-player minimum is required to book a tournament.

Directions: From I-680 in San Ramon, take the Crow Canyon exit east. Turn left on El Capitan and right on Silver Lake Drive.

Contact: 711 Silver Lake Drive, Danville, CA 94526, pro shop 925/735-8300, www.crow-canyon.com.

80 CANYON LAKES COUNTRY CLUB

Architect: Ted Robinson Sr., 1987
18 holes   **Public**   **$52.50–82.50**

East Bay Detail map, page 133

In the foothills of San Ramon, this course has lots of water, trees, bunkers, contoured fairways, and undulating greens. The 405-yard eighth and 392-yard ninth are strong holes, but the 287-yard fourth, with its green surrounded by water, is a lot of fun. The 526-yard 14th, a par-5 that plays over a creek, requires a precise 250-yard shot to a narrow fairway. It's possible to reach the green in two shots, but the green is severely sloped and fast—home of the four-putt. The par-5 17th is an uphill shot into the prevailing wind—a maddening hole. The 435-yard 18th has a blind second shot.

Play Policy and Fees: Green fees are $52.50 Tuesday and Wednesday, $67.50 Thursday, and

$82.50 Friday–Sunday, mandatory carts included. Nine-hole and twilight rates are offered. The course is closed on Monday.

Tees and Yardage: *Men:* Blue: yardage 6373, par 71, rating 71.4, slope 129; White: yardage 5970, par 71, rating 69.7, slope 126; *Women:* Red: yardage 5191, par 71, rating 70.6, slope 123.

Tee Times: Reservations can be booked seven days in advance.

Dress Code: Shirts must have collars and sleeves. No blue jeans are allowed.

Tournaments: Shotgun tournaments are available weekdays only. You must have 16 players to book a tournament. Events can be booked 12 months in advance. The banquet facility holds 140 people.

Directions: From I-680 in San Ramon, take the Bollinger Canyon exit east over the freeway. Turn left on Canyon Lakes Drive and left again on Bollinger Canyon Way to the course.

Contact: 640 Bollinger Canyon Way, San Ramon, CA 94583, pro shop 925/735-6511.

81 SAN RAMON ROYAL VISTA GOLF COURSE

Architect: Clark Glasson, 1962
18 holes   Public $32–42

🏌 📷 ⛳ 🏌 🚗 ⛳

East Bay Detail map, page 133

This is a relatively flat course with plenty of wildlife, even though homes line almost every fairway. More than 300 new trees were planted several years ago and are now becoming mature, which adds to the character. The course is usually in great condition, thanks to on-site well water, which is also used to create some pretty fountains and waterways. The 341-yard ninth hole is the signature on this course, featuring an island green. The 11th hole requires a layup off the tee due to a hazard halfway down the hole. The 16th doglegs right and has out-of-bounds on the right. Most greens are generous in size. The driving range is lighted.

Play Policy and Fees: Green fees are $32 weekdays and $42 weekends. Carts are additional.

Twilight, super twilight, junior (weekdays only), and senior (weekdays only) rates are available.

Tees and Yardage: *Men:* Blue: yardage 6452, par 72, rating 71.1, slope 122; White: yardage 6163, par 72, rating 70.1, slope 119; *Women:* Red: yardage 5782, par 72, rating 73.5, slope 124.

Tee Times: Reservations can be booked seven days in advance.

Dress Code: Shirts with collars are required. No tee shirts or tank tops are allowed on the course or at the driving range. Nonmetal spikes are required.

Tournaments: A 12-player minimum is required to book a tournament. Carts are required. A banquet facility can accommodate 250 people.

Directions: Driving south on I-680 in San Ramon, take the Alcosta Boulevard exit. Cross back over the freeway and drive one mile east. Turn left on Fircrest Lane to the course.

Contact: 9430 Fircrest Lane, San Ramon, CA 94583, pro shop 925/828-6100, fax 925/833-1779, www.sanramonroyalvista.com.

82 THE BRIDGES GOLF CLUB

Architect: Pascuzzo & Graves and Johnny Miller, 1999
18 holes   Public $75–95

🏌 📷 ⛳ 🏌 🚗 ⛳

East Bay Detail map, page 133

The Bridges is a links-style course, inspired by the great courses in Scotland. It plays deep in a valley with a natural creek running throughout. Incorporating the natural surroundings and landscape, the design offers a blend of narrowly sloped fairways, vast bunkers, quick greens, and heavily landscaped hillsides. Distinguishing features include two split fairways, elevation changes, and an 85-yard-long 18th green. One of the better and more difficult courses in California.

Play Policy and Fees: Green fees are $75 Monday–Thursday and $95 Friday–Sunday. Twilight, junior, and senior rates are available. All prices include a cart.

Tees and Yardage: *Men:* Black: yardage 6965, par 72, rating 75.0, slope 148; Blue: yardage 6625, par 72, rating 73.5, slope 146; White:

yardage 6229, par 72, rating 71.9, slope 142; *Women:* Gold: yardage 5730, par 73, rating 74.5, slope 130; Red: yardage 5229, par 73, rating 71.4, slope 123.

Tee Times: Reservations may be made 30 days in advance.

Dress Code: Collared shirts and soft spikes are required. No denim allowed.

Tournaments: Events may be booked one year in advance. The banquet facility can accommodate up to 150 people indoors and 250 indoors and out.

Directions: From Pleasanton, drive north on I-680. Take the Bollinger Canyon exit and travel east about three miles to South Gale Ridge. Turn right to the course entrance.

Contact: 9000 South Gale Ridge Road, San Ramon, CA 94583, pro shop 925/735-4253, fax 925/735-4256, www.thebridgesgolf.com.

83 DUBLIN RANCH GOLF CLUB
Architect: Robert Trent Jones Jr., 2004
18 holes　　　**Public**　　　**$47–65**

East Bay Detail map, page 133

A rolling course within a residential community, this layout is spotted with many bunkers, but no water hazards. There are spectacular views of Mount Diablo. With undulating greens and dramatic elevation changes throughout, this unique shorter course is designed to play quickly yet with substantial challenge, and will give advanced and novice players alike a chance to use every club in the bag.

Play Policy and Fees: Green fees are $47 Monday–Thursday and $65 Friday, weekends, and holidays. Twilight and junior rates are available.

Tees and Yardage: *Men:* Blue: yardage 4820, par 63, rating 63.4, slope 107; White: yardage 4350, par 63, rating 61.9, slope 105; *Women:* Red: yardage 3877, par 63, rating 62.0, slope 100; Gold: yardage 3412, par 63, rating 59.3, slope 95.

Tee Times: Reservations can be made seven days in advance.

Dress Code: Appropriate golf attire is required. Soft spikes only.

Tournaments: Tournaments of all types welcome. Minimum of 16 players.

Directions: Take I-580 east from Oakland, exit onto Fallon/Charro Road and go north. Follow the signs to the golf course.

Contact: 3700 Fallon Road, Dublin, CA 94568, 925/556-7040, fax 925/556-7045, www.dublinranchgolf.com.

84 MISSION HILLS OF HAYWARD GOLF COURSE
Architect: David Rainville and Gary Bye, 1999
9 holes　　　**Public**　　　**$14–19**

East Bay Detail map, page 133

This par-30 course is 1720 yards long, with six par-3s and three par-4s. Both the fairways and greens are undulating. The greens are extremely large, averaging over 7000 square feet. The course is challenging enough for the good golfer, yet accessible to the entire family. An extensive practice area is onsite, featuring a lighted, two-tier driving range, plus 10 grass stations.

Play Policy and Fees: Weekday green fees are $14 for Hayward residents and $16 for nonresidents. On weekends, fees are $17 for residents and $19 for nonresidents. Senior and junior rates are also available.

Tees and Yardage: *Men:* yardage 1720, par 30, rating n/a, slope n/a; *Women:* yardage 1343, par 30, rating n/a, slope n/a.

Tee Times: Reservations can be booked seven days in advance.

Dress Code: Appropriate golf attire is required.

Tournaments: This course is available for tournaments. Outside events should be scheduled at least 10 days in advance.

Directions: From Oakland, take I-880 south to Industrial Boulevard. Go east on Industrial. The course is at the corner of Industrial and Mission Boulevards.

Contact: 275 Industrial Parkway, Hayward, CA 94544, pro shop 510/888-0200.

85 CASTLEWOOD COUNTRY CLUB

Architect: William P. Bell, 1923 (Hill Course), 1954 (Valley Course)

36 holes   **Private**   **$102**

East Bay Detail map, page 133

The Valley Course is now one of the best in the East Bay. Robert Muir Graves added contours and mounds to define the fairways, and also redesigned all of the greens in the late 1990s. This course is a tough, demanding test. The men's course record is held by former PGA Tour winner Ron Cerrudo, who scored 62 on both courses in 1962. Don't expect to see anyone break that record—the course is tougher now because the trees are taller and the fairways aren't as hard as they were in '62. The Hill Course is a classic design from the 1920s. It's shorter but with smaller greens.

Play Policy and Fees: Reciprocal play is accepted with prior approval, at a rate of $102.

Tees and Yardage: Hill Course—*Men:* Blue: yardage 6240, par 70, rating 71.1, slope 127; White: yardage 5956, par 70, rating 69.9, slope 126; *Women:* Red: yardage 5483, par 73, rating 72.9, slope 131. Valley Course—*Men:* Blue: yardage 6678, par 72, rating 72.4, slope 128; White: yardage 6363, par 72, rating 71.1, slope 126; *Women:* Red: yardage 5918, par 74, rating 74.5, slope 131.

Tee Times: Reciprocal players should have their home professional call to make arrangements.

Dress Code: Collared shirts and soft spikes are required. No jeans are allowed.

Tournaments: Tournaments may be held on Monday only.

Directions: From I-680 in Pleasanton, take the Sunol/Castlewood Drive exit. Drive one block. The Valley Course is on the right, and the Hill Course is farther up the hill.

Contact: 707 Country Club Circle, Pleasanton, CA 94566, pro shop 925/485-2250, fax 925/485-2251, www.castlewoodcc.org.

86 PLEASANTON FAIRWAYS GOLF COURSE

Architect: Roland Curtola, 1974

9 holes   **Public**   **$12.50–25**

East Bay Detail map, page 133

This short, flat course is in the middle of the racetrack at the Alameda County Fairgrounds. This is not a course for beginners. The greens are all elevated, and a driver is needed on three holes. You must be accurate to hold the par-3 greens. The Curtola family owns a large driving range on the west end of the fairgrounds, about one-half mile from the course. Irons only on the driving range.

Play Policy and Fees: Green fees are $12.50 for nine holes and $19 for 18 holes weekdays, $15.50 for nine holes and $25 for 18 holes weekends. Senior and junior rates are available. The course is closed during the Alameda County Fair in late June and early July.

Tees and Yardage: *Men and Women:* yardage 1714, par 30, rating n/a, slope n/a.

Tee Times: Reservations can be booked seven days in advance.

Dress Code: Appropriate attire and soft spikes are required.

Tournaments: Limited tournaments accepted. Please inquire.

Directions: From I-680 in Pleasanton driving south, take the Bernal exit to the right, make a loop, and head east on Bernal. Turn left on Pleasanton Avenue and left again at the fairgrounds entrance.

Contact: P.O. Box 123, Pleasanton, CA 94566, pro shop 925/462-4653.

87 LAS POSITAS GOLF COURSE

Architect: Robert Muir Graves, 1967

27 holes   **Public**   **$15–38**

East Bay Detail map, page 133

There is an 18-hole championship layout and a nine-hole executive course. Both are fairly level, tree-lined courses generally in very good condition. The championship design has four lakes and a creek that come into play on seven holes. The greens are large and the fairways are wide and lush. The par-4 fifth hole doglegs around a lake and tempts long hitters to go for the green on the tee shot. But with a carry of at least 235 yards—good luck. The executive course has four par-4s, five par-3s.

Play Policy and Fees: Green fees for residents of Livermore are $27 for the 18-hole course weekdays, $33 weekends. Nonresident green fees are $30 weekdays, $38 weekends. Carts are additional. Rates on the executive course are $15 weekdays for residents, $17 for nonresidents, and $17 weekends for residents, $18 for non-residents. Twilight, junior, and senior rates available. The course is closed on Christmas.

Tees and Yardage: Championship—*Men:* Blue: yardage 6677, par 72, rating 72.1, slope 127; White: yardage 6331, par 72, rating 70.8, slope 123; *Women:* Red: yardage 5270, par 72, rating 70.7, slope 117. Executive—*Men:* Blue: yardage 2034, par 31, rating n/a, slope n/a; White: yardage 1830, par 31, rating n/a, slope n/a; *Women:* Red: yardage 1537, par 31, rating n/a, slope n/a.

Tee Times: Reservations can be booked seven days in advance beginning at 5 A.M.

Dress Code: Appropriate attire and soft spikes are required.

Tournaments: Tournaments are welcome and may be scheduled 12 months in advance. A banquet facility is available that can accommodate 150 people.

Directions: Driving east on I-580 at Livermore, exit on Airway Boulevard. This course is near Livermore Airport on the south side of the street.

Contact: 917 Clubhouse Drive, Livermore, CA 94550, pro shop 925/455-7820, fax 925/455-7838, www.lospositasgolf.com.

88 SPRINGTOWN GOLF COURSE
Architect: William F. Bell, 1963
9 holes   **Public**   **$14–25**

East Bay Detail map, page 133

This short course is well maintained, with water on two holes, undulating greens, and two long par-3s of 190 and 202 yards. This is a test for golfers of all skill levels. The third hole is perhaps the most memorable, with a large palm tree and bunker next to the par-4 green.

Play Policy and Fees: Green fees are $14 for nine holes and $22 for 18 holes on weekdays, $16 for nine holes and $25 for 18 holes on weekends. Carts are $22 for 18 holes. The course is closed Christmas Day.

Tees and Yardage: *Men:* White/Blue: yardage 5723, par 70, rating 67.0. slope 116; *Women:* White/Red: yardage 5126, par 70, rating 68.8, slope 110.

Tee Times: Reservations can be booked seven days in advance.

Dress Code: Shirts must be worn.

Tournaments: There is a 100-player minimum for shotgun tournaments and 24-player minimum for regular tournaments.

Directions: From I-580 in Livermore, take the Springtown Boulevard exit north. Turn right on Bluebell, which turns into Larkspur Drive.

Contact: 939 Larkspur Drive, Livermore, CA 94550, pro shop 925/455-5695.

89 SUNOL VALLEY GOLF CLUB
Architect: Clark Glasson, 1969
36 holes   **Public**   **$27–55**

East Bay Detail map, page 133

Nestled in the Mission Hills, both of these courses are geared to the mid- to high-handicapper. The Cypress Course is shorter but offers a solid test of the game. The Palm Course, with palm trees lining the wide fairways, is aptly named. At times you feel as if you are in Palm Springs. There's plenty to worry about on both courses: tight, rolling hills; lots of trees; water hazards; and bunkers. The greens are true but tricky.

Play Policy and Fees: Green fees are $27 to walk Monday–Friday, or $39 with a cart. Weekend fees are $55 when carts are mandatory and included. Sunrise, junior (twilight only), and twilight rates are available.

Tees and Yardage: Cypress Course—*Men:* Blue: yardage 6195, par 72, rating 69.8, slope 120; White: yardage 5801, par 72, rating 68.1, slope 117; *Women:* Red: yardage 5458, par 72, rating 70.1, slope 115. Palm Course—*Men:* Blue: yardage 6843, par 72, rating 72.4, slope 126; White: yardage 6409, par 72, rating 70.4, slope 120; *Women:* Red: yardage 5997, par 74, rating 74.4, slope 124.

Tee Times: Reservations can be booked seven days in advance. For an additional $3 per player, reservations can be booked 8–28 days in advance.

Dress Code: Nonmetal spikes are required.

Tournaments: A 16-player minimum is needed to book a tournament. Carts are required weekends and holidays only.

Directions: From I-680 in Sunol, exit on Andrade Road North. The course is adjacent to the freeway.

Contact: 6900 Mission Road, Sunol, CA 94586, pro shop 925/862-0414, fax 925/862-0428, www.sunolvalley.com.

90 RUBY HILL GOLF CLUB

Architect: Jack Nicklaus, 1996
18 holes   Private

East Bay Detail map, page 133

A design for tournaments if there ever was one, Ruby Hill is very long, with 10 par-4s over 400 yards from the back tees. If that isn't challenging enough, there are two lakes and creeks running throughout. The highlight of Ruby Hills is the greens, which are some of the best in Northern California.

Play Policy and Fees: Members and guests only. No reciprocal play is accepted. The course is closed on Monday.

Tees and Yardage: *Men:* Nicklaus: yardage 7448, par 72, rating 76.7, slope 138; Championship: yardage 7017, par 72, rating 74.2, slope 136; Members: yardage 6541, par 72, rating 72.4, slope 130; Seniors: yardage 5948, par 72, rating 69.2, slope 128; *Women:* Yellow: yardage 5846, par 73, rating 74.4, slope

129; Red: yardage 5279, par 72, rating 71.3, slope 123.

Tee Times: Not applicable.

Dress Code: Appropriate golf attire and nonmetal spikes are required. No denim is allowed.

Tournaments: Selected outside events are held on Monday only.

Directions: From I-680 in Pleasanton, take the Bernal Road exit east. Make a right on Vineyard Road, and the course is on the right.

Contact: 3404 West Ruby Hill Drive, Pleasanton, CA 94566, pro shop 925/417-5850, fax 925/417-5857, www.rubyhill.com.

91 THE COURSE AT WENTE VINEYARDS

Architect: Greg Norman, 1998
18 holes   Public $65–90

East Bay Detail map, page 133

This is one of the most beautiful and rewarding courses you will ever play. This challenging course allows golfers a chance to play every shot in their bags—and maybe a few in someone else's. The excellent use of land, varied terrain, and thoughtful design make this one of the more interesting and demanding courses in Northern California. Some hillside tee boxes command panoramic views. Some holes play beside working vineyards. Suggestion: When you're done with golf, tour the lovely vineyard facilities.

Play Policy and Fees: Green fees are $65 Monday–Thursday and $90 Friday, weekends, and holidays, including range balls and carts. Twilight rates available.

Tees and Yardage: *Men:* Black: yardage 6934, par 72, rating 74.0, slope 146; Gold: yardage 6710, par 72, rating 72.8, slope 142; Blue: yardage 6236, par 72, rating 70.9, slope 132; White: yardage 5684, par 72, rating 68.4, slope 122; *Women:* Red: yardage 4967, par 72, rating 73.4, slope 122.

Tee Times: Reservations are recommended and may be made 30 days in advance. For an additional $25 per player, tee times may be booked 31–60 days in advance.

Dress Code: Nonmetal spikes and appropriate golf attire are required. Shorts may not be shorter than four inches above the knee, and no denim is permitted.

Tournaments: Outside events are allowed and may be scheduled up to 12 months in advance. The banquet facility holds up to 144 people.

Directions: From San Jose, take I-680 north. Take the Livermore/Highway 84 exit east. Drive 7.7 miles to the first stoplight. Take a right on Concannon Road and another right on Arroyo Road. The course is on the left.

Contact: 5050 Arroyo Road, Livermore, CA 94550, pro shop 925/456-2475, fax 925/456-2490, www.wentegolf.com.

92 POPPY RIDGE GOLF COURSE

Architect: Rees Jones, 1996

27 holes **Public** **$36–78**

East Bay Detail map, page 133

 This facility, the second built by the Northern California Golf Association (the first was Poppy Hills), is a links-style golf course. Greens are open in front, allowing players to run the ball onto the putting surfaces. There is only one tree on the site, but several lakes and sidehill lies will test the skills of every golfer. The three nines, Merlot, Chardonnay, and Zinfandel, are similar in character; in fact, any combination you play has the same ratings. But the elevation changes, beautifully sculpted greens, and strategically located bunkers make any combination a memorable golf experience.

Play Policy and Fees: Outside play is welcome. If you are a member of the NCGA, green fees are $36 Monday–Thursday and $48 Friday–Sunday and holidays. Guests of members are $46 Monday–Thursday and $63 Friday–Sunday and holidays. Nonmember green fees are $56 Monday–Thursday and $78 Friday–Sunday and holidays. Nine-hole and twilight rates are available. Carts are $28.

Tees and Yardage: Merlot—*Men:* Black: yardage 3593, par 36, rating 74.8, slope 141; Blue:

yardage 3396, par 36, rating 72.8, slope 136; White: yardage 3187, par 36, rating 70.6, slope 129; *Women:* Gold: yardage 2633, par 36, rating 70.2, slope 120; Chardonnay—*Men:* Black: yardage 3513, par 36, rating 74.8, slope 141; Blue: yardage 3290, par 36, rating 72.8, slope 136; White: yardage 3072, par 36, rating 70.6, slope 129; *Women:* Gold: yardage 2607, par 36, rating 70.2, slope 120; Zinfandel—*Men:* Black: yardage 3535, par 36, rating 74.8, slope 141; Blue: yardage 3323, par 36, rating 72.8, slope 136; White: yardage 3062, par 36, rating 70.6, slope 129; *Women:* Gold: yardage 2660, par 36, rating 70.2, slope 120.

Tee Times: Reservations can be booked 30 days in advance.

Dress Code: Collared shirts are required, and nonmetal spikes are mandatory.

Tournaments: Outside events need board approval and should be booked two months to two years in advance. Carts are required.

Directions: From Livermore, take I-580 to the Greenville Road exit. Take Greenville Road five miles south to the course.

Contact: 4280 Greenville Road, Livermore, CA 94550, pro shop 925/456-8202, fax 925/455-2020, www.poppyridgegolf.com.

93 FREMONT PARK GOLF COURSE

Architect: Pete Dye, 2001

9 holes **Public** **$10–17**

East Bay Detail map, page 133

Serving the needs of the residents of the Fremont area, this nine-hole facility is a perfect venue for tuning your game, consisting mainly of short par-4s and par-3s. A lake adds beauty to the course. The driving range is popular, and the course offers a teaching academy. Fremont Park is a low-cost alternative for everyday golf and family outings.

Play Policy and Fees: Green fees are $10 weekdays, $17 weekends and holidays. Carts are additional. Twilight, junior, and senior rates are available, as are local rates.

Tees and Yardage: *Men:* Black: yardage 2350, par 33, rating 31.5, slope 112; White: yardage 2174, par 33, rating 30.9, slope 109; Yellow: yardage 1733, par 33, rating n/a, slope n/a; *Women:* Red: yardage 1903, par 33, rating 31.3, slope 108.

Tee Times: Reservations can be made seven days in advance.

Dress Code: No metal spikes are allowed on the course.

Tournaments: Tournaments welcome.

Directions: From I-680, take Mission Boulevard to Stevenson Boulevard and turn left onto Stevenson Place to the course.

Contact: 39751 Stevenson Place, Fremont, CA 94539, golf shop 510/790-1919, fax 510/790-0405, www.ci.fremont.ca.us/Recreation/Golfing.

94 SHORELINE GOLF LINKS

Architect: Robert Trent Jones Jr., 1983
18 holes   Public $36–52

San Jose and Vicinity Detail map, page 134

This sprawling, flat, links-style course demands accuracy with the long irons. The greens are large and undulating, the fairways are narrow, and there are more than 80 bunkers. Water guards the fourth, 11th, and 17th holes, all par-3s. The wind can blow here, but it's a fun course. The driving range has grass and mats, and there's a short-game practice area.

Play Policy and Fees: Green fees are $36 Monday–Thursday, $42 Friday, and $52 weekends and holidays. Special rates are available for juniors, seniors, and Mountain View residents. Carts are $22.

Tees and Yardage: *Men:* Blue: yardage 6632, par 72, rating 72.5, slope 125; White: yardage 6083, par 72, rating 70.2, slope 120; *Women:* Red: yardage 5400, par 72, rating 71.0, slope 123.

Tee Times: Reservations can be booked seven days in advance.

Dress Code: Shirts and shoes are necessary. Nonmetal spikes are required.

Tournaments: Tournaments can be scheduled six months in advance. A 12-player minimum is required to book a tournament. There is a premium charge for shotgun tournaments. The banquet facility accommodates up to 200 people.

Directions: From U.S. 101 in Mountain View, take the Shoreline Boulevard exit north and drive toward the bay. Follow Shoreline Boulevard to Shoreline Park. The golf course is just inside the park.

Contact: 2940 North Shoreline Boulevard, Mountain View, CA 94043, pro shop 650/969-2041, fax 650/969-8383, www.cityofmountainview.gov.

95 MOFFETT FIELD GOLF COURSE

Architect: Course designed, 1959
18 holes   Military $9–28

San Jose and Vicinity Detail map, page 134

This course is mostly flat, with more than 7000 pine, poplar, and cedar trees. Three lakes come into play. The course is easily walkable. Kikuyu grass makes the course distinctive, and it tends to create flier lies, requiring the golfer to pick the ball clean for best results. This isn't a demanding course, but out-of-bounds areas come into play on several holes.

Play Policy and Fees: Active and retired military personnel, reservists, Department of Defense personnel, federal employees, NASA employees, and sponsored guests only. Rates vary according to military status.

Tees and Yardage: *Men:* Blue: yardage 6524, par 72, rating 70.8, slope 119; White: yardage 6334, par 72, rating 70.6, slope 116; *Women:* Red: yardage 5964, par 73, rating 74.3, slope 122.

Tee Times: Tee times can be made three days in advance.

Dress Code: Appropriate golf attire and non-metal spikes are required.

Tournaments: This course is not available for outside events.

Directions: From U.S. 101 in Mountain View, take the Moffett Field exit. Drive north to the main gate of Moffett Field for instructions.

Contact: 1080 Lockhead Way, Sunnyvale, CA

94089 (750 MSS/SVBG-Box 42, Onizuka Air Station, CA 94089), pro shop 650/603-8026.

LOS ALTOS GOLF & COUNTRY CLUB

Architect: Tom Nicoll, 1923

18 holes   **Private**   **$125**

San Jose and Vicinity Detail map, page 134

The course is tight and tree-lined, with undulating greens. The course is beautifully manicured year-round. With the Santa Cruz Coastal Range as a backdrop, the vistas are some of the most spectacular in the entire Bay Area. Three-time U.S. Amateur champion and LPGA standout, Juli Inkster, holds the women's record of 68; head pro Brian Inkster, her husband, grew up on the course.

Play Policy and Fees: Reciprocal play is accepted with members of other selected private clubs at a rate of $125, plus $24 for a cart.

Tees and Yardage: *Men:* Blue: yardage 6534, par 71, rating 71.7, slope 132; White: yardage 6250, par 71, rating 70.4, slope 129; *Women:* Red: yardage 5911, par 74, rating 75.0, slope 132.

Tee Times: Have your club pro call for arrangements.

Dress Code: Appropriate golf attire and nonmetal spikes are required.

Tournaments: Shotgun tournaments are Monday only, May–October. Carts are required. A 100-player minimum is needed to book a tournament.

Directions: From I-280 in Los Altos, take the Magdelena Avenue exit northeast. Turn right on the Foothill Expressway and continue to Loyola Drive. Turn right on Loyola. Turn right onto Country Club Drive and then turn left 100 yards up the road into the course driveway.

Contact: 1560 County Club Drive, Los Altos, CA 94024, pro shop 650/947-3110, fax 650/948-4267, www.lagcc.com.

97 SUNNYVALE GOLF COURSE

Architect: Clark Glasson, 1968

18 holes   **Public**   **$31–41**

San Jose and Vicinity Detail map, page 134

This short, flat course boasts several long par-3s. Conspiring trees, wind, lakes, and doglegs all demand good positioning. Beware of the 18th hole, a short par-4 over water with a three-tiered green guarded by bunkers; it plays longer than its yardage. This public course features one of the largest pro shops in the country, offering full-service sales and repairs. This is a popular course with area residents.

Play Policy and Fees: Green fees are $31 weekdays and $41 weekends. Twilight rates are available. Senior monthly passes available. Optional carts are $12 per rider.

Tees and Yardage: *Men:* Black: yardage 6226, par 70, rating 70.4, slope 121; White: yardage 5736, par 70, rating 68.7, slope 114; *Women:* Gold: yardage 5261, par 71, rating 70.3, slope 116.

Tee Times: Reservations can be booked seven days in advance for weekdays and on Monday for weekends.

Dress Code: Appropriate attire and soft spikes are required.

Tournaments: No shotgun tournaments are allowed. A 24-player minimum is needed to book a tournament. Events should be booked 24 months in advance. A banquet facility is available that can accommodate 200 people.

Directions: From U.S. 101 in northern Sunnyvale, exit onto Mathilda Avenue south. Turn right on Maude Avenue and right again on Macara Lane.

Contact: 605 Macara Lane, Sunnyvale, CA 94086, pro shop 408/738-3666.

98 SANTA CLARA GOLF & TENNIS CLUB

Architect: Robert Muir Graves, 1986

18 holes   **Public**   **$20–41**

San Jose and Vicinity Detail map, page 134

This popular course has rolling hills and is long

and open, with a links-style rough on the fairway. It's walkable. There are doglegs and blind shots, and the wind can blow. The par-4 15th is brutal in the afternoon wind. Water comes into play on two par-4s on the front nine.

Play Policy and Fees: Green fees for residents of the city of Santa Clara are $20 weekdays and $26 weekends. Nonresident green fees are $33 weekdays and $41 weekends. Carts additional. Twilight rates are available.

Tees and Yardage: *Men:* Championship: yardage 6704, par 72, rating 72.4, slope 118; Men: yardage 6329, par 72, rating 70.5, slope 116; Senior: yardage 5918, par 72, rating 68.5, slope 111; *Women:* Forward: yardage 5492, par 72, rating 70.4, slope 112.

Tee Times: Residents can reserve tee times eight days in advance, and nonresidents can reserve tee times seven days in advance. Residents must have an ID card issued by the pro shop.

Dress Code: Appropriate attire and soft spikes are required.

Tournaments: Tournaments are accepted and may be scheduled 12 months in advance. The banquet facility can accommodate 400 people.

Directions: From Sunnyvale, take U.S. 101 south to the Great America Parkway exit. Go east on Tasman Drive and the course is on the left.

Contact: 5155 Stars and Stripes Drive, Santa Clara, CA 95054, pro shop 408/980-9515, fax 408/980-0479.

99 SUMMITPOINTE GOLF COURSE

Architect: Course designed, 1978
18 holes   Public $31–49

San Jose and Vicinity Detail map, page 134

The front nine is open but very hilly, while the back nine is flat and tight, with water on nearly every hole. The greens are tough and fast. The 16th hole, a 199-yard par-3, is described as one of the best holes in Northern California. The short, par-4 11th hole is a member of the Bay Area's "Dream 18." The course record is 64, held by PGA Tour professional Esteban

Toledo. The course boasts very nice views. A Nike Golf Learning Center is located here.

Play Policy and Fees: Green fees are $31 weekdays and $49 weekends and holidays. Carts are additional. Twilight, junior, and senior rates are available. The course often runs dining and golf specials as well. Please call for details.

Tees and Yardage: *Men:* Back: yardage 6331, par 72, rating 71.1, slope 131; Middle: yardage 6063, par 72, rating 69.7, slope 130; *Women:* Forward: yardage 5496, par 72, rating 70.6, slope 121.

Tee Times: Reservations can be booked seven days in advance.

Dress Code: Collared shirts are required. Blue jeans are not allowed. Nonmetal spikes are encouraged.

Tournaments: A 16-player minimum is required to book a tournament. Tournaments should be booked 3–6 months in advance. The banquet facility can accommodate 150 people.

Directions: From I-680 in Milpitas, take the Jacklin Road exit east to Park Victoria. Turn left and then right onto Country Club Drive.

Contact: 1500 Country Club Drive, Milpitas, CA 95035, pro shop 408/262-8813.

100 SPRING VALLEY GOLF COURSE

Architect: Ray Anderson, 1953
18 holes   Public $21–52

San Jose and Vicinity Detail map, page 134

This rolling course is in the foothills outside Milpitas. It's a gambler's paradise. Doglegs and water plus cypress, pine, and elm trees all come into play. There aren't many bunkers, but as a consolation they made the bunkers that do exist extra tricky. Stay below the pin. There are three holes over water, including the 182-yard 11th. A new clubhouse was completed here in 1998.

Play Policy and Fees: Green fees for 18 holes are $34 weekdays and $52 weekends. Fees for the back nine are $21 in the morning all week, $23 on weekend and holiday mornings. Evening, clergy, senior, and junior rates are available. Carts are $24.

Tees and Yardage: *Men:* Back: yardage 6073, par 70, rating 68.8, slope 112; Regular: yardage 5847, par 70, rating 68.8, slope 110; *Women:* Forward: yardage 5599, par 73, rating 71.2, slope 120.

Tee Times: Weekday reservations may be made seven days in advance. For weekend reservations, call at 7 A.M. on the Monday prior.

Dress Code: Appropriate attire and soft spikes are required.

Tournaments: Shotgun and standard tournaments may be arranged. See the course website for information on how to plan your event. The banquet facility can accommodate 150 people.

Directions: From I-880 or I-680 in Milpitas, exit on Highway 237/Calaveras Boulevard and drive east to the course.

Contact: 3441 East Calaveras Boulevard, Milpitas, CA 95035, pro shop 408/262-1722, fax 408/262-3260, www.springvalleygolfcourse.com.

101 SUNKEN GARDENS GOLF COURSE

Architect: Robert Dean Putman, 1959
9 holes   Public $14–17.50

San Jose and Vicinity Detail map, page 134

This mostly flat course borders a former quarry and is somewhat tight. There are two par-4s, and the rest are par-3s. The course is an excellent layout for beginners, juniors, and seniors.

Play Policy and Fees: Green fees are $14 weekdays and $17.50 weekends. Replay discounts offered. Power carts may be used only by physically challenged players.

Tees and Yardage: *Men and Women:* yardage 1502, par 29, rating n/a, slope n/a.

Tee Times: Weekend reservations must be made on Monday prior to the weekend.

Dress Code: Shirts must be worn, and no tank tops are allowed.

Tournaments: A 16-player minimum is needed to book a tournament.

Directions: This course is between U.S. 101

and I-280 in Sunnyvale. Exit on Wolfe Road toward El Camino Real. The course is on the east side of the street.

Contact: 1010 South Wolfe Road, Sunnyvale, CA 94086, pro shop 408/739-6588, clubhouse 408/732-2046.

102 BLACKBERRY FARM GOLF COURSE

Architect: Robert Muir Graves, 1962
9 holes   Public $13–15

San Jose and Vicinity Detail map, page 134

This flat, narrow course has lots of water and trees. It's relatively short, with dome-shaped greens. The 120-yard, par-3 eighth hole is over water.

Play Policy and Fees: Green fees are $13 weekdays and $15 weekends. Residents receive a $1 discount off the regular rates.

Tees and Yardage: *Men and Women:* yardage 1544, par 29, rating n/a, slope n/a.

Tee Times: Reservations are accepted one week in advance starting at 7 A.M.

Dress Code: Shirts must be worn.

Tournaments: Shotgun tournaments are not allowed. A 16-player minimum is required to book a tournament.

Directions: From I-280 in Cupertino, take Highway 85 south to the Stevens Creek Boulevard exit. Go west and drive one-third mile to the course, which is on the left.

Contact: 22100 Stevens Creek Boulevard, Cupertino, CA 95041, pro shop 408/253-9200, fax 408/255-5235, www.blackberryfarm.org.

103 DEEP CLIFF GOLF COURSE

Architect: Clark Glasson, 1960
18 holes   Public $25–35

San Jose and Vicinity Detail map, page 134

This mid-length course has three par-4s on the front nine and three par-4s on the back nine. It requires good placement shots because of the narrow corridor-type fairways. Stevens Creek bisects the course and comes into play on several holes.

Play Policy and Fees: Green fees are $25 weekdays and $35 weekends. Early bird, twilight, and senior rates are available.

Tees and Yardage: *Men:* Blue: yardage 3358, par 60, rating 59.2, slope 101; *Women:* White: yardage 2929, par 60, rating 56.8, slope 91.

Tee Times: Reservations can be booked seven days in advance.

Dress Code: Shirts and shoes are necessary. Nonmetal spikes are encouraged.

Tournaments: This course is available for outside events. Tournaments should be booked one year in advance. A 16-player minimum is required.

Directions: From I-280 in Sunnyvale, take the Foothill Expressway exit south to McClellan Road. Turn left and then turn right onto Clubhouse Lane.

Contact: 10700 Clubhouse Lane, Cupertino, CA 95014, pro shop 408/253-5357, fax 408/253-4521, www.playdeepcliff.com.

104 SAN JOSE MUNICIPAL GOLF COURSE

Architect: Robert Muir Graves, 1968

18 holes   **Public**   **$31-44**

San Jose and Vicinity Detail map, page 134

This course expanded holes 12 and 18 with new tee boxes in 2003, adding more than 100 yards in overall length. It is a relatively flat and forgiving layout, making it a good intermediate test of golf. There are several long par-4s. Most fairways are wide, but watch out for doglegs and large, undulating greens. The course is usually in excellent condition, and it is one of the busiest in Northern California. San Jose has a complete club-fitting center.

Play Policy and Fees: Green fees are $31 weekdays and $44 weekends. Call for special afternoon, student, senior, and twilight rates. Carts are additional.

Tees and Yardage: *Men:* Blue: yardage 6710, par 72, rating 71.2, slope 118; White: yardage 6309, par 72, rating 69.6, slope 116; *Women:* Red: yardage 5594, par 72, rating 71.0, slope 116.

Tee Times: Reservations can be booked seven days in advance for weekdays and on Tuesday for the upcoming weekend.

Dress Code: Appropriate attire and soft spikes are required.

Tournaments: This course is available for outside tournaments. A 20-player minimum is needed. Tournaments should be booked at least one month in advance.

Directions: From U.S. 101 heading south in San Jose, take the 13th Street exit and cross back over the freeway on Oakland Road. Follow it for one mile to the course on your right.

Contact: 1560 Oakland Road, San Jose, CA 95131, pro shop 408/441-4653, fax 408/453-8541, sjmuni.com.

105 SARATOGA COUNTRY CLUB

Architect: Course designed, 1962

9 holes   **Private**   **$24-60**

San Jose and Vicinity Detail map, page 134

Two holes have been added to lengthen the course, and a driving range opened in 1992. This hilly course has extremely narrow, tree-lined fairways. The par-4 seventh and 199-yard, par-3 ninth are unarguably the best holes on the course.

Play Policy and Fees: Reciprocal play is accepted with members of other private clubs. Reciprocal fees are $24 for nine holes and $36 for 18 holes Tuesday–Thursday, and $40 for nine holes and $60 for 18 holes Friday–Sunday and holidays. Carts are $13 for nine holes and $26 for 18 holes.

Tees and Yardage: *Men (18 holes):* yardage 4825, par 68, rating 65.0, slope 125; *Women:* yardage 4825, par 68, rating 69.8, slope 118.

Tee Times: Reciprocal players should have their home professional call to make arrangements up to 14 days in advance.

Dress Code: Collared shirts and nonmetal spikes are encouraged.

Tournaments: The course is available for outside events on Monday only.

Directions: From I-280 in Cupertino, take the Highway 85/Sunnyvale Road exit south to the Saratoga city line. Turn right on Prospect Road to the course.

Contact: 21990 Prospect Road (P.O. Box 2759), Saratoga, CA 95070, pro shop 408/253-5494, fax 408/253-0340, www.saratogacc.com.

106 PRUNERIDGE GOLF CLUB

Architect: Robert Trent Jones Jr., 1977

9 holes　　　**Public**　　　**$16**

🏃 📷 🍴 🛍 🍺

San Jose and Vicinity Detail map, page 134

This short, flat, and walkable course was redesigned in 1977 by Robert Trent Jones Jr. Watch out for ducks on the lake at the ninth hole. They can get aggressive if they aren't fed on the spot. This is a tight, high-quality executive course featuring four par-4s; 100,000 rounds are played here each year.

Play Policy and Fees: Green fees are $16. Senior and junior rates are available weekdays only.

Tees and Yardage: *Men (18 holes):* White: yardage 3628, par 62, rating 58.0, slope 92; *Women (18 holes):* Red: yardage 3256, par 62, rating 60.0, slope 75.

Tee Times: Reservations can be booked seven days in advance.

Dress Code: Appropriate attire and soft spikes are required.

Tournaments: This course is available for outside tournaments. Tournaments can be booked one month in advance. The banquet facility can hold 60 people.

Directions: The course is between U.S. 101 and I-280 in Santa Clara on Saratoga Avenue, which is off the San Tomas Expressway. From I-280, take the Saratoga Avenue exit north.

Contact: 400 North Saratoga Avenue, Santa Clara, CA 95050, pro shop 408/248-4424, fax 408/985-7340, www.pruneridgegolfclub.com.

107 PIN HIGH FAMILY GOLF CENTER

Architect: Course designed, 1994

3 holes　　　**Public**　　　**$5**

🏃 📷 🍴

San Jose and Vicinity Detail map, page 134

This is a three-hole course perfect for beginners and those who want to sneak out and play a little bit. Heck, if you have a long layover at San Jose International, take a cab, play three holes, and be back in time to find out the flight has been delayed. There are no tricks. The holes are all straight away. There are two par-3s and one par-4. If you don't like your score on the first go around, play eighteen holes and you'll have five more chances. This facility was designed to introduce people to golf and has PGA-trained teaching professionals on staff. Pin High has a lighted driving range that is open until 10 P.M. on weekdays and 9 P.M. on weekends.

Play Policy and Fees: Green fees are $5 for the first round, $4 for the next time around, and $3 for every round thereafter.

Tees and Yardage: *Men and Women (9 holes):* Back: yardage 1974, par 30, rating n/a, slope n/a; Middle: yardage 1893, par 30, rating n/a, slope n/a; Forward: yardage 1818, par 30, rating n/a, slope n/a.

Tee Times: Reservations are not accepted. Play is on a first-come, first-served basis.

Dress Code: Tank tops are not allowed on the golf course.

Tournaments: This course is available for outside events. The banquet facility can hold 50–75 people.

Directions: From San Jose, take I-880 north to Highway 237. Travel west on Highway 237 for two miles, then exit at North First Street. Take a right on North First Street. The course is one-quarter mile on the left side.

Contact: 4701 North Street (P.O. Box 280), Alviso, CA 95002, pro shop 408/934-1111.

108 LOS LAGOS GOLF COURSE

Architect: JMP Golf Design, 2002

18 holes   **Public**   **$29–42**

San Jose and Vicinity Detail map, page 134

This short city course is a fun round for mid-level golfers and families. Four lakes (hence the name, Los Lagos) come into play on five holes. The approach and green of the ninth hole is guarded by a lake on the left, to give you something to think about as you make the turn. The fourth hole, too, is an interesting hole, a short par-4 (291 yards all the way back), but with water protecting the right side of the fairway and a bevy of bunkers guarding the green. Go for it if your confidence is high, but be prepared to pay the consequences if you miss. An additional set of gold tees is offered for juniors, measuring 3903 yards. The two-tiered driving range is lighted and open late.

Play Policy and Fees: Green fees are $29 Monday–Thursday and $42 Friday–Sunday. Carts cost an additional $13 per rider. Twilight, junior, and senior rates also offered.

Tees and Yardage: *Men:* Blue: yardage 5393, par 68, rating 65.4, slope 112; White: yardage 4922, par 68, rating 63.0, slope 107; *Women:* Red: yardage 4490, par 68, rating 61.7, slope 103.

Tee Times: Reservations can be made seven days in advance.

Dress Code: No running shorts, gym shorts, or sleeveless shirts. Soft spikes only.

Tournaments: Tournaments for 20–144 players are welcomed.

Directions: From U.S. 101 in San Jose, exit on Capitol Expressway/Yerba Buena Road. Keep right. Merge onto Capitol Expressway and head west. Turn right at Tuers Road. The course is on your left.

Contact: 2995 Tuers Road, San Jose, CA 95121, golf shop 408/361-0250, fax 408/361-0255, www.playloslagos.com.

109 SAN JOSE COUNTRY CLUB

Architect: Tom Nichol, 1915

18 holes   **Private**   **$65**

San Jose and Vicinity Detail map, page 134

Situated in the foothills overlooking the Santa Clara Valley, this course is one of the oldest in Northern California. The course is short, hilly, and tight. The small greens require accurate iron play and a deft short game. From the tee on the fourth hole, you have a view of much of the course. On a clear day, you can see San Francisco. The course has two of the finest finishing holes in the region: the 17th, a par-5 across a ravine, at 516 yards; and the 18th, a 367-yard par-4 requiring a layup shot off the tee. Both greens are heavily bunkered. Precise approach shots are needed.

Play Policy and Fees: Reciprocal play is accepted with members of other private clubs at a rate of $65 to walk, plus $13 for a cart.

Tees and Yardage: *Men:* Blue: yardage 6201, par 70, rating 70.5, slope 127; White: yardage 5926, par 70, rating 69.4, slope 124; *Women:* Red: yardage 5477, par 73, rating 71.9, slope 126.

Tee Times: Reciprocal players should have their home professional call to make arrangements.

Dress Code: Appropriate golf attire and non-metal spikes are required. The dress code is strictly enforced.

Tournaments: Shotgun tournaments are available on Monday. An 80-player minimum is needed to close the course. Carts are required.

Directions: From I-680 in San Jose, take the Alum Rock Avenue exit east. Drive 2.5 miles to the course entrance.

Contact: 15571 Alum Rock Avenue, San Jose, CA 95127, pro shop 408/258-3636.

110 BOULDER CREEK GOLF & COUNTRY CLUB

Architect: Jack Fleming, 1961

18 holes   **Resort**   **$22–40**

San Jose and Vicinity Detail map, page 134

This scenic course sits in the midst of redwoods. It is well maintained, short, slightly rolling, and tight. The immaculate and demanding greens are the great neutralizer for the lack of length. The front nine has five par-3s, and the back nine plays as a regular nine-hole course. A hole in one was made on the first shot on the first hole on opening day in June 1961.

For condominium reservations and golf package information, call 408/338-2111.

Play Policy and Fees: Green fees are $22 Monday–Thursday, $26 Friday, and $40 weekends. Carts are $19. Twilight, senior, and junior rates are offered.

Tees and Yardage: *Men:* White: yardage 4396, par 65, rating 61.5, slope 98; *Women:* Red: yardage 4027, par 67, rating 63.3, slope 98.

Tee Times: Reservations can be booked seven days in advance.

Dress Code: No tank tops are allowed.

Tournaments: Shotgun tournaments are available weekdays only. A 16-player minimum is required for tournament play. Events can be booked up to two years in advance.

Directions: From Santa Cruz, drive 12 miles north on Highway 9 to Boulder Creek. In Boulder Creek, take Highway 236 three miles northwest to the course on the left.

Contact: 16901 Big Basin Highway, Boulder Creek, CA 95006, pro shop 831/338-2121, clubhouse 831/338-2111, fax 831/338-7862, www .bouldercreekgolf.com.

111 LA RINCONADA COUNTRY CLUB

Architect: Opened 1929;
redesign Robert Muir Graves, 1972
18 holes   Private $130

San Jose and Vicinity Detail map, page 134
This mature layout is short and narrow, with tree-lined fairways and undulating greens. A lake comes into play on the 14th and 15th holes. In the foothills of Los Gatos, this course offers a scenic view of the southern Santa Clara Valley. The best hole is the uphill, 418-yard, par-4 ninth.

Play Policy and Fees: Reciprocal play is accepted with members of other private clubs Tuesday, Thursday, and Friday at a rate of $130 including mandatory cart. Advance arrangements are required. The course is closed on Monday.

Tees and Yardage: *Men:* Blue: yardage 6123, par 70, rating 69.8, slope 131; White: yardage 5918, par 70, rating 68.9, slope 130; *Women:* Red: yardage 5545, par 72, rating 71.6, slope 125; Gold: yardage 5098, par 71, rating 68.9, slope 121.

Tee Times: Reciprocal players should have their home professional call to make arrangements.

Dress Code: Appropriate golf attire and nonmetal spikes are required.

Tournaments: All outside events must have board approval.

Directions: From Highway 17 in San Jose, take the Lark Avenue exit. Turn left on Winchester Boulevard. Turn right on La Rinconada Drive and follow it to Clearview Drive. Turn left to the course.

Contact: 14597 Clearview Drive, Los Gatos, CA 95030, pro shop 408/395-4220, fax 408/395-2169, www.larinconadacc.com.

112 THE GOLF CLUB AT BOULDER RIDGE

Architect: Bradford Benz, 2001
18 holes   Private $125

San Jose and Vicinity Detail map, page 134
This spectacular hilltop course is carved into an old stone quarry, and it features panoramic views of San Jose on one side and the Santa Teresa hills on the other. On clear days, one can see all the way to San Francisco from the 14th tee. Holes play up, down, and through the quarry site. Where there is a change in elevation, it generally shifts from tee down to green, making the layout very playable. In some areas you feel like you're in Arizona, with huge boulders dotting the landscape. Other holes are more like Scotland, with its wide-open playability.

Play Policy and Fees: Reciprocal play is accepted with members of other private clubs at a rate of $125, which includes a cart. Otherwise, members and guests only.

Tees and Yardage: *Men:* Obsidian: yardage 6923, par 72, rating 73.4, slope 139; Gold: yardage 6530, par 71, rating 71.4, slope 136; Silver: yardage 6157, par 71, rating 69.7, slope 132; *Women:* Copper: yardage 5716, par 72, rating 72.2, slope 124; Jade: yardage 5005, par 71, rating 68.6, slope 117.

Tee Times: Reciprocal players should have their home professional call to make arrangements.

Dress Code: Traditional golf attire and non-metal spikes are required.

Tournaments: This course is available for outside events. Please inquire.

Directions: Take the Almaden Expressway to the Winfield Boulevard exit. Turn right on Cross Springs Drive, then take a left on Mazzone Drive. Turn right at Crossview Circle; the course is on the right.

Contact: 6039 Crossview Circle, San Jose, CA 95120, pro shop 408/323-9900, www.thegolfclubatboulderridge.com.

113 PLEASANT HILLS GOLF COURSE

Architect: Henry Duino Sr., 1959; Joseph Soto, 1965
27 holes   **Public**   **$23–31**

San Jose and Vicinity Detail map, page 134
At the base of the foothills, this course has a half million trees (or so it seems), including fig, apple, and eucalyptus, which all come into play. A flat course dominated by trees, it's always in good shape. This public facility has an 18-hole course and a nine-hole executive course. The par-3 executive course is 2600 yards and not rated.

Play Policy and Fees: Green fees are $23 weekdays and $31 weekends. Twilight rates are available. Cash or checks only.

Tees and Yardage: *Men:* Blue: yardage 6510, par 72, rating 70.6, slope 123; White: yardage 6198, par 72, rating 69.2, slope 120; *Women:* Red: yardage 5800, par 73, rating 71.1, slope 114.

Tee Times: Reservations can be booked seven days in advance.

Dress Code: No tank tops or tee shirts are allowed on the course.

Tournaments: This course is available for outside tournaments.

Directions: From U.S. 101 in San Jose, take the Tully Road East exit. Drive northeast past Capitol Expressway and turn left on South White Road to the course.

Contact: 2050 South White Road, San Jose, CA 95152, pro shop 408/238-3485.

114 THE RANCH GOLF CLUB AT SILVER CREEK

Architect: Casey O'Callaghan, 2004
18 holes   **Public**   **$80–100**

San Jose and Vicinity Detail map, page 134
In the hills just south and east of San Jose, set within a 580-acre real estate community, this course is a pleasure to play. It combines a serene ambience with some solid hole design to create a memorable experience. The signature hole is the 15th, a 150-yard, downhill par-3 with a treacherous bunker in the middle of the green and large oak trees and native hillsides serving as the backdrop. Equally enjoyable is the dramatic home hole, a challenging 400-yard, par-4 with a two-acre lake to avoid. Note: The course had not yet been rated at press time.

Play Policy and Fees: Green fees are $80 Monday–Thursday and $100 Friday–Sunday and holidays. Carts included in green fees. Resident, twilight, junior, and senior rates are available.

Tees and Yardage: *Men:* Black: yardage 6747, par 72, rating n/a, slope n/a; Blue: yardage 6389, par 72, rating n/a, slope n/a; White: yardage 5808, par 72, rating n/a, slope n/a; *Women:* Red: yardage 4900, par 72, rating n/a, slope n/a.

Tee Times: Reservations can be made 14 days in advance.

Dress Code: Appropriate golf attire is required. Soft spikes only. No cutoffs, denim, or tank tops allowed.

Tournaments: Tournaments of all types welcome. Please call for details.

Directions: Exit U.S. 101 at Yerba Buena Avenue. Drive east and turn right on Silver Creek Valley Road. Follow it around to Hassler Parkway and turn right. Follow signs to the clubhouse entrance.

Contact: 4601 Hill Top View Lane, San Jose, CA 95138, golf shop 408/270-0557, www.the ranchgc.com.

115 SILVER CREEK VALLEY COUNTRY CLUB

Architect: Ted Robinson Sr., 1992

18 holes **Private** **$75–125**

🏃 📷 🍽 🎣 🍺

San Jose and Vicinity Detail map, page 134

The golf course takes you from a panoramic ridge to a valley floor and ends on a high plateau, where a waterfall plummets into a serene but treacherous lake guarding the signature 18th hole. Natural rock outcroppings, groves of eucalyptus trees, and majestic oaks protect many of the landing areas, while sculpted rock walls hold back armies of flowers surrounding the greens. The par-4 14th hole requires a well-played tee shot around a grove of oaks to a contoured fairway guarded left, right, and long by lateral hazards. The green is nestled at the base of a rocky canyon wall and is tiered, requiring a short, accurate approach. The capper on the front nine is the ninth hole, which offers breathtaking views of the Santa Clara Valley and the entire golf course.

Play Policy and Fees: Reciprocal play is accepted. Guest fees range $75–125, including cart. The course is closed on Monday.

Tees and Yardage: *Men:* Gold: yardage 6929, par 72, rating 73.5, slope 135; Blue: yardage 6527, par 72, rating 71.5, slope 131; White: yardage 6098, par 72, rating 69.6, slope 128; *Women:* Silver: yardage 5701, par 72, rating 72.8, slope 132; Red: yardage 5197, par 72, rating 70.7, slope 125.

Tee Times: Reciprocal players should have their home professional call to make arrangements.

Dress Code: Appropriate golf attire and nonmetal spikes are required.

Tournaments: All tournaments must be approved. The banquet facility can accommodate 275 people.

Directions: From San Jose, take U.S. 101 south to the Silver Creek Valley Road/Blossom Hill exit. Turn east onto Silver Creek Valley Road and follow the signs to the club.

Contact: 5460 Country Club Parkway, San Jose, CA 95138, pro shop 408/239-5775, fax 408/239-5777, www.scvcc.com.

116 THE VILLAGES GOLF & COUNTRY CLUB

Architect: Robert Muir Graves, 1970

27 holes **Private** **$75**

🏃 📷 🍽 🔧 🎣 🍺 ③

San Jose and Vicinity Detail map, page 134

This residential community has two courses, a championship 18-hole layout and a shorter nine-hole course. The championship course has water hazards on 10 holes, and bunkers come into play for the longer hitters. The 17th and 18th are long par-4s, with out-of-bounds left. The 17th has water on the right, and the 18th has water in front of the green. All three nines are enjoyable and usually in excellent shape. The nine-hole course is a par-27. The course record for the championship course is 63, by Roger Maltbie.

Play Policy and Fees: Reciprocal play is accepted after noon only with members of other private clubs, and fees are $75.

Tees and Yardage: *Men:* Blue: yardage 6701, par 72, rating 71.6, slope 130; White: yardage 6332, par 72, rating 69.7, slope 125; *Women:* Red: yardage 5849, par 73, rating 73.2, slope 120.

Tee Times: Reciprocal players should have their home professional call to make arrangements.

Dress Code: No denim is allowed, and shorts must be longer than four inches above the knee. Collared shirts are required.

Tournaments: Ten outside tournaments per year are held on Monday only. The banquet facility can accommodate 350 people.

Directions: From U.S. 101 in eastern San Jose, take Yerba Buena Avenue northeast about four miles. Turn right on San Felipe Road and drive 2.5 miles to the Villages Parkway. Turn left and drive to Cribari Lane and the course.

Contact: 5000 Cribari Lane, San Jose, CA 95135, pro shop 408/274-3220, fax 408/274-1405.

117 SANTA TERESA GOLF CLUB
Architect: George Santana, 1963
27 holes　　**Public**　　　　**$11–50**

🚶 🛒 🍴 🏌 🚙 🍽 **3**

San Jose and Vicinity Detail map, page 134
There are two layouts here, a championship 18-hole course and a par-3 nine-hole course. The challenging championship course, the pride of the South Bay public courses, is long, with tree-lined fairways. The front nine is flat and the back nine is hilly. This course has been voted the best municipal course in Santa Clara Valley. The testy 16th hole is one reason why: It's a tough par-3 of 220 yards, into a strong prevailing wind. The winds make various holes more difficult. A renovation of all 18 greens was completed in 2003, and the tee boxes in 2004.

Play Policy and Fees: Green fees are $35 weekdays and $50 weekends. Carts are additional. Afternoon, twilight, senior (weekdays only), and student (weekdays only) rates are offered. The short-course fees are $11 on weekdays and $15 weekends.

Tees and Yardage: *Men:* Blue: yardage 6742, par 71, rating 72.7, slope 129; White: yardage 6430, par 71, rating 71.3, slope 126; *Women:* Red: yardage 6032, par 73, rating 73.5, slope 129.

Tee Times: Reservations can be booked seven days in advance for weekdays and the Monday prior for weekends. Tee times for the short course are first-come, first-served.

Dress Code: Shirts and shoes are necessary.

Tournaments: A 20-player minimum is needed to book a tournament. Tournaments may start after 10 A.M. on weekdays and 11 A.M. on weekends and holidays. Shotgun tournaments are not allowed on weekends.

Directions: From U.S. 101 in San Jose, take the Bernal Road exit west. Drive two miles to the course.

Contact: 260 Bernal Road, San Jose, CA 95199, pro shop 408/225-2650, fax 408/226-9598.

118 COYOTE CREEK GOLF CLUB
Architect: Jack Nicklaus, 1999
36 holes　　**Public**　　　　**$59–98**

🚶 🛒 🍴 🏌 🚙 🍽

San Jose and Vicinity Detail map, page 134
The Tournament Course at Coyote Creek is demanding. Off the tee you will find plenty of room, and there are few mature trees to get in your way, but many of the greens are multi-tiered and guarded by deep pot bunkers. The front nine is characterized by rolling terrain, while the back nine is relatively flat. Water comes into play on several of the closing holes. A Champions Tour event was played here several years ago. The Valley Course is less demanding, a nice complement to the Tournament Course. Four lakes and two waterfalls beautify the finishing holes.

Play Policy and Fees: Green fees are $75 Monday–Thursday on the Tournament Course, $90 Friday, and $98 Saturday and Sunday, including cart. Fees for the Valley Course are $59 Monday–Thursday (not including cart) and $75 Friday–Sunday (including cart). Afternoon, twilight, junior, and senior rates are also available.

Tees and Yardage: Tournament Course—*Men:* Black: yardage 7027, par 72, rating 75.2, slope 140; Blue: yardage 6633, par 72, rating 73.1, slope 136; White: yardage 6420, par 72, rating 72.3, slope 132; Gold: yardage 5907, par 72, rating 69.9, slope 126; *Women:* Red: yardage 5184, par 72, rating 70.4, slope 124. Valley Course—*Men:* Blue: yardage 7066, par 72, rating 75.2, slope 133; White: yardage 6558, par 72, rating 72.0, slope 130; Gold: yardage 6173, par 72, rating 68.9, slope 124; *Women:* Red: yardage 5187, par 72, rating 69.8, slope 117.

Tee Times: Reservations can be booked 14 days in advance.

Dress Code: Appropriate golf attire and non-metal spikes are required.

Tournaments: Tournaments can be booked two years in advance. Shotgun tournaments are available weekdays only. A 20-player minimum is needed to book a tournament. Carts are required.

Directions: From U.S. 101 in Morgan Hill, take the Cochrane Road exit. From U.S. 101 in San Jose, exit at Bernal Road. Turn onto Monterey Road heading south toward Morgan Hill. Turn at Palm Avenue and look for the signs.

Contact: 9770 Monterey Road, Coyote, CA 95013, pro shop 408/463-1400, www.coyote creekgolf.com.

119 ALMADEN GOLF & COUNTRY CLUB

Architect: Jack Fleming, 1955
18 holes   **Private**   **$65**

🏌️ 📷 🍴 🏌️ 🚗 🍺

San Jose and Vicinity Detail map, page 134

This scenic, demanding course in the Silicon Valley has a tree-lined, rolling terrain. The greens are undulating. The difficult par-4 16th requires a strong tee shot, and trees on the right guard a heavy slope down to "Death Valley." The dogleg-left 17th forces most players to bail out again into "Chicken Alley" on the right. Almaden has been the site of several LPGA events. The women's course record is 62, set by Palo Alto native Vicki Fergon during the 1984 San Jose Classic.

Play Policy and Fees: Reciprocal play is accepted with members of other private clubs Tuesday and Thursday at a rate of $65. Carts additional. The course is closed on Monday.

Tees and Yardage: *Men:* Black: yardage 6960, par 72, rating 74.1, slope 132; Blue: yardage 6571, par 72, rating 72.4, slope 126; White: yardage 6202, par 72, rating 71.0, slope 121; Yellow: yardage 5717, par 72, rating 68.6, slope 115; *Women:* Red: yardage 5532, par 73, rating 72.6, slope 128.

Tee Times: Reciprocal players should have their home professional call to make arrangements.

Dress Code: Appropriate golf attire and non-metal spikes are required.

Tournaments: Outside events are accepted with board approval.

Directions: From U.S. 101 in San Jose, take Highway 85 to the Almaden Expressway. Take Almaden Expressway to Crown Boulevard. Turn right to Hampton Drive.

Contact: 6663 Hampton Drive, San Jose, CA 95120, pro shop 408/268-3959, www.alma dengcc.com.

120 CINNABAR HILLS GOLF CLUB

Architect: John Harbottle, 1998
27 holes   **Public**   **$60–100**

🏌️ 📷 🍴 🏕️ 🍺

San Jose and Vicinity Detail map, page 134

Cinnabar Hills Golf Club is a collection of three well-maintained and distinctive nine-hole golf courses: Lake, Canyon, and Mountain. The Canyon Course is a tight, undulating course surrounded by trees, with creeks running throughout. The Mountain Course features several elevated tee boxes, spacious landing areas, and well-protected greens. The Lake Course has a four-acre lake and two creeks, bringing water into play on eight of nine holes. Inside the clubhouse, make sure you visit the Brandenburg Historic Golf Museum.

Play Policy and Fees: Green fees Monday–Thursday are $60 walking, $80 riding. They are $100 Friday–Sunday and holidays, cart included and mandatory. Twilight and super twilight rates are available.

Tees and Yardage: Mountain/Canyon—*Men:* Hawk: yardage 6641, par 72, rating 72.5, slope 137; Cinnabar: yardage 6269, par 72, rating 70.8, slope 131; Quicksilver: yardage 5713, par 72, rating 68.1, slope 126; *Women:* Oak: yardage 4859, par 72, rating 68.1, slope 118; Lake/Mountain—*Men:* Hawk: yardage 6853, par 72, rating 73.6, slope 142; Cinnabar: yardage 6397, par 72, rating 71.2, slope 134; Quicksilver: yardage 5850, par 72, rating 68.6, slope 127; *Women:* Oak: yardage 5010, par 72, rating 68.1, slope 120; Canyon/Lake—*Men:* Hawk: yardage 6688, par 72, rating 72.9, slope 138; Cinnabar: yardage 6318, par 72, rating 71.0, slope 132; Quicksilver: yardage 5827, par 72, rating 68.9, slope 128; *Women:* Oak: yardage 4959, par 72, rating 68.4, slope 121.

Tee Times: Reservations can be made 14 days in advance without a fee. Golfers can make tee times 15–90 days in advance for an additional charge. For automated reservations, call 408/323-7880.

Dress Code: Nonmetal spikes are required.

Tournaments: Tournaments of 21 players or more are welcome and reservations can be made up to one year in advance.

Directions: From San Francisco, take I-280 to Highway 85 south. Exit at the Almaden Expressway and head south for five miles to Harry Road. Turn right on Harry Road and left on McKean Road. Follow McKean Road for five miles around the Calero Reservoir to the golf course on the left.

Contact: 23600 McKean Road, San Jose, CA 95141, pro shop 408/323-5200, fax 408/323-9512, www.cinnabarhills.com.

Chapter 8

PEBBLE BEACH GOLF LINKS © GEORGE FULLER

Monterey Peninsula and Vicinity

Monterey Peninsula and Vicinity

I f the United States has an answer to Scotland's collection of top-ranked golf courses, it is found at Pebble Beach and on the Monterey Peninsula.

If Scotland's Saint Andrews' Old Course is the Vatican, Cypress Point Club in Pebble Beach is the Sistine Chapel of Golf. It's the best course in the nation. It's designer Alister Mackenzie's masterwork, his Beethoven's Ninth, his Brandenburg Concertos, the one course on which he truly collaborated with divinity.

But before you throw your golf bag into the Pacific and take up tiddlywinks because Cypress Point is so exclusive it takes an act of God to play there, consider that you can play quite a few other excellent courses both inside and outside the gates at Pebble Beach.

Inside the Del Monte Forest gates there are Pebble Beach Golf Links, Spyglass Hill, Spanish Bay, and Poppy Hills. Put that collection against anything in the world and you'll come out in front.

At the head of the class is Pebble Beach Golf Links. Like the Pacific Ocean it is built adjacent to, Pebble Beach can be benign or monstrous, depending on the weather. Witness the famous par-3 seventh, a short hole of only 107 yards from the back tees. But when the wind comes from the water, it can play as many as five clubs longer.

PGA Tour great Tom Watson likes the nearby Links at Spanish Bay. Given the fact that he was one of the triumvirate who designed the course, one should hope so. He says, "Spanish Bay is so much like Scotland, you can almost hear the bagpipes." Those *are* bagpipes, Tom. They play every day at dusk.

Of all the courses in the forest you can and want to play, Spyglass

Hill Golf Course must be near the top of the list. It is one of Robert Trent Jones Sr.'s best designs, nestled into the deep trees above the coast.

Outside the forest gates, too, there are plenty of fine golfing choices. Pacific Grove Golf Course has been called the "poor man's Pebble Beach" more than once because of its location next to the Pacific. And in Carmel Valley, the courses you can play include the always-enjoyable Quail Lodge and Carmel Valley Ranch layouts.

Farther up the bay in Seaside, Bayonet & Black Horse golf courses have made quite a name for themselves. Long difficult to play because they were behind the gates of Fort Ord, they are now open for public play. Designed by an army general named "Bourbon Bob" McClure and opened in 1954, Bayonet is the older and more classic of the two designs. With some very nice ocean views, these two courses would be much more renowned (and much more expensive) if they were inside the gates of Pebble.

Another regional standout that should be on your play list is San Juan Oaks Golf Club next to the old Spanish Mission town of San Juan Bautista, about a 45-minute drive north from the Monterey Peninsula.

So you see, there are alternatives to tiddlywinks in this golf rich re gion after all.

Of course, while you're in the area, Carmel still charms visitors with its cobblestone streets and art galleries, Pacific Grove beckons with its Victorian architecture and lounging sea otters, and downtown Monterey and Cannery Row offer history, a fun wharf, good food, and the world-class Monterey Bay Aquarium.

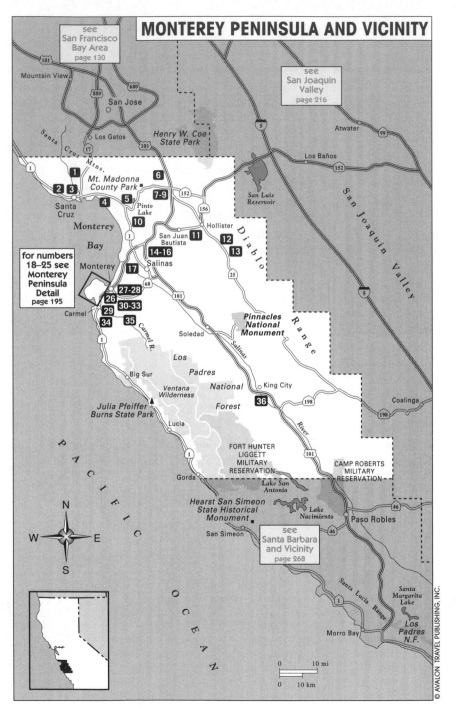

see
San Francisco
Bay Area
page 130

Mountain View

see
San Joaquin
Valley
page 216

San Jose

Los Gatos

Atwater

Henry W. Coe
State Park

Los Baños

Santa Cruz Mtns.

1

Mt. Madonna
County Park

6

2 **3**

4 **5**

Pinto Lake

7-9

Santa
Cruz

10

San Luis
Reservoir

Monterey
Bay

San Juan
Bautista

11

12

14-16

Salinas

13

for numbers
18-25 see
Monterey
Peninsula
Detail
page 195

Monterey

17

Hollister

Diablo

27-28

26

30-33

29

34 **35**

Carmel

Carmel R.

Soledad

**Pinnacles
National
Monument**

Range

San Joaquin Valley

Big Sur

Los
Padres

National

King City

Ventana
Wilderness

Forest

36

Coalinga

Julia Pfeiffer
Burns State Park

Lucia

Salinas River

FORT HUNTER
LIGGETT
MILITARY
RESERVATION

CAMP ROBERTS
MILITARY
RESERVATION

Gorda

Lake San
Antonio

P A C I F I C

Hearst San Simeon
State Historical
Monument

Lake
Nacimiento

Paso Robles

San Simeon

see
Santa Barbara
and Vicinity
page 268

N
W   E
S

Santa Lucia Range

Santa
Margarita
Lake

Los
Padres
N.F.

O C E A N

Morro Bay

0   10 mi
0   10 km

© AVALON TRAVEL PUBLISHING, INC.

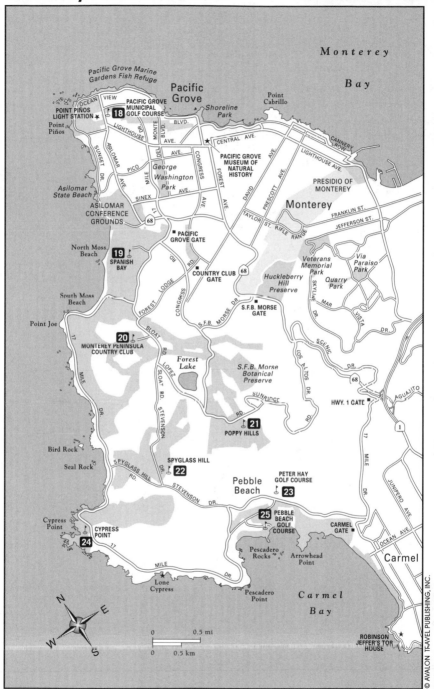

1 VALLEY GARDENS GOLF COURSE

Architect: Bob Baldock, 1971
9 holes **Public** **$13–15**

Monterey Peninsula and Vicinity map, page 194

This course is short, tight, and flat; 27 different varieties of trees come into play. Beginners, juniors, and seniors will find it an excellent layout. PGA professional Hal Wells holds the course record with a 23.

Play Policy and Fees: Green fees are $13 weekdays and $15 weekends for nine holes. Pull carts are $2.50. Senior and junior rates are available.

Tees and Yardage: *Men:* White: yardage 1781, par 31, rating n/a, slope n/a; *Women:* Red: yardage 1534, par 32, rating n/a, slope n/a.

Tee Times: Reservations may be booked one week in advance.

Dress Code: Shirts and shoes are required. No tank tops are allowed.

Tournaments: This course is available for outside events. Call for more information.

Directions: From Highway 17 in Scotts Valley, drive one mile west on Mount Hermon Road to the course.

Contact: 263 Mount Hermon Road, Scotts Valley, CA 95066, pro shop 831/438-3058.

2 PASATIEMPO GOLF COURSE

Architect: Alister Mackenzie, 1929
18 holes **Semiprivate** **$135–170**

Monterey Peninsula and Vicinity map, page 194

This course opened in 1929 and still ranks **BEST** as one of the best in the nation. The par-4 16th was course architect Alister Mackenzie's favorite hole in golf. It's a blind driving hole that requires a difficult uphill approach across a creek to a three-tiered green. There are hazards and out-of-bounds on both sides of the fairway, which doglegs to the left. The 18th is a famous par-3 that calls for a carry off the tee over a gully to a difficult, back-to-front green where you're best to be below the pin. Mackenzie spent the last years of his life living in a home on Pasatiempo and tinkering with the design. There is a great deal of memorabilia in the clubhouse. Pasatiempo, overlooking the Pacific Ocean and Monterey Bay, is one California golf experience that should not be missed.

Play Policy and Fees: Public play is accepted. Monday–Thursday, public green fees are $135 to walk and $155 with a cart. Friday–Sunday and holidays, public green fees are $150 to walk and $170 with a cart.

Tees and Yardage: *Men:* Blue: yardage 6445, par 70, rating 72.5, slope 136; White: yardage 6128, par 70, rating 71.0, slope 132; *Women:* Red: yardage 5629, par 72, rating 73.5, slope 133.

Tee Times: Weekday tee times may be reserved one week in advance, with calls accepted at 7 A.M. Weekend tee times may be reserved on the Monday prior starting at 10 A.M.

Dress Code: Collared shirts and soft spikes are mandatory, and shorts are acceptable. No denim is permitted.

Tournaments: A 16-player minimum is required to book a tournament. Tournaments may be booked a year in advance. Shotgun tournaments are available Monday and Thursday only. The banquet facility can accommodate 200 people.

Directions: From San Francisco, drive south on I-280. Take Highway 17 toward Santa Cruz. Exit onto Pasatiempo Drive and follow the signs.

Contact: 20 Clubhouse Road, Santa Cruz, CA 95060, pro shop 831/459-9155, www.pasatiempo.com.

3 DE LAVEAGA GOLF COURSE

Architect: Bert Stamps, 1970
18 holes **Semiprivate** **$39–49.50**

Monterey Peninsula and Vicinity map, page 194

This tight, rolling course in the Santa Cruz mountains has lateral hazards on nearly every hole. Staying in the fairways off the tee is vital. The course may give the appearance of birdie opportunities, but they don't come easily.

Play Policy and Fees: Green fees are $39 weekdays and $49.50 weekends. Resident, twilight, and super twilight rates are available. Carts are $17 per rider.

Tees and Yardage: *Men:* White: yardage 6010, par 72, rating 70.0, slope 136; *Women:* Red: yardage 5331, par 72, rating 71,2, slope 124.

Tee Times: Reservations can be booked six days in advance. Reservations are possible 60 days in advance on the website for a $5 per player service fee.

Dress Code: Traditional or ceramic-tipped spikes are not allowed.

Tournaments: A 16-player minimum is needed to book a tournament. Carts are required. Events should be scheduled 12 months in advance. A banquet facility is available that can accommodate up to 150 people.

Directions: From San Francisco, take I-280 to Highway 17 toward Santa Cruz. Take Highway 1 south to the Morrisey exit. Turn right on Fairmount and right again on Branciforte Avenue. Turn left on Upper Park Road and proceed to the course.

Contact: 401 Upper Park Road, Box A, Santa Cruz, CA 95065, pro shop 831/423-7212, fax 831/458-1309, www.delaveagagolf.com.

4 SEASCAPE GOLF CLUB

Architect: Course designed, 1927

18 holes   **Semiprivate**   **$45-70**

🏌️📷💲🏌️🛒⛳

Monterey Peninsula and Vicinity map, page 194

This scenic course has rolling, oceanside character, although you can't actually see the ocean. Cypress trees and bunkers border every hole. The course is tight, and accuracy is vital. Par-3s are the key to success here. The 180-yard driving range is for iron practice only. In 1999 the course underwent major renovations, including upgrades to the irrigation and drainage systems, bunker renovations, a

new pro shop, bar and grill, snack bar, and locker rooms.

Play Policy and Fees: Green fees are $45 Monday–Thursday, $55 Friday, and $70 weekends and holidays. Twilight rates and monthly junior cards are available, as are memberships. Carts are additional.

Tees and Yardage: *Men:* Black: yardage 6034, par 71, rating 70.2, slope 129; Gold: yardage 5813, par 71, rating 69.2, slope 127; *Women:* Silver: yardage 5514, par 72, rating 72.6, slope 127.

Tee Times: Reservations can be booked seven days in advance. For a $5 charge, reservations can be made 30 days out.

Dress Code: Appropriate attire and soft spikes are preferred.

Tournaments: A 20-player minimum is required to book a tournament. Events should be scheduled 12 months in advance. The banquet facility can accommodate up to 350 people.

Directions: From Santa Cruz, drive seven miles south on Highway 1. Exit on Rio Del Mar and go right. Turn left on Clubhouse Drive.

Contact: 610 Clubhouse Drive, Aptos, CA 95003, pro shop 831/688-3214, fax 831/688-3587.

5 SPRING HILLS GOLF CLUB

Architect: Hank Schimpeler, 1965

18 holes   **Public**   **$30-40**

🏌️📷💲🏌️🛒⛳

Monterey Peninsula and Vicinity map, page 194

Situated in the foothills, this challenging course is tight with lots of trees. The many doglegs make placement important. The back nine is rolling and scenic. During your round you may see deer, bobcats, rabbits, quail, coyotes, foxes, and hawks in this country setting. The clubhouse is an old farmhouse built in 1911. Some of the tees were rebuilt in 2004.

Play Policy and Fees: Green fees are $30 Monday–Thursday, $33 Friday, and $40 weekends and holidays. Twilight and senior rates are available. Carts are additional.

Tees and Yardage: *Men:* Blue: yardage 6015, par 71, rating 70.0, slope 127; White: yardage 5883,

par 71, rating 69.6, slope 125; *Women:* Red: yardage 5407, par 71, rating 74.9, slope 128.

Tee Times: Reservations can be booked one month in advance.

Dress Code: Shirts and nonmetal spikes are required.

Tournaments: Shotgun tournaments are available weekdays only. A 16-player minimum is required to book a tournament.

Directions: From south of Watsonville on Highway 1, take the Green Valley Road exit, drive four or five miles to Casserly Road, and turn right. Drive one mile to Smith Road and turn left. From north of Watsonville on Highway 1, take the Airport Boulevard exit. Go two miles and turn left onto Green Valley Road. Go two miles and turn right on Casserly Road. Turn left on Smith Road.

Contact: 501 Spring Hills Drive, Watsonville, CA 95076, pro shop 831/724-1404, fax 831/724-1474.

6 CORDEVALLE

Architect: Robert Trent Jones Jr., 1999
18 holes   Private/Resort $85–195

Monterey Peninsula and Vicinity map, page 194

Set in rolling hills dotted with native oaks, this course is truly inspiring. There is nothing fancy about it—what you see is what you get. The fairways are wide enough to hit driver and even provide players with ample bail-out areas. But if you cut a corner or miss the fairway in the wrong spot, you'll find yourself in a fairway bunker, a creek, or the thick native grasses. The greens are subtle and roll true, but leave the ball in the wrong spot and you'll have to work for a two-putt. Although the rough isn't long around the greens, it's dense and tricky. Hitting it over the side of the green will spell disaster. With multiple sets of tees, this is a layout every skill level can enjoy. The golf course is a treat in and of itself, but combined with the excellent lodge, dining, and spa here, the overall resort experience at CordeValle is one of the best in the state.

Play Policy and Fees: Guests of the Lodge at CordeValle can play here for $155. Otherwise, members and guests only. Green fees for accompanied guests are $85, while unaccompanied guests are $195. Carts or caddies are additional. Individual and corporate memberships are available.

Tees and Yardage: *Men:* Black: yardage 7169, par 72, rating 75.1, slope 138; Green: yardage 6703, par 72, rating 73.1, slope 134; Silver: yardage 6096, par 72, rating 70.0, slope 127; *Women:* Gold: yardage 5385, par 72, rating 71.0, slope 120.

Tee Times: Lodge guests should make arrangements through the concierge.

Dress Code: Appropriate golf attire and nonmetal spikes are required.

Tournaments: Only member-sponsored tournaments are allowed.

Directions: From San Jose, take U.S. 101 south to Morgan Hill. Take the San Martin exit and head west. Turn left on Monterey Avenue, then right on Highland Drive to the course.

Contact: 1 CordeValle Club Drive, San Martin, CA 95046, pro shop 408/695-4590, www.cordevalle.com.

7 EAGLE RIDGE GOLF CLUB

Architect: Golf Plan and Johnny Miller, 1999
18 holes   Public $65–90

Monterey Peninsula and Vicinity map, page 194

This course is set against the hills and features rolling fairways, native oaks, and dramatic fairway and greenside bunkers. There are no long carries for the average player, but for the low handicapper the course will play close to 7000 yards. On some holes, golfers can rip the driver without fear of needing pinpoint accuracy; on other holes, players would be foolish to even think about pulling a driver out of the bag. Around the greens, you are given friendly areas for errant shots, but if you bail out and miss the green on the wrong side, trouble awaits. The greens are undulating but not overly sloped.

The course features a 25,000-square-foot club-house that can hold banquets, business meetings, and special events.

Play Policy and Fees: Green fees are $65 Monday–Thursday and $90 Friday–Sunday and holidays. Twilight, super twilight, senior, and junior rates available. Carts are additional and required on weekends and holidays.

Tees and Yardage: *Men:* Black: yardage 7005, par 72, rating 74.2, slope 143; Blue: yardage 6665, par 72, rating 73.0, slope 138; White: yardage 6290, par 72, rating 71.6, slope 129; Yellow: yardage 5959, par 72, rating 70.1, slope 126; *Women:* Green: yardage 5546, par 72, rating 72.2, slope 128; Burgundy: yardage 5102, par 72, rating 69.6, slope 119.

Tee Times: Reservations may be made up to 30 days in advance.

Dress Code: Collared shirts and nonmetal spikes are required. Walking shorts are permitted.

Tournaments: Outside events are welcome. A full-time employee is on hand to assist, and the banquet facility can accommodate 240 people. Tournaments may be booked up to a year in advance.

Directions: From San Jose, follow U.S. 101 to Gilroy, take the Masten exit, and head west. Take a left on Santa Teresa and follow it for three miles. Turn right on Club Drive to the course.

Contact: 2951 Club Drive, Gilroy, CA 95020, pro shop 408/846-4531, fax 408/846-4532, www.eagleridgegc.com.

8 GILROY GOLF COURSE

Architect: Course designed, 1920

9 holes   **Public**   **$22–32**

🏌️ 🏆 🍴 ⛳ 🛺 🏌️

Monterey Peninsula and Vicinity map, page 194

This mature nine-hole course sits in oak-studded foothills. The terrain is rolling and hilly, with tricky, small greens. There are some very nice panoramic views of the valley. No water comes into play, but significant elevation change keeps play lively.

Play Policy and Fees: Green fees are $22 weekdays and $32 weekends and holidays. Twilight, senior, and junior rates are available.

Tees and Yardage: *Men:* Regular: yardage 3009, par 35, rating 34.3, slope 114; White: *Women:* Forward: yardage 2701, par 36, rating 35.1, slope 110.

Tee Times: Reservations can be booked seven days in advance.

Dress Code: Appropriate attire and soft spikes are required.

Tournaments: This course is available for outside tournaments.

Directions: From U.S. 101, drive two miles west on Hecker Pass Highway (Highway 152) in Gilroy. The course is on the right.

Contact: 2695 Hecker Pass Highway, Gilroy, CA 95020, pro shop 408/848-0490, fax 408/848-1382, www.gilroygolfcourse.com.

9 GAVILAN GOLF COURSE

Architect: Bob Ewing, 1969

9 holes   **Public**   **$13–23**

🏌️ 🏆 🍴 ⛳ 🛺 🏌️

Monterey Peninsula and Vicinity map, page 194

This course, owned by Gavilan Community College, dates back to the 1960s. It is a short, mostly flat course and excellent for beginners. The greens are small, tricky, and challenging.

Play Policy and Fees: Green fees are $13 for nine holes and $18 for 18 holes weekdays, $17 for nine holes and $23 for 18 holes weekends. Senior and junior rates are available. Carts additional.

Tees and Yardage: *Men (18 holes):* White/Blue: yardage 3794, par 60, rating 60.1, slope 100; *Women (18 holes):* Red/Yellow: yardage 3578, par 62, rating 59.5, slope 92.

Tee Times: Reservations can be booked seven days in advance.

Dress Code: Shirts must be worn.

Tournaments: This course is available for outside tournaments.

Directions: From U.S. 101 in Gilroy, take the Castro Valley exit and follow it until it dead-ends.

Turn right on Santa Teresa Boulevard. Enter at the south gate at the Gavilan Community College campus. **Contact:** 5055 Santa Teresa Boulevard, Gilroy, CA 95020, pro shop 408/846-4920, fax 408/846-4919, www.gavilangolf.com.

10 PAJARO VALLEY GOLF CLUB

Architect: Floyd McFarland, 1926

| 18 holes | Semiprivate | $45-65 |

Monterey Peninsula and Vicinity map, page 194

The serene and verdant Pajaro Valley provides an exquisite setting for this beautiful course. Dating back to the late 1920s, Pajaro Valley is short and wide, with rolling fairways. Several holes were lengthened in 2002, adding more than 200 yards of overall length to the layout. Mature groves of Monterey cypress trees present a challenge for every golfer. The 12th hole, a long par-4, features a three-tiered green surrounded by bunkers. Golfers are always pleased with their experience here.

Play Policy and Fees: Green fees are $45 Monday–Thursday and $65 Friday–Sunday and holidays. Twilight and junior rates are available. Carts are $17 per rider. Memberships are available.

Tees and Yardage: *Men:* Blue: yardage 6488, par 72, rating 69.5, slope 118; White: yardage 6237, par 72, rating 68.3, slope 116; *Women:* Red: yardage 5747, par 72, rating 72.3, slope 121.

Tee Times: Reservations for weekends and holidays are taken a week in advance.

Dress Code: Nonmetal spikes are mandatory.

Tournaments: This course is available for outside tournaments. Events may be scheduled 12 months in advance. The banquet facility can accommodate 100 people.

Directions: Take Highway 1 south past Watsonville. After the Riverside Drive exit, head to the top of the hill where the lanes merge. Turn left at the flashing yellow lights on Salinas Road and go three-fourths of a mile to the course on the right.

Contact: 967 Salinas Road, Royal Oaks, CA 95076, pro shop 831/724-3851, fax 831/724-9394.

11 SAN JUAN OAKS GOLF CLUB

Architect: Fred Couples and Gene Bates, 1996

| 18 holes | Public | $55-80 |

Monterey Peninsula and Vicinity map, page 194

Every hole of this well-designed, old-style **BEST** course is different. The layout meanders through rolling hills, where players encounter native oaks, plenty of bunkers, and undulating, well-paced greens. Don't let the scenic beauty of San Juan Oaks fool you; it is a good, fair test of golf. Some of Fred Couples's mementos are featured in the clubhouse. A second course has been planned here for some time.

Play Policy and Fees: Green fees are $55 Monday–Friday, $80 weekends and holidays. Carts are additional. Twilight, junior, and senior rates are available, as are special rates for San Benito County residents.

Tees and Yardage: *Men:* Black: yardage 7133, par 72, rating 75.6, slope 145; Blue: yardage 6712, par 72, rating 73.3, slope 139; White: yardage 6342, par 72, rating 71.7, slope 133; Gold: yardage 5785, par 72, rating 69.2, slope 127; *Women:* Red: yardage 4770, par 72, rating 68.1, slope 120.

Tee Times: Reservations can be booked one month in advance.

Dress Code: Collared shirts and nonmetal spikes are required. No denim; slacks preferred. No tank tops or cutoffs are allowed.

Tournaments: Shotgun tournaments are available weekdays only. A 24-player minimum is needed to book an event. Carts are mandatory. Events should be scheduled six months in advance. A spectacular mission-style clubhouse is available for banquets, weddings, and conferences and can accommodate 300 people.

Directions: From San Jose, take U.S. 101 to Highway 156 east. Follow Highway 156 four miles east of San Juan Bautista. Turn right on Union Road. The golf course entry road is one-quarter mile along on the right.

Contact: 3825 Union Road, Hollister, CA 95023 (P.O. Box 1060, San Juan Bautista, CA 95045), pro shop 831/636-6113, fax 831/636-6114, www.sanjuanoaks.com.

12 RIDGEMARK GOLF & COUNTRY CLUB

Architect: Richard Bigler, 1972

36 holes   Semiprivate   **$55–67**

> **Monterey Peninsula and Vicinity map, page 194**

These par-72 courses hug the rolling terrain of the Hollister-area foothills and feature large, contoured greens. The Diablo Course is steeper and requires more placement. It's shorter than the Gabilan Course and also has more water hazards. The Gabilan Course is flatter and less deceptive. Both provide a nice round of golf in a pleasant setting.

Ridgemark has 32 lodging units overlooking the golf course. For reservations, call 800/637-8151.

Play Policy and Fees: Green fees are $55 Monday–Friday, $67 weekends and holidays. Twilight rates are available after 3 P.M. Courses rotate daily between membership and public play. Call to find out which course is open for public play.

Tees and Yardage: Gabilan Course—*Men:* Blue: yardage 6721, par 72, rating 72.8, slope 131; White: yardage 6336, par 72, rating 71.0, slope 128; *Women:* Gold: yardage 5949, par 72, rating 73.7, slope 124; Red: yardage 5542, par 72, rating 71.3, slope 118. Diablo Course—*Men:* Blue: yardage 6582, par 72, rating 72.6, slope 126; White: yardage 6099, par 71, rating 70.3, slope 124; *Women:* Gold: yardage 5807, par 72, rating 73.6, slope 126; Red: yardage 5441, par 72, rating 71.8, slope 122.

Tee Times: Reservations can be booked 30 days in advance.

Dress Code: Collared shirts are required, and

slacks are preferred. No jeans are allowed on the course.

Tournaments: A 16-player minimum is needed to book an event. Tournaments should be scheduled 10 months in advance. The banquet facility holds 250 people.

Directions: From U.S. 101 south, take the Highway 25 exit and drive 13 miles to the golf course. The course is five miles south of Hollister.

Contact: 3800 Airline Highway, Hollister, CA 95023, pro shop 831/637-1010, fax 831/636-3168, www.ridgemark.com.

13 BOLADO PARK GOLF COURSE

Architect: W. I. Hawkins and Col. George E. Sikes, 1928; rebuilt George Santana, 1958

9 holes   Public   **$15–20**

> **Monterey Peninsula and Vicinity map, page 194**

This flat course in rural San Benito County is great for practice and as a place for locals to play. Although it was established in 1928, the course was rebuilt in 1958 in its present location by George Santana. Set in a quiet valley, the course offers nice views of the surrounding mountains.

Play Policy and Fees: Green fees are $15 weekdays and $20 weekends. This fee allows you to play as many holes as you like. Student and senior rates are available. Carts are $12 for nine holes and $20 for 18 holes.

Tees and Yardage: *Men (18 holes):* yardage 5985, par 70, rating 67.9, slope 114; *Women (18 holes):* yardage 5636, par 70, rating 70.2, slope 111.

Tee Times: Reservations are not accepted. All play is on a first-come, first-served basis.

Dress Code: Nonmetal spikes are encouraged.

Tournaments: This course is available for outside tournaments.

Directions: This course is five miles south of Hollister on Highway 25/Airline Highway in Tres Pinos.

Contact: 7777 Airline Highway 25 (P.O. Box 419), Tres Pinos, CA 95075, pro shop 831/628-9995.

14 SALINAS GOLF & COUNTRY CLUB

Architect: Opened 1929

18 holes   **Private**   **$60–70**

Monterey Peninsula and Vicinity map, page 194

This short course is tight and hilly, with small, tricky greens. It has lots of trees. Many up-and-down holes require finesse shots from side-hill lies. It's a good test for the irons and the short game. This course was the site of a battle fought by General Fremont during the Mexican-American War. In 2004, new tee boxes were constructed to provide additional length to the layout.

Play Policy and Fees: Reciprocal play is accepted with members of other private clubs. On weekdays, guest fees are $60, on weekends $70. Carts are additional. The course is closed on Monday.

Tees and Yardage: *Men:* Blue: yardage 6102, par 72, rating 69.4, slope 123; White: yardage 6017, par 72, rating 69.0, slope 122; *Women:* Red: yardage 5621, par 72, rating 72.5, slope 125.

Tee Times: Reciprocators should have their club pro call to make arrangements.

Dress Code: No blue jeans are allowed, and shirts must have collars. Nonmetal spikes are required.

Tournaments: Shotgun tournaments are available some weekdays only. Carts are required. A 50-player minimum is required to book a tournament.

Directions: From U.S. 101 in Salinas, take the Boronda Road exit. Turn right on Main Street (the first stoplight) and follow it to San Juan Grade Road. Turn left on San Juan Grade Road and drive 2.5 miles to the course.

Contact: 475 San Juan Grade Road, Salinas, CA 93912 (P.O. Box 4277, Salinas, CA 93906), pro shop 831/449-1527, clubhouse 831/449-1526, www.salinascountryclub.com.

15 TWIN CREEKS GOLF COURSE

Architect: Halsey Daray Golf, 2000

9 holes   **Public**   **$17–22**

Monterey Peninsula and Vicinity map, page 194

Twin Creeks is a nine-hole, executive-length course with a par of 31. Most greens are large and user-friendly. The course has five par-3s and four par-4s, making it an excellent choice for families, beginners, and any golfer wishing to practice his or her short game.

Play Policy and Fees: Fees for county residents are $17 weekdays, $20 weekends. Nonresident fees are $20 weekdays, $22 weekends. Call for other rates.

Tees and Yardage: *Men:* Back: yardage 1859, par 31, rating n/a, slope n/a; *Women:* Forward: yardage 1291, par 31, rating n/a, slope n/a.

Tee Times: Reservations recommended for weekend tee times only. Otherwise, first-come, first-served.

Dress Code: The dress code is casual, but no tank tops are allowed.

Tournaments: Tournaments and other events are welcome with a minimum of 10 days advance notice.

Directions: In Salinas, take the Laurel Drive exit off Highway 101. Drive east to Constitution Boulevard. Turn left, then take a right on Beacon Hill Drive, which dead-ends into the course.

Contact: 1551 Beacon Hill Drive, Salinas, CA 93905, pro shop 831/758-7333.

16 SALINAS FAIRWAYS GOLF COURSE

Architect: Jack Fleming, 1953; Steve Halsey, 1998

18 holes   **Public**   **$25–35**

Monterey Peninsula and Vicinity map, page 194

Situated on 140 acres adjacent to Salinas Municipal Airport, the terrain is mostly flat with some nice tree cover. This is a popular course for local residents. It is not too long, not too tough. It is pretty straightforward from the tees. What you see is what you get.

Play Policy and Fees: Fees for county residents are $25 weekdays, $30 weekends. Nonresident fees are $30 weekdays, $35 weekends. Call for other rates.

Tees and Yardage: *Men:* Blue: yardage 6479, par 71, rating 69.8, slope 115; White: yardage 6230, par 71, rating 68.7, slope 113; *Women:* Gold: yardage 5460, par 71, rating 69.7, slope 109, Red: yardage 5121, par 71, rating 67.9, slope 105.

Tee Times: Reservations recommended for weekend tee times only. Otherwise, first-come, first-served.

Dress Code: The dress code is casual.

Tournaments: Tournaments welcome. Please inquire

Directions: In Salinas, take the Airport Boulevard exit off Highway 101. Turn left on Skyway in one-half mile to the course.

Contact: 45 Skyway Boulevard, Salinas, CA 93905, pro shop 831/758-7300, fax 831/758-7162, www.golfsalinas.com.

17 BAYONET & BLACK HORSE GOLF COURSES

Architect: Gen. Robert McClure, 1954 (Bayonet); Gen. Edwin Carns, 1963 (Black Horse)

36 holes   Public $57–97

Monterey Peninsula and Vicinity map, page 194

Both of these are excellent choices and should be on your play list when in the area. They will both challenge even the top professional from the back tees, and have done so in various tournaments over the years. The Bayonet Course is long and difficult. The front nine is longer and more open, while the back nine has several tight doglegs and tricky greens. The Black Horse Course is shorter and somewhat more forgiving. It has a meandering layout bordered by tall trees and bunkers. Both courses offer ocean views, rolling fairways, and lots of trees. They are always in great condition and well run.

Play Policy and Fees: November–March green fees are $57 Monday–Friday, $77 weekends and holidays. April–October green fees are $72 Monday–Friday, $97 weekends and holidays. Twilight, junior, and senior rates are available. Carts are additional.

Tees and Yardage: Bayonet—*Men:* Gold: yardage 7117, par 72, rating 75.6, slope 136; Patriot: yardage 6831, par 72, rating 74.0, slope 134; Pearl: yardage 6496, par 72, rating 72.5, slope 131; *Women:* Crimson: yardage 5763, par 72, rating 69.2, slope 123. Black Horse—*Men:* Gold: yardage 7009, par 72, rating 74.9, slope 137; Patriot: yardage 6527, par 72, rating 72.4, slope 135; Pearl: yardage 6175, par 72, rating 70.8, slope 131; *Women:* Crimson: yardage 5628, par 72, rating 73.0, slope 126.

Tee Times: Reservations can be made 14 days in advance with no fee, and 15–29 days in advance for a fee of $10 per player.

Dress Code: Collared shirts are required. Nonmetal spikes are preferred.

Tournaments: These courses are available for tournaments and events. The clubhouse includes a full restaurant and banquet facility that accommodates 144 people.

Directions: The main gate of Fort Ord is off Highway 1 at Light Fighter Drive. Drive through the gate and turn right on North South Road. Follow North South Road and turn right on McClure Way.

Contact: 1 McClure Way, Seaside, CA 93955, pro shop 831/899-7271, fax 831/393-3008, www.bayonetblackhorse.com.

18 PACIFIC GROVE GOLF COURSE

Architect: Jack Neville, 1932

18 holes   Public $32–38

Monterey Peninsula Detail map, page 195

This tight, scenic, oceanside course has a Scottish links-style flavor and is fun to play. The front nine weaves through the forest and is flanked by trees, while the back nine is bordered by sand dunes and an ice plant.

An old lighthouse stands guard over the course. The course used to be one of Monterey Peninsula's best-kept secrets, but with more and more rounds played each year, these days you may want to make reservations.

Play Policy and Fees: Green fees are $32 Monday–Thursday and $38 Friday–Sunday and holidays. Twilight, senior, junior, and nine-hole rates are available. Carts are $30 and optional.

Tees and Yardage: *Men:* Blue: yardage 5732, par 70, rating 67.5, slope 118; White: yardage 5571, par 70, rating 66.8, slope 116; *Women:* Red: yardage 5305, par 70, rating 70.2, slope 116.

Tee Times: Reservations are recommended seven days in advance.

Dress Code: Casual attire is acceptable.

Tournaments: A 20-player minimum is required to book a tournament. Carts are required. Events should be scheduled 18 months in advance.

Directions: From Highway 1 in Monterey, take Highway 68/W. R. Holman (Pacific Grove Highway) west. Remain in the left lane after the second stoplight and continue on Highway 68 to Asilomar. Turn right at Asilomar Avenue and follow it to the cemetery and lighthouse. The clubhouse is across from the lighthouse.

Contact: 77 Asilomar Boulevard, Pacific Grove, CA 93950, pro shop 831/648-5777.

19 THE LINKS AT SPANISH BAY

Architect: Tom Watson, Robert Trent Jones Jr., and Sandy Tatum, 1987

18 holes   Resort $215–240

Monterey Peninsula Detail map, page 195

The most underrated of the Pebble Beach courses, Spanish Bay is a fast-rolling layout tailored in the pure Scottish fashion, complete with fescue grass fairways, pot bunkers, and mounds. Here the architects want golfers to hit run-up shots, keeping the ball low. Several holes flank the ocean, so this strategy is especially advantageous when the wind kicks up. This is one of the most authentic Scottish-links courses in America. One of the gems of California golf.

For reservations at the Lodge at Pebble Beach or the Inn at Spanish Bay, call 800/654-9300.

Play Policy and Fees: Green fees are $215 for Pebble Beach Resort guests and $240 (cart included) for the public. Players may carry their own bag, and caddies are available.

Tees and Yardage: *Men:* Blue: yardage 6821, par 72, rating 74.1, slope 146; Gold: yardage 6422, par 72, rating 72.0, slope 137; White: yardage 6043, par 72, rating 70.3, slope 129; *Women:* Red: yardage 5332, par 72, rating 72.1, slope 129.

Tee Times: Resort guests may make tee times with their room reservations 18 months in advance. Outside players (two or more) may make reservations 60 days in advance. For tee times, call 800/654-9300.

Dress Code: No cutoffs are allowed, and collared shirts are required. Soft spikes are preferred.

Tournaments: A 16-player minimum is required for a tournament. Events should be scheduled 24 months in advance. The banquet facility can accommodate 900 people.

Directions: From Highway 1 in Monterey, exit at Highway 68/W. R. Holman (Pacific Grove/Carmel Highway) west. The highway becomes Forest Avenue. Turn left at Sunset Drive and drive to 17-Mile Drive. Turn left and drive one-eighth mile to the gate. The course is 500 yards past the gate on the right.

Contact: 2700 17-Mile Drive (P.O. Box 658), Pebble Beach, CA 93953, pro shop 831/647-7495, fax 831/644-7956, www.pebblebeach.com.

20 MONTEREY PENINSULA COUNTRY CLUB

Architect: Seth J. Raynor, 1926 (Dunes), redesign Rees Jones, 1999; Bob Baldock, 1959 (Shore), redesign Michael Strantz, 2004

36 holes   Private

Monterey Peninsula Detail map, page 195

These meandering, scenic courses are flanked by pine trees, the ocean, and sand dunes. The greens are tricky and immaculate, with a lot of undulation. Keep the ball below the hole. The picturesque Dunes Course is longer and situated farther inland. It was used for the Bing Crosby National Pro-Am for 18 years. The Shore Course is shorter and tighter; it was completely redesigned by Mike Strantz in 2004. The land on which this course resides flanks the ocean and is more exposed to the elements. At press time, the Shore Course was under construction.

Play Policy and Fees: All guests must be member-sponsored. No reciprocal play is accepted.

Tees and Yardage: Dunes—*Men:* Gold: yardage 6762, par 72, rating 73.7, slope 135; Black: yardage 6430, par 72, rating 72.2, slope 131; Blue: yardage 6108, par 72, rating 70.5, slope 127; *Women:* White: yardage 5866, par 74, rating 74.4, slope 134; Red: yardage 5582, par 72, rating 72.8, slope 130.

Tee Times: Not applicable.

Dress Code: No denim is allowed, and skirts must be knee-length. Women may wear knee-length shorts. Nonmetal spikes are required.

Tournaments: These courses are not available for outside events.

Directions: From Highway 1 in Monterey, take Highway 68/W.R. Holman (Pacific Grove exit) to David Avenue. Turn left on David Avenue and drive less than one-quarter mile. Turn right on Congress Avenue. Turn left at Forest Lodge Road and drive to the entrance gate of 17-Mile Drive. Head south on Sloat Road and turn right on Club Road.

Contact: 3000 Club Road, Pebble Beach, CA 93953, pro shop 831/372-8141, fax 831/655-4765.

21 POPPY HILLS GOLF COURSE

Architect: Robert Trent Jones Jr., 1986
18 holes   Public $50–160

🏌️ 📷 🍴 🛏️ 🚙 🏊 ♨️

Monterey Peninsula Detail map, page 195

This pretty course is long and tight, with **BEST** plenty of trees, water, and sand. The large, undulating greens are well guarded by bunkers. Many of the greens are flanked by areas that give the player an option to chip or

putt. On most holes a golfer can play it safe or go for broke, especially on the par-5 ninth and 18th holes. This is the home of the Northern California Golf Association. This course is one of three in rotation for the annual AT&T Pebble Beach National Pro-Am.

Play Policy and Fees: Public green fees are $130 Monday–Thursday, $160 Friday–Sunday and holidays. NCGA member green fees are $50 Monday–Thursday, $62 Friday–Sunday and holidays. SCGA members receive a discount from the public rates. Carts are additional.

Tees and Yardage: *Men:* Blue: yardage 6833, par 72, rating 74.6, slope 144; White: yardage 6237, par 72, rating 71.5, slope 138; *Women:* Gold: yardage 5403, par 72, rating 71.6, slope 131.

Tee Times: Reservations are available one month in advance, or call the pro shop for available tee times.

Dress Code: Collared shirts and nonmetal spikes are required. Shorts are acceptable, but jeans are not permitted.

Tournaments: Group reservations are available one year in advance. The banquet facility can accommodate 120 people.

Directions: From Highway 1, take the Pebble Beach exit and proceed to the gate for instructions.

Contact: 3200 Lopez Road, Pebble Beach, CA 93953, pro shop 831/622-8239, www.poppy hillsgolf.com.

22 SPYGLASS HILL GOLF COURSE

Architect: Robert Trent Jones Sr., 1966
18 holes   Resort $265–290

🏌️ 📷 🍴 🛏️ 🚙 🏊 ♨️

Monterey Peninsula Detail map, page 195

This long, demanding, classic design is **BEST** both a beauty and a beast. Used annually for the AT&T Pebble Beach National Pro-Am, it almost always produces the highest scoring average. The first five holes wind through sand dunes and offer magnificent ocean views. It's surrounded by Monterey pines. The sometimes-small, undulating greens are well protected. The names given to each of the holes were derived from Robert Louis Stevenson's classic, *Treasure Island*. You'll find Treasure Island on the first hole, Long John Silver on the 14th (a double dogleg par-5), and Black Dog on the 16th (an infamous par-4). Spyglass is part of the AT&T Pebble Beach Pro-Am and the annual site of the NCGA Amateur Championship. It hosted qualifying rounds for the 1999 U.S. Amateur and is annually ranked in the country's top 100 courses. It should certainly be near the top of your list of "must-play" courses in California.

For reservations at the Lodge at Pebble Beach or the Inn at Spanish Bay, call 800/654-9300.

Play Policy and Fees: Green fees are $265 for Pebble Beach Resort guests and $290 for others. Carts are included.

Tees and Yardage: *Men:* Blue: yardage 6862, par 72, rating 75.2, slope 146; Gold: yardage 6480, par 72, rating 73.0, slope 144; White: yardage 6117, par 72, rating 71.4, slope 137; *Women:* Red: yardage 5380, par 72, rating 72.9, slope 132.

Tee Times: Resort guests may book tee times 18 months ahead, and nonguests may book 30 days ahead. For tee times, call 800/654-9300.

Dress Code: Golf attire is encouraged. No blue jeans are allowed. Soft spikes are preferred.

Tournaments: Please inquire.

Directions: From Highway 1, take the Pebble Beach exit and drive to the Highway 1 gate for instructions and a map.

Contact: Spyglass Hill Road (P.O. Box 658), Pebble Beach, CA 93953, pro shop 831/625-8563, fax 831/622-1308, www.pebblebeach.com.

23 PETER HAY GOLF COURSE

Architect: Peter Hay, 1957

9 holes   Public $20

Monterey Peninsula Detail map, page 195

This par-3 course provides an excellent opportunity to sharpen your short game. It is short and tight, with some hills and lots of trees; the longest hole is 118 yards. The course is named for the late Peter Hay, the designer and longtime pro at Pebble Beach Golf Links. It's fun, and besides, not much else at Pebble Beach is only $20!

For reservations at the Lodge at Pebble Beach or the Inn at Spanish Bay, call 800/654-9300.

Play Policy and Fees: Green fees are $20 for all-day play. Juniors under 12 golf free when accompanied by an adult.

Tees and Yardage: *Men and Women:* yardage 819, par 27, rating n/a, slope n/a.

Tee Times: Reservations are not accepted. All play is on a first-come, first-served basis.

Dress Code: Soft spikes are preferred.

Tournaments: A 16-player minimum is needed to book an event. Tournaments should be scheduled three months in advance. The banquet facility can accommodate 400 people.

Directions: From Highway 1, take the Pebble Beach exit. The guard will give you instructions and a map. The course is across from Pebble Beach Golf Links.

Contact: P.O. Box 658, Pebble Beach, CA 93953, pro shop 831/625-8518, clubhouse 831/622-8799, fax 800/644-7960, www.pebble beach.com.

24 CYPRESS POINT CLUB

Architect: Alister Mackenzie, 1928

18 holes   Private

Monterey Peninsula Detail map, page 195

This spectacular course is the best-known work of Scottish architect Alister Mackenzie, who designed it in 1928. Flanked by sand and sea, the course makes the most of its natural resources. The greens are fast and undulating. The famous par-3 16th hole requires a scenic and spectacular 200-yard carry over the ocean. The shorter par-3 15th hole flanks the ocean and is one of the prettiest in the world. Equally phenomenal is the par-4 17th, with the ocean to the right. The club is very exclusive. The course was used for the AT&T Pebble Beach National Pro-Am from 1947 to 1990.

Play Policy and Fees: Members and guests only. No reciprocal play is accepted.

Tees and Yardage: *Men:* Blue: yardage 6524, par 72, rating 72.1, slope 146; White: yardage 6332, par 72, rating 71.3, slope 136; *Women:* Green: yardage 5816, par 75, rating 74.9, slope 138.

Tee Times: Not applicable.

Dress Code: Appropriate golf attire is required.

Tournaments: This course is not available for outside events.

Directions: From Highway 1, take the Pacific Grove exit. At the first stop sign, drive to the Carmel Hill gate leading into Pebble Beach. Ask for instructions and a map at the gate.

Contact: 3150 17-Mile Drive (P.O. Box 466), Pebble Beach, CA 93953, pro shop 831/624-2223, fax 831/624-5057.

25 PEBBLE BEACH GOLF LINKS
Architect: Jack Neville, 1919
18 holes   **Resort**   **$380–405**

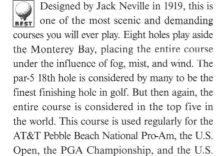

Monterey Peninsula Detail map, page 195

Designed by Jack Neville in 1919, this is one of the most scenic and demanding courses you will ever play. Eight holes play aside the Monterey Bay, placing the entire course under the influence of fog, mist, and wind. The par-5 18th hole is considered by many to be the finest finishing hole in golf. But then again, the entire course is considered in the top five in the world. This course is used regularly for the AT&T Pebble Beach National Pro-Am, the U.S. Open, the PGA Championship, and the U.S. Amateur. Play it with a caddie; it's worth the money for the experience.

For reservations at the Lodge at Pebble Beach or the Inn at Spanish Bay, call 800/654-9300.

Play Policy and Fees: Green fees for Pebble Beach Resort guests are $380, including cart. Fees for nonguests are also $405, including cart. Caddies are available.

Tees and Yardage: *Men:* Blue: yardage 6737, par 72, rating 73.8, slope 142; Gold: yardage 6348, par 72, rating 72.3, slope 137; White:

yardage 6116, par 72, rating 71.2, slope 134; *Women:* Red: yardage 5198, par 72, rating 71.9, slope 130.

Tee Times: Reservations are required. They may be booked 18 months in advance for lodge guests and one day in advance for the general public. Call 800/654-9300 to book tee times. The pro shop does not make reservations.

Dress Code: Collared shirts are required. Nonmetal spikes are recommended, and no jeans are allowed.

Tournaments: Tournament groups must stay on-site, and three years advance booking is recommended.

Directions: From Highway 1, take the Pebble Beach exit and drive to the Pebble Beach Resort gate for instructions and a map.

Contact: P.O. Box 658, Pebble Beach, CA 93953, pro shop 831/622-8723, fax 831/622-8795, www.pebblebeach.com.

26 DEL MONTE GOLF COURSE
Architect: Charles Maud, 1897
18 holes   **Public**   **$95**

Monterey Peninsula and Vicinity map, page 194

Originally built as a nine-hole course in 1897, Del Monte was expanded to 18 holes in 1901. It was reported in the early days to be the first course in the world to have green fairways throughout the seasons. This inland course offers a meandering, hilly layout with lots of trees and tight doglegs. The short but infuriating par-4 18th hole looks like an easy birdie, but don't count on it. It will drive you crazy. In 1997, Del Monte Golf Course celebrated its 100th birthday. This is thought to be the oldest course west of the Mississippi in continuous use. Many tees were rebuilt and extensive work was done around the course in 2003, and it is now in very good condition. The forward tees have been shortened, making the design more friendly to women golfers.

For reservations at the Lodge at Pebble Beach or the Inn at Spanish Bay, call 800/654-9300.

Play Policy and Fees: Green fees are $95 to walk. Carts are $20 per rider. The course has special arrangements with other hotels in the area, and guests of those hotels receive courtesy discount rates. Please inquire. Caddies are available upon request.

Tees and Yardage: *Men:* Blue: yardage 6339, par 72, rating 70.8, slope 123; White: yardage 6069, par 72, rating 69.5, slope 115; *Women:* Red: yardage 5429, par 72, rating 70.8, slope 115.

Tee Times: Reservations can be booked 60 days in advance.

Dress Code: Golf attire is encouraged. No cutoff shorts or tank tops allowed. Nonmetal spikes are preferred.

Tournaments: A 16-player minimum is required to book a tournament. Carts are required. The banquet facility can accommodate 180 people. Events can be booked 24 months in advance.

Directions: In Monterey heading south on Highway 1, take the central Monterey exit. Go left on Aguajito Road and go back under the highway. Turn left at Mark Thomas Drive and turn right at Sylvan Road to the course.

Contact: 1300 Sylvan Road, Monterey, CA 93940, pro shop 831/373-2700, fax 831/655-8792, www.pebblebeach.com.

27 PASADERA COUNTRY CLUB

Architect: Jack Nicklaus, 2000

18 holes   Private $250

Monterey Peninsula and Vicinity map, page 194

This course is built on the rolling, oak-studded hills typical of Central California. With its big landing areas and demanding greens, Pasadera is typical of newer Nicklaus designs. Some green complexes drop off sharply into yawning arroyos. Strong par-3s and some dramatically elevated tee boxes also enhance play on this beautiful course.

Play Policy and Fees: Pasadera is a private club, but it does accept limited public play for a fee of $250. Otherwise, members and guests only. No reciprocal play is accepted. Closed Monday.

Tees and Yardage: *Men:* Gold: yardage 6801, par 71, rating 72.8, slope 142; Combo: yardage 6417, par 71, rating 71.7, slope 140; Blue: yardage 6299, par 71, rating 71.0, slope 138; White: yardage 6009, par 71, rating 69.8, slope 132; *Women:* Red: yardage 5006, par 72, rating 69.6, slope 124.

Tee Times: Public tee times may be booked up to 10 days in advance by calling 831/647-2402.

Dress Code: Traditional golf attire and nonmetal spikes are required.

Tournaments: Some outside tournaments are accepted. They may be booked up to one year in advance.

Directions: Follow Highway 68, which runs between Salinas and Monterey. Turn north on York Road. This runs into Pasadera Drive and the golf club.

Contact: 100 Pasadera Drive, Monterey, CA 93940, pro shop 831/333-9590, fax 831/372-4486, www.pasadera.com.

28 LAGUNA SECA GOLF CLUB

Architect: Robert Trent Jones Sr. and Jr., 1970

18 holes   Public $65

Monterey Peninsula and Vicinity map, page 194

This challenging course has a number of elevated tees and greens. It's a sprawling course that follows the oak-studded coastal hills, and it will require every club in your bag—a great challenge! Laguna Seca is known as the "Sunshine Golf Course" because it has some of the best weather on the Monterey Peninsula. An extensive new driving range and practice area was completed in 2003.

Play Policy and Fees: Green fees are $65 every day. Twilight rates are $35. Carts cost $34. Annual memberships and "mini-memberships" are available.

Tees and Yardage: *Men:* Blue: yardage 6161, par 71, rating 70.7, slope 127; White: yardage 5739, par 71, rating 68.9, slope 122; *Women:* Red: yardage 5210, par 72, rating 70.2, slope 122.

Tee Times: Reservations can be booked at any time.

Dress Code: Appropriate golf attire is required. Nonmetal spikes are mandatory.

Tournaments: A 20-player minimum is required to book a tournament. Events should be scheduled 12 months in advance. A banquet facility is available that holds 200 people.

Directions: On the east side of Monterey off Highway 68, exit north on York Road and drive to the end.

Contact: 10520 York Road, Monterey, CA 93940, pro shop 831/373-3701, clubhouse 888/524-8629, fax 831/373-3899, www.laguna secagolf.com.

29 RANCHO CANADA GOLF CLUB

Architect: Robert Dean Putman, 1970
36 holes **Public** **$65–80**

Monterey Peninsula and Vicinity map, page 194

Nestled in the scenic Carmel River Valley, these beautiful courses are tight, with plenty of mature pine and oak trees. Both courses offer excellent greens that hold your approach shot and roll true. The West Course is tougher, tighter, and longer. The 15th hole is one of the tightest par-4s you'll ever play. The East Course is shorter, surrounded by trees, and crosses the Carmel River five times. Yard for yard, these are two of the better public courses in the area. Although they are similar in terrain, they complement each other well by providing distinct options in difficulty and length, so players of varying abilities are nicely accommodated.

Play Policy and Fees: Green fees are $80 for the West Course and $65 for the East Course. Carts are $34. Twilight rates available, as are yearly memberships, a popular option with locals.

Tees and Yardage: West Course—*Men:* Blue: yardage 6357, par 71, rating 71.4, slope 125; White: yardage 6121, par 71, rating 69.7, slope 121; *Women:* Red: yardage 5600, par 72, rating 71.9, slope 118. East Course—*Men:* Blue: yardage 6123, par 71, rating 69.8, slope 122; White: yardage 5843, par 71, rating 68.0, slope

118; *Women:* Red: yardage 5278, par 72, rating 69.4, slope 114.

Tee Times: Reservations are recommended but not required. They may be booked seven days in advance for weekends and holidays, and up to 30 days in advance for weekdays.

Dress Code: Collared shirts and nonmetal spikes are required.

Tournaments: This course is available for outside events that include a minimum of 20 players. The banquet facility can accommodate 400 people.

Directions: From Highway 1 in Carmel, take the Carmel Valley Road exit. Drive 1.5 miles east to the course. The entrance is on the right.

Contact: P.O. Box 22590, Carmel, CA 93922, pro shop 831/624-0111, fax 831/624-6635, www.ranchocanada.com.

30 MONTEREY PINES GOLF COURSE

Architect: Robert Muir Graves, 1962
18 holes **Public** **$12–24**

Monterey Peninsula and Vicinity map, page 194

This short, level course has narrow fairways and lots of trees. Four lakes come into play. The course has greatly improved conditions and has some of the best greens on the Monterey Peninsula. Monterey Pines is a good value for those wanting to play in this area. The course, formerly known as the U.S. Navy Course, is still operated by the military, but anyone can play here now.

Play Policy and Fees: Green fees for military personnel are $12. Green fees for civilians are $24. Carts are $12 per rider. Twilight rates available. No children under eight years of age are permitted.

Tees and Yardage: *Men:* Blue: yardage 5629, par 69, rating 66.9, slope 114; White: yardage 5413, par 69, rating 65.9, slope 112; *Women:* Red: yardage 5164, par 71, rating 69.3, slope 110.

Tee Times: Reservations can be made seven days in advance.

Dress Code: Appropriate golf attire and non-metal spikes are required.

Tournaments: This course is available for tournaments. A 24-player minimum is needed to book a tournament. Tournaments can be booked six months in advance.

Directions: From Highway 1 in Monterey, take the Casa Verde Way exit south to Fairgrounds Road. Turn right on Fairgrounds and continue to Garden Road, then turn left. The course is immediately on the left.

Contact: 1250 Garden Road, Monterey, CA 93943, pro shop 831/656-2167, fax 831/656-4516.

🟥31 TEHAMA GOLF CLUB

Architect: Jay Morrish, 1999
18 holes   **Private**

Monterey Peninsula and Vicinity map, page 194

Tehama is one of the more challenging courses to open in years. Off the tee on many holes, players must confront narrow, undulating fairways. There are few level lies anywhere and severe penalties await for those who miss the short grass. The tricky greens have breaks that even local knowledge doesn't help read.

Play Policy and Fees: Members and guests only. No reciprocal play is accepted.

Tees and Yardage: *Men:* Black: yardage 6498, par 72, rating 72.4, slope 139; Blue: yardage 6204, par 72, rating 71.2, slope 134; White: yardage 5911, par 72, rating 69.8, slope 131; *Women:* Red: yardage 5133, par 71, rating 70.8, slope 124.

Tee Times: Not applicable.

Dress Code: Appropriate golf attire is required.

Tournaments: Outside events are not allowed.

Directions: From Highway 1 near Carmel, take Highway 68 east toward Salinas. Make a right on Olmstead Road and a left on Via Malpaso to the front gate.

Contact: 25000 Via Malpaso, Carmel, CA 93923, pro shop 831/622-2250, fax 831/622-2201.

🟥32 QUAIL LODGE

Architect: Robert Muir Graves, 1963
18 holes   **Resort**   **$120–180**

Monterey Peninsula and Vicinity map, page 194

This is one of the most scenic courses in the Monterey Bay area, with weeping willows, lakes, and scenic plantings all around. The front nine is level, with generous landing areas off the tee—but most greens are usually well protected, requiring an accurate second shot. On the back nine you will find the fairways and greens getting smaller as your chances of hitting into a trap or water hazard become greater. Quail Lodge gives the average golfer a chance to score well, yet still remains a challenge for low handicappers. In July 2003, this classic Carmel Valley property reopened after a $25 million renovation that included rooms, common areas, and the clubhouse. The work done has elevated Quail Lodge once again into the elite status of California golf resorts.

For reservations at Quail Lodge, call 831/624-2888.

Play Policy and Fees: April–October, green fees for resort guests are $150. November–March, green fees for resort guests are $120. For nonguests, green fees April–October are $160 Monday–Thursday and $180 Friday–Sunday and holidays. November–March, green fees for nonguests are $130 Monday–Thursday and $150 Friday–Sunday and holidays. Carts and range balls are included in all prices. Junior, nine-hole, and twilight rates are available.

Tees and Yardage: *Men:* Blue: yardage 6449, par 71, rating 71.4, slope 128; Gold: yardage 6091, par 71, rating 69.6, slope 124; *Women:* Red: yardage 5488, par 71, rating 72.0, slope 127.

Tee Times: Reservations can be made 180 days in advance.

Dress Code: Tasteful golf attire—collared or sports shirts, skirts, walking shorts, or slacks—and nonmetal spikes are required.

Tournaments: This course is available for tournaments. The banquet facility can accommodate 200 people.

Directions: From Highway 1 in Carmel, take the Carmel Valley Road exit. Drive 3.5 miles to Valley Greens Drive. Turn right on Valley Greens Drive and follow it to the course.

Contact: 8000 Valley Greens Drive, Carmel, CA 93923, pro shop 831/620-8808, fax 831/624-3726, www.quaillodge.com.

33 CORRAL DE TIERRA COUNTRY CLUB

Architect: Bob Baldock, 1959; renovated J. Michael Poellot, 2000

18 holes   Private $105

Monterey Peninsula and Vicinity map, page 194

This challenging, rolling, tree-lined course has undulating greens. Water comes into play on several holes. The par-4 first hole starts from a scenic, elevated tee. The par-5s are tight but reachable in two for long hitters. The setting is peaceful, nestled in the valley between Monterey and Salinas.

Play Policy and Fees: Reciprocal play is accepted with members of other USGA country clubs at a rate of $105.

Tees and Yardage: *Men:* Black Oak: yardage 6683, par 72, rating 72.4, slope 134; Blue Spruce: yardage 6340, par 72, rating 70.9, slope 130; White Birch: yardage 5885, par 72, rating 69.2, slope 127; *Women:* Redwood: yardage 5392, par 72, rating 71.7, slope 125.

Tee Times: Club members may reserve tee times one week in advance.

Dress Code: No blue jeans may be worn, and standard country club attire is required.

Tournaments: Outside events require board approval and are held on Monday only. The banquet facility can accommodate 300 people.

Directions: From Highway 68 between Salinas and Monterey, take the Corral de Tierra Road exit south. Drive three-quarters of a mile to the course.

Contact: 81 Corral de Tierra Road, Salinas,

CA 93908, pro shop 831/484-1325, fax 831/484-0118, www.corraldetierracc.com.

34 THE PRESERVE

Architect: Tom Fazio and Sandy Tatum, 2000

18 holes   Private

Monterey Peninsula and Vicinity map, page 194

This course sits in a residential community on 20,000 private acres in the coastal foothills of the Santa Lucia Mountains adjoining Carmel and Pebble Beach. It is distinguished by rolling hills, old oak trees, and a picturesque design by Tom Fazio and Sandy Tatum. One of the more interesting holes is the fourth, a double-dogleg par-5 requiring a precise second shot, leaving a short uphill approach to a green surrounded by sentrylike oaks. There is some water in play, but generally the challenge is in the hilly terrain.

Play Policy and Fees: Members and guests only.

Tees and Yardage: *Men:* Black: yardage 7067, par 72, rating 74.5, slope 143; Gold: yardage 6555, par 72, rating 72.2, slope 138; White: yardage 6038, par 72, rating 70.0, slope 128; *Women:* Red: yardage 5148, par 72, rating 70.1, slope 123.

Tee Times: Not applicable.

Dress Code: Traditional golf attire, such as slacks and collared shirts, is required. Shorts are acceptable. Nonmetal spikes are required.

Tournaments: This course is not available for outside tournaments.

Directions: Take Carmel Valley Road east from the mouth of Carmel Valley. Turn right after two miles on Rancho San Carlos Road. The club can be seen from the road just after Valley Greens Drive.

Contact: 19 Pronghorn Run, Carmel, CA 93923, pro shop 831/626-8200, fax 831/626-8282, www.santaluciapreserve.com.

35 CARMEL VALLEY RANCH

Architect: Pete Dye, 1981

18 holes **Resort** **$150–180**

Monterey Peninsula and Vicinity map, page 194

This imaginative Pete Dye design features large greens and deep bunkers. Most holes are tight and unforgiving. The back nine is especially hilly and creative. Wonderful mature oak trees populate the course, and several lakes come into play. Elevation changes of up to 350 feet on several holes create interesting golf shots and spectacular views. Accommodations here are relaxing and luxurious.

Play Policy and Fees: Green fees are $150 for resort guests Monday–Thursday, $165 Friday–Sunday and holidays. Green fees for nonguests are $160 Monday–Thursday, $180 Friday–Sunday and holidays. Carts are included and mandatory. Twilight and junior rates available.

Tees and Yardage: *Men:* Blue: yardage 6234, par 70, rating 70.8, slope 138; White: yardage 5563, par 70, rating 67.8, slope 129; *Women:* Red: yardage 5046, par 70, rating 69.6, slope 124; Gold: yardage 4337, par 70, rating 65.8, slope 116.

Tee Times: After receiving hotel confirmation, guests can book a tee time at their convenience.

Dress Code: Golf attire is the only acceptable dress on the course. No blue jeans, tank tops, or short shorts may be worn. Nonmetal spikes are required.

Tournaments: An eight-player minimum is required to book a tournament. Carts are required. The banquet facility can accommodate up to 280 people.

Directions: From Highway 1 in Carmel, take the Carmel Valley Road exit and drive seven miles. Turn right on Robinson Canyon Road and left on Old Ranch Road.

Contact: 1 Old Ranch Road, Carmel, CA 93923, pro shop 831/625-9500, fax 831/626-2503, www.wyndham.com.

36 KING CITY GOLF COURSE

Architect: Course designed, 1953; redesign Robert Dean Putman, 1976

9 holes **Public** **$10–20**

Monterey Peninsula and Vicinity map, page 194

King City's only golf course opened in 1953. Robert Dean Putman redesigned it in 1976. It is a flat, short course that has tree-lined fairways and small, tricky greens. A creek meanders through the terrain and comes into play on four holes.

Play Policy and Fees: Green fees are $10 for nine holes and $15 for 18 holes on weekdays, $15 for nine holes and $20 for 18 holes on weekends and holidays. Twilight, senior, and junior rates are available.

Tees and Yardage: *Men (18 holes):* White/Blue: yardage 5573, par 70, rating 66.9, slope 117; *Women (18 holes):* Yellow/Red: yardage 5094, par 70, rating 69.7, slope 116.

Tee Times: Reservations can be booked seven days in advance but are not generally required except on weekends.

Dress Code: Appropriate attire and soft spikes are required.

Tournaments: This course is available for outside tournaments.

Directions: From U.S. 101 in King City, take the Canal Street exit. Turn right on Division Street. At the second stop sign, turn right on South Vanderhurst Street and drive to the course.

Contact: 613 South Vanderhurst Street, King City, CA 93930, pro shop 831/385-4546.

Chapter 9

COURTESY OF RIVERBEND GOLF CLUB

San Joaquin Valley

San Joaquin Valley

The San Joaquin Valley comprises a large section of land smack dab in the middle of California, and yet in many ways it is forgotten when people think about the state's landmass. The region extends from above Stockton to below Bakersfield, from the mountains west of I-5 to the mountains east of Fresno and Visalia.

I-5 and Highway 99 are the main arteries running north and south through this big territory, and most of us have zipped up and down the state dozens of times using one or the other. But unless you live or have business in one of the cities or towns along the route—Bakersfield, Fresno, Merced, Modesto, Stockton—there is little reason to stop except to gas up. Right?

Not exactly. There are long miles of flat nothing, to be sure, but there are also many acres of fertile land being used for the food crops that contribute to feeding the nation and the world. And, particularly along the eastern edge of the region, there are some areas of great interest and beauty.

East of Stockton and Modesto, for example, as the land leads into the Sierra Nevada foothills along Highway 49, there are some historic towns and villages dating back to gold-mining and frontier days. These are fun to explore. Several lakes and reservoirs provide recreational opportunities, and the terrain is hilly and heavily wooded. The golf courses in this area, such as Saddle Creek Golf Club, Hidden Hills Resort, and Pine Mountain Lake Country Club, are built in this golf-perfect terrain.

Farther south, clustered around Fresno, some very good designs are available for play. These include the award-winning Riverbend Golf Club, a 1999 Gary Roger Baird design, and the classic Riverside Golf Course of Fresno (1939).

Around Bakersfield, where the terrain is flatter, the courses include The Links at Riverlakes Ranch (1999) and Wasco Valley Rose. One resort course in this area that will surprise you is Horse Thief Golf & Country Club in Tehachapi, a 6700-yard layout at an elevation of 4000 feet. It's not the fanciest resort course in the state, but it sure provides a fun round of golf at a reasonable rate.

The weather can vary wildly in this big region. Be prepared for tule fog in February, sweltering heat in summer months, snow in Tehachapi, and cold in the Sierra Nevada foothills. But you know that old saying, "A day on the golf course beats a day in the office." In this region of the Golden State, add to that, ". . . in any weather."

The San Joaquin Valley does, after all, offer some incentive to stop longer than it takes to fill your car with fuel, and for golfers, any reason to play is a good one.

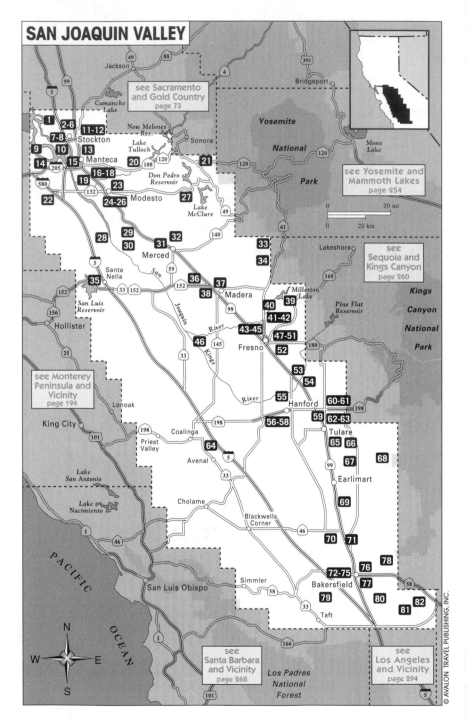

SAN JOAQUIN VALLEY

see Sacramento
and Gold Country
page 73

see Yosemite and
Mammoth Lakes
page 254

see
Sequoia and
Kings Canyon
page 260

see Monterey
Peninsula and
Vicinity
page 194

see Santa Barbara
and Vicinity
page 268

see
Los Angeles
and Vicinity
page 294

Jackson
Bridgeport
Stockton
Sonora
Lake Tulloch
Mono Lake
Manteca
Lakeshore
Modesto
Merced
Santa Nella
Madera
Millerton Lake
Pine Flat Reservoir
San Luis Reservoir
Hollister
Fresno
King City
Hanford
Lonoak
Coalinga
Priest Valley
Tulare
Avenal
Earlimart
Cholame
Blackwells Corner
Bakersfield
San Luis Obispo
Simmler
Taft

Yosemite National Park
Kings Canyon National Park
Los Padres National Forest

New Melones Res.
Camanche Lake
Don Pedro Reservoir
Lake McClure
Lake San Antonio
Lake Nacimiento

PACIFIC OCEAN

San Joaquin River
Kings River

0   20 mi
0   20 km

© AVALON TRAVEL PUBLISHING, INC.

216   California Golf

1 THE RESERVE AT SPANOS PARK

Architect: Andy Raugust, 1999

18 holes   **Public**   **$51–66**

🏃 📷 🍽 🚗 🍺

San Joaquin Valley map, page 216

Spanos Park is part of a planned residential community and working farm, and you will find corn fields throughout. This is a links-style course, with eight lakes that come into play on 12 holes. The fairways give you plenty of room for error, and there are plenty of places to bail out, but if you miss the fairways and greens badly, trouble awaits. Many of the greens are protected by well-placed pot bunkers, but they allow players to approach in a variety of ways. The greens are small, with subtle undulations.

Play Policy and Fees: Green fees are $51 Monday–Thursday, $55 Friday, and $66 weekends and holidays. All rates include cart. Midday, early bird, twilight, and super twilight rates are offered.

Tees and Yardage: *Men:* Gold: yardage 7000, par 72, rating 74.2, slope 133; Blue: yardage 6550, par 72, rating 71.8, slope 130; White: yardage 6060, par 72, rating 69.4, slope 125; *Women:* Red: yardage 5294, par 72, rating 68.9, slope 118.

Tee Times: Reservations can be made seven days in advance.

Dress Code: Collared shirts and nonmetal spikes are required. No denim is allowed.

Tournaments: At least 16 players are required for an event. The banquet facility can accommodate 160 people.

Directions: From Stockton, take I-5 north to the Eight Mile Road exit. Go west on Eight Mile Road for one-quarter mile to the course on the north side of the road.

Contact: 6301 West Eight Mile Road, Stockton, CA 95219, pro shop 209/477-4653, ext. 21, fax 209/477-0169, www.agl.com.

2 ELKHORN COUNTRY CLUB

Architect: Bert Stamps, 1963

18 holes   **Private**   **$30–50**

🏃 📷 🍽 🏌 🚗

San Joaquin Valley map, page 216

This tough course rewards accuracy over distance. More than 63 bunkers guard the fairways and the elevated greens. Trees abound.

Play Policy and Fees: Reciprocal play is accepted with members of other private clubs; otherwise, members and guests only. Reciprocal fees are $30 on weekdays and $50 on weekends and holidays. Twilight rates available.

Tees and Yardage: *Men:* Blue: yardage 6559, par 71, rating 72.5, slope 129; White: yardage 6125, par 71, rating 70.6, slope 126; Gold: yardage 5794, par 69, rating 69.2, slope 121; *Women:* Red: yardage 4656, par 73, rating 67.5, slope 116.

Tee Times: Reciprocal players should have their home professional call to make arrangements.

Dress Code: Appropriate golf attire is required, including collared shirts for men.

Tournaments: This course is available Monday only. A 72-player minimum is required for an afternoon shotgun start. A 48-player minimum is required for a morning start. Tournaments should be booked 12 months in advance. The banquet facility can accommodate 375 people.

Directions: From I-5, take the Eight Mile Road exit and drive three miles east. Turn right on Davis Road and drive one-quarter mile. Turn left on Elkhorn Drive.

Contact: 1050 Elkhorn Drive, Stockton, CA 95209, pro shop 209/477-0252, fax 209/477-9122.

3 SWENSON PARK GOLF COURSE

Architect: Jack Fleming, 1952

18 holes   **Public**   **$19.50–25**

🏃 📷 🍽 🏌 🚗 🍺 3

San Joaquin Valley map, page 216

Swenson Park offers some of the lowest green fees in Northern California for a regulation track. It is a wide-open layout with fewer than a dozen traps and just two water holes. The 15th and 16th holes, however, feature extremely demanding tee shots through narrow chutes. It is not exactly a field day for women. Check out the rating. There is also a par-27 executive course measuring 2760 yards. It is dotted with water hazards, though only two holes are longer than 150 yards.

Play Policy and Fees: Green fees are $19.50 weekdays and $25 weekends for 18 holes. Carts are $21. Twilight rates available.

Tees and Yardage: *Men:* White: yardage 6407, par 72, rating 69.8, slope 113; *Women:* Red: yardage 6266, par 74, rating 75.2, slope 125.

Tee Times: Reservations can be booked seven days in advance.

Dress Code: Appropriate golf attire and soft spikes are required.

Tournaments: This course is available for outside tournaments.

Directions: Heading north on I-5 on the north side of Stockton, take the Benjamin Holt Drive exit east. Turn left on Alexandria Place and drive to the course on the left.

Contact: 6803 Alexandria Place, Stockton, CA 95207, pro shop 209/937-7360, fax 209/937-7382.

4 VENETIAN GARDENS COMMUNITY GOLF COURSE

Architect: Course opened, 1975
9 holes **Private**

San Joaquin Valley map, page 216

This short par-3 course is in Venetian Gardens, a private residential community. None of the holes are longer than 100 yards, but water hazards come into play on all but one of them.

Play Policy and Fees: Members and guests only. No outside or reciprocal play is accepted. Guests play at no charge when accompanied by a member.

Tees and Yardage: *Men and Women:* yardage 777, par 27, rating n/a, slope n/a.

Tee Times: Not applicable.

Dress Code: Appropriate attire and soft spikes are required.

Tournaments: This course is not available for outside events.

Directions: From I-5 in Stockton, turn onto March Lane and drive one mile east to Venetian Drive North. Turn right on Mosaic Way to the Venetian Gardens Community Golf Course.

Contact: 1555 Mosaic Way, Stockton, CA 95207, pro shop 209/477-3871.

5 BROOKSIDE COUNTRY CLUB

Architect: Robert Trent Jones Jr., 1990
18 holes **Private** **$35–50**

San Joaquin Valley map, page 216

Brookside is a links-style layout that offers a spellbinding view of ocean freighters floating down the inland channel to the Port of Stockton, as well as some nice vistas of Mount Diablo in the distance. Water comes into play on 10 of 18 holes, the most notorious being the 16th, a double dogleg of 559 yards. The holes here offer a nice change of pace, from the 450-yard uphill ninth to the chip-shot 12th of 131 yards. Some new tee boxes were built and additional trees were planted in 2003.

Play Policy and Fees: This course accepts reciprocal play with members of other clubs. The reciprocal fee is $35 weekdays, $50 on weekends. Optional carts are $11 per rider.

Tees and Yardage: *Men:* Blue: yardage 6720, par 72, rating 72.1, slope 126; White: yardage 6244, par 72, rating 69.5, slope 123; Gold: yardage 5681, par 72, rating 67.4, slope 120; *Women:* Red: yardage 5022, par 72, rating 69.9, slope 124.

Tee Times: Reciprocal players should have their home professional call to make arrangements.

Dress Code: Appropriate golf attire, including collared shirts and nonmetal spikes, is required. No denim allowed.

Tournaments: Outside events are booked for Monday only. A 100-player minimum is needed to reserve a tournament.

Directions: Take I-5 to the March Lane exit on the north end of Stockton. Follow March Lane west into the Brookside real estate development. The entrance is on the left.

Contact: 3603 St. Andrews Drive, Stockton, CA 95219, pro shop 209/956-7888, www.brooksidegolf.net.

6 OAKMOORE GOLF COURSE

Architect: Donald A. Crump, 1959
9 holes   **Public**   **$35–45**

San Joaquin Valley map, page 216

The course is wooded, with three lakes and mostly elevated greens. A separate set of tees is used to create 18 holes. Groups seem to enjoy this unique opportunity to have full access to the golf course and clubhouse facility. Many return year after year.

Play Policy and Fees: At Oakmoore, there is always a tournament in progress. This is an unusual course—it is used solely for tournaments. No individual play. The approximate cost to each member of a visiting group is $35 Monday–Friday, $45 on weekends, which includes a cart and use of the clubhouse.

Tees and Yardage: *Men (18 holes):* yardage 6517, par 72, rating 72.0, slope n/a.

Tee Times: This is a very popular tournament course where previous events receive the first rights for the same date. Call in January for open dates.

Dress Code: None.

Tournaments: For tournaments there is a 48-player minimum Monday–Friday and a 60-player minimum on weekends.

Directions: From Highway 99 in Stockton, exit at Business 99/Wilson Way south and drive to the course.

Contact: 3737 North Wilson Way, Stockton, CA 95205, pro shop 209/943-1983.

7 LYONS GOLF COURSE

Architect: Captain Lyons, 1967
9 holes   **Public**   **$11.50–13**

San Joaquin Valley map, page 216

This is a level executive course with ponds that come into play on two holes. It's a good loop for beginners and those wishing to practice their games.

Play Policy and Fees: Green fees for nine holes are $11.50 on weekdays and $13 on weekends.

Replay is $2. Senior, student, and twilight rates are available. Carts additional.

Tees and Yardage: *Men (18 holes):* Blue: yardage 4220, par 64, rating 60.4, slope 94; White: yardage 4000, par 64, rating 59.6, slope 92; *Women (18 holes):* Red: yardage 3776, par 64, rating 60.4, slope 99.

Tee Times: Tee times can be made seven days in advance.

Dress Code: No tank tops or cutoff shorts are allowed on the course.

Tournaments: Tournaments welcome. Please inquire.

Directions: From Lodi, travel south on I-5. Take the Fresno Avenue exit. Go right on Fresno Avenue, take the first left on Washington, and continue until you cross over the bridge. You will see the course on the right. Take the first right into the course.

Contact: 3303 Navy Drive, Stockton, CA 95203, pro shop 209/937-7905.

8 STOCKTON GOLF & COUNTRY CLUB

Architect: Alister Mackenzie, 1914
18 holes   **Private**   **$75**

San Joaquin Valley map, page 216

The flavor of Alister Mackenzie's original design remains on this classic course, which is bordered by Stockton's deep-water channel. Like all of Mackenzie's best work, there is nothing complicated here. If you are hitting the ball well, you'll enjoy the course. If you're all over the map, you pay a price. It is a tight course with countless eucalyptus trees. The par-3s are outstanding, three of them measuring close to 200 yards. The first hole is bordered by the channel. A new $12 million clubhouse opened in 2004.

Play Policy and Fees: Reciprocal play is accepted with members of other private clubs. Reciprocal fees are $75. Optional carts are an additional $10. The course is closed on Monday.

Tees and Yardage: *Men:* Blue: yardage 6470, par 71, rating 71.2, slope 129; White: yardage 6286,

par 71, rating 70.5, slope 127; *Women:* Red: yardage 6030, par 72, rating 75.8, slope 130.

Tee Times: Reciprocal players should have their home professional call to make arrangements.

Dress Code: Collared shirts and nonmetal spikes are required. No denim is allowed on the course.

Tournaments: Outside events are allowed on Monday only with board and manager approval. A 72-player minimum is required to book a tournament, and carts are required.

Directions: From I-5 in Stockton, take the Country Club Boulevard exit west and drive 1.5 miles to the course.

Contact: 3800 West Country Club Boulevard, Stockton, CA 95204, pro shop 209/466-6221, clubhouse 209/466-4313.

9 DISCOVERY BAY

Architect: Ted Robinson Sr., 1986

18 holes   **Private**   **$75**

🚶 📷 🍴 🛍 🚗 🍺

San Joaquin Valley map, page 216

Water can be—and often is—found on 16 of 18 holes. Set in rolling terrain, Discovery Bay is wide open, with undulating greens. The par-3 17th hole features an island green, though there is room to bail out left on the 178-yard hole.

Play Policy and Fees: Reciprocal play is accepted with members of other private clubs on weekdays only at a rate of $75. The course is closed on Monday.

Tees and Yardage: *Men:* Blue: yardage 6518, par 71, rating 71.9, slope 126; White: yardage 6067, par 71, rating 69.7, slope 118; *Women:* Red: yardage 5279, par 71, rating 71.1, slope 125.

Tee Times: Reciprocal players should have their home professional call to make arrangements.

Dress Code: Appropriate golf attire and nonmetal spikes are required.

Tournaments: Tournament play is on Monday only. A 100-player minimum is needed to book a shotgun tournament.

Directions: From Highway 4, take the Discovery Bay Boulevard exit. Take the first right onto Clubhouse Drive.

Contact: 1475 Clubhouse Drive, Byron, CA

94514, pro shop 925/634-0704, fax 925/634-9033, www.discoverybaycc.com.

10 VAN BUSKIRK GOLF COURSE

Architect: Larry Nordstrom, 1961

18 holes   **Public**   **$19.50–25**

🚶 📷 🍴 🛍 🚗 🍺

San Joaquin Valley map, page 216

This flat, open course has three ponds, with water coming into play on nearly every hole on the front nine. Notable is the seventh hole, a long par-5 with out-of-bounds on the left and water on the right. On the back nine the greens are somewhat elevated. The Stockton City Championship is held here each August. Women say it plays long but not too nasty.

Play Policy and Fees: Green fees are $19.50 weekdays and $25 weekends. Twilight rates are available during the summer. Carts are $21 for 18 holes.

Tees and Yardage: *Men:* Blue: yardage 6928, par 72, rating 72.2, slope 118; White: yardage 6502, par 72, rating 70.1, slope 116; *Women:* Red: yardage 5871, par 73, rating 73.0, slope 122.

Tee Times: Reservations can be booked seven days in advance.

Dress Code: Golf attire is required.

Tournaments: A 24-player minimum is required to book a tournament. Events can be scheduled up to 12 months in advance.

Directions: From I-5 in Stockton, exit at 8th Street west to Fresno Street. Turn left and drive to the course.

Contact: 1740 Houston Avenue, Stockton, CA 95206, pro shop 209/937-7357.

11 J. B. GOLF COURSE

Architect: Kenneth Roberts, 1990

9 holes   **Public**   **$7–10**

📷 🍴 🛍 🍺 3

San Joaquin Valley map, page 216

This family-oriented par-3 golf course is a good tune-up for your iron game. A creek comes into play on two holes. There is an airstrip on-site.

Play Policy and Fees: Green fees are $7 for nine holes and $10 for 18 holes.

Tees and Yardage: *Men and Women:* yardage 888, par 27, rating n/a, slope n/a.

Tee Times: Reservations are not required; play is on a first-come, first-served basis.

Dress Code: Casual attire is acceptable.

Tournaments: No tournaments accepted.

Directions: Driving north on Highway 99 from Modesto, take the Farmington Road exit, Highway 4, and head east. The course is on the left-hand side.

Contact: 24305 East Highway 4, Farmington, CA 95230, pro shop 209/886-5670.

12 SADDLE CREEK GOLF CLUB

Architect: Carter Morrish, 1996

18 holes   Semiprivate $70–105

San Joaquin Valley map, page 216

The centerpiece of a 900-acre gated resort and residential community, this scenic, traditional-style course is characterized by rolling terrain, mature oak trees, ponds, lakes, and natural wetlands. The goal was to blend the course and land together naturally, and the owners succeeded. Water comes into play on eight holes. The layout is nicely balanced, enabling golfers to use every club in their bag, and five sets of tees provide a challenging course for players of all skill levels. This is the home course of the Northern California PGA. Saddle Creek was ranked the seventh best upscale public access course in the country by *Golf Digest*. This facility is expertly run and provides a wonderful golf experience.

Play Policy and Fees: Members receive priority for tee times, but public play is accepted. Green fees are $70 Monday–Friday, $105 weekends and holidays. Fees include optional cart and range balls. Twilight rates are offered. Memberships are available.

Tees and Yardage: *Men:* Black: yardage 6828, par 72, rating 73.1, slope 137; Blue: yardage 6434, par 72, rating 71.2, slope 127; White: yardage 6049, par 72, rating 69.7, slope 122; *Women:* Gold: yardage 5326, par 72, rating 71.3, slope 128; Red: yardage 4488, par 72, rating 66.7, slope 117.

Tee Times: Reservations can be booked 14 days in advance without a fee, up to 60 days in advance for a fee. Call 888/852-5787 for reservations.

Dress Code: Appropriate golf attire and non-metal spikes are required.

Tournaments: A 20-player minimum is required to book an event. Tournaments should be booked 12 months in advance. The banquet facility holds 300 people. Call for special winter rates.

Directions: From Stockton, take Highway 4 east to Copperopolis and Obyrnes Ferry Road. Turn right and follow the signs to the course. From Oakdale, take Highway 108/120 east to Obyrnes Ferry Road. Turn left and follow the signs to the course.

Contact: 1001 Saddle Creek Drive, Copperopolis, CA 95228, pro shop 209/785-3700, www.saddlecreek.com.

13 FRENCH CAMP GOLF COURSE & RV PARK

Architect: Lloyd Zastre, 1995 and 2001

18 holes   Public $15–17

San Joaquin Valley map, page 216

French Camp is an RV park with a longish executive golf course at its core. From the back tees, three of the five par-4s are over 400 yards long. Water comes into play on every hole on this well-maintained golf course. If you love golf and recreational vehicles are your thing, this is the place for you. French Camp has 197 landscaped spaces with full hookups, a swimming pool, a clubhouse with kitchen, showers, laundry room, an 18-hole putting course, and lighted driving range.

Play Policy and Fees: Green fees are $15 weekdays and $17 weekends. Junior, senior, camper, and twilight rates are available. Carts are $20.

Tees and Yardage: *Men:* Blue: yardage 3656, par 60, rating n/a, slope n/a; White: yardage 3363, par 60, rating n/a, slope n/a; *Women:* Red: yardage 2817, par 60, rating n/a, slope n/a.

Tee Times: Reservations can be booked seven

days in advance for the general public and one year in advance for RVers.

Dress Code: Shirts must be worn, and nonmetal spikes are required.

Tournaments: An eight-player minimum is needed to book a tournament. The banquet facility can accommodate 200 people.

Directions: From Stockton, take Highway 99 south five miles. From Manteca, take Highway 99 three miles north. The course is at the junction of Highway 99 and French Camp Road.

Contact: 3919 East French Camp Road (P.O. Box 1500), French Camp, CA 95231, pro shop 209/234-3030, fax 209/983-8993, www.french camp.com.

14 OLD RIVER GOLF COURSE
Architect: Hiram Sibley, 1999 and 2004
18 holes   **Public**

San Joaquin Valley map, page 216

Old River Golf Course has water coming into play on several holes. The course lets golfers use their creativity when approaching the green, giving them several different options. The greens are undulating. The course was expanding to 18 holes at press time.

Play Policy and Fees: Not available at press time.

Tees and Yardage: Note: At press time nine new holes were being added to this course, bringing the total to 18.

Tee Times: Reservations can be made seven days in advance for nonresidents and nine days in advance for residents of Tracy.

Dress Code: Casual attire is okay, but nonmetal spikes are required.

Tournaments: A 16-player minimum is required to book an event. Shotgun tournaments are allowed.

Directions: From Stockton, take I-5 south to Highway 205 west. Exit at MacArthur Road and head north for three miles. The course is on the left.

Contact: 18007 MacArthur, Tracy, CA 95376, pro shop 209/830-8585.

15 MANTECA GOLF COURSE
Architect: Jack Fleming, 1966
18 holes   **Public**   **$17–27**

San Joaquin Valley map, page 216

A magnificent clubhouse makes this municipal course seem like a country club. The golf course is both fun and demanding. The 11th hole is probably the most difficult, a 430-yard par-4 that used to be a par-5. The 18th hole is an excellent finisher, a long dogleg of 413 yards, and the par-3s offer variety. The 17th is a tough, 168-yarder to a sloping, bunkered green.

Play Policy and Fees: Green fees are $17 weekdays and $20 weekends for residents of Manteca. Fees for nonresidents are $20 weekdays and $27 weekends. Nine-hole rates are available. Carts are additional.

Tees and Yardage: *Men:* Blue: yardage 6478, par 72, rating 71.3, slope 121; White: yardage 6131, par 72, rating 69.7, slope 117; *Women:* Red: yardage 5564, par 72, rating 71.3, slope 122.

Tee Times: Reservations can be booked seven days in advance with a credit card.

Dress Code: None.

Tournaments: This course is available for outside tournaments. A banquet facility is available that holds 160 people.

Directions: The course is in Manteca off Highway 120 between I-5 and Highway 99. From Highway 120, take the Union Road exit heading north. The course is on the left, past Center Street.

Contact: 305 North Union Road, Manteca, CA 95337, pro shop 209/825-2500, fax 209/825-2506.

16 SPRING CREEK GOLF & COUNTRY CLUB
Architect: Jack Fleming, 1976
18 holes   **Private**

San Joaquin Valley map, page 216

This flat course is tight, with lots of oak trees, two of which are stationed in the middle of narrow fairways. The ninth hole is a notable par-4 that crosses water. At 432 yards, it places a premium on accuracy.

Play Policy and Fees: Reciprocal play is accepted with members of other private clubs. Reciprocal fees match those of the visitor's home club.

Tees and Yardage: *Men:* Championship: yardage 6461, par 72, rating 70.9, slope 124; Regular: yardage 6169, par 72, rating 69.7, slope 121; *Women:* Forward: yardage 5656, par 72, rating 73.1, slope 126.

Tee Times: Reciprocal players should have their home professional call to make arrangements.

Dress Code: Appropriate golf attire and nonmetal spikes are required.

Tournaments: This course is available for outside tournaments on Monday only. An 80-player minimum is needed to book an event. Tournaments should be scheduled five months in advance. The banquet facility can accommodate 175 people.

Directions: From Highway 99 in Ripon (north of Modesto), take the Ripon exit to the east side of the freeway. Drive two miles to Spring Creek Drive and the course.

Contact: 16436 East Spring Creek Drive (P.O. Box 535), Ripon, CA 95366, pro shop 209/599-3630.

🔟 ESCALON GOLF COURSE
Architect: Ken Roberts, 1985
9 holes   **Public**   **$6–13**

🏌️ 🏨 🍸 🏌️ 🍽️

San Joaquin Valley map, page 216

This executive course is flat and has one pond. There are four par-4 and five par-3 holes. It is easy to walk and is particularly popular among seniors. The course record is 25 for nine holes. See if you can beat it!

Play Policy and Fees: Green fees are $6 for nine holes and $11 for 18 holes weekdays, $7 for nine holes and $13 for 18 holes weekends. Power carts are available only for disabled players.

Tees and Yardage: *Men and Women:* yardage 1520, par 31, rating n/a, slope n/a.

Tee Times: Reservations can be made at any time.

Dress Code: Golf attire is requested.

Tournaments: This course is available for outside tournaments.

Directions: From Highway 99, take the Mariposa exit east. Drive about 15 miles through Collegeville (Mariposa Road turns into Escalon-Bellota Road). The course is on the right.

Contact: 17051 South Escalon-Bellota Road, Escalon, CA 95320, pro shop 209/838-1277.

🔢 DEL RIO COUNTRY CLUB
Architect: William P. Bell, 1947;
Pascuzzo & Graves, 1996; John Harbottle, 1999
27 holes   **Private**   **$150**

🏌️ 🏨 🍸 🏌️ 🛺 🍽️

San Joaquin Valley map, page 216

The three nines at Del Rio are challenging, rolling country courses that demand good shot placement. The greens are fast and undulating, with subtle breaks. The layouts feature gorgeous old oak trees, lakes and fountains, and colorful plantings. In 1999, John Harbottle renovated the greens on the original 18 holes, using William P. Bell's original design. This is a very pleasant facility.

Play Policy and Fees: Reciprocal play with members of other private clubs is accepted on weekdays only. On weekends, members and guests only. Reciprocal fees are $150. Optional carts are $24.

Tees and Yardage: Oaks/Bluff—*Men:* Black: yardage 6839, par 72, rating 73.0, slope 129; Blue: yardage 6506, par 72, rating 71.5, slope 127; White: yardage 6017, par 72, rating 69.0, slope 123; *Women:* Gold: yardage 5274, par 72, rating 70.7, slope 122. Oaks/River—*Men:* Black: yardage 6950, par 72, rating 73.5, slope 134; Blue: yardage 6534, par 72, rating 71.6, slope 131; White: yardage 6046, par 72, rating 68.9, slope 128; *Women:* Gold: yardage 5290, par 72, rating 70.5, slope 121. Bluff/River— *Men:* Black: yardage 6823, par 72, rating 73.1, slope 128; Blue: yardage 6362, par 72, rating 70.9, slope 126; White: yardage 5895, par 72, rating 68.7, slope 123; *Women:* Gold: yardage 5198, par 72, rating 70.4, slope 122.

Tee Times: Reciprocal players should have their home professional call to make arrangements.

Dress Code: Appropriate golf attire and nonmetal spikes are required.

Tournaments: This course is available for limited outside tournaments. Events may be booked up to a year in advance. The banquet facility can accommodate 250 people.

Directions: From Highway 99 in Modesto, take the Salida exit onto Kerinin Avenue north. Turn left at Dale Road and follow it to the T intersection. Turn right on Ladd, drive one mile to Saint John, and turn left up to the club.

Contact: 801 Stewart Road, Modesto, CA 95356, pro shop 209/545-0013, clubhouse 206/545-0723, fax 209/545-5133, www.delrio countryclub.com.

19 JACK TONE GOLF COURSE

Architect: George Buzzini, 1996

| 18 holes | Public | $16–19 |

San Joaquin Valley map, page 216

Jack Tone is an executive golf course featuring 11 par-3s, sand traps around the greens, and one water hazard. The 12th hole is a tricky 473-yard par-5, with out-of-bounds areas on the left and traps surrounding the green.

Play Policy and Fees: Green fees are $16 weekdays and $19 weekends. Carts are $13 weekdays and $18 weekends. Resident, twilight, senior, and junior rates are available.

Tees and Yardage: *Men:* Blue: yardage 3715, par 62, rating 58.8, slope 88; White: yardage 3510, par 62, rating 58.1, slope 87; *Women:* Red: yardage 3292, par 62, rating 57.5, slope 84.

Tee Times: Reservations may be booked one week in advance over the phone, or two weeks in advance over the Internet.

Dress Code: No tank tops are allowed on the course. Nonmetal spikes are required.

Tournaments: This course is available for outside events.

Directions: From Manteca, drive south on Highway 99. Take the Jack Tone Road exit and turn right. Follow Jack Tone Road until it dead-ends. Turn right and take the first left to the course.

Contact: 1500 Ruess Road, Ripon, CA 95366, pro shop 209/599-2973, www.jacktonegolf.com.

20 OAKDALE GOLF & COUNTRY CLUB

Architect: Bob Baldock, 1961

| 18 holes | Private | $55 |

San Joaquin Valley map, page 216

Long and rolling, Oakdale Country Club is medium tight with average-sized greens. A number of the tees and greens are elevated. The par-3 ninth is 200 yards downhill to a well-bunkered green with water on the right. The fifth hole is a 600-yard par-5 that doglegs left with a large elevated green.

Play Policy and Fees: Reciprocal play is accepted with members of other private clubs at a rate of $55; otherwise, members and guests only. Optional carts are $25.

Tees and Yardage: *Men:* Championship: yardage 6744, par 72, rating 72.7, slope 130; Regular: yardage 6462, par 72, rating 71.4, slope 128; *Women:* Forward: yardage 5690, par 72, rating 73.9, slope 127.

Tee Times: Reciprocal players should have their home professional call to make arrangements.

Dress Code: Appropriate golf attire and nonmetal spikes are required.

Tournaments: Outside events can be held Monday only, with board approval.

Directions: Driving east on Highway 108, turn left on Stearns Road. The course is north of Oakdale.

Contact: 243 North Stearns Road, Oakdale, CA 95361, pro shop 209/847-2924, www.oak dalecc.com.

21 PINE MOUNTAIN LAKE COUNTRY CLUB

Architect: William F. Bell, 1969

18 holes   Semiprivate   **$65–75**

🏌 📷 🍽 🏌 🛺 🍹

San Joaquin Valley map, page 216

Pine Mountain Lake is a hilly course at 3500 feet. The fairways are outlined by trees, and the greens are large, with pronounced undulation. Hitting the driver straight is the key to scoring well here. The par-4 11th hole measures a long 475 yards. It plays shorter, however, due to a 75-foot drop in elevation. Another set of forward tees was built in 2004 to make this course more friendly to women golfers. (They were not yet measured or rated at press time.)

Play Policy and Fees: Green fees are $65 weekdays, $75 weekends, including cart. Twilight rates are offered. Memberships available.

Tees and Yardage: *Men:* Blue: yardage 6382, par 70, rating 70.1, slope 125; White: yardage 6125, par 70, rating 69.0, slope 123; *Women:* Red: yardage 5731, par 72, rating 73.3, slope 128.

Tee Times: Reservations are taken 14 days in advance for members and 10 days in advance for public play.

Dress Code: Appropriate golf attire (including collared shirts) and nonmetal spikes are required. No blue jeans.

Tournaments: All tournaments must be approved by the golf professional. A 16-player minimum is needed to book a tournament. A banquet facility is available that holds 200 people.

Directions: From I-5 in Manteca, take Highway 120 east to Groveland. The course is north of Groveland on Mueller Drive.

Contact: 19228 Pine Mountain Drive, Groveland, CA 95321, pro shop 209/962-8620, clubhouse 209/962-8638, fax 209/962-8658, www.pinemountainlake.com.

22 TRACY GOLF & COUNTRY CLUB

Architect: Robert Trent Jones Sr., 1956

18 holes   Private   **$30–50**

🏌 📷 🍽 🏌 🛺 🍹

San Joaquin Valley map, page 216

This flat course has rolling terrain, fast, elevated greens, four ponds, and numerous bunkers. The original nine holes were designed by Robert Trent Jones Sr. The front nine is tight, while the newer back side is more wide open. The first hole is a monster, 429 yards into the wind. The par-5 fifth hole (497 yards) is excellent as well. All out-of-bounds areas are on the left, so big hooks are deadly.

Play Policy and Fees: Reciprocal play is accepted with members of other private clubs. Reciprocal rates are $30 weekdays, $50 weekends (including cart).

Tees and Yardage: *Men:* Blue: yardage 6619, par 72, rating 72.5, slope 118; White: yardage 6227, par 72, rating 70.7, slope 115; *Women:* Red: yardage 5772, par 72, rating 73.7, slope 125.

Tee Times: Reciprocal players should have their home professional call to make arrangements.

Dress Code: Collared shirts are required.

Tournaments: Outside tournaments accepted weekdays only. Carts are mandatory for tournament play.

Directions: From I-580, take the Chrisman Road exit. The course is next to the highway.

Contact: 35200 South Chrisman Road, Tracy, CA 95376, pro shop 209/835-9463, www.tracy countryclub.com.

23 CREEKSIDE GOLF COURSE

Architect: Stephen Halsey, 1991

18 holes   Public   **$19–28**

🏌 📷 🍽 🏌 🛺 🍹

San Joaquin Valley map, page 216

This course is not overly long or tough. It plays relatively flat, with two holes playing into a creek side, thus the name. Three ponds come into play on six holes. There are also several two-tiered greens. The par-4 18th hole is 392 yards from the white tees, with water on both sides of the fairway. It's a good test of golf for intermediate golfers.

Play Policy and Fees: Green fees are $19 weekdays and $28 weekends. Twilight and super twilight rates are available. Carts are $24.

Tees and Yardage: *Men:* Blue: yardage 6610, par 72, rating 71.4, slope 117; White: yardage 6021, par 72, rating 68.6, slope 111; *Women:* Red: yardage 5496, par 72, rating 69.5, slope 108.

Tee Times: Reservations can be booked seven days in advance. For tee times, call 209/491-4653.

Dress Code: A six-inch inseam on shorts is required, and shoes are mandatory.

Tournaments: A 28-player minimum is needed to book a tournament.

Directions: From Highway 99 in Modesto, take Highway 132 to Lincoln Avenue. Turn left on Lincoln and follow it to the course.

Contact: 701 Lincoln Avenue, Modesto, CA 95354, pro shop 209/571-5123.

24 DRYDEN PARK GOLF COURSE

Architect: William F. Bell, 1959

18 holes   **Public**   **$19–25**

San Joaquin Valley map, page 216

The Tuolumne River runs adjacent to this course. The front nine is flat, and the back nine is somewhat hilly. Numerous pine trees make Dryden a nice test despite its relatively modest length. Dryden Park has a lighted golf range.

Play Policy and Fees: Green fees are $19 weekdays and $25 weekends. Twilight rates are available. Carts are $12 for nine holes and $24 for 18 holes.

Tees and Yardage: *Men:* Blue: yardage 6574, par 72, rating 70.9, slope 122; White: yardage 6278, par 72, rating 69.5, slope 120; *Women:* Red: yardage 5900, par 72, rating 73.4, slope 121.

Tee Times: Reservations can be booked seven days in advance by calling the tee-time reservations number at 209/491-4653.

Dress Code: A six-inch inseam on shorts is required. Collared shirts and shoes are mandatory.

Tournaments: A 28-player minimum is needed to book a tournament. Events should be scheduled at least six months in advance. The banquet facility can accommodate 80 people.

Directions: This course is right off Highway 99 in Modesto. Take the Tuolumne Boulevard/B Street exit and make a right on Tuolumne.

Contact: 920 Sunset Boulevard, Modesto, CA 95351, pro shop 209/577-5359.

25 MODESTO MUNICIPAL GOLF COURSE

Architect: Course designed, 1959

9 holes   **Public**   **$12–14**

San Joaquin Valley map, page 216

This course is walkable and fairly flat. The fairways are narrow, and the trees are mature. The ninth is considered one of the top holes in the area. At 424 yards, it's a par-4 dogleg right with out-of-bounds on the right and trees on both sides. You can't see the green from the tee, but there is a bunker to the left front and a cart path to the right. The green will hold well-struck shots. This is a nice nine-hole layout.

Play Policy and Fees: Green fees are $12 for nine holes weekdays and $14 for nine holes on weekends. Afternoon, twilight, senior, and junior rates are available.

Tees and Yardage: *Men:* White: yardage 2989, par 35, rating 34.3, slope 116; *Women:* Red: yardage 2885, par 36, rating 34.3, slope 116.

Tee Times: Reservations can be booked seven days in advance.

Dress Code: A six-inch inseam on shorts is required, and shoes are mandatory.

Tournaments: A 28-player minimum is needed to book a tournament.

Directions: On Highway 99 off Tuolumne Boulevard, take the B Street off-ramp and make a right at the stop sign. Drive one-half block on Neece Drive and stay left along the river to the course.

Contact: 400 Tuolumne Boulevard, Modesto, CA 95351, pro shop 209/577-5360.

26 RIVER OAKS GOLF COURSE

Architect: Jim D. Phipps, 1979

18 holes   **Public**   **$15–18**

San Joaquin Valley map, page 216

This tree-lined executive course runs along the Tuolumne River. It has some ponds and no bunkers. The front nine is all par-3s, while the back nine has four short par-4s. The longest hole is the 12th, measuring around 350 yards. Most of the holes play around 100–170 yards. River Oaks has a junior golf program that enrolls more than 500 kids each summer. In this regard, it is the kind of course there should be more of.

Play Policy and Fees: Green fees are $15 weekdays and $18 weekends and holidays.

Tees and Yardage: *Men:* White: yardage 2855, par 58, rating 55.5, slope 83; *Women:* Red: yardage 2640, par 58, rating 54.3, slope 83.

Tee Times: Reservations can be booked seven days in advance.

Dress Code: Appropriate golf attire is required. Nonmetal spikes would be appreciated.

Tournaments: An 80-player minimum is needed to book a shotgun tournament.

Directions: From Modesto, drive south on Highway 99. Take the Hatch Road exit east. The course is on the left past Mitchell Road.

Contact: 3441 East Hatch Road (P.O. Box 97), Ceres, CA 95307, pro shop 209/537-4653, fax 209/537-4705.

27 HIDDEN HILLS RESORT AND GOLF CLUB

Architect: William F. Bell, 1970

18 holes   **Public**

San Joaquin Valley map, page 216

At press time, this facility was undergoing renovation. It was slated to reopen by early 2005. Please call to inquire.

Play Policy and Fees: Not available at press time.

Tees and Yardage: Not available at press time.

Tee Times: Reservations can be booked seven days in advance.

Dress Code: Appropriate attire and soft spikes are required.

Tournaments: Not available at press time.

Directions: From Highway 99 in Modesto, drive 30 miles east on Highway 132 to La Grange. After six miles, exit on Hayward Road south and follow it a mile. Turn left on Ranchito (where the pavement ends) and follow it to the course.

Contact: 7643 Fachada Way, La Grange, CA 95329, pro shop 209/852-2242, fax 209/852-2445.

28 DIABLO GRANDE GOLF CLUB

Architect: Dennis Griffiths (Ranch Course), 1996; Jack Nicklaus and Gene Sarazen (Legends West Course), 1996

36 holes   **Semiprivate**   **$60–120**

San Joaquin Valley map, page 216

Amid the rolling terrain of western Stanislaus County, the Ranch Course rolls by 400-year-old oak trees with the beautiful Salado Creek meandering throughout. On the Ranch Course, each hole is named after a breed of horse. Sounds peaceful, but beware of the par-5 12th, Mustang Hole. If the length doesn't stop you from going for it in two, the thought of hitting in the ravine that lies in wait should. Take your par and move on. The Legends West Course is just as scenic and well designed, but easier. Legends West is the first-ever design collaboration between Gene Sarazen and Jack Nicklaus. This facility is respected for its excellent teaching staff. Note: Hotel accommodations are planned for 2005 at this property.

Play Policy and Fees: Green fees for the Ranch Course are $60 Monday–Friday, $80 weekends and holidays, including cart. The Legends West Course is $80 Monday–Friday, $120 weekends and holidays. A 36-hole special is sometimes offered, as well as winter, senior, and other rates. Check website or call for details.

Tees and Yardage: Legends West—*Men:* Championship: yardage 7112, par 72, rating 74.4, slope 147; Blue: yardage 6680, par 72, rating 72.4, slope 137; White: yardage 6057, par 72, rating 69.7, slope 129; *Women:* Gold: yardage 5512, par 72, rating 72.3, slope 131; Red: yardage 4905, par 72, rating 69.3, slope 123. Ranch— *Men:* Championship: yardage 7243, par 72, rating 75.8, slope 144; Blue: yardage 6915, par 72, rating 74.3, slope 142; White: yardage 6378, par 72, rating 71.8, slope 133; *Women:* Gold: yardage 5291, par 72, rating 71.4, slope 120; Red: yardage 5026, par 72, rating 69.5, slope 120.

Tee Times: Reservations can be booked seven days in advance.

Dress Code: Collared shirts and nonmetal spikes are encouraged. Slacks or Bermuda-type shorts are preferred.

Tournaments: A 24-player minimum is needed to book a tournament.

Directions: Traveling north on I-5, take the Crows Landing Road exit east and turn left onto Ward Avenue. Head north on Ward about two miles until you reach Oak Flat Road. Turn left and go six miles to the course.

Contact: 10001 Oak Flat Road (P.O. Box 655), Patterson, CA 95363, pro shop 209/892-4653, fax 209/892-7403, www.diablogrande.com.

29 TURLOCK GOLF & COUNTRY CLUB

Architect: Robert Dean Putman, 1959; Andy Raugust, 1995

18 holes   **Private**   **$40–50**

San Joaquin Valley map, page 216

This flat course is deceiving. It's tight and the rough is difficult. The 14th hole is a rugged test. At 365 yards, this par-4 requires a carry over water and then doglegs 90 degrees. It's primarily a placement course with tricky greens. A new irrigation system was installed in 2003 that has helped improve conditioning.

Play Policy and Fees: Reciprocal play is accepted with members of other private clubs. Reciprocal fees are $40 weekdays, $50 weekends. Optional carts are $22.

Tees and Yardage: *Men:* Blue: yardage 6641, par 72, rating 72.5, slope 129; White: yardage

6301, par 72, rating 70.7, slope 127; *Women:* Red: yardage 5775, par 74, rating 73.5, slope 127.

Tee Times: Reciprocal players should have their home professional call to make arrangements.

Dress Code: Collared shirts and nonmetal spikes are required.

Tournaments: Tournaments are limited to Monday and Friday with board approval.

Directions: From Highway 99 south in Turlock, exit on Lander Avenue south and turn left on Bradbury. Turn right onto Golf Links Road.

Contact: 10532 Golf Links Road, Turlock, CA 95380, pro shop 209/634-4976, fax 209/634-5471, www.turlockcountryclub.com.

30 STEVINSON RANCH GOLF CLUB

Architect: John Harbottle and George H. Kelley, 1995

18 holes   **Public**   **$65–85**

San Joaquin Valley map, page 216

Former San Francisco Giants owner Bob Lurie is a partner in this John Harbottle design. The course has a links feel and is characterized by large tees and greens and distinctive bunkering. Greens have extended collars, giving golfers the option of chipping or putting. It is one tough cookie, particularly as you go farther back in tee selection. Still, if you play from the proper set of tees for your game, you will enjoy a round of golf on this scenic, open design. *Golf Digest* gave the course a four-star rating in 1998, and it was included in that magazine's 1997 top-25 listing of the best courses in California. This facility is expertly run and well maintained. A second course is in the talking stages.

On-site cottages can be used for meetings or overnight accommodations. A conference facility is available.

Play Policy and Fees: Green fees are $65 weekdays and $85 weekends, including cart. Winter and twilight rates are offered.

Tees and Yardage: *Men:* Black: yardage 7206, par 72, rating 74.7, slope 138; Gold: yardage

7060, par 72, rating 74.3, slope 136; Blue: yardage 6646, par 72, rating 72.7, slope 127; White: yardage 6093, par 72, rating 69.6, slope 122; *Women:* Red: yardage 5461, par 72, rating 71.9, slope 124.

Tee Times: Reservations can be booked 30 days in advance, or 60 days with accommodations reservations. Online tee times are available.

Dress Code: Collared shirts and nonmetal spikes are mandatory. No tank tops or cutoffs are allowed.

Tournaments: This course is available for outside tournaments. A 16-player minimum is needed.

Directions: From Turlock, drive south on Highway 99 to the Lander Avenue/Highway 165 exit. Drive south 10 miles to Stevinson. At the center of Stevinson, take a left on 3rd Avenue. Proceed one mile east to the entrance of the course.

Contact: 2700 North Van Clief Road (P.O. Box 96), Stevinson, CA 95374, pro shop 209/668-8200, fax 209/668-6909, www.stevinson ranch.com.

31 RANCHO DEL REY GOLF CLUB

Architect: Bob Baldock, 1963
18 holes   Semiprivate $27–30

San Joaquin Valley map, page 216

This course is mostly level, with lots of trees and water. The signature hole is the 17th, a par-3 with two willows and large bunkers framing the green. A complete overhaul of the greens and fairways was completed in 2004.

Play Policy and Fees: Green fees are $27 weekdays and $30 on weekends. Optional carts are $10 per rider. Nine-hole and twilight rates are offered.

Tees and Yardage: *Men:* Blue: yardage 6703, par 72, rating 72.5, slope 124; White: yardage 6314, par 72, rating 70.6, slope 121; *Women:* Red: yardage 5987, par 75, rating 73.6, slope 125.

Tee Times: Reservations can be made seven days in advance.

Dress Code: Shirts must be worn at all times. Nonmetal spikes are required.

Tournaments: A 20-player minimum is needed to book an event. The banquet facility can accommodate 100 people.

Directions: From Highway 99 in Atwater, exit north onto Buhach Road. Turn left on Green Sands Avenue and follow it to the course.

Contact: 5250 Green Sands Avenue, Atwater, CA 95301, pro shop 209/358-7131, fax 209/358-3803.

32 MERCED GOLF & COUNTRY CLUB

Architect: Bob Baldock, 1961; Robert Muir Graves, 1998
18 holes   Private $35

San Joaquin Valley map, page 216

Redesigned by Robert Muir Graves, this quiet valley course is short and challenging, with rolling hills and lots of trees. Merced Golf & Country Club is home to the Merced County Amateur and has hosted the U.S. Amateur Qualifying, the NCGA San Joaquin Valley Amateur, the Oldsmobile Sectional Qualifier, and the Player's West Merced Women's Classic.

Play Policy and Fees: Reciprocal play is accepted with members of other private clubs at a rate of $35; otherwise, members and guests only. Optional carts are $11 per rider.

Tees and Yardage: *Men:* Blue: yardage 6519, par 72, rating 71.4, slope 131; White: yardage 6206, par 72, rating 70.0, slope 129; *Women:* Red: yardage 5996, par 72, rating 73.1, slope 129.

Tee Times: Reciprocal players should have their home professional call to make arrangements.

Dress Code: Appropriate golf attire and non-metal spikes are required.

Tournaments: An 80-player minimum is needed to book a tournament. Carts are required. Events should be booked 12 months in advance.

Directions: From Highway 99 in Merced, take G Street north. Follow it to Bellevue Road; turn right and then turn left onto North Golf Road.

Contact: 6333 North Golf Road, Merced, CA 95340, pro shop 209/722-3357.

33 SIERRA MEADOWS RANCH GOLF CLUB

Architect: Alan Thomas, 1988; John Sirman, 1997
18 holes   Public $44–49

San Joaquin Valley map, page 216

This course closed for several months in 2004 for renovations, including new greens and an upgraded irrigation system. It is a mountain course that demands shot-making accuracy. Good iron play is essential for a successful round. The course has small greens, but they are fast and challenging.

Play Policy and Fees: Green fees are $44 Monday–Thursday and $49 Friday–Sunday, carts included. Senior, junior, and twilight rates are available.

Tees and Yardage: *Men:* Blue: yardage 6547, par 72, rating 71.1, slope 135; White: yardage 6270, par 72, rating 68.4, slope 126; *Women:* Red: yardage 5076, par 72, rating 68.6, slope 119.

Tee Times: Reservations can be booked one week in advance. They can also be booked online.

Dress Code: Collared shirts and nonmetal spikes are required.

Tournaments: Booking tournaments requires a 30-day minimum lead time. The banquet facility can accommodate 200 people.

Directions: From Mariposa, take Highway 49 for 28 miles heading to Oakhurst. Turn left on Harmony Lane and continue 2.7 miles to the course.

Contact: 46516 Opah Drive, Oakhurst, CA 93614, pro shop 559/642-1343, www.sierra meadows.com.

34 YOSEMITE LAKES PARK GOLF COURSE

Architect: Bob Baldock, 1970
9 holes   Private $12

San Joaquin Valley map, page 216

This is a fun executive course. Hills and water come into play on five holes, and the fairways are narrow. Don't expect this to be an easy stroll in the park. It can bite!

Play Policy and Fees: Reciprocal play is accepted with members of other private clubs at a rate of $12; otherwise, members and guests only.

Tees and Yardage: *Men:* Blue/White: yardage 3524, par 62, rating 59.2, slope 103; *Women (18 holes):* Red/Gold: yardage 3023, par 62, rating 57.9, slope 98.

Tee Times: Reservations are recommended.

Dress Code: Golf attire is encouraged.

Tournaments: This course is available for outside tournaments.

Directions: Driving toward Yosemite National Park on Highway 41 before Coarsegold, turn left on Yosemite Springs Parkway. Drive three miles to the course.

Contact: 30250 Yosemite Springs Parkway, Coarsegold, CA 93614, pro shop 559/642-2562.

35 FOREBAY GOLF COURSE

Architect: Joe Sontor, 1964
9 holes   Public $11.75–20.50

San Joaquin Valley map, page 216

On your way up or down I-5? It can get pretty long and monotonous out there. Forebay is a nice, quick, low-cost way to stretch those car-weary legs. It is a level, nine-hole course just off the interstate at Santa Nella. A creek runs through and some shade trees have been growing in for a couple of years. The testy, 424-yard, par-4 ninth hole requires a second-shot carry over the creek. It's nothing fancy, but it breaks up your journey!

Play Policy and Fees: Green fees are $11.75 for nine holes and $14.75 for 18 holes weekdays, $16.50 for nine holes and $20.50 for 18 holes weekends and holidays. Senior and twilight rates are available. Carts are $14 for nine holes and $18 for 18 holes.

Tees and Yardage: *Men (18 holes):* White/Blue: yardage 6465, par 72, rating 70.2, slope 111; *Women (18 holes):* Yellow/Red: yardage 5314, par 74, rating 69.4, slope 109.

Tee Times: Reservations are recommended one week in advance.

Dress Code: Appropriate golf attire is requested.

Tournaments: This course is available for outside tournaments.

Directions: In Santa Nella on I-5, exit onto Highway 33 south. Turn right on Bayview Road and continue to the course.

Contact: 29500 Bayview Road, Santa Nella, CA 95322, pro shop 209/826-3637, clubhouse 209/826-4858, www.forebaygolfcourse.com.

36 PHEASANT RUN GOLF CLUB

Architect: Richard Bigler, 1998 and 1999

18 holes   Public $23–33

🏌 📷 🍸 🏌 🛺 ⛳

San Joaquin Valley map, page 216

This is a desert-style course that acts as the recreational centerpiece of a residential community. It has a stadium feel, with palm trees and plenty of water in play. The greens are fairly fast and undulating. A prevailing breeze can be a factor, particularly in the afternoons. It plays long for women at almost 5900 yards, with a rating of 75.6.

Play Policy and Fees: Green fees are $23 Monday–Thursday, $26 Friday, and $33 weekends and holidays. Twilight, senior, and junior rates are available. Carts are $12 per rider.

Tees and Yardage: *Men:* Black: yardage 7322, par 72, rating 74.8, slope 126; Blue: yardage 6851, par 72, rating 72.6, slope 119; White: yardage 6288, par 72, rating 69.9, slope 115; *Women:* Gold: yardage 5864, par 73, rating 75.6, slope 127.

Tee Times: Reservations can be made seven days in advance.

Dress Code: Shirts and nonmetal spikes are required.

Tournaments: The course is available for outside events.

Directions: From Madera, drive 12 miles north on Highway 99. Take the Chowchilla Robertson exit. Make a right on Robertson and follow it to the course. From the north, take the same exit and make a left onto Robertson.

Contact: 19 Clubhouse Drive, Chowchilla, CA 93610, pro shop 866/475-2525, www.pheasantrungolfclub.com.

37 MADERA GOLF & COUNTRY CLUB

Architect: Bob Baldock, 1955

18 holes   Private $35

🏌 📷 🍸 🏌 🛺 ⛳

San Joaquin Valley map, page 216

This sporty course has lots of rolling hills. Tall eucalyptus trees come into play on the front nine, maturing pine trees on the back nine. It's easily walkable.

Play Policy and Fees: Reciprocal play is accepted with members of other private clubs. Green fees for reciprocators are $35. Carts are $14. The course is closed on Monday.

Tees and Yardage: *Men:* Blue: yardage 6647, par 72, rating 71.7, slope 126; White: yardage 6450, par 72, rating 70.8, slope 124; *Women:* Red: yardage 5903, par 73, rating 74.0, slope 120.

Tee Times: Reciprocal players should have their home professional call to make arrangements at least seven days in advance.

Dress Code: Collared shirts are a must, and shorts must be mid-thigh or longer. Nonmetal spikes are required.

Tournaments: This course is available for outside events on a very limited basis.

Directions: From Highway 99 north of downtown Madera, take the Avenue 17 exit east. Turn left onto County Road 26. The course is at Avenue 19.

Contact: 19297 Road 26, Madera, CA 93638, pro shop 559/674-2682, clubhouse 559/674-1527.

38 MADERA MUNICIPAL GOLF COURSE

Architect: Robert Dean Putman, 1991

18 holes   Public $17–22

🏌 📷 🍸 🏌 🛺 ⛳

San Joaquin Valley map, page 216

Robert Dean Putman tested his course on opening day, June 8, 1991, and shot a 68. He has designed a course with wide appeal. The greens are large, undulating, and well bunkered. The fairways are bunkered, too, and four lakes come into play on eight holes.

Play Policy and Fees: Green fees are $17 for 18 holes weekdays and $22 for 18 holes weekends. Nine-hole, twilight, and senior rates are available.

Tees and Yardage: *Men:* Blue: yardage 6831, par 72, rating 72.0, slope 121; White: yardage 6369, par 72, rating 69.7, slope 118; *Women:* Red: yardage 5519, par 72, rating 70.6, slope 112.

Tee Times: Reservations are recommended, though not required, and may be booked seven days in advance.

Dress Code: Appropriate attire and soft spikes are required.

Tournaments: This course is available for tournaments. The banquet facility can hold 275 people.

Directions: From Highway 99 north of Madera, take the Avenue 17 exit and follow it west one mile to the course.

Contact: 23200 Avenue 17, Madera, CA 93637, pro shop 559/675-3504, clubhouse 559/675-3533, fax 559/675-1936, www.maderagolf.com.

39 BRIGHTON CREST GOLF & COUNTRY CLUB

Architect: Johnny Miller, 1990

18 holes   Semiprivate $40–50

San Joaquin Valley map, page 216

At the 800-foot elevation, the course is above the winter fog level and is somewhat cooler during the summer months. The terrain is rolling, and the course is dotted with native blue and valley oaks. The greens, which Miller sized to fit the difficulty of the hole, are subtle but undulating. One of Miller's favorite holes is the par-5, 505-yard third. There is a slight dogleg right, and the second shot must negotiate two oaks. There is also a lateral hazard down the entire left side. Water runs in front of the small, two-tiered green. This was the first Johnny Miller–designed course in California.

Play Policy and Fees: Green fees are $40 Monday–Thursday, $45 Friday, and $50 weekends, carts included. Twilight rates are available.

Tees and Yardage: *Men:* Blue: yardage 6788, par 72, rating 71.2, slope 124; White: yardage 6298,

par 72, rating 70.9, slope 129; *Women:* Red: yardage 5195, par 72, rating 71.2, slope 124.

Tee Times: Reservations can be booked 14 days in advance.

Dress Code: Appropriate golf attire is required. Nonmetal spikes are optional.

Tournaments: A 24-player minimum is required to book an event. Carts are required. Events should be scheduled six months in advance.

Directions: From Fresno, take Highway 41 north to the Friant Road/Millerton Lake exit. The course is five miles past the town of Friant on Friant Road.

Contact: 21722 Fairway Oaks Lane, Friant, CA 93626, pro shop 559/299-8586, fax 559/299-8586, www.brightoncrest.com.

40 RIVERBEND GOLF CLUB

Architect: Gary Roger Baird, 1999

18 holes   Public $40–60

San Joaquin Valley map, page 216

Riverbend is a links-style course featuring large greens, old native oaks, and attractive bunkering that allows players several options in attacking the greens. The hardest hole on the course, the ninth, is a long par-4. The rolling fairway is fairly open, but don't overlook the bunkers to the right. Long hitters who can get over the second hill are looking at a nice 150-yard shot to a deep green. The rest of us are looking at a long-iron or a wood into the green that is guarded by a lake to the right with three bunkers in between. Translation: Take a bogey if you can, be happy, get something to eat at the snack bar, and enjoy the back nine. In the future, Riverbend hopes to add an 18-hole championship course and a nine-hole executive course, designed by Peter Jacobson. Plans also call for a resort hotel. Note: Some work was being done on this layout at press time, and the new yardage and ratings were not known.

Play Policy and Fees: Green fees are $40 Monday–Thursday, $60 Saturday, and $50 Friday and Sunday. Carts are included in green fees. Twilight rates are offered.

Tees and Yardage: *Men:* Black: yardage 7267, par 72, rating 72.7, slope 130; Blue: yardage 6530, par 72, rating 70.0, slope 122; White: yardage 5909, par 72, rating 66.8, slope 111; *Women:* Red: yardage 5136, par 72, rating 69.0, slope 112.

Tee Times: Reservations can be made seven days in advance.

Dress Code: No denim is allowed on the course. Collared shirts and nonmetal spikes are required.

Tournaments: A 20-player minimum is required to book an event, and shotgun tournaments are allowed.

Directions: From Highway 99 in Fresno, take the Avenue 12 exit and head east for 10 miles to the golf course.

Contact: 43369 Avenue 12, Fresno, CA 93638, pro shop 559/432-3020, fax 559/822-4653, www.riverbendgolfclub.com.

41 FORT WASHINGTON GOLF & COUNTRY CLUB

Architect: Willie Watson, 1923
18 holes   Private $125

San Joaquin Valley map, page 216

This is a classic valley course, and it ranks among the top courses in Central California. It is a walkable course with rolling hills, tree-lined fairways, and fast, undulating greens. The Pro-Scratch is played here annually in May. Fort Washington hosted the USGA mid-amateur in 2000.

Play Policy and Fees: Reciprocal play is accepted with members of other private clubs at a rate of $125.

Tees and Yardage: *Men:* Blue: yardage 6729, par 72, rating 73.0, slope 130; White: yardage 6461, par 72, rating 71.8, slope 126; *Women:* Red: yardage 6158, par 72, rating 75.8, slope 131; Gold: yardage 5603, par 72, rating 72.6, slope 124.

Tee Times: Reciprocal players should have their home professional call to make arrangements.

Dress Code: Collared shirts and nonmetal spikes are required. Bermuda shorts must be knee-length, and no denim is allowed.

Tournaments: A 100-player minimum is required to book a tournament. Carts are required. Events should be booked 12 months in advance. The banquet facility can accommodate 300 people.

Directions: From Highway 99 in Fresno, take the Herndon Avenue exit east. Turn left on Blackstone Avenue. Turn right on Friant Road and then turn right again on Fort Washington, which leads to the course.

Contact: 10272 North Millbrook, Fresno, CA 93720, pro shop 559/434-9120, fax 559/434-6160.

42 COPPER RIVER COUNTRY CLUB

Architect: David Pfaff, 1995
18 holes   Private

San Joaquin Valley map, page 216

This links-style course is driver-friendly, but bring a light touch because the greens are fast. There is water on seven holes. It is a peaceful setting with no parallel fairways, which lends a private feel.

Play Policy and Fees: Reciprocal play is accepted with members of other private clubs; otherwise, members and guests only.

Tees and Yardage: *Men:* Black: yardage 7043, par 72, rating 73.7, slope 130; Blue: yardage 6620, par 72, rating 71.7, slope 128; White: yardage 6262, par 72, rating 70.1, slope 125; *Women:* Gold: yardage 5819, par 72, rating 73.9, slope 128; Red: yardage 5374, par 72, rating 71.4, slope 123.

Tee Times: Reciprocal players should have their home professional call to make arrangements.

Dress Code: Appropriate golf attire and nonmetal spikes are required.

Tournaments: This course is available for outside tournaments. A banquet facility is available that can accommodate 280 people.

Directions: From Fresno, take Highway 41 toward Yosemite to the North Friant Road exit. Follow North Friant to the golf course on the right.

Contact: 11500 North Friant Road, Fresno, CA 93720, pro shop 559/434-5200, fax 559/434-8962, www.copperrivercountryclub.com.

43 RIVERSIDE GOLF COURSE

Architect: William P. Bell, 1939

18 holes   Public $16–20

San Joaquin Valley map, page 216

This rolling, classic design is long and well guarded by trees. It's testy, with a number of sidehill lies to medium-sized greens. Bring every club. Notable is the par-4 10th hole, which tees off from a bluff and requires a difficult second shot to a green guarded on the right by an overhanging tree. Riverside is one of the best courses in California in its price range.

Play Policy and Fees: Green fees are $16 weekdays, $20 weekends and holidays. Senior, junior, and twilight rates are offered. Carts are $11 per rider.

Tees and Yardage: *Men:* Blue: yardage 6636, par 72, rating 71.3, slope 125; White: yardage 6416, par 72, rating 70.3, slope 122; *Women:* Red: yardage 5915, par 72, rating 73.6, slope 123.

Tee Times: Reservations may be booked seven days in advance.

Dress Code: Shirts and shoes must be worn.

Tournaments: Outside events may be booked up to one year in advance. A 16-player minimum is required.

Directions: From Highway 99 in Fresno, exit onto Herndon Avenue east. Cross the railroad tracks and turn left on Van Buren. Turn right on Josephine Avenue and follow it to the course.

Contact: 7672 North Josephine Avenue, Fresno, CA 93711, pro shop 559/275-5900, fax 559/275-0492, www.playriverside.com.

44 SAN JOAQUIN COUNTRY CLUB

Architect: Bob Baldock, 1961

18 holes   Private $100

San Joaquin Valley map, page 216

This is a long, rolling course with lots of trees.

The San Joaquin River comes into play on the north side of three holes. The course boasts well-maintained greens, which are fast and tricky.

Play Policy and Fees: Reciprocal play is accepted with members of other private clubs at a rate of $100; otherwise, members and guests only.

Tees and Yardage: *Men:* Blue: yardage 6840, par 72, rating 73.4, slope 133; White: yardage 6346, par 72, rating 71.6, slope 129; Gold: yardage 6100, par 72, rating 70.5, slope 126; *Women:* Red: yardage 5715, par 72, rating 73.4, slope 129.

Tee Times: Reciprocal players should have their home professional call to make arrangements.

Dress Code: Appropriate golf attire and non-metal spikes are required.

Tournaments: This course is not available for outside tournaments.

Directions: From Highway 99 in Herndon, take the West Herndon Avenue exit. Drive east to North Marks Avenue and turn left. North Marks Avenue will take you to the course driveway.

Contact: 3484 West Bluff Avenue, Fresno, CA 93711, pro shop 559/439-3359, clubhouse 559/439-3483, fax 559/439-6456.

45 FIG GARDEN GOLF COURSE

*Architect: Nick Lombardo, 1958;
Robert Dean Putman, 1973*

18 holes   Semiprivate $60

San Joaquin Valley map, page 216

Robert Dean Putman redesigned this course in 1973. It's a tight course and has two lakes and a river. The 406-yard, par-4 16th hole is a monster, with the river flanking the left side. It is fairly level with mature trees flanking fairways and surrounding greens.

Play Policy and Fees: Green fees are $60. Nine-hole, twilight, and junior rates are offered. Carts are $16 per rider.

Tees and Yardage: *Men:* Blue: yardage 6700, par 72, rating 70.6, slope 117; White: yardage 6305, par 72, rating 68.7, slope 113; *Women:* Red: yardage 5510, par 72, rating 70.4, slope 117.

Tee Times: Reservations can be booked seven days in advance.

Dress Code: Appropriate golf attire is required.

Tournaments: A 24-player minimum is needed to book an event. Carts are required. Events should be scheduled 12 months in advance. An outdoor banquet facility can accommodate 150 people.

Directions: Heading south toward Fresno on Highway 99, take the Herndon exit east. Turn left on North Van Ness Boulevard and drive one mile to the course.

Contact: 7700 North Van Ness Boulevard, Fresno, CA 93711, pro shop 559/439-2928, fax 559/439-2129, www.figgardengolf.com.

46 JAVIER'S FRESNO WEST GOLF COURSE

Architect: Bob Baldock, 1966

18 holes   **Public**   **$18–23**

San Joaquin Valley map, page 216

This is a very quiet championship golf course. It's long, flat, and often windy. There's water on eight holes. Among the tougher holes is the 192-yard, par-3 eighth, which features water to the left and behind the green.

Play Policy and Fees: Green fees are $18 Monday–Friday, $23 weekends and holidays, including cart. Twilight and senior rates are available.

Tees and Yardage: *Men:* Blue: yardage 6959, par 72, rating 72.5, slope 119; White: yardage 6607, par 72, rating 70.8, slope 116; *Women:* Red: yardage 6000, par 73, rating 74.1, slope 122.

Tee Times: Reservations may be booked seven days in advance.

Dress Code: Soft spikes are required.

Tournaments: This course is available for outside tournaments. The banquet facility can accommodate 180 people.

Directions: From Highway 99 in Fresno, take the Highway 180/Whitesbridge Road exit. Drive past Kerman to the course.

Contact: 23986 West Whitesbridge Road, Kerman, CA 93630, pro shop 559/846-8655, fax 559/846-8694.

47 PALM LAKES GOLF COURSE

Architect: Richard Bigler, 1986

18 holes   **Public**   **$12.25**

San Joaquin Valley map, page 216

This short, walkable executive course has one large lake, which comes into play on four holes.

Play Policy and Fees: Green fees are $12.25 any day. Senior, junior, and nine-hole rates are offered.

Tees and Yardage: *Men:* yardage 4082, par 62, rating 60.2, slope 93; *Women:* yardage 4082, par 62, rating 62.8, slope 97.

Tee Times: Reservations can be booked seven days in advance.

Dress Code: Appropriate attire and soft spikes are required.

Tournaments: This course is available for outside tournaments.

Directions: Driving south on Highway 99 from Madera, take the Shaw exit east past California State University Fresno. Turn right on Willow and then left at East Dakota Avenue. The course is across from the airport.

Contact: 5025 East Dakota Avenue, Fresno, CA 93727, pro shop 559/291-4050.

48 HANK'S SWANK PAR 3

Architect: Henry Bocchini Jr., 1983

9 holes   **Public**   **$8–10**

San Joaquin Valley map, page 216

This pretty little par-3 course features rolling terrain, plenty of sand, and large, well-kept, undulating greens. If your clubs are in need of repair, you're in luck. Hank Bocchini can repair your clubs on-site. For the golf purist, he also custom-makes persimmon woods.

Play Policy and Fees: Green fees for nine holes are $8 weekdays and $10 on weekends. Senior and junior rates are available. A repeat round is $5.

Tees and Yardage: *Men and Women:* yardage 1330, par 27, rating n/a, slope n/a.

Tee Times: Reservations are not accepted. All play is on a first-come, first-served basis.

Dress Code: Appropriate attire and soft spikes are required.

Tournaments: This course is available for outside tournaments.

Directions: The course is one mile east of Fresno Airport on East Olive Avenue.

Contact: 6101 East Olive Avenue, Fresno, CA 93727, pro shop 559/252-7077.

49 AIRWAYS GOLF COURSE

Architect: Bert Stamps, 1948

18 holes   **Public**   **$13.50–28.25**

San Joaquin Valley map, page 216

This flat, tree-lined course is short and sporty. It's a mature course and excellent for beginners and intermediate players. Rounds are usually completed in less than four hours.

Play Policy and Fees: Green fees are $13.50 to walk, $18 to ride weekdays, and $16.25 to walk, $28.25 to ride weekends and holidays. Senior, junior, and twilight rates are offered, and monthly cards are available.

Tees and Yardage: *Men:* White: yardage 5286, par 69, rating 64.2, slope 108; *Women:* Red: yardage 5258, par 71, rating 69.2, slope 115.

Tee Times: Reservations may be booked a week in advance.

Dress Code: Shirts and shoes are required.

Tournaments: Outside tournaments are welcome.

Directions: From Highway 99 in Fresno, exit on Ashlon Avenue and drive east for eight miles. Turn right on Peach Avenue and proceed one-half mile to the course entrance on the right.

Contact: 5440 East Shields Avenue, Fresno, CA 93727, pro shop 559/291-6254, fax 559/291-8413, www.airways-golf.com.

50 VILLAGE GREEN GOLF COURSE

Architect: Robert Dean Putman, 1959

9 holes   **Public**   **$8–12**

San Joaquin Valley map, page 216

There are three par-4s and six par-3s on this executive course. All holes are bunkered from tee to green. The course is nicely maintained, with lots of trees. On the seventh hole, the ball must carry over trees and a duck pond to the green. You can barely see the green.

Play Policy and Fees: Green fees are $8 for nine holes and $11 for 18 holes weekdays, $9 for nine holes and $12 for 18 holes weekends. Carts are $9 for nine holes and $15 for 18 holes. Junior and senior rates are available.

Tees and Yardage: *Men and Women:* yardage 3429, par 60, rating 56.8, slope 109.

Tee Times: Reservations are not accepted. All play is on a first-come, first-served basis.

Dress Code: Appropriate attire and soft spikes are required.

Tournaments: This course is available for outside tournaments, and shotgun tournaments are welcome. A 12-player minimum is needed to book an event.

Directions: From Highway 99 in Fresno, take the Belmont Avenue exit east to Clovis Avenue. Go south on Clovis just past Tulare Street. The course is in the Village Green Country Club Apartments.

Contact: 236 South Clovis Avenue, Fresno, CA 93727, pro shop 559/456-4653.

51 BELMONT COUNTRY CLUB

Architect: Bert Stamps, 1956

18 holes   **Private**   **$50**

San Joaquin Valley map, page 216

This course is well maintained, short, and tight, with big greens and lots of trees. It's a good test of irons and your short game. Additions and renovations include new water features and rebuilt tee boxes.

Play Policy and Fees: Reciprocal play is accepted with members of other private clubs at a rate of $50. Carts are $22. The course is closed on Monday.

Tees and Yardage: *Men:* Blue: yardage 6503, par 72, rating 70.4, slope 128; White: yardage 6241, par 72, rating 69.5, slope 126; Gold: yardage 5880, par 72, rating 67.9, slope 122; *Women:* Red: yardage 5036, par 72, rating 68.8, slope 116.

Tee Times: Reciprocal players should have their club professional call to make arrangements.

Dress Code: Collared shirts are required for men, and the inseam of shorts must be at least six inches for men and women. No blue denim shorts or pants are permitted. Soft spikes only.

Tournaments: This course is available for outside tournaments Monday, Thursday, and Friday. Events may be booked six months to a year in advance.

Directions: In Fresno on Highway 99, take the Belmont Avenue exit east. Drive 13.5 miles to the course on the right.

Contact: 8253 East Belmont, Fresno, CA 93727, pro shop 559/251-5076, fax 559/251-2713, www.belmontcountryclub.net.

52 SUNNYSIDE COUNTRY CLUB
Architect: William P. Bell, 1911
18 holes   **Private**   **$100**

San Joaquin Valley map, page 216

This long, demanding course has tight fairways and lots of sand and trees. Be careful of the greens—they look innocent, but they're small, fast, and tricky. This is the oldest course in the San Joaquin Valley and one of the original four clubs to start the California State Golf Association. The women's record of 67 is owned by LPGA golfer Shelly Hamlin.

Play Policy and Fees: Reciprocal play is accepted with members of other private clubs at a rate of $100, plus $12 for a cart. The course is closed on Monday.

Tees and Yardage: *Men:* Blue: yardage 6803, par 72, rating 72.5, slope 130; White: yardage 6470, par 72, rating 71.2, slope 128; Gold: yardage 6096, par 72, rating 69.6, slope 124; *Women:* Red: yardage 5548, par 72, rating 71.9, slope 126.

Tee Times: Reciprocal players should have their club professional call to make arrangements.

Dress Code: No denim of any kind may be worn. Shorts must have a six-inch inseam, and shirts must have collars. Nonmetal spikes are required.

Tournaments: All tournaments must be member-sponsored. A 20-player minimum is needed. Tournaments can be booked six months in advance. The banquet facility can hold 300 people.

Directions: From Highway 99 in Fresno, take the Ventura Avenue/Kings Canyon Road exit east for seven miles to Clovis Avenue. Turn right on Clovis Avenue and turn left on East Butler Avenue to the course.

Contact: 5704 East Butler, Fresno, CA 93727, pro shop 559/255-6871, clubhouse 559/251-6011, fax 559/251-3090.

53 SELMA VALLEY GOLF COURSE
Architect: Robert Dean Putman, 1956
18 holes   **Public**   **$14–18**

San Joaquin Valley map, page 216

This mostly flat course is short, with many doglegs and tree-lined fairways. It's easy to walk and is particularly good for beginning and intermediate players. It's a fast course to play. Most rounds can be completed in fewer than four hours on a weekend—a rarity.

Play Policy and Fees: Green fees are $14 weekdays and $18 weekends and holidays. Carts are $22.

Tees and Yardage: *Men:* Back: yardage 5332, par 69, rating 65.3, slope 112; *Women:* Forward: yardage 5038, par 70, rating 68.9, slope 116.

Tee Times: Reservations may be booked seven days in advance.

Dress Code: The course requests respectful appearance and conduct.

Tournaments: This course is available for outside tournaments year-round.

Directions: From Highway 99 in Selma (20 miles south of Fresno), take the Floral Avenue exit for two miles to Bethel. Turn right on Bethel and drive one-half mile to Rose Avenue. Turn left on Rose Avenue and drive one-quarter mile to the course on the right.

Contact: 12389 East Rose Avenue, Selma, CA 93662, pro shop 559/896-2424, fax 559/896-4896.

**KINGS RIVER GOLF &
COUNTRY CLUB**
Architect: Bob Baldock, 1955;
Nick Lombardo and Robert Dean Putman, 1957
18 holes   Private

San Joaquin Valley map, page 216

This course is tight, mostly flat, and walkable.
The Kings River borders the course. The signature hole is the 519-yard, par-5 16th, which
crosses the Kings River. Bold players can cut
as much yardage as they dare off the tee to
reach the green in two shots. The greens are
small, fast, and usually in good shape.

Play Policy and Fees: Reciprocal play is accepted with members of other private clubs.
Fee is based on what Kings River members
would be charged at reciprocator's club.

Tees and Yardage: *Men:* Blue: yardage 6695, par
72, rating 72.2, slope 132; White: yardage 6431,
par 72, rating 71.1, slope 129; *Women:* Red:
yardage 6022, par 72, rating 75.1, slope 129.

Tee Times: Reciprocal players should have their
home professional call to make arrangements.

Dress Code: Appropriate golf attire and nonmetal spikes are required.

Tournaments: This course is available for a limited number of outside events. Please inquire.

Directions: This course is between Fresno and
Visalia. From Highway 99, take the Canejo exit
east for four miles to the course on the left.

Contact: 3100 Avenue 400, Kingsburg, CA
93631, pro shop 559/897-2077.

55 **KINGS COUNTRY CLUB**
Architect: William Lock, 1923
18 holes   Private $35–65

San Joaquin Valley map, page 216

This tough course plays longer than the yardage
suggests. Towering oak trees and two lakes con-
spire against the golfer. Don't take the 615-
yard, par-5 15th for granted. It may appear to
be a dull straightaway stretch, but it usually
gives players all they can handle.

Play Policy and Fees: Reciprocal play is ac-

cepted with members of other private clubs.
Green fees for reciprocators are $35 weekdays
and $65 weekends. Carts are additional.

Tees and Yardage: *Men:* Blue: yardage 6656, par
72, rating 72.8, slope 129; White: yardage 6411,
par 72, rating 71.6, slope 127; *Women:* Red:
yardage 5976, par 72, rating 74.9, slope 130.

Tee Times: Reciprocal players should have their
home professional call to make arrangements.

Dress Code: Appropriate golf attire and nonmetal spikes are required.

Tournaments: This course is available for a limited number of outside events.

Directions: Driving south on Highway 99 from
Fresno, take the Highway 43 exit south and turn
right on Dover Avenue. Drive two miles to 12th
Avenue, turn right, and follow it to the end.

Contact: 3529 12th Avenue, Hanford, CA 93230,
pro shop 559/582-0740, clubhouse 559/582-
2264.

56 **LEMOORE GOLF COURSE**
Architect: Bob Baldock, 1963
18 holes   Public $17–22

San Joaquin Valley map, page 216

Originally opened in 1928 as a nine-hole course,
this facility was expanded in 1991 to its present 18-hole layout. Thus, the two sides have
completely different personalities, with the
newer nine designed to have a linkslike feel. It
is within a residential neighborhood. The older
front nine is characterized by narrow fairways
and lots of trees and lakes.

Play Policy and Fees: Green fees are $17 week-
days and $22 weekends. Optional carts are
$11 per rider. Twilight, senior, and junior rates
are available.

Tees and Yardage: *Men:* Blue: yardage 6431, par
72, rating 70.8, slope 121; White: yardage 6001,
par 72, rating 68.8, slope 115; *Women:* Red:
yardage 5126, par 72, rating 69.0, slope 119.

Tee Times: Reservations can be booked seven
days in advance.

Dress Code: Appropriate golf attire and soft
spikes requested.

Tournaments: A 20-player minimum is required to book an event. Tournaments should be scheduled 4–8 months in advance.

Directions: Take Highway 198 west from Visalia to the 18th Avenue exit in Lemoore. Take 18th Avenue south to Iona Avenue. Turn right on Iona and drive to the course.

Contact: 350 West Iona Avenue, Lemoore, CA 93245, pro shop 559/924-9658, fax 559/924-4131, www.lemooregolfcourse.com.

57 FARMERS GOLF COURSE & PAINTBALL

Architect: Bob Baldock, 1960

9 holes	Public	$7–15

San Joaquin Valley map, page 216

This course, formerly known as Harvest Valley and before that Jackson Lakes, reduced from 18 holes to nine holes in 2002. The former back nine is now used for paintball games. It was bound to happen somewhere, sometime. But look on the bright side—now you can do a new sort of Olympic game: nine holes of golf followed by shooting the guy who won.

Play Policy and Fees: Weekday green fees are $7 for nine holes and $10 for 18 holes, and weekend fees are $12 for nine holes and $15 for 18 holes. All prices include a cart.

Tees and Yardage: *Men:* yardage 3000, par 34, rating n/a, slope n/a; *Women:* yardage 2500, par 34, rating n/a, slope n/a.

Tee Times: Reservations may be booked seven days in advance.

Dress Code: Shirts and shoes are required.

Tournaments: Outside tournaments are welcome and may be booked six weeks to one year in advance.

Directions: From Highway 99, take Highway 198 west to Lemoore. From Lemoore, follow 18th Avenue south three miles to the course, which is on the corner of 18th and Jackson.

Contact: 14868 18th Avenue, Lemoore, CA 93245, pro shop 559/925-1237, fax 559/925-1274.

58 LAKEVIEW GOLF CLUB

Architect: Kurt Nichols, 2001

9 holes	Public	$7–8

San Joaquin Valley map, page 216

This fun course is built on fairly flat terrain, with young trees still growing in. It features bent-grass greens that are generally in great shape. There is water on several holes, including in front of the second, to the left of the third, and on both sides of the sixth. It also offers some nice Sierra mountain views.

Play Policy and Fees: Green fees are $7 weekdays, $8 weekends and holidays. Carts are additional.

Tees and Yardage: *Men (18 holes):* Blue: yardage 6098, par 70, rating 65.8, slope 108; White: yardage 5418, par 70, rating 64.0, slope 104; *Women (18 holes):* Red: yardage 5034, par 70, rating 62.2, slope 96.

Tee Times: Reservations can be made 30 days in advance.

Dress Code: No metal spikes are allowed on the course.

Tournaments: Tournaments welcome.

Directions: Exit onto Highway 198 (heading west from Highway 99, east from I-5). Turn onto 9th Avenue, heading south. In one mile, turn left onto Hanford-Armona Road. The course is on your right.

Contact: 8945 Hanford-Armona Road, Hanford, CA 93230, golf shop 559/583-7888.

59 VALLEY OAKS GOLF COURSE

Architect: Robert D. Putman, 1972; Cary Bickler, 1984; J. Michael Poellot, 1996

27 holes	Public	$22–27

San Joaquin Valley map, page 216

There are three nine-hole courses: Valley, Oaks, and Lakes. The Lakes layout is the newest of the three and is more of a links-style design. Valley and Oaks are more traditional designs with mature oak trees and water, featuring fast, large, well-maintained greens. Good putting is essential. They are all fairly level layouts, so walking is a joy.

Play Policy and Fees: Green fees are $22 weekdays and $27 weekends. Optional carts are $11 per rider. Twilight, senior, and junior rates are available.

Tees and Yardage: Valley/Oaks—*Men:* Blue: yardage 6564, par 72, rating 70.8, slope 125; White: yardage 6228, par 72, rating 69.1, slope 121; *Women:* Red: yardage 5692, par 72, rating 72.4, slope 123. Oaks/Lakes—*Men:* Blue: yardage 6575, par 72, rating 71.0, slope 126; White: yardage 6213, par 72, rating 69.0, slope 122; *Women:* Red: yardage 5491, par 72, rating 71.5, slope 123. Lakes/Valley—*Men:* Blue: yardage 6471, par 72, rating 70.2, slope 122; White: yardage 6209, par 72, rating 68.5, slope 118; *Women:* Red: yardage 5597, par 72, rating 71.5, slope 122.

Tee Times: Reservations are not required, but they may be booked five days in advance.

Dress Code: Appropriate attire and soft spikes are required.

Tournaments: Tournaments may be booked 12 months in advance. The banquet facility holds 180 people.

Directions: In Visalia on Highway 99, take the Highway 198 turnoff east. Drive one mile and exit at South Plaza Drive. Continue to the course, which is next to the airport.

Contact: 1800 South Plaza Drive, Visalia, CA 93277, pro shop 559/651-1441.

🔟 VISALIA COUNTRY CLUB
Architect: Course designed, 1922;
Desmond Muirhead, 1964

18 holes　　　**Private**　　　**$75**

🏌 📷 🍴 🏌 🚜 🍺

San Joaquin Valley map, page 216

This level course has lots of trees and bunkers, with water on eight holes. Visalia demands accuracy off the tee, and the well-kept greens are large and tricky, requiring a deft putting touch. This is one of the few valley courses that overseeds in the winter months.

Play Policy and Fees: Reciprocal play is accepted with members of other private clubs at a rate of $75, including cart. The course is closed on Monday.

Tees and Yardage: *Men:* Blue: yardage 6634, par 72, rating 72.2, slope 131; White: yardage 6293, par 72, rating 70.7, slope 125; *Women:* Red: yardage 5823, par 72, rating 74.2, slope 131.

Tee Times: Reciprocal players should have their home professional call to make arrangements.

Dress Code: Nonmetal spikes are required; check with golf shop for apparel regulations.

Tournaments: The course is available for outside events on Monday only. A 100-player minimum is required to book an event. Events should be scheduled 12 months in advance. The banquet facility can accommodate 250 people.

Directions: From Highway 99, take Highway 198 east. In Visalia, take the Mooney Boulevard exit and turn left. Turn left again on West Main Street and turn right on Ranch Road. Follow it to the end and the club.

Contact: 625 Ranch Road, Visalia, CA 93291, pro shop 559/734-1458, fax 559/734-4635.

🔢 OAK PATCH GOLF COURSE
Architect: Tex Vanderwenter, 1992

9 holes　　　**Public**　　　**$7–15**

📷 🍴 🏌 🍺

San Joaquin Valley map, page 216

One par-4 on this short course has been called "the toughest hole in the valley," according to former pro Harry Harrison. This course runs along the Kaweah River.

Play Policy and Fees: Green fees are $7 for nine holes and $13 for 18 holes on weekdays, $8 for nine holes and $15 for 18 holes on weekends. Pull carts are $1.50. Closed Monday.

Tees and Yardage: *Men and Women:* yardage 1349, par 29, rating n/a, slope n/a.

Tee Times: Reservations are not accepted. All play is on a first-come, first-served basis.

Dress Code: Appropriate attire and soft spikes are required.

Tournaments: This course is available for outside tournaments.

Directions: From Visalia, drive seven miles

east on Highway 198 to Ivanhoe. Turn off on County Road 158. Follow signs under the bridge, turn right after the bridge, and continue to the course.

Contact: 30400 Road 158, Visalia, CA 93292, pro shop 559/733-5000.

62 SIERRA VIEW GOLF COURSE

Architect: Robert Dean Putman, 1956;
Bob Baldock, 1966

18 holes **Public** **$18–23**

San Joaquin Valley map, page 216

Originally a nine-hole course, Sierra View was filled out to 18 holes in 1966 by architect Bob Baldock. Situated in the San Joaquin Valley, this course has fast greens and lots of trees and bunkers. The layout is mostly flat, and the four par-5s measure under 500 yards and are easily reachable for long hitters. Sierra View's signature 14th hole requires a tee shot over a lake to an elevated green. Built in 1956, this is the oldest course in Visalia.

Play Policy and Fees: Green fees are $18 weekdays and $23 weekends. Carts are $22.

Tees and Yardage: *Men:* Blue: yardage 6388, par 72, rating 70.0, slope 119; White: yardage 6169, par 72, rating 69.1, slope 117; *Women:* Red: yardage 5886, par 73, rating 72.5, slope 118.

Tee Times: Reservations may be made any time.

Dress Code: Appropriate golf attire and non-metal spikes are required.

Tournaments: A 16-player minimum is needed for regular tournaments. Tournaments should be booked at least one month in advance, and packages are available.

Directions: On Highway 99 in south Visalia, take the Avenue 264 exit (Tagus exit) east. Continue four miles to the course.

Contact: 12608 Avenue 264, Visalia, CA 93277, pro shop 559/732-2078.

63 EXETER PUBLIC GOLF COURSE

Architect: Bob Baldock, 1963

9 holes **Public** **$6–12**

San Joaquin Valley map, page 216

A lot of water comes into play on this tree-lined, mature course. Three of the holes are par-4s; the longest is the 400-yard fifth.

Play Policy and Fees: Green fees weekdays are $6 for nine holes, $11 for 18 holes; weekend fees are $7 for nine holes, $12 for 18 holes.

Tees and Yardage: *Men and Women:* yardage 1528, par 30, rating n/a, slope n/a.

Tee Times: Reservations are not accepted. All play is on a first-come, first-served basis.

Dress Code: Appropriate attire and soft spikes are required.

Tournaments: This course is available for outside tournaments.

Directions: From Highway 99 in Visalia, drive east on Highway 198 (toward Three Rivers). Turn right on Anderson Road (Highway 180). Follow it to Visalia Road and turn left to the course.

Contact: 510 West Visalia Road, Exeter, CA 93221, pro shop 559/592-4783.

64 LONESOME DOVE GOLF COURSE

Architect: Bob Baldock, 1963

9 holes **Public** **$10–17**

San Joaquin Valley map, page 216

This hilly course is walkable. Mature trees and two lakes come into play on two holes. The course is a good exercise for players of all abilities. A few holes to watch out for are the second and fourth. The second hole, a par-3, is a long iron into a small green with water guarding three sides. The fourth hole is a par-4 that dares you to cut off as much of the dogleg as possible. Lonesome Dove (formerly Polvadero) sits next to I-5 between Los Angeles and the San Francisco Bay area. Many people like to take a break from the grueling drive and play a round.

Play Policy and Fees: Green fees are $10 for nine holes and $15 for 18 holes weekdays, $12 for nine holes and $17 for 18 holes weekends. Carts are $20 for 18 holes. Call for special rates that are always available.

Tees and Yardage: *Men (18 holes):* White/Blue combo: yardage 6490, par 72, rating 70.4, slope 119; *Women (18 holes):* White/Blue combo: yardage 6490, par 72, rating 70.2, slope 115.

Tee Times: Reservations can be booked seven days in advance.

Dress Code: Appropriate attire and soft spikes are required.

Tournaments: A 16-player minimum is required to book a tournament.

Directions: From I-5 near Coalinga, take the Jayne Avenue exit west to Sutter Avenue. Turn left, and the course is on the right.

Contact: 41605 Sutter Avenue, Coalinga, CA 93210, pro shop 559/935-3578.

65 TULARE GOLF COURSE

Architect: Bob Baldock, 1956

18 holes　　　**Public**　　　**$13–25**

San Joaquin Valley map, page 216

This course is mostly flat and open, with several lakes. This course prides itself on staying in top condition. Greens and fairways are constantly being maintained and rebuilt as needed. This care shows, and makes the course very popular with local golfers and tournaments.

Play Policy and Fees: Green fees are $13 for nine holes and $20 for 18 holes on weekdays, $16 for nine holes and $25 for 18 holes on weekends. Carts are $12 for nine holes and $20 for 18. Monthly tickets are available for juniors and seniors.

Tees and Yardage: *Men:* Blue: yardage 6762, par 72, rating 71.8, slope 124; White: yardage 6542, par 72, rating 71.0, slope 120; *Women:* Gold: yardage 5975, par 72, rating 74.1, slope 124; Red: yardage 5626, par 72, rating 71.9, slope 120.

Tee Times: Reservations are not necessary except for holidays and weekend play.

Dress Code: Appropriate attire and soft spikes are required.

Tournaments: This course is available for outside tournaments. Events may be booked up to one year in advance.

Directions: From Highway 99 in Tulare, head east on Avenue 200. Turn left on South Laspina. The course is on the right.

Contact: 5310 South Laspina, Tulare, CA 93274, pro shop 559/686-5300.

66 LINDSAY MUNICIPAL GOLF COURSE

Architect: Bob Baldock, 1961

9 holes　　　**Public**　　　**$5–9**

San Joaquin Valley map, page 216

This is a short course that you can play twice. Set in Lindsay City Park, it's flat, with lots of trees and small greens. It's a good course for beginners, seniors, and players wanting to work on their irons. The driving range is for irons only.

Play Policy and Fees: Green fees are $5 for nine holes and $8 for 18 holes weekdays, and $5 for nine holes and $9 for 18 holes weekends. Pull carts are $1.

Tees and Yardage: *Men and Women:* yardage 1090, par 27, rating n/a, slope n/a.

Tee Times: Reservations are not accepted. All play is on a first-come, first-served basis.

Dress Code: Appropriate attire and soft spikes are required.

Tournaments: This course is available for outside tournaments.

Directions: This course is in the city park eight blocks east of Highway 65 between Exeter and Porterville.

Contact: 801 North Elmwood, Lindsay, CA 93247, pro shop 559/562-1144.

67 PORTERVILLE GOLF COURSE

Architect: Course designed, 1920

9 holes　　　**Public**　　　**$10–15**

San Joaquin Valley map, page 216

This course is mostly flat and narrow, with out-of-bounds on every hole. The greens are quite small. It's a short layout where irons should be the clubs of choice.

Play Policy and Fees: Green fees are $10 for nine holes and $15 for 18 holes. Carts are $9 for nine holes and $18 for 18 holes. Junior rates are offered. The course is closed on Monday.

Tees and Yardage: *Men (18 holes):* Blue: yardage 5622, par 70, rating 67.0, slope 112; *Women (18 holes):* Red: yardage 5548, par 72, rating 70.2, slope 115.

Tee Times: Reservations on weekdays are not accepted. All play is on a first-come, first-served basis. Tee times for Saturday can be made starting Tuesday and tee times for Sunday can be made starting Wednesday.

Dress Code: Nonmetal spikes are required.

Tournaments: No shotgun starts are allowed.

Directions: From Highway 99 or Highway 65, take exit 190 east to Plano Road in Porterville. Turn left onto Plano and then right on Date Street. Drive to Leggett Road and turn left. Continue to Isham Avenue and the course.

Contact: 702 East Isham Avenue, Porterville, CA 93257, pro shop 559/784-9468.

68 RIVER ISLAND COUNTRY CLUB

Architect: Robert Dean Putman, 1964

18 holes   Private $30

San Joaquin Valley map, page 216

This long, sprawling course wanders through old oak trees and offers a variety of holes. The Tule River flows through the terrain. You cross the river 11 times, and it comes into play on nine holes. The course is walkable, but there is a lot of distance between holes.

Play Policy and Fees: Outside play is welcome after noon. The course is closed on Monday. Reciprocal play is accepted with members of other private clubs at a rate of $30. Optional carts are $13.

Tees and Yardage: *Men:* Blue: yardage 6910, par 72, rating 73.5, slope 133; White: yardage 6364,

par 72, rating 70.7, slope 127; *Women:* Red: yardage 5665, par 72, rating 73.2, slope 128.

Tee Times: Reciprocal players should have their home professional call to make arrangements.

Dress Code: Collared shirts and nonmetal spikes are required. Shorts must be to mid-thigh, and no blue jeans are allowed on the course.

Tournaments: This course is available for outside tournaments.

Directions: Take Highway 190 and drive past Porterville for 10 miles. The entrance to this private country club resort course is on the right.

Contact: 31989 River Island Drive, Porterville, CA 93257, pro shop 559/784-9425, www.river islandcc.com.

69 DELANO PUBLIC GOLF COURSE

Architect: Bert Stamps, 1962

9 holes   Public $6–8

San Joaquin Valley map, page 216

This level course offers undulating fairways. Ponds come into play on the first, eighth, and ninth holes. The third hole is a 209-yard par-3 with trees on the left and right, making for tight play. This traditional design boasts eucalyptus trees along the fairways.

Play Policy and Fees: Green fees are $6 for nine holes weekdays, $8 for nine holes weekends and holidays. Carts are $12 for nine holes. Senior, junior, and twilight rates are available.

Tees and Yardage: *Men (18 holes):* Blue: yardage 4642, par 64, rating 61.6, slope 102; White: yardage 4354, par 64, rating 61.6, slope 102; *Women (18 holes):* Red: yardage 3986, par 64, rating 65.8, slope 102.

Tee Times: Reservations can be booked seven days in advance.

Dress Code: Nonmetal spikes are mandatory.

Tournaments: This course is available for outside tournaments. A minimum of 20 players is needed to book a tournament. Tournaments may be booked 12 months in advance.

Directions: Take Highway 99 north to the

Woollomes Avenue exit. Head east to Lexington and take a left. The course is on the right. **Contact:** 104 South Lexington Street (P.O. Box 927), Delano, CA 93216, pro shop 661/725-7527, fax 661/725-8388.

70 WASCO VALLEY ROSE GOLF COURSE

Architect: Robert Dean Putman, 1991
18 holes   **Public**   **$16–18**

San Joaquin Valley map, page 216

Six lakes come into play on this course. There are several undulating fairways, elevated tees, and spectacular greens. The ninth provides an exciting finish to the front nine, particularly if you survive the sloping fairway, a large lake, and a bunker, all of which come into play off the tee. The men's course record is 65. You can beat that!

Play Policy and Fees: Green fees are $16 weekdays and $18 weekends. Twilight and senior rates are available. Carts are $10 per rider.

Tees and Yardage: *Men:* Blue: yardage 6862, par 72, rating 74.1, slope 126; White: yardage 6230, par 72, rating 70.8, slope 122; *Women:* Red: yardage 5356, par 72, rating 70.5, slope 119.

Tee Times: Reservations can be booked seven days in advance.

Dress Code: Nonmetal spikes are required.

Tournaments: A 30-player minimum is needed to book an event, and a 144-player field is required for a shotgun start.

Directions: From Highway 99, take the Highway 46 exit west. Drive two miles west of Wasco and take the Leonard Avenue exit to the course. The course is about 20 miles northwest of Bakersfield.

Contact: 301 North Leonard Avenue, Wasco, CA 93280, pro shop 661/758-8301, fax 661/758-3547.

71 NORTH KERN GOLF COURSE

Architect: Kermit Styber, 1953
18 holes   **Public**   **$16.50–20**

San Joaquin Valley map, page 216

This course is packed with trees and bunkers. Nevertheless, the fairways are wide and level, leading to small greens. The sixth hole is a devil. It's a 442-yard par-4 that plays uphill and into the wind. The green is heavily bunkered in front, leaving only a narrow opening. Pin placement can add more yardage to an already long hole. Several holes were remodeled in 2004, including new tees and rebuilt greens.

Play Policy and Fees: Green fees are $16.50 weekdays and $20 holidays and weekends. Carts are $10.50 per rider. Junior and senior rates are offered.

Tees and Yardage: *Men:* Blue: yardage 6754, par 72, rating 71.8, slope 123; White: yardage 6521, par 72, rating 70.8, slope 121; Gold: yardage 5700, par 72, rating 67.3, slope 113; *Women:* Red: yardage 5582, par 72, rating 71.4, slope 113.

Tee Times: Reservations may be booked seven days in advance.

Dress Code: Shorts and tee shirts are acceptable, and nonmetal spikes are required.

Tournaments: This course is available for outside tournaments. They should be booked one month in advance.

Directions: From Bakersfield, travel north on Highway 99 for 12 miles to the Shafter exit. Head east for 2.5 miles on Laredo Highway to Quality Road. Turn north on Quality Road and continue half a mile to the course.

Contact: 17412 Quality Road, Bakersfield, CA 93308, pro shop 661/399-0347, fax 661/399-5938.

72 THE LINKS AT RIVERLAKES RANCH

Architect: Ron Fream and Golf Plan, 1999
18 holes   **Public**   **$35–50**

San Joaquin Valley map, page 216

This course plays over 200 acres featuring existing almond orchards, redwoods, Canary Island pines, and 12 lakes. Bunker placement and green design make this course challenging for players of all skill levels.

Play Policy and Fees: Green fees are $35 Monday–Thursday, $40 Friday, and $50 weekends and holidays. Twilight, resident, senior, and junior rates are also available. Fees include cart.

Tees and Yardage: *Men:* Black: yardage 6800, par 72, rating 73.3, slope 134; Blue: yardage 6379, par 72, rating 71.4, slope 130; White: yardage 5891, par 72, rating 69.2, slope 126; *Women:* Red: yardage 5180, par 72, rating 70.4, slope 120.

Tee Times: Reservations can be made seven days in advance.

Dress Code: This is a nonmetal spike facility.

Tournaments: A 20-player minimum is required to book an event.

Directions: In Bakersfield from Highway 99, take the Oliver Street exit and head west to Riverlakes Drive. Go left on Riverlakes Drive. The course is on the right.

Contact: 5201 Riverlakes Drive, Bakersfield, CA 93312, pro shop 661/587-5465, fax 661/587-8885, www.riverlakesranchgolf.com.

73 SEVEN OAKS COUNTRY CLUB

Architect: Robert Muir Graves, 1992

27 holes   Private $100

🏌 📷 🍴 🛒 ☕

San Joaquin Valley map, page 216

A new nine was added to this facility in 2002, bringing the total number of holes to 27. They are fairly flat courses, set within a master-planned residential community. Water comes into play on several holes in the form of lakes. They are nicely manicured layouts with old oak trees, rocks, and colorful plantings everywhere.

Play Policy and Fees: Limited reciprocal play is accepted by prior arrangement only. Reciprocal fees are $100, plus an optional cart at $12 per rider.

Tees and Yardage: Island/Oaks—*Men:* Blue: yardage 7146, par 72, rating 74.1, slope 127;

White: yardage 6608, par 72, rating 71.1, slope 121; Gold: yardage 5962, par 72, rating 68.2, slope 113; *Women:* Red: yardage 5477, par 72, rating 72.0, slope 123. Lake/Island—*Men:* Blue: yardage 7079, par 72, rating 73.7, slope 127; White: yardage 6549, par 72, rating 70.9, slope 120; Gold: yardage 5960, par 72, rating 68.1, slope 112; *Women:* Red: yardage 5458, par 72, rating 71.9, slope 121. Oaks/Lake—*Men:* Blue: yardage 6959, par 72, rating 73.0, slope 126; White: yardage 6459, par 72, rating 70.4, slope 117; Gold: yardage 5874, par 72, rating 67.1, slope 107; *Women:* Red: yardage 5365, par 72, rating 71.1, slope 122.

Tee Times: Reciprocal players should have their home professional call to make arrangements.

Dress Code: Appropriate golf attire and nonmetal spikes are required.

Tournaments: Outside events are limited to charity events on Monday. Carts are mandatory. An 80-player minimum is required. The banquet facility can accommodate 325 people.

Directions: From Highway 99 in Bakersfield, take the Ming Avenue exit west. Continue about five miles to the intersection with Grand Lakes Avenue. The course is on the left.

Contact: 2000 Grand Lakes Avenue, Bakersfield, CA 93311, pro shop 661/664-6474, fax 661/664-6472, www.sevenoakscountryclub.com.

74 STOCKDALE COUNTRY CLUB

Architect: Lloyd Tevis, 1925

18 holes   Private $100

🏌 📷 🍴 🪣 🛒 ☕

San Joaquin Valley map, page 216

This course has numerous trees and a few water hazards on a traditional layout. First opened in 1925, it is one of the older clubs in the area.

Play Policy and Fees: Reciprocal play is accepted with members of other private clubs at a rate of $100; otherwise, members and guests only. Carts are $11 per rider.

Tees and Yardage: *Men:* Blue: yardage 6410, par 71, rating 70.6, slope 121; White: yardage 6172, par 71, rating 69.7, slope 118; *Women:* Red: yardage 5885, par 71, rating 74.3, slope 127.

Tee Times: Reciprocal players should have their home professional call to make arrangements.
Dress Code: Appropriate golf attire and non-metal spikes are required.
Tournaments: This course is not available for outside events.
Directions: From the north, take the Stockdale exit off Highway 99 in Bakersfield. Travel west to Stockdale Highway. Turn right and drive one-half mile to the club entrance.
Contact: 7001 Stockdale Highway (P.O. Box 9727), Bakersfield, CA 93309, pro shop 661/832-0587, clubhouse 661/832-0310, fax 661/832-6590, www.stockdalecountryclub.com.

75 SUNDALE COUNTRY CLUB
Architect: Del Webb, 1962
18 holes   Private $30

San Joaquin Valley map, page 216

Formerly a public course known as Kern City, this layout is mostly flat, with water and mature trees. The front nine has no parallel holes. Water can be found on six holes, and there is one long par-3. The course is deceptively difficult because the par-4 holes are long and the par-3 holes are tough.
Play Policy and Fees: Reciprocal play is accepted with members of other private clubs at a rate of $30; otherwise members and guests only.
Tees and Yardage: *Men:* Blue: yardage 6801, par 72, rating 71.8, slope 120; White: yardage 6589, par 72, rating 70.7, slope 115; Gold: yardage 6317, par 72, rating 69.2, slope 112; *Women:* Red: yardage 5743, par 73, rating 72.7, slope 124.
Tee Times: Reciprocal players should have their home professional call to make arrangements.
Dress Code: Shorts must come to mid-thigh. Collared shirts and nonmetal spikes are required. No tee shirts or jeans are allowed.
Tournaments: This course is not available for tournaments.
Directions: Take the Ming Avenue exit off Highway 99 in Bakersfield, and travel west to New Stine Road. Turn right. Drive one-quarter mile to Sundale Avenue. Turn left and drive one-half mile to the club.
Contact: 6218 Sundale Avenue, Bakersfield, CA 93309, pro shop 661/831-5224, clubhouse 661/831-4200.

76 BAKERSFIELD COUNTRY CLUB
Architect: William F. Bell, 1950
18 holes   Private $100

San Joaquin Valley map, page 216

This well-maintained, mature course spreads across a hill. The layout requires good shot-making ability. Every club in the bag comes into play. Several long par-4s highlight the course. The course record is 63.
Play Policy and Fees: Reciprocal play is accepted with members of other private clubs; otherwise, members and guests only. Green fees for reciprocators are $100. Carts are $20. Reservations are required. The course is closed on Monday.
Tees and Yardage: *Men:* Blue: yardage 6819, par 72, rating 72.5, slope 127; White: yardage 6458, par 72, rating 70.8, slope 123; *Women:* Red: yardage 6156, par 72, rating 76.0, slope 132.
Tee Times: Reciprocal players should have their home professional call to make arrangements.
Dress Code: Appropriate golf attire and non-metal spikes are required.
Tournaments: Shotgun tournaments are available weekdays only. Carts are required. An 80-player minimum is required to book a tournament. Tournaments should be booked six months in advance. The banquet facility can hold 250 people.
Directions: From Highway 99 at Bakersfield, go east on Highway 178 about six miles. Take the Oswell Street exit and turn right. Turn left on Country Club Drive.
Contact: 4200 Country Club Drive, Bakersfield, CA 93306; P.O. Box 6007, Bakersfield, CA 93306, pro shop 661/871-4121, clubhouse 661/871-4000, www.bakersfieldcountryclub.com.

77 PEPPERTREE GOLF CLUB

Architect: Eddie Novak

18 holes   **Public**   **$18–20**

🚶 📷 🍴 🏌 🛺

San Joaquin Valley map, page 216

Formerly called Valle Grande, this course is level and appears simple to play, but don't be fooled. Out-of-bounds and an abundance of trees make accuracy a must. Two water channels run through the fairways, adding to the course's charm and difficulty.

Play Policy and Fees: Green fees are $18 on weekdays and $20 on weekends. Twilight, junior, and senior rates are offered. Carts are $10 per rider.

Tees and Yardage: *Men:* Blue: yardage 6331, par 72, rating 68.7, slope 112; White: yardage 6070, par 72, rating 67.5, slope 109; *Women:* Red: yardage 5218, par 72, rating 68.4, slope 109.

Tee Times: Reservations can be booked 14 days in advance.

Dress Code: Collared shirts and nonmetal spikes are required.

Tournaments: A 44-player minimum is required to book a tournament. Carts are required. Events should be scheduled two months in advance.

Directions: Travel east on Highway 58 from Bakersfield, turn right on Cottonwood Road, and drive 1.25 miles. Turn left on Watts Drive to the club.

Contact: 1119 Watts Drive, Bakersfield, CA 93307, pro shop 661/832-2259, fax 661/832-2324.

78 RIO BRAVO COUNTRY CLUB

Architect: Robert Muir Graves, 1981

18 holes   **Private**   **$75**

🚶 📷 🍴 🛺 ⛳

San Joaquin Valley map, page 216

This is a beautiful championship layout in the foothills of the Tehachapi Mountains. Two new lakes were built in 2004 to add to the enjoyment. It plays long and has excellent greens. The hole to watch for is the 11th, affectionately known as "Big Bertha." It's par-5 and

616 yards uphill to a difficult green. There is no flat lie on this hole. The green, the most difficult on the course, is severely sloped left to right and tough to read. Rio Bravo has been the site of the PGA Tour Qualifying School, U.S. Open qualifying, and the Southern California Open.

Play Policy and Fees: Reciprocal play is accepted with members of other private clubs; otherwise, members and guests only. Fees are $75 for reciprocators, including carts. The course is closed on Monday and Christmas.

Tees and Yardage: *Men:* Blue: yardage 7000, par 72, rating 73.1, slope 131; White: yardage 6521, par 72, rating 70.4, slope 125; Gold: yardage 6116, par 72, rating 68.3, slope 119; *Women:* Red: yardage 5694, par 72, rating 73.3, slope 124.

Tee Times: Reciprocal players should have their home professional call to make arrangements.

Dress Code: Tee shirts, denim, and metal spikes are not allowed.

Tournaments: A 75-player minimum is needed to book an event. A 100-player minimum is needed to book a tournament on a Monday. The banquet facility can accommodate 300 people.

Directions: From Highway 99 in Bakersfield, take Highway 178 east and drive about 15 miles to the Rio Bravo Country Club. Continue past the airport and turn right on Mira Monte to the course.

Contact: 15200 Casa Club Drive, Bakersfield, CA 93306, pro shop 661/871-4653, clubhouse 661/871-4900, fax 661/871-4930, www.rio bravocountryclub.com.

79 BUENA VISTA GOLF COURSE

Architect: George Mifflin, 1953

18 holes   **Public**   **$25.50–29**

🚶 📷 🍴 🏌 🛺 ⛳

San Joaquin Valley map, page 216

Originally a nine-hole layout, this course is the only green spot in the whole area, thanks to irrigation from an on-site well. The course begins with a 355-yard par-4. This is not a mirage. The green sits on top of a hill 50 yards up, the highest point on the golf course. Hit your tee shot to the flat area of the fairway to avoid an uphill lie, and then go for the large, flat green at the top. Overall, the course offers a rolling layout dotted with many palm trees.

Play Policy and Fees: Green fees are $25.50 weekdays and $29 weekends. Carts are $10.50 per rider. Resident, senior, and junior rates are offered. The course is closed Christmas Day.

Tees and Yardage: *Men:* Blue: yardage 6668, par 72, rating 71.0, slope 118; White: yardage 6318, par 72, rating 69.8, slope 113; *Women:* Red: yardage 5726, par 72, rating 71.7, slope 117.

Tee Times: Reservations can be booked seven days in advance.

Dress Code: Nonmetal spikes are required.

Tournaments: A 24-player minimum is required to book an outside event.

Directions: Take I-5 to Highway 119. Drive west on Highway 119 for about five miles and turn left onto Golf Course Road (just past the California Aqueduct).

Contact: 10256 Golf Course Road, Taft, CA 93268, pro shop 661/763-5124, fax 661/763-1191.

80 SYCAMORE CANYON GOLF CLUB

Architect: Robert Dean Putman, 1989

18 holes   Public $25–29

San Joaquin Valley map, page 216

Twenty acres of water come into play on 14 holes. Beware of the 548-yard ninth hole. It doglegs around a lake that runs 300 yards parallel to the hole. This par-5 is the number-one handicap hole on this course. This demanding course is made up of long par-4 and par-3 holes, and every green has at least two bunkers.

Play Policy and Fees: Green fees are $25 weekdays and $29 weekends. Fees include cart. Twilight, junior, and senior rates are available.

Tees and Yardage: *Men:* Blue: yardage 7100, par 72, rating 74.2, slope 123; White: yardage 6428, par 72, rating 69.9, slope 117; *Women:* Red: yardage 5744, par 73, rating 71.6, slope 120.

Tee Times: Reservations can be booked seven days in advance.

Dress Code: No tank tops or sweats are allowed. Nonmetal spikes are required.

Tournaments: Tournaments welcome. Please inquire.

Directions: Take Highway 99 south of Bakersfield to the Bear Mountain/Arvin exit. Go 10 miles east to South Derby Street, then south 3.5 miles to Kenmar Lane. Turn left and drive to the course.

Contact: 500 Kenmar Lane, Arvin, CA 93203, pro shop 661/854-3163.

81 OAK TREE COUNTRY CLUB

Architect: Ted Robinson Sr., 1972

9 holes   Private $10–20

San Joaquin Valley map, page 216

The course, at 4000 feet, is rimmed by mountains. It's a level layout surrounding a small lake, and trees dot the fairways. Jutting rocks add to the mountainous look of the course, but they rarely come into play.

Play Policy and Fees: Reciprocal play is accepted with members of other private clubs. Green fees are $10 for nine holes and $15 for 18 holes on weekdays. Weekend green fees are $15 for nine holes and $20 for 18 holes. Carts are $10 for nine holes and $16 for 18 holes.

Tees and Yardage: *Men (18 holes):* Back: yardage 6298, par 72, rating 70.3, slope 120; *Women (18 holes):* Forward: yardage 5606, par 72, rating 72.1, slope 126.

Tee Times: Reciprocal players should have their home professional call to make arrangements.

Dress Code: Collared shirts are required, and shorts must be at least to mid-thigh.

Tournaments: This course is not available for outside tournaments.

Directions: From Bakersfield, travel east on Highway 58 for 38 miles to the town of Tehachapi and take the Highway 202 exit. Follow the signs for about 14 miles to Bear Valley Springs.

Contact: 29541 Rolling Oak Drive, Tehachapi, CA 93561, pro shop 661/821-5144, fax 661/821-5406.

82 HORSE THIEF GOLF & COUNTRY CLUB

Architect: Bob Baldock, 1974

18 holes   **Resort**   **$23–50**

🏌 📷 🍴 🛏 🪝 🛺 🍽

San Joaquin Valley map, page 216

Horse Thief is a mountain course, elevation 4000 feet. Although it is not particularly long, it requires accuracy. The most prominent features are the oak trees and rocks that come into play. Water is also a factor on four holes.

Play Policy and Fees: Green fees are $23 to walk, $35 to ride weekdays, and $38 to walk, $50 to ride weekends. Call for seasonal rates. Twilight and senior rates are also offered.

Tees and Yardage: *Men:* Blue: yardage 6719, par 72, rating 72.0, slope 131; White: yardage 6348, par 72, rating 70.2, slope 127; *Women:* Gold: yardage 5677, par 72, rating 73.1, slope 129.

Tee Times: Reservations can be booked 10 days in advance.

Dress Code: Collared shirts are required. No short shorts are allowed.

Tournaments: A 20-player minimum is required to book a tournament. The banquet facility can accommodate 40 people.

Directions: From Bakersfield, travel east on Highway 58 for 38 miles to Tehachapi and take the Highway 202 exit. Follow the signs for 16 miles to the Resort at Stallion Springs.

Contact: 18100 Lucaya Way (P.O. Box 1487), Tehachapi, CA 93561, pro shop 661/823-8571, fax 661/823-8337.

Chapter 10

COURTESY OF WAWONA HOTEL GOLF COURSE

Yosemite and Mammoth Lakes

Yosemite and Mammoth Lakes

Yosemite, of course, is never going to be a region that hosts the U.S. Open. But if it did, golf fans would see what adventurers, photographers, and nature lovers have seen for hundreds of years: It is an area of unmatched beauty and natural splendor.

Admirers of photographer Ansel Adams are undoubtedly aware of his stunning images of Yosemite. They are among his very best work, depicting the bold rock face of El Capitan, the majesty of the high forests and mountains, and the magic that everyone who visits comes to know.

There will never be an abundance of golf courses in this setting, and thankfully so. But the few that do exist are quite nice. The old stone and wood hotel called Wawona has nine holes attached to it, designed by the master architect Alister Mackenzie in 1918. The course is not long, but it sure is pretty, with tree-lined fairways and wildlife everywhere. The old hotel may not be for everyone, with no phones or televisions in the rooms, and no bathrooms in many, but if you might enjoy experiencing a throwback to what the region was like 100 years ago, this is it.

Ted Robinson contributed nine holes to the area with his design at Snowcreek Golf Course in 1991, and Cal Olson added nine holes at Sierra Star Golf Club in 1999. Like Wawona, these layouts feature lovely views, many trees, and the call of the wild.

Certainly no one wants to visit Yosemite only to golf. There is far too much in the way of hiking, swimming in streams, photographing nature, and enjoying quiet moments in the sun. But if you have your clubs with you, you sure can have a ball at any one of the three courses.

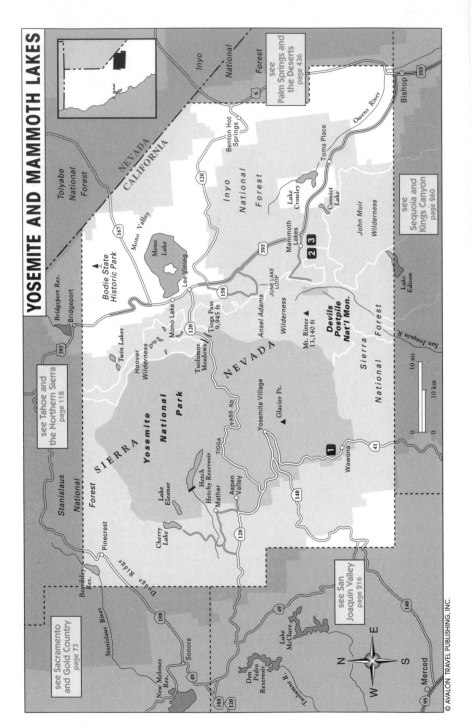

YOSEMITE AND MAMMOTH LAKES

see
Palm Springs and
the Deserts
page 436

see
Sequoia and
Kings Canyon
page 260

see Tahoe and
the Northern Sierra
page 118

see
San
Joaquin Valley
page 216

see
Sacramento
and Gold Country
page 73

NEVADA
CALIFORNIA

Toiyabe National Forest

Inyo National Forest

Bridgeport Res.
Bridgeport

Bodie State Historic Park

Mono Valley

Mono Lake

Lee Vining

Benton Hot Springs

Lake Crowley

Convict Lake

Toms Place

Mammoth Lakes

John Muir Wilderness

Lake Edison

Twin Lakes

Hoover Wilderness

Mono Lake

Tioga Pass 9,945 ft

JUNE LAKE LOOP

Ansel Adams Wilderness

Mt. Ritter 13,140 ft

Devils Postpile Nat'l Mon.

Sierra National Forest

SIERRA

Yosemite National Park

Tuolumne Meadows

NEVADA

Yosemite Village

Glacier Pt.

TIOGA PASS RD.

Wawona

Lake Eleanor

Hetch Hetchy Reservoir

Mather

Aspen Valley

Cherry Lake

Stanislaus National Forest

Pinecrest

Beardsley Res.

Dodge Ridge

Stanislaus River

New Melones Res.

Sonora

Lake McClure

Don Pedro Reservoir

Tuolumne R.

Merced

Owens River

Bishop

San Joaquin R.

10 mi
10 km

N
W   E
S

© AVALON TRAVEL PUBLISHING, INC.

1 WAWONA HOTEL GOLF COURSE

Architect: Alister Mackenzie, 1918
9 holes   **Resort**   **$14.50–23.60**

Yosemite and Mammoth Lakes map, page 254

This is a short, scenic course in Yosemite National Park. There are lots of trees, and the course is nicely maintained. Deer and other wildlife abound. The adjacent Wawona Hotel is a wonderful and historic place to stay and dine.

For reservations at the hotel, call the Yosemite reservations office at 559/252-4848.

Play Policy and Fees: Green fees are $14.50 for nine holes and $23.60 for 18 holes. Carts are $12.50 for nine holes and $20 for 18 holes. The course is open April–October.

Tees and Yardage: *Men:* yardage 3021, par 35, rating n/a, slope n/a; *Women:* yardage 2724, par 35, rating n/a, slope n/a.

Tee Times: Reservations are not required.

Dress Code: Appropriate golf attire and soft spikes are required.

Tournaments: This course is available for outside tournaments. Events should be booked three months in advance.

Directions: This course is between Oakhurst and Yosemite on Highway 41 at the south end of the park.

Contact: P.O. Box 2005, Wawona, CA 95389, pro shop 209/375-6572, www.yosemitepark.com.

2 SIERRA STAR GOLF CLUB

Architect: Cal Olson, 1999
18 holes   **Resort**   **$95–115**

Yosemite and Mammoth Lakes map, page 254

This tree-lined mountain course offers spectacular views on nearly every hole. Recognizing the narrow fairways and high elevation, the smart player will keep the driver in the bag, or better yet, take it out and leave it in the trunk of the car. The greens are firm, holding shots well; with five sets of tee boxes, Sierra Star can accommodate players of all skill levels. Because of the high elevation, the course

is open approximately five and a half months a year starting mid-May.

Play Policy and Fees: Green fees are $115 weekends, $95 weekdays. Nine-hole and twilight rates are available. All green fees include a cart. Pull carts are available for those who prefer to walk.

Tees and Yardage: *Men:* Back: yardage 6708, par 70, rating 71.0, slope 133; Regular: yardage 6617, par 70, rating 70.6, slope 133; *Women:* Forward: yardage 4912, par 70, rating 68.7, slope 128.

Tee Times: Reservations can be made six months in advance.

Dress Code: Alternative spikes are preferred, and golf attire is required.

Tournaments: A 36-player minimum is needed to book an event. Shotgun tournaments must have a minimum field of 120 players.

Directions: From Los Angeles, take U.S. 395 to Highway 203. Head west on 203 to Mammoth Lake, turn left on Minaret, then right on Meridian. The course is on the right-hand side.

Contact: 2001 Sierra Star Parkway (P.O. Box 1942), Mammoth Lakes, CA 93546, pro shop 760/924-GOLF.

3 SNOWCREEK GOLF COURSE

Architect: Ted Robinson Sr., 1991
9 holes   **Resort**   **$28–50**

Yosemite and Mammoth Lakes map, page 254

Golfers tend to be overcome by the scenery, but the course itself is also an eyeful. The fairways are narrow, and water comes into play on nearly every hole. The greens are relatively large for a course of this distance, which is a plus. A real treat if you're in the area. Like the other courses at this elevation, Snowcreek Golf Course is open from spring until around November 1.

Condominiums and attached townhouses are available for rent. Call 800/544-6007 for information and reservations.

Play Policy and Fees: Green fees are $28 for nine holes and $50 for 18 holes. Twilight rates are available. Snowcreek rental guests, seniors, juniors, and frequent players are entitled to discounted rates. Certain discounted rates are not offered during holiday periods. Power carts are $7 per person for nine holes and $13 per person for 18 holes. Pull carts are available for those who wish to walk.

Tees and Yardage: *Men (18 holes):* Black: yardage 6644, par 70, rating 70.6, slope 128; Blue: yardage 6262, par 70, rating 69.0, slope 125; White: yardage 5892, par 70, rating 67.6, slope 120; *Women (18 holes):* Red: yardage 5290, par 70, rating 69.0, slope 120.

Tee Times: Reservations may be booked one week in advance or at the time of accommodations booking at Snowcreek Resort.

Dress Code: Nonmetal spikes are mandatory; collared shirts are required.

Tournaments: This course is available for outside tournaments.

Directions: From U.S. 395, take Highway 203 west to Old Mammoth Road. Turn left on Old Mammoth Road and drive about one mile to the course. The course is on the left side.

Contact: Old Mammoth Road (P.O. Box 569), Mammoth Lakes, CA 93546, pro shop 760/934-6633, fax 760/934-7499, www.snowcreek resort.com.

Chapter 11

COURTESY OF SHERWOOD FOREST GOLF CLUB

Sequoia and Kings Canyon

Sequoia and Kings Canyon

There are few golf courses in this large region of national parks, mountains, and high desert. Most of the land is enveloped by Sierra National Forest, Kings Canyon National Park, Sequoia National Park, and Sequoia National Forest. So while golf may not be the priority item on your sports list, there sure are plenty of other fantastic things to do. Those who enjoy hiking will be happy in any of the national parks or forests, just as those who enjoy river sports will be happy on the south fork of the Kern River, which flows through the region.

Where golfers do find some play is where the Kern River opens into Isabella Lake at the southern end of Sequoia National Forest.

Both Kern Valley Country Club and Kern River Golf Course are found in this area, and both are public 18-hole facilities.

Running along the Kings River east of Fresno is the 18-hole Sherwood Forest Golf Club, a scenic loop of golf with mature trees and some nice views. And the newest course in the area is Woodlake Ranch Golf Course, off Highway 198 east of Visalia. An 18-hole con-course, Woodlake Ranch also offers pleasing Sierra views.

So while there are few opportunities to wield your sticks in this very rural segment of California, you won't have to go completely cold turkey. Besides, after spending a few days in a national park, you'll have a whole new perspective on golf.

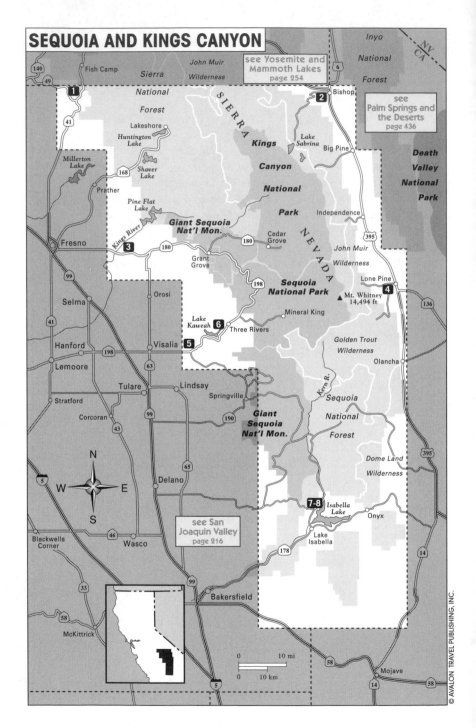

SEQUOIA AND KINGS CANYON

see Yosemite and
Mammoth Lakes
page 254

see
Palm Springs and
the Deserts
page 436

see San
Joaquin Valley
page 216

0   10 mi
0   10 km

© AVALON TRAVEL PUBLISHING, INC.

1 SIERRA MEADOWS AT RIVER CREEK

Architect: John Hilborn, 1991
9 holes **Public** **$20–37**

🚶 📷 🍽 🏌 🚗 ⛳

Sequoia and Kings Canyon map, page 260

Trees guard many holes on this scenic and challenging course. Water comes into play on three holes. The par-4 fourth hole is a 387-yard tester.

Play Policy and Fees: Green fees are $20 for nine holes Monday–Thursday and $22 for 18 holes, $32 for nine holes and $37 for 18 holes Friday and weekends. Carts are $12 for 18 holes.

Tees and Yardage: *Men (18 holes):* Blue: yardage 6304, par 72, rating 69.6, slope 128; White: yardage 6028, par 72, rating 68.6, slope 126; *Women (18 holes):* Gold: yardage 5568, par 72, rating 70.4, slope 121; Red: yardage 5124, par 72, rating 67.8, slope 117.

Tee Times: Reservations can be booked seven days in advance.

Dress Code: Appropriate attire and soft spikes are required.

Tournaments: Tournaments should be scheduled 12 months in advance.

Directions: From Fresno, take Highway 41 to Oakhurst. Take a left on Highway 49 for five miles to Road 600. Take a right on Road 600 for one-half mile to the course.

Contact: 41709 Road 600, Ahwahnee, CA 93607, pro shop 559/683-3388.

2 BISHOP COUNTRY CLUB

Architect: Course designed, 1952/1984
18 holes **Semiprivate** **$27–43**

🚶 📷 🍽 🏌 🚗 ⛳

Sequoia and Kings Canyon map, page 260

The first nine opened for play in 1952, and the second nine opened in 1984. This difficult course has lots of trees and bunkers. Water hazards spice up 15 holes. Keep the ball out of the rough. This course demands accuracy. During the summer the driving range is lighted.

Play Policy and Fees: Outside play is accepted. Green fees are seasonal. Winter rates are $27 any day, while summer rates are $43 weekdays

for locals. Please call for current rates. Senior and twilight rates offered. Carts are additional.

Tees and Yardage: *Men:* Blue: yardage 6576, par 71, rating 71.1, slope 126; White: yardage 6084, par 71, rating 69.0, slope 122; *Women:* Red: yardage 5453, par 71, rating 70.8, slope 123.

Tee Times: Reservations can be booked seven days in advance.

Dress Code: Golf attire is encouraged, and no tank tops are allowed.

Tournaments: This course is available for outside tournaments.

Directions: This course is one mile south of Bishop on U.S. 395.

Contact: South Highway 395, Bishop, CA 93515 (P.O. Box 1586, Bishop, CA 93514), pro shop 760/873-5828.

3 SHERWOOD FOREST GOLF CLUB

Architect: Bob Baldock, 1968
18 holes **Public** **$19–23**

🚶 📷 🍽 🏌 🚗 ⛳

Sequoia and Kings Canyon map, page 260

Owned and managed by the Hansen family, longtime PGA members, this scenic and well-run course runs along the Kings River and offers views of the mountains throughout. True to its name, the course has trees on every hole. The short par-4 18th is a great finishing hole. An iron or fairway wood off the tee is the smart play to avoid the lake short of the green. If played properly, this hole allows you to finish your round with a birdie. In 2003, some of the forward tees were shortened to make the course more women-friendly.

Play Policy and Fees: Green fees are $19 Monday–Thursday and $23 Friday, weekends, and holidays. Carts are $11 per rider.

Tees and Yardage: *Men:* Blue: yardage 6247, par 71, rating 69.8, slope 126; White: yardage 6050, par 71, rating 68.9, slope 124; *Women:* Red: yardage 5487, par 72, rating 71.3, slope 124.

Tee Times: Reservations can be booked seven days in advance.

Dress Code: No tank tops are allowed. Soft spikes only.

Tournaments: Tournaments welcome. Events should be booked six months in advance.

Directions: From north of Fresno, take Highway 99 south to Jensen Avenue. Follow Jensen east to McCall Avenue. Take McCall Avenue north to Kings Canyon/Highway 180 east to Frankwood Avenue, then follow Frankwood north one mile to the course.

Contact: 79 North Frankwood Avenue, Sanger, CA 93657, pro shop 559/787-2611, www.sherwoodforestgolf.com.

4 MOUNT WHITNEY GOLF CLUB

Architect: Bob Baldock, 1958

9 holes	Public	$17–26

🏌 📷 🍽 🏌 🛺 🍺

Sequoia and Kings Canyon map, page 260

This scenic course is at the base of Mount Whitney, and consequently has some exquisite views. It's flat, with some water, bunkers, trees, and narrow fairways. Accurate iron play is essential. A handsome new bridge was added in 2003 between the first and ninth holes. This course is proud to claim it has "the fastest greens in the West."

Play Policy and Fees: Green fees are $17 for nine holes and $24 for 18 holes weekdays, $19 for nine holes and $26 for 18 holes weekends and holidays. Carts are $12 per rider for 18 holes. The course is closed Thanksgiving and Christmas.

Tees and Yardage: *Men (18 holes):* Blue/White: yardage 6534, par 72, rating 70.6, slope 126; *Women (18 holes):* Red/Yellow: yardage 5692, par 72, rating 66.2, slope 111.

Tee Times: Reservations not needed.

Dress Code: Soft spikes only.

Tournaments: This course is available for outside tournaments.

Directions: Drive north on U.S. 395 to Lone Pine. The course is on the left.

Contact: 1225 South Pine Road, Lone Pine, CA 93545, pro shop 760/876-5795.

5 WOODLAKE RANCH GOLF COURSE

Architect: Ed Dobson and Hank Bocchini, 1998 and 2004

18 holes	Public	$16–18

🏌 📷 🍽 🏌 🛺 🍺

Sequoia and Kings Canyon map, page 260

A flat course with some elevated greens, this course features nice Sierra mountain views, on land that was once a walnut orchard. Plenty of walnut trees still line the fairways. A river runs next to some holes on the front nine but doesn't come into play. Note: Yardages listed may not be accurate when you get to the course, as some lengthening was taking place at press time.

Play Policy and Fees: Green fees are $16 weekdays, $18 weekends and holidays. Carts are additional. Nine-hole, monthly, junior, and senior rates are available.

Tees and Yardage: *Men:* Black: yardage 6700, par 72, rating n/a, slope n/a; White: yardage 6520, par 72, rating n/a, slope n/a; *Women:* Yellow: yardage 5677, par 74, rating n/a, slope n/a.

Tee Times: Reservations can be made five days in advance.

Dress Code: No metal spikes are allowed on the course. Collared golf shirts are required.

Tournaments: Tournaments welcome. Call for information.

Directions: From Highway 99 south of Fresno, get onto Highway 198 east. Turn left on Road 245 just east of Visalia, then right onto Avenue 322. The course is on the left.

Contact: 21730 Avenue 322, Woodlake, CA 93286, golf shop 559/564-1503, www.woodlakeranchgolf.com.

6 THREE RIVERS GOLF COURSE

Architect: Robert Dean Putman, 1962

9 holes	Public	$13–27

📷 🍽 🏌 🛺 🍺

Sequoia and Kings Canyon map, page 260

Located about 800 feet above sea level in the sequoias, this course is packed with trees and hilly, but walkable. This course reopened in 1999 after considerable renovation, including all new fairways and greens. Three Rivers has added a new clubhouse and restaurant.

Play Policy and Fees: Green fees are $13 for nine holes and $20 for 18 holes on weekdays and $16 for nine holes and $27 for 18 holes on weekends. Carts additional. Twilight, senior, and junior rates are available.

Tees and Yardage: *Men:* Blue: yardage 5478, par 70, rating 66.8, slope 109; White: yardage 5208, par 70, rating 65.8, slope 107; *Women:* Red: yardage 4042, par 70, rating n/a, slope n/a.

Tee Times: Tee times are not required but are recommended for weekends and holidays.

Dress Code: Nonmetal spikes are required.

Tournaments: This course is available for outside events.

Directions: From Highway 99 in Tulare, take Highway 198 east through Visalia to Three Rivers. The course is next to the highway.

Contact: 41117 Sierra Drive (P.O. Box 839), Three Rivers, CA 93271, pro shop 559/561-3133, fax 559/561-4179.

7 KERN VALLEY COUNTRY CLUB
Architect: Jack Ewing, 1957
9 holes   Public $11–25

🏌️ 🏌️ 🍴 🎣 🚗 🍷

Sequoia and Kings Canyon map, page 260

Kern Valley is a well-maintained, fairly flat, short course. Many trees line the narrow fairways, demanding accuracy off the tees and a good short game.

Play Policy and Fees: Green fees are $11 for nine holes and $18 for 18 holes weekdays, $15 for nine holes and $25 for 18 holes weekends. Call for special rates. Carts are additional.

Tees and Yardage: *Men (18 holes):* Blue/White: yardage 6255, par 72, rating 69.0, slope 116; *Women (18 holes):* Red/Yellow: yardage 5549, par 72, rating 71.4, slope 122.

Tee Times: Please call ahead.

Dress Code: Proper golf attire is encouraged, and nonmetal spikes are required.

Tournaments: Tournaments welcome. The banquet facility can accommodate 120 people.

Directions: From Bakersfield, travel northeast on Highway 178 for 50 miles. The course is one-half mile south of Kernville on Highway 155.

Contact: 9472 Burlando Road (P.O. Box 888), Kernville, CA 93238, pro shop 760/376-2828.

8 KERN RIVER GOLF COURSE
Architect: William P. Bell, 1953
18 holes   Public $25.50–29

🏌️ 🏌️ 🍴 🎣 🚗 🍷

Sequoia and Kings Canyon map, page 260

This public facility, one of two courses in the area that are rated over par, will test your golf skill. Kern River originally was designed in the 1920s as a nine-hole course, then nine more holes were added in the 1950s. The course features rolling terrain and an abundance of mature trees. A word of caution: There are two long par-3 holes on the back nine that can ruin your day. A hole to remember is the 11th, which is 235 yards from the back tees. If you miss the green to the right, you're stymied behind trees. The green is sharply sloped downhill and difficult to putt—don't leave the ball above the hole. The course record is 62 for men, held by Ron Baker, and 71 for women, held by Jacque Servadio.

Play Policy and Fees: Green fees are $25.50 weekdays and $29 weekends. Carts are $10.50 per rider. Special rates for resident seniors are available, as are junior and twilight rates.

Tees and Yardage: *Men:* Blue: yardage 6458, par 70, rating 70.7, slope 120; White: yardage 6258, par 70, rating 69.6, slope 118; *Women:* Red: yardage 5971, par 73, rating 73.5, slope 122.

Tee Times: Reservations are suggested and may be booked seven days in advance.

Dress Code: Shirt required.

Tournaments: Events may be booked one year in advance.

Directions: From Highway 99 in Bakersfield, take Highway 178 east to Alfred Herrall Highway. Follow the signs to Lake Ming.

Contact: P.O. Box 6339, Bakersfield, CA 93306, pro shop 661/872-5128, fax 661/872-4965.

Chapter 12

ALISAL GUEST RANCH AND RESORT, RANCH COURSE © GEORGE FULLER

Santa Barbara
and Vicinity

Santa Barbara and Vicinity

The Santa Barbara region incorporates some beautiful land on the Central California coast, as well as some peaceful rolling hills and inland valleys.

From Paso Robles and San Luis Obispo in the north, to Ventura and Oxnard in the south, this is a region of great geographic reach and topographic diversity. It incorporates many miles of Pacific shoreline along Highway 1, as well as scenic golden valleys that stretch out on either side of U.S. 101. Thus, visitors can choose from many recreational activities, including surfing, horseback riding, wine tasting, back-road exploration, and much more. One word of caution, though: Some of the coast, particularly around Vandenberg Air Force Base, is controlled by the United States military and is off-limits to the public.

Luckily, the golf courses along the coast near Santa Barbara represent some of the best layouts in the state. These include the historic and private 1929 Alister Mackenzie design at The Valley Club of Montecito, the acclaimed public courses La Purisima and Sandpiper, and the wonderful daily fee layout in Goleta called Glen Annie. And from a scenic standpoint, there are few more beautiful vistas in the entire state than the spring fields around Goleta bright with yellow flowers, complemented by the sparkling waters of the Pacific Ocean in the other direction.

One of the best experiences families can have in this region is a stay at Alisal Guest Ranch in the Santa Ynez Valley, 35 miles north of

Santa Barbara, where 36 holes of golf complement a stay that can include horseback riding, wine-tasting, and shopping in the cute little Danish town of Solvang.

Although it does not get much recognition as a golf destination, the northern section of the region—Paso Robles, Atascadero, San Luis Obispo—has over the past several years gained some very nice new courses. Hunter Ranch, The Links Course at Paso Robles, Dairy Creek, and Cypress Ridge all have been built since 1994, giving golfers new reason to keep their clubs packed in the trunk.

The southern part of this region—around Ventura and Camarillo—does not offer golfers much because there are so few courses here. By 2006, though, enthusiasts can expect to be playing a completely re-modeled Olivas Park Golf Course, a Ventura favorite since 1969, which is being fashioned into a links-style layout to take advantage of the breezes from the nearby Pacific.

The area does boast one of the state's best golf resorts, just northeast of Ventura, Ojai Valley Inn & Spa. After completing a multimillion dollar renovation in 2004, this venerable property is again among the state's elite destinations. Guests here are treated to a 1923 George C. Thomas design that is as fun to play as it is lovely.

There is great golf to be played in the Santa Barbara region, and a whole lot of exploration to be done.

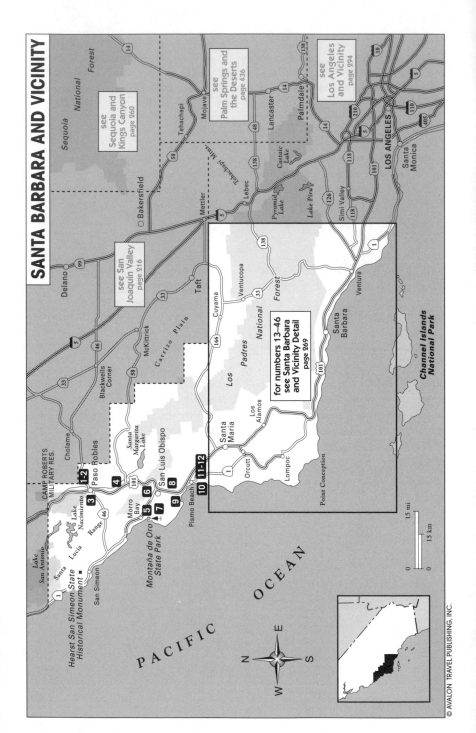

SANTA BARBARA AND VICINITY

see Sequoia and Kings Canyon
page 260

see Palm Springs and the Deserts
page 436

see Los Angeles and Vicinity
page 294

see San Joaquin Valley
page 216

for numbers 13–46
see Santa Barbara
and Vicinity Detail
page 269

PACIFIC OCEAN

Channel Islands National Park

Hearst San Simeon State Historical Monument

CAMP ROBERTS MILITARY RES.

Montaña de Oro State Park

Los Padres National Forest

Sequoia National Forest

© AVALON TRAVEL PUBLISHING, INC.

Santa Barbara and Vicinity Detail   Courses 13–46

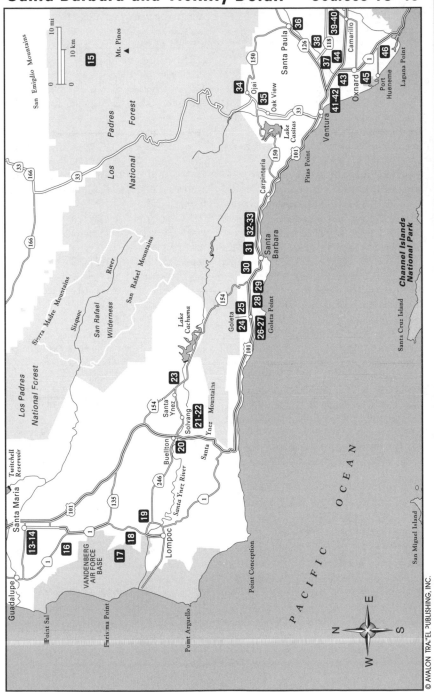

© AVALON TRAVEL PUBLISHING, INC.

1 LINKS COURSE AT PASO ROBLES

Architect: Rudy Duran, 1996

18 holes **Public** **$18–24**

🏃 📷 🍴 🏌 🚗 🥤

Santa Barbara and Vicinity map, page 268

This is a traditional Scottish links–style course. The fairways are generous, and wind is a factor. The course gives you plenty of options for several types of shots. Course management is a must if you are going to score well.

Play Policy and Fees: Green fees are $18 Monday–Friday and $24 weekends and holidays. Carts are $22 for 18 holes. Annual card, twilight, and senior rates are offered.

Tees and Yardage: *Men:* Gold: yardage 6937, par 72, rating 72.8, slope 117; Blue: yardage 6642, par 72, rating 71.3, slope 113; White: yardage 6220, par 72, rating 69.5, slope 109; *Women:* Red: yardage 5610, par 72, rating 72.1, slope 121.

Tee Times: Reservations can be booked seven days in advance.

Dress Code: Shirt and shoes are required. Soft spikes are preferred.

Tournaments: This course is available for outside tournaments.

Directions: On U.S. 101, take the 46 East exit and follow it to Jardine Road. Take a left on Jardine Road. The course is 1.5 miles along on the left.

Contact: 5151 Jardine Road, Paso Robles, CA 93446, pro shop 805/227-4567, www.linkscourse atpasorobles.com.

2 HUNTER RANCH GOLF COURSE

Architect: Hunter Resources, 1994

18 holes **Public** **$50–75**

🏃 📷 🍴 🏌 🚗 🥤

Santa Barbara and Vicinity map, page 268

This heavily bunkered course has rolling hills and an abundance of mature oak trees. This is a championship layout where water comes into play on four holes, and several greens are tiered. The tricky stretch of holes 11–14 is Hunter Ranch's version of Amen Corner at Augusta National Golf Club. Hunter Ranch was designed by Kenneth Hunter, Mike McGinnis, and Paul Casas. The course features an excellent practice facility.

Play Policy and Fees: The green fees are $50 Monday–Thursday to walk, $65 to ride; weekend and holiday green fees are $60 to walk, $75 to ride.

Tees and Yardage: *Men:* Blue: yardage 6741, par 72, rating 72.6, slope 136; White: yardage 6292, par 72, rating 70.7, slope 131; *Women:* Red: yardage 5639, par 72, rating 72.0, slope 128.

Tee Times: Reservations can be booked seven days in advance.

Dress Code: Collared shirts are preferred; no tank tops or cutoffs are allowed. Nonmetal spikes are required.

Tournaments: A 16-player minimum is needed to book a tournament. Tournaments can be booked 12 months in advance. The banquet facility holds 200 people.

Directions: From U.S. 101, drive east on Highway 46 for 3.5 miles to the course.

Contact: 4041 Highway 46 East, Paso Robles, CA 93446, pro shop 805/237-7444, fax 805/237-7430, www.hunterranchgolf.com.

3 PASO ROBLES GOLF CLUB

Architect: Bert Stamps, 1960

18 holes **Public** **$18–24**

🏃 📷 🍴 🏌 🚗

Santa Barbara and Vicinity map, page 268

Formerly a country club, this is a very walkable course. Paso Robles is a shot-maker's course, with water coming into play on 15 holes. Don't let the yardage fool you—this course will test your golf skills.

Play Policy and Fees: Green fees are $18 weekdays and $24 weekends. Twilight and senior rates available. Carts are $22.

Tees and Yardage: *Men:* Blue: yardage 6260, par 71, rating 71.0, slope 122; White: yardage 6032, par 71, rating 69.9, slope 120; *Women:* Red: yardage 5748, par 73, rating 73.5, slope 126.

Tee Times: Reservations may be booked up to seven days in advance.

Dress Code: Tasteful dress is requested. Soft spikes are preferred.

Tournaments: A 24-player minimum is required to book a tournament. Events may be booked up to one year in advance. The banquet facility can accommodate 200 people.

Directions: Travel 27 miles north of San Luis Obispo on U.S. 101 to the Spring Street exit in Paso Robles. Turn right onto Niblick Bridge and proceed to Country Club Drive.

Contact: 1600 Country Club Drive, Paso Robles, CA 93447 (P.O. Box 517, Paso Robles, CA 93446), pro shop 805/238-4722, www.centralcoast.com/pasoroblesgolfclub.

4 CHALK MOUNTAIN GOLF COURSE

Architect: Robert Muir Graves, 1980
18 holes   **Public**   **$28–33**

Santa Barbara and Vicinity map, page 268

This is a short, narrow course set in the mountains among groves of oak trees. It's the kind of course you have to play a few times before you can actually score well. A hole to watch out for is the fourth, a par-4. Known as "Cardiac Hill," it plays straight uphill. You can see the green from the tee, but it isn't much help. The hole is deceptive in its distance, and the tendency is to come up short. Accuracy off the tee is a must. As a nice gesture, this course offers you a free round of golf on your birthday! See website for details.

Play Policy and Fees: Green fees are $28 weekdays and $33 weekends. Senior (weekdays only), junior, and twilight rates are offered. Carts are $12 per rider.

Tees and Yardage: *Men:* Blue: yardage 6299, par 72, rating 70.9, slope 126; White: yardage 5926, par 72, rating 69.2, slope 122; *Women:* Red: yardage 5330, par 72, rating 71.4, slope 119.

Tee Times: Reservations can be booked seven days by phone or 14 days in advance on the website.

Dress Code: Soft spikes are preferred.

Tournaments: This course is available for outside tournaments. A 20-player minimum is needed to book an event. Tournaments should be scheduled 12 months in advance.

Directions: Off U.S. 101 at the south end of Atascadero, exit at Santa Rosa Avenue heading east. Follow the Heilman Regional Park signs out El Camino Real and El Bordo Road to the course.

Contact: 10000 El Bordo Road, Atascadero, CA 93422, pro shop 805/466-8848, fax 805/466-6238, www.chalkmountaingolf.com.

5 MORRO BAY GOLF COURSE

Architect: Russell Neyes, 1929; Al Lape, 1949
18 holes   **Public**   **$32–40**

Santa Barbara and Vicinity map, page 268

This picturesque layout is in Morro Bay State Park and has fantastic ocean views from almost every hole. It's slightly hilly, with tree-lined fairways. It is one of the busiest courses in the state. The long, undulating greens remind some of Poppy Hills and Spyglass Hill. To speed up play, most of the bunkers were removed in the 1960s. There are only four traps on the course. Wildlife is part of this course, which has an Audubon certification.

Play Policy and Fees: Green fees are $32 weekdays and $40 weekends and holidays. Senior and junior rates available. Carts are additional.

Tees and Yardage: *Men:* Blue: yardage 6360, par 71, rating 72.7, slope 115; White: yardage 6073, par 71, rating 69.6, slope 112; *Women:* Gold: yardage 5633, par 72, rating 72.9, slope 118; Red: yardage 5055, par 72, rating 69.7, slope 111.

Tee Times: For weekend tee times, reservations must be made the preceding week of play starting at 6:15 A.M.

Dress Code: Nonmetal spikes are recommended.

Tournaments: This course is available for outside tournaments.

Directions: Heading north from San Luis Obispo, take U.S. 101 and exit on Highway 1 to Morro Bay. Follow the Morro Bay State Park signs to the course.

Contact: 201 State Park Road, Morro Bay, CA 93442, pro shop 805/782-8060, www.slocountyparks.com.

6 DAIRY CREEK GOLF COURSE

Architect: John Harbottle, 1997

18 holes   Public $32–40

Santa Barbara and Vicinity map, page 268

This links-style course is defined by rolling hills, large greens, and plenty of wind. The number-one handicap hole is the par-5, 549-yard double-dogleg fifth hole with a creek running through the fairway.

Play Policy and Fees: Green fees are $32 weekdays and $40 weekends and holidays. Senior and junior rates available. Carts are additional.

Tees and Yardage: *Men:* Gold: yardage 6548, par 71, rating 72.0, slope 127; Blue: yardage 6103, par 71, rating 69.9, slope 124; White: yardage 5561, par 71, rating 67.5, slope 115; *Women:* Red: yardage 4965, par 71, rating 70.5, slope 121.

Tee Times: Reservations can be booked seven days in advance starting at 6:15 A.M.

Dress Code: Come as you are.

Tournaments: A 16-player minimum is needed to book a tournament.

Directions: On Highway 1 just north of San Luis Obispo, exit at El Chorro Regional Park. Take a right and make your first left. The course is on the left.

Contact: 2990A Dairy Creek Road, San Luis Obispo, CA 93405, pro shop 805/782-8060, www.slocountyparks.com.

7 SEA PINES GOLF RESORT

Architect: Course designed, 1954; Glenn Setting, 1995

9 holes   Public/Resort $9–12.50

Santa Barbara and Vicinity map, page 268

This well-maintained course has more than 200 trees lining the narrow fairways. Most of the pine trees are more than 25 years old. The first fairway has been removed and relocated to make way for a parking lot, so watch out for the row of small connecting ponds along the left side.

The Sea Pines Golf Resort is at the course. Call 805/528-5252 for reservations. Play-and-stay packages are available September–June.

Play Policy and Fees: Green fees for resort guests are $9 anytime. Public fees Monday–Thursday are $10.50, and Friday–Sunday fees are $12.50. Carts are $12 for nine holes and $18 for 18 holes.

Tees and Yardage: *Men:* Blue: yardage 4004, par 62, rating 62.2, slope 100; White: yardage 3772, par 62, rating 60.3, slope 96; *Women:* Red: yardage 3088, par 61, rating 58.4, slope 93.

Tee Times: Reservations are suggested and may be booked seven days in advance. If booked online, tee times may be made 30 days in advance.

Dress Code: Casual golf attire is acceptable.

Tournaments: This course is available for tournaments. The banquet facility can accommodate up to 100 people.

Directions: Off U.S. 101 in Los Osos, take the Los Osos Valley Road exit and drive west to the course, which is about 11 miles from the highway. Take the entrance to Montana de Oro State Park.

Contact: 1945 Solano Avenue, Los Osos, CA 93402, pro shop 805/528-4653, fax 805/528-5262, www.seapinesgolfresort.com.

8 SAN LUIS OBISPO COUNTRY CLUB

Architect: Bert Stamps, 1957

18 holes   Private $95

Santa Barbara and Vicinity map, page 268

This rolling course along the central coast plays longer than it looks because of the lush fairways that provide little roll. Thick stands of pine trees line the fairways, waiting for errant tee shots. The greens are protected by strategically placed bunkers. The course record is 64, held by PGA Tour professional Loren Roberts. A new clubhouse was completed in 2000.

Play Policy and Fees: Reciprocal play is ac-

cepted with members of other private clubs; otherwise, members and guests only. Fees for reciprocators are $95. Carts are $12 per rider.
Tees and Yardage: *Men:* Blue: yardage 6738, par 72, rating 73.6, slope 129; White: yardage 6391, par 72, rating 72.2, slope 127; Gold: yardage 5819, par 72, rating 69.5, slope 125; *Women:* Black: yardage 5315, par 74, rating 71.8, slope 123.
Tee Times: Reciprocators should have their club pro call to make arrangements.
Dress Code: Appropriate golf attire and non-metal spikes are required.
Tournaments: This course is available for outside tournaments on Monday with board approval.
Directions: Take the Marsh Street exit off U.S. 101 in San Luis Obispo and turn right. Travel to Broad Street (Highway 227) and turn right. Drive 4.5 miles to Los Ranchos Road, then right to Country Club Drive and right again to the club.
Contact: 255 Country Club Drive, San Luis Obispo, CA 93401, pro shop 805/543-4035, clubhouse 805/543-3400.

🤊 AVILA BEACH GOLF RESORT
Architect: Desmond Muirhead, 1968
18 holes   Public $47–62

🕴 📷 🗄 🔌 🚗 🍽 ≋

Santa Barbara and Vicinity map, page 268
In the heart of California's Central Coast, this course is both beautiful and challenging. The front nine is nestled in an oak-lined canyon bisected by a gentle, flowing creek. Accuracy and club selection are important. The back nine calls for distance and placement, as it traverses back and forth across San Luis Creek and a tidal lagoon.

Play-and-stay packages are available. Call for more information.
Play Policy and Fees: Green fees are $47 on weekdays and $62 on weekends and holidays. Twilight and senior rates are available. Carts are $16 per rider. Super twilight and early bird rates are available on a limited basis—call the course for details.

Tees and Yardage: *Men:* Blue: yardage 6513, par 71, rating 72.0, slope 137; White: yardage 6053, par 71, rating 69.6, slope 130; *Women:* Red: yardage 5041, par 71, rating 70.3, slope 121.
Tee Times: Reservations may be made up to two weeks in advance, and up to 30 days if booked through participating local hotels.
Dress Code: Collared shirts and soft spikes are required.
Tournaments: Tournaments and outside events are welcome. The banquet facility can accommodate 100–1500 people.
Directions: Take the Avila Beach exit off U.S. 101 north of Pismo Beach and drive west for three miles to the entrance of the San Luis Bay Inn. Turn right and follow the signs to the club.
Contact: Avila Beach Road (P.O. Box 2140), Avila Beach, CA 93424, pro shop 805/595-4000, ext. 1, fax 805/595-4002, www.avila beachresort.com.

🔟 PISMO STATE BEACH GOLF COURSE
Architect: Course designed, 1967
9 holes   Public $8.50–9.50

📷 🗄 🔌 🍽 ③

Santa Barbara and Vicinity map, page 268
This walkable par-3 course has water on seven holes, including a 160-yard pond carry on the seventh and a creek to the side of the eighth. There are no sand traps. Monterey pines line the fairways and get a lot of action. This is a good course for beginners.
Play Policy and Fees: Green fees are $8.50 weekdays and $9.50 weekends for nine holes. Senior and junior rates are available.
Tees and Yardage: *Men and Women:* yardage 1465, par 27, rating n/a, slope n/a.
Tee Times: Reservations are not accepted. All play is on a first-come, first-served basis.
Dress Code: Appropriate attire and soft spikes are required.
Tournaments: This course is available for outside tournaments.
Directions: On Highway 1 in Grover City, turn

right on Grand Avenue toward the beach and follow it to the course.

Contact: 25 Grand Avenue, Grover Beach, CA 93433, pro shop 805/481-5215.

11 CYPRESS RIDGE

Architect: Peter Jacobsen and Jim Hardy, 1999
18 holes   Public $50–60

Santa Barbara and Vicinity map, page 268

Cypress Ridge is a links-style course with excellent ocean views. It winds through 100-year-old cypress trees, giving you the feeling the course has been around for decades. Off-the-tee landing areas are ample, although fairly deep fairway bunkers come into play. If you miss the fairway, you will be playing out of thick native grass or possibly out-of-bounds. The greens are smallish with subtle slopes. All but two holes have bunkers, but players still have the opportunity to use a variety of shots around the green, including putting. Cypress Ridge is an Audubon International Signature Sanctuary facility.

Play Policy and Fees: Green fees are $50 Monday–Thursday and $60 Friday–Sunday and holidays. Twilight rates available. Carts are $15 per person.

Tees and Yardage: *Men:* Black: yardage 6803, par 72, rating 72.9, slope 134; Blue: yardage 6443, par 72, rating 71.2, slope 129; Combo: yardage 6140, par 72, rating 70.0, slope 126; White: yardage 5838, par 72, rating 68.5, slope 124; *Women:* Red: yardage 5087, par 72, rating 70.3, slope 120.

Tee Times: Reservations can be made 10 days in advance.

Dress Code: Appropriate golf attire and non-metal spikes are mandatory.

Tournaments: A 24-player minimum is needed to book an event.

Directions: Going south on U.S. 101 in San Luis Obispo, take the El Campo exit. Stay on El Campo until you cross Los Berros Road. The next intersection will be Halcyon. Turn left; the course is 400 yards along on the right.

Contact: 780 Cypress Ridge Parkway, Arroyo Grande, CA 93421 (P.O. Box 179, Arroyo Grande, CA 93420), pro shop 805/474-7979, www.cypressridge.com.

12 BLACKLAKE GOLF RESORT

Architect: Ted Robinson Sr., 1965; Garret Gill, 1996
27 holes   Public $46–61

Santa Barbara and Vicinity map, page 268

These well-designed nine-hole courses offer tree-lined fairways, several lakes, and a rolling terrain. Between Santa Maria and Pismo Beach, Blacklake Golf Resort is the Central Coast's only 27-hole golf resort. As might be expected on a Ted Robinson design, golfers encounter water features aplenty on these scenic nonets. The Lake/Canyon loop is the original layout.

Play-and-stay packages are available with several nearby inns. Call the course for details.

Play Policy and Fees: Weekday green fees are $46, weekends and holidays $61. Carts are $16 per rider. Senior, twilight, and super twilight rates are offered.

Tees and Yardage: Canyon/Oaks—*Men:* Back: yardage 6034, par 71, rating 69.3, slope 121; Middle: yardage 5719, par 71, rating 67.8, slope 117; *Women:* Forward: yardage 4908, par 71, rating 69.5, slope 116. Lake/Canyon—*Men:* Back: yardage 6401, par 72, rating 70.9, slope 123; Middle: yardage 6056, par 72, rating 69.2, slope 118; *Women:* Forward: yardage 5161, par 72, rating 72.0, slope 120. Lake/Oaks—*Men:* Back: yardage 6158, par 71, rating 69.7, slope 121; Middle: yardage 5813, par 71, rating 68.0, slope 116; *Women:* Forward: yardage 5161, par 71, rating 69.7, slope 117.

Tee Times: Reservations may be booked 14 days in advance.

Dress Code: Appropriate golf attire is required.

Tournaments: Events may be scheduled up to a year in advance. The banquet facility can accommodate 300 people.

Directions: From Los Angeles, travel north on U.S. 101 past Santa Maria to the Tefft Street exit in Nipomo. Turn left over the highway to

Pomeroy. Turn left onto Willow and right to the golf course.

Contact: 1490 Golf Course Lane, Nipomo, CA 93444, pro shop 805/343-1214, fax 805/343-6317, www.blacklake.com.

13 SANTA MARIA COUNTRY CLUB

Architect: Course designed, 1921

18 holes   Private $75

Santa Barbara and Vicinity Detail map, page 269

This is a fairly level course, but don't let that fool you. It is heavily wooded, and more than one golfer has claimed to have lost a ball to a hungry chipmunk. The original nine holes were built in the 1920s, and the second nine holes were added in the 1950s. A set of gold tees was added recently to make the course more women-friendly.

Play Policy and Fees: Reciprocal play is accepted with members of other private clubs. Otherwise, members and guests only. Reciprocal green fees are $75 or equal to what a member would be charged at the reciprocating club. Carts are $14 per rider.

Tees and Yardage: *Men:* Blue: yardage 6505, par 72, rating 71.3, slope 129; White: yardage 6256, par 72, rating 70.0, slope 125; *Women:* Red: yardage 5834, par 72, rating 74.3, slope 126; Gold: yardage 5200, par 72, rating 70.8, slope 120.

Tee Times: Reciprocators should have their club pro call to make arrangements.

Dress Code: Collared shirts and nonmetal spikes are required.

Tournaments: Outside events are available on Monday only and must be board approved.

Directions: Travel south of Santa Maria on U.S. 101 to the Betteravia exit. Turn west and drive to Broadway, then south to Waller Lane. From there go right to the club.

Contact: 505 West Waller Lane, Santa Maria, CA 93455, pro shop 805/937-2027, fax 805/937-4175.

14 SUNSET RIDGE GOLF COURSE

Architect: Tom Howell, 1994

9 holes   Public $8–14

Santa Barbara and Vicinity Detail map, page 269

This is a par-3 executive course with one par-4. Five of the par-3s are over 160 yards.

Play Policy and Fees: Green fees are $8 for nine holes and $12 for 18 holes on weekdays. Green fees on weekends and holidays are $10 for nine holes and $14 for 18 holes. Senior and junior rates are $6 for nine holes and $9 for 18 holes on weekdays and $8 for nine holes and $10 for 18 holes on weekends. Carts are additional.

Tees and Yardage: *Men and Women (18 holes):* White: yardage 3046, par 56, rating 56.1, slope 84.

Tee Times: Reservations can be made the day of play.

Dress Code: Appropriate attire and soft spikes are required.

Tournaments: This course is available for outside tournaments. A 12-player minimum is needed to book an event. Tournaments should be booked 12 months in advance. The banquet facility can accommodate 50 people.

Directions: From U.S. 101 in Santa Maria, take the Betteravia exit and head west to Skyway Drive. Turn left on Skyway Drive. Take Skyway Drive to Fairway Drive, turn right, and go to the end of the street. Sunset Ridge is on the left.

Contact: 1424 Fairway Drive, Santa Maria, CA 93455, pro shop 805/347-1070.

15 PINE MOUNTAIN CLUB

Architect: William F. Bell, 1971

9 holes   Private $8–15

Santa Barbara and Vicinity Detail map, page 269

This is an interesting course set at 5500 feet and nestled among the beautiful pine trees. (You may want to pack mountaineering boots.) The

fifth hole is known as "Cardiac Hill," obviously because it is very steep. This hole is one of the reasons that the club now has power carts.
Play Policy and Fees: Guests must be accompanied by a member. Guest fees are $8 for nine holes and $13 for 18 holes weekdays, and $10 for nine holes and $15 for 18 holes weekends and holidays. Carts are $11 for nine holes and $17 for 18 holes.
Tees and Yardage: *Men (18 holes):* Back: yardage 3610, par 60, rating 58.8, slope 100; *Women (18 holes):* Forward: yardage 3156, par 60, rating 57.2, slope 95.
Tee Times: No outside play is accepted.
Dress Code: No tank tops or halter tops allowed. Soft spikes only.
Tournaments: This course is not available for outside events.
Directions: Travel 40 miles south of Bakersfield on I-5 and take the Frazier Park exit to Frazier Mountain Road. Drive west five miles and continue west on Cuddly Valley Road for another six miles to the top of the mountain. Turn right on Mil Potrero Road and drive five miles to the course.
Contact: 2524 Beechwood Way (P.O. Box P), Pine Mountain, CA 93222, pro shop 661/242-3734, clubhouse 661/242-3788, www.frazmtn.com/pmcpoa.

16 RANCHO MARIA GOLF CLUB

Architect: Bob Baldock, 1965
18 holes   Public $24–30

🚶 📷 🍴 🏌 🚙 🍺

Santa Barbara and Vicinity Detail map, page 269

This course is in the foothills southwest of Santa Maria. There are no parallel fairways, and the rolling greens can be very fast. Watch for the 13th hole in the afternoon. This par-4 is dangerous in a confronting wind. The green, which slopes to the right, is also heavily bunkered on that side.
Play Policy and Fees: Green fees are $24 weekdays and $30 weekends. Senior and twilight fees are available. Carts are $10 per rider.

Tees and Yardage: *Men:* Blue: yardage 6541, par 72, rating 70.7, slope 124; White: yardage 6148, par 72, rating 69.7, slope 120; *Women:* Red: yardage 5504, par 72, rating 70.9, slope 119.
Tee Times: Reservations are not required but can be booked seven days in advance.
Dress Code: Appropriate attire and soft spikes are required.
Tournaments: A 24-player minimum is required to book a tournament. Tournaments should be booked two months in advance.
Directions: Take the Orcutt/Clark Avenue exit off U.S. 101 in Santa Maria and drive west on Clark Avenue for 2.5 miles to Highway 1. Turn right and drive two miles to the course.
Contact: 1950 Casmalia Road, Santa Maria, CA 93455, pro shop 805/937-2019, www.ranchomariagolf.com.

17 MARSHALLIA RANCH GOLF COURSE

Architect: Robert Dean Putman, 1965
18 holes   Military $10–45

🚶 📷 🍴 🏌 🚙 🍺

Santa Barbara and Vicinity Detail map, page 269

Set three miles from the ocean, this tight and heavily wooded course becomes increasingly difficult as the prevailing winds pick up. Each hole is separated by dense stands of trees. The course is fairly flat and walkable. The ninth and 16th holes are rated among the best in Santa Barbara County. The ninth is a par-4 through a chute to a narrow landing area and onto a green guarded by two large bunkers and surrounded by ice plant. The 16th is a par-4 straight uphill and into the wind. For most golfers it's unreachable in two. Morning and evening fog can cut short a day's play.
Play Policy and Fees: Public play is allowed on a limited basis. Member green fees range $10–31, depending on military personnel status. Civilian green fees are $45 every day. Twilight rates available. Carts are $20 for 18 holes. The course is closed on Monday.

Tees and Yardage: *Men:* Blue: yardage 6845, par 72, rating 73.4, slope 130; White: yardage 6388, par 72, rating 71.1, slope 124; *Women:* Red: yardage 5404, par 72, rating 72.5, slope 124.

Tee Times: Civilian play is on a space-available basis. No reservations are accepted.

Dress Code: No tank tops or short shorts are allowed.

Tournaments: This course is available for outside tournaments.

Directions: Follow U.S. 101 north to Highway 1 and take the Lompoc-Vandenberg exit (just beyond Gaviota coming from the south) north to Vandenberg AFB. Drive past the main gate about four miles to the exit for Marshallia Ranch. Go left to the course.

Contact: P.O. Box 5938, Vandenberg AFB, CA 93437, pro shop 805/734-1333.

18 VILLAGE COUNTRY CLUB

Architect: Ted Robinson Sr., 1964

18 holes   Private $50–60

Santa Barbara and Vicinity Detail map, page 269

Gently rolling terrain and fairways lined with mature pine and oak trees mark this interesting course. Driving accuracy is rewarded. The par-4 and par-5 holes are doglegs. The greens are mostly contoured and can be challenging. The par-4 15th is a tough water-hazard hole. Water is on the left within the landing zone. If you stray too far to the right, you're in the creek. Your second shot should be 130–140 yards uphill to a two-tiered green. Pin placement makes all the difference here. The green is fast and will hold if you find the top tier. If you find the lower tier, your ball will roll back.

Play Policy and Fees: Reciprocal play is accepted with members of other private clubs. The fees for reciprocators are $50 weekdays and $60 weekends. Carts are $13 per rider.

Tees and Yardage: *Men:* Blue: yardage 6561, par 72, rating 71.7, slope 127; White: yardage 6269, par 72, rating 70.3, slope 122; *Women:* Red:

yardage 5701, par 72, rating 73.0, slope 127; Gold: yardage 5106, par 72, rating 69.7, slope 117.

Tee Times: Reciprocators should have their home professional make the arrangements.

Dress Code: Appropriate golf attire is required. Soft spikes are preferred.

Tournaments: Shotgun starts must have permission of the golf committee. An 18-player minimum is needed to book a tournament.

Directions: Travel north from Lompoc on Harris Grade Road to Burton Mesa Boulevard and turn left. At Clubhouse Road, turn right and drive three-quarters of a mile to the club.

Contact: 4300 Clubhouse Road, Lompoc, CA 93436, pro shop 805/733-3537, clubhouse 805/733-3535.

19 LA PURISIMA GOLF COURSE

Architect: Robert Muir Graves, 1986

18 holes   Public $50–60

Santa Barbara and Vicinity Detail map, page 269

This is a highly rated public, pure golf facility. Overlooking Lompoc Valley, this scenic course meanders among the oak groves over rolling terrain. Three lakes come into play here, not to mention the wind, which can pick up in the afternoon. La Purisima hosted the 1996 PGA Tour final qualifying tournament and ranks among the state's top designs. No pushover, even par wins most professional events here. This would be a wonderful site for a future U.S. Open.

Play Policy and Fees: Green fees are $50 weekdays and $60 weekends and holidays. Twilight rates available. Carts are $30.

Tees and Yardage: *Men:* Black: yardage 7105, par 72, rating 75.6, slope 143; Blue: yardage 6670, par 72, rating 73.1, slope 136; White: yardage 6187, par 72, rating 71.1, slope 131; *Women:* Red: yardage 5763, par 72, rating 75.6, slope 135.

Tee Times: Reservations can be booked seven days in advance.

Dress Code: Collared shirts are required. Soft spikes only.

Tournaments: A 16-player minimum is required to book a tournament. Events can be scheduled 2–24 months in advance. The banquet facility can accommodate 100 people.

Directions: The course is 12 miles west of Buellton and four miles east of Lompoc on Highway 246.

Contact: 3455 State Highway 246, Lompoc, CA 93436, pro shop 805/735-8395, fax 805/736-0246, www.lapurisimagolf.com.

20 ZACA CREEK GOLF COURSE
Architect: Course designed, 1985
9 holes   Public $9–10

Santa Barbara and Vicinity Detail map, page 269

Nestled in the Santa Ynez Valley, this flat course offers seven par-3s and two par-4s that will test every club in your bag. The holes range 90–285 yards.

Play Policy and Fees: Green fees are $9 weekdays, $10 weekends. Replays are $6. Pull carts are $2.

Tees and Yardage: *Men:* yardage 1560, par 29, rating n/a, slope n/a; *Women:* yardage 1544, par 31, rating n/a, slope n/a.

Tee Times: Reservations are recommended.

Dress Code: Appropriate attire and soft spikes are required.

Tournaments: This course is available for outside tournaments.

Directions: Travel 37 miles northwest of Santa Barbara on U.S. 101 to the Highway 246 exit and turn east. Drive to the Avenue of Flags and go left. Continue to Shadow Mountain Drive and turn right.

Contact: 223 Shadow Mountain Drive, Buellton, CA 93463, pro shop 805/688-2575.

21 ALISAL GUEST RANCH AND RESORT, RANCH COURSE
Architect: William F. Bell, 1955; Stephen Halsey, 1995
18 holes   Private/Resort $80–90

Santa Barbara and Vicinity Detail map, page 269

Located on the 10,000-acre Alisal Guest Ranch, a working cattle ranch, this scenic course is set in a valley. When you're not watching for native birds and deer, keep an eye out for the fifth, a par-3, 161-yard hole that provides a view of Solvang and the Santa Ynez Valley from its elevated tee. Players hit across Alisal Creek to a green heavily bunkered on the front left. The tight fairways are lined with mature oaks and sycamores. The course is nicely maintained and usually uncrowded. An early morning round offers the chance to see numerous birds and other wildlife on this pleasant and walkable course. Try the best hamburger in the area at the Ranch Course clubhouse restaurant.

For reservations at Alisal Guest Ranch, call 800/425-4725. Golf packages are available with a stay of two or more nights.

Play Policy and Fees: Reciprocal play is accepted with members of other private clubs. Otherwise, members and resort guests only. Green fees are $80 for 18 holes, with carts available for $30. The fee for reciprocators is $90, including cart.

Tees and Yardage: *Men:* Blue: yardage 6551, par 72, rating 72.0, slope 133; White: yardage 6101, par 72, rating 70.1, slope 127; *Women:* Red: yardage 5752, par 73, rating 75.1, slope 133.

Tee Times: Reciprocators should have their club pro call to make arrangements. Resort guests must have a room reservation to book a tee time at the course.

Dress Code: Soft spikes and collared shirts with a pocket are required. No tee shirts or jeans are permitted.

Tournaments: This course is not available for outside tournaments.

Directions: From U.S. 101 in Solvang, take Mission Drive (in downtown Solvang). Turn south on Alisal Road and drive 1.75 miles to the course.

Contact: 1054 Alisal Road (P.O. Box 26), Solvang, CA 93463, pro shop 805/688-4215, clubhouse 805/688-6411, fax 805/688-6411, www.alisal.com.

22 ALISAL GUEST RANCH AND RESORT, RIVER COURSE

Architect: Halsey/Daray Design Group, 1992

18 holes   **Public**   **$25–55**

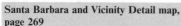

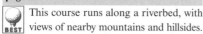

> Santa Barbara and Vicinity Detail map, page 269

This course runs along a riverbed, with views of nearby mountains and hillsides. The signature hole is the seventh, a 438-yard par-4 with a lake on the left and out-of-bounds on the right. The eighth plays with a winery paralleling the right side of the fairway and a view of the old mission up on the hill. Great quality for the price asked, making this is one of California's best values.

For reservations at Alisal Guest Ranch, call 800/425-4725. Golf packages are available with a stay of two or more nights.

Play Policy and Fees: Green fees for 18 holes are $45 weekdays and $55 weekends and holidays. For nine holes and for twilight play (after 2 P.M.), weekday fees are $25 and weekend and holiday fees are $30. Carts are $26 for 18 holes and $16 for nine holes. Senior, junior, and annual rates are available.

Tees and Yardage: *Men:* Gold: yardage 6830, par 72, rating 73.1, slope 126; Blue: yardage 6451, par 72, rating 70.6, slope 120; White: yardage 6099, par 72, rating 68.7, slope 115; *Women:* Red: yardage 5710, par 72, rating 73.1, slope 122.

Tee Times: Reservations may be booked seven days in advance.

Dress Code: Collared shirts and nonmetal spikes are mandatory. Shorts must be Bermuda length.

Tournaments: Events may be scheduled up to one year in advance. The banquet facility can hold 150 people.

Directions: From U.S. 101, drive three miles east on Highway 246 into Solvang. Turn right on Alisal Road and drive one-quarter mile to the course on the left.

Contact: 150 Alisal Road (P.O. Box 1589), Solvang, CA 93463, pro shop 805/688-6042, fax 805/688-8229, www.rivercourse.com.

23 RANCHO SAN MARCOS GOLF COURSE

Architect: Robert Trent Jones Jr., 1998

18 holes   **Public**   **$85–145**

> Santa Barbara and Vicinity Detail map, page 269

This course, in Los Padres National Forest, offers centuries-old oak trees and views of the Santa Ynez River and Lake Cachuma. The front nine is fairly flat and easy to walk, but the back nine has some severe elevation changes. Pull out a driver with caution. A premium is placed on accuracy off the tee. Because of the plentiful mounding, chances are you will not have a level lie. It is always a pleasure to play a course like this with a caddie who can help read some of the tricky greens and offer local knowledge on the blind shots. The facility also includes a 15-acre practice area with all-grass tees.

Play Policy and Fees: Green fees for tri-county residents are $85 Monday–Thursday and $115 Friday–Sunday. Nonresident daily fees are $125 Monday–Friday and $145 Friday–Sunday. Carts and range balls included in fees. Caddies are available with 24 hours advance notice. Twilight, junior, and replay rates are also available.

Tees and Yardage: *Men:* Black: yardage 6817, par 71, rating 73.2, slope 136; White: yardage 6245, par 71, rating 70.3, slope 127; *Women:* Green: yardage 5004, par 71, rating 69.8, slope 119.

Tee Times: Reservations may be booked seven days in advance.

Dress Code: Golf attire, collared shirts, and soft spikes are required. No denim is permitted.

Tournaments: A 12-player minimum is required

to book an event. At least a three-month lead time is preferred.

Directions: Take U.S. 101 to Santa Barbara and the State Street–San Marcos Pass exit. Cross State Street and turn toward the mountains on San Marcos Pass, Highway 154. The golf course entrance is 12.5 miles along on the right.

Contact: 4600 Highway 154, Santa Barbara, CA 93105, pro shop 805/683-6334, fax 805/692-8805, www.rsm1804.com.

24 GLEN ANNIE GOLF CLUB

Architect: Damion Pascuzzo and Robert Muir Graves, 1997

18 holes　　　**Public**　　　**$59–74**

Santa Barbara and Vicinity Detail map, page 269

Glen Annie is one of California's hidden gems. It offers excellent views of the Pacific Ocean and the Channel Islands, especially on the back nine, which takes the player up into the hills. This is a challenging course where fescue grass penalizes players who miss the fairways and greens. Because of the proximity to the ocean, wind can be a factor, as it is on the long, 447-yard, uphill par-4 first hole, which plays into its teeth. The greens roll true with subtle undulations that make them tricky to read. The course is surrounded by environmentally sensitive areas (ESA). Golfers are not allowed to play out of an ESA and must take a drop. Don't let the sweeping views off the first hole distract you; this is a tough, long, uphill par-4 that demands two well-hit shots to reach the green. Take the time to visit and play this course.

Play Policy and Fees: Green fees are $59 Monday–Friday and $74 weekends and holidays. Carts are $11 per rider. Twilight, monthly, and resident rates are available.

Tees and Yardage: *Men:* Green: yardage 6420, par 71, rating 71.2, slope 130; White: yardage 5940, par 71, rating 68.8, slope 125; *Women:* Burgundy: yardage 5036, par 71, rating 69.4, slope 123.

Tee Times: Tee times can be made seven days in advance.

Dress Code: Guests are asked to wear collared shirts, and no denim is allowed on the course. This is a nonmetal spike facility.

Tournaments: Shotgun tournaments are available. A 20-player minimum is needed to book a tournament.

Directions: From Santa Barbara, take U.S. 101 north to the Glen Annie off-ramp north. Continue for one-half mile to the entry gate on the left.

Contact: 405 Glen Annie Road, Goleta, CA 93117, pro shop 805/968-6400, fax 805/968-6140, www.glenanniegolf.com.

25 TWIN LAKES GOLF & LEARNING CENTER

Architect: Robert Muir Graves, 1985

9 holes　　　**Public**　　　**$11–12**

Santa Barbara and Vicinity Detail map, page 269

This is a par-29 course that has seven par-3s and two par-4s. Two lakes and a creek come into play on four holes. The course is tight and will test all iron play. The course record is 23.

Play Policy and Fees: Green fees are $11 weekdays and $12 weekends. Replays are $5. Senior and junior discounts are available.

Tees and Yardage: *Men:* yardage 1500, par 29, rating n/a, slope n/a; *Women:* yardage 1292, par 29, rating n/a, slope n/a.

Tee Times: Reservations can be booked seven days in advance but are not necessary except on weekends.

Dress Code: Shirts and soft spike shoes are necessary.

Tournaments: This course is available for outside tournaments.

Directions: Take the Fairview exit off U.S. 101 north of Santa Barbara and drive west to the course.

Contact: 6034 Hollister Avenue, Goleta, CA 93117, pro shop 805/964-1414, fax 805/964-8457, www.twinlakesgolf.com.

26 SANDPIPER GOLF COURSE

Architect: William F. Bell, 1971

18 holes **Public** **$135–145**

Santa Barbara and Vicinity Detail map, page 269

Championship golf takes you to the edge of the Pacific Ocean at this beautiful, challenging, and inspiring course. Sandpiper features beautiful, rolling fairways and challenging greens in a seaside links-style layout with breathtaking ocean and mountain views from every hole. Step off the green of the beautiful par-3 11th hole and onto the sand of the scenic Santa Barbara coastline. Sandpiper has been rated among the top 25 public golf courses in the nation and hosted the final stage of the 1997 PGA Tour Qualifying.

Play Policy and Fees: Green fees are $135 Monday–Thursday and $145 Friday, weekends, and holidays. Twilight and replay rates are available. Carts are $15.

Tees and Yardage: *Men:* Black: yardage 7068, par 72, rating 73.9, slope 131; Silver: yardage 6597, par 72, rating 71.6, slope 126; *Women:* Copper: yardage 5701, par 72, rating 73.7, slope 126.

Tee Times: Reservations can be made seven days in advance.

Dress Code: Collared shirts and nonmetal spikes are required. No denim is allowed on the course.

Tournaments: A 16-player minimum is required to book a tournament. Tournaments should be booked 12 months in advance.

Directions: Travel 12 miles north of Santa Barbara on U.S. 101 and exit at the Winchester Canyon Road/Hollister Avenue exit. Turn left at the stop sign and drive one-quarter mile on Hollister Avenue to the course on the right.

Contact: 7925 Hollister Avenue, Goleta, CA 93117, pro shop 805/968-1541, www.sandpipergolf.com.

27 OCEAN MEADOWS GOLF CLUB

Architect: Harry Rainville and David Rainville, 1964

9 holes **Public** **$16–30**

Santa Barbara and Vicinity Detail map, page 269

This relatively flat course has tree-lined fairways and mountain views. It is built within the boundaries of an ecologically rich ocean slough and consequently has numerous lateral water hazards. Bird-watchers (not to be confused with birdie watchers) might want to bring binoculars to view the beautiful and abundant wildlife in the area, which includes blue herons and snowy egrets. It'll take more than binoculars to see an eagle.

Play Policy and Fees: Green fees are $16 for nine holes and $26 for 18 holes weekdays, $18 for nine holes and $30 for 18 holes weekends and holidays. Carts are $12 for nine holes and $16 for 18 holes. Senior rates available.

Tees and Yardage: *Men (18 holes):* White/Blue: yardage 6275, par 72, rating 69.4, slope 115; *Women (18 holes):* Red/White: yardage 5691, par 72, rating 73.4, slope 119.

Tee Times: Reservations can be booked seven days in advance.

Dress Code: Soft spikes are preferred.

Tournaments: A 16-player minimum is required to book a tournament.

Directions: Go north of Santa Barbara on U.S. 101 to the Storke–Glen Annie exit. Drive south one mile to Whittier Drive.

Contact: 6925 Whittier Drive, Goleta, CA 93117, pro shop 805/968-6814, fax 805/968-0816.

28 HIDDEN OAKS GOLF COURSE

Architect: Billy Casper, 1975

9 holes **Public** **$11–22**

Santa Barbara and Vicinity Detail map, page 269

This short course is all par-3s. There are bentgrass greens and lush, narrow fairways. A well on the course provides year-round water, and in the drought years the course was the only green spot in the Santa Barbara area. The longest hole is the ninth at 173 yards. The sixth hole is tricky, shooting down 122 yards from an elevated tee to the green.

Play Policy and Fees: Green fees are $11 weekdays and $12 weekends and holidays for nine holes. For 18 holes, fees are $20 weekdays and $22 weekends. Senior and junior rates are available every day. Pull carts are $2.

Tees and Yardage: *Men:* yardage 1170, par 27, rating n/a, slope n/a; *Women:* yardage 854, par 27, rating n/a, slope n/a.

Tee Times: All play is on a first-come, first-served basis.

Dress Code: Shirts must be worn.

Tournaments: A 36-player minimum is required to book a tournament. Events should be scheduled two months in advance.

Directions: Off U.S. 101 heading south to Santa Barbara, take the Turnpike exit and turn left on Hollister. Turn right on Puente and follow it to Calle Camarade. Take a right turn to the course.

Contact: 4760-G Calle Camarade, Santa Barbara, CA 93110, pro shop 805/967-3493.

29 LA CUMBRE COUNTRY CLUB

Architect: Tom Bendelow, 1918; William P. Bell, 1920; William F. Bell, 1957; Robert Muir Graves, 1988
18 holes   Private $135

Santa Barbara and Vicinity Detail map, page 269

This is a well-maintained course with a 30-acre lake coming into play on the back nine. Five holes border the lake. The course predates the surrounding homes of the Hope Ranch residential development. Al Geiberger holds the course record with a 61.

Play Policy and Fees: Reciprocal play is accepted with members of other private clubs; otherwise, members and guests only. Green fee for reciprocators is $135. Carts are $35.

Tees and Yardage: *Men:* Blue: yardage 6414,

par 71, rating 71.5, slope 130; White: yardage 6113, par 71, rating 70.1, slope 126; Gold: yardage 5697, par 71, rating 68.2, slope 122; *Women:* Red: yardage 5697, par 72, rating 73.9, slope 135.

Tee Times: Reciprocators should have their club pro call to make arrangements.

Dress Code: Appropriate golf attire and non-metal spikes are required.

Tournaments: This course is available for a limited number of outside events. Please inquire of the general manager.

Directions: Heading into Santa Barbara on U.S. 101, take the Hope Avenue/La Cumbre Road exit. Turn left on Frontage Road and then left on La Cumbre Road and continue one-quarter mile past the arched entrance to Hope Ranch Park and Via Laguna. The club is on the left.

Contact: 4015 Via Laguna, Santa Barbara, CA 93110, pro shop 805/682-3131, fax 805/687-3964.

30 SANTA BARBARA GOLF CLUB

Architect: Lawrence Hughes, 1958
18 holes   Public $30–40

Santa Barbara and Vicinity Detail map, page 269

This course in the foothills above Santa Barbara offers a nice view of the Channel Islands. Trees border the holes, and the fairways are made up of kikuyu grass, which can get gnarly on the club face. The course plays long. The Santa Barbara City Championship, the Santa Barbara Classic, the Santa Barbara Women's Open, and the Santa Barbara City Seniors tournaments are held here. This is a popular course with local players.

Play Policy and Fees: Nonresident green fees are $30 weekdays and $40 weekends. Resident twilight, senior, junior, and nine-hole rates are available. Carts are additional.

Tees and Yardage: *Men:* Blue: yardage 6037, par 70, rating 69.3, slope 126; White: yardage 5785,

par 70, rating 68.1, slope 123; *Women:* Red: yardage 5535, par 72, rating 72.2, slope 124.

Tee Times: Reservations can be booked seven days in advance.

Dress Code: Appropriate attire and soft spikes are required.

Tournaments: Shotgun tournaments are available weekdays only. A 24-player minimum is required to book a tournament. Events can be scheduled up to 12 months in advance. The banquet facility can accommodate 100 people.

Directions: Exit U.S. 101 at Las Positas Road in Santa Barbara and drive east for three-quarters of a mile to McCaw Avenue. Turn left and continue one-quarter mile to the course.

Contact: 3500 McCaw Avenue, Santa Barbara, CA 93105, pro shop 805/687-7087, fax 805/687-1651, www.sbgolf.com.

31 MONTECITO COUNTRY CLUB

Architect: Max Behr, 1922
18 holes   **Private**   **$90–110**

Santa Barbara and Vicinity Detail map, page 269

This classic club features a challenging golf course that emphasizes shot-making. Ocean and mountain views are abundant from the rolling, tree-lined fairways and well-kept, undulating greens. The course plays much longer than yardage indicates. Accuracy and the ability to recover from troublesome lies are needed to score well here. Memorable holes include the par-4 third hole and the 18th, which is a top-notch finishing par-5.

Play Policy and Fees: Reciprocal play is accepted with members of other private clubs. The reciprocator fee is $90 walking, $110 riding.

Tees and Yardage: *Men:* Blue: yardage 6239, par 71, rating 70.6, slope 124; White: yardage 6032, par 71, rating 69.7, slope 122; *Women:* Red: yardage 5794, par 73, rating 75.1, slope 134.

Tee Times: Guests should have their club professional make reservations with the Montecito pro shop. Tee times can be made three days in advance.

Dress Code: Appropriate golf attire is required.

Tournaments: Not available for outside tournaments.

Directions: From U.S. 101, take the Cabrillo Boulevard exit north and drive through the underpass, bearing right to Hot Springs Road (the first street). Turn left and drive one-half mile to Summit Road. Turn left and drive to the club.

Contact: 920 Summit Road, Santa Barbara, CA 93102 (P.O. Box 1170, Santa Barbara, CA 93108), pro shop 805/969-0800, fax 805/969-3906, www.montecitocc.com.

32 BIRNAM WOOD GOLF CLUB

Architect: Robert Trent Jones Sr., 1967
18 holes   **Private**

Santa Barbara and Vicinity Detail map, page 269

This is a short course that rewards accuracy. There are numerous out-of-bounds markers to the left and right. Barrancas are found in front of the greens, making it impossible to roll the ball on. Sharpen up your iron play before tackling this well-maintained, Robert Trent Jones Sr. beauty.

Play Policy and Fees: Members and guests only.

Tees and Yardage: *Men:* Blue: yardage 6035, par 70, rating 69.3, slope 125; White: yardage 5822, par 70, rating 68.3, slope 123; *Women:* Red: yardage 5363, par 71, rating 71.9, slope 128.

Tee Times: No reservations are taken.

Dress Code: Appropriate golf attire and non-metal spikes are required.

Tournaments: All outside events must have a member sponsor.

Directions: Take the Sheffield Drive exit off U.S. 101 in Santa Barbara and drive to the end. Turn left on East Valley Road and drive up the hill to the club entrance.

Contact: 2031 Packing House Road, Santa Barbara, CA 93108, pro shop 805/969-0919, fax 805/969-5037.

33 THE VALLEY CLUB OF MONTECITO

Architect: Alister Mackenzie, 1929
18 holes   **Private**

Santa Barbara and Vicinity Detail map, page 269

This classic Alister Mackenzie design features small greens and a natural setting. A creek runs through about half the holes, and the narrow fairways are bordered by large cypress and pine trees. The ocean is visible from many holes. The club is very exclusive. Fewer than 100 members use it regularly. The Valley Club is rated among the top 20 courses in the state, and there have been no modifications to it since it opened in 1929.

Play Policy and Fees: Members and guests only.
Tees and Yardage: *Men:* Blue: yardage 6612, par 72, rating 72.2, slope 133; White: yardage 6336, par 72, rating 71.1, slope 129; *Women:* Red: yardage 5813, par 73, rating 74.4, slope 133.
Tee Times: Not applicable.
Dress Code: Collared shirts and soft spikes are required. No blue jeans are allowed.
Tournaments: This course is not available for outside events.
Directions: Take the San Ysidro Road exit off U.S. 101 and travel north to East Valley Road. Turn right and drive one mile to Valley Club Road, then turn right to the club.
Contact: 1901 East Valley Road, Santa Barbara, CA 93150 (P.O. Box 5640, Santa Barbara, CA 93108), pro shop 805/969-4681, fax 805/969-6174.

34 SOULE PARK GOLF COURSE

Architect: William F. Bell, 1962
18 holes   **Public**   **$28–40**

Santa Barbara and Vicinity Detail map, page 269

This course is at the base of the mountains in the Ojai Valley and traverses a rolling terrain. A creek runs through the course, and mature trees line the fairways. A hole that will stagger many a golfer is the 568-yard, par-5 seventh. This is a three-shot hole with a creek running in front of the green, requiring a 120-yard carry. The green is guarded by a huge oak tree. It is definitely a position hole.

Play Policy and Fees: On weekdays, green fees are $28. On weekends, fees are $40. Midday, twilight, super twilight, junior (weekdays only), and senior (weekdays only) rates are offered.
Tees and Yardage: *Men:* Blue: yardage 6436, par 72, rating 70.3, slope 121; White: yardage 6172, par 72, rating 69.2, slope 118; *Women:* Red: yardage 5636, par 73, rating 72.0, slope 123.
Tee Times: Reservations may be booked seven days in advance starting at 7 A.M.
Dress Code: Soft spikes only.
Tournaments: This course is available for tournaments. The banquet facility holds 150 people.
Directions: From Ventura, travel north 16 miles on Highway 33 to the town of Ojai. Turn right on East Ojai Avenue and drive two miles to the course.
Contact: 1033 East Ojai Avenue (P.O. Box 758), Ojai, CA 93023, pro shop 805/646-5633.

35 OJAI VALLEY INN & SPA

Architect: George C. Thomas Jr., 1923; renovated Jay Morrish, 1988
18 holes   **Resort**   **$59–118**

Santa Barbara and Vicinity Detail map, page 269

This beautiful mountainside course was built in the 1920s by George C. Thomas Jr. and renovated by Jay Morrish in 1988. In 1999, two "missing" holes of Thomas's were replaced. This course has been home to seven Senior PGA Tour events. Over the years, this venerable course has boasted Jimmy Demeret and Doug Sanders as host professionals. The course record of 61 was set by Buddy Allin in the 1996 FHP Health Care Classic. Note: In 2004, a $65 million facelift was completed on the resort, including the introduction of 100 new guest rooms, two new restaurants, a new golf clubhouse, a ballroom and conference center, new swimming pools, and an improved entrance and lobby. In addition, the nines were reversed on the golf course.

For resort reservations, call 800/422-6524.

Play Policy and Fees: For daily fee players, green fees are $69 for nine holes and $118 for 18 holes. For hotel guests, fees are $59 for nine holes and $103 for 18 holes. Twilight rates and junior rates are available. Carts are $10 for nine holes and $17 for 18 holes. (Note: Fees were expected to rise when renovations were complete, but had not been set at press time. Please call for current information.)

Tees and Yardage: *Men:* Blue: yardage 6305, par 70, rating 70.7, slope 125; White: yardage 5979, par 70, rating 69.0, slope 120; *Women:* Red: yardage 5235, par 71, rating 71.2, slope 130.

Tee Times: Daily fee players may book one week in advance.

Dress Code: Proper golf attire and nonmetal spikes are required.

Tournaments: This course is available for outside events. The banquet facility can accommodate 300 people.

Directions: From Ventura, travel north 13 miles on Highway 33 to Ojai. Turn right on Country Club Road.

Contact: 905 Country Club Road, Ojai, CA 93023, pro shop 805/646-5511, www.golfojai.com.

36 MOUNTAIN VIEW GOLF COURSE
Architect: Tony Pawlak and Paul McGrath, 1969
18 holes   Semiprivate $20–25

Santa Barbara and Vicinity Detail map, page 269

This is a short course in a narrow valley at the base of South Mountain. Mature trees border the fairways of this wandering course, and there is water in play on several holes. The course may be short on the scorecard, but it's difficult. Accuracy is essential to scoring well.

Play Policy and Fees: Green fees are $20 weekdays and $25 weekends. Twilight, senior (with card), and junior rates are available. Carts are additional.

Tees and Yardage: *Men:* White: yardage 5445, par 69, rating 65.0, slope 112; *Women:* Red: yardage 4778, par 70, rating 67.3, slope 115.

Tee Times: Reservations can be booked seven days in advance.

Dress Code: Appropriate golf attire. Soft spikes only.

Tournaments: Shotgun tournaments are available weekdays only.

Directions: Take the Highway 126 exit off U.S. 101 just south of Ventura and drive east to the 10th Street exit. Turn left under the freeway, drive to Harvard Boulevard, and turn right. At 12th Street, turn right and drive one-half mile to South Mountain Road. Turn right to the course.

Contact: 16799 South Mountain Road, Santa Paula, CA 93060, pro shop 805/525-1571, www.mountainviewgc.com.

37 SATICOY REGIONAL GOLF COURSE
Architect: George C. Thomas Jr., 1921; William F. Bell, 1964
9 holes   Public $11–20

Santa Barbara and Vicinity Detail map, page 269

This course was built in 1921 as the Saticoy Golf and Country Club. It has narrow fairways, gradual slopes, and quick, traditional greens. Water, bunkers, and trees make this a shot-maker's course from start to finish. The original George C. Thomas Jr. design has been whittled down and land has been taken away by Ventura County over the years, so that today there is still some of the original flavor, but it's fading.

Play Policy and Fees: Green fees are $11 for nine holes and $17 for 18 holes weekdays, $13 for nine holes and $20 for 18 holes weekends. Carts are $7 for nine holes and $10 for 18 holes. Seniors (over 60) pay $8 for nine holes and $11 for 18 holes.

Tees and Yardage: *Men (18 holes):* yardage 5358,

par 68, rating 65.4, slope 109; *Women (18 holes):* yardage 4768, par 68, rating 66.9, slope 107.

Tee Times: Reservations may be booked seven days in advance.

Dress Code: Appropriate golf attire is required.

Tournaments: A 20-player minimum is needed to book an event. Tournaments should be scheduled at least three months in advance.

Directions: Take the Central Avenue exit off U.S. 101 south of Ventura and continue for five miles until it dead-ends at Vineyard. Make a right turn and drive until Vineyard dead-ends at Highway 118. Turn left on Highway 118 and drive one mile to the course on the left.

Contact: 1025 South Wells Road, Ventura, CA 93004, pro shop 805/647-6678, fax 805/647-6691.

38 SATICOY COUNTRY CLUB
Architect: William F. Bell, 1964
18 holes   Private $128–148

Santa Barbara and Vicinity Detail map, page 269

Make sure your tee shots are accurate or you will be in for a long day. The fairways are tight and demanding, and the greens are large and undulating. Many of the greens are elevated. The par-3 10th is 174 yards from the back tees, dropping about 100 feet over water to the green. Situated on the side of a mountain, this is the course to play in Ventura County if you're looking for golf in a quiet setting.

Play Policy and Fees: Reciprocal play is accepted with members of other private clubs. Reciprocator fees are $128 on weekdays and $148 on weekends. Otherwise, members and guests only.

Tees and Yardage: *Men:* Championship: yardage 6883, par 72, rating 73.6, slope 136; Tournament: yardage 6563, par 72, rating 72.3, slope 133; Regular: yardage 6355, par 72, rating 71.2, slope 130; *Women:* Forward: yardage 5842, par 73, rating 75.5, slope 137.

Tee Times: Reciprocators should have their head pro call to make arrangements.

Dress Code: Collared shirts, golf slacks or Bermuda-length shorts, and nonmetal spikes are required.

Tournaments: This course is available for outside events on Monday on a limited basis. Call for details.

Directions: Take the Central Avenue exit off U.S. 101 just south of Ventura, then drive north for two miles to Santa Clara Avenue. Turn right and travel 1.25 miles to Los Angeles Avenue and turn left. Drive one-half mile to the club.

Contact: 4450 North Clubhouse Drive, Somis, CA 93066, pro shop 805/485-5216, www.saticoycountryclub.com.

39 LAS POSAS COUNTRY CLUB
Architect: Lawrence Hughes, 1958
18 holes   Private $50–70

Santa Barbara and Vicinity Detail map, page 269

The front nine is hilly with narrow fairways. The back nine is flatter but well bunkered. The greens are soft, quick, and true. PGA Tour professional Corey Pavin is an honorary member.

Play Policy and Fees: Reciprocal play is accepted with members of other private clubs; otherwise, members and guests only. Green fees are $50 weekdays, $70 weekends for reciprocators. Carts are $12 per person.

Tees and Yardage: *Men:* White: yardage 6211, par 71, rating 70.2, slope 123; Gold: yardage 5931, par 71, rating 68.9, slope 120; *Women:* Forward: yardage 5642, par 71, rating 73.8, slope 130.

Tee Times: Reciprocators should have their club pro call to make arrangements.

Dress Code: Appropriate golf attire is required. No metal spikes are allowed.

Tournaments: This course is available for outside tournaments on Monday only. A 72-player minimum is needed to book an event. Tournaments should be scheduled six months in advance. A banquet facility is available that can accommodate 300 people.

Directions: Take the Las Posas Road exit off

U.S. 101 in Camarillo and drive north for one-half mile to Crestview Avenue. Turn right and drive one-quarter mile to Valley Vista Drive and turn right. Continue one mile to Fairway Drive and turn left to the club.

Contact: 955 Fairway Drive, Camarillo, CA 93010, pro shop 805/482-4518, clubhouse 805/388-2901, fax 805/388-1378.

40 STERLING HILLS GOLF CLUB

Architect: Pascuzzo & Graves, 1999

18 holes   **Public**   **$39-75**

Santa Barbara and Vicinity Detail map, page 269

Sterling Hills is an 18-hole, par-71, upscale course that plays longer than its yardage. This is partly due to some severe undulation in the greens. Golfers have to be in the fairway here, because there is a premium on the approach shot. It is imperative to leave yourself in the right spot on the green or scoring will be tough. There is enough contour to the fairways to keep it from being flat, but it is a very walkable layout.

Play Policy and Fees: Weekday green fees are $39 without a cart and $56 with a cart. Green fees on weekends are $75 with a cart (riding is mandatory). Twilight, junior (weekdays only), and senior (weekdays only) rates are available.

Tees and Yardage: *Men:* Black: yardage 6813, par 71, rating 72.9, slope 133; Blue: yardage 6395, par 71, rating 70.9, slope 126; White: yardage 5906, par 71, rating 69.0, slope 121; *Women:* Red: yardage 5482, par 71, rating 72.0, slope 120.

Tee Times: Tee times can be booked up to seven days in advance. A $10 fee is charged for reservations made 8–30 days in advance.

Dress Code: Collared shirts and soft-spiked shoes are required. Denim is not allowed.

Tournaments: Outside events are welcome. The course features a 2900-square-foot banquet facility seating 180 people comfortably.

Directions: From Los Angeles, take U.S. 101 north to Camarillo and the Central Avenue exit. Turn right on Central Avenue and drive until you get to Beardsley Road. Take a right on Beardsley and another right on Sterling Hills Drive to the golf course.

Contact: 901 Sterling Hills Drive, Camarillo, CA 93010, pro shop 805/987-3446, fax 805/604-1873, www.sterlinghillsgolf.com.

41 BUENAVENTURA GOLF COURSE

Architect: William P. Bell and William F. Bell, 1949

18 holes   **Public**   **$18-25**

Santa Barbara and Vicinity Detail map, page 269

At press time, this course was being remodeled and shortened from par 72 to par 70. The remodel will take roughly 300 yards from the existing 6400-yard course. The design is highlighted by eight lakes; large cypress, pine, and eucalyptus trees; and narrow fairways. Greens and tees have recently been upgraded.

Play Policy and Fees: Green fees are $18 weekdays and $25 weekends and holidays. Carts are $22.

Tees and Yardage: Not available at press time.

Tee Times: Reservations can be made seven days in advance.

Dress Code: Collared shirts are required.

Tournaments: Shotgun tournaments are available. A 16-player minimum is required to book an event. Events should be booked 12 months in advance. The banquet facility can hold 280 people.

Directions: From U.S. 101 (Ventura Freeway) in Ventura, take the Victoria Avenue exit south for one mile to Olivas Park Drive. Turn left and go one-quarter mile to the course on the right.

Contact: 5882 Olivas Park Drive, Ventura, CA 93003, pro shop 805/642-2231, fax 805/642-5403.

42 OLIVAS PARK GOLF COURSE
Architect: William F. Bell, 1969;
Forrest Richardson 2005

18 holes   Public $20–27

**Santa Barbara and Vicinity Detail map,
page 269**

At press time, this course was being completely remodeled. It will be closed for roughly 16 months as it is being redesigned. When it re-opens in 2006 it will be a links-style layout with no trees, subject to the ocean breezes from the nearby Pacific. Please call for status.

Play Policy and Fees: During the week, Ventura City resident rates are $20 and nonresident rates are $22. On the weekends, resident fees are $25 and nonresident fees are $27. Carts are $12 per rider. Fivesomes are not allowed.

Tees and Yardage: Not available at press time.

Tee Times: Reservations may be made seven days in advance. If you have a Ventura City Reservation card, you may book nine days in advance.

Dress Code: Nonmetal spikes are encouraged. No tank tops or sandals are allowed.

Tournaments: This course is available for outside tournaments.

Directions: From Santa Barbara, drive about 26 miles south on U.S. 101 to the Seaward exit in Ventura. Turn left on Harbor Road and drive five miles to Olivas Park Drive. Turn left and drive 100 yards to the course.

Contact: 3750 Olivas Park Drive, Ventura, CA 93003, pro shop 805/677-6770, fax 805/642-7495.

43 RIVER RIDGE GOLF CLUB
Architect: William F. Bell, 1986

18 holes   Public $28–38

**Santa Barbara and Vicinity Detail map,
page 269**

This is a rolling, links-style course with nearly eight acres of water. The 191-yard, par-3 14th features an island green. You'll need every club in the bag because of the wind and hills. Note: River Ridge is expanding to 36 holes, with nine holes opened in 2004 and the other nine planned for summer 2005. The new holes will change the existing configuration and ratings.

Play Policy and Fees: Green fees are $28 weekdays and $38 weekends and holidays. Carts are $24. Local resident, twilight, senior, and junior rates are offered.

Tees and Yardage: *Men:* Blue: yardage 6777, par 72, rating 72.6, slope 122; White: yardage 6370, par 72, rating 70.6, slope 117; Gold: yardage 5990, par 72, rating 68.8, slope 113; *Women:* Red: yardage 5362, par 72, rating 71.3, slope 124.

Tee Times: Reservations can be booked seven days in advance.

Dress Code: Nonmetal spikes are required.

Tournaments: Tournaments welcome. Events should be booked 12 months in advance.

Directions: Take the Vineyard exit off U.S. 101 in Oxnard and drive west for three miles to the course.

Contact: 2401 West Vineyard Avenue, Oxnard, CA 93030, pro shop 805/983-4653, fax 805/981-4653, www.riverridge-golfclub.com.

44 SPANISH HILLS GOLF & COUNTRY CLUB
Architect: Robert Cupp, 1993

18 holes   Private $151

**Santa Barbara and Vicinity Detail map,
page 269**

This is a challenging but fair course with beautiful vistas and numerous changes in elevation. Architect Robert Cupp has made artistic use of water and bunkers. The talk of the course is the uphill, par-4 finishing hole, which features a green surrounded by water and flanked by a spectacular clubhouse.

Play Policy and Fees: Some reciprocal play is accepted with members of other private clubs at a rate of $151 per player, including cart. Otherwise, guests must be accompanied by a member.

Tees and Yardage: *Men:* Professional: yardage 6749, par 71, rating 72.9, slope 132; Championship: yardage 6310, par 71, rating 70.8, slope 126; Back: yardage 5895, par 71, rating 68.7, slope 121; *Women:* Middle: yardage 5375, par 71, rating 72.9, slope 129; Forward: yardage 5002, par 71, rating 70.5, slope 126.

Tee Times: Reciprocators should have their club pro call to make arrangements.

Dress Code: No denim is allowed. Women must wear either a collared or sleeved shirt. Men's shorts must be Bermuda-length. Nonmetal spikes are required.

Tournaments: Outside events are limited to Monday. A 100-player minimum is needed to book a tournament. Carts are a must. Events must be scheduled six months in advance. A banquet facility is available that can accommodate 240 people.

Directions: This course is 45 miles north of Los Angeles. Heading north on U.S. 101, exit on Las Posas Road. Turn right on Las Posas. Turn left on Ponderosa. Turn left on Crestview Avenue and continue to the course.

Contact: 999 Crestview Avenue, Camarillo, CA 93010, pro shop 805/388-5000, www.spanishhillscc.com.

45 SEEBEE GOLF COURSE OF PORT HUENEME
Architect: Jack Daray, 1957
18 holes   Military/Public $20–26

🏃 📷 🍺 🏌 🛺 ⛳

Santa Barbara and Vicinity Detail map, page 269

This is a deceptive course. Although flat, it plays tough because of green and bunker placement. The prevailing west wind off the ocean and numerous trees add to the challenge. Jack Daray built the original nine holes here in 1957. In mid-1990 the course was expanded to 18 holes. Give careful study to the 13th. It's a par-3, 179 yards from the championship tees. The large green appears to be surrounded by water, and it's tough getting there. The green is not only guarded by water, but there are also front bunkers, left and right, and out-of-bounds left and behind the green.

Play Policy and Fees: This was formerly a military-only course. The public now has access but must first obtain a base pass by calling the pro shop. Green fees for the public are $20 weekdays and $26 on weekends. Military green fees vary according to military status. Carts are $22 for two people. Closed Christmas.

Tees and Yardage: *Men:* Blue: yardage 6278, par 71, rating 70.1, slope 122; White: yardage 5971, par 71, rating 68.6, slope 118; *Women:* Red: yardage 5422, par 72, rating 71.5, slope 122.

Tee Times: Reservations can be booked seven days in advance for civilians and retired military. Active military can make reservations eight days in advance.

Dress Code: No tank tops are allowed. Nonmetal spikes are preferred.

Tournaments: This course is available for outside tournaments.

Directions: Take Ventura Road off U.S. 101 in Oxnard and drive south on Ventura Road to the Sunkist gate. Turn right and proceed to Pacific Street. Turn right on Pacific Street and drive to Port Hueneme Naval Base and the course.

Contact: 1000 23rd Avenue, Port Hueneme, CA 93043, pro shop 805/982-2620.

46 POINT MUGU GOLF CLUB
Architect: Marlin Cox, 1963
9 holes   Military $11–18

🏃 📷 🍺 🏌 🛺 ⛳

Santa Barbara and Vicinity Detail map, page 269

This short course is wide open and flat. The course has nine greens but 15 different tee boxes. Four water hazards line the course, but the biggest obstacle is the sound of low-flying aircraft going to and from the nearby airstrip. Bring ear plugs.

Play Policy and Fees: Public play is accepted with a base pass, which must be obtained in advance. Green fees for military personnel vary according to status. Green fees for public play are $11 for nine holes and $13 for 18 holes on weekdays. On weekends, green fees are $15 for nine holes and $18 for 18 holes. Twilight rates available.

Tees and Yardage: *Men (18 holes):* Blue/White: yardage 5858, par 70, rating 68.1, slope 112; *Women (18 holes):* Red/Yellow: yardage 5432, par 72, rating 72.6, slope 119.

Tee Times: Reservations can be booked seven days in advance.

Dress Code: Collared shirts and nonmetal spikes are encouraged.

Tournaments: This course is available for out-side tournaments. A 48-player minimum is needed to book a tournament. Tournaments should be booked two months in advance.

Directions: Take the Wood Road–USN Point Mugu exit off Highway 1 north of Camarillo Beach. Obtain a guest pass from the Visitor Information Center and enter the base at Mugu Road. Turn right at Third Street and drive to the course.

Contact: NAWS, Building 153, Point Mugu, CA 93042, pro shop 805/989-7109, fax 805/989-0856.

Chapter 13

THE TOURNAMENT PLAYERS CLUB (TPC) AT VALENCIA © GEORGE FULLER

Los Angeles and Vicinity

Los Angeles and Vicinity

Southern California may be better known as home to Hollywood than as a great place to use your 3-wood, but when you take a closer look at this varied region, it's not all that bad for golfers after all.

If you are visiting, you'll want to do what the locals do: take advantage of the great beaches, visit attractions such as Universal Studios and Disneyland, hang out and gawk at Hollywood and Vine, and keep an eye peeled for movie stars at the many, many restaurants and shopping venues. But you should also come equipped to play some good golf.

Used to be that visitors to and residents of Southern California had precious slim pickings of quality golf courses. You could play the Wilson or Harding Course at Griffith Park, and Rancho Park was not always as busy as it is today. The San Fernando Valley held out some promise, with Van Nuys Golf Course, Woodley Lakes, and Sepulveda Golf Course providing municipal golf options. Members at Riviera Country Club, Los Angeles Country Club, Bel-Air, Wilshire Country Club, or one of the other fine private clubs were set, of course. But those looking for public golf—that was a different story.

South of Los Angeles, things were a little better. Palos Verdes Golf Club has been in play since 1924, and nearby Los Verdes in Rancho Palos Verdes opened in 1964. Always scenic and always affordable, Los Verdes is one of the best bargains for an ocean view course in the United States at $20–25. Farther south still in Orange County, golfers could choose from several designs, including 36 holes at Costa Mesa Golf & Country Club (1967) and 18 popular holes of executive play at Casta Del Sol in Mission Viejo (1963).

Over the past 20 years, though, many new courses have been constructed within an hour's radius of the city center. That's great news for golfers looking for a round in the sprawling Los Angeles and Orange County areas.

In 1991, the face of upscale daily fee golf changed in the region with the opening of 36 holes of ocean-view, Tom Fazio–designed golf at Pelican Hill in Newport Beach, followed in 1996 by another Fazio design in Irvine, Oak Creek. More recently, the Pete Dye–designed Trump National Golf Club Los Angeles opened its full 18 holes. Formerly Ocean Trails Golf Club, this course perched above the Pacific coastline played as a 15-hole course (three holes were forced out of play because of a landslide in 1999) until late 2004.

One of the very newest designs is Arroyo Trabuco Golf Club in Mission Viejo. This facility opened in summer 2004. Designed by Casey O'Callaghan and Tom Lehman, the course is laid out around Trabuco Creek and Ladera Open Space Reserve. Its concept is to provide a "high-end golfing experience at a competitive price."

The Riverside area has also seen some very good new courses open in recent years, including Oak Quarry Golf Club (2000) and PGA of Southern California Golf Club (2000).

North of Los Angeles, the areas around Valencia, Moorpark, and Simi Valley have been the hotbed of new course openings over the past several years. In the Moorpark area, two excellent courses are now available for play, Moorpark Country Club and Rustic Canyon Golf Club. And in 2003, the Tournament Players Club at Valencia opened. A hilly layout with some tough carries from the tees and to the greens, it is designed, as are all TPC courses, for tournament play, which means that the farther back you play the tougher the angles. While much of the course overlooks the burgeoning Santa Clarita Valley, there are also some nice mountain views.

Golfers are getting some very good options with all this new course development, and that's just fine. It has been a long time coming.

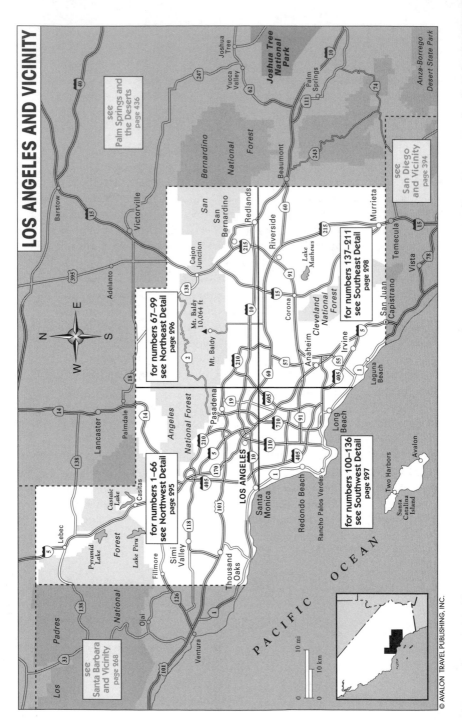

LOS ANGELES AND VICINITY

see
**Palm Springs and
the Deserts**
page 436

*Joshua Tree
National Park*

Joshua
Tree

Yucca
Valley

Palm
Springs

*Anza-Borrego
Desert State Park*

Barstow

Victorville

*San
Bernardino
National
Forest*

Beaumont

see
**San Diego
and Vicinity**
page 394

Adelanto

Cajon
Junction

San
Bernardino

Redlands

Riverside

Lake
Mathews

Murrieta

Temecula

Vista

for numbers 67–99
see Northeast Detail
page 296

Mt. Baldy
10,064 ft

Mt. Baldy

Corona

Cleveland
National
Forest

San Juan
Capistrano

Lancaster

Palmdale

*Angeles
National Forest*

Pasadena

Anaheim

Irvine

Laguna
Beach

Long
Beach

for numbers 137–211
see Southeast Detail
page 298

for numbers 1–66
see Northwest Detail
page 295

LOS ANGELES

Santa
Monica

Redondo Beach

Rancho Palos Verdes

for numbers 100–136
see Southwest Detail
page 297

Two Harbors

Avalon

*Santa
Catalina
Island*

Castaic
Lake

Casitas

Lebec

Pyramid
Lake

Padres

National

Lake Piru

Forest

Fillmore

Simi
Valley

Thousand
Oaks

PACIFIC OCEAN

Los

see
**Santa Barbara
and Vicinity**
page 268

Ojai

Ventura

10 mi

10 km

© AVALON TRAVEL PUBLISHING, INC.

Northwest Detail

Courses 1–66

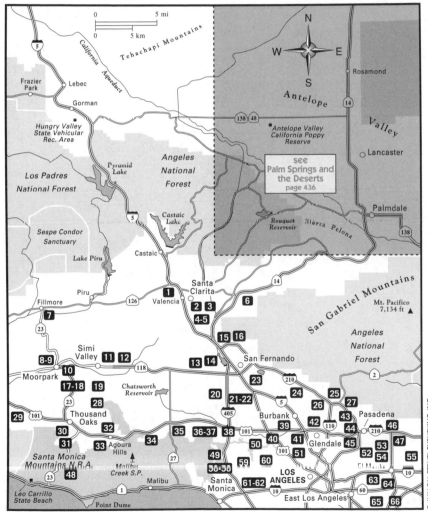

Northeast Detail

Courses 67–99

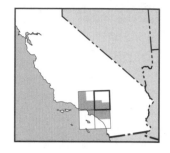

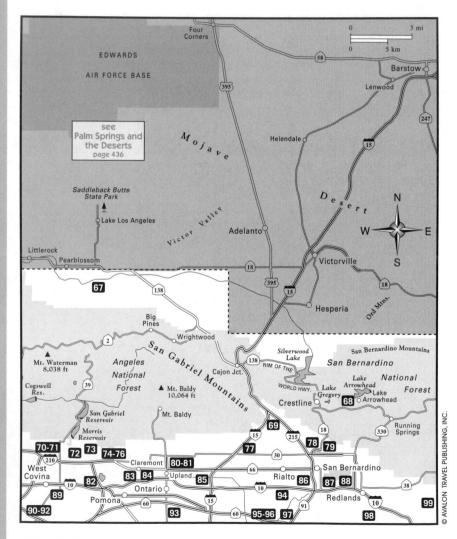

Southwest Detail

Courses 100–136

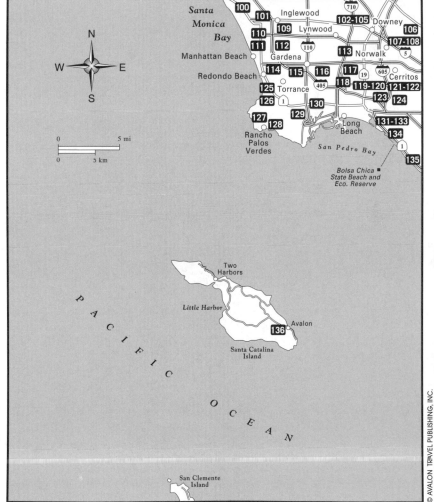

Santa Monica Bay

100
101 Inglewood
102–105 Downey
106
107–108
110 109 Lynwood
111 112
113 Norwalk
Manhattan Beach
Gardena
Redondo Beach
114 115 116 117 118
Cerritos
125 Torrance
119–120 121–122
126
123 124
127 128
129 130
131–133
134
Rancho Palos Verdes
Long Beach
135
San Pedro Bay
Bolsa Chica State Beach and Eco. Reserve

Two Harbors

Little Harbor

PACIFIC

136 Avalon

Santa Catalina Island

OCEAN

San Clemente Island

© AVALON TRAVEL PUBLISHING, INC.

Southeast Detail

Courses 137–211

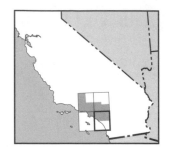

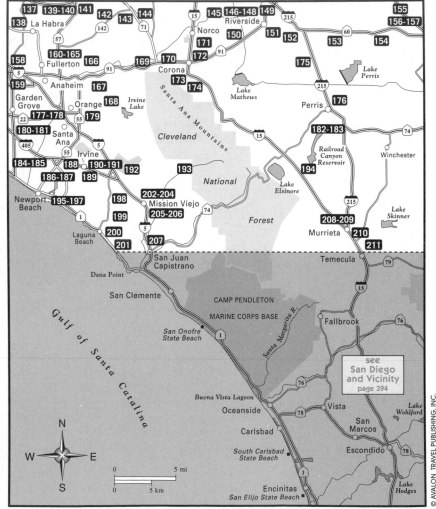

137 139-140 141 142 143 144 145 146-148 149 155
138 La Habra 156-157
57
142 71 Riverside
Norco 150 151 152 153 154
158 160-165 166 169 170 171 91 175
Fullerton Corona 172
5 91 173
159 Anaheim 167 174 Lake Lake
Garden 168 Mathews Perris
Grove Irvine 182-183 176
22 177-178 Orange Lake Perris Winchester
180-181 179 Railroad
Santa Santa Ana Mountains Canyon
405 Ana Cleveland Reservoir
55 184-185 188 190-191 192 193 194 Lake
Irvine Skinner
186-187 189 National Elsinore
Newport 195-197 198 202-204 Lake
Beach Mission Viejo Forest 208-209
199 205-206 74 Murrieta 210
Laguna 200 5 211
Beach 201 207
San Juan Temecula 79
Capistrano
Dana Point 15

San Clemente CAMP PENDLETON
MARINE CORPS BASE
San Onofre Fallbrook 76
State Beach

see
San Diego
and Vicinity
page 394

Buena Vista Lagoon 76
Oceanside 78 Vista Lake
Carlsbad San Wohlford
Marcos
South Carlsbad Escondido 78
State Beach
Encinitas Lake
San Elijo State Beach Hodges

N
W E
S
0 5 mi
0 5 km

© AVALON TRAVEL PUBLISHING, INC.

1 THE TOURNAMENT PLAYERS CLUB (TPC) AT VALENCIA

Architect: Chris Gray and Mark O'Meara, 2003
18 holes   Public $100–130

🚶 📷 🍽️ 🚜 🛏️

Northwest Detail map, page 295

⛳ This is the best newer public facility in
BEST the Los Angeles area. Owned and operated by the PGA Tour, TPC at Valencia is
a hilly course with some tough carries from
the tees and to the greens. It is designed, as
are all TPC courses, for tournament play,
which means that the farther back you play
the tougher the angles. While much of the
course overlooks the burgeoning Santa Clarita Valley, there are also some nice mountain
views. But players come here for the golf experience. Expertly run and always in immaculate condition, TPC Valencia will put your
skills to the test. Large putting surfaces feature a variety of pin positions, and it is a good
idea to be on the same tier as the flag. The
back nine narrows up a lot. The 14th and 15th
holes are back-to-back par-5s that will keep
you talking about the blind tee shots, narrow
landing zones, and tough greens. So tighten
up your golf glove and go play the only TPC
course in California.

Play Policy and Fees: Green fees are $100 Tues-
day–Thursday and $130 Friday–Sunday. Ju-
nior rates are offered, as are replay rates.

Tees and Yardage: *Men:* TPC: yardage 7220,
par 72, rating 75.8, slope 140; Player: yardage
6747, par 72, rating 73.6, slope 133; Medal:
yardage 6440, par 72, rating 71.7, slope 127;
Executive: yardage 6076, par 72, rating 69.7,
slope 122; *Women:* Forward: yardage 5141, par
72, rating 67.2, slope 122.

Tee Times: Reservations can be made nine days
in advance.

Dress Code: Appropriate golf attire is required:
collared shirt, no work-type jeans. No metal
spikes are allowed on the course.

Tournaments: Tournaments welcome. Call for
details.

Directions: Take I-5 north out of Los Angeles
to the Valencia Boulevard exit and go left over
the freeway past the Old Road to Heritage
View Lane. Turn left to the club.

Contact: 26550 Heritage View Lane, Valencia,
CA 91380, pro shop 661/288-7925, fax 661/288-
1912, www.tpc.com.

2 THE GREENS AT VALENCIA

Architect: Ted Robinson Sr., 1999
27 holes   Public $10–14

🍽️ 🛏️

Northwest Detail map, page 295

This is a unique 27-hole putting course designed
by Ted Robinson. The course describes itself
as "golf in miniature," as opposed to miniature
golf. Only 18 holes are used at one time. The
course features lots of water and sand. The signature hole features a waterfall and an island
green. The course is lighted and open until
9 P.M. Sunday–Thursday, until 11 P.M. Friday
and Saturday. Fun for families.

Play Policy and Fees: Green fees are $10 Mon-
day–Thursday and $14 Friday–Sunday. Dis-
count memberships are available.

Tees and Yardage: Not available.

Tee Times: Reservations can be made but are
not necessary.

Dress Code: Appropriate attire and soft spikes
are required.

Tournaments: Call the pro shop for information on tournaments. A banquet facility is available that can accommodate up to 350 people.

Directions: From Los Angeles, take I-405 north
to I-5 north. Exit at Valencia Boulevard and
turn right (east). Make a left on McBean Parkway. The course is right across from the Valencia Town Center.

Contact: 26501 McBean Parkway, Valencia,
CA 91355, pro shop 661/222-2900, fax 661/222-
2904, www.thegreens.com.

3 FRIENDLY VALLEY GOLF COURSE

9 holes   **Private**

Northwest Detail map, page 295

This is a good opportunity for members to practice up on their short game. It features eight par-3s and is walkable. Friendly Valley also has a pitch-and-putt course.

Play Policy and Fees: Members and guests only. This is a private retirement village.

Tees and Yardage: Not available.

Tee Times: Not applicable.

Dress Code: Appropriate golf attire is required.

Tournaments: This course is not available for outside events.

Directions: Take Highway 126 off I-5 and follow it to San Fernando Road. From there travel 1.5 miles to Avenue of the Oaks. Turn left and look for the course.

Contact: 19345 Avenue of the Oaks, Newhall, CA 91321, pro shop 661/252-9859.

4 VALENCIA COUNTRY CLUB

Architect: Robert Trent Jones Sr., 1965

18 holes   **Private**

Northwest Detail map, page 295

This Robert Trent Jones Sr. design offers a scenic, natural layout with lots of trees. Water comes into play on eight holes. It's always a love/hate relationship with Jones, so take your pick on the third. There is no bailout on this 180-yard par-3 from the back tees. Watch out for water and bunkers on the right and trees on the left. It's considered one of the toughest par-3 holes in Southern California. From the championship tees, the course record is 63, held by Bob Burns. From the tournament tees, the course record is 67, held by Jeff Flesher.

Play Policy and Fees: Members and guests only. Limited reciprocal play. While playing, guests must be accompanied by a member.

Tees and Yardage: *Men:* Gold: yardage 7076, par 72, rating 74.7, slope 138; Blue: yardage

6723, par 72, rating 73.0, slope 134; White: yardage 6305, par 72, rating 71.1, slope 129; *Women:* Red: yardage 5702, par 74, rating 74.1, slope 133.

Tee Times: Not applicable.

Dress Code: Appropriate golf attire and non-metal spikes are required.

Tournaments: Outside events are scheduled on Monday only. Carts are required. A 72-player minimum is needed to book a shotgun tournament.

Directions: From San Fernando, travel north on I-5 for 12 miles to Magic Mountain Parkway and turn east on Tourney Road to the club.

Contact: 27330 North Tourney Road, Valencia, CA 91355, pro shop 661/287-1880, fax 661/254-5863, www.heritagegolfgroup.com.

5 VISTA VALENCIA GOLF COURSE

Architect: Terry Van Gorder, 1963

18 holes   **Public**   **$23–42**

Northwest Detail map, page 295

This is a short course that requires good iron play. Five lakes, 88 bunkers, and one island green are found on the layout. The course is always in good condition. There is also a par-3 course at the facility, along with a Nike Golf Learning Center.

Play Policy and Fees: Green fees are $23 to walk and $35 to ride Monday–Thursday, $25 to walk and $37 to ride Friday, and $30 to walk and $42 to ride weekends. Twilight, super twilight, and senior (with card) discounts are available.

Tees and Yardage: *Men:* Blue: yardage 4366, par 61, rating 61.4, slope 104; White: yardage 4064, par 61, rating 60.5, slope 102; *Women:* Silver: yardage 3758, par 64, rating 62.1, slope 103.

Tee Times: Reservations can be booked seven days in advance.

Dress Code: Shirts must be worn; no tank tops are allowed.

Tournaments: A 12-player minimum is needed to book a tournament. Carts are required.

Directions: In Valencia traveling north on I-5,

exit at Lyons Avenue. Drive east for one-half mile to Wiley Canyon Road. Turn left and then left again at Tournament Road. Drive one-half mile to Trevino Road and turn left again; then drive one-half mile to the club.

Contact: 24700 West Trevino Drive, Valencia, CA 91355, pro shop 661/253-1870, fax 661/253-2164.

6 ROBINSON RANCH
Architect: Ted Robinson Sr. and Ted Robinson Jr., 2000
36 holes   Public $87–132

Northwest Detail map, page 295

 There are two lovely courses here, the Mountain Course and the Valley Course, just north of Los Angeles. They are very scenic and well maintained, and play—as the names suggest—quite differently from one another. The Mountain Course, while shorter, has many more elevation changes. The Valley Course is a classic example of how to use water, sand, and mounding to create a challenging layout on a relatively flat lie. The six finishing holes are very challenging and have thus been named "Death Row."

Play Policy and Fees: If starting times are booked within eight days of play, then green fees are $87 Monday–Thursday and $117 Friday, weekends, and holidays. If starting times are booked 9–60 days in advance, premium rates are $102 Monday–Thursday and $132 Friday, weekends, and holidays. Carts are included in all fees. Twilight and junior rates are also available. Ranch Club memberships are offered.

Tees and Yardage: Mountain—*Men:* Black: yardage 6508, par 71, rating 72.3, slope 137; Blue: yardage 6172, par 71, rating 70.7, slope 134; White: yardage 5773, par 71, rating 68.8, slope 129; *Women:* Gold: yardage 5076, par 71, rating 69.5, slope 121; Valley—*Men:* Black: yardage 6903, par 72, rating 74.4, slope 149; Blue: yardage 6469, par 72, rating 72.4, slope 141; White: yardage 6024, par 72, rating 70.0, slope 135; *Women:* Gold: yardage 5417, par 72, rating 72.2, slope 126.

Tee Times: Reservations may be booked up to 60 days in advance.

Dress Code: Soft spikes, collared shirts, and appropriate golf attire are required. No denim is allowed.

Tournaments: Events are welcome, with a minimum of 20 players. Reservations may be booked up to one year in advance.

Directions: From I-5, take Highway 14 north to the Sand Canyon Road exit. Turn right and proceed approximately three-quarters of a mile to Robinson Ranch on the left.

Contact: 27734 Sand Canyon Road, Santa Clarita, CA 91351, pro shop 661/252-7666, fax 661/252-8666, www.robinsonranchgolf.com.

7 ELKINS RANCH GOLF COURSE
Architect: William Tucker Jr., 1962
18 holes   Public $24–30

Northwest Detail map, page 295

This course is set in a canyon in the country. There are lots of water holes and few parallel fairways. It's a very challenging course with five lakes, elevated tees, and demanding greens. Fun for all levels of play, it's quiet and scenic. It's a great getaway course that sees quite a few rounds a year. The forward tees were lengthened in 2004.

Play Policy and Fees: Green fees are $24 weekdays and $30 weekends. Twilight, junior, and senior (weekdays only) rates are available. Carts are $24.

Tees and Yardage: *Men:* Blue: yardage 6302, par 71, rating 69.9, slope 117; White: yardage 6011, par 71, rating 68.3, slope 112; *Women:* Red: yardage 5700, par 73, rating 72.7, slope 123.

Tee Times: Reservations are recommended and should be made 10 days in advance.

Dress Code: Golfers must wear collared shirts. Bermuda shorts are allowed, but no cutoffs.

Tournaments: Shotgun tournaments are available weekdays only. Carts are required. A 28-player minimum is required to book a regular tournament. The outside banquet facility can accommodate 200 people. Events should be booked 12 months in advance.

Directions: Take I-5 north to Highway 126 and turn west. Drive 19 miles to Fillmore. At Highway 23, the third stoplight, turn left. The course is 1.5 miles along on the left.

Contact: 1386 Chambersburg Road, Fillmore, CA 93016 (P.O. Box 695, Fillmore, CA 93015), pro shop 805/524-1440, fax 805/524-1296, www.elkinsranchgc.com.

8 MOORPARK COUNTRY CLUB

Architect: Jacobsen/Hardy Golf Design, 2002

27 holes   Public $75–95

Northwest Detail map, page 295

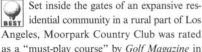 Set inside the gates of an expansive residential community in a rural part of Los Angeles, Moorpark Country Club was rated as a "must-play course" by *Golf Magazine* in 2004. Its 27 holes meander through canyons and arroyos, along creeks and ridgelines. Many of the challenges and shot values are created by this varied terrain. The course features some nice views of the surrounding valleys, and the Pacific Ocean and the Channel Islands can be seen in the distance on very clear days. The par-5 fifth hole of the Ridgeline nine is one of the longest golf holes in the United States. Named "Long Canyon," it measures 676 yards from the tips, though it is possible to get home in two with a little help from the wind. The par-4 13th hole of Creekside, named "La Bruha Verde," forces you to carry a canyon wall and then traverse another arroyo to reach an elevated green. Play conservatively and you might make par; go for birdie and you could add a few more strokes to your score.

Play Policy and Fees: Green fees are $75 Monday–Thursday, $85 Friday, and $95 weekends and holidays, cart included. Twilight and accompanied junior rates also available.

Tees and Yardage: Ridgeline/Creekside Course— *Men:* Black: yardage 7010, par 72, rating 73.8, slope 142; Blue: yardage 6535, par 72, rating 71.5, slope 137; White: yardage 6011, par 72,

rating 69.2, slope 128; *Women:* Red: yardage 5419, par 72, rating 72.1, slope 128; Gold: yardage 4717, par 72, rating 68.3, slope 116. Canyon Crest Course—*Men:* Black: yardage 3512, par 36, rating n/a, slope n/a; Blue: yardage 3266, par 36, rating n/a, slope n/a; White: yardage 3031, par 36, rating n/a, slope n/a; *Women:* Red: yardage 2591, par 36, rating n/a, slope n/a; Gold: yardage 2499, par 36, rating n/a, slope n/a.

Tee Times: Reservations can be made seven days in advance.

Dress Code: Appropriate golf attire is required. No denim is allowed. Soft spikes only.

Tournaments: This course is available for outside tournaments.

Directions: North from Los Angeles, take either U.S. 101 to Highway 23 North or Highway 118 West to Highway 23 South. Exit at New Los Angeles Avenue (Highway 118) and travel roughly four miles west to Grimes Canyon Road and turn right (north) onto Grimes Canyon Road. Travel 2.5 miles to Country Club Estates. Turn right onto Championship Drive.

Contact: 11800 Championship Drive, Moorpark, CA 93021, phone 805/532-2834, fax 805/532-2866, www.moorparkcountryclub.com.

9 RUSTIC CANYON GOLF CLUB

Architect: Gil Hanse, 2002

18 holes   Public $35–50

Northwest Detail map, page 295

Highly rated by several national magazines as a quality, affordable course when it opened in 2002, this is a flat, links-style layout in a valley. The design features big, undulating greens that players can roll the ball onto. The fact that they are big also means you'll get some long, curving putts. Chipping and putting aprons surround every hole, making it friendly for beginning or occasional golfers. Not too much trouble off the tee, and there are no trees or water, but lots of bunkers keep you honest. Due to the affordable prices, this is a very popular course. Make reservations early.

Play Policy and Fees: Green fees are $35 Monday–Thursday, $40 Friday, and $50 weekends and holidays. Carts cost an additional $12. Twilight rates available.

Tees and Yardage: *Men:* Player: yardage 6906, par 72, rating 73.1, slope 130; Back: yardage 6585, par 72, rating 71.3, slope 125; Middle: yardage 6011, par 72, rating 68.3, slope 120; *Women:* Forward: yardage 5273, par 72, rating 69.4, slope 113.

Tee Times: Reservations can be made seven days in advance.

Dress Code: Collared shirts required. No denim is allowed. Soft spikes only.

Tournaments: Limited tournaments welcome.

Directions: From Los Angeles, take Highway 118 west, take the Princeton Avenue exit, and proceed north to Campus Park Drive. Turn left to the club entrance.

Contact: 15100 Happy Camp Canyon Road, Moorpark, CA 93021, phone 805/530-0221, fax 805/530-0289.

10 TIERRA REJADA GOLF CLUB

Architect: Robert Cupp, 1999
18 holes **Public** **$70–90**

Northwest Detail map, page 295

This course has a little of everything: rolling hills, multiple tees, elevation change, lakes, and fairway bunkers. You'll need a strong bump-and-run game on some holes and a strong aerial game on others. Many a match will be settled on the finishing hole, which features a tight tee shot to a blind fairway, and a lake in front of the green.

Play Policy and Fees: Green fees are $70 Monday–Thursday, $80 Friday, and $90 on the weekends. Carts are mandatory and are included in all prices. Midday, twilight, and senior rates are available.

Tees and Yardage: *Men:* Black: yardage 7015, par 72, rating 73.3, slope 132; Blue: yardage 6557, par 72, rating 71.0, slope 126; White: yardage 6005, par 72, rating 68.5, slope 121; *Women:* Gold: yardage 5148, par 72, rating 69.4, slope 123.

Tee Times: Reservations may be made up to a week in advance.

Dress Code: Collared shirts and soft spikes are required. No denim is permitted.

Tournaments: Tournaments are welcome and may be booked up to one year in advance.

Directions: From U.S. 101, take Highway 23 north. Exit on Tierra Rejada Road and make a right. In half a block, you'll see the course on your left.

Contact: 15187 Tierra Rejada Road, Moorpark, CA 91320, pro shop 805/531-9300, fax 805/531-9303, www.tierrarejada.com.

11 LOST CANYONS GOLF CLUB

Architect: Pete Dye with Fred Couples, 2000
36 holes **Public** **$95–120**

Northwest Detail map, page 295

Lost Canyons is one of the best new golf facilities in the state. The upscale club boasts two courses, the Sky Course and the Shadow Course, both set in the foothills of the Santa Susana Mountains. Rolling hills and yawning canyons require a confident player to traverse the carries and handle the typical Pete Dye trouble. Some deep bunkers and sharp falloffs protect the greens.

Play Policy and Fees: Including cart, green fees are $95 Monday–Thursday and $120 Friday–Sunday. Twilight, senior, junior, and resident rates are available.

Tees and Yardage: Sky Course—*Men:* Black: yardage 7250, par 72, rating 76.1, slope 149; Gold: yardage 6770, par 72, rating 73.6, slope 143; Silver: yardage 6205, par 72, rating 70.3, slope 135; White: yardage 5605, par 72, rating 72.9, slope 127; *Women:* Copper: yardage 4885, par 72, rating 70.0, slope 120. Shadow Course—*Men:* Black: yardage 7005, par 72, rating 75.0, slope 149; Gold: yardage 6530, par 72, rating 72.4, slope 144; Silver: yardage 6055, par 72, rating 70.5, slope 136; White: yardage 5420, par 72, rating 67.1, slope 127; *Women:* Copper: yardage 4795, par 72, rating 69.1, slope 125.

Tee Times: Reservations may be made up to

30 days in advance. For an additional $10 charge, premium tee times may be reserved up to 60 days in advance.

Dress Code: Collared shirts, Bermuda shorts or golf pants, and nonmetal spikes are required. Denim, beachwear, and tee shirts are not permitted.

Tournaments: Tournaments are available for groups of 36–288 players. Reservations may be booked up to one year in advance.

Directions: This course is 35 minutes northwest of downtown Los Angeles. Take Highway 118 and exit at Tapo Canyon Road. Drive two miles north to Lost Canyons Drive, then travel one mile west to the clubhouse.

Contact: 3301 Lost Canyons Drive, Simi Valley, CA 93063, pro shop 805/522-4653, fax 805/955-9726, www.lostcanyons.com.

12 SIMI HILLS GOLF COURSE

Architect: Ted Robinson Sr., 1981

18 holes   **Public**   **$28–53**

🏌 📷 🍴 🎣 🚗 🍺

Northwest Detail map, page 295

The course makes use of the natural terrain and is set on what was once a Chumash Indian reservation. Many of the ancient trees were kept in place to enhance the beauty and increase the difficulty of the course, parts of which wind through hills and valleys. Three lakes add to the beauty.

Play Policy and Fees: Green fees are $28 to walk weekdays, $41 to ride, and $39 to walk weekends, $53 to ride.

Tees and Yardage: *Men:* Blue: yardage 6509, par 71, rating 70.6, slope 125; White: yardage 6133, par 71, rating 69.1, slope 121; *Women:* Red: yardage 5505, par 71, rating 71.1, slope 120.

Tee Times: Reservations can be booked seven days in advance on weekdays and five days in advance on weekends. Residents can call at 7 A.M., nonresidents at 9 A.M.

Dress Code: Collared shirts must be worn on the course.

Tournaments: Shotgun tournaments are available weekdays only. Carts are required. A 16-player minimum is required to book a regular tournament. Tournaments can be booked 11 months in advance.

Directions: From I-5 north of Los Angeles, travel west on Highway 118 for about 15 miles to the Stearns Street exit and turn right. Drive to Alamo Street and turn left to the course.

Contact: 5031 Alamo Street, Simi Valley, CA 93063, pro shop 805/522-0803, fax 805/520-9379.

13 PORTER VALLEY COUNTRY CLUB

Architect: Ted Robinson Sr., 1968

18 holes   **Private**   **$55–75**

🏌 📷 🍴 🛏 🚗 🍺

Northwest Detail map, page 295

This is a short course with tight fairways and well-bunkered greens. There are a few water hazards. The course sits up in the hills, offering golfers a beautiful view of the entire San Fernando Valley. But the course itself is especially hilly. It is a fun little challenge that can be more difficult than it looks.

Play Policy and Fees: Limited reciprocal play accepted. Guest fees are $55 Tuesday–Thursday and $75 on Friday and weekends.

Tees and Yardage: *Men:* Blue: yardage 6090, par 70, rating 70.6, slope 129; White: yardage 5769, par 70, rating 69.2, slope 126; *Women:* Red: yardage 5476, par 70, rating 73.6, slope 129.

Tee Times: Reservations may be booked seven days in advance.

Dress Code: No denim is allowed, and shirts must have collars. Nonmetal spikes are required.

Tournaments: This course is available for outside tournaments on Monday only. The banquet facility can accommodate 300 people.

Directions: Take I-5 or I-405 to Highway 118 and travel west to Northridge. Exit at Tampa Road and drive north to the first light. Make a right turn on Rinaldi Drive, and take a left onto Porter Valley Drive to the club.

Contact: 19216 Singing Hills Drive, Northridge, CA 91326, pro shop 818/368-2919, clubhouse 818/360-1071, www.portervalley.com.

14 KNOLLWOOD COUNTRY CLUB

Architect: William F. Bell, 1956
18 holes   Public $21.50–40

Northwest Detail map, page 295

There are no parallel holes on this course. Instead, they run single file through a string of homes. Many approach shots are uphill, making it tough to judge distance. This course was originally built and owned by Bob Hope and Dean Martin. Dave Berganio holds the men's course record of 64. Donna Caponi holds the women's record of 70.

Play Policy and Fees: Green fees are $21.50 to walk weekdays, $33.50 to ride. Weekend fees are $28 to walk, $40 to ride.

Tees and Yardage: *Men:* Blue: yardage 6376, par 72, rating 70.8, slope 124; White: yardage 6054, par 72, rating 68.9, slope 119; *Women:* Silver: yardage 5714, par 72, rating 73.1, slope 126.

Tee Times: Reservations can be booked seven days in advance.

Dress Code: No tank tops are allowed.

Tournaments: Shotgun tournaments are available weekdays only. Carts are required. A 24-player minimum is required to book a tournament. Events should be scheduled 12 months in advance. The banquet facility holds 500 people.

Directions: From Los Angeles, take I-5 north to Highway 118. Go west and exit at Balboa Boulevard and go north three-quarters of a mile to the course.

Contact: 12040 Balboa Boulevard, Granada Hills, CA 91344, pro shop 818/363-8161, fax 818/368-0136.

15 THE CASCADES GOLF CLUB

Architect: Steve Timm, Robert Cupp, 1999
18 holes   Public $60–85

Northwest Detail map, page 295

The Cascades course has a traditional layout with lots of elevation changes. The bent-grass greens allow players with a good touch to make putts. However, for golfers who choose not to use the fairways, getting to the putting surface and scoring well is a challenge. Waterways and ravines come into play on several holes, but the shots required are not overly tough. It is a nicely maintained layout in a scenic setting.

Play Policy and Fees: Green fees are $60 weekdays and $85 weekends, cart included. Twilight, super twilight, early bird, senior, and other special rates are available.

Tees and Yardage: *Men:* Black: yardage 6610, par 71, rating 72.6, slope 139; Blue: yardage 6132, par 71, rating 70.7, slope 134; White: yardage 5593, par 71, rating 68.1, slope 127; *Women:* Red: yardage 5080, par 71, rating 64.4, slope 124.

Tee Times: Reservations can be booked one week in advance free of charge, or one week to one month in advance for a fee of $10 per player.

Dress Code: Collared shirts and nonmetal spikes are required.

Tournaments: This course is available for tournaments.

Directions: From West Los Angeles, take I-405 north until it turns into I-5. Take I-5 to I-210. Take I-210 east and get off at the Yarnell exit. Go right on Foothill for one mile and take another right on Balboa. Follow Balboa to Silver Oaks Drive. Turn right to the course.

Contact: 16325 Silver Oak Drive, Sylmar, CA 91342, pro shop 818/833-8900, www.cascades golf.com.

16 EL CARISO GOLF COURSE

Architect: Robert Muir Graves, 1977
18 holes   Public $18–23

Northwest Detail map, page 295

A well-placed tee shot is important on this executive course. Five lakes come into play, and each green is well bunkered. The fifth hole is a tough 389-yard par-4 that doglegs left and has water to the right. El Cariso is usually very well maintained. It is one of the tougher executive courses around. The course record is

54, held by PGA Tour professional David Berganio, who grew up playing at El Cariso.

Play Policy and Fees: Green fees are $18 weekdays and $23 weekends. Call ahead for special twilight and senior rates. Carts are $17 per person.

Tees and Yardage: *Men:* Blue: yardage 4493, par 62, rating 61.1, slope 97; White: yardage 4085, par 62, rating 59.7, slope 92; *Women:* Red: yardage 3540, par 62, rating 59.3, slope 89.

Tee Times: Reservations can be booked seven days in advance.

Dress Code: Shirts and shoes are required.

Tournaments: A 24-player minimum is required to book a tournament. Events should be booked nine months in advance. The banquet facility can hold up to 150 people.

Directions: Take I-210 to Hubbard and exit right. Go east for one mile. At Eldridge Avenue, turn right and go one block to the course. The course is on the left.

Contact: 13100 Eldridge Avenue, Sylmar, CA 91342, pro shop 818/367-6157, clubhouse 818/367-2140, fax 818/362-8651.

17 WOOD RANCH GOLF CLUB

Architect: Ted Robinson Sr., 1985
18 holes   Private $90–103

Northwest Detail map, page 295

Wood Ranch is considered one of the toughest courses in the Los Angeles area. This is an excellent target golf course, with water hazards on 11 holes, lots of deep pot bunkers, few trees, and deep rough. It is long and demanding, with a links-style flavor. The pride of this course is the 410-yard, par-4 16th hole. It drops 120 feet from the tee and requires a testy second shot to a severe, two-tiered green.

Play Policy and Fees: Reciprocal play is accepted at a rate of $90 walking, $103 riding.

Tees and Yardage: *Men:* Gold: yardage 6972, par 72, rating 75.2, slope 146; Blue: yardage 6552, par 72, rating 73.1, slope 140; White: yardage 6126, par 72, rating 71.5, slope 133; *Women:* Silver: yardage 5392, par 72, rating 72.6, slope 139.

Tee Times: Reservations are recommended. Reciprocators should have their club pro call to make arrangements.

Dress Code: Collared shirts and slacks or Bermuda-style shorts are required. No denim whatsoever is allowed on the course. Soft spikes only.

Tournaments: This course is available for outside tournaments on Monday only.

Directions: From Los Angeles, travel north on U.S. 101 to Highway 23. Head north to the Olsen Road exit and turn right. At Wood Ranch Parkway, turn right and drive to the club.

Contact: 301 Wood Ranch Parkway, Simi Valley, CA 93065, pro shop 805/522-7262, fax 805/526-6679.

18 SUNSET HILLS COUNTRY CLUB

Architect: Ted Robinson Sr., 1974
18 holes   Private $52–74

Northwest Detail map, page 295

This well-maintained course offers narrow fairways, fast greens, and blind tee shots. All the holes are fun but challenging. It is not a long course, but it has a lot of character. There is some elevation change, and the greens have been compared in quality to those at Sherwood Country Club.

Play Policy and Fees: Reciprocal play is accepted with members of other private clubs, at a rate of $52 weekdays and $74 weekends, including cart.

Tees and Yardage: *Men:* Black: yardage 6066, par 71, rating 69.3, slope 121; White: yardage 5804, par 71, rating 68.0, slope 118; *Women:* Red: yardage 5543, par 71, rating 73.2, slope 125.

Tee Times: Reciprocators should have their home professional call to make the arrangements.

Dress Code: Golfers must wear collared shirts. No jeans are allowed. Shorts must have a six-inch inseam. Nonmetal spikes are encouraged.

Tournaments: This course is available for outside tournaments on Monday only. The banquet facility can accommodate 250 people.

Directions: From U.S. 101 (Ventura Freeway), take the Fillmore exit (Highway 23) and drive north for 4.5 miles to Olsen Road. Turn left and drive one-half mile to Erbes Road. Turn left to the club.

Contact: 4155 Erbes Road North, Thousand Oaks, CA 91360, pro shop 805/495-5407, clubhouse 805/495-6484, fax 805/523-7574.

19 SINALOA GOLF COURSE

Architect: Opened, 1994

9 holes   **Public**   **$9-17.50**

Northwest Detail map, page 295

This is a fun par-3 course. The fifth hole is patterned after the 12th hole at Augusta National. The eighth hole is patterned after the 10th hole at Winged Foot West. Sharpen your short game or bring the family.

Play Policy and Fees: Green fees are $9 for nine holes and $14 for 18 holes weekdays, $11 for nine holes and $17.50 for 18 holes weekends. Call for special rates.

Tees and Yardage: *Men and Women:* yardage 1088, par 27, rating n/a, slope n/a.

Tee Times: Reservations can be booked seven days in advance.

Dress Code: Appropriate attire and soft spikes are required.

Tournaments: Shotgun tournaments are available weekdays only. A 12-player minimum is needed to book an event.

Directions: From Simi Valley, drive west on Highway 118 to the Madera Road exit. Go south and follow the road for about two miles to the course.

Contact: 980 Madera Road, Simi Valley, CA 93065, pro shop 805/581-2662, fax 805/581-4549.

20 MISSION HILLS LITTLE LEAGUE GOLF COURSE

9 holes   **Public**   **$5-6**

Northwest Detail map, page 295

This short, flat course is good for beginners.

A few trees dot the course, but there are no traps. All nine holes are par-3s.

Play Policy and Fees: Green fees are $5 weekdays and $6 weekends. Replays are $2.50 Monday–Friday, $4 weekends. Inquire about senior and junior discounts.

Tees and Yardage: *Men and Women:* yardage 1150, par 27, rating n/a, slope n/a.

Tee Times: Reservations are not accepted. All play is on a first-come, first-served basis.

Dress Code: Appropriate attire and soft spikes are required.

Tournaments: This course is available for outside tournaments.

Directions: Off I-405, take the Nordoff exit west. Turn right on Woodley and you'll see the course near the Veterans Administration Hospital.

Contact: P.O. Box 2642, Mission Hills, CA 91343, pro shop 818/892-3019.

21 VAN NUYS GOLF COURSE

Architect: Joe Novak

27 holes   **Public**   **$9-13**

Northwest Detail map, page 295

There are 27 holes here: an 18-hole par-3 course, and a nine-hole executive layout. The executive course is one of the better short courses in the area. It measures around 1600 yards, and the average playing time is under two hours. The 18-hole course is a par-3 layout. It is lined with trees and is relatively flat, with lakes and ducks. The course is good for beginners.

Play Policy and Fees: Green fees for the 18-hole par-3 course are $11 weekdays and $13 weekends. Nine-hole rates are available. Green fees for the nine-hole executive course are $9 weekdays and $11 weekends. Ask about other discounts.

Tees and Yardage: 18-hole course—*Men and Women:* yardage 2100, par 54, rating n/a, slope n/a.

Tee Times: Reservations can be booked seven days in advance for the executive course

Dress Code: Appropriate attire and soft spikes are required.

Tournaments: A 12- to 16-player minimum is needed to book an event. No shotgun tournaments are allowed.

Directions: From I-405 in Van Nuys, take the Victory exit west. Drive about one mile to Odessa Avenue. Turn right onto Odessa and drive to the course.

Contact: 6550 Odessa Avenue, Van Nuys, CA 91406, starting times 818/785-8871, pro shop 818/785-3685.

22 WOODLEY LAKES GOLF COURSE

Architect: Ray Goates, 1965
18 holes   **Public**   **$22–28.50**

Northwest Detail map, page 295

This is a relatively long and flat course with large greens. Many of the greens are elevated. The course is not too demanding unless you hit into one or more of its six lakes. The course record is 62, set by former UCLA and PGA Tour professional Duffy Waldorf.

Play Policy and Fees: Green fees are $22 weekdays and $28.50 weekends. Carts are $24 for two people.

Tees and Yardage: *Men:* Blue: yardage 6803, par 72, rating 71.7, slope 114; White: yardage 6523, par 72, rating 70.3, slope 111; *Women:* Red: yardage 6224, par 72, rating 74.6, slope 120.

Tee Times: Reservations can be made up to seven days in advance with a Los Angeles Recreation and Parks reservation card (818/291-9980). Cards can be obtained at any city golf facility or by writing to City of Los Angeles, Department of Recreation and Parks, 200 North Main Street, Room 1380, City Hall East, Los Angeles, CA 90012-4172.

Dress Code: Nonmetal spikes are encouraged.

Tournaments: A 24-player minimum is needed to book a tournament.

Directions: From I-405 in Van Nuys, exit at Victory Boulevard and drive half a mile to Woodley Avenue. Turn left to the course. The course is about two miles from Van Nuys Airport.

Contact: 6331 Woodley Avenue, Van Nuys, CA 91406, starting times 818/780-6886, pro shop 818/787-8163.

23 HANSEN DAM GOLF COURSE

Architect: Course designed, 1963
18 holes   **Public**   **$23–28**

Northwest Detail map, page 295

This course plays longer than it looks. Big hitters must be careful about staying on the fairways. The greens tend to be small, so chipping skills are important. Some changes have taken place in recent years, including shifting the hole routing some on the back nine. Instead of ending on a par-3, as it originally did, the 18th is now a par-4, using the old 17th green.

Play Policy and Fees: Green fees are $23 weekdays and $28 weekends. Early bird and twilight rates are available. Carts are additional.

Tees and Yardage: *Men:* Blue: yardage 6662, par 72, rating 71.1, slope 118; White: yardage 6361, par 72, rating 68.5, slope 114; *Women:* Red: yardage 6084, par 72, rating 74.0, slope 123.

Tee Times: Reservations can be made up to seven days in advance with a Los Angeles Recreation and Parks reservation card (818/291-9980). Cards can be obtained at any city golf facility or by writing to City of Los Angeles, Department of Parks & Recreation, 200 North Main Street, Room 1380, City Hall East, Los Angeles, CA 90012-4172.

Dress Code: Shirts must be worn. Nonmetal spikes are preferred.

Tournaments: No shotgun tournaments are allowed. A 24-player minimum is needed to book an event.

Directions: From I-5, take Osborne and go east 1.5 miles to Glenoaks Boulevard and turn right. Turn left to Montague and turn left to the course.

Contact: 10400 Glenoaks Boulevard, Pacoima, CA 91331, pro shop 818/896-0050.

24 VERDUGO HILLS GOLF COURSE

Architect: Bill Hairston, 1959
18 holes **Public** **$9–13**

Northwest Detail map, page 295

This hilly, well-kept par-3 course has lots of trees and small greens. There are no bunkers or water hazards to slow you down. It's walkable. The longest hole is 140 yards. This course is considered to be one of the best-conditioned par-3 courses in Southern California. The course and range are lighted in the evening, and both are open until 9:30 P.M. in the fall and winter and 10:30 P.M. in the spring and summer.

Play Policy and Fees: Green fees are $9 for nine holes and $11 for 18 holes on weekdays. Green fees for weekends are $11 for nine holes and $13 for 18 holes. Senior and junior rates available.

Tees and Yardage: *Men and Women:* yardage 1805, par 54, rating n/a, slope n/a.

Tee Times: Reservations can be booked 30 days in advance.

Dress Code: Soft spikes are preferred.

Tournaments: This course is available for outside tournaments.

Directions: From I-210 in Tujunga, take the Lowell Avenue exit. Drive one block and turn left on La Tuna Canyon Road. Veer left to the course, which is at the junction of La Tuna Canyon Road and Tujunga Canyon Road.

Contact: 6433 La Tuna Canyon Road, Tujunga, CA 91042, pro shop 818/352-3161.

25 LA CANADA–FLINTRIDGE COUNTRY CLUB

Architect: Lawrence Hughes, 1962
18 holes **Private**

Northwest Detail map, page 295

This short and narrow course makes up for lack of length with hills and tight fairways. Cart use is mandatory. On the back nine, watch for the par-3 12th. You tee off from an elevated tee to a narrow landing area, but first you must

clear at least 160 yards of brush. The hole then opens up and is reachable in two shots for longer hitters. In 2004, a new stream was created on the 17th hole to help with runoff, although it also added to the fun of the hole.

Play Policy and Fees: Reciprocal play is accepted with members of other private clubs; otherwise, members and guests only.

Tees and Yardage: *Men:* Blue: yardage 5773, par 70, rating 68.5, slope 125; White: yardage 5566, par 70, rating 67.4, slope 122; *Women:* Red: yardage 5230, par 70, rating 70.9, slope 127.

Tee Times: Reciprocators should have their home professional make the arrangements.

Dress Code: Appropriate golf attire is mandatory. Soft spikes only.

Tournaments: A 72-player minimum is needed to book a tournament. All shotgun starts are on Monday only. Carts are required.

Directions: From Pasadena, drive west on I-210 (Foothill Freeway) and take the Angeles Crest Highway exit. Drive north for 1.5 miles to Starlight Crest Drive. Turn right and drive one-quarter mile to Godbey Drive. Turn right to the club.

Contact: 5500 Godbey Drive, La Canada, CA 91011, pro shop 818/790-0155.

26 OAKMONT COUNTRY CLUB

Architect: Max Behr, 1924
18 holes **Private** **$125**

Northwest Detail map, page 295

Set on land that was originally a vineyard, this mature course has tight fairways and well-maintained, tricky greens. Good ball placement is a must because of an abundance of trees. The LPGA Tour and Senior PGA Tour have held tournaments here in the past.

Play Policy and Fees: Reciprocal play is accepted with members of other private clubs at a rate of $125, plus $13 for a cart. Otherwise, members and guests only.

Tees and Yardage: *Men:* Blue: yardage 6736, par 72, rating 72.8, slope 131; White: yardage 6413, par 72, rating 71.2, slope 127; *Women:* Red: yardage 5785, par 72, rating 74.6, slope 134.

Tee Times: Reciprocators should have their home professional make the arrangements.

Dress Code: Appropriate golf attire and non-metal spikes are required.

Tournaments: Outside tournaments are limited to Monday only.

Directions: From the Ventura Freeway, take the Glendale Avenue exit and drive north on Verdugo/Canada Road for 3.5 miles to Country Club Drive. Turn left and drive half a mile to the club.

Contact: 3100 Country Club Drive, Glendale, CA 91208, pro shop 818/542-4292, www.oakmontcc.com.

27 ALTADENA GOLF COURSE

Architect: William P. Bell, 1939
9 holes   Public $13.50–16.50

Northwest Detail map, page 295

This is a flat, wide-open golf course with tree-lined fairways and very challenging greens. The San Gabriel Mountains provide a pleasant backdrop, with Mount Wilson as the focal point.

Play Policy and Fees: Green fees for nine holes are $13.50 weekdays, with a replay at $7. On weekends and holidays, green fees are $16.50, with replays at $9. Carts are additional. Senior, junior, and twilight rates are available.

Tees and Yardage: *Men (18 holes):* Back: yardage 5990, par 72, rating 67.4, slope 108; *Women (18 holes):* Forward: yardage 5418, par 74, rating 66.0, slope 104.

Tee Times: Reservations are not required, but they are strongly recommended.

Dress Code: Shirts and shoes are necessary. Nonmetal spikes are encouraged.

Tournaments: This course is open for tournaments booked at least two weeks in advance.

Directions: Travel on I-210 to the Lake Avenue exit in Pasadena. Drive 2.5 miles to Mendocino. Turn right, and the course is 1.5 miles along on the right.

Contact: 1456 East Mendocino Drive, Altadena, CA 91001, pro shop 626/797-3821, fax 626/797-6071, www.dcgolf.info.

28 NORTH RANCH COUNTRY CLUB

Architect: Ted Robinson Sr., 1975
27 holes   Private

Northwest Detail map, page 295

This private club has 27 holes, which break into three nines. The design is known for its smooth, fast greens and tight fairways. Players who miss the fairway can find themselves in big trouble. The 1988 Men's NCAA Championship was held here. The Southwest Intercollegiate Championships have also been held here.

Play Policy and Fees: Select reciprocal play is accepted with members of other private clubs; otherwise, members and guests only. The course is closed on Monday.

Tees and Yardage: Oak/Lakes—*Men:* Blue: yardage 6936, par 72, rating 74.4, slope 136; White: yardage 6456, par 72, rating 71.9, slope 133; *Women:* Red: yardage 5830, par 72, rating 74.9, slope 132; Yellow: yardage 5355, par 72, rating 71.7, slope 124. Valley/Lakes—*Men:* Blue: yardage 6656, par 71, rating 73.9, slope 136; White: yardage 6361, par 72, rating 71.9, slope 132; *Women:* Red: yardage 5876, par 72, rating 75.2, slope 137; Yellow: yardage 5262, par 72, rating 71.2, slope 126. Valley/Oaks—*Men:* Blue: yardage 6656, par 71, rating 73.3, slope 138; White: yardage 6242, par 72, rating 71.2, slope 131; *Women:* Red: yardage 5696, par 72, rating 74.8, slope 138; Yellow: yardage 5391, par 72, rating 72.7, slope 134.

Tee Times: Reciprocators should have their home professional make the arrangements.

Dress Code: Appropriate golf attire and non-metal spikes are required.

Tournaments: This course is available for outside tournaments on Monday only.

Directions: From Westlake, travel north on U.S. 101 to the Westlake Boulevard exit and drive north for two miles to Valley Spring Drive. Turn right and drive one mile to the club.

Contact: 4761 Valley Spring Drive, Westlake Village, CA 91362, pro shop 818/889-9421, clubhouse 818/889-3531.

29 CAMARILLO SPRINGS GOLF COURSE

Architect: Ted Robinson Sr., 1972
18 holes   **Public**   **$27-52**

Northwest Detail map, page 295

This is a well-maintained, easily walkable course with lots of trees. Water comes into play on 14 holes. The sixth is a knockout. This par-5 aims toward a beautiful mountain range. There are two lakes on the left; one is not visible. Out-of-bounds is on the right and so are two fairway bunkers. Note: Some new tee boxes were added in 2004, which lengthened the course and added some new challenge.

Play Policy and Fees: Green fees are $27 to walk, $36 to ride weekdays and $52 weekends, including mandatory cart. Twilight, senior, and junior rates are available.

Tees and Yardage: *Men:* Blue: yardage 6375, par 72, rating 70.8, slope 128; White: yardage 5931, par 72, rating 68.9, slope 121; *Women:* Red: yardage 5297, par 72, rating 65.6, slope 114.

Tee Times: Reservations can be booked seven days in advance.

Dress Code: Collared shirts are required. Soft spikes are preferred.

Tournaments: A 16-player minimum is need to book a tournament. Carts are mandatory, and events should be scheduled 12 months in advance. The banquet facility can accommodate 120 people.

Directions: In Camarillo, take the Camarillo Springs Road exit off U.S. 101 and drive south to the course.

Contact: 791 Camarillo Springs Road, Camarillo, CA 93012, pro shop 805/484-1075, fax 805/484-3970, www.camarillospringsgolf.com.

30 LOS ROBLES GREENS GOLF COURSE

Architect: Bob Baldock, 1964
18 holes   **Public**   **$29-37**

Northwest Detail map, page 295

This is a moderately hilly course with three lakes and fairways flanked by trees. The course features a nice variety of holes, requiring players to both fade and draw the ball. It is a scenic course with many old oak trees. The course is in excellent condition, considering the large number of rounds played here annually.

Play Policy and Fees: Green fees are $29 weekdays and $37 weekends. Carts are $12.50 per rider. Afternoon and twilight rates are offered. Call for other specials.

Tees and Yardage: *Men:* Black: yardage 6274, par 70, rating 70.1, slope 125; Blue: yardage 5693, par 70, rating 68.7, slope 119; White: yardage 5626, par 70, rating 67.0. slope 117; *Women:* Red: yardage 5206, par 70, rating 70.5, slope 118.

Tee Times: Reservations can be booked seven days in advance.

Dress Code: Soft spikes are preferred.

Tournaments: A 24-player minimum is required to book a tournament. Carts required. Tournaments should be booked 12 months in advance. The banquet facility holds 250 people.

Directions: Travel north on U.S. 101 (Ventura Freeway) to the Moorpark Road exit and turn left under the freeway. Drive one block and turn right to the club.

Contact: 299 South Moorpark Road, Thousand Oaks, CA 91361, pro shop 805/495-6421.

31 SHERWOOD COUNTRY CLUB

Architect: Jack Nicklaus, 1989
18 holes   **Private**

Northwest Detail map, page 295

Sherwood was built on a site used for the original movie *Robin Hood*, a spectacular setting with huge oak trees that have been there for more than 100 years. This is a typical Nicklaus layout, featuring flawless bentgrass greens and fairways, several holes that favor left-to-right players (of which Nicklaus is one), and tiered greens surrounded by severe slopes and mounds certain to penalize those who miss them with approach shots. The course's signature hole is the par-3 15th.

From an elevated tee, the tee shot must carry a series of seven ponds, pools, and waterfalls and hold a wide but shallow green. Sherwood is the site of the annual PGA Tour Target World Challenge.

Play Policy and Fees: Reciprocal play is accepted on a very limited basis; otherwise, members and guests only.

Tees and Yardage: *Men:* Gold: yardage 7025, par 72, rating 74.3, slope 142; Blue: yardage 6594, par 72, rating 72.3, slope 136; White: yardage 6003, par 72, rating 69.7, slope 129; *Women:* Red: yardage 5248, par 72, rating 72.4, slope 133.

Tee Times: Reciprocators should have their home professional make the arrangements.

Dress Code: Appropriate golf attire and nonmetal spikes are required.

Tournaments: This course is available on Monday for charity events.

Directions: Take U.S. 101 to Westlake Boulevard. Drive south two miles to Potrero Road. Turn right and drive three miles to Stafford Road and go left to the club.

Contact: 320 West Stafford Road, Thousand Oaks, CA 91361, pro shop 805/496-3036, fax 805/230-1286, www.sherwoodcc.com.

32 LINDERO COUNTRY CLUB

Architect: Ted Robinson Sr., 1976

9 holes   Semiprivate $11–20

Northwest Detail map, page 295

New management spent some money in 2003 to get this nine-hole course in great shape. They also added some water features and colorful plantings. It is a tight but rolling course with lots of trees and relatively small greens. Don't expect to tear it up. Accuracy is important. The toughest hole is the par-3 third. You hit from a slightly elevated tee to a small green guarded on the right by a huge oak and bunker. To the left is a creek that flows through the course. If your tee shot strays on this course, you're in trouble. The driving range is covered and lighted.

Play Policy and Fees: Green fees are $11 for nine holes and $15 for 18 holes weekdays, $15 for nine holes and $20 for 18 holes weekends.

Tees and Yardage: *Men (18 holes):* Blue: yardage 3334, par 58, rating 58.4, slope 95; White: yardage 3114, par 58, rating 58.1, slope 94; *Women:* Red: yardage 2906, par 58, rating 55.0, slope 87.

Tee Times: Reservations can be booked six days in advance.

Dress Code: Golf attire is encouraged, and collared shirts and nonmetal spikes are required.

Tournaments: This course is available for tournaments.

Directions: Travel north on U.S. 101 (Ventura Freeway) to the Reyes Adobe exit. Turn right and drive to Thousand Oaks Boulevard. Turn left and continue to Lake Lindero Drive. The course will be on your right.

Contact: 5719 Lake Lindero Drive, Agoura Hills, CA 91301, pro shop 818/889-1158, fax 818/889-6935.

33 WESTLAKE VILLAGE GOLF COURSE

Architect: Ted Robinson Sr., 1967

18 holes   Public $23–33

Northwest Detail map, page 295

This course offers well-kept greens, three lakes, and scenic, tree-lined fairways. The trees make this course competitive and tough. Slice or hook, and you'll be forced to execute a recovery shot. There are seven par-3s, nine par-4s, and two par-5s. The par-5s, thank goodness, are straight.

The course is adjacent to the Westlake Inn. Call 818/889-0230 for information and reservations.

Play Policy and Fees: Green fees are $23 weekdays and $33 weekends. Carts are $22. Call for specials and other rates.

Tees and Yardage: *Men:* Blue: yardage 5053, par 67, rating 63.4, slope 104; White: yardage 4641, par 67, rating 61.2, slope 95; *Women:* Red: yardage 4641, par 67, rating 66.0, slope 111.

Tee Times: Reservations may be booked seven days in advance.

Dress Code: Collared shirts and soft spike shoes are required.

Tournaments: Events should be booked at least 10 days in advance. The banquet facility can accommodate 100 people.

Directions: Travel north on U.S. 101 (Ventura Freeway) and take the Lindero Canyon Road exit. Drive south to Agoura Road and turn right. Continue three-quarters of a mile to Lakeview Canyon Road and turn right to the course.

Contact: 4812 Lakeview Canyon Road, Westlake Village, CA 91361, pro shop 818/889-0770, fax 818/889-0406.

34 CALABASAS GOLF & COUNTRY CLUB

Architect: Robert Trent Jones Sr. and Jr., 1968
18 holes   **Private**   **$58–88**

Northwest Detail map, page 295

This challenging layout is in a rapidly developing residential area. It is nicely maintained, with trees, lakes, and rolling terrain. Although the course isn't especially long for men at under 6500 yards, it can be difficult. From the women's tees—more than 5600 yards—length is the biggest factor.

Play Policy and Fees: Reciprocal play is accepted with members of other private clubs at a rate of $58 weekdays, $88 weekends; otherwise, members and guests only. The course is closed on Monday.

Tees and Yardage: *Men:* Blue: yardage 6323, par 72, rating 70.4, slope 125; White: yardage 6082, par 72, rating 69.2, slope 122; *Women:* Red: yardage 5602, par 72, rating 73.3, slope 135.

Tee Times: Prior arrangements are required for reciprocal play. Reservations can be booked seven days in advance by the reciprocator's home professional.

Dress Code: Collared shirts and nonmetal spikes are required. Shorts must be Bermuda-length, and no jeans or tank tops are allowed on the course.

Tournaments: This course is available for outside tournaments on Monday.

Directions: Travel north on U.S. 101 (Ventura Freeway) from Los Angeles to Parkway Calabasas, turn at the first right, and drive to the club.

Contact: 4515 Park Entrada, Calabasas Park, CA 91302, pro shop 818/222-3222, clubhouse 818/222-3200.

35 WOODLAND HILLS COUNTRY CLUB

Architect: William P. Bell, 1924
18 holes   **Private**   **$45–65**

Northwest Detail map, page 295

In a parklike setting, this course features rolling hills and oak trees. The greens are among the most severe in Southern California. It is advisable to leave the ball below the hole or you probably will pay a penalty of three putts.

Play Policy and Fees: Reciprocal play is accepted with members of other private clubs at a rate of $45 weekdays, $65 weekends; otherwise, members and guests only. Carts are additional. The course is closed on Monday.

Tees and Yardage: *Men:* Blue: yardage 6203, par 70, rating 70.7, slope 127; White: yardage 5947, par 70, rating 69.6, slope 125; *Women:* Red: yardage 5698, par 72, rating 74.0, slope 133; Yellow: yardage 5222, par 72, rating 71.7, slope 128.

Tee Times: Reciprocal players should have their home professional call.

Dress Code: Appropriate golf attire is strictly enforced. Nonmetal spikes are required.

Tournaments: Shotgun tournaments are available on Monday. Carts are required. A 72-player minimum is needed to book a tournament. Tournaments should be booked 12 months in advance.

Directions: Travel north on U.S. 101 (Ventura Freeway) in Woodland Hills to the DeSoto Avenue exit. Drive south past Ventura Boulevard three-quarters of a mile and turn right on Dumetz Road. Drive one-quarter mile to the club.

Contact: 21150 Dumetz Road, Woodland Hills, CA 91364, pro shop 818/347-1476.

36 BRAEMAR COUNTRY CLUB

Architect: Ted Robinson Sr., 1963
36 holes   **Private**

Northwest Detail map, page 295

Both courses are short, tight, and hilly. There are mature trees and a few parallel fairways. There is virtually no room for error because of a plethora of out-of-bounds, water hazards, and other assorted obstacles. The Guldahl Course is named in honor of its first head professional, Ralph Guldahl, former Masters champion (1939) and U.S. Open champion (1937 and 1938). Guldahl spent 28 years at Braemar as director of golf and revered teacher until 1987. A statue and some of his golf memorabilia are on display at the club.

Play Policy and Fees: Reciprocal play is accepted with members of other ClubCorp. facilities, at a cart-fee-only rate of $13 per rider. Otherwise, members and guests only.

Tees and Yardage: East Course—*Men:* Blue: yardage 6061, par 70, rating 69.8, slope 131; White: yardage 5772, par 70, rating 68.4, slope 128; *Women:* Red: yardage 5360, par 70, rating 72.3, slope 132. Guldahl Course—*Men:* Blue: yardage 5839, par 71, rating 68.7, slope 126; White: yardage 5530, par 71, rating 67.4, slope 122; *Women:* Red: yardage 5227, par 71, rating 71.0, slope 127.

Tee Times: Not applicable.

Dress Code: No jeans or short shorts are allowed on the course. Men must wear collared shirts.

Tournaments: This course is available for outside tournaments on Monday.

Directions: Travel north on U.S. 101 (Ventura Freeway) and take the Reseda Boulevard exit. Drive south for 2.5 miles to the club entrance on the right.

Contact: 4001 Reseda Boulevard (P.O. Box 570217), Tarzana, CA 91357, pro shop 818/345-6520, www.braemarclub.com.

37 EL CABALLERO COUNTRY CLUB

Architect: William H. Johnson, 1957; remodel Robert Trent Jones Sr., 1964
18 holes   **Private**

Northwest Detail map, page 295

This rolling course is a caddie club, where members most often walk. It is long and challenging, with large, receptive greens. Most fairways are flanked by trees. The course was remodeled by Robert Trent Jones Sr. in 1964.

Play Policy and Fees: Reciprocal play is accepted with members of other private clubs; otherwise, members and guests only. Reciprocal fees are worked out between the head professionals of each club. The course is closed on Monday.

Tees and Yardage: *Men:* Blue: yardage 6830, par 71, rating 73.1, slope 135; White: yardage 6418, par 71, rating 71.3, slope 131; *Women:* Red: yardage 5903, par 72, rating 75.4, slope 139.

Tee Times: Reciprocators should have their home professional call to make arrangements.

Dress Code: Collared shirts and nonmetal spikes are required.

Tournaments: This course is available for charity tournaments on Monday only. Carts are required.

Directions: Traveling north on U.S. 101 (Ventura Freeway) in Tarzana, exit on Reseda Boulevard south (it becomes Mecca Avenue). At Tarzana Drive, turn left to the club.

Contact: 18300 Tarzana Drive, Tarzana, CA 91356, pro shop 818/345-2770, fax 818/345-3486.

38 SEPULVEDA GOLF COURSE

Architect: William P. Bell, 1953
36 holes   **Public**   **$22–28.50**

Northwest Detail map, page 295

The Balboa Course is the shorter of Sepulveda's two layouts, with small greens and tight fairways. Shot placement is crucial. The greens are heavily bunkered, and there are overhanging trees. The Encino Course, although longer, is much easier for men because it's wide open. For women, on the other hand, the course is very long at 6192 yards, par 75, with a rating of 74.3. They are both popular, heavily played municipal courses.

Play Policy and Fees: Green fees are $22 weekdays and $28.50 weekends. Carts are $24. Twilight, super twilight, senior, junior, and nine-hole rates are offered.

Tees and Yardage: Balboa Course—*Men:* Blue: yardage 6359, par 70, rating 69.3, slope 111; White: yardage 6125, par 70, rating 68.2, slope 109; *Women:* Red: yardage 5912, par 72, rating 73.5, slope 120. Encino Course—*Men:* Blue: yardage 6764, par 72, rating 70.8, slope 112; White: yardage 6458, par 72, rating 69.3, slope 109; *Women:* Red: yardage 6192, par 75, rating 74.3, slope 118.

Tee Times: Reservations are recommended one week in advance but can only be made by holders of a Los Angeles Recreation and Parks reservation card (818/291-9980). Cards can be obtained at any city golf facility or by writing to City of Los Angeles, Department of Parks & Recreation, 200 North Main Street, Room 1380, City Hall East, Los Angeles, CA 90012-4172.

Dress Code: Appropriate attire and soft spikes are required.

Tournaments: All events must be booked through the Los Angeles reservations office, 213/485-5515.

Directions: Take Highway 134 to the Burbank Boulevard exit in Encino and turn right. Go about one-half mile to the course.

Contact: 16821 Burbank Boulevard, Encino, CA 91436, pro shop 818/986-4560, www.laparks.org.

39 DE BELL GOLF COURSE
Architect: William F. Bell, 1958
18 holes   **Public**   **$20–36**

🚶 🏌 🍴 ⛳ 🚗 🍽

Northwest Detail map, page 295

This is a fairly straight course with a minimum of sand traps and no water hazards. Although

it is a short course, it is demanding, and course management is important. It has been called a thinking person's course.

Play Policy and Fees: Green fees are $20 weekdays to walk, $31 to ride, and $25 weekends to walk, $36 to ride. Burbank residents with a card receive a discount. Call for other rates.

Tees and Yardage: *Men:* Blue: yardage 5631, par 71, rating 68.8, slope 114; White: yardage 5353, par 71, rating 65.7, slope 112; *Women:* Red: yardage 5004, par 71, rating 72.5, slope 123.

Tee Times: Reservations can be booked five days in advance.

Dress Code: Nonmetal spikes are preferred.

Tournaments: A 24-player minimum is needed to book an event. Tournaments can be scheduled up to 10 months in advance. The banquet facility can accommodate up to 150 people.

Directions: From I-5 in Burbank, take the Olive Avenue exit east about 2.5 miles to Walnut Avenue. Turn right on Walnut and follow it to the course.

Contact: 1500 Walnut Avenue, Burbank, CA 91504, pro shop 818/845-5052, fax 818/845-8124.

40 LAKESIDE GOLF CLUB
Architect: Max Behr, 1926
18 holes   **Private**   **$100**

🏌 🍴 ⛳ 🚗 🍽

Northwest Detail map, page 295

Built in 1926, this traditional rolling course has small, undulating greens. Although short in yardage, it plays longer and demands accuracy. These fairways were once a haven for Hollywood's heroes and rogues: Bing Crosby, Dean Martin, Bob Hope—just about anybody who ever had a golf tournament named for him.

Play Policy and Fees: Reciprocal play is accepted with members of some other private clubs at a rate of $100, plus $12 for a cart. Otherwise, members and guests only.

Tees and Yardage: *Men:* Blue: yardage 6534, par 70, rating 72.4, slope 127; White: yardage 6272, par 70, rating 71.1, slope 124; *Women:* Red: yardage 5983, par 74, rating 75.3, slope 134.

Tee Times: Reciprocators should have their home pro call to make the arrangements.

Dress Code: Appropriate golf attire and non-metal spikes are required.

Tournaments: This course is available for outside tournaments on Monday. Carts are required.

Directions: Travel north on U.S. 101 (Hollywood Freeway) to the Barham Boulevard exit and drive north to Lakeside Drive. Turn left and drive to the club. Or take Ventura Boulevard (Highway 134) to Pass Avenue south, crossing Riverside to Lakeside Drive. Turn right to the club.

Contact: 4500 Lakeside Drive, Toluca Lake, CA 91610 (P.O. Box 2386, Burbank, CA 91602), pro shop 818/985-3335.

41 GRIFFITH PARK GOLF COURSE

Architect: (Wilson Course) Tom Bendelow, 1914, renovated George C. Thomas Jr., 1923, William H. Johnson, 1948; (Harding Course) George C. Thomas Jr., 1926, renovated William H. Johnson, 1948

54 holes   **Public**   **$22–28.50**

Northwest Detail map, page 295

Both championship designs at this sprawling park are fairly open driving courses, with lots of mature trees guarding angles in the fairways. You'll have no trouble keeping the ball in play, but to score well, intelligent course management is a must. The old-school greens are in great shape. They generally slope from side to side or back to front. A little water comes into play on both, but mostly they are parklike in nature. The Wilson Course is the more difficult of the two championship courses. They both receive substantially heavy play as they are the best of the Los Angeles area municipal courses. Both have excellent lineage, as George C. Thomas Jr. also designed Riviera Country Club, Bel-Air Country Club, and others, and William H. Johnson, who began his career on the construction crew of Willie Watson, also designed many courses throughout Southern California in the 1950s and '60s. The 1065-yard nine-hole Los Feliz Course (par 27) and the 2478-yard executive course (Roosevelt), par 33, are Johnson's designs.

Play Policy and Fees: Green fees are $22 weekdays and $28.50 weekends for 18 holes on the Wilson and Harding courses. Fees for the executive course are $10 weekdays and $13 weekends. The par-3 course is $4 weekdays and $5 weekends. Twilight rates are also available. Reservations are recommended.

Tees and Yardage: Wilson Course—*Men:* Blue: yardage 6947, par 72, rating 72.9, slope 122; White: yardage 6695, par 72, rating 71.8, slope 119; *Women:* Red: yardage 6483, par 73, rating 76.6, slope 128. Harding Course—*Men:* Blue: yardage 6536, par 72, rating 70.8, slope 123; White: yardage 6317, par 72, rating 69.8, slope 121; *Women:* Red: yardage 6096, par 73, rating 74.3, slope 121.

Tee Times: A Los Angeles Recreation and Parks reservation card (818/291-9980) is required to make reservations. Cards can be obtained at any city golf facility or by writing to City of Los Angeles, Department of Parks & Recreation, 200 North Main Street, Room 1380, City Hall East, Los Angeles, CA 90012-4172. Otherwise, same day play is accepted by showing up and placing your name on the waiting list.

Dress Code: Appropriate attire and soft spikes are required.

Tournaments: All tournaments are weekdays only. A 24-player minimum is needed to book an event.

Directions: Take I-5 north and exit at Griffith Park. Turn right and drive two blocks and turn left. Follow the road for 1.5 miles to the parking lot.

Contact: 4730 Crystal Springs Drive, Los Angeles, CA 90027, pro shop 323/664-2255, www.ci.la.ca.us/RAP/grifmet/gpact.htm.

42 SCHOLL CANYON GOLF & TENNIS CLUB

Architect: George Williams, 1994

18 holes   **Public**   **$17–32**

Northwest Detail map, page 295

This short 18-hole course has exceptional character, bent-grass greens, and tremendous views. On the back nine you are hitting from elevated boxes over canyons. This course was built on a landfill. There are six par-4s and 12 par-3s. The course record is 51.

Play Policy and Fees: Green fees are $17 to walk weekdays, $28 to ride, and $21 to walk weekends, $32 to ride. Twilight rates offered.

Tees and Yardage: *Men:* Back: yardage 3039, par 60, rating n/a, slope n/a; *Women:* Red: yardage 2400, par 60, rating n/a, slope n/a.

Tee Times: Reservations can be booked seven days in advance.

Dress Code: Shirts must be worn.

Tournaments: A 16-player minimum is required to book a tournament.

Directions: From Highway 134 in Glendale, take the Harvey Drive exit and head north to Glenoaks. Turn right onto Glenoaks Boulevard. Drive three miles to the club.

Contact: 1300 East Glenoaks Boulevard, Glendale, CA 91206, pro shop 818/243-4100.

43 CHEVY CHASE COUNTRY CLUB

Architect: William P. Bell, 1927

9 holes   **Private**   **$25–50**

Northwest Detail map, page 295

This course has a long history. It was built in 1927 by the ubiquitous Billy Bell and features a variety of holes that traverse the rolling terrain of this area. The layout is short and extremely tight, with out-of-bounds on virtually every hole. In 2000, under new ownership, significant changes and improvements were made to the course, including building some new tees and bunkers, as well as a new clubhouse to replace the old one that had been destroyed by fire.

Play Policy and Fees: Some reciprocal play is accepted with members of other private clubs, at a rate ranging $25–50. Otherwise, members and guests only.

Tees and Yardage: *Men (18 holes):* Black/Blue: yardage 5200, par 67, rating 66.1, slope 124; *Women (18 holes):* Blue/White: yardage 4843, par 72, rating 69.4, slope 123.

Tee Times: Reciprocators should have their home professional make the arrangements.

Dress Code: Appropriate golf attire and non-metal spikes are required.

Tournaments: Outside events are held on Monday only. A 40-player minimum is needed to book a tournament. Tournaments should be booked six months in advance.

Directions: From Highway 134 in Glendale, take the Harvey exit and travel north for three blocks to Chevy Chase Drive. Turn right and drive two miles to the club.

Contact: 3067 East Chevy Chase Drive, Glendale, CA 91206, pro shop 818/244-8461, clubhouse 818/246-5566, www.chevychasecc.com.

44 BROOKSIDE GOLF COURSE

Architect: William P. Bell, 1928

36 holes   **Public**   **$31–41**

Northwest Detail map, page 295

Water comes into play on quite a few holes on these courses. They play on fairly flat terrain next door to the Rose Bowl in Pasadena. Quite a few mature trees dot both layouts. The first holes were built here in 1928, making it one of the area's oldest golf facilities. The Pasadena City Amateur is played here. These are very popular courses with area residents. The number-one course (C. W. Koiner) is particularly long for women at 6114 yards, and it's deservedly a par 75.

Play Policy and Fees: Green fees are $31 weekdays and $41 weekends. Twilight, local resident, and senior rates are available. Cart fees are $12 per rider.

Tees and Yardage: Course 1 (C. W. Koiner)– *Men:* Gold: yardage 7037, par 72, rating 74.0, slope 133; Blue: yardage 6732, par 72, rating 72.7, slope 129; White: yardage 6372, par 72, rating 70.9, slope 126; *Women:* Silver: yardage 6114, par 75, rating 74.9, slope 128. Course 2 (E. O. Nay)—*Men:* Blue: yardage 6046, par 70, rating 68.9, slope 122; White: yardage 5735, par 70, rating 67.5, slope 118; *Women:* Silver: yardage 5377, par 71, rating 70.7, slope 123.

Tee Times: Reservations can be booked seven days in advance on weekdays. A special reservation system is set up for weekends. Reservations: 818/585-3595 or 800/468-7952.

Dress Code: Bermuda-type shorts are allowed. Soft spikes only.

Tournaments: A 16-player minimum is needed to book a tournament on weekdays, 24 players on weekends. Shotgun tournaments on the weekend are booked on a very limited basis.

Directions: From I-210 in Pasadena, take the Seco/Mountain exit. Travel south on Seco to Rosemont; the course is adjacent to the Rose Bowl.

Contact: 1133 Rosemont Avenue, Pasadena, CA 91103, pro shop 626/796-8151, fax 626/796-0195.

45 ANNANDALE GOLF COURSE
Architect: William P. Bell, 1906; Brian Curley, 1999
18 holes   **Private**   **$70–90**

Northwest Detail map, page 295

This classic, hilly, and narrow course is known for its fast, sloping greens and uneven fairway lies. The memorable 14th and 16th holes are set in a canyon. A lake fronts the 16th green. It is a long and challenging course for women, as the rating of 75.6 indicates. This course has one of the Los Angeles region's best caddie programs.

Play Policy and Fees: Reciprocal play is accepted with members of other private clubs at a weekday rate of $70 and a weekend rate of $90. Otherwise, members and guests only.

Tees and Yardage: *Men:* Back: yardage 6462, par 70, rating 71.9, slope 132; Middle: yardage 6109, par 70, rating 70.2, slope 129; *Women:* Forward: yardage 5732, par 73, rating 75.6, slope 138.

Tee Times: Reciprocators should have their home professional call to make arrangements.

Dress Code: Appropriate golf attire is required, and nonmetal spikes are encouraged.

Tournaments: This course is not available for outside events.

Directions: Take the San Rafael exit off Highway 134 in Pasadena. Turn left to the entrance gate.

Contact: 1 North San Rafael Avenue, Pasadena, CA 91105, pro shop 626/795-8253, clubhouse 626/796-6125.

46 EATON CANYON GOLF COURSE
Architect: William F. Bell, 1959
9 holes   **Public**   **$13.50–16.50**

Northwest Detail map, page 295

The first four holes are flat and the last five are hilly on this tight course. There are lots of trees. The longest hole measures 483 yards.

Play Policy and Fees: Green fees for nine holes are $13.50 weekdays, with a replay at $7. On weekends and holidays, green fees are $16.50, with replays at $9. Carts are additional. Senior, junior, and twilight rates are available.

Tees and Yardage: *Men (18 holes):* Blue: yardage 5724, par 70, rating 67.2, slope 122; White: yardage 5320, par 70, rating 65.5, slope 119; *Women (18 holes):* Red: yardage 5100, par 70, rating 69.3, slope 114.

Tee Times: Reservations can be booked seven days in advance.

Dress Code: Soft spikes are preferred.

Tournaments: A 20-player minimum is needed to book an event. Carts are mandatory for shotgun tournaments.

Directions: Heading east of Pasadena on I-210, take the Madre exit and turn left (north) on Madre Avenue. Then turn right onto North Sierra Madre Villa Avenue.

Contact: 1150 North Sierra Madre Villa Avenue, Pasadena, CA 91107, pro shop 626/794-6773, www.dcgolf.info.

47 SANTA ANITA GOLF COURSE

Architect: William P. Bell, 1938

18 holes   **Public**   **$21.50–28**

Northwest Detail map, page 295

This is a well-maintained course with tight fairways, undulating and smallish greens, and several well-placed bunkers. It is long and challenging. It has rolling terrain and is more of a links-style course without the ocean. The Santa Anita Racetrack is next door, and the San Gabriel Mountains provide a pleasant backdrop. Although it is long for women at 5908, it is a par 74 from the forward tees.

Play Policy and Fees: Green fees are $21.50 weekdays and $28 weekends. Twilight, senior, junior, and nine-hole rates are available. Carts are $12 per rider.

Tees and Yardage: *Men:* Back: yardage 6389, par 70/71, rating 70.1, slope 122; *Women:* Forward: yardage 5908, par 74, rating 73.3, slope 122.

Tee Times: Reservations can be booked seven days in advance.

Dress Code: No tank tops are allowed. Soft spikes are preferred.

Tournaments: No shotgun tournaments are allowed. A 24-player minimum is required to book a tournament.

Directions: Take Santa Anita Avenue off I-210 and drive south to the course.

Contact: 405 South Santa Anita Avenue, Arcadia, CA 91006, pro shop 626/447-7156.

48 MALIBU COUNTRY CLUB

Architect: William F. Bell, 1977

18 holes   **Public**   **$57–82**

Northwest Detail map, page 295

Nestled in the Santa Monica Mountains, this scenic, hilly course features two natural lakes and interesting, sloping topography. The weather stays fair and warm at this course because the hills block the ocean breezes. Bring your best driving game since some holes are a bit tight from the tee, and expect a bunch of hill-

side lies. Still, this course is fun to play and lovely in its canyon setting. Note: There is a small hitting area into a net, but no driving range.

Play Policy and Fees: Green fees are $57 Monday–Thursday and $82 Friday–Sunday. Twilight rates available. Carts are included and mandatory. Players should check in 20 minutes prior to teeing off.

Tees and Yardage: *Men:* Blue: yardage 6631, par 72, rating 72.5, slope 132; White: yardage 6156, par 72, rating 70.0, slope 125; *Women:* Red: yardage 5523, par 72, rating 71.4, slope 120.

Tee Times: Reservations can be booked 10 days in advance.

Dress Code: Men must wear collared shirts. No jeans, sweat suits, or cutoffs are allowed. Shorts must be Bermuda-length.

Tournaments: A 12-player minimum is needed to book an event. Shotgun tournaments are available weekdays only with a minimum of 72 players. The staff can help arrange catering.

Directions: Off U.S. 101 in Malibu, exit on Kanan Road and drive six miles toward the beach. After the second tunnel, turn right on Mulholland Highway. When the road forks, stay left. The course is two miles along on the right, on Encinal Canyon Road. If coming from Pacific Coast Highway, head east on Kanan, left on Mulholland, and left at the Encinal Canyon fork.

Contact: 901 Encinal Canyon Road, Malibu, CA 90265, pro shop 818/889-6680.

49 MOUNTAINGATE COUNTRY CLUB

Architect: Ted Robinson Sr., 1974

27 holes   **Private**   **$125**

Northwest Detail map, page 295

There are three nine-hole layouts here. All are characterized by rolling fairways and difficult, undulating greens. Overall, the South is the most challenging of the three courses. There are elevated greens and rolling hills on most every hole. Wherever you hit, don't expect to get a flat lie. The PGA Champions Tour has held tournaments here in the past, including the Johnny Mathis Classic and the GTE Senior Classic.

Play Policy and Fees: Reciprocal play is accepted with members of other private clubs at a rate of $125, plus $15 cart fee. Otherwise, members and guests only.

Tees and Yardage: Lake/North—*Men:* Gold: yardage 6450, par 72, rating 72.2, slope 133; Blue: yardage 6111, par 72, rating 70.4, slope 129; Players: yardage 5972, par 72, rating 70.0, slope 128; *Women:* White: yardage 5541, par 72, rating 73.9, slope 128. North/South—*Men:* Gold: yardage 6719, par 72, rating 73.2, slope 134; Blue: yardage 6358, par 72, rating 71.6, slope 132; Players: yardage 6268, par 72, rating 71.4, slope 130; *Women:* White: yardage 5667, par 72, rating 74.7, slope 129. South/Lake—*Men:* Gold: yardage 6765, par 72, rating 73.9, slope 137; Blue: yardage 6395, par 72, rating 71.9, slope 133; Players: yardage 6244, par 72, rating 71.6, slope 131; *Women:* White: yardage 5624, par 72, rating 74.4, slope 129.

Tee Times: Reciprocators must have their head pro call to make arrangements at least 24 hours in advance.

Dress Code: Collared shirts and nonmetal spikes are preferred. Bermuda-length shorts are permitted, but no denim is allowed.

Tournaments: This course is available for outside tournaments on Monday only. The banquet facility can hold 200 people.

Directions: Travel north on I-405 to the Getty Center exit. Follow the exit to Sepulveda Boulevard and turn left, driving 1.5 miles to Mountaingate Drive. From there, turn left to the club.

Contact: 12445 Mountaingate Drive, Los Angeles, CA 90049, pro shop 310/476-2800, fax 310/476-8145.

50 STUDIO CITY GOLF COURSE

9 holes   Public $8–9

Northwest Detail map, page 295

This is a nine-hole, par-3 course with no hole longer than 135 yards. The adjoining driving range is open until 11 P.M. For those interested in a quick set of tennis, a tennis club is affiliated with the golf course.

Play Policy and Fees: Green fees are $8 weekdays and $9 weekends and holidays. The senior rate is $7.

Tees and Yardage: *Men and Women:* yardage 975, par 27, rating n/a, slope n/a.

Tee Times: Reservations are not accepted. All play is on a first-come, first-served basis.

Dress Code: Appropriate attire and soft spikes are required.

Tournaments: This course is not available for outside events.

Directions: Take U.S. 101 west to Coldwater Canyon. Turn right and drive to the first light (Moorpark Road). Turn left and drive to Whitsett Avenue. Turn right onto Whitsett and drive two blocks to the course.

Contact: 4141 Whitsett Avenue, Studio City, CA 91604, pro shop 818/761-3250.

51 ROOSEVELT MUNICIPAL GOLF COURSE

Architect: Course designed, 1966

9 holes   Public $11.50–15

Northwest Detail map, page 295

This nine-hole executive course is lined by trees and surrounded by hillside terrain. The longest hole is number two, a 392-yard par-4.

Play Policy and Fees: Green fees are $11.50 weekdays and $15 weekends and holidays. Senior, junior, and twilight rates are available.

Tees and Yardage: *Men:* Back: yardage 2478, par 33, rating n/a, slope n/a; *Women:* Forward: yardage 2274, par 33, rating n/a, slope n/a.

Tee Times: A Los Angeles Recreation and Parks reservation card (818/291-9980) is required to make reservations, up to seven days in advance. Cards can be obtained at any city golf facility or by writing to City of Los Angeles, Department of Parks & Recreation, 200 North Main Street, Room 1380, City Hall East, Los Angeles, CA 90012-4172. Otherwise, same day play is accepted by showing up and placing your name on the waiting list.

Dress Code: A neat appearance is requested.

Tournaments: This course is available for tournaments.

Directions: From I-5, take the Los Feliz Boulevard exit. Travel west on Los Feliz and turn right on Vermont Avenue, then drive to Griffith Park. The golf course is on the right soon after entering the park.

Contact: 2650 North Vermont Avenue, Los Angeles, CA 92007, pro shop 323/665-2011.

52 ARROYO SECO GOLF COURSE

Architect: William B. Johnson, 1955

18 holes　　　　**Public**　　　　**$11–14**

Northwest Detail map, page 295

This flat par-3 course has a small creek near the 15th hole. The holes range in distance from 91 yards (14th) to 143 yards (15th). The course is lighted, which makes for a fun before or after work round. It's also a fun family outing or a course to practice your short game.

Play Policy and Fees: Green fees are $11 for nine holes and $14 for 18 holes. Early bird, twilight, and senior rates are available.

Tees and Yardage: *Men and Women:* yardage 2185, par 54, rating n/a, slope n/a.

Tee Times: Reservations can be booked seven days in advance by calling 213/255-1506.

Dress Code: Nonmetal spikes are required.

Tournaments: This course is available for outside tournaments. Events should be scheduled 2–3 months in advance.

Directions: On Highway 110 (Pasadena Freeway) in South Pasadena, take the Orange Grove Boulevard exit south. Turn right on Mission Street. On Mission Street, stay in the right lane. Go down the hill and around to the right. Turn left at the tennis courts.

Contact: 1055 Lohman Lane, South Pasadena, CA 91030, pro shop 323/257-0475, fax 323/255-1507, www.arroyoseco.com.

53 SAN GABRIEL COUNTRY CLUB

Architect: Norman Macbeth, 1919; renovated Robert Trent Jones Jr., 1972

18 holes　　　　**Private**　　　　**$70**

Northwest Detail map, page 295

This historic course was built in 1919, then renovated in 1972 by Robert Trent Jones Jr. It plays longer than it looks because of the bunkers. Lots of mature trees line the fairways, and the greens are well maintained. Fairways are seeded with kikuyu grass. Among the notable holes is the 437-yard seventh, which features a dogleg right. Both sides of the fairway are out-of-bounds. The 420-yard 10th hole, which features an uphill second shot to a heavily bunkered green, will test the skills of any player.

Play Policy and Fees: Reciprocal play is accepted with members of other private clubs with the approval of the head professional, at a rate of $70, plus cart and caddie. Otherwise, members and accompanied guests only.

Tees and Yardage: *Men:* Gold: yardage 6518, par 71, rating 71.7, slope 129; Silver: yardage 6254, par 71, rating 70.3, slope 124; Blue: yardage 5981, par 71, rating 69.0, slope 120; *Women:* Green: yardage 5615, par 73, rating 73.8, slope 131.

Tee Times: Reciprocators should have their club pro call to make arrangements.

Dress Code: Golfers must wear collared shirts, and nonmetal spikes are required. No denim is allowed, but Bermuda-length shorts are acceptable.

Tournaments: San Gabriel hosts several outside tournaments per year.

Directions: Travel on I-10 to San Gabriel and take the San Gabriel Boulevard exit. Drive north to Las Tunas Drive and turn left to the club.

Contact: 411 East Las Tunas Drive, San Gabriel, CA 91776, pro shop 626/287-6052, fax 626/287-4129.

54 ALHAMBRA GOLF COURSE

Architect: William F. Bell, 1956; Tom Johnson, 2004
18 holes   **Public**   **$14.50–24**

🚶 📷 🍴 🏌 🚗 ☕

Northwest Detail map, page 295

Extensive bunker and tee renovations were completed in 2004 on this short regulation course. The front nine is flat and easy to walk, with large groves of eucalyptus and black acacias. The back nine is composed of rolling hills, with more sand and water. The two nines are distinctly different, although both have well-maintained greens. The greens are small and quick, requiring a soft touch. One unique feature of this course is the three-tiered, night-lighted driving range, believed to be America's first. This is a shot-maker's layout. Alhambra also offers a strong junior program.

Play Policy and Fees: Green fees are $19.50 weekdays and $24 weekends for 18 holes, $14.50 weekdays and $15.50 weekends for nine holes. Carts are $8 per person for nine holes and $11 per person for 18 holes. Senior, junior, twilight, and super twilight rates are available. There is also a discount for Alhambra residents.

Tees and Yardage: *Men:* Blue: yardage 5197, par 70, rating 64.3, slope 107; White: yardage 4863, par 70, rating 63.1, slope 102; *Women:* Red: yardage 4501, par 71, rating 64.7, slope 105.

Tee Times: Reservations can be booked seven days in advance.

Dress Code: No tank tops, gym shorts, or metal spikes are allowed. Collared shirts are preferred.

Tournaments: This course is available for tournaments. Shotgun tournaments are permitted on weekdays only. Events may be booked a year in advance, with a deposit required to reserve and full payment required two weeks prior to the day of the event.

Directions: From downtown Los Angeles, take I-10 east to the Garfield Avenue exit to Alhambra. Turn right on Valley Boulevard and travel one-half mile to Almansor Street. Turn left on Almansor and drive three-quarters of a mile.

Contact: 630 South Almansor Street, Alhambra, CA 91801, pro shop 626/570-5059, fax 626/570-0385, www.alhambragolf.com.

55 ARCADIA PAR-3

Architect: Course designed, 1959
18 holes   **Public**   **$10–13**

🚶 📷 🍴 🏌 ☕ 3

Northwest Detail map, page 295

This flat, 18-hole par-3 course has no bunkers or water. You tee off from mats. It's good practice for irons. The course is lighted for night play and is open until 10 P.M. The last tee time is 8 P.M. There is a Nike Golf Learning Center here for those wishing to learn the game or improve.

Play Policy and Fees: Green fees are $10 weekdays and $13 weekends. Twilight, senior, and junior rates are available.

Tees and Yardage: *Men:* Back: yardage 1947, par 54, rating n/a, slope n/a; *Women:* Forward: yardage 1876, par 54, rating n/a, slope n/a.

Tee Times: Reservations can be booked 21 days in advance.

Dress Code: Collared shirts are required. No short shorts are allowed on the course.

Tournaments: This course is available for outside tournaments.

Directions: Off I-10 in Arcadia, exit on Santa Anita Avenue and drive south for two miles until you reach Live Oak. Follow Live Oak east 1.5 miles to the course on the right.

Contact: 620 East Live Oak, Arcadia, CA 91006, pro shop 626/443-9367, fax 626/443-2537.

56 RIVIERA COUNTRY CLUB

Architect: George C. Thomas Jr., 1926
18 holes   **Private**   **$350**

🚶 📷 🍴 🏁 🚗 ☕

Northwest Detail map, page 295

This well-maintained club course is one of the golf world's classic designs. Many of Hollywood's rich and famous are members here. George C. Thomas Jr. designed this long, tough layout in 1926, using some of the best architectural techniques of his era.

He was not only a master of strategy, devising a course that demands precise placement of every shot, but he included deception bunkers that from the fairway look like they are next to greens, when in fact they are 30 yards short. Plus, the fairways and rough are planted with kikuyu grass, so there's not much roll. The 165-yard, par-3 sixth hole features a bunker in the middle of the green that has occasionally been copied on other courses. If that doesn't frighten you, maybe the par-4 18th will. With a narrow, deceptively sloping green, it is considered one of the toughest holes in golf. The 1948 U.S. Open was played at Riviera and won by the great Ben Hogan. After Hogan won the Los Angeles Open here in 1947 and 1948, the course became known as Hogan's Alley. The Los Angeles Open is played here annually. Changes to the course have included a rebuild of an alternate fairway on the eighth; it was part of Thomas's original course design.

Riviera Country Club has hotel rooms available for guests and reciprocal members.

Play Policy and Fees: Very limited reciprocal play is accepted with members of other private clubs at a rate of $350 plus caddie. Please call in advance.

Tees and Yardage: *Men:* Black: yardage 7157, par 71, rating 75.6, slope 137; Blue: yardage 7013, par 71, rating 74.6, slope 135; White: yardage 6531, par 71, rating 72.2, slope 130; Gold: yardage 6094, par 71, rating 70.0, slope 124; *Women:* Red: yardage 5844, par 74, rating 75.6, slope 143.

Tee Times: Reciprocators should have their home professional call to make arrangements.

Dress Code: Appropriate golf attire and non-metal spikes are required.

Tournaments: This course is available for outside tournaments on Monday only. A 100-player minimum is needed to book an event. Events should be scheduled 18–24 months in advance. A banquet facility is available that can accommodate 125 people.

Directions: Take the Sunset Boulevard exit off I-405 and travel west three miles to Capri Drive, then turn left to the club.

Contact: 1250 Capri Drive, Pacific Palisades, CA 90272, pro shop 310/459-5395, clubhouse 310/454-6591, fax 310/454-8351.

57 BRENTWOOD COUNTRY CLUB

Architect: Willie Watson, 1910

18 holes   **Private**   **$55–70**

Northwest Detail map, page 295

Accurate tee shots are important here. The course is fairly tight, with lots of trees. The back nine is especially narrow and long. A small lake borders nine holes. The course also gets hilly in spots. The greens make this a particularly good course: They are fast and true.

Play Policy and Fees: Reciprocal play is accepted with members of other private clubs; otherwise, members and guests only. Reciprocator fees are $55 Monday–Thursday and $70 Friday–Sunday. Carts are additional.

Tees and Yardage: *Men:* Black: yardage 6757, par 72, rating 72.8, slope 129; Blue: yardage 6510, par 72, rating 71.7, slope 126; White: yardage 6021, par 72, rating 69.1, slope 122; Silver: yardage 5875, par 72, rating 66.7, slope 117; *Women:* Red: yardage 5534, par 73, rating 73.7, slope 128.

Tee Times: Reciprocators should have their home professional make the arrangements.

Dress Code: Appropriate golf attire and non-metal spikes are required.

Tournaments: This course is not available for outside events.

Directions: Take the Sunset Boulevard exit off I-405 north of L.A. and travel west for 1.5 miles to Burlingame Avenue. Turn left and travel half a mile to the club.

Contact: 590 South Burlingame Avenue, Los Angeles, CA 90049, pro shop 310/451-8011, fax 310/656-3393.

58 BEL-AIR COUNTRY CLUB

Architect: George C. Thomas Jr., 1926

18 holes   **Private**

Northwest Detail map, page 295

A George C. Thomas Jr. classic, this prestigious, hilly course has narrow fairways and lots of trees. It's nicely bunkered, has small greens, and places a premium on accuracy. One of the landmark holes is the 10th, a par-3, 200-yard nerve-racker known as the "Swinging Bridge." You park your cart on one side of a canyon, walk back to the tee, and hope your drive clears the canyon. The tee is next to the club grill, where there is always a gallery. This club attracts many of Los Angeles's rich and famous. Bel-Air was the site of the 1976 U.S. Amateur Championship and is the home course of the UCLA Bruins golf team.

Play Policy and Fees: Members and guests only.

Tees and Yardage: *Men:* Black: yardage 6754, par 70, rating 73.8, slope 137; Blue: yardage 6482, par 70, rating 72.0, slope 134; White: yardage 6210, par 70, rating 70.8, slope 130; *Women:* Red: yardage 5778, par 74, rating 75.2, slope 138.

Tee Times: Not applicable.

Dress Code: Appropriate golf attire and nonmetal spikes are required. No denim is permitted.

Tournaments: This course is not available for outside events.

Directions: Take the Sunset Boulevard exit off I-405 and travel east for three-quarters of a mile to Bellagio Road. Turn left and bear right. You'll shortly find the club entrance on the right.

Contact: 10768 Bellagio Road, Los Angeles, CA 90077, pro shop 310/440-2444, fax 310/472-7044.

59 THE LOS ANGELES COUNTRY CLUB

Architect: George C. Thomas Jr., 1921

36 holes   **Private**

Northwest Detail map, page 295

This private club in the heart of Los Angeles has two 18-hole courses. They are beautiful layouts, showcasing both the landscape design skills and classic golf strategy of architect George C. Thomas Jr. With its sharp doglegs, surprising elevation changes, and fairways populated with mature trees, the North Course is often ranked the number-one course in Southern California and has been the home of numerous Los Angeles Open championships. It is regarded as among the best courses in the country. For all golfers, it is a solid test, but particularly for women as the 78.4/145 ratings indicate. The South Course is shorter and more forgiving, but every bit as lovely.

Play Policy and Fees: Members and guests only.

Tees and Yardage: North Course—*Men:* Blue: yardage 6909, par 71, rating 74.1, slope 140; White: yardage 6601, par 71, rating 72.5, slope 137; *Women:* Red: yardage 6205, par 74, rating 78.4, slope 145. South Course—*Men:* White: yardage 5970, par 70, rating 68.6, slope 122; *Women:* Red: yardage 5638, par 71, rating 67.3, slope 117.

Tee Times: Not applicable.

Dress Code: No shorts are allowed on the golf course. Women must wear skirts. Nonmetal spikes are required.

Tournaments: This course is not available for outside events.

Directions: Take the Wilshire Boulevard exit off I-405 and drive east to the club.

Contact: 10101 Wilshire Boulevard, Los Angeles, CA 90024, pro shop 310/276-6104, fax 310/246-2650.

60 THE WILSHIRE COUNTRY CLUB

Architect: Norman Macbeth, 1919

18 holes **Private** **$150**

Northwest Detail map, page 295

Built in 1919, this course was used for the Los Angeles Open in 1926. The mostly level fairways are lined with mature trees, and the greens are well maintained. A barranca runs through 14 of the 18 fairways.

Play Policy and Fees: Approved reciprocal play is accepted with members of other private clubs at a rate of $150, plus caddie or cart; otherwise, members and guests only.

Tees and Yardage: *Men:* Blue: yardage 6527, par 71, rating 71.6, slope 131; White: yardage 6299, par 71, rating 70.5, slope 129; *Women:* Red: yardage 6011, par 74, rating 75.8, slope 143.

Tee Times: Reciprocators should have their club pro call to make arrangements.

Dress Code: Appropriate golf attire and non-metal spikes are required.

Tournaments: All outside events must be approved by the general manager.

Directions: Take the Santa Monica Boulevard exit off U.S. 101 (Hollywood Freeway) and travel west for one mile to Vine Street. Turn left and drive one mile (Vine becomes Rossmore Avenue) to the club on the right.

Contact: 301 North Rossmore Avenue, Los Angeles, CA 90004, pro shop 323/934-1121.

61 RANCHO PARK GOLF COURSE

Architect: William P. Bell, 1947; William H. Johnson

27 holes **Public** **$22–28.50**

Northwest Detail map, page 295

This course is one of the most heavily played courses in the country, so expect slow play. The course features many trees and rolling terrain. This facility also offers a nine-hole, par-3 course. Par is 27. Rancho Park was once the site of the Ralphs Senior Classic, an October stop on the Champions Tour. Arnold Palmer once made a 12 on the par-5 18th hole (ninth hole during professional events) here during the Los Angeles Open. Asked how he made 12, he replied, "I missed a three-footer for 11." A plaque is near the tee at the 18th to commemorate the event. Because of the heavy play, each hole on the championship course has an alternate green.

Play Policy and Fees: Green fees are $22 weekdays and $28.50 weekends for 18 holes. Twilight rates are offered. Pull carts are $3, electric $20, and personal remote control $6.

Tees and Yardage: *Men:* Blue: yardage 6628, par 71, rating 71.7, slope 126; White: yardage 6300, par 71, rating 70.1, slope 123; *Women:* Red: yardage 6036, par 73, rating 74.5, slope 124.

Tee Times: Reservations can be made one week in advance, but only by holders of a Los Angeles Recreation and Parks reservation card (818/291 9980). Cards can be obtained at any city golf facility or by writing to City of Los Angeles, Department of Parks & Recreation, 200 North Main Street, Room 1380, City Hall East, Los Angeles, CA 90012-4172. Standbys are welcome for noncardholders.

Dress Code: Appropriate attire and soft spikes are required.

Tournaments: All reservations must be made through the Los Angeles Recreation and Parks Department. Call 818/291-9980.

Directions: Take the Santa Monica Freeway to the Overland exit. Travel north on Overland approximately 1.5 miles to Pico Boulevard. Turn right and drive one-half mile to the course.

Contact: 10460 West Pico Boulevard, Los Angeles, CA 90064, pro shop 310/839-4374.

62 HILLCREST COUNTRY CLUB

Architect: Willie Watson, 1920

18 holes **Private**

Northwest Detail map, page 295

This is a relatively short, classic design by Willie Watson, who designed several of California's best courses, including nearby Brentwood Country Club and Harding Park, as well as Sonoma

Golf Club in Northern California. Hillcrest is a tree-lined course, and it can be testy. The fairways are lush and nicely maintained. There is also a pitch-and-putt, six-hole, par-3 course.

Play Policy and Fees: Members and guests only.

Tees and Yardage: *Men:* Black: yardage 6461, par 71, rating 71.6, slope 129; Blue: yardage 6194, par 71, rating 70.5, slope 126; White: yardage 5795, par 71, rating 68.5, slope 122; *Women:* Red: yardage 5528, par 73, rating 73.4, slope 132.

Tee Times: Not applicable.

Dress Code: Appropriate golf attire and non-metal spikes are required.

Tournaments: No outside tournaments.

Directions: Take the Pico Boulevard exit off I-405 southbound and travel east to the club. From northbound on I-405, take the Venice Boulevard exit to Motor Street, which turns into Pico Boulevard, and drive to the club.

Contact: 10000 West Pico Boulevard, Los Angeles, CA 90064, pro shop 310/553-8911, ext. 246, fax 310/277-4728.

63 MONTEREY PARK GOLF COURSE

Architect: Course designed, 1973
9 holes   **Public**   **$8–9**

Northwest Detail map, page 295

This is an executive course consisting of seven par-3s and two par-4s. The course and adjoining driving range are lighted for night play.

Play Policy and Fees: Daytime green fees are $8 weekdays and $9 weekends. Night rates are $9. Call for special rates.

Tees and Yardage: *Men and Women:* yardage 1400, par 29, rating n/a, slope n/a.

Tee Times: Reservations can be booked seven days in advance.

Dress Code: Soft spikes required.

Tournaments: Shotgun tournaments are not available. A 16-player minimum is needed to book an event.

Directions: From I-710 (Long Beach Freeway) in Monterey Park, take the Ramona Boule-

vard exit. The course is directly off the freeway on Ramona Boulevard.

Contact: 3600 Ramona Boulevard, Monterey Park, CA 91754, pro shop 323/266-4632.

64 WHITTIER NARROWS GOLF COURSE

Architect: William F. Bell, 1960
27 holes   **Public**   **$27–40**

Northwest Detail map, page 295

These popular courses are flat and narrow, with lots of trees and elevated greens. The main course is the River/Pines combo, with the Mountain nine used more as a nine-hole course, although it can be played in combination with the Pines nine. No loop is particularly difficult, and therefore this is a good facility for beginning golfers.

Play Policy and Fees: Green fees are $27 to ride weekdays and $40 to ride weekends and holidays. Walking, nine-hole, senior, and twilight rates are available. Call for other special rates.

Tees and Yardage: Pines/Mountain—*Men:* Blue: yardage 6328, par 72, rating 68.4, slope 114; White: yardage 6083, par 72, rating 67.9, slope 112; River/Pines—*Men:* Blue: yardage 6819, par 72, rating 72.3, slope 121; White: yardage 6670, par 72, rating 71.4, slope 119; *Women:* Red: yardage 5965, par 72, rating 73.6, slope 117.

Tee Times: Reservations can be booked seven days in advance.

Dress Code: Soft spikes only.

Tournaments: Please call for information.

Directions: Off Highway 60 in Rosemead, take the San Gabriel Boulevard exit and drive north to Walnut Grove Street. Drive to Rush Street and turn right to the course.

Contact: 8640 East Rush Street, Rosemead, CA 91770, pro shop 626/288-1044, http://parks.co.la.ca.us/whittier.html.

65 MONTEBELLO COUNTRY CLUB

Architect: Max Behr, 1928,
renovation David Rainville, 1999

18 holes   **Public**   **$28–38**

Northwest Detail map, page 295

Built in 1928, this flat course is one of the better-maintained courses in the area. Trees line many of the fairways, placing a premium on accuracy off the tee. The course underwent major renovations in 1999. Three new lakes were added, as well as many new bunkers and all new greens.

Play Policy and Fees: Green fees are $28 weekdays and $38 weekends. Carts are $12.

Tees and Yardage: *Men:* Black: yardage 6528, par 71, rating 71.2, slope 122; Blue: yardage 6462, par 71, rating 70.8, slope 121; White: yardage 5941, par 71, rating 68.4, slope 118; *Women:* Red: yardage 5543, par 71, rating 71.2, slope 120.

Tee Times: Reservations can be booked seven days in advance on weekdays and on Monday morning for the following weekend.

Dress Code: Collared shirts and nonmetal spikes are required.

Tournaments: A 24-player minimum is needed for a tournament, and events should be booked four to six months in advance. The banquet facilities can accommodate up to 1200 people.

Directions: In Montebello, traveling on Highway 60 (Pomona Freeway), exit at Garfield Avenue and drive south for one block. Turn right on Via San Clemente at the club sign.

Contact: 901 Via San Clemente, Montebello, CA 90640, pro shop 323/887-4565.

66 PICO RIVERA GOLF COURSE

Architect: Course designed, 1966

9 holes   **Public**   **$9–11**

Northwest Detail map, page 295

All the greens are elevated on this short executive course. The longest hole is 270 yards, which is the fifth. Finishing holes eight and nine are surrounded by lakes. The course is lighted for night play.

Play Policy and Fees: Green fees are $9 weekdays and $11 weekends and holidays. Senior, junior, and twilight rates are offered.

Tees and Yardage: *Men:* Back: yardage 1430, par 29, rating n/a, slope n/a; *Women:* Forward: yardage 1294, par 29, rating n/a, slope n/a.

Tee Times: Reservations can be made seven days in advance. Walk-on play is okay.

Dress Code: No tank tops or boots are allowed on the course.

Tournaments: This course is available for outside tournaments. A 16-player minimum is required to book an event. A banquet facility is available that can accommodate up to 130 people.

Directions: From I-605, take the Beverly Boulevard exit onto San Gabriel River Parkway to Fairway Drive. The course is off Fairway Drive.

Contact: 3260 Fairway Drive, Pico Rivera, CA 90660, pro shop 562/692-9933.

67 CRYSTALAIRE COUNTRY CLUB

Architect: William F. Bell, 1956

18 holes   **Private**   **$45–67**

Northeast Detail map, page 296

This scenic country course sits in the high desert, surrounded by mountains. The terrain is rolling to hilly, with lots of mature trees and three lakes. Watch for the par-3 sixth. Players must carry the lake to reach the hole. This hole has been the downfall of many, but it has also recorded more holes-in-one than any other hole on the course. The course elevation is 3500 feet, but it is usually open in the winter.

Play Policy and Fees: Reciprocal play is accepted with members of other private clubs. Reciprocal fees are $45 weekdays plus optional cart, and $67 weekends including mandatory cart.

Tees and Yardage: *Men:* Blue: yardage 6962, par 72, rating 72.8, slope 131; White: yardage 6621, par 72, rating 71.3, slope 127; *Women:* Red: yardage 6612, par 74, rating 76.9, slope

138; Gold: yardage 5277, par 72, rating 71.7, slope 127.

Tee Times: Reciprocators should have their club pro call to make arrangements or present their home club card.

Dress Code: Appropriate golf attire and non-metal spikes are required.

Tournaments: This course is available for outside tournaments Monday and Tuesday. Tournaments should be scheduled six months in advance. The banquet facility can accommodate 120 people.

Directions: Heading south of Lancaster, take the Pearblossom exit off Highway 14 and travel about 16 miles east to the town of Llano. Turn south on 165th Street and drive one mile to Crystalaire Drive. Take Crystalaire to Boca Raton Avenue and turn right to the course.

Contact: 15701 Boca Raton Avenue, Llano, CA 93544, pro shop 661/944-2111, clubhouse 661/944-2112, www.crystalairecc.com.

68 LAKE ARROWHEAD COUNTRY CLUB

Architect: William F. Bell, 1963
18 holes   Private $80

🚶 📷 🍴 🛺 🍽

Northeast Detail map, page 296

Originally a 1930s nine-hole course, Lake Arrowhead became 18 holes in 1963. The front nine is level and open, while the back nine is hilly. A small lake comes into play. All the holes are dotted with bunkers. This is a fun and serene course to play in the true mountain tradition. Note: This course is at high elevation and closes in winter months due to snow on the ground. John Daly holds the course record with 63.

Play Policy and Fees: Reciprocal play with members of other private clubs is generally accepted, although occasionally weekends are booked with members. Otherwise, no outside play is accepted. Reciprocal fees are $80, including cart and range.

Tees and Yardage: *Men:* Blue: yardage 6231, par 71, rating 69.6, slope 128; White: yardage 6035, par 71, rating 68.5, slope 125; *Women:*

Red: yardage 5558, par 73, rating 73.6, slope 137; Gold: yardage 4933, par 73, rating 69.9, slope 128.

Tee Times: Reciprocators should have their home professional make the arrangements.

Dress Code: Soft spikes only.

Tournaments: This course is not available for outside events.

Directions: Drive northeast of San Bernardino on I-215 to the Mountain Resorts exit. Continue to Highway 18 (Waterman Avenue) and turn left, following it to the Blue Jay exit. Bear left to the stop signal, turn left, and drive one-half mile to Grass Valley Road. Bear right and continue 1.5 miles to Golf Course Road. Turn left and drive 100 yards to the club.

Contact: 250 Golf Course Road (P.O. Box 670), Lake Arrowhead, CA 92352, pro shop 909/337-3515, www.lakearrowheadcc.com.

69 EL RANCHO VERDE ROYAL VISTA GOLF CLUB

Architect: Harry Rainville, 1957
18 holes   Public $18–45

🚶 📷 🍴 🛺 🍽

Northeast Detail map, page 296

This course offers gentle, rolling hills, with many pine and eucalyptus trees on the front nine and orange groves on the back nine. It boasts tough par-3s and lovely views of the San Bernardino Mountains. The 12th is a good example of both the testy par-3s and the setting: It's 226 yards uphill, with an orange grove to the left and out-of-bounds to the right. The facility includes a lighted driving range open to 10 P.M.

Play Policy and Fees: Green fees are $18 to walk and $28 to ride weekdays, $39 to walk and $45 to ride weekends. Twilight, senior, and junior rates are offered. Please call for other rates.

Tees and Yardage: *Men:* Black: yardage 7080, par 72, rating 73.4, slope 126; Blue: yardage 6746, par 72, rating 71.9, slope 122; White: yardage 6491, par 72, rating 71.1, slope 121; Gold: yardage 6147, par 72, rating 69.2, slope 116; *Women:* Red: yardage 5491, par 71, rating 72.0, slope 124.

Tee Times: Reservations can be booked seven days in advance.

Dress Code: No tank tops are allowed. Non-metal spikes are preferred.

Tournaments: This course is available for outside tournaments. A 24-player minimum is required to book a tournament. Events should be scheduled 12 months in advance. The banquet facility can accommodate 300 people.

Directions: From Los Angeles, drive east on I-10 (San Bernardino Freeway) to Riverside Avenue in the town of Rialto. Turn left and drive six miles to Country Club Drive.

Contact: 355 East Country Club Drive, Rialto, CA 92377, pro shop 909/875-5346, clubhouse 909/875-7111, www.elranchoverde.com.

70 RANCHO DUARTE GOLF CLUB

| 9 holes | Public | $11–15 |

Northeast Detail map, page 296

This well-bunkered course offers undulating fairways and greens. There are five par-3s and four par-4s. The longest hole is 329 yards.

Play Policy and Fees: Green fees are $11 weekdays and $15 weekends. Senior and twilight rates are available.

Tees and Yardage: *Men:* Back: yardage 1635, par 31, rating n/a, slope n/a; Middle: yardage 1518, par 31, rating n/a, slope n/a; *Women:* Forward: yardage 1341, par 31, rating n/a, slope n/a.

Tee Times: Reservations can be made seven days in advance.

Dress Code: Shirts and shoes are necessary.

Tournaments: A 72-player minimum is needed to book a shotgun tournament. Carts are required.

Directions: Driving on I-210 in Duarte, take Mount Olive Drive and go right on Huntington. At the first stoplight, turn left on Las Lomas and drive one-half block to the course on the right.

Contact: 1000 Las Lomas, Duarte, CA 91010, pro shop 626/357-9981.

71 AZUSA GREENS COUNTRY CLUB

Architect: Bob Baldock, 1965

| 18 holes | Public | $29–38 |

Northeast Detail map, page 296

At the base of the San Gabriel Valley foothills, this course is fairly level with straight, tree-lined fairways. Bunkers come into play on every hole, and the undulating greens will test players of all abilities. This course provides a well-maintained, scenic round of golf.

Play Policy and Fees: Green fees are $29 weekdays and $38 weekends, carts included. Senior (weekdays only), twilight, and nine-hole rates are offered. Call for specials.

Tees and Yardage: *Men:* Blue: yardage 6193, par 70, rating 69.0, slope 118; White: yardage 5953, par 70, rating 68.1, slope 117; *Women:* Red: yardage 5601, par 72, rating 71.3, slope 117.

Tee Times: Reservations can be booked seven days in advance.

Dress Code: Collared shirts are required. No cutoffs are allowed on the course.

Tournaments: A 16-player minimum is required to book an event. Tournaments can be scheduled 12 months in advance. The banquet facility can accommodate up to 250 people.

Directions: From Pasadena travel east on I-210 to the Azusa Avenue exit. Drive north three miles to Sierra Madre Avenue and turn left. Drive four blocks to the clubhouse on the right.

Contact: 919 West Sierra Madre Avenue, Azusa, CA 91702, pro shop 626/969-1727, fax 626/969-1413, www.azusagreenscountryclub.com.

72 GLENOAKS GOLF COURSE

| 9 holes | Public | $8–10 |

Northeast Detail map, page 296

This is a well-maintained par-3 course. The longest hole here is 151 yards, so leave your woods at home. Tennis and racquetball courts are nearby.

Play Policy and Fees: Green fees are $8 week-days and $10 weekends. Senior and junior rates are available.

Tees and Yardage: *Men and Women:* yardage 1078, par 27, rating n/a, slope n/a.

Tee Times: Reservations are not accepted. All play is on a first-come, first-served basis.

Dress Code: Appropriate attire and soft spikes are required.

Tournaments: This course is available for outside tournaments. A 36-player minimum is needed. Tournaments can be booked two months in advance.

Directions: From Highway 210 exit at Grand Avenue. Go one block to Glendora Avenue, turn right, and go to Dawson Avenue. Turn right and you're at the course.

Contact: 200 West Dawson Street, Glendora, CA 91740, pro shop 626/335-7565.

73 GLENDORA COUNTRY CLUB

Architect: E. Warren Beach, 1955;
Robert Trent Jones Jr., 1970

18 holes   Private

Northeast Detail map, page 296

This picturesque course nestles at the foot of the San Gabriel Mountains. The narrow, tree-lined fairways are fairly level and easy to walk. It is a traditional East Coast–type course, with gently rolling fairways, strategically placed bunkers, and small greens. Mature trees and mountain views make a round here very pleasant.

Play Policy and Fees: Limited reciprocal play is accepted with members of other area private clubs; otherwise, members and guests only.

Tees and Yardage: *Men:* Blue: yardage 6597, par 72, rating 72.2, slope 131; White: yardage 6377, par 72, rating 71.3, slope 128; *Women:* Red: yardage 5992, par 74, rating 75.6, slope 137.

Tee Times: Reciprocators should have their home professional call to make arrangements.

Dress Code: Appropriate golf attire and non-metal spikes are required.

Tournaments: This course is available for outside tournaments on Monday. A 120-player minimum is needed to book an event. Tournaments should be scheduled 12 months in advance. The banquet facility can accommodate 350 people.

Directions: Travel east on I-210. (Stay in the middle lane.) At the "End of Freeway/Foothill Boulevard" sign, take the Lone Hill exit and drive north for half a mile to Alosta Avenue. Turn right, drive half a mile to Amelia Avenue, and turn left to the club.

Contact: 310 South Amelia Avenue, Glendora, CA 91740, pro shop 626/335-3713, fax 626/335-6786, www.glendoracountryclub.com.

74 SAN DIMAS CANYON GOLF COURSE

Architect: Jeff Brauer, 1991

18 holes   Public $25–50

Northeast Detail map, page 296

This course offers a relatively level front nine and a back nine that plays through some hills. Four water hazards come into play on five holes. The par-3 16th hole is a real challenge: From an elevated tee, you hit over a lake to a green faced by a rock retaining wall and surrounded by mounds and pot bunkers.

Play Policy and Fees: Green fees are $25 to walk weekdays, $38 to ride, and $50 to ride weekends (mandatory before noon). Call for other rates.

Tees and Yardage: *Men:* Blue: yardage 6400, par 72, rating 70.3, slope 118; White: yardage 5929, par 72, rating 68.3, slope 113; *Women:* Silver: yardage 5483, par 73, rating 72.5, slope 128.

Tee Times: Reservations can be booked seven days in advance.

Dress Code: No tank tops or cutoff jeans are allowed. Soft spikes only.

Tournaments: Shotgun tournaments are available on weekdays. Carts are required. A 16-player minimum is needed to book an event. Tournaments should be scheduled 3–12 months in advance. A banquet facility holds 300 people.

Directions: Travel east on I-210 (Foothill Freeway) and Highway 30 to the San Dimas Avenue exit. Travel north to Foothill Boulevard and turn right. Drive three-quarters of a mile to San Dimas Canyon Road. Go left and continue one mile to the Terrebonne Avenue entrance to Gray Oaks, then turn left to the club. **Contact:** 2100 Terrebonne Avenue, San Dimas, CA 91773, pro shop 909/599-2313, www.americangolf.com.

75 SIERRA LA VERNE COUNTRY CLUB

Architect: Dan Murray, 1976
18 holes   **Private**

Northeast Detail map, page 296

Set in the foothills of the San Gabriel Mountains, this course is both picturesque and challenging. The front nine is more open and not as difficult as the back nine, which requires accuracy with irons and good putting on the well-manicured greens. The greens are severe, however, and it is difficult to read the break and speed.

Play Policy and Fees: Limited reciprocal play is accepted with members of other private clubs; otherwise, members and guests only.

Tees and Yardage: *Men:* Blue: yardage 6356, par 71, rating 70.6, slope 126; White: yardage 6021, par 71, rating 69.0, slope 122; *Women:* Red: yardage 5603, par 72, rating 74.4, slope 138.

Tee Times: Reciprocators should have their home professional call to make arrangements.

Dress Code: Appropriate golf attire and nonmetal spikes are required.

Tournaments: This course is available for outside tournaments on Monday and Thursday. A 72-player minimum is needed to book an event, and carts are mandatory. Tournaments should be scheduled six months to a year in advance. A banquet facility is available that can accommodate 200 people.

Directions: From Pasadena travel east on I-210. Exit at Foothill Boulevard heading east and drive to Wheeler Road north. Take Wheeler Road to Birdie and follow Birdie to Country Club Drive. Turn left on Country Club Drive and proceed to the clubhouse.

Contact: 6300 Country Club Drive, La Verne, CA 91750, pro shop 909/596-2100, fax 909/392-9514, www.sierralavernecc.com.

76 MARSHALL CANYON GOLF CLUB

Architect: Course designed, 1966
18 holes   **Public**   **$21.50–28**

Northeast Detail map, page 296

This course is in a canyon at the base of the San Gabriel Mountains, which offer a spectacular backdrop. The greens have a great deal of contour and are extremely tricky because of the mountains, which cause optical illusions. The par-3, 177-yard 11th hole plays over part of the canyon and is particularly scenic. Deer and other wildlife abound in this rustic setting and can often be seen grazing on the links.

Play Policy and Fees: Green fees are $21.50 weekdays and $28 weekends, carts additional. Twilight, super twilight, nine-hole, and senior rates are available.

Tees and Yardage: *Men:* Blue: yardage 6145, par 71, rating 69.2, slope 121; White: yardage 5903, par 71, rating 68.0, slope 117; *Women:* Red: yardage 5559, par 73, rating 71.3, slope 118.

Tee Times: Reservations can be booked seven days in advance.

Dress Code: Appropriate golf attire is required.

Tournaments: A 16-player minimum is needed to book a tournament.

Directions: Take I-210 east to Wheeler, then go north to Golden Hills. Go east on Golden Hills to Stephens Ranch Road and north to the course.

Contact: 6100 Stephens Ranch Road, La Verne, CA 91750, pro shop 909/593-6914, clubhouse 909/593-8211.

77 SIERRA LAKES GOLF CLUB

Architect: Ted Robinson Sr., 2000
18 holes   **Public**   **$46–72**

Northeast Detail map, page 296

This is a popular, big-hitters' course, with wide fairways and receptive greens. It is picturesque, featuring palm trees, fescue grasses, and views of the San Bernardino Mountains. There are also several lakes and plenty of sand in play. It is women-friendly and fun for golfers of all levels. **Play Policy and Fees:** Green fees are $46 Monday–Thursday, $52 Friday, and $72 weekends and holidays, all including cart. Twilight, early bird, and senior (weekdays only) rates are also available.

Tees and Yardage: *Men:* Black: yardage 6805, par 72, rating 73.0, slope 125; Blue: yardage 6535, par 72, rating 71.2, slope 121; White: yardage 6090, par 72, rating 69.7, slope 117; *Women:* Red: yardage 5324, par 72, rating 70.0, slope 118.

Tee Times: Reservations are accepted eight days in advance.

Dress Code: Appropriate golf attire and nonmetal spikes are mandatory.

Tournaments: Reservations for tournaments may be made up to one year in advance.

Directions: Exit I-15 at Summit Avenue and go north (left) at the top of the off-ramp. Travel two miles to Clubhouse Drive and take a right.

Contact: 16600 Clubhouse Drive, Fontana, CA 92335, pro shop 909/350-2500, fax 909/350-4600, www.sierralakes.com.

78 SHANDIN HILLS GOLF CLUB

Architect: Cary Bickler, 1982

18 holes   **Public**   **$24–35**

Northeast Detail map, page 296

This is a challenging course with 79 bunkers. The rough is kept shaggy, so accuracy is essential. Narrow, tree-lined fairways lead from elevated tees to elevated greens. I-215 bisects the two nines, but scenic views of the San Bernardino Mountains abound. PGA Tour pro Kirk Triplett set the course record of 61 while playing a Golden State Mini-Tour event in 1987.

Play Policy and Fees: Weekday green fees are $24, and weekends are $35. Carts are $11 per rider. Twilight and super twilight rates are available. Call for other rates.

Tees and Yardage: *Men:* Blue: yardage 6517, par 72, rating 71.9, slope 129; White: yardage 6192, par 72, rating 70.4, slope 122; *Women:* Silver: yardage 5592, par 72, rating 72.0, slope 123.

Tee Times: Reservations may be booked up to seven days in advance. Credit cards are required to reserve weekend tee times.

Dress Code: Collared shirts are required, and nonmetal spikes are preferred. Tank tops are not permitted.

Tournaments: This course is available for outside tournaments. The banquet facility holds up to 250 people. Call the course for more information.

Directions: From Los Angeles, travel east on I-10 to I-215. In San Bernardino take the Mount Vernon/27th Street off-ramp and turn right on 27th Street, then immediately turn left on Little Mountain. Travel one mile to the club.

Contact: 3380 Little Mountain Drive, San Bernardino, CA 92407, pro shop 909/886-0669, fax 909/881-2138, www.americangolf.com.

79 ARROWHEAD COUNTRY CLUB

Architect: Clark Glasson, 1970

18 holes   **Private**   **$60**

Northeast Detail map, page 296

This course, in one form or another, has been around since the 1920s. It first opened for memberships in 1944. It has level terrain, mature trees, and water hazards. It is at the foot of the mountains in a desert area, so the heat can be a factor in summer months. In the winter, several ski areas are open 30 minutes away in the San Bernardino Mountains.

Play Policy and Fees: Reciprocal play is accepted with members of other private clubs; otherwise, members and guests only. Guest and reciprocal fees are $60, including range. Optional carts are additional.

Tees and Yardage: *Men:* Blue: yardage 6573, par 72, rating 71.8, slope 127; White: yardage 6247, par 72, rating 70.2, slope 124; *Women:* Red: yardage 5752, par 72, rating 74.3, slope 128.

Tee Times: Reciprocators should have their club pro call to make arrangements.

Dress Code: Collared shirts and nonmetal spikes are required. No blue jeans or short shorts are allowed on the course.

Tournaments: This course is not available for outside events.

Directions: From San Bernardino, travel east on Highway 30 to Waterman Avenue north. Drive half a mile and turn right on 34th Street. Continue to Parkside Drive and the entrance to the club.

Contact: 3433 Parkside Drive, San Bernardino, CA 92404, pro shop 909/882-1638, clubhouse 909/882-1735.

80 UPLAND HILLS COUNTRY CLUB

Architect: David Rainville, 1983
18 holes   Semiprivate   **$24–48**

Northeast Detail map, page 296

This course in the foothills is fairly flat and easy to walk. Six lakes and fast greens make it a challenge. It is short and tight, causing lots of trouble, but it's always in good condition. Out-of-bounds line both sides of the fairways on 15 holes.

Play Policy and Fees: Monday–Thursday green fees are $24 walking and $35 with a cart. Friday green fees are $26 walking and $37 with a cart. Green fees are $48 weekends and holidays, including mandatory cart. Twilight rates are available.

Tees and Yardage: *Men:* Blue: yardage 5938, par 70, rating 68.6, slope 121; White: yardage 5549, par 70, rating 66.7, slope 118; *Women:* Silver: yardage 5004, par 70, rating 68.2, slope 115.

Tee Times: Reservations can be booked nine days in advance.

Dress Code: No jeans or cutoffs are allowed on the course; collared shirts are mandatory.

Tournaments: A 16-player minimum is required to book a tournament.

Directions: Travel east on I-10 (San Bernardino Freeway) to Euclid Avenue in Upland. Turn

north to 16th Street, then drive east for one mile to the club.

Contact: 1231 East 16th Street, Upland, CA 91786, pro shop 909/946-4711, clubhouse 909/946-3057.

81 RED HILL COUNTRY CLUB

Architect: George C. Thomas Jr., 1921
18 holes   Private   **$55**

Northeast Detail map, page 296

This deceptive course offers a challenging test. It's a traditional layout, void of railroad ties or other gimmicks. There are lots of trees and undulating greens. Watch out for the two ponds that have been incorporated into the seventh and eighth holes.

Play Policy and Fees: Reciprocal play is accepted with members of other private clubs at the guest rate of $55 plus an optional cart at $11. Otherwise, members and guests only.

Tees and Yardage: *Men:* Blue: yardage 6621, par 72, rating 71.6, slope 124; Middle: yardage 6463, par 72, rating 70.9, slope 123; White: yardage 6373, par 72, rating 70.5, slope 122; *Women:* Red: yardage 6019, par 74, rating 76.0, slope 137.

Tee Times: Reciprocators should have their home professional call to make arrangements.

Dress Code: Appropriate golf attire and nonmetal spikes are required.

Tournaments: This course authorizes 20 outside events a year. A 100-player minimum is needed to book an event.

Directions: Take I-10 (San Bernardino Freeway) to the Euclid Avenue exit (west of San Bernardino) and drive north to Foothill Boulevard. Turn right and drive 1.5 miles to Red Hill Country Club Drive and turn left to the club.

Contact: 8358 Red Hill Country Club Drive, Rancho Cucamonga, CA 91730, pro shop 909/982-1358.

82 VIA VERDE COUNTRY CLUB

Architect: Lawrence Hughes and William F. Bell, 1970
18 holes **Private** **$46–66**

Northeast Detail map, page 296

This scenic course on a hill is well bunkered, with narrow fairways and rolling terrain. It is within a residential community. The greens are extremely fast and usually in excellent condition. Water comes into play on two holes. It is primarily a target golf course; accuracy is imperative.

Play Policy and Fees: Reciprocal play is accepted with members of other private clubs at a rate of $46 weekdays, $66 weekends, including cart. Otherwise, members and guests only.

Tees and Yardage: *Men:* Blue: yardage 6443, par 72, rating 70.9, slope 124; White: yardage 6215, par 72, rating 69.3, slope 120; Gold: yardage 5770, par 72, rating 67.3, slope 115; *Women:* Red: yardage 5686, par 72, rating 74.7, slope 130.

Tee Times: Reservations may be made seven days in advance. Reciprocators should have their club pro call to make arrangements.

Dress Code: Appropriate golf attire is required. Soft spikes are preferred.

Tournaments: This course is available for occasional outside tournaments on Monday. A 72-player minimum is required to book an event. The banquet facility can accommodate 400 people.

Directions: From San Bernardino, drive west on I-10 (San Bernardino Freeway) to the Via Verde exit. Drive north one mile to Avenida Entrada and turn left. Drive three-fourths of a mile to the end and turn left to the club.

Contact: 1400 Avenida Entrada, San Dimas, CA 91773, pro shop 909/599-8486, fax 909/599-0304, www.viaverdecountryclub.com.

83 MOUNTAIN MEADOWS GOLF COURSE

Architect: Ted Robinson Sr., 1975
18 holes **Public** **$21.50–28**

Northeast Detail map, page 296

This is a hilly course with numerous trees flank-ing the fairways. For scenery and difficulty, watch out for the 13th. It's a 213-yard par-3 over a canyon, overlooking part of the San Gabriel Valley. This scenic and well-maintained layout has been awarded the Los Angeles County Course of the Year several times.

Play Policy and Fees: Green fees are $21.50 weekdays and $28 weekends. Optional carts are $12 per rider.

Tees and Yardage: *Men:* Blue: yardage 6440, par 72, rating 70.4, slope 131; White: yardage 6113, par 72, rating 69.0, slope 128; *Women:* Silver: yardage 5519, par 72, rating 72.1, slope 127.

Tee Times: Reservations can be booked seven days in advance.

Dress Code: No tank tops or short shorts are allowed.

Tournaments: Shotgun tournaments are available. A 24-player minimum is needed to book a regular tournament. Events should be booked 12 months in advance. The banquet facility holds 300 people.

Directions: Travel on I-10 (San Bernardino Freeway) to the Fairplex Drive exit. Go north on Fairplex for about one mile to the club.

Contact: 1875 Fairplex Drive, Pomona, CA 91768, pro shop 909/623-3704.

84 CLAREMONT GOLF COURSE

Architect: Course designed, 1959
9 holes **Public** **$12–14**

Northeast Detail map, page 296

This fun nine-hole executive course has two sets of tee boxes, so the course can be played as 18 holes. The longest hole on the course is the sixth, which can play as a 426-yard par-4 dogleg left.

Play Policy and Fees: Green fees are $12 for nine holes weekdays and $14 for nine holes weekends. Replay rates offered. Senior and junior rates are available all week, and other special rates are often available. Carts are reserved for seniors and disabled persons.

Tees and Yardage: *Men (18 holes):* Back: yardage 3820, par 58, rating 57.4, slope 86; *Women (18* *holes):* Forward: yardage 3350, par 62, rating 60.5, slope 90.

Tee Times: Reservations can be made seven days in advance.

Dress Code: Casual attire is okay, but no tank tops or short shorts are allowed on the course.

Tournaments: Claremont is available for outside events. Tournaments should be scheduled at least one month in advance.

Directions: The course is 40 miles east of Los Angeles. From Los Angeles, take I-10 east to Indian Hill Boulevard exit. Drive north on Indian Hill Boulevard for three miles to the course.

Contact: 1550 North Indian Hill Boulevard, Claremont, CA 91711, pro shop 909/624-2748, www.claremontgolf.com.

85 EMPIRE LAKES GOLF COURSE

Architect: Arnold Palmer, 1996

18 holes　　　**Public**　　　**$60–90**

Northeast Detail map, page 296

This popular course plays host to a PGA Nationwide Tour event. It is characterized by gorgeous mountain views, undulating fairways, and greens with finger-shaped bunkers throughout. If you're hitting your driver remotely straight, bring it on, because the fairways are wide open. For those with a driver that refuses to do anything but hook or slice, keep it in the bag, or you'll find yourself trying to hack back into the fairway. A new set of yellow tees was added in 2004, and the course was lengthened from the black tees at the same time to accommodate professional play, to more than 7000 yards.

Play Policy and Fees: Green fees are $60 Monday–Thursday, $75 Friday, and $90 weekends and holidays. Twilight, midday, nine-hole, senior, and junior rates are available. Carts are included in all green fees.

Tees and Yardage: *Men:* Black: yardage 7034, par 72, rating 74.1, slope 136; Blue: yardage 6628, par 72, rating 72.1, slope 133; Yellow: yardage 6340, par 72, rating 70.9, slope 130; White: yardage 6024, par 72, rating 69.4, slope

126; *Women:* Red: yardage 5200, par 72, rating 70.5, slope 125.

Tee Times: Reservations can be booked seven days in advance.

Dress Code: Collared shirts and nonmetal spikes are required. No blue jeans are allowed on the course.

Tournaments: A 12-player minimum is needed to book a tournament. The banquet facility can accommodate 200 people.

Directions: From I-10 in Ontario, take the Haven exit. Follow Haven north one mile to 6th Street. Take a right on 6th; the course is on the right.

Contact: 11015 6th Street, Rancho Cucamonga, CA 91730, pro shop 909/481-6663, fax 909/481-6763.

86 COLTON GOLF CLUB

Architect: Robert Trent Jones Sr., 1963

18 holes　　　**Public**　　　**$12–20**

Northeast Detail map, page 296

This is an executive course designed for those who want to test almost every club in the bag. The Robert Trent Jones Sr. layout offers all his usual challenges in short form, including sculpted, well-protected greens. It's short, but still a championship course. Colton Golf Club was once owned by Sam Snead.

Play Policy and Fees: Green fees are $12 to walk weekdays, $20 to ride, and $14 to walk weekends, $20 to ride. Senior, nine-hole, and other special rates are available. Call for more information.

Tees and Yardage: *Men:* Back: yardage 3108, par 57, rating 54.6, slope 82; *Women:* Forward: yardage 2626, par 57, rating n/a, slope n/a.

Tee Times: Reservations can be booked seven days in advance.

Dress Code: Shirts must be worn.

Tournaments: Shotgun tournaments are available weekdays only. A 20-player minimum is required to book a tournament.

Directions: Take I-10 to Colton and exit at Riverside Avenue. Follow Riverside to Valley

Boulevard, turn right, and go about one mile to the course. Alternatively, take the Pepper exit off I-10 and proceed to Valley Boulevard. **Contact:** 1901 Valley Boulevard, Colton, CA 92324, pro shop 909/877-1712, fax 909/877-2226.

87 SAN BERNARDINO GOLF CLUB

Architect: Dan Brown, 1968
18 holes   **Public**   **$19–39**

Northeast Detail map, page 296

This busy course has only four bunkers, but five holes have water. Don't be fooled by the apparent short length. Typically, scores here are higher on average than on neighboring courses. Stay in the fairways or you're in tall rough. The San Bernardino County Men's Amateur Championships are held here the last weekend in August.

Play Policy and Fees: On weekdays, green fees are $19 walking and $29 riding. On weekends and holidays, green fees are $29 walking and $39 riding. A variety of daytime rates are offered, including senior, student, afternoon, and twilight. Please call for details.

Tees and Yardage: *Men:* Blue: yardage 5778, par 70, rating 67.5, slope 111; White: yardage 5543, par 70, rating 66.4, slope 109; *Women:* Red: yardage 5356, par 73, rating 69.9, slope 114.

Tee Times: Reservations can be booked seven days in advance.

Dress Code: No tank tops or bathing suits are allowed. Nonmetal spikes are preferred.

Tournaments: A 144-player minimum is needed to book a shotgun tournament. Carts are required.

Directions: In San Bernardino, take I-10 (San Bernardino Freeway) to the Waterman Avenue exit north and travel three-quarters of a mile to the course.

Contact: 1494 South Waterman Avenue, San Bernardino, CA 92408, pro shop 909/885-2414.

88 PALM MEADOWS GOLF CLUB

Architect: William F. Bell, 1958
18 holes   **Public**   **$14–32**

Northeast Detail map, page 296

This well-manicured course is on the old Norton Air Force Base. It has gentle, rolling fairways surrounded by a unique combination of eucalyptus and palm trees. Palm Meadows is an ideal course for golfers of all skill levels.

Play Policy and Fees: Green fees during the week are $14 walking and $22 riding. On weekends, fees are $17 walking, $32 riding. Senior and other rates are available. Please call for details.

Tees and Yardage: *Men:* Blue: yardage 6674, par 72, rating 71.5, slope 124; White: yardage 6404, par 72, rating 70.4, slope 120; *Women:* Red: yardage 5851, par 73, rating 72.9, slope 124.

Tee Times: Reservations may be booked seven days in advance.

Dress Code: No cutoffs or tank tops are allowed. Soft spikes are preferred.

Tournaments: This course is available for outside tournaments. Events may be booked up to two years in advance. The banquet facility accommodates up to 180 people.

Directions: Drive southeast of San Bernardino on I-10 to the Tippecanoe exit. Turn north and proceed 1.5 miles. Turn right on Palm Meadows Drive.

Contact: 1964 East Palm Meadows Drive, San Bernardino, CA 92408, pro shop 909/382-2002.

89 SOUTH HILLS COUNTRY CLUB

Architect: William P. Bell and William F. Bell, 1954
18 holes   **Private**   **$60–100**

Northeast Detail map, page 296

This old-style course requires solid shot-making ability. It requires precision iron play and a great imagination on and around the greens. The fairways are medium-width over rolling terrain. A fair number of bunkers surround the well-groomed, fast greens. It is a right-to-left course, favoring players who draw the ball (or fade it, for you lefties).

Play Policy and Fees: Reciprocal play is accepted with members of other private clubs at a green fee that ranges $60–100, depending on the club. Fee includes cart. Otherwise, members and guests only. The course is closed on Monday.

Tees and Yardage: *Men:* White: yardage 6301, par 72, rating 70.0, slope 121; *Women:* Red: yardage 5603, par 72, rating 74.1, slope 134.

Tee Times: Reciprocators should have their home pro call to make arrangements.

Dress Code: Appropriate golf attire and non-metal spikes are mandatory.

Tournaments: A 100-player minimum is required to book a tournament. Carts are required. Tournament fees are $140 per person. Events should be booked four months in advance.

Directions: From Los Angeles, travel on I-10 (San Bernardino Freeway) to the Citrus Avenue exit and drive south for one mile to the club at the Lark Hill Drive intersection.

Contact: 2655 South Citrus Avenue, West Covina, CA 91791, pro shop 626/332-3222, clubhouse 626/339-1231.

90 INDUSTRY HILLS GOLF CLUB

Architect: William F. Bell, 1979 and 1980

36 holes   Public/Resort $63–93

Northeast Detail map, page 296

This public facility has two highly regarded 18-hole courses, named after President Dwight D. Eisenhower and golfer/Olympian Babe Zaharias. The Eisenhower Course is long and extremely demanding, and it has been rated as one of the best public facilities in the United States by major golf publications. The greens are huge, but they're often tiered and undulating. Although shorter by about 100 yards, the Zaharias Course places a premium on accuracy. A shot-maker will excel here. Both courses cover rolling and hilly terrain and make use of a funicular, imported from Switzerland, to transport players. Qualifying rounds for the U.S. Open have frequently been held here.

The courses are affiliated with Pacific Palms Conference Resort, which offers golf packages. The resort can be reached at 800/524-4557.

Play Policy and Fees: Green fees are $63 Monday–Thursday and $93 Friday, weekends, and holidays. Fees include carts. Twilight, senior (50-plus), and other rates are offered. Registered guests at Pacific Palms Conference Resort receive member rates.

Tees and Yardage: Eisenhower Course—*Men:* Black: yardage 7199, par 72, rating 75.3, slope 143; Blue: yardage 6750, par 72, rating 72.9, slope 136; White: yardage 6272, par 72, rating 70.4, slope 130; *Women:* Red: yardage 5620, par 73, rating 74.1, slope 139. Zaharias Course—*Men:* Black: yardage 6821, par 71, rating 73.9, slope 135; Blue: yardage 6600, par 71, rating 72.9, slope 132; White: yardage 6124, par 71, rating 70.5, slope 126; *Women:* Red: yardage 5363, par 71, rating 73.3, slope 129.

Tee Times: Reservations can be booked seven days in advance.

Dress Code: Appropriate golf attire and non-metal spikes are required.

Tournaments: These courses are available for outside tournaments.

Directions: Travel on Highway 60 (Pomona Freeway) to the Azusa Avenue exit north. Drive 1.5 miles and turn left on Industry Hills Parkway and continue to the club. From I-10 (San Bernardino Freeway), take the Azusa Avenue exit; drive south on Azusa for three miles and turn right on Industry Hills Parkway to the club.

Contact: 1 Industry Hills Parkway, City of Industry, CA 91744, pro shop 626/810-4653, www.pacificpalmsresort.com.

91 CALIFORNIA COUNTRY CLUB

Architect: William F. Bell, 1956

18 holes   Private

Northeast Detail map, page 296

This is a mostly flat course except for a few elevated tees. Water hazards are minimal. In a traditional style, one finds an abundance of parallel fairways separated by mature trees. It plays extremely long, even though the landing zones are fairly wide open. It is always in excellent condition.

Play Policy and Fees: Members and guests only, although reciprocal play is accepted on a limited basis.

Tees and Yardage: *Men:* Blue: yardage 6804, par 72, rating 72.6, slope 129; White: yardage 6531, par 72, rating 71.3, slope 127; *Women:* Red: yardage 6098, par 74, rating 75.7, slope 136.

Tee Times: Reciprocators should have their club pro call to make arrangements.

Dress Code: Appropriate golf attire is required, and nonmetal spikes are encouraged.

Tournaments: This course is available for outside tournaments on Monday, Thursday, and Friday. A minimum of 24 players is required to book an event.

Directions: From Los Angeles, travel on Highway 60 (Pomona Freeway) east to the Crossroads Parkway exit. Head left over the freeway. Turn left at the stoplight onto Workman Mill Road. Turn right and go to Coleford Avenue, then turn left to the club.

Contact: 1509 South Workman Mill Road, Whittier, CA 90680 (P.O. Box 31, Whittier, CA 90601), pro shop 626/968-4222, clubhouse 626/333-4571, www.golfccc.com.

92 WILDWOOD MOBILE COUNTRY CLUB

Architect: Course designed, 1971
9 holes   **Private**

Northeast Detail map, page 296

This mostly flat par-3 course can be intimidating because it is so narrow. There's a fence on one side and mobile homes on the other. Only two holes measure more than 150 yards, so it's a good chance for members to fine-tune their short-iron play.

Play Policy and Fees: Members and guests only. This is a resident course.

Tees and Yardage: *Men and Women:* yardage 1190, par 27, rating n/a, slope n/a.

Tee Times: Not applicable.

Dress Code: Appropriate attire and soft spikes are required.

Tournaments: Not available for outside events.

Directions: This course is off Highway 60 (Pomona Freeway) in Hacienda Heights. Take the 7th Avenue exit north. At the first light, turn left on Clark Street, which runs into the course.

Contact: 901 South 6th Avenue, Hacienda Heights, CA 91745, pro shop 626/968-2338.

93 WHISPERING LAKES GOLF COURSE

Architect: William Tucker Jr., 1959
18 holes   **Public**   **$30–34**

Northeast Detail map, page 296

This course has level terrain, mature trees, and wide-open fairways. The driving range has lights. Some investment was made in 2004 to improve the condition of the layout.

Play Policy and Fees: Green fees are $30 weekdays and $34 weekends, including cart. Local resident, senior, student, and twilight rates are available.

Tees and Yardage: *Men:* Blue: yardage 6726, par 72, rating 71.4, slope 120; White: yardage 6310, par 72, rating 69.0, slope 114; *Women:* Red: yardage 6006, par 72, rating 73.0, slope 118.

Tee Times: Reservations can be booked seven days in advance for weekdays.

Dress Code: No tank tops are allowed on the course. Nonmetal spikes are required.

Tournaments: A 20-player minimum is needed to book an event.

Directions: Travel east of Los Angeles on Highway 60 (Pomona Freeway) to the Vineyard exit near Ontario. Turn left on Riverside Drive, travel two blocks, and turn left to the club.

Contact: 2525 Riverside Drive, Ontario, CA 91761, pro shop 909/923-3673, clubhouse 909/923-3675.

94 EL RIVINO COUNTRY CLUB

Architect: Joseph Calwell, 1956

18 holes   **Public**   **$20–33**

⬛ 🎏 🚗

Northeast Detail map, page 296

Built in 1956, this wide-open course has five lakes, level terrain, and mature trees. The first hole is a long, 626-yard par-6 designed to scare off the fainthearted. If the first hole doesn't send you packing, wait until the fourth. The green is surrounded on three sides by water.

Play Policy and Fees: Green fees are $20 weekdays and $33 weekends. Optional carts are $13 per rider.

Tees and Yardage: *Men:* Blue: yardage 6437, par 73, rating 70.3, slope 115; White: yardage 6142, par 73, rating 69.0, slope 111; *Women:* Red: yardage 5863, par 73, rating 71.8, slope 116.

Tee Times: Reservations can be booked 14 days in advance on weekdays and seven days in advance on weekends.

Dress Code: Golfers must wear sleeved shirts. Short shorts are not allowed. Nonmetal spikes are required.

Tournaments: No shotgun tournaments are allowed. Tournaments should be booked at least four months in advance.

Directions: From Los Angeles, travel east on I-10 (San Bernardino Freeway) to the Cedar Avenue exit in Bloomington. Head south on Cedar Avenue for three miles to El Rivino Road and then turn east on El Rivino Road to the club.

Contact: 5530 El Rivino Road (P.O. Box 3369), Riverside, CA 92519, pro shop 909/684-8905.

95 THE COUNTRY VILLAGE GOLF COURSE

Architect: Course designed, 1967

9 holes   **Private**

⬛ 🏌 3

Northeast Detail map, page 296

This short par-3 course has plenty of trees and sand traps, but no water as it winds through a senior apartment complex.

Play Policy and Fees: This course is part of a private senior residential community; residents and guests only.

Tees and Yardage: *Men:* Back: yardage 1073, par 27, rating n/a, slope n/a; *Women:* Forward: yardage 878, par 27, rating n/a, slope n/a.

Tee Times: Not applicable.

Dress Code: Appropriate attire and soft spikes are required.

Tournaments: This course is available for outside events. The banquet facility can accommodate 300 people.

Directions: From Los Angeles, take Highway 60 east for 50 miles and take the Country Village exit. Turn left; the apartment complex is on the left.

Contact: 10301 Country Club Drive, Mira Loma, CA 91752, pro shop 909/685-7466.

96 OAK QUARRY GOLF CLUB

Architect: Gil Morgan and Schmidt Curley Golf Design, 2000

18 holes   **Public**   **$65–95**

🏌 ⬛ 🎏 🚗 ⛳

Northeast Detail map, page 296

Situated in the Jurupa Mountains, this magnificent course winds its way through the white-faced, jagged terrain of the abandoned Jensen Quarry. The fourth, fifth, sixth, ninth, 13th, 14th, and 15th holes play right down in the old quarry itself, with the balance of the holes along the perimeter. If played from all the way back, this course can challenge even the best golfers.

Play Policy and Fees: Green fees are $65 Monday–Thursday, $75 Friday, and $95 weekends and holidays. Twilight rates are also available. All fees include cart and range balls.

Tees and Yardage: *Men:* Tournament: yardage 7002, par 72, rating 73.9, slope 137; Championship: yardage 6600, par 72, rating 71.9, slope 133; Regular: yardage 6028, par 72, rating 69.0, slope 126; *Women:* Red: yardage 5408, par 72, rating 75.4, slope 131.

Tee Times: Reservations are available up to two weeks in advance.

Dress Code: Collared shirts and nonmetal spikes are required.

Tournaments: Events may be booked up to one year in advance.

Directions: From I-10, exit at Sierra Avenue. Drive south three miles to the club entrance on the right. From Highway 60, exit at Valley Way north to Sierra Avenue. Turn left, and the clubhouse entrance will be on the left.

Contact: 7151 Sierra Avenue, Riverside, CA 92509, pro shop 909/685-1440, fax 909/685-5966, www.oakquarry.com.

97 RIVERSIDE GOLF CLUB

Architect: Charles Maud, 1948

18 holes　　　**Public**　　　**$20–37**

Northeast Detail map, page 296

This course is long but fairly level. It is lined with pine and mulberry trees. It is wide open, as are its mostly level greens. A clubhouse offers complete banquet facilities.

Play Policy and Fees: Green fees are $20 to walk weekdays, $32 to ride, and $25 to walk weekends, $37 to ride. Twilight, senior, and other rates are offered.

Tees and Yardage: *Men:* Blue: yardage 6760, par 72, rating 71.4, slope 112; White: yardage 6494, par 72, rating 70.0, slope 110; *Women:* Red: yardage 6203, par 73, rating 74.8, slope 120.

Tee Times: Reservations can be booked seven days in advance.

Dress Code: Collared shirts must be worn. Nonmetal spikes are required.

Tournaments: A 24-player minimum is needed to book a tournament. Shotgun tournaments are available. Tournaments should be booked 6–12 months in advance.

Directions: Driving toward Riverside, take the Columbia Avenue exit off the Riverside Freeway (Highway 91) and travel north on Orange Street to the club.

Contact: P.O. Box 391, Riverside, CA 92502, pro shop 909/682-3748, fax 909/682-9567.

98 REDLANDS COUNTRY CLUB

Architect: A. E. Sterling and J. H. Fisher, 1896; Alister Mackenzie, 1927

18 holes　　　**Private**　　　**$50–60**

Northeast Detail map, page 296

This course has a colorful history. It was originally built as a nine-hole layout just before the 20th century. In 1927, it was expanded to an 18-hole course under the direction of club member Raven Hornby with the consultation of Alister Mackenzie, according to club records. It has similar characteristics to the Lakeside Course at the Olympic Club and Cherry Hills Country Club near Denver, Colorado. There are lots of oaks and many tall cypress and pine trees.

Play Policy and Fees: Limited reciprocal play is accepted with members of other private clubs at a rate of $50 weekdays, $60 weekends, including cart; otherwise, members and guests only.

Tees and Yardage: *Men:* Blue: yardage 6228, par 70, rating 70.3, slope 124; White: yardage 6027, par 70, rating 69.3, slope 122; *Women:* Red: yardage 5709, par 73, rating 73.7, slope 127.

Tee Times: Reciprocators should have their club pro call to make arrangements.

Dress Code: Collared shirts and nonmetal spikes are required. Shorts can be no more than four inches above the knee. No denim is allowed on the course.

Tournaments: This course is available for limited outside events on Monday.

Directions: Take the Ford exit off I-10 east of San Bernardino and travel south for 1.5 miles. Bear right at the fork on Garden Hill and turn left on Garden Street to the club.

Contact: 1749 Garden Street, Redlands, CA 92373, pro shop 909/793-1295, clubhouse 909/793-2661.

99 YUCAIPA VALLEY GOLF CLUB

Architect: Rainville-Bye, 1999

18 holes　　　**Public**　　　**$29–52**

Northeast Detail map, page 296

This strategically bunkered course features dramatic mountain views and elevated greens. With several long greens, some severely sloping, Yucaipa Valley demands careful club selection. Long hitters will enjoy this course.

Play Policy and Fees: Weekday green fees are $29 to walk and $39 to ride. Weekend green fees are $41 to walk and $52 to ride. Midday, twilight, and senior rates are available.

Tees and Yardage: *Men:* Black: yardage 6803, par 72, rating 72.8, slope 128; Blue: yardage 6446, par 72, rating 71.2, slope 124; White: yardage 6066, par 72, rating 69.4, slope 120; *Women:* Red: yardage 5273, par 72, rating 70.9, slope 119.

Tee Times: Reservations can be made seven days in advance.

Dress Code: Soft spikes only. No tank tops, tube tops, tee shirts, cutoff shorts, swim trunks, or sandals are allowed.

Tournaments: This course is available for tournaments anytime on Monday, and after 11 A.M. on all other days of the week. Shotgun starts are permitted, and carts are not required.

Directions: Exit I-10 at Yucaipa Boulevard East to Oak Glen Road. Turn north on Oak Glen Road to Chapman Heights Road. Turn left (west) to the course.

Contact: 33725 Chapman Heights Road, Yucaipa, CA 92399, pro shop 909/790-6522, www.yvgc.com.

100 PENMAR GOLF COURSE

Architect: Course designed, 1962

| 9 holes | Public | $11.50–15 |

Southwest Detail map, page 297

This popular nine-hole course offers an interesting and challenging layout. You think the course should be a pushover, but the rough can twist your clubface and cause some higher scores. Good practice for your short game, plus, considering the dearth of public facilities in the immediate area, a welcome addition to the Venice/Santa Monica communities.

Play Policy and Fees: Green fees are $11.50 for nine holes weekdays and $15 weekends.

Tees and Yardage: *Men:* White: yardage 2496, par 33, rating 68.0, slope 107; *Women:* Yellow: yardage 2311, par 34, rating 66.0, slope 104.

Tee Times: Reservations can be booked seven days in advance with a City of Los Angeles Recreation and Parks membership card.

Dress Code: Nonmetal spikes are encouraged.

Tournaments: This course is available for outside tournaments, but shotgun starts are not allowed. A 24-player minimum is needed to book an event. Tournaments should be scheduled 12 months in advance.

Directions: In Venice, drive north on Lincoln Boulevard (Highway 1) to Rose Avenue, turn right, and go two blocks to the course.

Contact: 1233 Rose Avenue, Venice, CA 90291, pro shop 310/396-6228, fax 310/575-8251.

101 WESTCHESTER GOLF COURSE

Architect: Course designed, 1967

| 15 holes | Public | $16–21 |

Southwest Detail map, page 297

This very popular, 15-hole facility is adjacent to Los Angeles International Airport. Slow play is the norm out here, and walk-up waits are also considerable most times, particularly mornings when the regulars show up. A little squirrelly, the course begins with a short par-3, squeezed by the driving range on the right. Westchester features a large driving range and practice facility from which six teaching professionals operate. A club repair shop is also on-site.

Play Policy and Fees: Green fees are $16 Monday–Thursday and $21 Friday and weekends. Twilight and nine-hole rates are available. Carts are $16 (two people). Pull carts are $3.

Tees and Yardage: *Men and Women:* yardage 3470, par 53, rating n/a, slope n/a.

Tee Times: Reservations can be booked seven days in advance.

Dress Code: Appropriate attire and soft spikes are required.

Tournaments: A 12-player minimum is needed to book an event.

Directions: From I-405 in Westchester (near Inglewood), exit on Manchester Boulevard heading west and drive to the course on the left. From I-105 west, take the Sepulveda Boulevard exit heading north, under the airport runway. Turn left (west) on Manchester Boulevard, and the course is on the left.

Contact: 6900 West Manchester, Los Angeles, CA 90045, pro shop 310/649-9168.

102 RIO HONDO GOLF CLUB

Architect: John Duncan Dunn, 1923; Gerry Perkl, 1994
18 holes   **Public**   **$35–45**

Southwest Detail map, page 297

This is a level course with narrow, tree-lined fairways. Architect Gerry Perkl directed an extensive remodeling program in 1994 that included the addition of four lakes and a new irrigation system, making it one of the more popular designs in the area.

Play Policy and Fees: Green fees are $35 weekdays and $45 weekends. Optional carts are $11 per rider.

Tees and Yardage: *Men:* Blue: yardage 6360, par 71, rating 70.5, slope 122; White: yardage 6030, par 71, rating 68.9, slope 118; Gold: yardage 5657, par 71, rating 67.1, slope 114; *Women:* Red: yardage 5103, par 71, rating 69.4, slope 117.

Tee Times: Reservations can be booked seven days in advance.

Dress Code: Collared shirts and nonmetal spikes are required.

Tournaments: Shotgun tournaments are available weekdays only. Carts are required. A 24-player minimum is required to book a regular tournament. Events should be scheduled 12 months in advance. The banquet facility can accommodate 400 people.

Directions: Take I-710 (Long Beach Freeway) in Downey to the Firestone Boulevard exit. Drive east for one mile to Old River School Road. Turn left and continue one-half mile to the club.

Contact: 10629 Old River School Road,

Downey, CA 90241, pro shop 562/927-2329, fax 562/928-6245.

103 FORD PARK GOLF COURSE

Architect: Course designed, 1975
9 holes   **Public**   **$3.75–4**

Southwest Detail map, page 297

This is a short par-3 course, excellent for working on your short game. Leave your woods and long irons at home. Kids welcome!

Play Policy and Fees: Green fees are $3.75 weekdays and $4 weekends. Juniors and seniors receive discounts weekdays.

Tees and Yardage: *Men and Women:* yardage 1017, par 27, rating n/a, slope n/a.

Tee Times: Reservations are not accepted. All play is on a first-come, first-served basis.

Dress Code: Appropriate attire and soft spikes are required.

Tournaments: This course is available for outside tournaments.

Directions: In Bell Gardens, take the Garfield Avenue exit off I-5 and travel west about three miles to Park Lane. From there, take a right and you'll see the course.

Contact: 8000 Park Lane, Bell Gardens, CA 90201, pro shop 562/927-8811.

104 LOS AMIGOS COUNTRY CLUB

Architect: Ron Riege, 1965
18 holes   **Public**   **$21.50–28**

Southwest Detail map, page 297

This is a well-maintained public golf facility with large greens. It plays long, requiring significant approach shots to reach the greens in regulation. The greens can be quick when baked under the hot summer sun. Water comes into play frequently. This is one of the busier courses in Southern California.

Play Policy and Fees: Green fees are $21.50 weekdays and $28 weekends. Senior rates are available. Carts are $22.

Tees and Yardage: *Men:* Blue: yardage 5937, par

70, rating 68.1, slope 116; White: yardage 5763, par 70, rating 67.4, slope 113; *Women:* Red: yardage 5653, par 71, rating 72.0, slope 121.

Tee Times: Reservations can be booked seven days in advance.

Dress Code: No tank tops are allowed. Soft spikes are preferred.

Tournaments: Shotgun tournaments are available weekdays only. A 24-player minimum is required to book a tournament.

Directions: From the Long Beach Freeway (I-710) take the Imperial Highway east to Old River School Road. Turn left to the course on Quill Drive.

Contact: 7295 Quill Drive, Downey, CA 90242, pro shop 562/862-1717.

105 SOUTH GATE PAR-3 GOLF COURSE

Architect: William H. Johnson, 1948

9 holes   Public $5–6.25

Southwest Detail map, page 297

This short par-3 course is excellent for sharpening your short game. The longest hole, the eighth, measures 156 yards. Several large trees come into play.

Play Policy and Fees: Green fees are $5 weekdays and $6.25 weekends for nine holes. Senior bargain rates are available on Thursday and Friday. Call for information.

Tees and Yardage: *Men and Women:* yardage 1010, par 27, rating n/a, slope n/a.

Tee Times: Reservations are not accepted. All play is on a first-come, first-served basis.

Dress Code: Appropriate attire and soft spikes are required.

Tournaments: A 36-player minimum is needed to book a tournament.

Directions: From I-710 in South Gate, take the Imperial Highway off-ramp to Wright Road. The road merges into Atlantic Avenue. Turn left on Tweedy Boulevard, then right onto Pinehurst Avenue. The course is on the left.

Contact: 9615 Pinehurst Avenue, South Gate, CA 90280, pro shop 323/357-9613.

106 CANDLEWOOD COUNTRY CLUB

Architect: Harry Rainville and David Rainville, 1952

18 holes   Private $45

Southwest Detail map, page 297

Lots of mature trees line the narrow fairways, and a canal runs through the back nine. This course is not especially long, but it can be difficult in spots. Beware of the seventh hole, a par-5, 555-yarder, a double dogleg with water in front of the green. The most difficult shot on this hole is the approach, which most likely will require a short iron over water to the sizable green. But you're hitting downhill with out-of-bounds to the right and left— so beware. Candlewood was the first course to host an LPGA event in 1958. The winner was Patty Berg.

Play Policy and Fees: Reciprocal play is accepted with members of other private clubs at a rate of $45 weekdays to walk, plus $12 for an optional cart. Otherwise, members and guests only.

Tees and Yardage: *Men:* Back: yardage 6177, par 70, rating 70.4, slope 133; Middle: yardage 5894, par 70, rating 69.2, slope 131; *Women:* Forward: yardage 5708, par 70, rating 74.4, slope 135.

Tee Times: Tee times are first-come, first-served on weekdays, and there is a card draw on weekends. Reciprocators should have their club pro call to make arrangements.

Dress Code: Appropriate golf attire is required. Soft spikes are preferred.

Tournaments: This course is available for outside events on Monday. A 72-player minimum is needed to book a tournament. Events should be scheduled a year in advance. The banquet facility can accommodate 300 people.

Directions: Travel on I-605 to the Telegraph Road exit east and drive about 3.5 miles to the club.

Contact: 14000 East Telegraph Road, Whittier, CA 90604, pro shop 562/941-5310, fax 562/941-7160, www.candlewoodcc.com.

107 LA MIRADA GOLF COURSE

Architect: William F. Bell, 1961

18 holes   Public $21.50–28

Southwest Detail map, page 297

This is a well-maintained course with some trees. The greens are bunkered on most holes. Water comes into play on one hole, the 10th. The par-5s generally are reachable in two shots for longer hitters. This course permits fivesomes. Play can be slow, even during the week, taking up to five hours. The course record of 61 is held by Blaine McAllister. The tournament record of 63 belongs to Tiger Woods.

Play Policy and Fees: Green fees are $21.50 weekdays and $28 weekends. Senior, twilight, and junior rates are available. Carts are $12 per rider.

Tees and Yardage: *Men:* Blue: yardage 6056, par 70, rating 68.6, slope 114; White: yardage 5806, par 70, rating 67.4, slope 111; *Women:* Silver: yardage 5641, par 71, rating 71.8, slope 117.

Tee Times: Reservations can be booked seven days in advance.

Dress Code: No tank tops are allowed. Soft spikes only.

Tournaments: Shotgun tournaments are available weekdays only. A 24-player minimum is required to book a tournament.

Directions: From I-5, take Highway 39 east to Norwalk Boulevard. Go left on Norwalk for about one mile to La Mirada and follow it to the course.

Contact: 15501 East Alicante Road, La Mirada, CA 90638, pro shop 562/943-7123, clubhouse 562/943-3731.

108 NORWALK GOLF CENTER

Architect: Course designed, 1963

9 holes   Public $5.25–5.75

Southwest Detail map, page 297

This par-3 course is excellent for beginners, seniors, and those wishing to practice their short game. The longest hole is 130 yards. This course is lighted for night play.

Play Policy and Fees: Green fees are $5.25 weekdays and $5.75 weekends. Junior and senior rates are offered.

Tees and Yardage: *Men and Women:* yardage 1000, par 27, rating n/a, slope n/a.

Tee Times: Reservations are not accepted. All play is on a first-come, first-served basis.

Dress Code: The dress can be casual but should always be appropriate.

Tournaments: A 36-player minimum is needed to book an event.

Directions: Off I-5 in Norwalk, exit on Rosecrans Avenue. Go east on Rosecrans to Shoemaker Avenue and turn left to the course.

Contact: 13717 Shoemaker Avenue, Norwalk, CA 90650, pro shop 562/921-6500, fax 562/921-8830.

109 CHESTER WASHINGTON GOLF COURSE

18 holes   Public $21.50–28

Southwest Detail map, page 297

This is a wide-open course for free swingers and a confidence booster for everyone. There are few hazards to worry about.

Play Policy and Fees: Green fees are $21.50 weekdays and $28 weekends. Junior, senior, twilight, and super twilight rates are available. Carts are $12 per rider.

Tees and Yardage: *Men:* Blue: yardage 6320, par 70, rating 69.8, slope 119; White: yardage 6007, par 70, rating 68.3, slope 115; *Women:* Red: yardage 5680, par 73, rating 72.7, slope 121.

Tee Times: Reservations can be booked seven days in advance.

Dress Code: Collared shirts are required.

Tournaments: A 12-player minimum is needed to book an event. Tournaments should be booked 12 months in advance. The banquet facility can hold 250 people seated and 300 people for cocktails.

Directions: From I-405 driving south (near Inglewood and Hawthorne), take the Imperial Highway exit and drive west. Turn right on Western Avenue to the course.

Contact: 1930 West 120th Street, Los Angeles, CA 90047, pro shop 323/756-6975, clubhouse 213/756-2516, fax 213/779-7289.

110 THE LAKES AT EL SEGUNDO

Architect: Martin and Fred Hawtree, 1994

9 holes   **Public**   **$9–11**

Southwest Detail map, page 297

At LAX with a wait between flights? How about nine holes or a quick session on the range? This executive course just south of the airport has two par-4s, the longest of which is the 269-yard fourth hole. Three lakes and many sand bunkers make this course a challenge. Greens are big and mostly forgiving. The course features a superb, two-tiered, lighted driving range and practice facility that is open until 11 P.M. Tip: Try the tuna melt at the restaurant; it's far better than airplane food!

Play Policy and Fees: Green fees are $9 weekdays and $11 weekends. Senior and junior rates are available. No power carts, but pull carts are $2 with a $1 deposit.

Tees and Yardage: *Men:* White: yardage 1340, par 29, rating n/a, slope n/a; Women: Red: yardage 1268, par 29, rating n/a, slope n/a.

Tee Times: Reservations can be booked seven days in advance.

Dress Code: No tank tops are allowed on the golf course. Nonmetal spikes are required.

Tournaments: This course is available for outside tournaments.

Directions: From Los Angeles International Airport, take Sepulveda Boulevard south. Follow Sepulveda Boulevard half a mile past El Segundo Boulevard to the course. The course is on Sepulveda between El Segundo and Rosecrans Avenue.

Contact: 400 South Sepulveda Boulevard, El Segundo, CA 90245, pro shop 310/322-0202.

111 MANHATTAN BEACH MARRIOTT GOLF COURSE

Architect: Course designed, 1980

9 holes   **Public**   **$10–12**

Southwest Detail map, page 297

This short par-3 course near Los Angeles International Airport is next to the Manhattan Beach Marriott Hotel. It is hilly but walkable. There are few flat lies. Lake Kathleen comes into play on the first and eighth holes. The latter measures 177 yards and is the longest hole on the course. If you are in Los Angeles on business and enjoy golf, this is a nice stay-and-play option.

The Manhattan Beach Marriott owns the course, and reservations can be made by calling 310/546-7511.

Play Policy and Fees: Green fees are $10 weekdays and $12 weekends and holidays. Power carts are not available. Pull carts are $2.

Tees and Yardage: *Men and Women:* yardage 1220, par 27, rating n/a, slope n/a.

Tee Times: Reservations can be booked seven days in advance.

Dress Code: Proper golf attire is required.

Tournaments: This course is available for outside tournaments.

Directions: From Los Angeles International Airport, take I-405 south. Exit at Rosecrans Avenue. Drive west approximately five minutes to the course. The course is directly behind the Manhattan Beach Marriott Hotel.

Contact: 1400 Parkview Avenue, Manhattan Beach, CA 90267, pro shop 310/546-4551.

112 ALONDRA PARK GOLF COURSE

Architect: William P. Bell and William H. Johnson, 1947; Cecil B. Hollingsworth, 1950

36 holes   **Public**   **$10–28**

Southwest Detail map, page 297

There are two 18-hole courses at this facility, a regulation-length course and a par-3 course. The regulation course is level and open with ocean breezes from two miles away. It is not a difficult course, and there are very few places where golfers can get into trouble. The par-3 course is also flat and offers a good practice round. It is a good course for beginners and seniors. Architect Cecil B. Hollingsworth built the executive course in 1950.

Play Policy and Fees: Green fees are $21.50 weekdays and $28 weekends and holidays for the main course, $10 weekdays and $11.50 weekends for the par-3 executive course. Carts are additional.

Tees and Yardage: Regulation Course—*Men:* Blue: yardage 6577, par 72, rating 71.2, slope 118; White: yardage 6308, par 72, rating 69.8, slope 116; *Women:* Red: yardage 5976, par 72, rating 74.2, slope 117. Par-3 Course—*Men and Women:* yardage 2252, par 54, rating n/a, slope n/a.

Tee Times: Reservations may be booked seven days in advance.

Dress Code: Appropriate golf attire is required. Spikes are allowed.

Tournaments: Events may be booked 30 days in advance.

Directions: Off I-405 in Redondo Beach, take the Redondo Beach Boulevard exit and drive northeast. The course is on the corner of Prairie and Redondo Beach Boulevard.

Contact: 16400 South Prairie, Lawndale, CA 90260, pro shop 310/217-9915.

113 COMPTON GOLF COURSE

Architect: John Hilbur, 1958
9 holes   Public $3.50–7.50

Southwest Detail map, page 297

Although all the holes are par-3s, this is not a pitch-and-putt. The holes average 170 yards in length. Every Saturday, Compton Golf Course offers a junior program for children 7–14 years of age. Children are given a golf lesson, and 9–10 A.M. a teacher volunteers time in assisting students with classwork.

Play Policy and Fees: Green fees are $3.50 for nine holes and $6.50 for 18 holes on weekdays. Weekend green fees are $4 for nine holes and $7.50 for 18 holes.

Tees and Yardage: *Men and Women:* yardage 2600, par 27, rating n/a, slope n/a.

Tee Times: Reservations are on a first-come, first-served basis.

Dress Code: Appropriate attire and soft spikes are required.

Tournaments: This course is available for outside tournaments.

Directions: From Los Angeles, take I-405 south to the Alondra exit in Compton. Go west on Alondra Boulevard until you reach Atlantic Avenue. Go north on Atlantic Avenue until you reach Compton Boulevard. Take Compton Boulevard back over the freeway to the course.

Contact: 6400 East Compton Boulevard, Compton, CA 90221, pro shop 562/633-6721.

114 NEW HORIZONS GOLF COURSE

Architect: Ray Watts, 1964
9 holes   Private

Southwest Detail map, page 297

The very short par-3 course has narrow fairways and undulating greens. Its members enjoy it as a good course for a fun round of low-key golf.

Play Policy and Fees: This is a private course for residents of the surrounding development only.

Tees and Yardage: *Men and Women:* yardage 552, par 27, rating n/a, slope n/a.

Tee Times: Not applicable.

Dress Code: Appropriate attire and soft spikes are required.

Tournaments: This course is not available for outside events.

Directions: Take I-110 north to Torrance Boulevard. Follow Torrance Boulevard about one mile to Maple Avenue. Turn right and go about three-quarters of a mile to the club.

Contact: 22727 Maple Avenue, Torrance, CA 90505, pro shop 310/325-8926.

115 DOMINGUEZ GOLF COURSE

Architect: Course designed, 1960

18 holes   **Public**   **$14–16**

Southwest Detail map, page 297

This tight course has a lot of gullies and some bunkers. It's a tough par-3 course with undulating greens. The course has lights and is open 6 A.M.–10 P.M.

Play Policy and Fees: Green fees are $14 weekdays, $16 on weekends and holidays. Nine-hole, twilight, senior, and junior rates are available.

Tees and Yardage: *Men and Women:* yardage 1991, par 54, rating n/a, slope n/a.

Tee Times: Reservations can be booked seven days in advance.

Dress Code: Soft spikes are preferred.

Tournaments: This course is available for outside tournaments.

Directions: From I-405 north, exit on Main Street in Carson. The course is south of the freeway on the left.

Contact: 19800 South Main Street, Carson, CA 90745, pro shop 310/719-1942.

116 THE LINKS AT VICTORIA

Architect: Edwin H. Ripperdan, 1966, remodel Casey O'Callaghan, 2000

18 holes   **Public**   **$21.50–28**

Southwest Detail map, page 297

This facility reopened after a complete renovation in 2000. Environmental areas were added or enhanced for wildlife, new cart paths were added, and five feet of topsoil was replaced throughout the course. Most greens are protected by sand. There are no water holes. The 515-yard first hole may foil you right off the bat if you're not aware of the fairway bunkers. It is an easy course to walk. The course features large greens and wide fairways. The wind usually comes up in the afternoon.

Play Policy and Fees: Green fees are $21.50 weekdays and $28 for weekends. Nine-hole, senior, junior, twilight, and super twilight rates

are offered. Carts are additional. Specials including breakfast or lunch are often offered. Please call for details.

Tees and Yardage: *Men:* Blue: yardage 6804, par 72, rating 72.7, slope 119; White: yardage 6360, par 72, rating 70.8, slope 117; *Women:* Red: yardage 4862, par 72, rating 68.3, slope 115.

Tee Times: Reservations can be made at any time.

Dress Code: Soft spikes only.

Tournaments: This course is available for outside tournaments.

Directions: Take I-405 south of Los Angeles International Airport to the Avalon exit. Go north on Avalon to 192nd Street. Turn left on 192nd Street to the course.

Contact: 340 East 192nd Street, Carson, CA 90746, pro shop 310/323-6981.

117 SKYLINKS/LONG BEACH LEGENDS GOLF COURSE

Architect: William F. Bell, 1959; Cal Olson, 2004

18 holes   **Public**

Southwest Detail map, page 297

At press time this course (formerly Skylinks—the new name was thought to be Long Beach Legends, but final decisions had not been made) was closed for renovations. New elevated tees, enlarged greens, rerouted fairways, new grass, 475 yards of additional length, four new lakes, upgrades to the bunkers and drainage, new cart paths, 660 new trees, 1000 new shrubs, renovations to the clubhouse, and a new name are all part of the year-long renovation to this Long Beach facility. It is scheduled to reopen by early 2005. Note: The course can be noisy because it is across the street from the Long Beach Airport.

Play Policy and Fees: Green fees were not available at press time.

Tees and Yardage: Not available at press time.

Tee Times: Reservations can be made seven days in advance.

Dress Code: Appropriate golf attire is requested.

Tournaments: This course is available for tournaments.

Directions: Take I-405 south to Long Beach. Exit onto Lakewood Boulevard north. The course is three blocks down on the right, across from Long Beach Airport.

Contact: 4800 Wardlow Road, Long Beach, CA 90808, phone 562/421-3388.

118 VIRGINIA COUNTRY CLUB

Architect: William P. Bell, 1923;
renovated John Harbottle, 2002

18 holes   **Private**

Southwest Detail map, page 297

This is an old-style, medium-length, testy course. Golf history buffs will enjoy it for that reason alone. Mature trees line the fairways and putting is always tricky. It has been remodeled several times over the years, most recently in 2002 when John Harbottle renovated the greens and bunkers.

Play Policy and Fees: Reciprocal play is accepted with members of other private clubs; otherwise, members and guests only. Reciprocal rates are determined by what Virginia members would be charged at the reciprocating club.

Tees and Yardage: *Men:* Virginia: yardage 6629, par 71, rating 72.8, slope 130; Member: yardage 6251, par 71, rating 71.1, slope 126; *Women:* Club: yardage 5758, par 72, rating 74.3, slope 133.

Tee Times: Reciprocators should have their home professional call to make arrangements.

Dress Code: Appropriate golf attire and soft spikes are required.

Tournaments: All outside events must be member-sponsored.

Directions: Travel on I-405 to Long Beach Boulevard north. Turn left on San Antonio Road and right on Virginia Road to the course.

Contact: 4602 Virginia Road, Long Beach, CA 90807, pro shop 562/424-5211, clubhouse 562/427-0924.

119 LAKEWOOD COUNTRY CLUB

Architect: William P. Bell, 1933

18 holes   **Public**   **$21.50-28**

Southwest Detail map, page 297

This is a fairly flat course, built alongside an 11-acre lake that brings water into play on the second, third, sixth, ninth, 10th, 11th, and 12th holes. This course can be noisy because it is near Long Beach Airport. It is the site of the annual Queen Mary Open.

Play Policy and Fees: Greens fees are $21.50 weekdays and $28 weekends. Twilight, senior, and junior rates are offered. Carts are additional.

Tees and Yardage: *Men:* Gold: yardage 7033, par 72, rating 72.9, slope 124; Blue: yardage 6720, par 72, rating 71.4, slope 121; White: yardage 6423, par 72, rating 70.1, slope 117; *Women:* Silver: yardage 5926, par 72, rating 74.0, slope 126.

Tee Times: Reservations can be made seven days in advance. Be persistent and call early.

Dress Code: No tank tops are allowed on the course.

Tournaments: Shotgun tournaments are available weekdays only. A 24-player minimum is required to book a tournament.

Directions: Take the Lakewood Boulevard (Highway 19) exit off I-405 near the Long Beach Airport and head north. At Carson Street, turn left and drive about two miles to the club.

Contact: 3101 Carson Street, Lakewood, CA 90712, pro shop 562/429-9711, fax 562/429-7295.

120 HEARTWELL GOLF COURSE

Architect: William F. Bell, 1962

18 holes   **Public**   **$12-13**

Southwest Detail map, page 297

This well-conditioned course has elevated greens. The longest holes are the eighth and ninth at 140 yards. The course and driving range are lighted for night play. Tiger Woods began playing golf here as a child.

Play Policy and Fees: Green fees are $12 week-days and $13 weekends. Discounts available for Long Beach residents. Nine-hole rates are offered. Carts are additional.

Tees and Yardage: *Men and Women:* yardage 2143, par 54, rating n/a, slope n/a.

Tee Times: Reservations can be booked seven days in advance.

Dress Code: Golf attire is encouraged.

Tournaments: All shotgun tournaments must have approval of the golf commission. A 16-player minimum is needed to book a tournament.

Directions: Off I-405 in Long Beach, take the Lakewood Boulevard exit north. Follow Lakewood two miles to Carson Street and turn right. The course is 1.5 miles along on the right.

Contact: 6700 East Carson Street, Long Beach, CA 90808, pro shop 562/421-8855.

121 CYPRESS GOLF CLUB
Architect: Dye Designs, 1992

18 holes   Public $55–75

Southwest Detail map, page 297

Cypress is a spectacular and challenging championship 18-hole golf course. Water hazards, bunkers, and mounds have been used to create scenic and demanding holes. The greens are large with subtle breaks sure to challenge every golfer. The course record of 63 was set by Tiger Woods.

Play Policy and Fees: Green fees are $55 Monday–Thursday, $65 Friday, and $75 weekends. Twilight rates offered. All green fees include carts.

Tees and Yardage: *Men:* Blue: yardage 6510, par 71, rating 72.2, slope 134; White: yardage 6039, par 71, rating 69.5, slope 127; *Women:* Red: yardage 5188, par 71, rating 70.8, slope 129.

Tee Times: Reservations can be booked 14 days in advance.

Dress Code: Appropriate golf attire and non-metal spikes are required. No denim is allowed.

Tournaments: A 13-player minimum is needed to book a tournament. A banquet facility is available that can accommodate 200 people.

Directions: From I-605 near I-405, take the Katella Avenue exit to the racetrack and turn left.

Contact: 4921 Katella Avenue, Los Alamitos, CA 90720, pro shop 714/527-1800, fax 714/527-5749.

122 NAVY GOLF COURSE SEAL BEACH
Architect: Joseph B. Williams, 1966

27 holes   Military $9–36

Southwest Detail map, page 297

There are two courses here: a regulation-length 18-hole course called Destroyer and a nine-hole executive course called Cruiser. Tree-lined fairways, numerous water hazards, and offshore breezes add to the character and challenge of the Destroyer Course. Beware of the par-3, 186-yard ninth hole. Tee shots must carry over water to a bunker-lined green. Cruiser is a par-32, nine-hole executive course. Tiger Woods often played here; his father, Earl, was a career army officer. These are busy courses, with many rounds played annually.

Play Policy and Fees: Military personnel and guests only. Green fees are $9–36 for military personnel, depending on rank.

Tees and Yardage: Destroyer Course—*Men:* Blue: yardage 6819, par 72, rating 72.6, slope 125; White: yardage 6505, par 72, rating 71.2, slope 121; *Women:* Red: yardage 5914, par 72, rating 74.1, slope 128.

Tee Times: Reservations can be made seven days in advance.

Dress Code: Appropriate golf attire is required.

Tournaments: This course is available for charity events. Reservations must be made one year in advance. No weekend shotguns are allowed.

Directions: Heading south on I-405 (San Diego Freeway), bear right at the intersection with the Garden Grove Freeway to the Cypress–Valley View exit. Drive north 1.5 miles to Orangewood Avenue, then left to the course.

Contact: 5660 Orangewood Avenue, Cypress, CA 90630, pro shop 714/373-9155.

123 EL DORADO PARK GOLF COURSE

Architect: Course opened, 1955; redesign Ted Robinson Sr., 1962

18 holes   **Public**   **$29–34**

Southwest Detail map, page 297

This course is mostly level, with lots of doglegs and mature trees lining most fairways. Water comes into play on five holes. The Long Beach Open is played here annually.

Play Policy and Fees: Green fees are $29 weekdays and $34 weekends to walk. Optional carts are $12 per rider. Resident and twilight rates are available. To obtain resident rates, players must purchase and present a discount card from Long Beach's Recreation and Parks Department.

Tees and Yardage: *Men:* Black: yardage 6900, par 72, rating 72.6, slope 130; Blue: yardage 6491, par 72, rating 70.9, slope 126; White: yardage 6189, par 72, rating 69.6, slope 123; *Women:* Silver: yardage 5625, par 72, rating 72.5, slope 125.

Tee Times: Reservations can be booked six days in advance with a Los Angeles Recreation and Parks reservation card (818/291-9980) and three days without. Cards can be obtained at any city golf facility or by writing to City of Los Angeles, Department of Parks & Recreation, 200 North Main Street, Room 1380, City Hall East, Los Angeles, CA 90012-4172.

Dress Code: Appropriate golf attire is required.

Tournaments: A 64-player minimum is needed to book a tournament. A few shotgun tournaments are allowed each year.

Directions: From Los Angeles, travel south on I-405 (San Diego Freeway) to the Studebaker Road exit. Turn north and drive three-quarters of a mile to the club.

Contact: 2400 Studebaker Road, Long Beach, CA 90815, pro shop 562/430-5411.

124 OLD RANCH COUNTRY CLUB

Architect: Ted Robinson Sr., 1965 and 2001

18 holes   **Private**   **$100**

Southwest Detail map, page 297

This course is fairly level, but don't let that fool you. Because of Old Ranch's proximity to the ocean, winds can greatly affect playing conditions. The best holes on the course are the four finishing holes. The course was completely redesigned by Ted Robinson in 2001 from his original 1965 design.

Play Policy and Fees: Reciprocal play is accepted with members of other private clubs at a rate of $100, including cart; otherwise, members and guests only.

Tees and Yardage: *Men:* Gold: yardage 6831, par 72, rating 72.9, slope 135; Blue: yardage 6384, par 72, rating 70.9, slope 129; White: yardage 5985, par 72, rating 69.1, slope 125; *Women:* Red: yardage 5346, par 72, rating 71.6, slope 124.

Tee Times: Reciprocators should have their home professional call to make arrangements.

Dress Code: Appropriate golf attire and nonmetal spikes are required.

Tournaments: Please inquire.

Directions: Near Long Beach, take the Seal Beach exit off I-405 (San Diego Freeway) and turn right. Drive one-half mile to Lampson Avenue. Turn right again and drive one-half mile to the club.

Contact: 3901 Lampson Avenue, Seal Beach, CA 90740, pro shop 562/596-4611, clubhouse 562/596-4425, fax 562/594-0414.

125 SEA AIRE PARK GOLF COURSE

Architect: Course designed, 1952

9 holes   **Public**   **$4–4.50**

Southwest Detail map, page 297

This is a very short par-3 course. So short, in fact, it used to have a rule that you could only bring three clubs. The longest hole is 84 yards.

It is a good practice course for your short iron game. The course caters to beginners, and the price is right.

Play Policy and Fees: Green fees are $4 for Torrance residents and $4.50 for nonresidents. Senior and junior rates are available.

Tees and Yardage: *Men and Women:* yardage 510, par 27, rating n/a, slope n/a.

Tee Times: Reservations are not accepted. All play is on a first-come, first-served basis.

Dress Code: Appropriate attire and soft spikes are required.

Tournaments: This course is available for outside tournaments.

Directions: In Torrance, drive west on Sepulveda. Cross Anza and turn left on Reynolds, then left on Lupine Drive to the course.

Contact: 22730 Lupine Drive, Torrance, CA 90505, pro shop 310/543-1583.

126 PALOS VERDES GOLF CLUB

Architect: William P. Bell and
George C. Thomas Jr., 1924

18 holes   Semiprivate $205

Southwest Detail map, page 297

This course offers spectacular views, tree-lined fairways, small, fast greens, and plenty of sand. Do not let the yardage fool you—Palos Verdes is a challenge! Most fairways have generous landing areas, but to score well, hitting it down the middle is not enough. You must know what side of the fairway to play to save strokes. Water comes into play on only one hole. A steady ocean breeze can be expected throughout your round. Average and low handicappers will enjoy this course, but beginners may struggle no matter which tees are chosen. An excellent driving range is offered with many targets and both grass and mats, depending on conditions.

Play Policy and Fees: Nonmember play is accepted after 10 A.M. on Monday and after 2 P.M. Tuesday–Friday. Green fees for nonresidents and nonmembers is $205, carts included. Other rates are offered, please call for information. Memberships are available, although there is a wait list of several years and one must live in Palos Verdes Estates.

Tees and Yardage: *Men:* Blue: yardage 6219, par 71, rating 70.5, slope 129; White: yardage 5718, par 71, rating 68.2, slope 123; *Women:* Red: yardage 5459, par 71, rating 74.1, slope 136.

Tee Times: Reservations can be booked three days in advance.

Dress Code: Appropriate golf attire and non-metal spikes are required.

Tournaments: Shotgun tournaments are available only on Monday on a limited basis, and carts are required. A 128-player minimum is required to book a shotgun tournament. Events should be scheduled 12 months in advance. The banquet facility can accommodate 250 people.

Directions: From I-405 south of Los Angeles International Airport, take the Hawthorne Boulevard (Highway 107) exit. Go south six miles and take a right on Palos Verdes Drive. Stay on Palos Verdes Drive and take a left onto Via Campesina. The course is on the left.

Contact: 3301 Via Campesina, Palos Verdes Estates, CA 90274, pro shop 310/375-2759, clubhouse 310/375-2533, www.pvgc.org.

127 LOS VERDES GOLF CLUB

Architect: William F. Bell, 1964

18 holes   Public $20–25

Southwest Detail map, page 297

This course offers one of the best golf values in the state. It has wide views of the Pacific Ocean from most holes. The course is well maintained, with excellent putting surfaces. The 13th, 14th, and 15th present a tough three-hole sequence in addition to offering spectacular views of Catalina Island on clear days. Elevated greens from many fairways require more club than you think, and the wind can be a factor so close to the water. The only drawback here is that it is so popular a round can take a long time to play.

Play Policy and Fees: Green fees are $20 weekdays and $25 weekends. Twilight, senior, and junior rates are available. Carts are $22.

Tees and Yardage: *Men:* Back: yardage 6617, par 71, rating 71.7, slope 121; Middle: yardage 6234, par 71, rating 69.9, slope 117; *Women:* Forward: yardage 5772, par 72, rating 67.7, slope 113. Junior tees available.

Tee Times: Reservations can be booked seven days in advance.

Dress Code: No tank tops are allowed.

Tournaments: Shotgun tournaments are available weekdays only. A 24-player minimum is required for tournament play.

Directions: Travel on I-405 to Hawthorne Boulevard, turn south, and drive 11 miles to Los Verdes Drive. Turn right and follow it to the club. Or take I-110 (Harbor Freeway) south to Pacific Coast Highway (Highway 1), then west to Hawthorne Boulevard. Turn south and drive 5.5 miles to Los Verdes Drive. Turn right and follow Los Verdes Drive around to the course.

Contact: 7000 West Los Verdes Drive, Rancho Palos Verdes, CA 90275, pro shop 310/377-7888.

128 TRUMP NATIONAL GOLF CLUB LOS ANGELES

Architect: Pete Dye, 1999

18 holes   Public $99-195

Southwest Detail map, page 297

Formerly Ocean Trails Golf Club, this course played as a 15-hole layout until 2004 due to a landslide in June of 1999 that devastated three holes. The complete 18-hole route had long delays in reopening. The design features spectacular ocean views and several long, narrow greens. It is a demanding course with sloped, often narrow landing areas. Shots can be affected by ocean winds. Bring your "A" game to this course. The clubhouse contains an executive meeting room, award-winning dining, and banquet facilities that can accommodate around 300 people.

There are plans to construct 75 home sites at Ocean Trails. The residential community is named Costa Verde.

Play Policy and Fees: Green fees Monday-Thursday are $99-145, and fees Friday-Sunday are $145-195. All rates include a cart. Fees were expected to increase when the full 18 holes opened.

Tees and Yardage: *Men:* Black: yardage 7153, par 71, rating n/a, slope n/a; Blue: yardage 6561, par 71, rating n/a, slope n/a; White: yardage 6026, par 71, rating n/a, slope n/a; *Women:* Yellow: yardage 5319, par 72, rating n/a, slope n/a; Green: yardage 4631, par 72, rating n/a, slope n/a.

Tee Times: Reservations may be made up to three weeks in advance.

Dress Code: For men, collared shirts are required. For women, appropriate golf attire is requested. No denim is allowed, but shorts are permitted. Soft spikes only.

Tournaments: Groups of 8-16 players may book events three weeks in advance, groups of 16-50 may book six months in advance, and groups of more than 50 may book a year in advance.

Directions: From Los Angeles, take I-405 south to I-110. Head west on I-110 to Gaffey Street. Follow Gaffey Street west to 25th Street. Take a right on 25th Street, which turns into Palos Verdes Drive south. The course is on the ocean side.

Contact: 1 Ocean Trails Drive, Rancho Palos Verdes, CA 90275, pro shop 310/303-3241, clubhouse 310/265-5525, fax 310/265-5522, www.oceantrails.com.

129 ROLLING HILLS COUNTRY CLUB

Architect: Ted Robinson Sr., 1969

18 holes   Private $150

Southwest Detail map, page 297

This well-manicured course appears short, but it's tricky because of narrow, tree-lined fairways. Watch out for the 181-yard 11th hole. The green is surrounded by a pond that's filled with errant golf balls. Many holes feature large double greens and rolling fairways. The men's course record is 63, held by PGA Tour regular John Cook, and the women's record is 67, held by Mary Enright.

Play Policy and Fees: Reciprocal play is accepted with members of other private clubs at a rate of $150 including cart; otherwise, members and guests only.

Tees and Yardage: *Men:* Back: yardage 6112, par 70, rating 69.4, slope 122; Middle: yardage 5821, par 70, rating 67.9, slope 119; *Women:* Front: yardage 5432, par 70, rating 73.3, slope 131.

Tee Times: Reciprocators should have their home professional call to make arrangements.

Dress Code: No jeans, halter tops, or short shorts are allowed on the course. Walking shorts are acceptable (17 inches minimum length). Men must wear collared shirts. Nonmetal spikes are required.

Tournaments: This course is available for outside tournaments Monday only. A banquet facility accommodates 250 people.

Directions: South of Carson on I-110, turn onto the Pacific Coast Highway west (Highway 1) and drive for 2.25 miles to Narbonne. Turn left and drive one mile to the club.

Contact: 27000 Palos Verdes Drive, Rolling Hills Estates, CA 90274, pro shop 310/326-7731, clubhouse 310/326-4343, fax 310/326-4036, www.rollinghillscc.com.

130 HARBOR PARK GOLF COURSE

Architect: William H. Toomey, 1957
9 holes   **Public**   **$11.50–15**

🏌 📷 ⛳ 🎒 🚗 🍽

Southwest Detail map, page 297

This is a long nine-hole course. Those who find the fairway can tame this course, but the greens can be difficult, especially in summer when they tend to dry out. Harbor Park is under a National Bird Migration flight path; more than 260 different species of birds can be seen and occasionally felt.

Play Policy and Fees: Green fees are $11.50 weekdays and $15 weekends and holidays. Senior, junior, and twilight rates are available.

Tees and Yardage: *Men:* Back: yardage 3161, par 36, rating n/a, slope n/a; *Women:* Forward: yardage 3010, par 37, rating n/a, slope n/a.

Tee Times: A Los Angeles Recreation and Parks reservation card (818/291-9980) is required to make reservations, up to seven days in advance. Cards can be obtained at any city golf facility or by writing to City of Los Angeles, Department of Parks & Recreation, 200 North Main Street, Room 1380, City Hall East, Los Angeles, CA 90012-4172. Otherwise, same day play is accepted by showing up and placing your name on the waiting list.

Dress Code: Nonmetal spikes are recommended.

Tournaments: This course is available for outside tournaments. Call the Los Angeles City Recreation and Parks Department at 213/473-7055 for more information.

Directions: Take the Anaheim Street exit from I-110 south of Los Angeles. Turn right and drive two blocks north. The course is on the left.

Contact: 1235 North Figueroa Place, Wilmington, CA 90744, pro shop 310/549-4953, fax 310/549-4954.

131 RECREATION PARK GOLF COURSE

Architect: William F. Bell, 1969
18 holes   **Public**   **$22–29**

🏌 📷 ⛳ 🎒 🚗 🍽

Southwest Detail map, page 297

This course features rolling terrain and undulating greens. The course is fairly wide open and features many trees. It is usually nicely maintained. PGA Tour professional Paul Goydos holds the course record with 62.

Play Policy and Fees: Green fees for 18 holes are $22 weekdays and $29 weekends. Carts additional. Resident and twilight rates are available.

Tees and Yardage: *Men:* Blue: yardage 6405, par 72, rating 69.9, slope 111; White: yardage 6155, par 72, rating 68.8, slope 108; *Women:* Silver: yardage 5900, par 74, rating 73.3, slope 123.

Tee Times: Reservations can be booked six days in advance with a Los Angeles Recreation and Parks reservation card (818/291-9980) and three days in advance without. Cards can be obtained at any city golf facility or by writing to City of

Los Angeles, Department of Parks & Recreation, 200 North Main Street, Room 1380, City Hall East, Los Angeles, CA 90012-4172.

Dress Code: Soft spike shoes are preferred.

Tournaments: This course is available for outside tournaments and offers a full banquet facility that can accommodate 200 people. A 64-player minimum is needed to book a tournament. Events should be booked 12 months in advance.

Directions: Follow the Pacific Coast Highway (Highway 1) north from Seal Beach and exit at 7th Street. Drive half a mile on 7th to the course entrance. From I-405, take the Highway 22 exit west. Highway 22 becomes 7th Street. Follow signs to the course.

Contact: 5001 Deukmejian Drive, Long Beach, CA 90804, pro shop 562/494-5000, fax 562/498-4313.

132 BIXBY VILLAGE GOLF COURSE

Architect: Course opened, 1979
9 holes   **Public**   **$9–10.75**

Southwest Detail map, page 297

This hilly course has undulating greens and two lakes. The longest hole is the par-4 eighth at 322 yards.

Play Policy and Fees: Green fees are $9 weekdays and $10.75 weekends. Replay discounts offered. Senior and junior rates are also available.

Tees and Yardage: *Men:* Back: yardage 1567, par 29, rating n/a, slope n/a; *Women:* Forward: yardage 1417, par 29, rating n/a, slope n/a.

Tee Times: Reservations are not required, but they may be booked seven days in advance.

Dress Code: Shirts and shoes are necessary. Nonmetal spikes are encouraged.

Tournaments: Tournaments should be booked at least four weeks in advance.

Directions: On I-405 south in Long Beach, exit on Bellflower Boulevard and drive south. Veer left on the Pacific Coast Highway (Highway 1). Turn left on Loynes Drive and drive one-quarter mile to Bixby Village Drive. Turn left on Bixby Village Drive toward the course.

Contact: 6180 Bixby Village Drive, Long Beach, CA 90803, pro shop 562/498-7003.

133 LEISURE WORLD GOLF COURSE

Architect: Course designed, 1960
9 holes   **Private**

Southwest Detail map, page 297

This par-3 residential course is flat, with some nice oak trees around many of the holes. A pond offers some excitement on several holes.

Play Policy and Fees: Members only. This is a resident course.

Tees and Yardage: *Men and Women:* yardage 829, par 27, rating n/a, slope n/a.

Tee Times: Not applicable.

Dress Code: Appropriate attire and soft spikes are required.

Tournaments: This course is not available for outside events.

Directions: On I-405 heading south to Seal Beach, exit on Seal Beach Boulevard east. Turn left (south) and drive two blocks to the course on the right.

Contact: 13580 St. Andrews Drive, Seal Beach, CA 90740, pro shop 562/431-6586.

134 MEADOWLARK GOLF CLUB

Architect: William P. Bell, 1922
18 holes   **Public**   **$28–38**

Southwest Detail map, page 297

Established in the early 1920s, this is a rolling course with narrow, tree-lined fairways. The greens are small, so shot placement is essential. There are several water hazards. The course is close to the ocean in Huntington Beach, so it is subject to ocean breezes. The upside is that the air is usually clean and clear. This is a busy course with a classic feel.

Play Policy and Fees: Green fees are $28 Monday–Friday and $38 weekends and holidays. Twilight, senior, and junior rates are available. Carts are $12 per person.

Tees and Yardage: *Men:* Blue: yardage 5609, par 70, rating 66.8, slope 113; *Women:* White: yardage 5221, par 71, rating 70.8, slope 120.

Tee Times: Reservations are available 21 days in advance beginning at 6 A.M.

Dress Code: No tank tops are allowed.

Tournaments: This course is available for outside tournaments.

Directions: From south Orange County, drive north on I-405 to the Warner Avenue exit and go west four miles to Graham Street. Turn right to the club.

Contact: 16782 Graham Street, Huntington Beach, CA 92649, pro shop 714/846-1364, clubhouse 714/846-4450.

135 SEACLIFF COUNTRY CLUB
Architect: Press Maxwell, 1965; remodel Ron Fream, 1985
18 holes **Private**

Southwest Detail map, page 297

This course plays quite long, particularly for women. It features mature tree-lined fairways, and some holes are tight in the landing zones. Its undulating greens require some local knowledge, and the course is subject to afternoon breezes off the Pacific, about a mile away. It is a well-maintained layout that members enjoy for its views and relaxed pace.

Play Policy and Fees: Reciprocal play is accepted with members of other private clubs; otherwise, members and guests only. Reciprocator green fees are based on what Seacliff members would be charged at the reciprocator's club.

Tees and Yardage: *Men:* Gold: yardage 6935, par 72, rating 73.9, slope 136; Blue: yardage 6567, par 72, rating 72.3, slope 130; White: yardage 6079, par 72, rating 70.1, slope 125; *Women:* Red: yardage 5585, par 72, rating 73.5, slope 136.

Tee Times: Reciprocators should have their home professional call to make arrangements.

Dress Code: Appropriate golf attire is required. Nonmetal spikes are encouraged.

Tournaments: This course is available for outside tournaments on Monday. A 100-player minimum is needed to book a tournament.

Directions: In Huntington Beach, travel south on I-405 (San Diego Freeway) to the Golden West exit. Turn right and drive seven miles to Palm Avenue. Turn right and drive to the club.

Contact: 6501 Palm Avenue, Huntington Beach, CA 92648, pro shop 714/536-7575, fax 714/536-2417.

136 CATALINA ISLAND GOLF COURSE
Architect: John Duncan Dunn, 1925
9 holes **Resort** **$27–48**

Southwest Detail map, page 297

A trip to Catalina can be done in a day, or accommodations can be found on the island. The golf course is in a canyon with an occasional ocean view. It is a short but demanding nine-hole layout requiring every club in the bag. Greens are small and surrounded by traps, offering a challenge to any adventurous golfer. William Wrigley, of chewing-gum fame, sponsored tournaments here in the 1920s. It was an 18-hole course until World War II, when some land was lost to government concerns. Plans have long been discussed to build another 18-hole course out on this fun, relaxed island offshore from Los Angeles.

Play Policy and Fees: Green fees are $27 for nine holes and $48 for 18 holes. Carts are $14 for nine holes and $28 for 18 holes.

Tees and Yardage: *Men (18 holes):* White: yardage 4311, par 64, rating 61.9, slope 110; *Women (18 holes):* Red: yardage 4131, par 64, rating 64.0, slope 100.

Tee Times: Reservations may be booked up to seven days in advance.

Dress Code: Soft spikes are required. Tank tops and cutoffs are not allowed.

Tournaments: Outside tournaments are welcome and should be booked as far in advance as possible.

Directions: Take the boat from San Pedro Bay or Long Beach (Catalina Express or Catalina

Cruises) to Catalina Island, 26 miles off the mainland. In the summer, boats leave from Redondo and Newport Beaches. Helicopters are available from Long Beach and San Pedro. For information or boat reservations, call 949/673-5245.

Contact: 1 Country Club Road (P.O. Box 2019), Avalon, CA 90704, pro shop 310/510-0530, www.catalina.com.

137 FRIENDLY HILLS COUNTRY CLUB

Architect: Jimmy Hines, 1968

18 holes   **Private**   **$125**

> Southeast Detail map, page 298

This club features rolling terrain, undulating greens, and fairways pinched by mature, overhanging trees. The course gets off to a fast start at the first hole, a par-5, 558-yard heavyweight. The hole tees off over a lake to an uphill fairway and green that bunkered on both sides. The greens are treacherous. Located in the hills above Whittier, this layout is usually in immaculate condition. It has hosted many qualifying tournaments over the years, including those for the U.S. Amateur and the U.S. Open.

Play Policy and Fees: Reciprocal play is accepted with members of other private clubs at a rate of $125 plus optional cart at $12; otherwise, members and guests only. The course is closed on Monday.

Tees and Yardage: *Men:* Blue: yardage 6412, par 70, rating 71.5, slope 136; White: yardage 6136, par 70, rating 70.3, slope 133; *Women:* Red: yardage 5659, par 71, rating 74.9, slope 134.

Tee Times: Reciprocators should have their home professional call to make arrangements.

Dress Code: Appropriate golf attire and nonmetal spikes are required.

Tournaments: This course is available for outside tournaments on Monday only, with a minimum of 100 players.

Directions: From the Pomona Freeway (Highway 60) in Whittier, take the Hacienda Boulevard South exit and go south for three miles to Colima Road. Turn right and drive 2.25 miles to Mar Vista. Go left to Villaverde Drive and the club.

Contact: 8500 Villaverde Drive, Whittier, CA 90605, pro shop 562/693-3623, fax 562/693-8601, www.friendlyhillscc.com.

138 WESTRIDGE GOLF CLUB

Architect: Graves & Pascuzzo, 1999

18 holes   **Public**   **$55–80**

> Southeast Detail map, page 298

This scenic course plays around large hills and valleys, with three lakes placed along fairways and near greens. The location and layout take full advantage of surrounding views of the San Gabriel Mountains. It is a well-maintained and popular course that provides a good round at a fair price.

Play Policy and Fees: Green fees are $55 Monday–Thursday, $65 Friday, and $80 on the weekends. Twilight and super twilight rates are offered. Memberships are available.

Tees and Yardage: *Men:* Black: yardage 6615, par 72, rating 72.7, slope 135; Blue: yardage 6267, par 72, rating 71.1, slope 134; White: yardage 5862, par 72, rating 68.6, slope 128; *Women:* Red: yardage 5150, par 72, rating 71.3, slope 125.

Tee Times: Reservations may be made up to a week in advance.

Dress Code: Collared shirts are required, and denim is not allowed. Soft spikes only.

Tournaments: A 20-player minimum is required to book an event. The banquet room holds 160 people, plus another 150 on the terrace.

Directions: From Los Angeles, head south on I-5. Take the Beach Boulevard exit and head north to the Imperial Highway. Take a right on the Imperial Highway and another right on La Habra Hills Drive, then follow it to the course.

Contact: 1400 South La Habra Hills Drive, La Habra, CA 90631, pro shop 562/690-4200, fax 562/690-4300, www.westridgegolfclub.com.

139 HACIENDA GOLF CLUB

Architect: Max Behr, 1920

18 holes   **Private**   **$75**

🏌 📷 🍽 🚗 🅿

Southeast Detail map, page 298

This course was built in 1920, during the Golden Age of course design. It is a classic, old-style layout, with narrow, tree-lined fairways that traverse a rolling terrain. The 16th hole is a gem. It's 194 yards over a lake to a two-tiered green. The USGA Women's Amateur Championship was held here in 1966. The course record is 62 for men, set by Tiger Woods.

Play Policy and Fees: Reciprocal play is accepted with members of other private clubs at a rate of $75, plus $11 for an optional cart; otherwise, members and guests only.

Tees and Yardage: *Men:* Blue: yardage 6660, par 71, rating 72.7, slope 133; White: yardage 6380, par 71, rating 71.3, slope 129; *Women:* Red: yardage 5833, par 72, rating 74.9, slope 138.

Tee Times: Reciprocators should have their home professional call to make arrangements.

Dress Code: Slacks or Bermuda-length shorts are required, and nonmetal spikes are mandatory.

Tournaments: This course is available for outside tournaments on Monday. Events should be booked 12 months in advance. The banquet facility can accommodate up to 280 people.

Directions: Travel on Highway 60 (Pomona Freeway) to La Habra Heights and exit on Hacienda Boulevard south. Drive four miles to East Road and turn left. Continue three-quarters of a mile to the club.

Contact: 718 East Road, La Habra Heights, CA 90631, pro shop 562/697-3610.

140 LOS ANGELES ROYAL VISTA GOLF COURSE

Architect: Ted Robinson Sr., 1965

27 holes   **Semiprivate**   **$25–36**

🏌 📷 🍽 ⛳ 🚗 🅿

Southeast Detail map, page 298

All three nonets are moderately hilly, with mature trees and some water. The shorter South Course is the narrowest, and the East Course plays the longest. On the South Course, watch out for the second hole. It's a par-3, 199-yarder that requires a delicate tee shot over a lake to a green tucked between two hills. The first hole on the East Course is a difficult starting hole. There is water on the left, a major dogleg left after the tee shot, and a straight, uphill approach to a shallow, extremely elevated green. Los Angeles Royal Vista used to be a private facility. It offers showers, banquets, and a sports bar.

Play Policy and Fees: Green fees are $25 weekdays and $36 weekends. Carts are $12 per person. Various other rates are offered; please call for details. Memberships are available.

Tees and Yardage: East/North—*Men:* Blue: yardage 6605, par 71, rating 70.6, slope 121; White: yardage 6034, par 71, rating 68.0, slope 114; *Women:* Red: yardage 5528, par 71, rating 71.2, slope 120. North/South—*Men:* Blue: yardage 6259, par 71, rating 69.3, slope 119; White: yardage 5716, par 71, rating 66.8, slope 114; *Women:* Red: yardage 5316, par 71, rating 69.9, slope 118. South/East—*Men:* Blue: yardage 6366, par 72, rating 69.5, slope 120; White: yardage 5884, par 72, rating 67.4, slope 116; *Women:* Red: yardage 5678, par 72, rating 71.1, slope 117.

Tee Times: Reservations can be booked seven days in advance by calling 800/334-6533.

Dress Code: No tank tops are allowed on the course.

Tournaments: Shotgun tournaments are available weekdays only. Carts are required before 11 A.M. on weekends. A 12-player minimum is required to book a tournament. The banquet facility can accommodate 500 people.

Directions: From Los Angeles, travel on Highway 60 (Pomona Freeway) east to the Fairway Drive exit and turn right on the Brea Canyon cutoff. At Colima Road, turn left to the club.

Contact: 20055 East Colima Road, Walnut, CA 91789, pro shop 909/595-7441, www.larv.com.

141 DIAMOND BAR GOLF COURSE

Architect: William F. Bell, 1962

18 holes　　**Public**　　**$21–27**

🏌 📷 🍽 🥢 🚗 🍴

Southeast Detail map, page 298

This is a tree-lined course with water hazards on four holes and doglegs on several others. The course is very open, so errant tee shots are salvageable. Golfers of all abilities are welcome and will enjoy this layout.

Play Policy and Fees: Green fees are $21 weekdays and $27 weekends. Twilight, super twilight, and nine-hole rates are offered. Carts are $11 per rider.

Tees and Yardage: *Men:* Blue: yardage 6810, par 72, rating 72.8, slope 124; White: yardage 6475, par 72, rating 70.4, slope 119; *Women:* Red: yardage 6014, par 73, rating 73.9, slope 122.

Tee Times: Reservations can be booked seven days in advance.

Dress Code: Collared shirts and nonmetal spikes are preferred.

Tournaments: Shotgun tournaments are available weekdays only. A 24-player minimum is required to book a tournament. Events can be scheduled 12 months in advance. The banquet facility can accommodate up to 250 people.

Directions: From downtown Los Angeles, take Highway 60 (Pomona Freeway) east 24 miles to Grand Avenue. Turn right, go to the next light, and turn left to the course.

Contact: 22751 East Golden Springs, Diamond Bar, CA 91765, pro shop 909/861-8282, clubhouse 909/861-5757, www.diamondbar golf.com.

142 WESTERN HILLS GOLF & COUNTRY CLUB

Architect: Harry Rainville and David Rainville, 1963

18 holes　　**Private**　　**$35**

🏌 📷 🍽 🚗 🍴

Southeast Detail map, page 298

This rolling course has mature trees and is well bunkered. There is a double green that serves two holes, the 12th and 14th. Water comes into

play on only one hole. The U.S. Amateur qualifier has been held here in the past.

Play Policy and Fees: Reciprocal play is accepted with members of other private clubs Monday–Friday; otherwise, members and guests only. Reciprocal fees are $35, plus optional cart at $11 per person.

Tees and Yardage: *Men:* Blue: yardage 6746, par 72, rating 72.8, slope 132; White: yardage 6401, par 72, rating 71.0, slope 128; *Women:* Red: yardage 5882, par 72, rating 75.9, slope 136.

Tee Times: Reciprocators should have their home professional call to make arrangements.

Dress Code: Collared shirts and nonmetal spikes are required. No jeans are allowed on the course.

Tournaments: The course is available for outside tournaments on Monday.

Directions: From Highway 71, take Chino Hills Parkway west to Carbon Canyon Road. Turn left and drive two miles to the club. From Highway 57, take Lambert Road east 11 miles to the club.

Contact: 1800 Carbon Canyon Road, Chino, CA 91709, pro shop 714/528-6400, fax 714/528-1513.

143 LOS SERRANOS GOLF & COUNTRY CLUB

Architect: John Duncan Dunn, 1925 (North Course); Zell Eaton, 1964 (South Course)

36 holes　　**Public**　　**$26–65**

🏌 📷 🍽 🥢 🚗 🍴

Southeast Detail map, page 298

There are two very nice golf courses at this facility, and the owners are continually improving and upgrading the facilities. That fact makes them two of the best and most popular public facilities in Southern California. The South Course is long and hilly and gets breezy in the afternoons. It is the longest golf course in California at more than 7400 yards, and it plays that long. The North Course is shorter and the more forgiving of the two. It was built in 1925 on scenic, rolling land that once was a horse ranch. The South Course has six par-5s, including the first two holes, each of them reachable in two for the longer hitter. Almost 2000 new trees were planted in 2003 to replace others that had been lost to disease. Tennis great Jack Kramer owns this facility, so tennis is also very popular at this public country club.

Play Policy and Fees: Green fees for the North Course are $26 Monday–Friday, $50 including mandatory cart weekends and holidays. Fees for the South Course are $32 Monday–Friday, $65 including mandatory carts on weekends and holidays. Twilight, senior, and junior rates are offered.

Tees and Yardage: North—*Men:* Blue: yardage 6430, par 72, rating 71.3, slope 129; White: yardage 6201, par 72, rating 70.2, slope 127; *Women:* Gold: yardage 5938, par 74, rating 73.9, slope 125. South—*Men:* Black: 7470, par 74, rating 76.1, slope 135; Blue: yardage 7104, par 74, rating 74.0, slope 134; White: yardage 6656, par 74, rating 71.4, slope 131; *Women:* Gold: yardage 5954, par 74, rating 73.9, slope 125.

Tee Times: Reservations are accepted seven days in advance.

Dress Code: No tank tops or cutoff shorts are allowed. Soft spikes only.

Tournaments: Tournaments welcome. A 20-player minimum is needed to book an event.

Directions: From Highway 60 (Pomona Freeway), take the Pomona/Corona Highway 71 exit and travel south on Highway 71 for five miles to the Soquel Canyon Parkway exit. Take a right on Soquel Canyon Parkway to Los Serranos Road. Turn right to the club.

Contact: 15656 Yorba Avenue, Chino, CA 91709, pro shop 909/597-1711, clubhouse 909/597-1769, www.losserranoscountryclub.com.

144 EL PRADO GOLF COURSES

Architect: Harry Rainville and David Rainville, 1976
36 holes   **Public**   **$24–34**

Southeast Detail map, page 298

There are two 18-hole championship courses here. The Chino Creek Course is a little longer and the more challenging of the two, with water hazards and several out-of-bounds. There are

rolling hills, but the course is very walkable. The Butterfield Stage Course is flatter and more forgiving, making it receptive to beginning golfers. It, too, has water. Greens are usually nicely maintained.

Play Policy and Fees: Green fees are $24 weekdays and $34 weekends. Senior rates are available.

Tees and Yardage: Butterfield Stage—*Men:* Blue: yardage 6508, par 72, rating 70.6, slope 116; White: yardage 6251, par 72, rating 68.9, slope 111; *Women:* Red: yardage 5503, par 72, rating 72.0, slope 118. Chino Creek—*Men:* Blue: yardage 6671, par 72, rating 71.5, slope 119; White: yardage 6296, par 72, rating 69.3, slope 114; *Women:* Red: yardage 5596, par 72, rating 72.1, slope 121.

Tee Times: Weekend reservations may be booked the Monday prior.

Dress Code: Nonmetal spikes are required.

Tournaments: Events should be scheduled at least six months in advance. The banquet facility can accommodate 400 people.

Directions: From Los Angeles, travel east on Highway 60 (Pomona Freeway) to the Corona Freeway/Highway 71 exit. Turn right and drive six miles to Euclid Avenue. Turn left on Euclid Avenue to Pine Street. Turn left to the course.

Contact: 6555 Pine Avenue, Chino, CA 91710, pro shop 909/597-1753, www.elpradogc.com.

145 PARADISE KNOLLS GOLF CLUB

Architect: Course designed, 1965
18 holes   **Public**   **$21–44**

Southeast Detail map, page 298

This is a pretty course, with an interesting mix of mature eucalyptus, palm, and pepper trees that act as natural dividers between the fairways. The course is fairly level, with parallel fairways and small greens. It is a women-friendly facility in that it is not overly long from the gray tees, and the ball can be played on the ground.

Play Policy and Fees: Green fees are $21 walking and $33 riding on weekdays, and $32 walking and $44 riding on weekends. Twilight and senior rates are available.

Tees and Yardage: *Men:* Blue: yardage 6281, par 72, rating 70.0, slope 122; *Women:* Gray: yardage 5863, par 72, rating 67.9, slope 116.

Tee Times: Reservations can be booked seven days in advance.

Dress Code: Appropriate attire and soft spikes are required.

Tournaments: A 16-player minimum is needed to book a tournament.

Directions: From Riverside, travel east on Highway 60 (Pomona Freeway) to I-15 south. Take the Limonite exit and turn left. Drive about three miles to the course.

Contact: 9330 Limonite Avenue, Riverside, CA 92509, pro shop 909/685-7034, fax 909/685-8504.

146 GOOSE CREEK GOLF CLUB
Architect: Brian Curley, 1999
18 holes   **Public**   **$35–55**

🧍 🏌 💼 🛍 🛺

Southeast Detail map, page 298

Goose Creek is an expertly run public course that has a links feel, giving players plenty of options for reaching the green. The front nine is shorter than the back, with a marsh coming into play on several holes. For the most part, the course is open off the tee, and although the bunkers are imposing, they are playable. Chipping aprons collect golf balls that miss the greens, from which players can putt or chip, depending on your preference and skill. The course is very enjoyable for everyone, including women and seniors. Goose Creek offers one of the largest practice facilities in Southern California.

Play Policy and Fees: Green fees are $35 Monday–Thursday, $45 Friday, and $55 weekends and holidays. Senior, junior, and twilight rates are offered. Optional carts are additional.

Tees and Yardage: *Men:* Blue: yardage 6520, par 70, rating 71.1, slope 127; White: yardage 6121, par 70, rating 69.4, slope 121; *Women:* Red: yardage: 5052, par 70, rating 69.4, slope

115; Gold: yardage 4545, par 70, rating 62.0, slope 103.

Tee Times: Reservations can be made seven days in advance.

Dress Code: Casual dress is okay, but shirts and shoes are required. Soft spikes are preferred.

Tournaments: Events can be booked one year in advance. A 20-player minimum is required to book an event. The banquet facility can accommodate up to 150 people.

Directions: From Anaheim, take Highway 91 east to I-15. Take I-15 north for five miles and exit at Limonite. Follow Limonite to Wineville and take a right. Wineville turns into 68th Street. The course is on the right-hand side.

Contact: 11418 68th Street, Mira Loma, CA 91752, pro shop 909/735-3982, fax 909/735-6721, www.goosecreekgolf.com.

147 INDIAN HILLS GOLF CLUB
Architect: Harold Heers and Jimmy Powell, 1964
18 holes   **Public**   **$30–48**

🏌 💼 🛺 🛍

Southeast Detail map, page 298

This is a rolling course with numerous mature trees and no parallel fairways. The two nines loop out and back from the clubhouse. The greens are undulating and can be tough. Walking on this hilly course is for the adventurous. The course record is 64.

Play Policy and Fees: Green fees are $30 weekdays and $48 weekends. Twilight and super twilight rates are offered. All fees include cart.

Tees and Yardage: *Men:* Championship: yardage 6104, par 70, rating 69.7, slope 125; Regular: yardage 5836, par 70, rating 68.5, slope 124; *Women:* Forward: yardage 5562, par 72, rating 72.5, slope 120.

Tee Times: Reservations can be booked seven days in advance by calling 909/360-2089.

Dress Code: Collared shirts are required.

Tournaments: Shotgun tournaments are available. Carts are required. A 20-player minimum is needed to book a regular tournament. Tournaments can be booked 12 months in advance.

Directions: From Los Angeles, take Highway

60 (Pomona Freeway) east to the Van Buren/Etiwanda Avenue exit in Riverside. Travel south on Van Buren Boulevard for 4.5 miles to Limonite Avenue and turn left. Drive to Clay Street and turn left, then right on Lakeside Drive. Follow the signs to the club on top of the hill.

Contact: 5700 Clubhouse Drive, Riverside, CA 92509, pro shop 909/360-2090, www.indian hillsgolf.com.

148 JURUPA HILLS COUNTRY CLUB

Architect: William F. Bell, 1960
18 holes   **Public**   **$31–50**

Southeast Detail map, page 298

Trees of all sizes outline this course in the Riverside foothills. Locally, the course is known for its well-kept, fast greens that can be difficult to judge because of the sloping terrain. There is surprising elevation change on some holes. It's a favorite spot for local tournaments. The SCPGA Senior's Championship is held here. Olin Dutra, the club's first pro, was a former U.S. Open champ. Dutra, Gary McCord, and Bill Lytle share the course record of 62.

Play Policy and Fees: Green fees are $31 weekdays and $50 weekends, including cart. Senior and twilight rates are available.

Tees and Yardage: *Men:* Back: yardage 6022, par 70, rating 68.5, slope 119; *Women:* Forward: yardage 5773, par 71, rating 73.4, slope 123.

Tee Times: Reservations are suggested and may be booked seven days in advance.

Dress Code: Collared shirts are required.

Tournaments: This course specializes in tournaments and golf outings. The banquet facility can accommodate 160 people.

Directions: From Ontario, take Highway 60 (Pomona Freeway) east to the Van Buren/Etiwanda Avenue exit in Riverside. Travel east on Van Buren Boulevard for 4.5 miles and turn left on Limonite Avenue. Drive 1.5 miles to Camino Real. Turn right and drive to Linares. Turn left to the club.

Contact: 6161 Moraga Avenue, Riverside, CA 92509, pro shop 909/685-7214, fax 909/685-4752.

149 FAIRMOUNT PARK GOLF CLUB

9 holes   **Public**   **$8–10**

Southeast Detail map, page 298

This is an older course, but it has character. Mature palm and cypress trees beautify the level fairways. It's a left-to-right course with some sharp doglegs. The first hole can be a tester thanks to a large tree in the middle of the fairway. The course includes a 60-stall, night-lighted driving range.

Play Policy and Fees: Green fees are $8 for nine holes weekdays, $10 weekends. Repeat rounds are $4. Carts are additional.

Tees and Yardage: *Men (18 holes):* Blue/White: yardage 6165, par 72, rating 68.6, slope n/a; *Women (9 holes):* Red: yardage 2610, par 36, rating n/a, slope n/a.

Tee Times: Reservations can be booked seven days in advance.

Dress Code: Casual dress is accepted, but shirts must worn at all times.

Tournaments: Shotgun tournaments are available weekdays only. A 72-player minimum is needed to book a shotgun tournament. A $2 surcharge is added for all events.

Directions: From Los Angeles, travel east on Highway 60 (Pomona Freeway) to Riverside. Take the Market Street exit to the course.

Contact: 2681 Dexter Drive, Riverside, CA 92501, pro shop 909/682-2202.

150 VAN BUREN GOLF CENTER

Architect: Murry Nonhoff, 1996
18 holes   **Public**   **$11–17**

Southeast Detail map, page 298

This is an 18-hole executive course, with 11 holes lighted for night play, but you get to go round on those holes twice at night for a 22-hole loop.

It is a straightforward layout that requires most clubs in the bag, although you can leave the woods at home. There are three par-4s, the rest par-3s. Water comes into play on two holes. It is a fun (if not scenic) course for beginning golfers. The driving range is also lighted for night use.

Play Policy and Fees: Weekday green fees are $11 during the day, $14 evenings. Weekend green fees are $17 until noon, $16 noon–5 P.M., and $14 evenings. Junior and early bird rates are offered.

Tees and Yardage: *Men:* Back: yardage 2588, par 57, rating n/a, slope n/a; Middle: yardage 2362, par 57, rating n/a, slope n/a; *Women:* Forward: yardage 2063, par 57, rating n/a, slope n/a.

Tee Times: Reservations can be made 14 days in advance.

Dress Code: Collared shirts are required.

Tournaments: A 16-player minimum is required to book an event. The banquet facility can accommodate 50 people.

Directions: From Los Angeles, take Highway 60 east and get off at Van Buren Boulevard. Turn right on Van Buren and drive 6.5 miles. The course is on the right, just past Central Avenue.

Contact: 6720 Van Buren Boulevard, Riverside, CA 92503, pro shop 909/688-2563, fax 909/688-6830, www.vanburengolf.com.

151 VICTORIA CLUB

Architect: Charles Maud, 1903; Max Behr, 1923; William P. Bell, 1949

18 holes   Private $100

Southeast Detail map, page 298

This course has that old-style look to it and no wonder—it was built in 1903. It has been revised many times over the years, with William P. Bell, Max Behr, and others working on it at one time or another. There are many interesting holes. There is a lake on the first hole, and a large creekbed meanders through the course. Accurate placement is crucial because of flanking trees.

Play Policy and Fees: Reciprocal play is ac-

cepted with members of other private clubs on Tuesday and Thursday; otherwise, members and guests only. Reciprocal fees are $100, plus optional cart.

Tees and Yardage: *Men:* Blue: yardage 6483, par 72, rating 71.3, slope 130; White: yardage 6256, par 72, rating 70.2, slope 128; *Women:* Red: yardage 5822, par 73, rating 74.3, slope 130.

Tee Times: Reciprocal players should have their home professional call to make arrangements.

Dress Code: Collared shirts and nonmetal spikes are required. Bermuda shorts must be 18 inches in length.

Tournaments: Outside events are limited to Monday.

Directions: In Riverside, take the Central Avenue exit off Highway 91 (Riverside Freeway), travel east for one mile to the first traffic light (Victoria), and turn left. From there, go one-half mile to Arroyo Drive and turn right to the club entrance.

Contact: 2521 Arroyo Drive, Riverside, CA 92506, pro shop 909/684-5035, clubhouse 909/683-5323.

152 CANYON CREST COUNTRY CLUB

Architect: Olin Dutra, 1964

18 holes   Private

Southeast Detail map, page 298

This course is very hilly, with lots of mature trees and numerous bunkers. Accurate shot placement is critical, or your round could become a nightmare. A brush-filled dry creekbed runs through the course, lining six holes. Homes line the perimeter, which means out-of-bounds on nearly every hole. Carts are advisable because the hills make for strenuous walking.

Play Policy and Fees: Reciprocal play with other private clubs is accepted; otherwise, members and guests only. The course is closed on Monday.

Tees and Yardage: *Men:* Blue: yardage 6565, par 72, rating 71.4, slope 124; White: yardage 6267,

par 72, rating 70.2, slope 121; *Women:* Red: yardage 5855, par 72, rating 75.6, slope 134.

Tee Times: Reciprocal players should have their home professional call to make arrangements.

Dress Code: Appropriate golf attire and non-metal spikes are required.

Tournaments: Outside events are on Monday only. A 72-player minimum is needed to book a tournament.

Directions: In Riverside, take the Martin Luther King Drive exit off Highway 60 (Pomona Freeway). Go west for about one-quarter mile to Canyon Crest Drive and turn left. Drive about 1.5 miles and turn right on Country Club Drive.

Contact: 975 Country Club Drive, Riverside, CA 92506, pro shop 909/274-7906, clubhouse 909/274-7900, www.canyoncrestcc.com.

153 MORENO VALLEY RANCH GOLF CLUB

Architect: Pete Dye, 1988

27 holes   **Public**   **$43–65**

Southeast Detail map, page 298

There are three nine-hole loops here. They are nicely maintained courses with fast, sloping greens and some great views of the surrounding mountains. The fairway landing zones are tight in some places, demanding accurate tee shots. The Valley and Lake Courses are rolling, with elevated tees and greens. The Mountain Course is tight, with many elevation changes. This facility hosted the Nike Inland Empire Open, a PGA-sponsored event, from 1994 to 1999.

Play Policy and Fees: Weekday green fees are $43, including cart. Weekend fees are $65 including cart. Twilight, senior, junior, and replay rates are available, and ladies play for $35 on Monday.

Tees and Yardage: Valley/Mountain—*Men:* Tournament: yardage 6880, par 72, rating 73.6, slope 146; Championship: yardage 6338, par 72, rating 70.9, slope 137; Regular: yardage 5833, par 72, rating 68.7, slope 128; *Women:* Forward: yardage 5196, par 72, rating 70.1, slope 122. Mountain/Lake—*Men:* Tournament:

yardage 6684, par 72, rating 73.2, slope 144; Championship: yardage 6361, par 72, rating 71.2, slope 140; Regular: yardage 5830, par 72, rating 68.6, slope 130; *Women:* Forward: yardage 5108, par 72, rating 69.6, slope 121. Lake/Valley—*Men:* Tournament: yardage 6898, par 72, rating 74.4, slope 141; Championship: yardage 6453, par 72, rating 71.5, slope 138; Regular: yardage 5907, par 72, rating 69.2, slope 127; *Women:* Forward: yardage 5246, par 72, rating 70.1, slope 122.

Tee Times: Reservations may be booked up to seven days in advance.

Dress Code: Collared shirts are required. No cutoff shorts are permitted. Soft spikes.

Tournaments: Tournaments welcome, and many tournament packages include a banquet afterward.

Directions: From Riverside, take Highway 60 (Pomona Freeway) east. Exit south on Moreno Beach Drive. Go two miles to John F. Kennedy Avenue and turn left to the course.

Contact: 28095 John F. Kennedy Avenue, Moreno Valley, CA 92555, pro shop 909/924-4444, www.mvrgolf.com.

154 QUAIL RANCH GOLF CLUB

Architect: Desmond Muirhead, 1969

18 holes   **Public**   **$25–38**

Southeast Detail map, page 298

This is a Scottish links–style course with rolling terrain and undulating greens. The Southern California Golf Association rated this course as one of its top 10 public golf facilities in 1988. The PGA Tour School qualifier and the U.S. Open qualifier have been held here. Craig Stadler impressed the locals once: He finished a round in the dark and asked the pro staff if they would park their cars around the 18th green with their headlights on so he could finish his round. CBS golf analyst Gary McCord holds the course record of 62.

Play Policy and Fees: Green fees are $25 weekdays and $38 weekends and holidays. Twilight rates are offered. Carts are included.

Tees and Yardage: *Men:* Black: yardage 6848, par 72, rating 73.4, slope 135; Blue: yardage 6603, par 72, rating 72.3, slope 132; White: yardage 6108, par 72, rating 70.0, slope 128; *Women:* Gold: yardage 5212, par 72, rating 71.0, slope 124.

Tee Times: Reservations can be booked seven days in advance.

Dress Code: Appropriate golf attire and non-metal spikes are required.

Tournaments: This course is available for outside tournaments.

Directions: From Moreno Valley, take Highway 91 to Highway 60 (Pomona Freeway). Take Highway 60 east about 14 miles to the Gilman Springs exit. Drive four miles south to the club.

Contact: 15960 Gilman Springs Road, Moreno Valley, CA 92355, pro shop 909/654-2727, fax 909/654-5692, www.quailranchgolf.com.

155 CALIMESA COUNTRY CLUB

Architect: William F. Bell, 1958
18 holes   Public $19–27

Southeast Detail map, page 298

This scenic little course is set in a canyon. It shows lots of character with its up-and-down layout and mature trees. You can have fun on this course.

Play Policy and Fees: Green fees are $19 weekdays and $27 weekends. Twilight and senior (weekdays only) rates are available. Midday rates offered. Optional carts are $11 per person.

Tees and Yardage: *Men:* Blue: yardage 5970, par 70, rating 68.3, slope 115; White: yardage 5608, par 70, rating 67.1, slope 106; *Women:* Red: yardage 5293, par 72, rating 70.8, slope 117.

Tee Times: Reservations can be booked seven days in advance.

Dress Code: Collared shirts are required.

Tournaments: This course is available for outside tournaments.

Directions: Travel eight miles east of Redlands on I-10 to Calimesa. Turn east on County Line Road to 3rd Street and travel south to the club.

Contact: 1300 South 3rd Street, Calimesa, CA 92320, pro shop 909/795-2488.

156 OAK VALLEY GOLF CLUB

Architect: Schmidt Curley Golf Design, 1988
18 holes   Public $60–85

Southeast Detail map, page 298

This is a links-style course with rolling terrain. The signature hole is the seventh, a 474-yard par-4. From the tee, you are hitting downhill. The next shot is uphill to a shelved green with traps guarding the left side and brush hovering off the right side. Oak Valley has received a four-star rating from *Golf Digest.*

Play Policy and Fees: Green fees are $60 weekdays and $85 weekends and holidays, cart included. Midday rates offered.

Tees and Yardage: *Men:* Blue: yardage 7003, par 72, rating 74.0, slope 138; White: yardage 6372, par 72, rating 71.0, slope 131; Gold: yardage 5860, par 72, rating 68.7, slope 126; *Women:* Red: yardage 5349, par 72, rating 71.9, slope 128.

Tee Times: Reservations may be booked up to seven days in advance.

Dress Code: Collared shirts, appropriate golf attire, and nonmetal spikes are required.

Tournaments: Events may be booked up to a year in advance. The banquet facility accommodates 144 people.

Directions: From I-10, take the San Timoteo exit north and drive one-third of a mile to the course.

Contact: 1888 Golf Club Drive, Beaumont, CA 92223, pro shop 909/769-7200, fax 909/769-1229, www.oakvalleygolf.com.

157 PGA OF SOUTHERN CALIFORNIA GOLF CLUB AT OAK VALLEY

Architect: Schmidt Curley Golf Design, 2000
36 holes   Public $66–92

Southeast Detail map, page 298

There are two courses here, the Legends and the Champions, as well as a full-service teaching operation. The facility is owned and operated by the PGA of Southern California, which has exerted every effort to make the experience affordable for everyone. The courses are well designed, expertly run, very nicely maintained, and are distinguished by some exciting holes, strong par-3s, and nice mountain vistas. They are heavily bunkered, and water comes into play on quite a few holes. There are enough tees from which to select that all golfers can find a distance to suit their skills. There is even a Learners Loop on each course that measures about 3700 yards—a very good idea. On the other hand, the courses are quite capable of giving professional golfers a run for their money from the back tees, which measure around 7400 yards.

Play Policy and Fees: Green fees are $66 on weekdays and $92 on weekends and holidays. Twilight, super twilight, and junior rates are offered. All fees include a cart. Memberships are available.

Tees and Yardage: The Legends—*Men:* Green: yardage 7442, par 72, rating 76.6, slope 144; Black: yardage 6803, par 72, rating 73.4, slope 136; Blue: yardage 6394, par 72, rating 71.6, slope 129; White: yardage 5871, par 72, rating 68.9, slope 125; *Women:* Red: yardage 5169, par 72, rating 70.9, slope 130. The Champions—*Men:* Green: yardage 7377, par 72, rating 76.5, slope 141; Black: yardage 6804, par 72, rating 73.7, slope 135; Blue: yardage 6348, par 72, rating 71.4, slope 129; White: yardage 5948, par 72, rating 69.4, slope 125; *Women:* Red: yardage 5274, par 72, rating 72.4, slope 128.

Tee Times: Reservations may be booked up to seven days in advance.

Dress Code: Soft spikes and collared shirts are required. No denim is permitted.

Tournaments: Tournaments are welcome and may be booked up to one year in advance.

Directions: Off Highway 10, exit at Cherry Valley and turn right. Turn left on Desert Lawn and travel 1.5 miles to Champions Drive. Turn right on Champions Drive and follow the road to the golf club entrance.

Contact: 36211 Champions Drive, Calimesa, CA 92320, pro shop 877/742-2500, fax 909/845-7790, www.scpgagolf.com.

158 LOS COYOTES COUNTRY CLUB

Architect: William F. Bell, 1958; Ted Robinson Sr., 1970
27 holes   **Private**   **$75**

Southeast Detail map, page 298

These courses are set around the top of a small hill. The rolling fairways are seeded with kikuyu grass, and the rough is tough. All three layouts are well bunkered and interesting. They play long from any set of tees. The Valley/Vista Course was the site of the annual Los Coyotes LPGA Classic from 1989 to 1992, won twice by Nancy Lopez and once by Pat Bradley.

Play Policy and Fees: Reciprocal play is accepted with members of other private clubs (weekdays only); otherwise, members and guests only. Fees for reciprocators are $75 including cart.

Tees and Yardage: Lake/Valley—*Men:* Black: yardage 6578, par 71, rating 71.9, slope 126, Blue: yardage 6289, par 71, rating 70.6, slope 123; White: yardage 6014, par 71, rating 69.2, slope 121; *Women:* Green: yardage 5499, par 71, rating 73.0, slope 130. Vista/Lake—*Men:* Black: yardage 6477, par 71, rating 71.5, slope 129; Blue: yardage 6452, par 71, rating 70.2, slope 127; White: yardage 5927, par 71, rating 68.9, slope 125; *Women:* Green: yardage 5619, par 71, rating 74.1, slope 135. Valley/Vista—*Men:* Black: yardage 7052, par 72, rating 74.3, slope 131; Blue: yardage 6757, par 72, rating 73.0, slope 128; White: yardage 6469, par 72, rating 71.8, slope 126; *Women:* Green: yardage 6090, par 72, rating 76.6, slope 139.

Tee Times: Reciprocal players should have their home professional call to make arrangements.

Dress Code: Appropriate golf attire and non-metal spikes are required.

Tournaments: This course is available for outside tournaments on Monday.

Directions: Take Highway 91 or I-5 to the Beach Boulevard exit. Drive north for three miles from Highway 91 or two miles from I-5 to Los Coyotes Drive and turn right, then continue one mile to the club.

Contact: 8888 Los Coyotes Drive, Buena Park,

CA 90621, pro shop 714/994-7788, www.amer
icangolf.com.

159 ANAHEIM "DAD" MILLER GOLF COURSE

Architect: Dick "Dad" Miller, 1961
18 holes   **Public**   **$23–35**

Southeast Detail map, page 298

A Tiger Woods Learning Center is being built
adjacent to this popular public course, slated
to open by 2006. Aimed at junior golfers, this
is a wonderful development for the Anaheim
area. The new center will include a practice
and teaching facility, and a par-3 golf course.
Its construction will cause the existing "Dad"
Miller Course to break up its long 17th hole,
which runs more than 600 yards and plays as
a par-6 for women. Several other changes will
simultaneously occur, including a new driving
range. This "Dad" Miller Course as it currently plays is not long, but it is challenging
for the average golfer. The tree-lined fairways
are level, and it is well kept for a public course.
It's flat and easy to walk. This course is close
to Disneyland and Knotts Berry Farm.

Play Policy and Fees: Green fees Monday–Friday are $23 to walk. Weekend fees are $35 to
walk. Optional carts are $12 per rider. Nine-
hole, twilight, and senior rates are available.

Tees and Yardage: *Men:* Blue: yardage 6040, par
71, rating 68.6, slope 116; White: yardage 5760,
par 71, rating 67.4, slope 113; *Women:* Red:
yardage 5362, par 72, rating 70.2, slope 116.

Tee Times: Tee times may be booked seven
days in advance through the computer reservations system. Call 714/765-GOLF (4653).

Dress Code: Casual attire is acceptable, but
nonmetal spikes are required.

Tournaments: This course is available for tournaments. The banquet facility holds 100 people.

Directions: Travel on I-5 (Santa Ana Freeway)
to the Brookhurst Street exit. Drive south one-
half mile to Crescent Avenue and turn right.
Continue one-half mile to Gilbert Street and
turn left to the course.

Contact: 430 North Gilbert Street, Anaheim,
CA 92801, pro shop 714/765-3481, www.ana
heim.net.

160 FULLERTON GOLF CLUB

Architect: William F. Bell, 1963
18 holes   **Public**   **$20–29**

Southeast Detail map, page 298

This is a short, narrow course with a creek
coming into play on 14 holes. The course is
generally in good condition. It is a fun course
for beginning to intermediate golfers to practice course management. It is important to
keep the ball in the fairways. This course also
features one of the best junior golf programs
in Southern California.

Play Policy and Fees: Green fees to walk are
$20 Monday–Friday and $29 weekends. Senior, junior, and twilight rates are available.
Carts are an additional $12.

Tees and Yardage: *Men:* Blue: yardage 5159,
par 67, rating 65.4, slope 114; *Women:* Silver:
yardage 5059, par 67, rating 70.3, slope 123.

Tee Times: Reservations can be booked seven
days in advance.

Dress Code: Golf attire is encouraged.

Tournaments: Shotgun tournaments are available weekdays only. A 120-player minimum is
needed for a shotgun start. For a regular tournament, a 16-player minimum is needed.

Directions: From Highway 91 in Fullerton, take
the Harbor Boulevard exit. Go north for three
miles to the course, just past the Greenview
Terrace condo development.

Contact: 2700 North Harbor Boulevard, Fullerton, CA 92635, pro shop 714/871-5141.

161 COYOTE HILLS GOLF COURSE

Architect: Cal Olson, Payne Stewart, 1996
18 holes   **Public**   **$90–110**

Southeast Detail map, page 298

Coyote Hills is in a wildlife preserve that features cascading streams and spectacular views.

Imagine standing on an elevated tee box at the ninth hole, looking down at a wildlife preserve. Now picture yourself hitting the ball down the middle of the fairway. If you don't, trouble awaits. The wildlife preserve along the left side turns into water, with sand guarding the front of the green. If you hit the ball too far to the right, you'll get to tee it up again, plus penalty. There are enough tee boxes here to suit anybody's game. This course has been recognized by *Golf For Women* as one of its "100 Women-Friendly Golf Courses."

Play Policy and Fees: Green fees are $90 Monday–Thursday and $110 Friday, weekends, and holidays. Price includes cart and driving range. Twilight, super twilight, junior, and nine-hole rates are available.

Tees and Yardage: *Men:* Coyote: yardage 6510, par 70, rating 72.2, slope 135; Back: yardage 6007, par 70, rating 69.4, slope 128; Regular: yardage 5618, par 70, rating 67.6, slope 124; Middle: yardage 5142, par 70, rating 65.3, slope 118; *Women:* Forward: yardage 4437, par 70, rating 67.6, slope 115.

Tee Times: Reservations can be booked 45 days in advance.

Dress Code: Collared shirts and nonmetal spikes are a must. No denim is allowed on the course, and shorts must be country club length.

Tournaments: A 16-player minimum is needed for a tournament. Carts are mandatory. Events should be booked 16 months in advance. The banquet facility can accommodate 250 people.

Directions: This course is five miles north of Disneyland. From Highway 57, take the Yorba Linda exit. Take a right on State College Boulevard and a left on Bastanchury Road. The course is on the left.

Contact: 1440 Bastanchury Road, Fullerton, CA 92835, pro shop 714/672-6800, fax 714/672-6808, www.coyotehillsgc.com.

162 BREA GOLF COURSE

Architect: William F. Bell, 1955

9 holes   **Public**   **$9.50–12**

Southeast Detail map, page 298

This mostly flat course has a storm channel running through its center. There are few trees. The course consists of two par-4s and seven par-3s.

Play Policy and Fees: Green fees to walk are $9.50 weekdays and $12 weekends. Senior and junior rates are available. Carts additional but not necessary.

Tees and Yardage: *Men:* Back: yardage 1733, par 29, rating n/a, slope n/a; *Women:* Forward: yardage 1412, par 29, rating n/a, slope n/a.

Tee Times: Reservations may be booked seven days in advance.

Dress Code: Appropriate attire and soft spikes are required.

Tournaments: This course is available for outside events.

Directions: From Highway 57 heading south toward Brea, take the Imperial Highway exit west to Brea Boulevard and turn left. At the second signal, turn right on West Fir, which dead-ends at the course.

Contact: 501 West Fir Street, Brea, CA 92621, pro shop 714/529-3003.

163 BIRCH HILLS GOLF COURSE

Architect: Harry Rainville, 1975

18 holes   **Public**   **$21–41**

Southeast Detail map, page 298

This short executive course is hilly and has good greens that can be tricky to putt. The course has five par-4s, and golfers can use their drivers. The fairways are fairly wide, and some water comes into play on the front nine. It is an excellent course for seniors and is walkable. Birch Hills offers an excellent practice facility.

Play Policy and Fees: Green fees are $21 to walk weekdays, $31 to ride, and $31 to walk weekends, $41 to ride. Senior, twilight, and super twilight rates are available.

Tees and Yardage: *Men:* Blue: yardage 3560, par 59, rating 57.7, slope 91; White: yardage 3410, par 59, rating 57.3, slope 90; *Women:* Red: yardage 3003, par 59, rating 55.9, slope 85.

Tee Times: Reservations can be booked seven days in advance.

Dress Code: Shirts must be worn.

Tournaments: A 16-player minimum is required to book a tournament.

Directions: Driving south on Highway 57 from Brea, exit at Imperial Highway east. Turn left on Associated Road and right on Birch Street to the course.

Contact: 2250 East Birch Street, Brea, CA 92621, pro shop 714/990-0201, www.mdjmgmt.com/birchhome.htm.

164 ALTA VISTA COUNTRY CLUB
Architect: Harry Rainville, 1961
18 holes   **Private**   **$60–70**

Southeast Detail map, page 298

This is a rolling course with mature trees, lots of out-of-bounds, and some lakes. Homes line the perimeter. The back nine was redesigned in 1992 to create a more challenging home stretch.

Play Policy and Fees: Reciprocal play is accepted with members of other private clubs at a rate of $60 weekdays, $70 weekends; otherwise, members and guests only. Optional carts are $11 per rider.

Tees and Yardage: *Men:* Black: yardage 6559, par 72, rating 71.1, slope 124; Blue: yardage 6305, par 72, rating 69.4, slope 117; White: yardage 5999, par 72, rating 68.8, slope 116; *Women:* Red: yardage 5523, par 72, rating 72.5, slope 127.

Tee Times: Reservations for reciprocal play can be booked four days in advance.

Dress Code: All shirts must have a collar. No blue jeans are allowed.

Tournaments: This course is available for outside tournaments on Monday. Carts are required. A 48-player minimum is needed to book a tournament. Events should be booked 12 months in advance.

Directions: Travel on Highway 91 to Placentia and take the Kraemer Boulevard exit. Drive north two miles to Alta Vista Street and turn right. Turn left on Sue Drive and continue one-half block to the club.

Contact: 777 East Alta Vista Street, Placentia, CA 92670, pro shop 714/528-1103, www.altavistacc.com.

165 BLACK GOLD GOLF CLUB
Architect: Arthur Hills, 2001
18 holes   **Public**   **$79–99**

Southeast Detail map, page 298

Getting here is not half the fun. But considering the dearth of good daily fee courses in the Los Angeles area, Black Gold has an important role. Once you get past the oil derricks and hazy views on this inland Los Angeles area course, it is actually a pretty solid test of the game. Designer Art Hills and team used the natural contours and hilly nature of the land to the fullest extent. This makes for some tight driving holes and some uneven fairway lies. One of the more memorable holes is the par-5 fourth, a "grip it and rip it" opportunity. It's a short, downhill par-5 that allows golfers to be as aggressive as they like. The green is guarded on the left by a deep hollow and some bunkers. A few lakes come into play, adding to the excitement.

Play Policy and Fees: Green fees are $79 Monday–Thursday for nonresidents of Yorba Linda, $89 Friday, and $99 weekends and holidays. Cart fees included. Resident, twilight, senior, and junior rates are also offered.

Tees and Yardage: *Men:* Black: yardage 6756, par 72, rating 73.1, slope 133; Blue: yardage 6439, par 72, rating 71.6, slope 130; White: yardage 6045, par 72, rating 69.8, slope 125; Gold: yardage 5564, par 72, rating 67.3, slope 118; *Women:* Red: yardage 4937, par 72, rating 69.3, slope 124.

Tee Times: Reservations can be made seven days in advance.

Dress Code: Appropriate golf attire is required. No metal spikes are allowed on the course.

Tournaments: Tournaments welcome. Call for details.

Directions: Take Imperial Highway (90) either eastbound from Highway 57 or northbound from Highway 91 to Valley View Road; go north one mile to Lakeview Avenue and turn right to the club entrance.

Contact: 17681 Lakeview Avenue, Yorba Linda, CA 92886, pro shop 714/961-0060, fax 714/993-9472, www.blackgoldgolf.com.

166 YORBA LINDA COUNTRY CLUB

Architect: Harry Rainville and David Rainville, 1957
18 holes   Private

Southeast Detail map, page 298

This old-style course nestles among numerous homes. There are tree-lined fairways, hills, bunkers, and a little water. It's walkable. Women golfers find it plays long and very difficult.

Play Policy and Fees: Members and guests only.

Tees and Yardage: *Men:* Black: yardage 6851, par 71, rating 73.5, slope 133; Blue: yardage 6527, par 71, rating 72.3, slope 130; White: yardage 6113, par 71, rating 70.8, slope 126; *Women:* Red: yardage 5848, par 73, rating 75.3, slope 138.

Tee Times: Not applicable.

Dress Code: Appropriate golf attire is required. No denim is allowed on the course. Nonmetal spikes are required.

Tournaments: This course is available for outside tournaments on Monday only, and carts are required. A 100-player minimum is needed. Tournaments should be scheduled 12 months in advance. The banquet facility can accommodate 200 people.

Directions: Take the Riverside Freeway (Highway 91) to Imperial Highway (Highway 90). Drive north to Kellogg and turn right to Mountain View and the club.

Contact: 19400 Mountain View, Yorba Linda, CA 92886, pro shop 714/779-2467, clubhouse 714/779-2461.

167 ANAHEIM HILLS GOLF COURSE

Architect: Richard Bigler, 1972
18 holes   Public $42.50-57.50

Southeast Detail map, page 298

Anaheim Hills offers great views and lots of wildlife. Most of the fairways are separated on this hilly course (only four are parallel). The greens are undulating and can be fast in the summer. The first hole is a short par-5, but because the tee is elevated, errant tee shots can easily wind up lost or out-of-bounds. Local knowledge is imperative. A very nice new clubhouse opened in 2004.

Play Policy and Fees: Green fees Monday–Thursday are $42.50, Friday $52.50, and weekends and holidays $57.50. Carts are mandatory and are included in all prices.

Tees and Yardage: *Men:* Blue: yardage 6249, par 71, rating 69.6, slope 117; White: yardage 6009, par 71, rating 68.4, slope 114; *Women:* Red: yardage 5331, par 72, rating 71.0, slope 119.

Tee Times: Reservations may be made seven days in advance.

Dress Code: No tank tops, short shorts, or cutoffs are allowed. Nonmetal spikes are required.

Tournaments: This course is available for tournaments. The banquet facility holds 150 people.

Directions: Take the Riverside Freeway (Highway 91) to the Imperial Highway exit south. Drive one-half mile to Nohl Ranch Road, turn left, and travel one-half mile to the club.

Contact: 6501 Nohl Ranch Road, Anaheim, CA 92807, pro shop 714/998-3041.

168 RIDGELINE EXECUTIVE GOLF COURSE

Architect: Course designed, 1950
9 holes   Public $12-18

Southeast Detail map, page 298

This slightly hilly executive course is popular among seniors, juniors, and families. Although not long in yardage, Ridgeline is a challenge and requires an accurate short game. This course also offers young players a chance to learn how to hit from uphill, downhill, and sidehill lies.

Play Policy and Fees: Green fees on weekdays are $12 for nine or 18 holes. Green fees on weekends are $12 for nine holes and $18 for 18 holes. Carts additional.

Tees and Yardage: *Men:* Back: yardage 1831, par 31, rating n/a, slope n/a; *Women:* Forward: yardage 1758, par 31, rating n/a, slope n/a.

Tee Times: Tee times can be made one week in advance.

Dress Code: Shirts and shoes are required.

Tournaments: This course is available for outside events. Events should be booked one month in advance. The banquet facility can accommodate 200 people.

Directions: From Highway 55 in Newport Beach, exit at Katella Avenue. Head east 3.5 miles and turn right on Meads Avenue. The course is three blocks on the left.

Contact: 1051 North Meads Avenue, Orange, CA 92869, pro shop 714/538-5030.

169 GREEN RIVER GOLF CLUB

Architect: Lawrence Hughes (Orange Course), 1958; Cary Bickler (Riverside Course), 1968

36 holes   Public $32–38

🏌️ 📷 🗄️ 🏌️ 🛺 🍴

Southeast Detail map, page 298

On a site where the television series *Tarzan* was filmed in the 1960s, Green River features two courses with gently rolling slopes, many trees, and several lakes. An errant tee shot means trouble. The Santa Ana River runs through both courses. The first hole on the Orange Course features trees down the right side and the river down the left side. These courses are in a narrow valley with the Chino Hills on each side, so they can get quite windy. This facility has a very active junior golf program. As a member of The Audubon Cooperative Sanctuary Program for golf courses, the 560-acre property is home to over 50 bird species, including the endangered golden eagle.

Play Policy and Fees: Green fees are $32 on weekdays and $38 on weekends and holidays. Carts are $12 per rider. Senior, junior, early bird, twilight, and super twilight rates are available.

Tees and Yardage: Orange Course–*Men:* Blue: yardage 6480, par 71, rating 71.1, slope 126; White: yardage 6256, par 71, rating 70.0, slope 124; *Women:* Red: yardage 5725, par 71, rating 72.8, slope 125. Riverside Course–*Men:* Blue: yardage 6383, par 71, rating 68.7, slope 117; White: yardage 6013, par 71, rating 67.4, slope 116; *Women:* Red: yardage 5467, par 71, rating 71.1, slope 121.

Tee Times: Reservations may be booked seven days in advance for weekdays. For weekend tee times, call at 6:30 A.M. on the Monday prior.

Dress Code: Collared shirts and nonmetal spikes are required.

Tournaments: With both courses, tournaments up to 340 players can be accommodated. The clubhouse can host a banquet for up to 500 people. Events may be scheduled up to one year in advance.

Directions: From the Riverside Freeway (Highway 91), take the Green River Drive exit north and travel one mile to the entrance.

Contact: 5215 Green River Road, Corona, CA 91720, pro shop 714/970-8411, clubhouse 714/737-5000, fax 714/737-7432, www.greenrivergolf.com.

170 MOUNTAIN VIEW COUNTRY CLUB

Architect: William F. Bell, 1955

18 holes   Public $25–45

🏌️ 📷 🗄️ 🏌️ 🛺 🍴

Southeast Detail map, page 298

This course has tight fairways, tiny greens, and lots of trees. The front nine winds through homes, while the back nine is hilly. It is a traditional course that offers a challenge to players of any skill level.

Play Policy and Fees: Green fees are $25 walking and $34 with a cart on weekdays, and $35 walking and $45 with a cart on weekends. Senior and twilight rates are available.

Tees and Yardage: *Men:* Blue: yardage 6433, par 72, rating 70.9, slope 129; White: yardage 6167,

par 72, rating 70.0, slope 126; *Women:* Red: yardage 5374, par 72, rating 71.9, slope 120.

Tee Times: Reservations can be booked seven days in advance.

Dress Code: Collared shirts and golf shoes are required.

Tournaments: A 144-player minimum is needed to book a shotgun tournament.

Directions: From the Riverside Freeway (Highway 91) east of Orange County, go south on Serfas Club Drive exit and travel east 400 yards to Pinecrest. Turn left and drive to the club entrance at the end of the street.

Contact: 2121 Mountain View Drive, Corona, CA 91720, pro shop 714/633-0282.

171 HIDDEN VALLEY GOLF CLUB

Architect: Casey O'Callaghan, 1997

18 holes   Public $60–95

Southeast Detail map, page 298

This target golf course, cut out of the hills, features constant elevation changes, rock outcroppings, and fair but challenging greens. Water comes into play on two holes. The signature hole is the 15th, a severe downhill, dogleg right that drops in elevation 220 feet from tee to green. Five sets of tees meet the needs of all golfers. Hidden Valley is one of the better new public designs in Southern California over the past 10 years; *Golf Magazine* and *Golf Digest* have both rated the course highly. It is particularly playable for women from the red tees.

Play Policy and Fees: Green fees are $60 Monday–Friday, $95 on Saturday, and $85 on Sunday. Twilight, early bird, and senior (weekdays only) rates are available. All prices include a cart.

Tees and Yardage: *Men:* Black: yardage 6751, par 72, rating 73.8, slope 145; Blue: yardage 6330, par 72, rating 71.5, slope 137; White: yardage 5826, par 72, rating 68.9, slope 130; *Women:* Silver: yardage 5330, par 71, rating 70.7, slope 124; Red: yardage 4698, par 71, rating 66.6, slope 116.

Tee Times: Reservations are recommended and may be booked 14 days in advance.

Dress Code: Collared shirts and nonmetal spikes are mandatory. No denim is permitted.

Tournaments: Events of up to 144 players may be booked up to one year in advance. The banquet facility can accommodate 150 people.

Directions: From Los Angeles, take Highway 91 east for 35 miles. Take the McKinley exit and head north through five stoplights. Turn right on Parkview Avenue to the course.

Contact: 10 Clubhouse Drive, Norco, CA 91760, pro shop 909/737-1010, fax 909/737-2424, www.hiddenvalleygolf.com.

172 CRESTA VERDE GOLF CLUB

Architect: Randolph Scott, 1927; redesign Jay Miller, 2002

18 holes   Public $29–39

Southeast Detail map, page 298

The course offers a rolling terrain with some steep slopes, many mature trees, and winding fairways. Although short at 5900 yards, it is not for the casual walker. The 17th hole has a 400-foot elevated tee. Here's a course with Hollywood history. Henry Fonda and Randolph Scott started this course back in 1927. In fact, Scott, who was a star attraction at the early Bing Crosby National Pro-Am at Pebble Beach, is credited with being the original architect. A new clubhouse was completed in 2004, as well as a triple-deck driving range. This facility is nicely maintained and perfect for practice or a fun round.

Play Policy and Fees: Green fees are $29 weekdays and $39 weekends, including cart. Various types of memberships and cards can be purchased. Please call for details.

Tees and Yardage: *Men:* Blue: yardage 5922, par 70, rating 69.0, slope 123; White: yardage 5922, par 70, rating 67.1, slope 118; *Women:* Red: yardage 5236, par 72, rating 71.1, slope 118.

Tee Times: Reservations can be booked seven days in advance.

Dress Code: No tank tops are allowed on the course.

Tournaments: This course is available for outside tournaments.

Directions: From the Riverside Freeway (Highway 91), take the Main Street North/Norco exit and travel north for one mile to Parkridge Avenue. Turn right and drive 1.25 miles to Cresta Road. Turn left and drive to the club entrance.

Contact: 1295 Cresta Road, Corona, CA 91719, pro shop 909/737-2255, fax 909/737-6410, www.crestaverdegolf.com.

173 TRILOGY GOLF CLUB AT GLEN IVY
Architect: Ted Robinson Sr., 2002

18 holes **Public** **$55–80**

Southeast Detail map, page 298

There are no parallel fairways on this scenic course, which contributes to the peaceful ambience. A few waterfalls beautify the design. Perhaps the most interesting hole is the 18th, which features a drop of more than 200 feet from tee to fairway, making you feel as though you could hit the ball a mile. The back nine has more elevation change from the front, with nice views of the surrounding mountains. Placement is more important than length on this fun course.

Play Policy and Fees: Green fees are $55 Monday–Thursday, $60 Friday, and $80 weekends and holidays. Twilight and junior rates are available. Carts included.

Tees and Yardage: *Men:* Black: yardage 6673, par 72, rating 72.0, slope 132; Blue: yardage 6332, par 72, rating 70.3, slope 129; White: yardage 6000, par 72, rating 68.8, slope 125; *Women:* Gold: yardage 5439, par 72, rating 72.4, slope 130.

Tee Times: Reservations can be made seven days in advance.

Dress Code: Appropriate golf attire is required. Soft spikes only.

Tournaments: Tournaments welcome.

Directions: Take I-15 to Temescal Canyon Road exit (six miles south of Highway 91), go west to Trilogy Parkway, and turn right to the club.

Contact: 24440 Trilogy Parkway, Glen Ivy, CA 92883, phone 909/277-7175, fax 909/277-7179.

174 EAGLE GLEN GOLF CLUB
Architect: Gary Roger Baird, 1999

18 holes **Public** **$80–105**

Southeast Detail map, page 298

Part of the continuing trend of upscale courses with wide fairways, minimal rough, and multilevel, undulating greens, Eagle Glen lies partially next to a new housing development and partially at the base of the Cleveland National Forest. It is a well-designed layout with a number of memorable holes: the ninth, which feels like you are on top of the world; the 14th, a long par-4 into a prevailing wind; and a reachable par-5 finishing hole that requires a carry over water on both shots. Walking is virtually impossible due to a 400-foot elevation gain on the front side.

Play Policy and Fees: Green fees are $80 Monday–Thursday and $105 Friday–Sunday. Fee includes cart and use of range. Twilight, senior, junior, police, clergy, and fire rates are available.

Tees and Yardage: *Men:* Black: yardage 6930, par 72, rating 73.3, slope 136; Gold: yardage 6290, par 72, rating 70.3, slope 129; Silver: yardage 5659, par 72, rating 67.3, slope 122; *Women:* Jade: yardage 4998, par 72, rating 67.7, slope 113.

Tee Times: Tee times may be booked 14 days in advance.

Dress Code: Proper golf attire and footwear is required. No denim permitted.

Tournaments: This course is available for tournaments for groups of 12 or more. The banquet facility accommodates 250 people.

Directions: Take Highway 91 to Corona. Turn south on I-15 to the Cajalco Road exit, then head west. Follow Eagle Glen Parkway to the clubhouse.

Contact: 1800 Eagle Glen Parkway, Corona, CA 91719, pro shop 909/272-4653, fax 909/278-1558, www.eagleglengc.com.

175 GENERAL OLD GOLF COURSE

Architect: Course designed, 1957

18 holes   **Public**   **$23–45**

Southeast Detail map, page 298

There are numerous doglegs and bunkers at this championship layout. Seven holes must be reached over or around water. The front nine is relatively flat, and the back nine is up and down. Recent changes include making the course more women-friendly by moving tee boxes into more favorable positions and softening angles.

Play Policy and Fees: This former military course in now open to public play. Green fees are $23 walking and $35 riding on weekdays. On weekends, the rate is $33 walking and $45 riding. Military, senior, and twilight rates are available.

Tees and Yardage: *Men:* Bluc: yardage 6797, par 72, rating 72.1, slope 120; White: yardage 6348, par 72, rating 70.1, slope 116; Gold: yardage 5608, par 72, rating 66.3, slope 110; *Women:* Red: yardage 5632, par 72, rating 72.3, slope 118.

Tee Times: Reservations can be booked seven days in advance.

Dress Code: Soft spikes are preferred.

Tournaments: A 24-player minimum is needed to book a tournament. Shotgun tournaments are not available. Tournaments can be booked 12 months in advance.

Directions: From Riverside, drive southeast on I-215 four miles to Van Buren Boulevard, the first exit past the main gate to March AFB. Turn right and drive one mile to Village West Drive and turn left to the golf course.

Contact: 6104 Village West Drive, Riverside, CA 92518, pro shop 909/697-6690.

176 MENIFEE LAKES COUNTRY CLUB

Architect: Ted Robinson Sr., 1989

36 holes   **Semiprivate**   **$35–65**

Southeast Detail map, page 298

There are two 18-hole championship layouts

here, The Palms and The Lakes, both within a residential development, with homes lining most holes. Nevertheless, they are scenic courses with nice views of the San Jacinto Mountains. The snowcapped peaks of Big Bear can be seen in winter. The courses are characterized by tight fairways and plenty of Ted Robinson–signature water. The greens are guarded by bunkers, and it seems like lakes come into play on every hole. The two designs are similar in length and feel

Play Policy and Fees: Green fees are $40 weekdays and $65 weekends for nonresidents, $35 weekdays and $55 weekends for area residents. Twilight rates offered. Carts are included in all prices. Memberships are available.

Tees and Yardage: The Lakes—*Men:* Blue: yardage 6516, par 72, rating 71.6, slope 125; White: yardage 6100, par 72, rating 69.6, slope 119; *Women:* Red: yardage 5455, par 72, rating 72.5, slope 123. The Palms—*Men:* Blue: yardage 6503, par 72, rating 71.1, slope 122; White: yardage 6115, par 72, rating 68.7, slope 116; *Women:* Red: yardage 5463, par 72, rating 72.2, slope 121.

Tee Times: Reservations may be booked eight days in advance.

Dress Code: Collared shirts are required, and no denim is allowed.

Tournaments: These courses are available for outside tournaments. Events may be booked up to two years in advance.

Directions: From Perris, take the Newport Road exit off I-215 south. Follow it about one-half mile to Menifee Lakes Drive. Turn left and follow the road to the course.

Contact: 29875 Menifee Lakes Drive, Menifee, CA 92584, pro shop 909/672-3090, fax 909/672-6154, www.menifee-lakes.com.

177 RIVER VIEW GOLF

Architect: David Pfaff, 1972

18 holes   **Public**   **$20–42**

Southeast Detail map, page 298

This challenging short course near Disneyland

and the John Wayne Orange County Airport crisscrosses the bed of the Santa Ana River. The front nine requires good ball placement, and the back nine is wide open. It is a populated area of Southern California, and the layout is bordered by homes, but it is convenient and generally in good condition.

Play Policy and Fees: Green fees are $20 to walk and $32 to ride on weekdays, $30 to walk and $42 to ride on weekends. Twilight and senior rates are available.

Tees and Yardage: *Men:* Back: yardage 6176, par 70, rating 67.8, slope 115; *Women:* Forward: yardage 5790, par 70, rating 71.0, slope 121.

Tee Times: Reservations can be booked 10 days in advance.

Dress Code: No tank tops are allowed on the course. Soft spikes are preferred.

Tournaments: This course welcomes tournaments of 20–150 people. Tournament packages include a post-golf barbecue.

Directions: Travel south from Los Angeles on I-5 (Santa Ana Freeway) to the Bristol exit. Head south to Santa Clara Street, then west to the club.

Contact: 1800 West Santa Clara Street, Santa Ana, CA 92706, pro shop 714/543-1115, www.riverviewgolf.com.

178 WILLOWICK GOLF COURSE
Architect: William P. Bell, 1928
18 holes   **Public**   **$23–47**

Southeast Detail map, page 298

This older design is wide open and level, with many trees and bunkers. It is an established course that has been a favorite of Southern Californians since the 1920s. It is short and walkable, good for exercising the legs. It provides an enjoyable round for all skill levels. A respected teaching program is in place.

Play Policy and Fees: Green fees are $23 to walk, $35 to ride weekdays, and $35 to walk, $47 to ride weekends. Twilight, super twilight, nine-hole, and early bird rates are available.

Tees and Yardage: *Men:* Back: yardage 6063,

par 71, rating 67.7, slope 110; *Women:* Forward: yardage 5742, par 71, rating 72.3, slope 118.

Tee Times: Reservations can be booked seven days in advance.

Dress Code: Soft spikes are preferred.

Tournaments: A 24-player minimum is needed to book a tournament.

Directions: In Santa Ana, take the Harbor exit off Highway 22 (Garden Grove Freeway) and travel one mile south to 5th Street. Turn left on 5th Street and drive one-half mile to the course on the left.

Contact: 3017 West 5th Street, Santa Ana, CA 92703, pro shop 714/554-0672, www.willow ickgolf.com.

179 TUSTIN RANCH GOLF CLUB
Architect: Ted Robinson Sr., 1989
18 holes   **Public**   **$95–145**

Southeast Detail map, page 298

Architect Ted Robinson took a flat parcel of land and sculpted an excellent public course from it. There is water on many holes, with mature trees and colorful flowerbeds beautifying the landscape. Carts are not permitted on fairways, so the course is maintained in country club–quality condition. The signature hole is the par-3 11th, which requires tee shots to carry a pond that includes waterscapes to an undulating green. This is one of the few public courses in Southern California to offer caddies, and it is a great experience for all golfers. Brent Geiberger holds the course record of 65.

Play Policy and Fees: Green fees are $95 Monday–Thursday, $115 Friday, and $145 weekends and holidays, including carts. Resident, cardholder, twilight, and senior rates are offered. Caddies are available and must be reserved 48 hours in advance.

Tees and Yardage: *Men:* Black: yardage 6803, par 72, rating 73.5, slope 134; Blue: yardage 6446, par 72, rating 72.0, slope 129; White: yardage 6064, par 72, rating 70.2, slope 123; *Women:* Gold: yardage 5263, par 72, rating 71.7, slope 132.

Tee Times: Reservations can be made seven days in advance. For reservations more than seven days in advance, a $20 fee per player is required.

Dress Code: Golf attire is encouraged, but absolutely no tee shirts are allowed. Nonmetal spikes are required.

Tournaments: A 13-player minimum is required to book a tournament.

Directions: Take I-5 to the Tustin Ranch Road exit. Go left 1.6 miles to Township Drive on the right. From Highway 55 near Tustin, take the 4th Street/Irvine Boulevard exit and go east. Drive three miles and turn left on Tustin Ranch Road. Turn right on Township Drive.

Contact: 12442 Tustin Ranch Road, Tustin, CA 92782, pro shop 714/730-1611, clubhouse 714/730-4725, www.tustinranchgolf.com.

180 DAVID L. BAKER MEMORIAL GOLF COURSE

Architect: Garret Gill and George Williams, 1989

18 holes **Public** **$21–27**

Southeast Detail map, page 298

Named in tribute to open-space proponent David L. Baker, this course has five lakes, which come into play on nine holes, and many well-placed bunkers. There are no par-5s. The course is within a scenic park and is lighted for night play. It's a short course that provides a fun round for all skill levels. A Nike Golf Learning Center is on-site.

Play Policy and Fees: Green fees are $21 to walk Monday–Friday and $27 to walk weekends and holidays. Carts are $12 per rider. Senior, junior, twilight, and super twilight rates are available.

Tees and Yardage: *Men:* Back: yardage 3847, par 62, rating 59.8, slope 97; *Women:* Forward: yardage 3118, par 62, rating 57.7, slope 91.

Tee Times: Reservations can be booked seven days in advance.

Dress Code: Soft spikes are preferred.

Tournaments: Shotgun tournaments are available weekdays only. A 12-player minimum is required to book a tournament.

Directions: Off I-405 near Fountain Valley, take the Brookhurst exit north for two miles and turn right on Edinger Avenue.

Contact: 10410 Edinger Avenue, Fountain Valley, CA 92708, pro shop 714/418-2152, fax 714/531-2478.

181 MILE SQUARE GOLF COURSE

Architect: Harry Rainville (Classic Course), 1969; David Rainville and Gary Bye (Players Course), 2001

36 holes **Public** **$30–60**

Southeast Detail map, page 298

These are fairly open and level courses. The newer Players Course opened in 2001 and is more of a links-style design with fewer trees and wider fairways. The Classic Course features numerous mature trees and a small creek. Quite a few lakes on both layouts add to the challenge and scenery. Afternoon breezes usually make play more challenging. Many fairways parallel one another, so errant tee shots can still be played. Red foxes inhabit the course. They are quite tame, but they've been known to steal golf balls and resell them in the pro shop. A summer camp for junior golfers is quite popular.

Play Policy and Fees: Green fees on the Classic Course are $30 Monday–Thursday, $32 Friday, and $40 weekends and holidays. Green fees on the Players Course are $35 Monday–Thursday, $45 Friday, and $60 weekends and holidays. Carts are $12 per rider. Nine-hole, twilight, and early bird rates are offered.

Tees and Yardage: Classic—*Men:* Championship: yardage 6714, par 72, rating 71.5, slope 123; Regular: yardage 6415, par 72, rating 70.1, slope 120; *Women:* Forward: yardage 5648, par 72, rating 72.4, slope 120. Players—*Men:* Championship: yardage 6759, par 72, rating 72.3, slope 125; Regular: yardage 6334, par 72, rating 70.5, slope 119; *Women:* Forward: yardage 5717, par 72, rating 73.3, slope 125.

Tee Times: Weekday reservations can be booked seven days in advance. Bookings are taken on

Monday for Saturday tee times and on Tuesday for Sunday tee times.

Dress Code: Proper golf attire is required. Soft spikes only.

Tournaments: This course does not allow shotgun starts. A 24-player minimum is needed to book a tournament.

Directions: In Fountain Valley, take the Brookhurst Street/Fountain Valley exit off I-405 (San Diego Freeway) and follow the Brookhurst Street north off-ramp. Continue north one mile to Warner Avenue and turn right. Drive one-half mile to Ward Street and turn left to the course.

Contact: 10401 Warner Avenue, Fountain Valley, CA 92708, pro shop 714/962-5541, fax 714/596-4748, www.milesquaregolfcourse.com.

182 NORTH GOLF COURSE

Architect: Del Webb, 1975
18 holes   Semiprivate $14.50–24

Southeast Detail map, page 298

This level, executive course in the middle of Sun City features small, well-maintained greens. It chiefly gets play from the Sun City community, but all golfers are welcome. There are seven par-4s and 11 par-3s. This course may be short, but it'll put up solid resistance to par.

Play Policy and Fees: Green fees are $18 on weekdays and $24 on weekends. Senior rates are $14.50 weekdays and $17.50 weekends. Twilight and super twilight rates are available. Carts are $3 per player. Memberships are available.

Tees and Yardage: *Men:* White: yardage 4007, par 61, rating 58.4, slope 94; *Women:* Red: yardage 3467, par 61, rating 59.0, slope 89.

Tee Times: Reservations may be booked seven days in advance by the public and 10 days in advance by members.

Dress Code: Appropriate golf attire preferred. Soft spikes required.

Tournaments: Events may be booked a year in advance. The banquet facility can accommodate 125 people.

Directions: From Riverside, take I-215 south

to Sun City. Exit at McCall Boulevard, take a right, and drive three blocks to the golf course. From San Diego, take I-15 to I-215 north to Sun City and exit at McCall Boulevard. Turn left and go three blocks to the golf course.

Contact: 26660 McCall Boulevard, Sun City, CA 92586, pro shop 909/679-5111.

183 CHERRY HILLS GOLF CLUB

Architect: Del Webb, 1962
18 holes   Semiprivate $27–37

Southeast Detail map, page 298

With five sets of tees from which to choose, this course will serve the needs of just about any skill level. It caters to a mature crowd in and around Sun City. The layout is fairly level, with trees providing cover and separating fairways. Cherry Hills prides itself on excellent course conditioning.

Play Policy and Fees: Green fees are $27 weekdays and $37 weekends and holidays. Carts are mandatory and included. Twilight rates are offered.

Tees and Yardage: *Men:* Blue: yardage 6938, par 72, rating 72.6, slope 124; White: yardage 6496, par 72, rating 70.5, slope 120; Gold: yardage 6011, par 72, rating 72.5, slope 125; *Women:* Red: yardage 5927, par 72, rating 72.5, slope 125; Silver: yardage 5308, par 72, rating 69.6, slope 119.

Tee Times: Reservations can be booked seven days in advance.

Dress Code: Collared shirts and nonmetal spikes are required.

Tournaments: Shotgun tournaments are available on a very limited basis. Carts are required. A 24-player minimum is needed to book a regular tournament. Tournaments can be booked one month in advance.

Directions: In Sun City, take the McCall Boulevard/Sun City exit off I-215 and travel west on McCall for one-quarter mile to Sun City Boulevard. Turn left and drive one-quarter mile to Cherry Hills Boulevard. Turn right and go one block to the club.

Contact: 26583 Cherry Hills Boulevard, Sun City, CA 92586, pro shop 909/679-1182.

184 MESA VERDE COUNTRY CLUB

Architect: William F. Bell, 1958

18 holes   **Private**   **$72**

Southeast Detail map, page 298

This mature course offers a variety of holes and hazards, and is easy walking. The 18th is a par-3, 200-yarder fronted by water with out-of-bounds left. It usually plays into the wind to a sizable green that slopes toward the water. Overall, the course is a fair challenge. The LPGA has played several tournaments here, including the Women's Kemper Open. LPGA Hall-of-Famer Nancy Lopez holds the women's course record with 66.

Play Policy and Fees: Reciprocal play is accepted with members of other private clubs; otherwise, members and guests only. Reciprocal fees are based on what Mesa Verde members would be charged at the reciprocate club, but the minimum fee is $72, optional cart included.

Tees and Yardage: *Men:* Blue: yardage 6733, par 71, rating 72.4, slope 130; White: yardage 6256, par 71, rating 69.9, slope 124; Yellow: yardage 5800, par 71, rating 67.5, slope 117; *Women:* Red: yardage 5467, par 71, rating 72.0, slope 130.

Tee Times: Reciprocal player's home professional should call to make arrangements.

Dress Code: Appropriate golf attire and non-metal spikes are required.

Tournaments: This course is available for outside tournaments on Monday only. Carts are required. A 100-player minimum is needed to book a tournament. Tournaments should be booked at least one year in advance. The banquet facility can accommodate 250 people.

Directions: Travel south on I-405 (San Diego Freeway) to Costa Mesa and take the Harbor Boulevard exit. Drive south and turn right on Adams Street. Continue three-quarters of a mile to Mesa Verde West and turn right on Club House Road.

Contact: 3000 Club House Road, Costa Mesa, CA 92626, pro shop 714/549-0522, clubhouse 714/549-0377.

185 COSTA MESA GOLF & COUNTRY CLUB

Architect: William F. Bell, 1967

36 holes   **Public**   **$20–39**

Southeast Detail map, page 298

Los Lagos is the older of these two popular public courses, and it features many trees, three lakes, and a rolling layout. When the wind comes up, as it often does, this course can be extremely difficult. Mesa Linda is shorter, and it's an excellent layout for seniors. Both are fairly level designs. The driving range is lighted for night practice.

Play Policy and Fees: Los Lagos green fees are $27 Monday–Thursday, $29 Friday, and $39 weekends and holidays. Mesa Linda green fees are $20 Monday–Thursday, $25 Friday, and $30 weekends and holidays. Resident, twilight, and senior rates are available. Carts are $24.

Tees and Yardage: Los Lagos—*Men:* Blue: yardage 6542, par 72, rating 71.1, slope 126; White: yardage 6233, par 72, rating 69.8, slope 123; *Women:* Red: yardage 5907, par 72, rating 73.5, slope 127. Mesa Linda—*Men:* Blue: yardage 5330, par 70, rating 66.7, slope 118; *Women:* Red: yardage 5098, par 70, rating 69.9, slope 115.

Tee Times: Reservations can be booked seven days in advance.

Dress Code: Soft spikes only.

Tournaments: Shotgun tournaments are available weekdays only. A 24-player minimum is needed to book a tournament.

Directions: Traveling south on I-405 (near Huntington Beach and Costa Mesa), exit on Harbor Boulevard. Continue south one mile to Adams Avenue and turn right. Drive one-quarter mile to Mesa Verde Drive; turn left and then right on Golf Course Drive.

Contact: 1701 Golf Course Drive, Costa Mesa, CA 92626, pro shop 714/540-7500.

186 THE NEWPORT BEACH COUNTRY CLUB

Architect: William P. Bell and William F. Bell, 1952; Ted Robinson Sr., 2000

18 holes   Private $125

Southeast Detail map, page 298

This is a scenic, traditional course, with trees lining both sides of most fairways and water coming into play on a few holes. It is about a mile from the beach and therefore is subject to ocean breezes, especially in the afternoon. Putts often break deceptively toward the Pacific Ocean. This is the home of the Toshiba Senior Classic, a PGA Senior Tour event. PGA Tour and Champions Tour standout Hale Irwin holds the course record with 62.

Play Policy and Fees: Reciprocal play is accepted with members of other private clubs Monday–Thursday only. The reciprocal fee is $125, including cart.

Tees and Yardage: *Men:* Blue: yardage 6584, par 71, rating 71.8, slope 126; White: yardage 6239, par 71, rating 70.2, slope 122; *Women:* Red: yardage 5702, par 71, rating 74.4, slope 134.

Tee Times: Reciprocal player's home professional should call to make arrangements.

Dress Code: Nonmetal spikes are mandatory.

Tournaments: This course is available for outside tournaments on Monday only. Carts are required. A 100-player minimum is needed to book a tournament.

Directions: Travel north from Laguna Beach on Highway 1, one-half mile past MacArthur Boulevard. The course is between Jamboree Road and MacArthur Boulevard on Pacific Coast Highway next to Fashion Island Shopping Center.

Contact: 1600 Pacific Coast Highway, Newport Beach, CA 92660, pro shop 949/644-9680, clubhouse 949/644-9550, www.newportbeachcc.com.

187 SANTA ANA COUNTRY CLUB

Architect: John Duncan Dunn, 1924

18 holes   Private

Southeast Detail map, page 298

This historic course is very scenic. Colorful plantings, mature trees, and five lakes make the site beautiful. Water comes into play on several holes. It is not long by today's standards, but it can put up a fight. The terrain is relatively flat, always exquisitely maintained. When PGA Tour star Fred Couples lived in Newport Beach, he played and practiced here frequently. In fact, Couples shares the course record of 63. Founded as Santiago Golf Club, and later called The Orange County Country Club, Santa Ana Country Club was one of the pioneers of golf in Southern California.

Play Policy and Fees: Members and guests only.

Tees and Yardage: *Men:* Black: yardage 6536, par 72, rating 71.7, slope 128; Blue: yardage 6165, par 72, rating 69.9, slope 123; White: yardage 5809, par 72, rating 67.8, slope 119; *Women:* Gold: yardage 5399, par 72, rating 73.0, slope 128.

Tee Times: Not applicable.

Dress Code: Appropriate golf attire and soft spikes are required. Jackets are required in the dining room at dinner.

Tournaments: This course is available for a limited number of outside events on Monday.

Directions: Travel south from Los Angeles on I-405 to the Newport Freeway (Highway 55). Exit at Mesa Drive, turn left, and drive 100 yards to Newport Boulevard. Turn left and drive 100 yards to the club.

Contact: 20382 Newport Boulevard, Santa Ana, CA 92707, pro shop 714/545-7260, clubhouse 714/556-3000, www.santaanacc.org.

188 RANCHO SAN JOAQUIN GOLF COURSE

Architect: William F. Bell, 1969

18 holes **Public** **$20–60**

Southeast Detail map, page 298

Located in a sprawling residential community, this is a fairly level layout with undulating greens and some water hazards. It is popular with local residents and students from nearby University of California Irvine.

Play Policy and Fees: Walking green fees are $35 Monday–Thursday and $40 Friday. On weekends, green fees are $57, including cart. Twilight and student rates available.

Tees and Yardage: *Men:* Blue: yardage 6180, par 72, rating 69.7, slope 125; *Women:* White: yardage 5771, par 72, rating 73.5, slope 126.

Tee Times: Reservations can be booked seven days in advance.

Dress Code: No tank tops are allowed on the course. Soft spikes are preferred.

Tournaments: This course is available for outside events.

Directions: Travel south on I-405 from Santa Ana to the Culver Drive exit west. Turn right and drive to the second traffic light on Ethel Coplen Way. Turn right again and drive to the course.

Contact: 1 Ethel Coplen Way, Irvine, CA 92715, pro shop 949/786-5522, clubhouse 949/786-1224.

189 SHADY CANYON GOLF CLUB

Architect: Tom Fazio, 2001

18 holes **Private**

Southeast Detail map, page 298

 An exclusive private club in a surprisingly serene environment just over the hill west of the busy I-405 freeway in Irvine, Shady Canyon is Tom Fazio at his finest. The course delivers a solid test, picture-postcard holes, and service excellence. Tough putting surfaces are generally sloped back-to-front, and

some will funnel the ball to the center, as well, but overall you'd best be below the hole. The greens are Bermuda, but they are often rolling in the 10–11 range. Downhill putts don't stand much of a chance, particularly given the slippery breaks. An abundance of acacia, pepper, and oak trees and critters of all sorts call the ravines and ridges of the course home. It is certainly among the top new courses in the state.

Play Policy and Fees: Members and guests only. No reciprocal play is accepted.

Tees and Yardage: *Men:* Black: yardage 7012, par 71, rating 74.5, slope 144; Gold: yardage 6582, par 71, rating 72.2, slope 137; Gold/Blue: yardage 6366, par 71, rating 71.1, slope 135; Blue: yardage 6150, par 71, rating 70.6, slope 131; White: yardage 5710, par 71, rating 68.1, slope 125; *Women:* White/Green: yardage 5415, par 71, rating 73.1, slope 135; Green: yardage 4966, par 71, rating 69.4, slope 126.

Tee Times: Reservations can be made seven days in advance.

Dress Code: Collared shirts required. No denim is allowed. Soft spikes only.

Tournaments: No outside tournaments accepted.

Directions: From I-405 south of Los Angeles, take the Shady Canyon exit; head west to the entrance gate.

Contact: 100 Shady Canyon Drive, Irvine, CA 92603, pro shop 949/856-7000, fax 949/856-7001, www.shadycanyon.com/golfclub.

190 STRAWBERRY FARMS GOLF CLUB

Architect: Jim Lipe, 1997

18 holes **Public** **$85–135**

Southeast Detail map, page 298

Situated around Sand Canyon Reservoir, this course is surrounded by lakes, wildlife, natural waterfalls, and vegetation. Most of the holes on the front nine are so tight you'll feel like teeing off with a 7-iron once you've gone OB a few times. Needless to say, accuracy is a must to score well, and wind can be a factor, especially in the afternoon. Bunkers front many putting surfaces, eliminating the ground game. It's not one of Jim Lipe's better courses. Strawberry Farms offers golf instruction for adults and juniors. In the summer months, free junior clinics are available. Call the pro shop for more information.

Play Policy and Fees: Green fees are $85 Monday and Tuesday, $95 Wednesday and Thursday, and $135 Friday–Sunday and holidays. Twilight rates are available after 3 P.M. during the summer. All green fees include golf carts with the Pro Shot GPS system.

Tees and Yardage: *Men:* Black: yardage 6700, par 71, rating 72.7, slope 134; Blue: yardage 6276, par 71, rating 70.4, slope 129; White: yardage 5808, par 71, rating 68.2, slope 122; *Women:* Gold: yardage 5243, par 72, rating 70.9, slope 121; Red: yardage 4832, par 72, rating 68.7, slope 114.

Tee Times: Reservations may be made seven days in advance. For an additional $10 fee, premium tee times may be booked 8–30 days in advance.

Dress Code: Collared shirts and nonmetal spikes are required. No jeans are permitted.

Tournaments: Tournaments may be scheduled up to a year in advance. The banquet facility can accommodate 150 people.

Directions: From I-405 in Irvine, take the University/Jeffrey exit and head west. The course is on the left.

Contact: 11 Strawberry Farms Road, Irvine, CA 92612, pro shop 949/551-1811, www.strawberryfieldsgolf.com.

191 OAK CREEK GOLF CLUB

Architect: Tom Fazio, 1996
18 holes   **Public**   **$95–135**

Southeast Detail map, page 298

Oak Creek is a picturesque course where good shots are rewarded and bad shots are penalized. Landing zones are generally wide open and driver-friendly. If you miss fairways, though, bring plenty of golf balls, because they get lost easily in the deep rough. To score well, you must hit the fairways off the tee, stay out of the well-placed bunkers, and survive the long par-3s—there are three over 200 yards. The course is particularly women-friendly, with the silver tees measuring under 5000 yards. It is an example of a design where Tom Fazio and company took a somewhat uninteresting piece of raw land and made a very good golf course.

Play Policy and Fees: Green fees are $95 Monday–Thursday and $135 Friday–Sunday. Twilight, senior, junior, and nine-hole rates are available.

Tees and Yardage: *Men:* Black: yardage 6850, par 71, rating 72.7, slope 132; Gold: yardage 6543, par 71, rating 71.3, slope 129; White: yardage 6187, par 71, rating 69.4, slope 125; *Women:* Copper: yardage 5621, par 70, rating 72.7, slope 126; Silver: yardage 4989, par 71, rating 69.0, slope 120.

Tee Times: Reservations can be made seven days in advance. Premium tee times can be made with a credit card 8–60 days in advance for a $15 nonrefundable fee.

Dress Code: No denim is allowed on the course. Collared shirts and nonmetal spikes are required.

Tournaments: A 36-player minimum is required to book a tournament. The banquet facility can accommodate 60 people. Events can be scheduled up to one year in advance.

Directions: From I-405 in Newport Beach, head south and take the Sand Canyon Avenue exit. Head east on Sand Canyon Avenue to Irvine Center Drive and take a left. The golf course is on the right.

Contact: 1 Golf Club Drive, Irvine, CA 92620, pro shop 949/653-7300, fax 949/653-5305, www.oakcreekgolfclub.com.

192 EL TORO GOLF COURSE

Architect: William P. Bell, 1949
18 holes   **Public**   **$32–55**

Southeast Detail map, page 298

A former military course, El Toro is now open to the public. Many plans are being discussed for what to do with this expansive facility, including the possibility of additional golf courses, recreational opportunities, and residential development. The existing course is relatively flat with mature trees and a few doglegs. There is also a nine-hole practice course available.

Play Policy and Fees: Green fees are $32 to walk, $45 to ride Monday–Thursday; $37 to walk, $50 to ride Friday; and $55 riding only on weekends. Twilight, super twilight, senior, junior, and military rates are offered.

Tees and Yardage: *Men:* Blue: yardage 6750, par 72, rating 71.8, slope 120; White: yardage 6468, par 72, rating 70.4 slope 117; *Women:* Red: yardage 5657, par 72, rating 71.9, slope 120.

Tee Times: Reservations accepted seven days in advance.

Dress Code: Soft spikes are preferred.

Tournaments: Please inquire.

Directions: From I-5, take the Alton exit; drive east 3.5 miles to Fairbanks and take a left. Go approximately 100 yards to Astor and turn right to the course.

Contact: El Toro Marine Memorial MCAS, Santa Ana, CA 92709, pro shop 949/726-2577, www.eltorogolf.com.

193 DOVE CANYON COUNTRY CLUB

Architect: Jack Nicklaus, 1990
18 holes   Private

Southeast Detail map, page 298

 This course backs up to Cleveland National Forest, so count on plenty of wildlife. There are both barrancas and bunnies. The course is rolling, with some water and beautiful old oaks. A lake and a waterfall flank the finishing hole. It is among Nicklaus's more user-friendly courses, although from the championship tees—combined with tough pin placements—the course can play extremely difficult. PGA Tour professional Paul Goydos holds the course record with 60. This is a nonsmoking course.

Play Policy and Fees: Members and guests only.

Tees and Yardage: *Men:* Black: yardage 6903,

par 71, rating 73.7, slope 136; Players: yardage 6660, par 71, rating 72.4, slope 133; Blue: yardage 6488, par 71, rating 71.5, slope 131; White: yardage 6047, par 71, rating 69.3, slope 127; *Women:* Gold: yardage 5575, par 71, rating 73.7, slope 133; Green: yardage 5263, par 71, rating 71.9, slope 129.

Tee Times: Reservations may be booked a week in advance.

Dress Code: Collared shirts and nonmetal spikes are required. No denim, jeans, or tee shirts are permitted.

Tournaments: This course is available for outside tournaments. The banquet facility can accommodate approximately 150 people.

Directions: From I-5 south, take the Alicia Road exit east. Drive to Santa Margarita Parkway. Turn south on Santa Margarita to Plano Trabuco and turn right. Take Plano Trabuco to Dove Canyon Drive and turn left. Follow Dove Canyon to the guard gate and the course.

Contact: 22682 Golf Club Drive, Dove Canyon, CA 92679, pro shop 949/858-2888, clubhouse 949/858-2800, fax 949/858-1910.

194 CANYON LAKE GOLF CLUB

Architect: Ted Robinson Sr., 1968
18 holes   Private $35–45

Southeast Detail map, page 298

This hilly course in a private community is short and tight, with many hidden greens. Watch for the 15th. It is a par-3, 183-yard hole with a drop of 200 feet. The green is surrounded by trees and bunkers.

Play Policy and Fees: Reciprocal play is accepted with members of other private clubs; otherwise, members and guests only. Reciprocal fees, including cart, are $35 on weekdays and $45 on weekends.

Tees and Yardage: *Men:* Blue: yardage 5949, par 71, rating 68.7, slope 121; White: yardage 5708, par 71, rating 67.6, slope 117; Red: yardage 5430, par 71, rating 66.5, slope 114; *Women:* Gold: yardage 5153, par 71, rating 72.0, slope 131.

Tee Times: Reservations are accepted seven

days in advance. Reciprocators should have their club pro call to make arrangements.

Dress Code: Collared shirts are required. No denim is allowed, and shorts must be no more than four inches above the knee.

Tournaments: Tournaments must be sponsored by a member and are limited to Monday and Thursday.

Directions: From Riverside, travel south on I-215 to Newport Road. Turn right, head west to the last stop, and turn left. The club entrance is 300 yards past the traffic light.

Contact: 32001 Railroad Canyon Road, Canyon Lake, CA 92587, pro shop 909/246-1782, fax 909/244-8376.

195 NEWPORT BEACH GOLF COURSE

Architect: Harry Rainville and David Rainville, 1966
18 holes   **Public**   **$15–22**

Southeast Detail map, page 298

This executive course offers well-maintained and well-contoured holes, with bunkers and water often coming into play. The course is lighted for night play, and players can start until 8 P.M. The course features five par-4s. The 18th hole is among the most difficult at 225 yards, downhill. There are no grass tees here; golfers tee off from mats.

Play Policy and Fees: Green fees are $15 Monday–Thursday, $17 Friday, and $22 weekends.

Tees and Yardage: *Men and Women:* yardage 3216, par 59, rating n/a, slope n/a.

Tee Times: Reservations can be booked seven days in advance.

Dress Code: Nonmetal spikes are required.

Tournaments: Shotgun tournaments are available weekdays only.

Directions: In Newport Beach from the Newport Freeway (Highway 55), exit at Highway 73/South Corona Del Mar and drive south to Irvine Avenue. Turn right and drive half a mile to the club.

Contact: 3100 Irvine Avenue, Newport Beach, CA 92660, pro shop 949/852-8681.

196 BIG CANYON COUNTRY CLUB

Architect: Robert Muir Graves, 1971
18 holes   **Private**

Southeast Detail map, page 298

This is a traditional layout with many trees and bunkers, along with several water hazards. It has rolling fairways and many blind shots to the greens. It is among the more exclusive country clubs in the state. Tiger Woods holds the course record of 61.

Play Policy and Fees: Reciprocal play is accepted on a very limited basis; otherwise, members and guests only.

Tees and Yardage: *Men:* Black: yardage 6876, par 72, rating 73.9, slope 135; Blue: yardage 6617, par 72, rating 72.7, slope 130; White: yardage 6163, par 72, rating 70.5, slope 126; *Women:* Red: yardage 5605, par 72, rating 75.1, slope 137.

Tee Times: Reciprocal applications are considered from the head professional of other private clubs.

Dress Code: Appropriate golf attire and nonmetal spikes are required.

Tournaments: This course is not available for outside events.

Directions: From I-405 at Newport Beach, take the MacArthur Boulevard exit south and drive five miles to San Joaquin Hills Road. Turn right and drive to Big Canyon Drive and the course.

Contact: 1 Big Canyon Drive, Newport Beach, CA 92660, pro shop 949/720-1003, clubhouse 949/644-5404.

197 PELICAN HILL GOLF CLUB

Architect: Tom Fazio, 1991
36 holes   **Resort**   **$175–250**

Southeast Detail map, page 298

 These two oceanfront gems are equally good but distinctly different. Both offer spectacular ocean views from every hole. Ocean South is a good test of golf and can be difficult when the ocean breezes are stiff. More often it is user-friendly, with generous fairway landing areas and big, tiered greens. You'll want to putt from below the hole, or your ball could just keep on rolling. The Ocean North Course is a longer, tighter, flatter design, often preferred by better players. It is more of a "links-style" course. These are two of the best courses in the West, excellently managed and run. A wonderful clubhouse serves great food. A lighted driving range and excellent instruction are available in a separate facility a block from the golf clubhouse.

Play Policy and Fees: Green fees are $175 Monday–Thursday and $250 Friday–Sunday and holidays, including cart. Twilight rates are available.

Tees and Yardage: Ocean South Course—*Men:* Tournament: yardage 6589, par 70, rating 72.1, slope 130; Championship: yardage 6283, par 70, rating 70.3, slope 125; Middle: yardage 5865, par 70, rating 68.1, slope 119; *Women:* Intermediate: yardage 5367, par 70, rating 72.7, slope 131; Forward: yardage 4710, par 70, rating 68.2, slope 119. Ocean North Course—*Men:* Tournament: yardage 6856, par 71, rating 73.3, slope 133; Championship: yardage 6516, par 71, rating 71.7, slope 129; Middle: yardage 6153, par 71, rating 69.7, slope 124; *Women:* Intermediate: yardage 5800, par 71, rating 74.5, slope 137; Forward: yardage 4950, par 71, rating 69.4, slope 124.

Tee Times: Reservations can be made seven days in advance without a charge. Tee times can be made up to 60 days in advance with a $20 fee per player. For reservations, call 949/760-0707.

Dress Code: Appropriate golf attire and nonmetal spikes are required. No denim is allowed.

Tournaments: A 36-player minimum is needed to book a tournament. Tournaments can be booked 12 months in advance. The banquet facility can accommodate 300 people.

Directions: Take I-405 or Highway 55 to Highway 73 (a toll road). Exit at Newport Coast Road. Turn right on Pelican Hill Road South. **Contact:** 22651 Pelican Hill Road South, Newport Coast, CA 92657, pro shop 949/760-0707, www.pelicanhill.com.

198 LAGUNA WOODS GOLF CLUB

Architect: Harry Rainville and David Rainville, 1974
27 holes   **Private**

🏌 📷 🍽 🏌 🚗 🍺

Southeast Detail map, page 298

There are three nine-hole rotations in the retirement community of Leisure World. They are rolling layouts with mature trees, great for the seniors who primarily play them. Each rotation varies in difficulty, so matching horses to courses is easy.

Play Policy and Fees: Members and guests only.

Tees and Yardage: Courses 1 and 2—*Men:* Blue: yardage 6070, par 71, rating 69.1, slope 116; White: yardage 6002, par 71, rating 68.8, slope 115; *Women:* Red: yardage 5557, par 71, rating 71.3, slope 120. Courses 2 and 3—*Men:* Blue: yardage 5574, par 71, rating 66.4, slope 114, White: yardage 5497, par 71, rating 66.1, slope 118; *Women:* Red: yardage 5214, par 71, rating 70.2, slope 118. Courses 3 and 1—*Men:* Blue: yardage 5718, par 71, rating 67.5, slope 114; White: yardage 5631, par 71, rating 67.1, slope 113; *Women:* Red: yardage 5299, par 71, rating 70.3, slope 120.

Tee Times: Not applicable.

Dress Code: Appropriate golf attire is required, and nonmetal spikes are recommended.

Tournaments: This course is not available for outside events.

Directions: Take the El Toro Road exit off I-5 at Laguna Hills and travel west to Moulton Parkway. Drive right one-quarter mile to the club.

Contact: 24112 Moulton Parkway (P.O. Box 2307), Laguna Hills, CA 92653, pro shop 949/597-4336, fax 949/380-4301.

199 ALISO VIEJO GOLF CLUB

Architect: Nicklaus Design, 1999
27 holes   **Public**   **$65–85**

🏌 📷 🍽 🚗 🍺

Southeast Detail map, page 298

Aliso Viejo is 27 holes of thoughtful, and at times inspired, design—not overly long (no nine measures more than 3300 yards), with wide fairways and large, contoured greens that guarantee a lot of three-putts if your approach is not accurate. Bunkers are well-placed and somewhat deep, though you can always see whatever trouble lies ahead. There are lots of holes you'll remember after the round. The three nines are named Valley, Creek, and Ridge. A clubhouse has been planned for some time, and will perhaps be complete in 2004. At that time, this course could become an 18-hole facility.

Play Policy and Fees: Green fees are $65 Monday–Thursday for 18 holes and $85 Friday–Sunday. Nine-hole, junior, senior, and twilight rates are also available. All green fees include a cart.

Tees and Yardage: Valley/Ridge Course—*Men:* Black: yardage 6268, par 71, rating 70.3, slope 132; Blue: yardage 6150, par 71, rating 69.5, slope 131; White: yardage 5781, par 71, rating 68.1, slope 128; *Women:* Red: yardage 4740, par 71, rating 67.5, slope 117. Creek/Valley Course: *Men:* Black: yardage 6435, par 71, rating 71.3, slope 134; Blue: yardage 6291, par 71, rating 70.5, slope 132; White: yardage 5928, par 71, rating 68.9, slope 129; *Women:* Red: yardage 4878, par 71, rating 68.6, slope 122. Ridge/Creek Course: *Men:* Black: yardage 6277, par 70, rating 70.7, slope 136; Blue: yardage 6131, par 70, rating 70.1, slope 135; White: yardage 5749, par 70, rating 68.3, slope 130; *Women:* Red: yardage 4736, par 70, rating 68.6, slope 121.

Tee Times: Reservations can be made up to seven days in advance. A $15 fee is charged for tee times made 8–14 days in advance, and a $20 fee is charged for tee times booked 15–30 days in advance.

Dress Code: No jeans are allowed on the course, and collared shirts are required. Dress shorts are okay. Soft spikes required.

Tournaments: A minimum of 12 players is required to book an event. All tournaments include a personal tournament coordinator, scoring, and unlimited advanced booking. The banquet facility can accommodate up to 320 people.

Directions: From San Clemente, head north on I-5 to the El Toro Road exit. Turn left on El Toro to Moulton Parkway. Turn left on Moulton Parkway to Glenwood Drive. Turn right on Glenwood to the golf course.

Contact: 25002 Golf Course Drive, Aliso Viejo, CA 92656, pro shop 949/598-9200, www.alisogolf.com.

200 ALISO CREEK INN AND GOLF COURSE

Architect: Course designed, 1951

9 holes   **Resort**   **$19–28**

Southeast Detail map, page 298

This traditional course is set in a heavily foliaged canyon with a meandering creek. There are 19 bunkers and lots of trees. With the ocean just 400 yards away, a sea breeze adds to the quiet atmosphere. Aliso Creek provides a pleasant round of golf.

Aliso Creek Inn offers 62 rooms in studios or townhouses. They are simple but clean. Please call 949/499-2271 for information.

Play Policy and Fees: Green fees are $19 for nine holes Monday–Thursday, $22 Friday, and $28 weekends. Replays are $13 weekdays only. Senior rates are offered. Carts additional.

Tees and Yardage: *Men:* Back: yardage 2221, par 32, rating n/a, slope n/a; Middle: yardage 1962, par 32, rating n/a, slope n/a; *Women:* Forward: yardage 1669, par 32, rating n/a, slope n/a.

Tee Times: Reservations can be booked seven days in advance.

Dress Code: Collared shirts and nonmetal spikes are required.

Tournaments: Shotgun tournaments are not allowed.

Directions: Take I-5 or I-405 southbound in Orange County to Highway 133 (Laguna Freeway). Take Highway 133 west to Highway 1 (Pacific Coast Highway). Drive south on Highway 1 almost three miles to the green overpass. Take an immediate left turn at Ben Brown's sign. From northbound I-5, take the Beach Cities exit. Drive north on Highway 1 about six miles. Turn right at the sign across from Aliso State Beach Pier.

Contact: 31106 Pacific Coast Highway, South Laguna Beach, CA 92677, pro shop 949/499-1919, www.alisocreekinn.com.

 EL NIGUEL COUNTRY CLUB

Architect: David Kent, 1963
18 holes   **Private**

Southeast Detail map, page 298

This is a challenging course that is heavily bunkered. It features level fairways and lots of trees. The greens are some of the toughest west of the Rocky Mountains. You'll need a fortune teller to help you read them. The par-3 holes are exceptionally good. Fairways and roughs are kikuyu grass, which makes them unwieldy. The course is beautifully maintained, and at one time it was considered the finest course in Orange County.

Play Policy and Fees: Reciprocal play is accepted with members of other private clubs; otherwise, members and guests only.

Tees and Yardage: *Men:* Black: yardage 7010, par 72, rating 73.8, slope 134; Blue: yardage 6629, par 72, rating 72.1, slope 128; White: yardage 6437, par 72, rating 71.1, slope 124; Gold: yardage 6108, par 72, rating 69.1, slope 119; *Women:* Red: yardage 5739, par 72, rating 74.8, slope 134.

Tee Times: Reciprocators should have their home professional call to make arrangements.

Dress Code: Appropriate golf attire and non-metal spikes are required.

Tournaments: This course is available for outside tournaments with board approval. Submit a request in writing to the general manager. A 100-player minimum is needed.

Directions: Take the Crown Valley Parkway exit off I-5 in Laguna Niguel, then drive west for 4.5 miles to Clubhouse Drive and turn left.

Contact: 23700 Clubhouse Drive, Laguna Niguel, CA 92677, pro shop 949/496-2023, fax 949/249-9455.

CASTA DEL SOL GOLF COURSE

Architect: Ted Robinson Sr., 1963
18 holes   **Public**   **$20–30**

Southeast Detail map, page 298

This rolling executive course has several streams and lakes. It can be testy, but this short course is a fun round for beginning and intermediate players.

Play Policy and Fees: Green fees are $20 on weekdays and $30 on weekends. Carts are $12 per person. Twilight rates are offered.

Tees and Yardage: *Men:* Back: yardage 3670, par 60, rating 58.1, slope 96; *Women:* Forward: yardage 3398, par 61, rating 60.0, slope 98.

Tee Times: Reservations may be booked seven days in advance.

Dress Code: Tank tops are not permitted. Soft spikes are preferred.

Tournaments: Events may be booked up to a year in advance. The banquet facility can accommodate 80 people.

Directions: Take the La Paz Road exit off I-5 and travel east for one mile to Marguerite Parkway. Turn left and drive 1.5 miles to Casta del Sol Road. Turn right and drive to the course.

Contact: 27601 Casta Del Sol Road, Mission Viejo, CA 92692, pro shop 949/581-9700, fax 949/581-5697, www.americangolf.com.

203 COTO DE CAZA GOLF CLUB

Architect: Robert Trent Jones Jr., 1987 (North Course) and 1995 (South Course)
36 holes   **Private**   **$110**

Southeast Detail map, page 298

Designed by Robert Trent Jones Jr. with Johnny Miller as a consultant, Coto is set in canyons in south Orange County and features native California oak trees. The North Course's par-5 first hole requires a tee shot through a chute and over one of the canyons, with trees and more canyon guarding the left side. The wonderful new South Course complements the

North Course. Most consider it several shots easier. Small, traditional greens have subtle mounding and offer straightforward putting. These are two delightful and well-kept designs.
Play Policy and Fees: Limited reciprocal play is accepted with members of other ClubCorp. facilities; otherwise, members and guests only. The green fee for reciprocal play is $110, cart included.
Tees and Yardage: North Course—*Men:* Black: yardage 7131, par 72, rating 75.5, slope 147; Gold: yardage 6752, par 72, rating 73.4, slope 140; Blue: yardage 6482, par 72, rating 72.1, slope 131; White: yardage 6110, par 72, rating 70.2, slope 131; *Women:* Red: yardage 5389, par 72, rating 72.5, slope 132. South Course— *Men:* Black: yardage 6943, par 72, rating 74.3, slope 140; Gold: yardage 6634, par 72, rating 72.8, slope 137; Blue: yardage 6336, par 72, rating 71.1, slope 133; White: yardage 5862, par 72, rating 69.1, slope 125; *Women:* Red: yardage 5326, par 72, rating 72.1, slope 129.
Tee Times: Reciprocal players should have their home professional call to make arrangements.
Dress Code: Appropriate golf attire and nonmetal spikes are required.
Tournaments: The courses are available for outside tournaments on Monday.
Directions: From Mission Viejo, take I-5 south to the Oso Parkway exit. Drive east for six miles until Oso Parkway ends. Turn left on Coto de Caza Drive. Turn right into the club.
Contact: 25291 Vista del Verde, Coto de Caza, CA 92679, pro shop 949/858-2770, clubhouse 949/858-4100.

TIJERAS CREEK GOLF CLUB
Architect: Ted Robinson Sr., 1990
18 holes **Public** **$80–115**

🏃 📷 🍽️ 🛺 🍺

Southeast Detail map, page 298

A very women-friendly design, this course has distinctly different nines. The front side winds through a housing development, while the back nine is built in a natural canyon terrain populated by old-growth sycamores, oaks, and na-

tive chaparral. Deer and other wildlife are frequently spotted on the back nine. Tijeras Creek is regarded as one of the best public courses in Orange County.
Play Policy and Fees: Regular green fees are $80 Monday–Thursday, $95 Friday and Sunday, and $115 on Saturday. Twilight, sunset, and replay rates are offered.
Tees and Yardage: *Men:* Black: yardage 6918, par 72, rating 73.4, slope 136; Blue: yardage 6559, par 72, rating 71.1, slope 129; White: yardage 6220, par 72, rating 69.1, slope 124; *Women:* Red: yardage 5130, par 72, rating 69.8, slope 120.
Tee Times: Reservations can be made seven days in advance.
Dress Code: Collared shirts and nonmetal spikes are required. No denim is allowed on the course.
Tournaments: This course is available for tournaments Monday–Thursday. Reservations may be made up to one year in advance.
Directions: From I-5, take the Oso Parkway exit east. Drive three miles to Antonio. Turn left on Antonio and drive two miles to Tijeras Creek Road. Turn left and follow the road to the golf club.
Contact: 29082 Tijeras Creek Road, Rancho Santa Margarita, CA 92688, pro shop 949/589-9793, fax 949/589-0219, www.tijerascreek.com.

 MISSION VIEJO COUNTRY CLUB
Architect: Robert Trent Jones Sr., 1967
18 holes **Private** **$125**

🏃 📷 🍽️ 🛺 🍺

Southeast Detail map, page 298

This is a long and demanding course with a stream running through eight holes. The fairways are hilly and parallel. The greens are well maintained, very fast, and usually elevated, just like RTJ Sr. liked them. This course was once dubbed "Mission Impossible" by Johnny Miller. Mission Viejo has twice been host to the local U.S. Open qualifying and has also hosted the U.S. Open women's qualifying. PGA Tour standout Mark O'Meara grew up in the area and learned to play golf at Mission Viejo. There is a lounge in the clubhouse named in his honor.

Play Policy and Fees: Reciprocal play is accepted with members of other private clubs; otherwise, members and guests only. Reciprocal fees are $125. Optional carts are $14 per person.

Tees and Yardage: *Men:* Black: yardage 6903, par 72, rating 73.8, slope 136; Blue: yardage 6552, par 72, rating 72.2, slope 133; White: yardage 6153, par 72, rating 70.3, slope 126; *Women:* Red: yardage 5607, par 72, rating 75.0, slope 140; Gold: yardage 4976, par 72, rating 64.9, slope 111.

Tee Times: Reciprocal players should have their home professional call to make arrangements.

Dress Code: All shirts must have collars. No jeans are allowed on the course, and shorts must have a 17-inch inseam. Metal spikes are prohibited.

Tournaments: This course is available for outside tournaments, requiring a 100-player minimum. Tournaments should be scheduled at least eight months in advance. The banquet facility can accommodate 200 people.

Directions: Take the Oso Parkway exit off I-5 near Mission Viejo, travel east half a mile to Country Club Drive, and turn right to the club.

Contact: 26200 Country Club Drive, Mission Viejo, CA 92691, pro shop 949/582-1020, clubhouse 949/582-1550, fax 949/582-3875, www.missionviejocc.com.

206 ARROYO TRABUCO GOLF CLUB

Architect: Casey O'Callaghan and Tom Lehman, 2004
18 holes   **Public**   **$55-85**

Southeast Detail map, page 298

Set amidst Trabuco Creek and Ladera Open Space Reserve, Arroyo Trabuco provides a "high-end golfing experience at a competitive price." The 240-acre site occupies an old gravel pit (whose operations were shut down in December 2000), and several holes play around the old facility. The layout encounters quite a bit of rolling topography, making for some fun and memorable holes. The facility includes a wedding garden and a 250-seat banquet hall.

Play Policy and Fees: Green fees are $55 Monday-Thursday, $75 Friday, and $85 weekends and holidays. Fees include power carts. Twilight rates are available.

Tees and Yardage: *Men:* Black: yardage 7011, par 72, rating 73.7, slope 134; Blue: yardage 6602, par 72, rating 71.3, slope 129; White: yardage 6115, par 72, rating 69.3, slope 125; *Women:* Red: yardage 5553, par 72, rating 67.0, slope 119; Gold: yardage 5045, par 72, rating 64.2, slope 112.

Tee Times: Reservations can be made seven days in advance.

Dress Code: Appropriate golf attire is required. Soft spikes only.

Tournaments: Tournaments of all types are welcome.

Directions: From I-5 south of Los Angeles, take the Avery Parkway exit. Drive east one-half mile to the course.

Contact: 26772 Avery Parkway, Mission Viejo, CA 92692, phone 949/364-1881, fax 949/364-1441, www.arroyotrabuco.com.

207 MARBELLA GOLF & COUNTRY CLUB

Architect: Tom Weiskopf and Jay Morrish, 1989
18 holes   **Private**   **$100**

Southeast Detail map, page 298

This long, hilly course features undulating fairways and large bent-grass greens. The front nine is mostly flat, while the back nine is hillier. The pride of the course is the 428-yard, par-4 18th hole. This downhill hole is guarded by water and is a test for any player. Masters and British Open Champion Mark O'Meara holds the course record with a 62.

Play Policy and Fees: Reciprocal play is accepted on a very limited basis with local clubs; otherwise, members and guests only. Reciprocal fees are $100, plus optional cart at $13.50 per person.

Tees and Yardage: *Men:* Gold: yardage 6563, par 70, rating 72.0, slope 133; Players: yardage 6366, par 70, rating 71.1, slope 131; Blue: yardage 6199, par 70, rating 70.4, slope 129; White: yardage 5773, par 70, rating 68.2, slope 124; *Women:* Red: yardage 5285, par 70, rating 72.1, slope 127.

Tee Times: Reciprocal players should have their home professional call to make arrangements.

Dress Code: Appropriate golf attire and nonmetal spikes are required.

Tournaments: This course is available for outside tournaments on Monday.

Directions: From I-5 in Los Angeles, drive south to the Ortega Highway/Highway 74 exit. Drive east to Rancho Viejo Road. Turn left on Rancho Viejo Road. Drive one mile to the club, which is on the right.

Contact: 30800 Golf Club Drive, San Juan Capistrano, CA 92675, pro shop 949/248-3700.

208 BEAR CREEK GOLF CLUB

Architect: Jack Nicklaus, 1983

18 holes   **Private**   **$101**

Southeast Detail map, page 298

This championship course is aptly named because it's a bear to play. It was designed by Jack Nicklaus in 1983 and features a natural rolling terrain with pot bunkers, mounds, and creeks. Water guards half the course, and the greens are large and tricky. Nicklaus's favorite hole is the 391-yard, par-4 fourth hole. It has a split-level fairway divided by grass bunkers. Bear Creek rates among the top courses in the state, although the wind picks up considerably in the afternoons, often making this an angry bear. Immaculately conditioned, this course was the site of the 1985 Skins Game and is used regularly for PGA Tour qualifying.

Play Policy and Fees: Limited reciprocal play is accepted with members of other private clubs; otherwise, members and guests only. Reciprocal fee is $101, including cart.

Tees and Yardage: *Men:* Gold: yardage 7003, par 72, rating 74.7, slope 141; Blue: yardage 6422, par 72, rating 71.8, slope 135; White: yardage 5990, par 72, rating 69.9, slope 129; *Women:* Red: yardage 5426, par 72, rating 73.3, slope 137; Green: yardage 5230, par 72, rating 72.5, slope 134.

Tee Times: Reciprocal players should have their home professional call to make arrangements.

Dress Code: Proper dress code is strictly enforced. Nonmetal spikes are required.

Tournaments: Shotgun tournaments are available Monday only. Carts are required. A 100-player minimum is required to book a tournament. Events should be scheduled 12 months in advance. A banquet facility is available that can accommodate up to 220 people.

Directions: From Temecula, take I-15 to the Clinton Keith exit in Murrieta, then travel west to Bear Creek Drive and turn north to the club.

Contact: 22640 North Bear Creek Drive, Murrieta, CA 92562, pro shop 909/677-8631, clubhouse 909/677-8621, www.bearcreekgc.com.

209 THE COLONY COUNTRY CLUB

Architect: David Rainville, 1989

18 holes   **Semiprivate**   **$20–30**

Southeast Detail map, page 298

Five lakes and a channel keep golfers honest on this executive course. Although the course is mostly flat, its trees and bunkers can be a problem for errant shots. The toughest hole is the par-4 seventh, which is bordered by trees on both sides of the fairway, with a large eucalyptus tree looming off the tee.

Play Policy and Fees: Weekday green fees are $20 walking and $25 riding; weekend fees are $25 walking, $30 riding. Senior, junior, and twilight rates are offered.

Tees and Yardage: *Men:* Blue: yardage 4681, par 65, rating 62.3, slope 108; White: yardage 4345, par 65, rating 60.5, slope 104; *Women:* Red: yardage 3843, par 65, rating 62.0, slope 100.

Tee Times: Reservations can be booked five days in advance.

Dress Code: Collared shirts and nonmetal spikes are required.

Tournaments: A 20-player minimum is needed to book a tournament.

Directions: From Temecula, take I-15 five miles north to California Oaks Road. The course is one block east of the freeway.

Contact: 40603 Colony Drive, Murrieta, CA 92562, pro shop 909/677-2221.

210 THE SCGA GOLF COURSE
Architect: Robert Trent Jones Sr., 1972
18 holes   Public $48-78

🚶 📷 🍴 🛺 ⛳

Southeast Detail map, page 298

Acquired by the Southern California Golf Association in February 1994, this classic Robert Trent Jones Sr. course is long, open, and traverses rolling terrain. The pride of the course is the par-4 third hole, which features an elevation drop of about 150 feet from tee to fairway. This hole also provides great views of the valley. The course has hosted numerous qualifiers for the U.S. PubLinks, SCGA, and U.S. Amateur. An innovative and well-respected junior golf program is in place.

Play Policy and Fees: Green fees for SCGA members are $48 Monday–Thursday, $53 Friday, and $63 weekends and holidays. Fees for nonmembers are $63 Monday–Thursday, $68 Friday, and $78 weekends and holidays. Fees include carts. Twilight and other special rates are available. Check the website or call for details.

Tees and Yardage: *Men:* Black: yardage 7066, par 72, rating 74.4, slope 137; Blue: yardage 6724, par 72, rating 73.0, slope 134; White: yardage 6294, par 72, rating 71.0, slope 128; *Women:* Red: yardage 5355, par 72, rating 71.7, slope 128.

Tee Times: Reservations can be booked seven days in advance for nonmembers and 10 days in advance for SCGA members.

Dress Code: Collared shirts and slacks are required. Bermuda shorts are okay. Nonmetal spikes are required.

Tournaments: A 16-player minimum is needed to book a tournament. Carts are required.

Directions: The course is in Murrieta, off I-15 and I-215. Take the Murrieta Hot Springs Road exit east for 1.5 miles to Via Princessa and the course.

Contact: 39500 Robert Trent Jones Parkway, Murrieta, CA 92563, pro shop 909/677-7446, www.scgagolfcourse.com.

211 TEMEKU HILLS GOLF AND COUNTRY CLUB
Architect: Ted Robinson Sr., 1995
18 holes   Public $43-59

🚶 📷 🍴 🛺 ⛳

Southeast Detail map, page 298

Carts are mandatory on this hilly course, which features multitiered greens and five lakes. As always, architect Ted Robinson has incorporated waterfalls (four), which are visually pleasing but also dangerous for those easily distracted. The pride of the course is the downhill 345-yard, par-4 10th hole, a dogleg right with water in front and behind the green. The nines were switched in 1999.

Play Policy and Fees: Green fees are $43 on weekdays, $59 on weekends, including cart. Twilight and super twilight rates are offered.

Tees and Yardage: *Men:* Gold: yardage 6636, par 72, rating 72.4, slope 131; Blue: yardage 6175, par 72, rating 70.3, slope 126; White: yardage 5825, par 72, rating 68.6, slope 123; *Women:* Red: yardage 5113, par 72, rating 70.0, slope 125.

Tee Times: Reservations can be booked seven days in advance.

Dress Code: Collared shirts and nonmetal spikes are required. No blue jeans or tank tops are allowed. Bermuda shorts are permitted.

Tournaments: A 16-player minimum is required to book a tournament. Events can be scheduled 12 months in advance. The banquet facility can accommodate 450 people.

Directions: From San Diego, take I-15 north. Exit at Rancho California Road. Drive east three miles to the course.

Contact: 41687 Temeku Drive, Temecula, CA 92591, pro shop 909/693-1440, clubhouse 909/694-9998, fax 909/693-1445, www.temeku hills.com.

Chapter 14

BARONA CREEK GOLF CLUB © GEORGE FULLER

San Diego and Vicinity

San Diego and Vicinity

Everybody loves San Diego. Around the world and in every corner of the United States, San Diego is known as the perfect Southern California city. It's not as big and busy as Los Angeles, its downtown is right at the lovely waterfront, the weather is supreme year-round . . . what's not to love?

Residents enjoy boating and ocean sports, surfing, hiking, horseback riding, and exploring the back roads of their home territory. They also golf like crazy. Their options are many, and they take advantage of them all.

The region stretches from San Clemente to the border with Mexico, from the Pacific Ocean and east across the desert toward the Salton Sea and El Centro. The landscape of the golf courses reflects this diversity. You will find courses on ocean bluffs, in rolling mountain valleys, perched on hillsides, and in fertile meadows bordered by crops.

Some of the fastest-growing communities in the country are in this wide region: Chula Vista, Rancho Santa Fe, Escondido, Temecula, and Fallbrook. Those areas are also where you'll find the most growth in the game of golf.

In Chula Vista, The Auld Course opened in 2001, and it serves up a popular round in a rolling landscape, with a welcome emphasis on pace of play. A little northeast of downtown San Diego in Lakeside, Barona Creek Golf Club is an inspired Gary Roger Baird design next to a gaming casino on the Barona Indian Reservation, a peaceful setting for golf.

Rancho Santa Fe, some 20 minutes north of downtown San Diego near the coast, has seen the opening of several excellent new courses in the past few years, including The Crosby at Rancho Santa Fe (2001), The Santaluz Club (2002), and The Bridges at Rancho Santa Fe (2000). All are private courses, part of gated residential communities, and like many coastal courses they are subject to afternoon winds.

In golf-rich Escondido, Maderas Golf Club opened in 2001; it draws raves from players and the golf media. Nearby, Reidy Creek opened a year later in 2002. Not your average par-3 course, this Cal Olson design is a real knockout.

A short drive up I-15 is Fallbrook and the new Golf Club of California (2001), another top-notch private design. Farther up I-15 in Temecula, CrossCreek Golf Club opened in 2001, an upscale daily fee course. Both of these courses are in warm, protected valley terrain.

When viewed in combination with the award-winning resort courses over on the coast—Four Seasons Aviara, La Costa, the new Lodge at Torrey Pines (adjacent to the 36 tremendous holes at Torrey Pines Golf Course), and many others—this is an area with much outstanding golf to offer.

San Diego is a crowd-pleasing region the whole family will enjoy, with lots of recreational activities for everyone. And thankfully for enthusiasts, it is one of California's fastest-growing areas for golf.

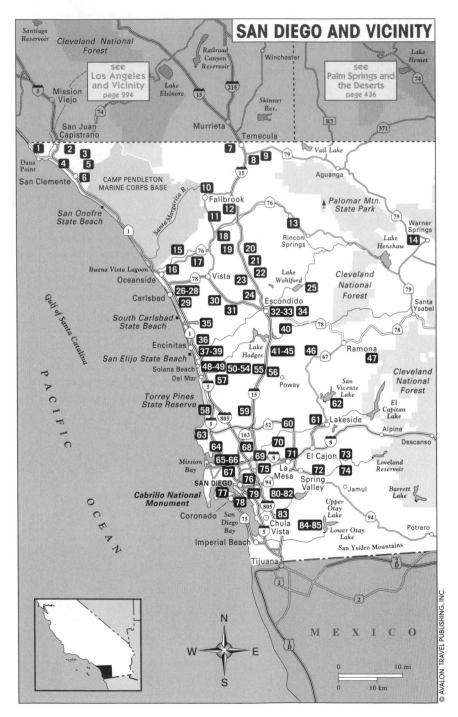

■ MONARCH BEACH GOLF LINKS

Architect: Robert Trent Jones Jr., 1983
18 holes   Public/Resort $160–185

San Diego and Vicinity map, page 394

Most of this course offers a nice view of the ocean, and a couple of holes run alongside it. The course was built to conform nicely to the terrain. Watch out for the seventh hole. It's a par-5, 602-yard twister with a creek intersecting the fairway. To reach the green in regulation, it is necessary to clear the creek twice. Long hitters might reach the green in two, but if they miss, they will be appropriately penalized. The course is on both sides of scenic Pacific Coast Highway. Note: There is no driving range here, but there are cages where players can loosen up. This is a very nice resort-style facility.

The lovely St. Regis Monarch Beach Resort & Spa is affiliated with the course and offers golf packages. For reservations or information, call 949/234-3200.

Play Policy and Fees: Green fees are $160 Monday–Thursday and $185 Friday–Sunday, including carts. Guests of The St. Regis Monarch Beach Resort receive discounted rates. Senior, twilight, and super twilight rates are offered.

Tees and Yardage: *Men:* Championship: yardage 6601, par 70, rating 72.8, slope 138; Back: yardage 6052, par 70, rating 70.0, slope 132; Middle: yardage 5612, par 70, rating 67.7, slope 125; *Women:* Forward: yardage 5050, par 70, rating 70.4, slope 125.

Tee Times: Reservations are required and may be booked 14 days in advance. For tee times 15–30 days in advance, there is a $15 advance booking fee. Resort guests may book times up to 60 days in advance.

Dress Code: Collared shirts are required, and no denim is allowed. Soft spikes only.

Tournaments: Tournaments may be booked up to a year in advance. A banquet facility holds 200 people.

Directions: Take the Crown Valley Parkway exit off I-5. Drive 3.5 miles to Niguel Road. Turn left and travel another three miles. Turn right into the entryway across from the tennis club.

Contact: 22 Monarch Beach Resort Drive North, Dana Point, CA 92629, pro shop 949/240-8247, www.troongolf.com.

■ SAN JUAN HILLS GOLF CLUB

Architect: Harry Rainville and David Rainville, 1966
18 holes   Public $32–63

San Diego and Vicinity map, page 394

Recent renovations have improved this 1966 design greatly, including rebuilt tee boxes and bunkers. The front and back nines are as different as night and day. The front nine is flat, with trees lining the fairway. The back nine is hilly, with an abundance of trees to get in your way. This course is fairly close to the ocean, so the air is clean, but afternoon winds can make the course testy.

Play Policy and Fees: Monday–Wednesday green fees are $32 walking, $47 riding. Carts are mandatory before twilight Thursday–Sunday. Green fees are $47 Thursday, $52 Friday, and $63 weekends and holidays. Twilight rates are available.

Tees and Yardage: *Men:* Blue: yardage 6295, par 71, rating 69.5, slope 117; White: yardage 5960, par 71, rating 67.7, slope 111; *Women:* Red: yardage 5402, par 71, rating 71.1, slope 124.

Tee Times: Reservations can be booked 10 days in advance.

Dress Code: Collared shirts are required. Soft spikes only.

Tournaments: A 24-player minimum is needed to book a tournament. Tournaments can be booked one month in advance. The banquet facility can accommodate 70 people.

Directions: From I-5 near San Juan Capistrano, take the exit for San Juan Creek Road. Go to the light and turn right. Take the next right and go one-quarter of a mile to the course.

Contact: 32120 San Juan Creek Road, San Juan Capistrano, CA 92675, pro shop 949/493-1167, fax 949/493-0866, www.sanjuanhillsgolf.com.

3 TALEGA GOLF CLUB

Architect: Fred Couples and
Schmidt Curley Golf Design, 2001

18 holes   **Public**   **$95–125**

San Diego and Vicinity map, page 394

Talega nestles in the foothills of the Coastal Range, giving the land a rolling character. It is a big-hitter's course, with generous fairways and receptive greens. The bunkers are filled with crushed white marble. Some lakes and water features beautify the design.

Play Policy and Fees: Fees are $95 Monday–Thursday, $115 Friday, and $125 weekends and holidays. Cart fees are included in all prices. Resident, senior, junior, early bird, and twilight rates are also available. Check the website for specials.

Tees and Yardage: *Men:* Copper: yardage 6951, par 72, rating 73.6, slope 137; Blue: yardage 6583, par 72, rating 71.8, slope 130; White: yardage 6187, par 72, rating 69.2, slope 124; *Women:* Red: yardage 5569, par 72, rating 71.1, slope 121.

Tee Times: Reservations may be made up to 10 days in advance.

Dress Code: Collared shirts are required, and shorts may not be more than five inches above the knee. No denim is permitted. Soft spikes only.

Tournaments: This course is available for outside events.

Directions: Take I-5 to the Pico exit in San Clemente. Drive east two miles, then turn left on Vista Hermosa. Continue approximately one-half mile to Avenida Talega. The club is on the left.

Contact: 990 Avenida Talega, San Clemente, CA 92673, pro shop 949/369-6226, fax 949/369-6227, www.talegagolfclub.com.

4 SHORECLIFFS GOLF COURSE

Architect: Joseph B. Williams, 1962

18 holes   **Public**   **$32–49**

San Diego and Vicinity map, page 394

This course demands accuracy. It is short and tight and meanders in and out of canyons.

Hook a tee shot and you might find yourself in a canyon with the coyotes. There are lots of out-of-bounds and several water hazards. The yardage of this course makes it look easier than it plays. This was one of President Nixon's favorite courses.

Play Policy and Fees: Green fees are $32 weekdays, $49 weekends. Carts are included and mandatory. Senior and twilight rates are offered.

Tees and Yardage: *Men:* Blue: yardage 6129, par 71, rating 70.7, slope 130; White: yardage 5822, par 71, rating 69.2, slope 126; *Women:* Red: yardage 5223, par 72, rating 71.1, slope 123.

Tee Times: Reservations can be booked seven days in advance.

Dress Code: Appropriate golf attire is required.

Tournaments: This course is available for outside tournaments.

Directions: Take the Camino de Estrella exit off I-5 and drive east to Avenida Vaquero. Turn right to the course.

Contact: 501 Avenida Vaquero, San Clemente, CA 92672, pro shop 949/492-1177, clubhouse 949/492-5216, www.pacificgc.com.

5 PACIFIC GOLF & COUNTRY CLUB

Architect: Gary Player and Carl Litton, 1988

27 holes   **Private**   **$100**

San Diego and Vicinity map, page 394

These three nine-hole rotas are named after each of the courses where Gary Player won his British Open Championships. But they are not links-style courses as one might think they were. Instead, they are scenic, traditional parkland layouts that roll through meadows. The first hole at Carnoustie/Muirfield gives some golfers a scare. It's an uphill par-4 to an undulating, sloping green. To make par, your second shot had better be a good one. All three nines are distinctly different. Wind can be a factor here. The course record is 66, set by Gary Player on opening day.

Play Policy and Fees: Reciprocal play with other private clubs is accepted; otherwise, members and guests only. Reciprocal green fees are $100.

Tees and Yardage: Royal Lytham/Carnoustie—*Men:* Championship: yardage 6484, par 72, rating 72.1, slope 138; Tournament: yardage 6147, par 72, rating 69.7, slope 135; Members: yardage 5615, par 72, rating 67.3, slope 127; *Women:* Forward: yardage 5208, par 72, rating 71.5, slope 130. Carnoustie/Muirfield—*Men:* Championship: yardage 6847, par 72, rating 73.8, slope 142; Tournament: yardage 6411, par 72, rating 71.7, slope 136; Members: yardage 5671, par 72, rating 68.1, slope 127; *Women:* Forward: yardage 5214, par 72, rating 72.0, slope 131. Muirfield/Royal Lytham—*Men:* Championship: yardage 6631, par 72, rating 72.2, slope 137; Tournament: yardage 6272, par 72, rating 70.3, slope 132; Members: yardage 5686, par 72, rating 67.6, slope 124; *Women:* Forward: yardage 5220, par 72, rating 71.2, slope 130.

Tee Times: Reciprocal players should have their home professional call to arrange starting times.

Dress Code: Appropriate golf attire is required.

Tournaments: A 12-player minimum is needed to book a tournament. Tournaments are on Monday only. Carts are required.

Directions: Take the Pico exit off I-5 in San Clemente and travel two miles east to Avenida La Pata. Turn right and drive one mile to the club.

Contact: 200 Avenida La Pata, San Clemente, CA 92673, pro shop 949/498-3771, clubhouse 949/498-6604, www.pacificgc.com.

6 SAN CLEMENTE GOLF COURSE

Architect: William P. Bell, 1928

18 holes	Public	$30–38

San Diego and Vicinity map, page 394

This is a scenic course offering delightful ocean views. Some improvements were made in 2003, including some new bunkers and rebuilt greens. The par-3 15th hole has an elevated tee with a spectacular view of the Pacific Ocean. The back nine is more enjoyable and challenging than the front nine. It is a popular and heavily played course.

Play Policy and Fees: Green fees are $30 weekdays and $38 weekends. Twilight rates and resident discounts are available. Carts are $12 per rider.

Tees and Yardage: *Men:* Blue: yardage 6413, par 72, rating 70.8, slope 124; White: yardage 6061, par 72, rating 69.3, slope 120; *Women:* Red: yardage 5708, par 73, rating 73.5, slope 123.

Tee Times: Reservations can be booked seven days in advance.

Dress Code: Nonmetal spikes are required.

Tournaments: Five shotgun tournaments are allowed per year. A 24-player minimum is required to book a tournament. Events should be booked 12 months in advance. The banquet facility can accommodate 25–175 people.

Directions: From San Diego, travel north on I-5 and take the Avenida Magdalena exit. Turn right on El Camino Real and go one block. Turn left on Magdalena to the course. Coming from Los Angeles on I-5, exit at Avenida Calfia and turn right. Take another right over the freeway, a right on El Camino Real for one block to Avenida Magdalena, and a left to the course.

Contact: 150 East Magdalena, San Clemente, CA 92672, pro shop 949/361-8380.

7 CROSSCREEK GOLF CLUB

Architect: Arthur Hills, 2001

18 holes	Public	$59–89

San Diego and Vicinity map, page 394

There is quite a bit of elevation change on this layout, often featuring greens severely higher than fairways. This is part of the challenge, as are the many mature oak and sycamore trees and native shrubs that line the fairways. Be cautious with your driver on the front nine, as there are some very tight driving holes. The course is generally in immaculate condition, and it features bent-grass greens. Views are of the nearby surrounding hills. Eventually there may be some homes built and memberships sold, but for now it is one of the better public facilities in the area. You'll also get a short, fun golf history lesson as you go to the first tee. It's a nice way to impart tradition.

Play Policy and Fees: Green fees are $59 Monday–Thursday, $69 Friday, and $89 weekends and holidays. Carts and range balls included. Twilight, senior, and junior rates available.

Tees and Yardage: *Men:* Black: yardage 6833, par 71, rating 74.1, slope 142; Gold: yardage 6310, par 71, rating 71.6, slope 136; Blue: yardage 5609, par 71, rating 68.5, slope 126; *Women:* Green: yardage 4606, par 71, rating 67.4, slope 118.

Tee Times: Reservations can be made 30 days in advance.

Dress Code: Collared shirts required. No denim is allowed. Soft spikes only.

Tournaments: Tournaments of 16 players or more may book up to six months in advance. A group contract is required.

Directions: Take I-15 to Rancho California Road and go west 4.5 miles to De Luz Road. Turn left and go one-quarter mile to Via Vaquero Road. Follow Via Vaquero Road to the club.

Contact: 43860 Glen Meadows Road, Temecula, CA 92590, pro shop 909/506-3402, fax 909/506-6802, www.crosscreekgolfclub.com.

8 TEMECULA CREEK INN GOLF COURSE

Architect: Dick Rossen, 1970; Ted Robinson Sr., 1989
27 holes   Resort $60–80

San Diego and Vicinity map, page 394

Temecula Creek features three distinctly different nines that can be played in three 18-hole combinations. The Creek Course is the flattest of the three, with a pond in play on one hole. The Oaks Course brings many trees into play, along with several ponds. The most recently designed nine, the Stonehouse Course, is the most varied in character, with several elevation changes. All of the courses are well kept and scenic.

The Temecula Inn has 80 rooms and 10 junior suites. For more information or reservations, call 800/698-9295.

Play Policy and Fees: Green fees are $60 on weekdays and $80 weekends and holidays. Carts are included. Play-and-stay packages are available.

Tees and Yardage: Creek Course—*Men:* Blue: yardage 3348, par 36, rating n/a, slope n/a; White: yardage 3183, par 36, rating n/a, slope n/a; *Women:* Red: yardage 2870, par 36, rating n/a, slope n/a. Oaks Course—*Men:* Blue: yardage 3436, par 36, rating n/a, slope n/a; White: yardage 3192, par 36, rating n/a, slope n/a; *Women:* Red: yardage 2867, par 36, rating n/a, slope n/a. Stonehouse Course—*Men:* Blue: yardage 3257, par 36, rating n/a, slope n/a; White: yardage 3103, par 36, rating n/a, slope n/a; *Women:* Red: yardage 2816, par 36, rating n/a, slope n/a.

Tee Times: Reservations may be booked seven days in advance.

Dress Code: Collared shirts are required. No jeans are allowed on the course, and nonmetal spikes are recommended.

Tournaments: Events should be booked 12 months in advance. The banquet facility can accommodate up to 200 people. Call 909/506-1777 for more information.

Directions: From the junction of I-15 and Highway 79 south, travel east one mile to Pala Road and turn right. Take Pala Road to Rainbow Canyon Road. Take a right and follow the road to the golf course.

Contact: 44501 Rainbow Canyon Road, Temecula, CA 92592, pro shop 909/676-2405, fax 909/506-9640, www.jcgolf.com.

9 REDHAWK GOLF CLUB

Architect: Ron Fream, 1991
18 holes   Public $50–70

San Diego and Vicinity map, page 394

New owner CSC Golf Management has made significant improvements to this course. This course's rolling terrain features several elevated tees and greens. There are generous landing areas, but tiered and sloping greens present a real challenge. Redhawk has the largest putting green in California. This course has been rated as high as seventh among public courses in the state.

Play Policy and Fees: Green fees are $50 Monday–Friday and $70 weekends and holidays. All prices include carts. Twilight and CSC Club rates are available, as is a juniors program.

Tees and Yardage: *Men:* Tour: yardage 7180, par 72, rating 75.7, slope 149; Competition: yardage 6755, par 72, rating 72.7, slope 137; Championship: yardage 6310, par 72, rating 69.5, slope 125; *Women:* Forward: yardage 5515, par 72, rating 72.0, slope 124.

Tee Times: Reservations may be booked seven days in advance.

Dress Code: Collared shirts and nonmetal spikes are required. No blue jeans are permitted.

Tournaments: A 16-player minimum is needed to book a tournament. Events may be booked up to a year in advance.

Directions: From Highway 15 in Temecula, take the Highway 79 south exit. Travel east on Highway 79 for 2.5 miles, turn right on Redhawk Parkway, and drive straight to the course.

Contact: 45100 Redhawk Parkway, Temecula, CA 92592, pro shop 909/302-3850, www.redhawkgolfcourse.com.

10 THE GOLF CLUB OF CALIFORNIA

Architect: Johnny Pott and Wade Cable, 2001
18 holes   Private

San Diego and Vicinity map, page 394

Far from city congestion, this wonderful track presents a terrific test of golf in the peaceful serenity of the country. The course is in the foothills of the San Luis Rey River Valley and features mature oak, towering sycamore, and fragrant eucalyptus trees, along with meandering creeks, wetlands, diverse natural vegetation, and acres of open space. The gentle foothills provide challenging elevation changes while also creating scenic backcountry views. Holes are framed by tall fescue and native grasses, which have been thinned to make the course

more playable for the average golfer. The par-3 sixth is influenced by the famous seventh hole at Riviera Country Club, with a bunker set in the middle of the green. Encased in dunes, the par-4 13th is a rendition of the 14th at Ireland's Lahinch. Good shots are rewarded, weak ones penalized. The par-5s are particularly strong.

Play Policy and Fees: Members and guests only. No outside play is accepted.

Tees and Yardage: *Men:* Black: yardage 6850, par 72, rating 73.7, slope 146; Blue: yardage 6497, par 72, rating 72.2, slope 140; White: yardage 6093, par 72, rating 70.2, slope 133; *Women:* Red: yardage 5224, par 72, rating 71.9, slope 135.

Tee Times: Reservations can be made seven days in advance.

Dress Code: Appropriate golf attire is required. Soft spikes only.

Tournaments: Please inquire.

Directions: From I-15, exit at Highway 76 and travel west approximately three miles to Flowerwood Lane; turn right and proceed one mile to the entrance. From I-5, exit at Highway 76, travel approximately 16 miles to Flowerwood Lane, turn left, and proceed one mile to the entrance.

Contact: 3742 Flowerwood Lane, Fallbrook, CA 92028, phone 760/451-8702, fax 760/451-8703, www.thegolfclubofcalifornia.com.

11 FALLBROOK GOLF CLUB

Architect: Harry Rainville, 1962
18 holes   Public $26–38

San Diego and Vicinity map, page 394

Fallbrook offers a great challenge to all skill levels. The course features greens tightly guarded by sand. Shot-makers will score well here, especially those with a good short game. Oak Creek runs through the layout. The creek and the hundreds of live oak trees add to the course's beauty and challenge. The back nine was built first here, the front a few years later. Some unexpected development of homes squeezed the front nine out of some yardage, creating a very short, uphill par-3 ninth hole.

Play Policy and Fees: Green fees are $26 weekdays and $38 weekends. Nine-hole, twilight, and membership rates are also available. Carts are $12 per person at all times.

Tees and Yardage: *Men:* White: yardage 6223, par 72, rating 69.9, slope 119; *Women:* Red: yardage 5597, par 72, rating 73.8, slope 130.

Tee Times: Reservations may be booked 10 days in advance.

Dress Code: Collared shirts and nonmetal spikes are required. Shorts may not be more than five inches above the knee, and no tank tops or tee shirts are allowed.

Tournaments: Events are welcome. The banquet facility can accommodate 175 people.

Directions: From I-15 north of Escondido, take Highway 76 west for two miles to Gird Road, then drive north two miles to the course.

Contact: 2757 Gird Road, Fallbrook, CA 92088 (P.O. Box 2167, Fallbrook, CA 92028), pro shop 760/728-8334, www.fallbrookgolf.com.

12 PALA MESA RESORT

Architect: Dick Rossen, 1964
18 holes   Resort $69–85

San Diego and Vicinity map, page 394

This scenic, mature course rolls through oak woodlands with tight fairways and fast greens. It's pretty, set against some hills, and a little more demanding than a garden-variety resort course. The par-3 holes are memorable.

For reservations at the resort, call 760/723-8292.

Play Policy and Fees: Green fees are $69 Monday–Thursday, $74 Friday, and $85 weekends. Carts are included. Resort guests receive a discount. Twilight and super twilight rates are offered.

Tees and Yardage: *Men:* Blue: yardage 6502, par 72, rating 72.0, slope 131; White: yardage 6172, par 72, rating 70.2, slope 127; *Women:* Red: yardage 5632, par 72, rating 74.0, slope 134.

Tee Times: Reservations can be booked seven days in advance.

Dress Code: Collared shirts and nonmetal spikes

are required. No denim, cutoffs, or halter tops are allowed on the course.

Tournaments: Carts are required. A 28-player minimum is required to book a tournament.

Directions: From San Diego, drive north on I-15 to Highway 76. Turn left to Old Highway 395. Turn right and drive two miles to the course.

Contact: 2001 Old Highway 395, Fallbrook, CA 92028, pro shop 800/722-4700, fax 760/723-8292, www.palamesa.com.

13 PAUMA VALLEY COUNTRY CLUB

Architect: Robert Trent Jones Sr., 1960
18 holes   Private

San Diego and Vicinity map, page 394

In a wonderful valley some 15 miles east **BEST** of Oceanside, Pauma Valley is a hidden gem and pleased to stay that way. It's very low-key and very private. The course is a bear. Pick your trap; they are everywhere. With more than 120 bunkers, this difficult design is considered a ball-striker's course. It's an original Robert Trent Jones Sr. layout and plays very long. It is generally regarded among the premier courses in San Diego County, as well as one of the top layouts in the state.

Play Policy and Fees: Members and guests only.

Tees and Yardage: *Men:* Blue: yardage 7077, par 71, rating 74.4, slope 133; Gold: yardage 6811, par 71, rating 73.1, slope 130; White: yardage 6465, par 71, rating 71.3, slope 125; *Women:* Red: yardage 5981, par 72, rating 76.2, slope 135; Green: yardage 5113, par 72, rating 70.9, slope 125.

Tee Times: Not applicable.

Dress Code: Standard country club attire is mandatory. Nonmetal spikes are required.

Tournaments: This course is not available for outside events.

Directions: From I-15, travel east on Highway 76 for 14 miles to the town of Pauma Valley. Turn right on Pauma Valley Drive and continue three-quarters of a mile to the club.

Contact: Pauma Valley Drive (P.O. Box 206), Pauma Valley, CA 92061, pro shop 760/742-1230, fax 760/742-1839.

14 WARNER SPRINGS RANCH GOLF COURSE

Architect: David Rainville, 1965

18 holes **Semiprivate** **$28–45**

San Diego and Vicinity map, page 394

Warner Springs meanders through the western foothills of San Diego's Cuyamaca Mountains at an elevation of 3000 feet. Picturesque mountain vistas and open grazing lands create the backdrop for a course that boasts some of the best greens in Southern California. They tend to be fast. The signature hole, the par-3 fifth, can play anywhere from 110 to 190 yards. Do not get greedy on the 13th hole off the tee, or you may lose a few balls.

Play Policy and Fees: Green fees are $28 Monday–Thursday, $35 Friday, and $45 weekends and holidays. Twilight and senior rates are available. Carts are included in the fees.

Tees and Yardage: *Men:* Championship: yardage 6892, par 72, rating 72.7, slope 128; Blue: yardage 6701, par 72, rating 71.9, slope 126; White: yardage 6252, par 72, rating 69.6, slope 120; *Women:* Red: yardage 5422, par 72, rating 70.8, slope 127.

Tee Times: Reservations can be booked seven days in advance.

Dress Code: Appropriate golf attire and non-metal spikes are required and strictly enforced.

Tournaments: Shotgun tournaments are available Monday–Thursday (excluding holidays), requiring a 60-player minimum. A 24-player minimum is needed for a regular tournament. Events can be scheduled 6–12 months in advance.

Directions: Take I-15 north from San Diego. Turn right on Scripps Poway Parkway and left on Highway 67. Follow Highway 67 to Santa Ysabel, Highway 79, and turn left.

Contact: 31652 Highway 79 (P.O. Box 10), Warner Springs, CA 92086, pro shop 760/782-4270, fax 760/782-9249.

15 OCEANSIDE MUNICIPAL GOLF COURSE

Architect: Richard Bigler, 1970

18 holes **Public** **$24–32**

San Diego and Vicinity map, page 394

This course has level terrain, but water comes into play on 13 holes. The greens are fairly large. Mature trees line the fairways. Work has been done on the course in recent years to improve conditions, including leveling tee boxes and rebuilding some greens. Oceanside allows fivesomes, which can make for some long rounds.

Play Policy and Fees: Green fees are $24 weekdays and $32 weekends. Carts are $10 per rider.

Tees and Yardage: *Men:* Blue: yardage 6450, par 72, rating 70.6, slope 122; White: yardage 6056, par 72, rating 68.8, slope 117; *Women:* Red: yardage 5398, par 72, rating 72.1, slope 124.

Tee Times: Reservations by phone can be booked eight days in advance, starting at 6 P.M. Credit cards are required for reservations Friday–Sunday.

Dress Code: Collared shirts are required.

Tournaments: A 16-player minimum is required to book a tournament. An outside banquet facility can accommodate up to 100 people. Events can be scheduled 12 months in advance.

Directions: From I-15 north of Escondido, travel west on Highway 76. Turn right onto Douglas Drive and go two miles to the course.

Contact: 825 Douglas Drive, Oceanside, CA 92054, pro shop 760/433-1360, fax 760/433-4143.

16 OCEANSIDE CENTER CITY GOLF COURSE

Architect: William H. Johnson, 1957

18 holes **Public** **$12–18**

San Diego and Vicinity map, page 394

Set in an older neighborhood, this course is executive length and includes 10 par-4s, seven par-3s, and one par-5. The layout is hilly with greens on the large side, and there is only one bunker on the site. It is popular with locals

looking for a low-key, inexpensive round. Nothing fancy here; just good-old community golf.
Play Policy and Fees: Green fees are $12 weekdays and $18 weekends. Carts are $15 weekdays and $20 weekends. Nine-hole and senior rates are available.
Tees and Yardage: *Men:* Blue: yardage 4797, par 66, rating 61.2, slope 94; White: yardage 5371, par 66, rating 60.3, slope 93; *Women:* Red: yardage 4203, par 66, rating 61.8, slope 99.
Tee Times: Reservations are not accepted.
Dress Code: No tank tops or short shorts are allowed.
Tournaments: This course is available for outside tournaments. Events may be booked 30 days in advance.
Directions: Take I-5 to Oceanside Boulevard in Oceanside. Drive inland. Stay in the left lane and turn left on Saratoga. The course is two blocks from the freeway.
Contact: Saratoga Street (P.O. Box 1088), Oceanside, CA 92054, pro shop 760/433-8590, fax 760/439-2288.

🔢17 MARINE MEMORIAL GOLF COURSE

Architect: William P. Bell, 1949
18 holes   Military $6–28

🏌️🏌️🏌️🏌️🏌️🏌️🔢3

San Diego and Vicinity map, page 394

This is a relatively level course in a peaceful valley. Some holes are strategically placed among the hills. The fairways are tight, and sand guards the greens.
Play Policy and Fees: Guests, with the exception of Department of Defense civilian employees, must be accompanied by military personnel. Military personnel are entitled to bring three guests. Fees vary according to military status.
Tees and Yardage: *Men:* Blue: yardage 6765, par 72, rating 72.3, slope 129; White: yardage 6443, par 72, rating 70.6, slope 126; *Women:* Red: yardage 5716, par 72, rating 73.1, slope 125.
Tee Times: Personnel on active duty can book reservations at noon on Friday for the follow-

ing Tuesday–Monday. Retired personnel can book reservations at 8 A.M. on Saturday.
Dress Code: No jeans are allowed on the course. Collared shirts and nonmetal spikes are required.
Tournaments: This course is available for some outside events. Contact Doug Blanshard (760/725-4390) for more information about tournaments.
Directions: From Highway 76 east of Oceanside, travel north on Douglas Drive for 1.25 miles. Turn right on North River Road and drive 3.5 miles to the San Luis Rey entrance. Drive one mile and turn left at the course sign.
Contact: Building 18415, Camp Pendleton, CA 92055, pro shop 760/725-4704.

🔢18 SAN LUIS REY DOWNS GOLF & COUNTRY CLUB

Architect: William F. Bell, 1965
18 holes   Resort $34–64

San Diego and Vicinity map, page 394

The San Luis Rey River snakes through this level course, and water comes into play on nine holes. Five par-3s and five par-5s add a twist to this tree-lined layout. Adjacent to the course is the San Luis Rey Downs Training Center, where top-notch thoroughbred horses are trained. This course provides a fun round in a tranquil setting.

San Luis Rey Downs Resort also includes a golf school and complete tennis facility. Play-and-stay packages are available. Call for reservations.

Play Policy and Fees: Green fees Monday–Thursday are $34 to walk and $44 to ride. Friday fees are $36 to walk and $46 to ride, and weekends and holidays are $64 to ride. Twilight rates are available. Weekend twilight rates are $45 with cart noon–2 P.M., $35 with cart 2–4 P.M., and $28 with cart after 4 P.M. Carts are mandatory on weekends and holidays.
Tees and Yardage: *Men:* Blue: yardage 6750, par 72, rating 73.0, slope 136; White: yardage 6365, par 72, rating 71.2, slope 132; *Women:* Red: yardage 5493, par 72, rating 72.1, slope 124.

Tee Times: Reservations may be booked up to seven days in advance.

Dress Code: Collared shirts are required, and no denim is permitted.

Tournaments: This course is available for tournaments, and the schedule tends to fill up a year in advance. The banquet facility can accommodate 150 people.

Directions: From I-15 north of Escondido, travel 4.5 miles west on Highway 76 to Camino Del Rey in the town of Bonsall. Turn left over the bridge and bear left at the sign for San Luis Rey Downs. Continue for three-quarters of a mile to the golf resort.

Contact: 31474 Golf Club Drive, Bonsall, CA 92003, pro shop 800/783-6967, fax 619/940-8509, www.slrd.com.

19 VISTA VALLEY COUNTRY CLUB

Architect: Ted Robinson Sr., 1978
18 holes   **Private**   **$60**

San Diego and Vicinity map, page 394

This course is nestled in a valley with a creek meandering through the hills. There are scenic mountain views. This is a good, challenging golf course for both the low- and high-handicapper.

Play Policy and Fees: Reciprocal play is accepted with members of the other private clubs at a rate of $60; otherwise, members and guests only. Optional cart is $12 per rider.

Tees and Yardage: *Men:* Blue: yardage 6345, par 71, rating 71.5, slope 135; White: yardage 6035, par 71, rating 70.1, slope 130; *Women:* Red: yardage 5460, par 71, rating 73.2, slope 134.

Tee Times: Reciprocal players should have their home professional call to arrange starting times seven days in advance.

Dress Code: Appropriate golf attire and nonmetal spikes are required.

Tournaments: This course is available for outside tournaments on Monday only.

Directions: From I-15, take the Gopher Canyon Road exit and travel west for 2.5 miles to Vista

Valley Drive. Turn left and drive one-half mile to the club.

Contact: 29354 Vista Valley Drive, Vista, CA 92084, pro shop 760/758-5275, clubhouse 760/758-3189, www.vistavalley.com.

20 CASTLE CREEK COUNTRY CLUB

Architect: Jack Daray, 1956
18 holes   **Semiprivate**   **$43–56**

San Diego and Vicinity map, page 394

Castle Creek meanders through this well-maintained course. The front nine is flat, and the back nine is hilly. There are more than 1000 trees lining the fairways. The green tees make this course very women-friendly.

Play Policy and Fees: Green fees are $43 Monday–Thursday, $45 Friday, and $56 weekends and holidays. Carts included. Midday and twilight rates are offered.

Tees and Yardage: *Men:* Blue: yardage 6372, par 72, rating 70.6, slope 129; White: yardage 5939, par 72, rating 68.6, slope 123; *Women:* Red: yardage 5396, par 72, rating 72.4, slope 124; Green: yardage 4813, par 72, rating 67.4, slope 114.

Tee Times: Reservations can be booked nine days in advance.

Dress Code: Collared shirts and nonmetal spikes are mandatory.

Tournaments: Carts are required. A 20-player minimum is needed to book a tournament.

Directions: From I-15, take the Old Castle Road/Gopher Canyon Road exit and travel east. Turn left and drive one-half mile to the club.

Contact: 8797 Circle "R" Drive, Escondido, CA 92026, pro shop 760/749-2422, clubhouse 760/749-2877, fax 760/749-8243, www.castlecreekcc.com.

21 WELK RESORT SAN DIEGO

Architect: David Rainville, 1986
36 holes   **Resort**   **$16–42**

San Diego and Vicinity map, page 394

There are two short courses here, an executive

course called The Fountain, and a par-3 course called The Oaks. The Fountain executive course has 10 par-3s and eight par-4s. It is up and down and features lots of water, trees, and large rocks. The par-3 first hole is guarded by a lake that features a fountain shaped like a champagne glass, perfect for a course at Lawrence Welk Resort. Cheers! The Oaks par-3 course is 1837 yards from the back tees and 1652 yards from the forward tees. They both offer fun, no-stress rounds in a scenic environment.

For reservations at the hotel, call 760/749-3000.

Play Policy and Fees: Green fees for the Fountain Course are $39 weekdays and $42 weekends, including carts. Twilight and early bird rates are available. The green fee for the Oaks Course is $16 any day. The Oaks is a walking course.

Tees and Yardage: Fountain—*Men:* Blue: yardage 4002, par 62, rating 58.9, slope 102; White: yardage 3581, par 62, rating 56.9, slope 96; *Women:* Red: yardage 3055, par 62, rating 57.7, slope 90.

Tee Times: Reservations can be booked seven days in advance for local residents, 14 days in advance for time-share owners or guests, and 30 days or more with a hotel package.

Dress Code: Collared shirts and nonmetal spikes are required.

Tournaments: These courses are available for outside tournaments. A 20-player minimum is needed to book an event. The banquet facility can accommodate 300 people.

Directions: On I-15 from San Diego, drive 33 miles north and take the Mountain Meadow Road exit. Turn north on Champagne Boulevard.

Contact: 8860 Lawrence Welk Drive, Escondido, CA 92026, pro shop 760/749-3225, fax 760/749-4619.

22 MEADOW LAKE GOLF COURSE

Architect: Tom Sanderson, 1965
18 holes   Semiprivate $38–55

San Diego and Vicinity map, page 394

This is a mountainous course with lots of doglegs. There are blind shots, but the variation between tight and open makes this a fair, sporting challenge. Don't be deceived by stated yardage—elevation changes call for every club in the bag.

Play Policy and Fees: Green fees are $38 Monday–Thursday, $40 Friday, and $55 Saturday and Sunday. Carts are included in fees and mandatory at certain times. Senior and twilight rates are available.

Tees and Yardage: *Men:* Back: yardage 6416, par 72, rating 71.5, slope 131; Middle: yardage 6007, par 72, rating 69.2, slope 125; *Women:* Forward: yardage 5419, par 74, rating 71.5, slope 130.

Tee Times: Reservations can be booked seven days in advance.

Dress Code: Collared shirts are required. No cutoffs are allowed on the course.

Tournaments: A 24-player minimum is needed to book a tournament. Carts are required. Events should be booked 12 months in advance. The banquet facility can hold 150 people.

Directions: Drive 33 miles north from San Diego on I-15 and take the Mountain Meadows exit. Travel east 1.5 miles to the club on Meadow Glen Way.

Contact: 10333 Meadow Glen Way East, Escondido, CA 92026, pro shop 760/749-1620, fax 760/749-4646.

23 TWIN OAKS GOLF COURSE

Architect: Ted Robinson Sr., 1993
18 holes   Public $55–75

San Diego and Vicinity map, page 394

Located in a tranquil valley, Twin Oaks features elevation changes and undulating greens. Water comes into play on four holes. The seventh hole is a 142-yard par-3 from the back tees, over water, with a small but well-placed bunker guarding the left side of the green. If the pin is tucked left, the smart player will hit to the middle of the green to take par. Twin Oaks is owned by JC Resorts, which owns and/or operates several other courses in the area, including Temecula Creek, Rancho Bernardo Inn, and the Encinitas Ranch Golf Course.

For reservations at the Rancho Bernardo Inn, call 800/542-6096.

Play Policy and Fees: Green fees are $55 Monday–Thursday, $60 Friday, and $75 weekends and holidays. Twilight (after 1 P.M.) rates are available. JC Card (members) discounts also available.

Tees and Yardage: *Men:* Blue: yardage 6535, par 72, rating 71.9, slope 130; White: yardage 6146, par 72, rating 70.1, slope 126; *Women:* Red: yardage 5424, par 72, rating 71.7, slope 128.

Tee Times: Tee times may be booked seven days in advance. Walk-ons are welcome.

Dress Code: Collared shirts are required, and no denim is permitted.

Tournaments: A 16-player minimum is required to book an event. The banquet facility holds 200 people.

Directions: Take I-5 south from Los Angeles to Highway 78 east. Take Highway 78 east for 11 miles and exit at Twin Oaks Valley Road. Turn north on Twin Oaks Valley Road for two miles; the course is on the right.

Contact: 1425 North Twin Oaks Valley Road, San Marcos, CA 92069, pro shop 760/591-4700, fax 760/591-3242, www.jcgolf.com.

24 ESCONDIDO COUNTRY CLUB

Architect: Harry Rainville and David Rainville, 1962
18 holes   **Private**   **$52–57**

San Diego and Vicinity map, page 394

Escondido is sneaky hard, with hills, wind, and subtle greens all in the mix—plus a stream that wanders through most of the course. Accuracy and patience pay off here. It doesn't look lethal, but it can be. The greens can drive you nuts: putts might look level, but they can just sail past the hole.

Play Policy and Fees: Reciprocal play is accepted with members of other private clubs; otherwise, members and guests only. Reciprocal fees are $52 weekdays and $57 weekends. Carts are $13 per rider.

Tees and Yardage: *Men:* Black: yardage 6140, par 70, rating 70.3, slope 124; Players: yardage 6012, par 70, rating 70.0, slope 123; Silver: yardage 5884, par 70, rating 69.2, slope 121; *Women:* Green: yardage 5593, par 72, rating 74.2, slope 130.

Tee Times: Reciprocal players should have their home professional call to make arrangements.

Dress Code: Appropriate golf attire and non-metal spikes are required

Tournaments: Outside tournaments accepted Monday only. Please inquire.

Directions: Take the Centre City Parkway exit off I-15 two miles north of Escondido. Turn left on Country Club Lane and drive one mile to the club.

Contact: 1800 West Country Club Lane, Escondido, CA 92026, pro shop 760/746-4212, clubhouse 760/743-3301.

25 SKYLINE RANCH COUNTRY CLUB

Architect: Course designed, 1975
9 holes   **Private**

San Diego and Vicinity map, page 394

Set within a mobile home park, this course is mostly level and walkable. Trees and water come into play on several holes, and there are two par-4s. There are front nine and back nine tees.

Play Policy and Fees: The course is restricted to members of the mobile home park and their guests. Guests must be accompanied by a member.

Tees and Yardage: *Men and Women:* yardage 3032, par 58 (M)/60 (W), rating n/a, slope n/a.

Tee Times: Not applicable.

Dress Code: Appropriate golf attire is required.

Tournaments: This course is not available for outside events.

Directions: From Escondido, take Valley Center Road north for 11 miles. Turn right on Lake Wolford Road. Turn right on Paradise Mountain Road to the club entrance.

Contact: 18218 Paradise Mountain Road, Valley Center, CA 92082, pro shop 760/749-3233.

26 EL CAMINO COUNTRY CLUB

Architect: William F. Bell, 1958

18 holes   **Private**   **$81.50**

San Diego and Vicinity map, page 394

This course features a flat layout with plenty of trees and narrow fairways that offer little trouble. The course plays long, so be prepared. It is not laid out in a circle, but pretty close to it, so there are out-of-bounds areas to the left of every hole.

Play Policy and Fees: Reciprocal play is accepted with members of other private clubs at a rate $81.50, including cart; otherwise, members and guests only.

Tees and Yardage: *Men:* Blue: yardage 6734, par 72, rating 72.8, slope 131; White: yardage 6362, par 72, rating 70.9, slope 126; *Women:* Red: yardage 5814, par 72, rating 75.0, slope 130.

Tee Times: Reciprocal players should have their home professional call to make arrangements.

Dress Code: Nonmetal spikes are required.

Tournaments: This course is available for outside events on Monday only.

Directions: Take I-5 to the Highway 78 exit in Oceanside. Drive to El Camino Real exit north and cross the overpass to Vista Way. Turn right and drive one-quarter mile to the club.

Contact: 3202 Vista Way, Oceanside, CA 92056, pro shop 760/757-0321, fax 760/966-7117, www.americangolfcountryclubs.com.

27 EMERALD ISLE GOLF

Architect: Mike Gandy, 1986

18 holes   **Public**   **$16–29**

San Diego and Vicinity map, page 394

This is a challenging executive course with two par-4s on the front nine, the longest measuring 245 yards. Water comes into play on seven holes, while trees, bunkers, and rolling terrain also keep golfers honest. If you are looking for a good executive course in the Oceanside area, this is one.

Play Policy and Fees: Green fees are $16 to walk weekdays, $25 to ride; weekends are $19 to walk, $29 to ride. Senior and twilight rates are offered.

Tees and Yardage: *Men:* Back: yardage 2398, par 56, rating n/a, slope n/a; *Women:* Forward: yardage 2137, par 56, rating n/a, slope n/a.

Tee Times: Reservations are recommended and can be made the same day.

Dress Code: Shirts must be worn.

Tournaments: Shotgun tournaments are available weekday mornings only. A 16-player minimum is needed to book a tournament.

Directions: Take I-5 south to Oceanside. Take the Highway 76 exit east and go two miles. Turn right on El Camino Real. Turn left at the first light, Vista Oceana, and drive one block to the course.

Contact: 660 South El Camino Real, Oceanside, CA 92054, pro shop 760/721-4700, fax 760/721-2542.

28 RANCHO CARLSBAD GOLF COURSE

Architect: Art Shipero, 1965

18 holes   **Public**   **$13.50–16.50**

San Diego and Vicinity map, page 394

This is a well-maintained executive course with flat terrain. It's challenging for any caliber of golfer. It's a tight, tree-lined course, but a good shot is rewarded. The greens tend to be fast and tricky to putt. The two par-4s are 260 and 225 yards.

Play Policy and Fees: Green fees are $13.50 weekdays and $16.50 weekends and holidays. Twilight, junior, nine-hole, and resident rates are also available.

Tees and Yardage: *Men:* Blue: yardage 2396, par 56, rating n/a, slope n/a; White: yardage 2158, par 56, rating n/a, slope n/a; *Women:* Red: yardage 1955, par 56, rating n/a, slope n/a.

Tee Times: Reservations can be booked seven days in advance.

Dress Code: No tank tops are allowed on the course.

Tournaments: A 72-player minimum is needed for a shotgun tournament. A 24-player minimum is needed for a regular tournament. Events should be booked three months in advance.

Directions: From I-5, take Highway 78 east to El Camino Real (County Road S-11). Drive south to Rancho Carlsbad Drive and turn left to the course.

Contact: 5200 El Camino Real, Carlsbad, CA 92008, pro shop 760/438-1772, fax 760/438-4750, www.ranchocarlsbad.com.

29 FOUR SEASONS RESORT AVIARA GOLF CLUB

Architect: Arnold Palmer and Ed Seay, 1991

18 holes   **Resort**   **$175–195**

San Diego and Vicinity map, page 394

An Arnold Palmer design, this course was rated by both *Golf Magazine* and *Golf Digest* as one of the best new resort courses in 1991 and 1992, and with good reason. It follows the coastal topography and features wide fairways and enormous greens. The course is always in top condition, making a round here very enjoyable. For average golfers the back tees are a whole lot of golf course. Many prefer to play it from the middle tees, which is still a substantial test of skills requiring several sizable carries from the tees. Aviara is one of the top resort courses in California.

For reservations at this award-winning resort, call 760/603-6900. Besides traditional play-and-stay packages, the Four Seasons Resort offers a golf and spa getaway.

Play Policy and Fees: Green fees, including a cart, are $175 Monday–Thursday and $195 Friday–Sunday. Twilight rates are offered.

Tees and Yardage: *Men:* Palmer: yardage 7007, par 72, rating 74.2, slope 137; Back: yardage

6591, par 72, rating 71.8, slope 130; Middle: yardage 6054, par 72, rating 68.9, slope 121; *Women:* Forward: yardage 5007, par 72, rating 69.3, slope127.

Tee Times: Reservations can be booked six days in advance. Resort guests can book up to 30 days in advance.

Dress Code: Appropriate golf attire and nonmetal spikes are required.

Tournaments: Outside events are allowed for guests of the hotel.

Directions: From I-5 at Carlsbad, take the Poinsettia Lane exit east for one mile to Aviara Parkway. Turn right and drive one mile to Batiquitos Drive.

Contact: 7447 Batiquitos Drive, Carlsbad, CA 92009, pro shop 760/603-6900, fax 760/603-3680, www.fourseasons.com.

30 SHADOWRIDGE COUNTRY CLUB

Architect: David Rainville, 1981

18 holes   **Private**

San Diego and Vicinity map, page 394

This is a rolling layout with eucalyptus-lined fairways and several picturesque lakes. The beautiful finishing hole features a stone-edged lake in front of the green.

Play Policy and Fees: Reciprocal play is accepted with members of other ClubCorp. facilities; otherwise, members and guests only.

Tees and Yardage: *Men:* Black: yardage 6943, par 72, rating 73.9, slope 129; Blue: yardage 6610, par 72, rating 72.7, slope 125; White: yardage 6280, par 72, rating 71.1, slope 123; Green: yardage 5704, par 72, rating 68.1, slope 115; *Women:* Red: yardage 5336, par 72, rating 72.8, slope 129.

Tee Times: Reciprocal players should have their home professional call to make arrangements.

Dress Code: Collared shirts and nonmetal spikes are required. No jeans or short shorts are allowed on the golf course.

Tournaments: Shotgun tournaments are available Monday only. Carts are required. A

72-player minimum is needed to book a tournament. Tournaments should be booked 12 months in advance. The banquet facility can hold 300 people.

Directions: Travel north from San Diego on I-5 or I-15 to Highway 78 west. Take the Sycamore exit off Highway 78 and go south to Shadowridge Drive. Turn right and continue to Gateway Drive.

Contact: 1980 Gateway Drive, Vista, CA 92083, pro shop 760/727-7706, clubhouse 760/727-7700.

31 LAKE SAN MARCOS COUNTRY CLUB

Architect: Harry Rainville and David Rainville, 1963
18 holes   Private/Resort $50-60

San Diego and Vicinity map, page 394

This gently rolling layout through a housing development is mature and well maintained. The 606-yard third hole is a double dogleg known as "The Monster." Greens tend to be elevated and contoured. It is an enjoyable walking course. There is also a 2700-yard, par-58 executive course on the property.

The Quails Inn is part of the Lake San Marcos Country Club. For reservations, call 760/744-0120.

Play Policy and Fees: Members, guests, and those staying at the hotel only. Hotel guest green fees are $50 weekdays and $60 weekends. Carts are included. Reservations are recommended.

Tees and Yardage: *Men:* Blue: yardage 6515, par 72, rating 72.8, slope 128; White: yardage 6272, par 72, rating 71.1, slope 125; *Women:* Red: yardage 5929, par 73, rating 73.6, slope 129.

Tee Times: Reservations can be booked three days in advance.

Dress Code: Appropriate golf attire is required.

Tournaments: A 12-player minimum is required to book an event. Carts are required. Tournaments should be booked at least one month in advance. The banquet facility can accommodate up to 500 people.

Directions: Take the Palomar Airport Road

exit from I-5 south of Oceanside. Travel seven miles east to Rancho Santa Fe Road and turn right. Continue to Lake San Marcos. To reach the executive course, continue to Camino del Arroyo. Turn left to the course.

Contact: 1750 San Pablo Drive, Lake San Marcos, CA 92069, pro shop 760/744-1310, clubhouse 760/744-9385, fax 760/744-5020, www.lakesanmarcosresort.com.

32 REIDY CREEK GOLF COURSE

Architect: Cal Olson Golf Architecture, 2002
18 holes   Public $23-28

San Diego and Vicinity map, page 394

This par-54 design is not your average executive course. In fact, despite its diminutive length, it is a good test of your skills. The rural setting is very nice, and the holes have all the fun and challenge you'd find on a full-size layout. But they're all par-3s. This course is excellent for all golfers, particularly juniors and beginners, to put their practice to a course setting.

Play Policy and Fees: Green fees are $23 Monday–Friday and $28 weekends and holidays. JC Players Card rates and other specials are also available. Carts not included.

Tees and Yardage: *Men:* Blue: yardage 2600, par 54, rating n/a, slope n/a; White: yardage 2049, par 54, rating n/a, slope n/a; *Women:* Red: yardage 1658, par 54, rating n/a, slope n/a.

Tee Times: Reservations can be made nine days in advance.

Dress Code: Shirts must have collars. No jeans or metal spikes are allowed on the course.

Tournaments: Tournaments welcome. Call for details.

Directions: Take I-15 to Highway 78 east, take the Broadway exit, and head north approximately two miles. Turn right into Reidy Creek Golf Course entrance.

Contact: 2300 North Broadway, Escondido, CA 92026, pro shop 760/740-2450, fax 760/743-6573, www.jcresorts.com.

33 MADERAS GOLF CLUB

Architect: Johnny Miller, Neal Meagher, and Robert Muir Graves, 2001

18 holes   Semiprivate $130–165

🚶 📷 🍴 🛒 🍽️

San Diego and Vicinity map, page 394

Maderas Golf Club offers beauty, challenge, and plenty of thrilling shots as it winds through the cliffs, rock outcroppings, creeks, and forests of the inland hill country of north San Diego. Golfers will discover three lakes, five waterfalls, and more than 40 acres of native wildflowers throughout the golf course, providing Maderas with 12 months of natural color. Dramatic natural rock features and sweeping elevation changes combine with superb playing conditions to make Maderas Golf Club one of California's better venues.

Play Policy and Fees: Green fees are $130 Sunday–Thursday and $165 Friday and Saturday. Carts included. Twilight and junior rates also offered.

Tees and Yardage: *Men:* Black: yardage 7115, par 72, rating 75.6, slope 145; Maderas: yardage 6840, par 72, rating 74.1, slope 140; Gold: yardage 6654, par 72, rating 73.1, slope 138; Silver: yardage: 6352, par 72, rating 71.1, slope 135; Copper: yardage 6057, par 72, rating 70.3, slope 131; *Women:* Jade: yardage 5100, par 72, rating 70.0, slope 128.

Tee Times: Reservations can be made 60 days in advance.

Dress Code: Appropriate golf attire is required. Soft spikes only.

Tournaments: Available for tournaments seven days per week, for 8–150 players.

Directions: From I-15, exit onto Rancho Bernardo Road east. Turn left onto Old Coach Road, approximately three miles. The course entrance comes up in roughly 1.5 miles.

Contact: 17750 Old Coach Road, Poway, CA 92064, golf shop 858/451-8100, fax 858/613-3897, www.maderasgolf.com.

34 EAGLE CREST GOLF CLUB

Architect: David Rainville, 1993

18 holes   Public $40–65

🚶 📷 🍴 🛒 🍽️

San Diego and Vicinity map, page 394

Eight lakes and rolling terrain make this course a challenge for any player. No other hole is visible from the one you're playing, a rarity these days. The signature hole is the 518-yard, par-5 sixth, where a lake and waterfall guard the left side of the green.

Play Policy and Fees: Green fees are $40 Monday–Thursday, $45 Friday, and $65 weekends and holidays. Carts are included and mandatory.

Tees and Yardage: *Men:* Back: yardage 6417, par 72, rating 71.2, slope 132; Middle: yardage 6035, par 72, rating 67.9, slope 126; *Women:* Forward: yardage 5012, par 72, rating 69.9, slope 123.

Tee Times: Reservations can be booked seven days in advance.

Dress Code: Appropriate golf attire and non-metal spikes are required.

Tournaments: This course is available for outside tournaments.

Directions: From San Diego, take Highway 78 to I-15 south. Exit at Via Rancho Parkway. Drive one mile east to San Pasqual Road. Turn right on San Pasqual Road and drive 5.5 miles to Rockwood. Drive one mile to the course.

Contact: 1656 Cloverdale Road, Escondido, CA 92027, pro shop 760/737-9762.

35 LA COSTA RESORT & SPA

Architect: Dick Wilson and Joe Lee, 1964

36 holes   Resort $185–195

🚶 📷 🍴 🛏️ 🛒 🍽️

San Diego and Vicinity map, page 394

There are two scenic, challenging, fun golf courses at La Costa. The North Course is wide open and rolling, while the South Course is tighter and more demanding. Water and tree-lined fairways make accuracy a must on both designs. If they feel a little like Florida courses, it's because courses by the designers,

Dick Wilson and Joe Lee, are everywhere in the Sunshine State. Nine holes of each course are used for the PGA Tour's Accenture Match Play World Golf Championship. A $140 million renovation in 2003-2004 brought new life to this classic California resort. The courses are now in better shape than ever.

To make reservations or for information, check the website or call 760/438-9111.

Play Policy and Fees: Green fees are $185 Monday-Thursday and $195 Friday, weekends, and holidays. Twilight rates are available. Resort guests receive a discount. Carts are included.

Tees and Yardage: North Course—*Men:* Black: yardage 7021, par 72, rating 74.9, slope 141; Blue: yardage 6608, par 72, rating 72.9, slope 135; White: yardage 6269, par 72, rating 71.4, slope 131; *Women:* Red: yardage 5939, par 72, rating 76.3, slope 137. South Course—*Men:* Black: yardage 7001, par 72, rating 74.8, slope 140; Blue: yardage 6524, par 72, rating 72.4, slope 135; White: yardage 6198, par 72, rating 70.8, slope 131; *Women:* Red: yardage 5612, par 72, rating 74.2, slope 134.

Tee Times: If staying at the resort, golfers can make tee times when reservations are made.

Dress Code: No denim, short shorts, or tee shirts are allowed on the course.

Tournaments: This course is not available for outside events. The banquet facility can accommodate up to 800 people.

Directions: Drive 20 miles north of San Diego on I-5 to the La Costa Avenue exit east. Go 1.5 miles to El Camino Real and turn left to the club.

Contact: Costa del Mar Road, Carlsbad, CA 92009, pro shop 760/438-9111, fax 760/931-7500, www.lacosta.com.

36 ENCINITAS RANCH GOLF COURSE

Architect: Cary Bickler, 1998
18 holes   **Public**   **$65-85**

🏌 📷 💰 🎣 🚗 ⛳

San Diego and Vicinity map, page 394

Offering up a solid test of golf, this scenic course is one-half mile inland from the coast and offers excellent views of the ocean from 14 holes. The greens are firm but roll true. The afternoon breeze can make this challenging course downright tough, but the setting is worth the visit. JC Resorts Golf School is here if you would like to hone your skills.

Play Policy and Fees: Green fees are $65 Monday-Thursday, $70 Friday, and $85 weekends and holidays. Twilight rates, JC Players Card rates, and other specials are also available. Carts are $10 per rider.

Tees and Yardage: *Men:* Blue: yardage 6523, par 72, rating 71.2, slope 127; White: yardage 5820, par 72, rating 67.9, slope 118; *Women:* Gold: yardage 5235, par 72, rating 70.0, slope 118; Silver: yardage 4690, par 72, rating 67.1, slope 110.

Tee Times: Reservations can be made seven days in advance.

Dress Code: Shirts must have collars, and shorts must be Bermuda-length. No jeans or metal spikes are allowed on the course.

Tournaments: A 16-player minimum is required to book an event. The banquet facility holds 200 people.

Directions: From I-5 in Encinitas, take the Lacadia Drive exit. Head east one mile on Lacadia to Quail Garden Drive.

Contact: 1275 Quail Garden Drive, Encinitas, CA 92024, pro shop 760/944-1936, fax 760/944-1948.

37 THE BRIDGES AT RANCHO SANTA FE

Architect: Robert Trent Jones Jr., 2000
18 holes   **Private**

🏌 📷 💰 🚗 ⛳

San Diego and Vicinity map, page 394

A scenic course in the rolling hills inland from the northern San Diego coast, this is a real treat for those who are members or are fortunate enough to be invited. There is quite a bit of elevation change, especially on the back nine, with tee shots over canyons and some harrowing approach shots into greens. Two unique "stress-ribbon" bridges give the course its name—

concrete and steel constructions with no pillars into the floor of the canyons over which they cross. The Battle at The Bridges, a two-man best-ball event that in 2003 featured the team of Ernie Els/Tiger Woods versus the team of Sergio Garcia/Phil Mickelson, is played here. Mickelson is a member. A 36,000-square-foot clubhouse is built in a grand Tuscan villa style.

Play Policy and Fees: No outside play is accepted. No reciprocal play is accepted. Guests must be accompanied by a member.

Tees and Yardage: *Men:* Black: yardage 6916, par 71, rating 73.7, slope 143; Gold: yardage 6561, par 71, rating 72.0, slope 138; Bridges: yardage 6401, par 71, rating 71.4, slope 136; Blue: yardage 6188, par 71, rating 70.3, slope 133; White: yardage 5773, par 71, rating 67.9, slope 125; *Women:* Red: yardage 5078, par 72, rating 70.7 slope 129.

Tee Times: Members and guests only. No tee times required.

Dress Code: Appropriate golf attire is required. Soft spikes only.

Tournaments: No outside tournaments.

Directions: From Los Angeles, take I-5 south to Encinitas Boulevard and turn left. Turn left again on Rancho Santa Fe Road, right on El Camino Del Norte, then left on Aliso Canyon Road. The community is at junction of Aliso Canyon Road and Avenida del Duque. For the main gate to the community, turn right; entry is on your left.

Contact: 18550 Seven Bridges Road, Rancho Santa Fe, CA 92067, pro shop 858/759-7200, fax 858/759-7216, www.thebridgesrsf.com.

38 THE CROSBY AT RANCHO SANTA FE

Architect: Schmidt Curley Golf Design, 2001
18 holes   **Private**   **$150**

🏃 📷 🍴 🛺 🥤

San Diego and Vicinity map, page 394

This course is on The Crosby Estate in Rancho Santa Fe, named in honor of Bing Crosby, who grew up in the Rancho Santa Fe area. The famous crooner's first "clambake" golf

tournament, now known as The AT&T Pebble Beach National Pro-Am, was held at nearby Rancho Santa Fe Golf Club. This layout features quite a bit of elevation change as it plays through some rolling hills and valleys. Mature trees and native vegetation line the fairways, placing a premium on position and accuracy. Some severely undulating greens add to the demand on the short game. Aesthetically outstanding with sweeping views, this is also one solid challenge of a course.

Play Policy and Fees: No outside play is accepted. Some reciprocal play is accepted; please inquire. Reciprocal fees are $150.

Tees and Yardage: *Men:* Black: yardage 6804, par 70, rating 73.2, slope 139; Crosby: yardage 6603, par 70, rating 72.2, slope 136; Blue: yardage 6358, par 70, rating 71.1, slope 133; White: yardage 5849, par 70, rating 68.6, slope 128; *Women:* Crosby: yardage 5608, par 72, rating 72.8, slope134; Red: yardage 4899, par 70, rating 68.9, slope 123.

Tee Times: Reciprocal players should have their home professional call to make arrangements 14 days in advance.

Dress Code: Appropriate golf attire is required. Soft spikes only.

Tournaments: Please inquire.

Directions: From I-5, exit Via de la Valle east; drive approximately five miles. Turn right on Paseo Delicias, which becomes Del Dios Highway; in 2.5 miles, turn right onto Bing Crosby Boulevard.

Contact: 16930 Bing Crosby Boulevard, San Diego, CA 92127, pro shop 858/756-6310, fax 858/759-6394, www.thecrosbyestate.com.

39 THE SANTALUZ CLUB

Architect: Rees Jones, 2002
18 holes   **Private**

🏃 📷 🍴 🛺 🥤 🌊

San Diego and Vicinity map, page 394

Opened for play in 2002, Santaluz is a private club within an upscale, family-oriented residential community. It is an open, fun layout to play. Rees Jones designed the course so golfers can see every shot clearly, and to reward position off the tee. But everyone should be able to keep the ball in play. Greens are generally open at the throat, so players can run the ball up. There are some picturesque, downhill par-3 holes. A 35,000-square-foot clubhouse has a spa, fitness center, etc. The restaurant serves a great burger!

Play Policy and Fees: Members and guests only. Closed Monday.

Tees and Yardage: *Men:* Championship: yardage 7112; par 71, rating 74.1; slope 135; Back: yardage 6622, par 71, rating 71.7, slope 130; Middle: yardage 6230, par 71, rating 69.9, slope 126; *Women:* Forward: yardage 5706, par 71, rating 73.1, slope 124; Front: yardage: 5131, par 71, rating 69.3, slope 118.

Tee Times: Reservations can be made 60 days in advance.

Dress Code: Appropriate golf attire is required. Soft spikes only.

Tournaments: Not available for outside tournaments.

Directions: From I-5, take Del Mar Heights Road and go east 1 mile; turn left on Camino Real and go three miles, then turn right on San Dieguito Road and drive just over four miles to the guard house.

Contact: 8170 Caminito Santaluz East, San Diego, CA 92127, golf shop 858/759-3131, fax 858/759-4266, www.santaluz.com.

40 THE VINEYARD AT ESCONDIDO

Architect: David Rainville, 1993
18 holes   **Public**   **$57–69**

San Diego and Vicinity map, page 394

This scenic layout winds past acres of wetlands with stunning mountain backdrops. Five lakes, more than 70 bunkers, well-defined fairways, and perfect greens make this course a must on everyone's list. A lighted practice area features a driving range with target and putting greens.

Play Policy and Fees: Green fees are $57 walk-

ing on weekdays and $69, including carts, on weekends. Twilight rates are offered

Tees and Yardage: *Men:* Blue: yardage 6531, par 70, rating 71.2, slope 127; White: yardage 6160, par 70, rating 69.4, slope 122; *Women:* Red: yardage 5073, par 70, rating 70.3, slope 117.

Tee Times: Reservations can be booked seven days in advance.

Dress Code: Appropriate golf attire and non-metal spikes are required.

Tournaments: A 16-player minimum is required to book a tournament. Carts are mandatory. Shotgun tournaments are available weekdays only. Events should be booked six months in advance. The banquet facility can accommodate 80 people.

Directions: From I-15 in Escondido, take the Via Rancho Parkway east to San Pasqual Road. Turn right and proceed one-quarter mile to the club entrance.

Contact: 925 San Pasqual Road, Escondido, CA 92025, pro shop 760/735-9545.

41 BERNARDO HEIGHTS COUNTRY CLUB

Architect: Ted Robinson Sr., 1983
18 holes   **Private**   **$45–60**

San Diego and Vicinity map, page 394

This well-maintained course is hilly with a few trees, some water, and fast greens. Homes and condos line many fairways but are not intrusive. It's a big course, with large, sloping greens. Bernardo Heights completed a remodel of all back nine greens in 2004.

Play Policy and Fees: Reciprocal play is accepted with members of other private clubs at a rate of $45 weekdays, $60 weekends. Optional carts are $13.

Tees and Yardage: *Men:* Blue: yardage 6679, par 72, rating 71.9, slope 124; White: yardage 6221, par 72, rating 69.7, slope 119; Gold: yardage 5839, par 72, rating 67.8, slope 113; *Women:* Red: yardage 5601, par 72, rating 73.9, slope 131.

Tee Times: Reciprocal players should have their home professional call to make arrangements.

Dress Code: Appropriate golf attire and non-metal spikes are required.

Tournaments: This course is available for outside events on Monday. Carts are required.

Directions: Take the Bernardo Center Drive exit off I-15 and drive east to Bernardo Heights Parkway, then turn right to the club.

Contact: 16066 Bernardo Heights Parkway, San Diego, CA 92128, pro shop 858/487-3440, fax 858/487-8607, www.bhcc.com.

42 THE COUNTRY CLUB OF RANCHO BERNARDO

Architect: William F. Bell, 1967;
renovated Ted Robinson Sr., 1984

18 holes   **Private**

San Diego and Vicinity map, page 394

This course is a fairly open layout where the short par-4s are uphill and the longer par-4s are downhill. It's known as hole-in-one paradise, although the par-3s range up to 190 yards.

Play Policy and Fees: Members and guests only. Guests must be accompanied by a member.

Tees and Yardage: *Men:* Black: yardage 6532, par 72, rating 71.2, slope 125; Silver: yardage 6163, par 72, rating 69.5, slope 121; *Women:* Green: yardage 5546, par 72, rating 72.5, slope 127.

Tee Times: Not applicable.

Dress Code: Appropriate golf attire and non-metal spikes are required.

Tournaments: This course is available for outside events on a limited basis. Reservations are required.

Directions: On I-15, travel eight miles south of the city of Escondido to Rancho Bernardo Road east. Drive one mile to Bernardo Oaks Drive and turn left to the club.

Contact: 12280 Green East Road, San Diego, CA 92128, pro shop 858/487-1212, clubhouse 858/487-1134, fax 858/487-7595, www.ccofrb.com.

43 OAKS NORTH GOLF COURSE

Architect: Ted Robinson Sr., 1971

27 holes   **Public**   **$30–34**

San Diego and Vicinity map, page 394

These popular executive courses are always in great condition. That makes them a favorite among local golfers. The nines feature tight fairways and undulating greens. The courses have regulation par-4s and par-3s, but no par-5s. Homes line some fairways. Greens are receptive—only two are tiered. Each 18-hole combination is par-60. For the price, you can't go wrong here.

Play Policy and Fees: Green fees are $30 weekdays, $34 weekends. Junior and twilight rates are offered, and memberships are available. Carts are additional to all rates.

Tees and Yardage: North—*Men:* White: yardage 1749, par 30, rating n/a, slope n/a; *Women:* Red: yardage 1564, par 30, rating n/a, slope n/a. East—*Men:* White: yardage 1668, par 30, rating n/a, slope n/a; *Women:* Red: yardage 1479, par 30, rating n/a, slope n/a. South—*Men:* White: yardage 1859, par 30, rating n/a, slope n/a; *Women:* Red: yardage 1651, par 30, rating n/a, slope n/a.

Tee Times: Reservations can be booked seven days in advance.

Dress Code: Collared shirts and Bermuda-length shorts or slacks are required for men; no tank tops or short shorts for women are allowed. Nonmetal spikes are encouraged.

Tournaments: A 72-player minimum is needed to book a tournament. Tournaments should be booked six months in advance. The banquet facility can hold 300 people.

Directions: From I-15 in San Diego, take Rancho Bernardo Road to Pomerado. Take a left on Pomerado to Oaks North Drive.

Contact: 12602 Oaks North Drive, San Diego, CA 92128, pro shop 858/487-3021, fax 858/487-0894.

44 RANCHO BERNARDO INN & COUNTRY CLUB

Architect: William F. Bell, 1962;
Schmidt Curley Golf Design, 1998

18 holes   **Resort**   **$85–110**

San Diego and Vicinity map, page 394

Set in a small, scenic valley and enclosed by homes, this course offers sloping fairways, a meandering creek, two lakes, natural vegetation areas, and fast greens. It is well maintained and challenging, offering four sets of tees. The par-5 18th is a beautiful signature hole featuring a cascading waterfall. The Rancho Bernardo Inn is also a top-ranked tennis resort and spa, and it has large, nicely appointed accommodations as well as some of the best food in San Diego. The Golf University Instructional Schools are also based here.

For reservations at the resort, call 858/675-8500.

Play Policy and Fees: Green fees are $85 Monday–Friday and $110 on weekends. Green fees include carts. Twilight rates are available, as are JC Players Card rates with discounts for frequent players. Discounts and packages are available to hotel guests.

Tees and Yardage: *Men:* Black: yardage 6631, par 72, rating 72.3, slope 133; Blue: yardage 6243, par 72, rating 70.4, slope 129; White: yardage 5780, par 72, rating 68.0, slope 124; *Women:* Gold: yardage 4945, par 72, rating 73.6, slope 129.

Tee Times: Reservations can be booked seven days in advance.

Dress Code: No jeans or running shorts are allowed. Shirts must have collars and sleeves. This is a nonmetal spike facility.

Tournaments: This course is available for outside tournaments. A 16-player minimum is needed. Tournaments should be booked 12 months in advance. The banquet facility can accommodate 300 people.

Directions: Travel eight miles south of Escondido on I-15 to Rancho Bernardo Road east.

Drive one mile to Bernardo Oaks Drive and turn left to the inn and golf course.

Contact: 17550 Bernardo Oaks Drive, San Diego, CA 92128, pro shop 858/675-8470, clubhouse 800/662-6439, fax 858/675-8541, www.jc resorts.com.

45 STONERIDGE COUNTRY CLUB

Architect: Ted Robinson Sr., 1972

18 holes   **Private**   **$80–85**

San Diego and Vicinity map, page 394

The front nine is level and the back nine is hilly on this well-maintained course. Frequent afternoon winds can stiffen the challenge here. Stoneridge hosted an LPGA tour event from 1988 to 1992.

Play Policy and Fees: Reciprocal play is accepted with members of other private clubs at a rate of $80 weekdays, $85 weekends; otherwise, members and guests only. Fee includes cart.

Tees and Yardage: *Men:* Black: yardage 6286, par 72, rating 70.9, slope 131; Gold: yardage 6042, par 72, rating 69.8, slope 128; *Women:* Silver: yardage 5696, par 72, rating 74.5, slope 133.

Tee Times: Reciprocators should have their club pro call to make arrangements.

Dress Code: Appropriate golf attire and nonmetal spikes are required.

Tournaments: This course is available for outside tournaments on Monday.

Directions: From I-15 south of Escondido, take the Rancho Bernardo Road exit and travel east for 2.5 miles to Stoneridge Country Club Lane.

Contact: 17166 Stoneridge Country Club Lane, Poway, CA 92064, pro shop 858/487-2117, clubhouse 858/487-2138.

46 MOUNT WOODSON GOLF CLUB

Architect: Schmidt Curley Golf Design, 1991

18 holes   **Public**   **$65–90**

San Diego and Vicinity map, page 394

Tucked away in the mountains of Ramona at

the base of Mount Woodson, this is a spectacular course in a natural setting. It is frequently voted by golfers as one of their top picks in San Diego County. There are boulders, lakes, ancient oaks, and numerous elevation changes. The 150-yard bridge that links the second green to the third tee is a landmark. Holes 13, 15, and 17 offer superb views. Six lakes come into play. Both the fairways and the undulating greens are well bunkered. There are no parallel fairways. Eventual plans call for adding a set of tees farther back at around 6100 yards. While here, peek inside Mt. Woodson Castle, a 27-room, 12,000-square-foot architectural treasure. This fabulous stone mansion, built in 1921, is recognized in the national historic registry.

Play Policy and Fees: Green fees are $65 Monday–Thursday, $85 Friday and Sunday, and $90 Saturday. San Diego County resident discounts are offered. Twilight rates are available. Fees include cart. Specials are often posted on the website.

Tees and Yardage: *Men:* Blue: yardage 5804, par 70, rating 68.3, slope 130; White: yardage 5265, par 70, rating 65.7, slope 124; *Women:* Red: yardage 4441, par 70, rating 65.9, slope 116.

Tee Times: Reservations can be booked seven days in advance.

Dress Code: Collared shirts and nonmetal spikes are required. Shorts must be Bermuda length. No denim is allowed.

Tournaments: A 16-player minimum is required to book a tournament. The banquet facility can accommodate 200 people.

Directions: From I-15, take Scripps Poway Parkway east to Highway 67. Turn left on Highway 67 and drive for seven miles to Archie Moore Road. Turn left to the club entrance.

Contact: 16422 North Woodson Drive, Ramona, CA 92065, pro shop 760/788-3555, fax 760/788-3565, www.mtwoodson.com.

47 SAN VICENTE INN & GOLF CLUB

Architect: Ted Robinson Sr., 1972
18 holes   **Semiprivate**   **$51–61**

San Diego and Vicinity map, page 394

This picturesque course in a valley follows the topography of the land. Four lakes come into play on 14 of the holes, many of which are shaded by ancient live oaks. The sixth is a challenge: 329 yards uphill to the directional flag, then down to a bunkered green. A 26-room, on-site lodge is packed with winter guests November–April.

Stay-and-play packages are offered at San Vicente Inn. For reservations or information, call 760/789-8290 or 800/776-1289.

Play Policy and Fees: Green fees are $51 Monday–Thursday and $61 Friday–Sunday, including cart. Twilight rates are available.

Tees and Yardage: *Men:* Blue: yardage 6633, par 72, rating 71.8, slope 132; White: yardage 6228, par 72, rating 69.9, slope 129; Gold: yardage 5759, par 72, rating 68.6, slope 126; *Women:* Red: yardage 5501, par 72, rating 72.9, slope 134.

Tee Times: Reservations can be booked five days in advance.

Dress Code: Collared shirts and nonmetal spikes are preferred. No short shorts are allowed.

Tournaments: Carts are required. A 100-player minimum is needed to book a shotgun tournament.

Directions: From Main Street in downtown Ramona, drive south on 10th Street and continue six miles to the San Diego Country Estates.

Contact: 24157 San Vicente Road, Ramona, CA 92065, pro shop 760/789-3477, fax 760/788-6115, www.sanvicenteresort.com.

48 LOMAS SANTA FE COUNTRY CLUB

Architect: William F. Bell, 1964
18 holes   **Private**

San Diego and Vicinity map, page 394

This is a well-maintained course in a beautiful

setting. The course offers rolling terrain with tight fairways.

Play Policy and Fees: Platinum members of other American Golf facilities receive reciprocal privileges here; otherwise, members and guests only.

Tees and Yardage: *Men:* Blue: yardage 6607, par 72, rating 72.4, slope 133; Players: yardage 6400, par 72, rating 71.5, slope 131; White: yardage 6208, par 72, rating 70.6, slope 129; *Women:* Red: yardage 5830, par 72, rating 76.1, slope 138.

Tee Times: Not applicable.

Dress Code: Appropriate golf attire and non-metal spikes are required. No denim is allowed on the course.

Tournaments: This course is available for outside events on Monday. Tournaments should be booked 12 months in advance. The banquet facility can accommodate 400 people.

Directions: Take the Lomas Santa Fe Drive exit off I-5 and drive east one mile to the club.

Contact: 1505 Lomas Santa Fe Drive (P.O. Box 1007), Solana Beach, CA 92075, pro shop 858/755-1547, fax 858/793-0299.

49 LOMAS SANTA FE EXECUTIVE COURSE

18 holes   Public $20–22

San Diego and Vicinity map, page 394

This fairly level but challenging executive course offers excellent greens and a chance to work on your short game.

Play Policy and Fees: Green fees are $20 Monday–Friday and $22 weekends. Carts are $20. Twilight rates are available.

Tees and Yardage: *Men and Women:* yardage 2431, par 56, rating n/a, slope n/a.

Tee Times: Reservations can be made at any time.

Dress Code: No tank tops are allowed on the course.

Tournaments: Outside events and a banquet facility are available.

Directions: From San Diego, take I-5 north to the Lomas Sante Fe Drive exit. Take Lomas Sante Fe Drive east one mile, turn left on Highland Drive, and then left on Sun Valley Road. The course is on the left.

Contact: 1580 Sun Valley Road, Solana Beach, CA 92075, pro shop 858/755-0195, fax 858/755-4259.

50 DEL MAR COUNTRY CLUB

Architect: Joseph Lee, 1991
18 holes   Private

San Diego and Vicinity map, page 394

This course features bent grass from tee to green, and four lakes come into play on four holes. Del Mar is situated in a valley, with natural timbers and stands of old eucalyptus and new plantings. There are also 80 bunkers to contend with—so bring your sand wedge. This is a rare California design by Joe Lee, who is prolific in Florida.

Play Policy and Fees: Members and guests only. Some reciprocal play is considered.

Tees and Yardage: *Men:* Blue: yardage 6950, par 72, rating 74.0, slope 138; White: yardage 6508, par 72, rating 71.8, slope 134; Gold: yardage 5972, par 72, rating 69.2, slope 126; *Women:* Red: yardage 5381, par 72, rating 72.5, slope 128.

Tee Times: Reciprocal players should have their home professional call to inquire.

Dress Code: Appropriate golf attire and non-metal spikes are required. No denim is permitted.

Tournaments: This course is available for outside tournaments. Please inquire.

Directions: Take the Via de la Valle exit off I-5 and drive east to El Camino Real south. At San Dieguito Road, travel one mile and turn east. The course is about 600 yards east of the entrance to the Fairbanks Country Club.

Contact: 6001 Clubhouse Drive, Rancho Santa Fe, CA 92067, pro shop 858/759-5520, fax 858/759-5995.

51 FAIRBANKS RANCH COUNTRY CLUB

Architect: Ted Robinson Sr., 1984
18 holes   **Private**

San Diego and Vicinity map, page 394

Ted Robinson designed this challenging course, which bears his trademarks: The greens are surrounded by mounds and palm trees, and there is quite a bit of water. In fact, there are 30 acres of lakes. The course can be about two shots tougher in the afternoon, but it's almost always in ideal condition. This course was the site of the 1984 Olympic equestrian endurance event, and several of the horse jumps are still in place around the course.

Play Policy and Fees: Members and guests only.

Tees and Yardage: *Men:* Black: yardage 7220, par 72, rating 74.0, slope 132; Blue: yardage 6455, par 72, rating 72.0, slope 128; White: yardage 6244, par 72, rating 70.7, slope 124; *Women:* Green: yardage 5571, par 72, rating 73.5, slope 131.

Tee Times: Reciprocal players should have their home professional call to inquire.

Dress Code: Appropriate golf attire and non-metal spikes are required.

Tournaments: Please inquire.

Directions: Take the Via de la Valle exit off I-5 and drive east to El Camino Real. Drive south to San Dieguito Road, then east for one mile to the club.

Contact: 15150 San Dieguito Road (P.O. Box 8586), Rancho Santa Fe, CA 92067, pro shop 858/259-8819, clubhouse 858/259-8811, fax 858/259-8593, www.fairbanksranch.com.

52 MORGAN RUN RESORT & CLUB

Architect: Jay Morrish, 1965
27 holes   **Resort**   **$100–120**

San Diego and Vicinity map, page 394

There are three nine-hole courses here, played in combos of two. They are flat and easy to walk, but the narrow fairways and long rough make them challenging. A river snakes through two of the nines. Known locally for its slow greens, Morgan Run is home to the internationally acclaimed San Diego Academy of Golf.

For reservations at the 90-room, boutique-style resort, call 858/756-2471.

Play Policy and Fees: Green fees are $100 Monday–Thursday, $120 Friday–Sunday and holidays. Rates include cart. Twilight rates are offered.

Tees and Yardage: East/South—*Men:* Blue: yardage 6427, par 72, rating 71.5, slope 126; White: yardage 6206, par 72, rating 70.3, slope 123; Gold: yardage 5858, par 72, rating 68.1, slope 118; *Women:* Red: yardage 5542, par 72, rating 72.9, slope 130. North/East—*Men:* Blue: yardage 6292, par 71, rating 70.3, slope 123; White: yardage 5985, par 71, rating 68.9, slope 119; Gold: yardage 5585, par 71, rating 67.0, slope 115; *Women:* Red: yardage 5249, par 71, rating 71.0, slope 125. South/North—*Men:* Blue: yardage 6469, par 71, rating 71.2, slope 123; White: yardage 6096, par 71, rating 69.6, slope 119; Gold: yardage 5669, par 71, rating 67.3, slope 115; *Women:* Red: yardage 5409, par 71, rating 72.4, slope 131.

Tee Times: Reservations can be booked seven days in advance.

Dress Code: Collared shirts are required, and no denim or metal spikes are allowed on the course.

Tournaments: This course is available for outside tournaments.

Directions: From I-5 in Del Mar, take the Via de la Valle exit. Drive east for three miles and turn right on Cancha de Golf.

Contact: 5690 Cancha de Golf, Rancho Santa Fe, CA 92067, pro shop 858/756-3255, fax 858/756-3013, www.morganrun.com.

53 RANCHO SANTA FE GOLF CLUB

Architect: Max Behr, 1929
18 holes   **Private**   **$200–220**

San Diego and Vicinity map, page 394

This classic course has a rolling layout among mature trees with very little water. Regarded locally as one of the top courses in the country—and certainly in Southern California—its design is a tribute to economy, demanding both strength and smarts. It is a true treasure. This course was the original site of the Bing Crosby National Pro-Am and the hangout of many Hollywood types during the 1940s and '50s.

The swanky Inn at Rancho Santa Fe has 87 guest rooms. For reservations, call 858/756-1131. **Play Policy and Fees:** Members and guests only. Guests at the Inn at Rancho Santa Fe are welcome to play in the afternoon for $200 weekdays and $220 on weekends, including cart. The course is closed Monday.

Tees and Yardage: *Men:* Black: yardage 7035, par 72, rating 74.7, slope 142; Blue: yardage 6904, par 72, rating 74.0, slope 140; White: yardage 6431, par 72, rating 71.9, slope 134; *Women:* Red: yardage 5831, par 72, rating 75.3, slope 137; Green: yardage 4970, par 72, rating 70.4, slope 128.

Tee Times: Reservations can be booked seven days in advance for guests at the inn.

Dress Code: Appropriate golf attire and non-metal spikes are required.

Tournaments: Outside play is limited to local charity events.

Directions: Take I-5 to Lomas Santa Fe Drive and travel east for four miles on Highway 8 to the inn. Turn left on Avenida de Acacias and drive half a mile to Via de la Cumbre. Go left one-quarter mile to the club.

Contact: 5827 Via de la Cumbre (P.O. Box 598), Rancho Santa Fe, CA 92067, pro shop 858/756-3094, www.rsfgc.com.

54 THE FARMS

Architect: John Fought and Tom Lehman, 1988
18 holes   **Private**

San Diego and Vicinity map, page 394

Members consider this maturing course a very private retreat. It is very hilly with three man-made lakes that come into play on five holes. This is one of the most scenic courses in the country. It demands accuracy to navigate rough-

lined fairways and tiered greens, as well as some strength when the wind blows.

Play Policy and Fees: Members and guests only.

Tees and Yardage: *Men:* Gold: yardage 6860, par 72, rating 73.9, slope 143; Blue: yardage 6460, par 72, rating 71.9, slope 139; White: yardage 6069, par 72, rating 69.9, slope 135; *Women:* Red: yardage 5619, par 72, rating 74.0, slope 137; Green: yardage 4593, par 72, rating 67.7, slope 124.

Tee Times: Not applicable.

Dress Code: Appropriate golf attire and non-metal spikes are required.

Tournaments: This course is not available for outside events.

Directions: From I-5, take the Carmel Valley Road exit and drive east 4–5 miles. Turn left on Rancho Santa Fe Road. At the dead end, turn right; the course is one-quarter mile farther.

Contact: 8500 Saint Andrews Road (P.O. Box 2769), Rancho Santa Fe, CA 92067, pro shop 858/756-5884.

55 DOUBLETREE GOLF RESORT SAN DIEGO

Architect: William F. Bell, 1964
18 holes   **Resort**   **$60–80**

San Diego and Vicinity map, page 394

This rolling course is well groomed with exceptional greens. Water comes into play on four holes. The par-5 sixth hole has a lateral water hazard running alongside the fairway and a pond in front of the green. The eighth hole is a long par-4 up a hill to a sloped green. It is a fun round of golf for all skill levels.

For reservations at the resort, call 858/672-9100.

Play Policy and Fees: Green fees for nonguests are $60 Monday–Thursday, $70 Friday, and $80 weekends and holidays. Hotel guests receive discounted rates. Early bird, twilight, super twilight, senior, and junior rates are available. Carts are included in fees.

Tees and Yardage: *Men:* Blue: yardage 6428, par 72, rating 71.4, slope 129; White: yardage 6018,

par 72, rating 69.4, slope 126; *Women:* Red: yardage 5361, par 72, rating 71.9, slope 125.

Tee Times: Reservations can be booked seven days in advance for public play and 30 days in advance for hotel guests.

Dress Code: Appropriate golf attire and non-metal spikes are required.

Tournaments: A 16-player minimum is needed to book a tournament. The banquet facility can accommodate 300 people.

Directions: Travel 23 miles north of San Diego on I-15 to the Carmel Mountain Road exit. Drive west for one-quarter mile to Penasquitos Drive and turn right to the club entrance.

Contact: 14455 Penasquitos Drive, San Diego, CA 92128, pro shop 858/485-4145, www .doubletreehotels.com.

56 CARMEL MOUNTAIN RANCH COUNTRY CLUB

Architect: Ron Fream, 1986
18 holes   Semiprivate $78–98

🏌 📷 🍴 🛺 ⛳

San Diego and Vicinity map, page 394

The holes on this rolling, narrow course follow the contours of the hills. There are no parallel fairways. The greens are nicely kept and fast. Homes line virtually every fairway, and there are some serious hills here, all of which demand accuracy and patience. The fifth hole has been rated the toughest par-4 in San Diego. The eighth features two lakes and a waterfall.

Play Policy and Fees: Green fees are $78 Monday–Thursday, $80 Friday, and $98 weekends and holidays. Carts are included. San Diego County residents receive a discount. Twilight, senior, junior, and military rates are available.

Tees and Yardage: *Men:* Blue: yardage 6404, par 71, rating 72.5, slope 132; White: yardage 6023, par 71, rating 70.8, slope 127; Gold: yardage 5626, par 71, rating 69.0, slope 123; *Women:* Red: yardage 5006, par 71, rating 71.0, slope 122.

Tee Times: Reservations can be booked 30 days in advance. An additional $5 per player reservation fee will apply to all reservations made

prior to seven days in advance. All reservations must be guaranteed with a credit card.

Dress Code: Collared shirts are required. No jeans are allowed on the course. Nonmetal spikes are required.

Tournaments: This course is available for tournaments. Carts are required. The banquet facility can accommodate 250 people.

Directions: Take I-15 to the Carmel Mountain Road east. Drive past three stoplights and take a right on Highland Ranch Road. Drive past three more stoplights and take a right on Carmel Ridge Road. Drive to the top of the hill.

Contact: 14050 Carmel Ridge Road, San Diego, CA 92128, pro shop 858/487-9224, clubhouse 858/451-8353, fax 858/487-9075, www.club cmr.com.

57 DEL MAR NATIONAL GOLF CLUB

Architect: Tom Fazio, 1999
18 holes   Public $125–155

🏌 📷 🍴 🛺

San Diego and Vicinity map, page 394

This course (formerly Meadows Del Mar) plays long for a par-71, and there are no adjoining fairways. The rolling coastal hills and valleys provide lots of variation in play, as well as some nice surroundings. Typical of a scenic Fazio design, Del Mar blends with the natural environment over more than 300 acres. It is a good course for all skill levels and considered women-friendly.

Play Policy and Fees: Green fees are $125 Monday–Thursday and $155 Friday–Sunday and holidays. Twilight rates are offered.

Tees and Yardage: *Men:* Championship: yardage 7054, par 71, rating 74.0, slope 136; Tournament: yardage 6424, par 71, rating 71.5, slope 131; Resort: yardage 5880, par 71, rating 68.9, slope 124; *Women:* Forward: yardage 4974, par 71, rating 68.3, slope 116.

Tee Times: Reservations may be booked up to 60 days in advance.

Dress Code: Collared shirts, along with Bermuda shorts or long pants, are required for male golfers. Nonmetal spikes are mandatory for all players. No denim is permitted.

Tournaments: For events of 36–100 players, reservations may be made up to six months in advance. For events of more than 100 players, reservations may be made up to one year in advance.

Directions: From I-5 north of San Diego, take Highway 56/Carmel Valley Road east to the Carmel Country Road exit. Turn right on Carmel Country Road, then proceed one-quarter mile to the club's entrance on the left.

Contact: 5300 Meadows Del Mar, San Diego, CA 92130, pro shop 858/792-6200, fax 858/792-0130, www.delmarnationalgolf.com.

58 TORREY PINES GOLF COURSE

Architect: William F. Bell, 1957; redesign Rees Jones (South Course), 2002

36 holes   **Public**   **$140–205**

San Diego and Vicinity map, page 394

 Among the very best public facilities in California, Torrey Pines offers two very popular championship 18-hole layouts. Both have some spectacular ocean views. The South Course is wide open but demanding. It plays more than 7600 yards for the pros! Players need to hit solid shots to score. There is no let up on the course, which gets particularly tough when the wind is blowing off the ocean. The North Course is shorter and more scenic, but still no stroll in the pines, particularly for women, as the forward tee rating of 76.4 indicates. The 12th hole on the South Course, more than 485 yards into the wind, has been rated one of the toughest holes in the country. The North Course is about two shots easier. Both courses are used for the PGA Tour's Buick Invitational. The 2008 U.S. Open will be held here.

For information on the Lodge at Torrey Pines, call 858/453-4420 or 800/656-0087.

Play Policy and Fees: South Course green fees are $185 Monday–Thursday and $205 Friday–Sunday. North Course green fees are $140

Monday–Thursday and $150 Friday–Sunday. All fees include cart.

Tees and Yardage: South Course—*Men:* Black: yardage 7607, par 72, rating 78.1, slope 143; Blue: yardage 7227, par 72, rating 76.1, slope 139; White: yardage 6885, par 72, rating 74.3, slope 136; Green: yardage 6542, par 72, rating 72.5, slope 133; *Women:* Red: yardage 5542, par 72, rating 73.6, slope 129. North Course—*Men:* Tournament: yardage 6828, par 72, rating 73.2, slope 130; Blue: yardage 6600, par 72, rating 72.1, slope 128; White: yardage 6325, par 72, rating 70.8, slope 125; *Women:* Red: yardage 6117, par 72, rating 76.4, slope 133.

Tee Times: Reservations can be made up to two months in advance. Guests of the Lodge at Torrey Pines have reserved tee times, and reservations can be made when booking accommodations.

Dress Code: Appropriate golf attire and soft spikes required.

Tournaments: A 32-player minimum is needed to book a tournament, and carts are required. The Lodge at Torrey Pines has banquet facilities.

Directions: Drive north from San Diego on I-5 to Genesse. Turn west to North Torrey Pines Road and turn north into the club.

Contact: 11480 North Torrey Pines Road, La Jolla, CA 92037, pro shop 800/985-4653, www.torreypinesgolfcourse.com.

59 MIRAMAR MEMORIAL GOLF CLUB

Architect: Jack Daray, 1963

18 holes   **Military**

San Diego and Vicinity map, page 394

Located on base at the Miramar Marine Corps Air Station, this course was originally built as an emergency landing area. Today it's lined with trees. The course is flat, but wind and rough make it a firm test. The par-5 ninth hole measures 640 yards, making it the longest par-5 in Southern California.

Play Policy and Fees: Active and retired military personnel and guests only. Green fees are based on military status.

Tees and Yardage: *Men:* Blue: yardage 6818, par 72, rating 72.2, slope 126; White: yardage 6402, par 72, rating 70.0, slope 120; *Women:* Red: yardage 5898, par 72, rating 73.9, slope 128.

Tee Times: Not applicable.

Dress Code: Appropriate golf attire is required.

Tournaments: This course is not available for outside events.

Directions: Take I-15 or State Road 163 for 12 miles north of San Diego to Miramar Way. Exit and drive west to the main gate.

Contact: MCAS Miramar, P.O. Box 45312, San Diego, CA 92145, pro shop 858/577-4155.

60 CARLTON OAKS COUNTRY CLUB & LODGE

Architect: Perry Dye, 1989

18 holes   Resort $55–80

San Diego and Vicinity map, page 394

This terrific layout has it all—water, wind, rough, and well-guarded greens. The 14th hole is one of the most challenging on the course. With a slight dogleg left to a narrow landing area, this hole demands accuracy off the tee. The second shot is a long iron to a green bunkered left and back. Oh, did we mention that the fairway is lined with trees? Good luck! In 2003, this course expanded its length to greater than 7200 yards from the back tees.

For information on the lodge, check the website or call 619/448-4242 or 800/831-6757.

Play Policy and Fees: Green fees are $55 Monday–Thursday, $60 Friday, $80 Saturday, and $70 Sunday. Twilight rates are offered. Carts are included.

Tees and Yardage: *Men:* Black: yardage 7225, par 72, rating 72.5, slope 146; Blue: yardage 6700, par 72, rating 72.5, slope 139; White: yardage 6140, par 72, rating 69.8, slope 132; Gold: yardage 5706, par 72, rating 67.9, slope 125; *Women:* Red: yardage 5044, par 72, rating 76.3, slope 143.

Tee Times: Reservations can be booked seven days in advance.

Dress Code: Collared shirts and nonmetal spikes are required. Bermuda-length shorts are okay.

Tournaments: This course is available for outside tournaments. Carts are required for tournament play.

Directions: Take Highway 52 east to the Mast Boulevard exit. Drive one mile on Mast and turn right on Pebble Beach Drive. Turn right on Carlton Oaks Drive and drive to the course on the left.

Contact: 9200 Inwood Drive, Santee, CA 92071, pro shop 619/448-8500, clubhouse 619/448-4242, fax 619/258-8736, www.carltonoaks golf.com.

61 WILLOWBROOK COUNTRY CLUB

Architect: Course designed, 1955; Jack Daray Jr., 1981

9 holes   Public $15–18

San Diego and Vicinity map, page 394

This level course has water on four holes, five for the slightly errant. The 500-yard fifth can be a real monster if the afternoon winds pick up, as they often do. The 447-yard ninth features rough and water left off the tee and trees straight ahead. Better have your power fade working here.

Play Policy and Fees: Green fees are $15 for nine holes weekdays, $18 for nine holes weekends. Twilight rates are offered.

Tees and Yardage: *Men (18 holes):* White: yardage 5891, par 72, rating 68.5, slope 123; *Women (18 holes):* Yellow/Red: yardage 4956, par 72, rating 68.1, slope 118.

Tee Times: Reservations can be booked seven days in advance.

Dress Code: No tank tops for men are allowed on the course.

Tournaments: A 72-player minimum is needed to book a shotgun tournament. A 16-player minimum is needed for a regular tournament. Events should be scheduled 2–3 months in advance.

Directions: Take I-8 east from San Diego to the Highway 67 exit in El Cajon. Travel north to the Riverford Road exit (bear left). Make a left on Riverford Road and then turn right on Riverside Drive. The club is on the right side about one-half mile along.

Contact: 11905 Riverside Drive, Lakeside, CA 92040, pro shop 619/561-1061, fax 619/561-2068.

62 BARONA CREEK GOLF CLUB

Architect: Gary Roger Baird, 2001
18 holes   Resort $80–100

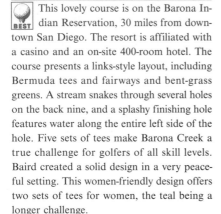

San Diego and Vicinity map, page 394

This lovely course is on the Barona Indian Reservation, 30 miles from downtown San Diego. The resort is affiliated with a casino and an on-site 400-room hotel. The course presents a links-style layout, including Bermuda tees and fairways and bent-grass greens. A stream snakes through several holes on the back nine, and a splashy finishing hole features water along the entire left side of the hole. Five sets of tees make Barona Creek a true challenge for golfers of all skill levels. Baird created a solid design in a very peaceful setting. This women-friendly design offers two sets of tees for women, the teal being a longer challenge.

For information on Barona Valley Ranch Resort, visit the website or call 888/7-BARONA (888/722-7662) or 619/443-2300.

Play Policy and Fees: Green fees are $80 weekdays, $100 weekends. Twilight rates available. Prices include cart and range balls.

Tees and Yardage: *Men:* Black: yardage 7088, par 72, rating 74.5, slope 139; Gold: yardage 6596, par 72, rating 72.1, slope 133; Silver: yardage 6231, par 72, rating 70.4, slope 129; *Women:* Teal: yardage 5813, par 72, rating 73.8, slope 130; Burgundy: yardage 5296, par 72, rating 70.6, slope 126.

Tee Times: Reservations may be booked seven days in advance.

Dress Code: Country club attire is expected. Collared shirts are required, and no denim is allowed. Soft spikes only.

Tournaments: This course is available for spe-

cial events. Contact the tournament director at 619/387-7018.

Directions: From I-8, take Highway 67 traveling north. Exit at Willow Road East, then turn left on Wildcat Canyon North.

Contact: 1932 Wildcat Canyon Road, Lakeside, CA 92040, pro shop 619/387-7018, fax 619/390-8931, www.barona.com.

63 LA JOLLA COUNTRY CLUB

Architect: William P. Bell, 1927
18 holes   Private

San Diego and Vicinity map, page 394

This is an older, traditional course perched on a bluff overlooking the Pacific. It is nicely maintained and relatively hilly with lots of trees and bunkers. When the wind picks up, it can be a tough course. The key here is accuracy and the ability to read the small, subtle, and quick greens. Gene Littler holds the course record with 63.

Play Policy and Fees: Members and guests only.

Tees and Yardage: *Men:* Black: yardage 6685, par 72, rating 72.9, slope 129; Silver: yardage 6437, par 72, rating 71.0, slope 127; Blue: yardage 6260, par 72, rating 71.0, slope 122; White: yardage 5937, par 72, rating 69.5, slope 122; *Women:* Green: yardage 5391, par 74, rating 72.7, slope 131.

Tee Times: Not applicable.

Dress Code: Appropriate golf attire and nonmetal spikes are required.

Tournaments: This course is not available for outside events.

Directions: Take the Ardath Road exit (it becomes Torrey Pines Road) off I-5 north of San Diego and drive 3.25 miles. Turn left on Girard Street and then left on Pearl Street. Drive two blocks to High Avenue and turn right. Continue one block to the club.

Contact: 7301 High Avenue Extension (P.O. Box 1760), La Jolla, CA 92038, pro shop 858/454-2505.

64 MISSION BAY GOLF COURSE

Architect: Ted Robinson Sr., 1964

18 holes   **Public**   **$12–19**

San Diego and Vicinity map, page 394

This is a nice executive course, providing a good round for families and beginning golfers. In fact it's a ball for anyone. Holes range 75–291 yards, including four par-4s. Water and sand come into play often. The course, which is lighted for play until 10 P.M., is beautifully landscaped and next to Mission Bay.

Play Policy and Fees: Green fees are $12 for nine holes and $19 for 18 holes. Senior and junior rates available.

Tees and Yardage: *Men:* yardage 2719, par 58, rating n/a, slope n/a; *Women:* yardage 2427, par 58, rating n/a, slope n/a.

Tee Times: Reservations can be booked seven days in advance.

Dress Code: Appropriate attire and soft spikes are required.

Tournaments: A 16-player minimum is required to book an event. Tournaments should be scheduled 2–6 months in advance. The banquet facility can accommodate up to 200 people.

Directions: Take I-5 from San Diego and go west on Clairmont Drive. Then drive north on Mission Bay Drive to the course.

Contact: 2702 North Mission Bay Drive, San Diego, CA 92109, pro shop 858/581-7880.

65 TECOLOTE CANYON GOLF COURSE

Architect: Robert Trent Jones Jr., 1964;
Robert Trent Jones Jr. and Sam Snead, 1998

18 holes   **Public**   **$19–24**

San Diego and Vicinity map, page 394

This well-maintained executive course is a great place for beginners and players of all skill levels. A 3.5-hour round is routine here during the week. A Nike Golf Learning Center is here.

Play Policy and Fees: Green fees are $19 weekdays and $24 weekends and holidays. Senior, junior, and twilight rates are offered. AGPA

members also receive a discount. Carts are additional.

Tees and Yardage: *Men and Women:* yardage 3166, par 58, rating n/a, slope n/a.

Tee Times: Reservations are suggested for weekdays. For weekend tee times, reservations are required at least four days in advance.

Dress Code: Nonmetal spikes and appropriate golf attire are required.

Tournaments: This course is available for tournaments with 30 days advance notice.

Directions: From downtown San Diego, head north on I-5 to the Clairmont Drive exit. Travel east one-quarter mile to Bueguer Street, then turn right. Take the first left on Field Street. Follow Field Street to the golf course.

Contact: 2755 Snead Avenue, San Diego, CA 92111, pro shop 858/279-1600, fax 858/279-2194, www.agpa.com.

66 RIVERWALK GOLF CLUB

Architect: Lawrence Hughes, 1947;
Ted Robinson Sr. and Jr., 1998

27 holes   **Public**   **$79–99**

San Diego and Vicinity map, page 394

This is a scenic, 27-hole facility that father and son Robinson transformed from a flat track to one that now features undulating fairways, waterfalls, and well-protected, bent-grass greens. The three nines are called Friars, Presidio, and Mission. Water comes into play on 13 of the 27 holes. The San Diego River is a prominent feature running through the course. The hardest hole on the Mission Course is the 542-yard par-5, with the San Diego River running in front of the green, making it risky for even the longest hitter to reach it in two. Formerly known as the Stardust Country Club, this course hosted the PGA Tour from 1955 until 1968.

The course is in Mission Valley's Hotel Circle and offers several play-and-stay packages with nearby hotels. Call the pro shop for more information.

Play Policy and Fees: Green fees are $79 Monday–Thursday, $89 Friday, and $99 weekends and holidays. Twilight, junior, early bird, and replay rates are also available. Area residents also receive discounted rates.

Tees and Yardage: Friars/Presidio—*Men:* Back: yardage 6627, par 72, rating 71.7, slope 129; Middle: yardage 6277, par 72, rating 70.0, slope 125; *Women:* Forward: yardage 5532, par 72, rating 70.9, slope 115. Mission/Friars—*Men:* Back: yardage 6383, par 72, rating 70.7, slope 129; Middle: yardage 6033, par 72, rating 68.9, slope 125; *Women:* Forward: yardage 5215, par 72, rating 69.5, slope 114. Presidio/Mission— *Men:* Back: yardage 6550, par 72, rating 71.9, slope 126; Middle: yardage 6156, par 72, rating 70.0, slope 123; *Women:* Forward: yardage 5427, par 72, rating 71.3, slope 115.

Tee Times: Reservations can be made up to 30 days in advance. All reservations beyond seven days require an additional $5 reservation charge and must be guaranteed with a credit card.

Dress Code: Collared shirts and nonmetal spikes are required. No denim is allowed, and shorts must be Bermuda-length.

Tournaments: Riverwalk is available for outside events, and banquet facilities are available that can accommodate 250 people. A 24-player minimum is needed to book a tournament.

Directions: Drive north on I-5 from San Diego. Take I-8 east and exit at Hotel Circle North. Go north on Fashion Valley Road. The course is on the left.

Contact: 1150 Fashion Valley Road, San Diego, CA 92108, pro shop 619/296-4653, fax 619/296-8011, www.riverwalkgc.com.

67 PRESIDIO HILLS GOLF COURSE

Architect: George Marston, 1932
18 holes   **Public**   **$10**

San Diego and Vicinity map, page 394

This is the one of the oldest courses in the San Diego area. It's been a family operation for many years. This is a fun little pitch-and-putt course for tuning up the short game. Full-grown

sycamore trees keep the course in welcome shade. The San Diego Junior Golf Association, one of the oldest and most successful in the nation, starts its youngsters here. Years after they made the PGA Tour, such players as Lon Hinkle and Morris Hatalsky returned here to polish their short games.

Play Policy and Fees: Green fees are $10 for 18 holes.

Tees and Yardage: *Men and Women:* yardage 1325, par 54, rating n/a, slope n/a.

Tee Times: Reservations are not accepted. All play is on a first-come, first-served basis.

Dress Code: Nonmetal spikes are required.

Tournaments: This course is available for outside tournaments.

Directions: Take the Taylor Street exit off I-8 in San Diego. Drive about one mile to Juan Street, turn left, and drive one block to the course, on the left.

Contact: 4136 Wallace Street, San Diego, CA 92110, pro shop 619/295-9476.

68 FOUR POINTS SHERATON SAN DIEGO

Architect: Course designed, 1998
9 holes   **Resort**   **$6-8**

San Diego and Vicinity map, page 394

This is a short par-3 course that is fun for the family. The longest hole is 140 yards.

For hotel rates and information, check the website or call 858/277-8888.

Play Policy and Fees: Green fees for hotel guests are $6 any day. For nonguests, green fees are $8. Twilight, junior, senior, military, and replay rates are available.

Tees and Yardage: *Men:* yardage 793, par 27, rating n/a, slope n/a; *Women:* yardage 724, par 27, rating n/a, slope n/a.

Tee Times: Reservations are made on a first-come, first-served basis.

Dress Code: Appropriate golf attire and soft spikes are required.

Tournaments: Outside events are allowed.

Directions: From the San Diego airport, take

I-805 north to Highway 163 north. Exit at Kearny Villa Road and take a right. Aero Drive is on the right.

Contact: 8110 Aero Drive, San Diego, CA 92123, pro shop 858/277-8888, ext. 5637, www.sd4points.com.

69 ADMIRAL BAKER GOLF COURSE

Architect: Jack Daray, 1957

| 36 holes | Military | $9–31 |

San Diego and Vicinity map, page 394

The North Course is the more interesting of the two courses and offers a variety of holes traversing rather hilly terrain. The South Course is shorter and more level. This facility was formerly known as Mission Gorge.

Play Policy and Fees: Active or retired military personnel and guests only. Green fees vary depending on status.

Tees and Yardage: North Course—*Men:* Blue: yardage 6801, par 72, rating 72.4, slope 127; White: yardage 6486, par 72, rating 70.8, slope 124; *Women:* Red: yardage 5844, par 72, rating 73.9, slope 126. South Course—*Men:* White: yardage 6061, par 72, rating 68.2, slope 116; *Women:* Red: yardage 5535, par 72, rating 71.4, slope 121.

Tee Times: Only military personnel are allowed to make reservations. For weekday tee times, active duty and retired military may call seven days in advance. For weekend times, active duty may call on Tuesday at 6 A.M., and retired military may call Tuesday after 10 A.M.

Dress Code: No tank tops or open-toed shoes are allowed. Soft spikes are required.

Tournaments: Nonmilitary groups may play only with proper military sponsorship.

Directions: Take I-5 from I-8 and drive one-quarter mile north to the Friars Road East exit. Drive east to Admiral Baker Road and turn left past the security gate to the club.

Contact: Friars Road and Admiral Baker Road, San Diego, CA 92021, pro shop 619/556 5520.

70 MISSION TRAILS GOLF COURSE

Architect: William F. Bell, 1966

| 18 holes | Public | $28–50 |

San Diego and Vicinity map, page 394

Set in a valley, this scenic course features a layout that follows the contours of the land, with two of the holes running alongside Lake Murray. Mature trees separate the fairways. A Nike Golf Learning Center is on the property.

Play Policy and Fees: Weekday green fees are $28 to walk and $40 to ride. Weekend fees are $38 to walk and $50 to ride. Twilight and super twilight rates are offered.

Tees and Yardage: *Men:* Blue: yardage 6004, par 71, rating 69.1, slope 126; White: yardage 5601, par 71, rating 67.7, slope 119; *Women:* Red: yardage 5119, par 71, rating 70.0, slope 122.

Tee Times: Reservations may be made seven days in advance.

Dress Code: Appropriate golf attire is required.

Tournaments: Outside tournaments should be booked a year in advance. Call 619/297-4431 for information.

Directions: Drive on I-8 in San Diego to College Avenue. Turn north and drive one mile to Navajo Road. Turn right and drive two miles to Golfcrest Drive. Turn right again and continue one-quarter mile to Golfcrest Place. Turn left into the club.

Contact: 7380 Golfcrest Place, San Diego, CA 92119, pro shop 619/460-5400.

71 SUN VALLEY GOLF COURSE

Architect: Course designed, 1950

| 9 holes | Public | $7–13 |

San Diego and Vicinity map, page 394

This hilly course has nice, open fairways. It's part of a larger municipal park in a suburban San Diego neighborhood. The longest hole is 131 yards; the shortest, 96. A major renovation several years ago included a new driving range, new tee-box locations on several holes, a new irrigation system, and a remodeled pro shop.

Play Policy and Fees: Green fees are $7 for nine holes and $11 for 18 holes Monday–Thursday. Friday–Sunday, green fees are $9 for nine holes and $13 for 18 holes.

Tees and Yardage: *Men and Women:* yardage 1013, par 27, rating n/a, slope n/a.

Tee Times: Reservations are accepted up to 30 days in advance.

Dress Code: Shirts are required at all times.

Tournaments: This course is available for outside tournaments.

Directions: Take I-8 east of San Diego to El Cajon Boulevard. Go left to La Mesa Boulevard and follow it to Memorial Drive and the course.

Contact: 5080 Memorial Drive, La Mesa, CA 92041, pro shop 619/466-6102, fax 619/466-6120.

72 COTTONWOOD AT RANCHO SAN DIEGO

Architect: O. W. Morman, 1960

36 holes   Public $28–45

San Diego and Vicinity map, page 394

These two scenic courses have a lot of trees, ponds, and lakes. A river runs through them in the winter. The name is derived from the fact that they play through large groves of cottonwood trees. The Ivanhoe Course has numerous doglegs and is one of the best-maintained public courses in the area. The Monte Vista Course has tight fairways and is shorter.

Play Policy and Fees: Green fees for the Ivanhoe Course are $31 Monday–Thursday, $35 Friday, and $45 weekends. Green fees for the Monte Vista Course are $28 Monday–Thursday, $32 Friday, and $42 weekends. Twilight, super twilight, and junior rates are available. Carts are $12 per person. Specials are often found on the website.

Tees and Yardage: Ivanhoe—*Men:* Championship: yardage 6764, par 72, rating 72.6, slope 126; Regular: yardage 6445, par 72, rating 70.5, slope 116; *Women:* Forward: yardage 5686, par 73, rating 72.4, slope 121. Monte Vista—*Men:*

Regular: yardage 6302, par 71, rating 69.6, slope 116; *Women:* Forward: yardage 5531, par 72, rating 70.4, slope 117.

Tee Times: Reservations are recommended and may be made two weeks in advance.

Dress Code: Collared shirts and soft spikes are required. No cutoffs or board shorts may be worn.

Tournaments: Tournaments of all kinds are welcome with two weeks advance notice.

Directions: From I-5 or I-805, take I-8 east to the 2nd Street exit in El Cajon. Drive south on 2nd Street for about four miles to Willow Glen Drive and turn left to the club.

Contact: 3121 Willow Glen Drive, El Cajon, CA 92019, pro shop 619/442-9891, fax 619/442-2361, www.cottonwoodgolf.com.

73 SINGING HILLS COUNTRY CLUB AT SYCUAN

Architect: Cecil Hollingsworth, 1956 (Willow Glen Course); Ted Robinson Sr., 1980

54 holes   Resort $16–55

San Diego and Vicinity map, page 394

Three 18-hole courses spread across 425 acres of scenic mountain terrain at Singing Hills, two of which are regulation length. They are called Willow Glen and Oak Glen. The third design is a fun par-3 course called Pine Glen. Mature trees line the flat, straight fairways on the Oak Glen Course. The Willow Glen Course offers a rolling layout and is known for its elevated tee on the fourth hole and for the par-3 12th with its tiered green beyond a lake ringed with flowers.

Singing Hills has 102 rooms and suites, plus a bustling casino. Most rooms have golf course views. The resort also features a tennis facility.

Play Policy and Fees: Green fees are $40 weekdays, $46 Friday on the Willow Glen and Oak Glen courses, and $50 weekends and holidays on Willow Glen, $55 on Oak Glen. Fees include use of a cart. Green fees for the Pine Glen course are $16 weekdays and $18 weekends and holidays, with an additional $16 for use of a cart.

Twilight rates are available. Senior rates are available only at the Pine Glen course.

Tees and Yardage: Willow Glen—*Men:* Blue: yardage 6605, par 72, rating 72.3, slope 129; White: yardage 6207, par 72, rating 70.2, slope 125; *Women:* Red: yardage 5585, par 72, rating 72.5, slope 127. Oak Glen—*Men:* Blue: yardage 6489, par 72, rating 71.1, slope 128; White: yardage 6044, par 72, rating 69.0, slope 123; *Women:* Red: yardage 5549, par 72, rating 71.4, slope 124. Pine Glen: *Men:* Back: yardage 2508, par 54, rating n/a, slope n/a; *Women:* Forward: yardage 2253, par 54, rating n/a, slope n/a.

Tee Times: Reservations can be booked seven days in advance Monday–Friday and five days in advance on weekends.

Dress Code: No tank tops are allowed on the course. Shorts must be mid-thigh in length. Nonmetal spikes are preferred.

Tournaments: Shotgun tournaments are available weekdays only. A 72-player minimum is required for a shotgun tournament, and carts are required. The banquet facility can accommodate 300 people.

Directions: From I-5 or I-805, take I-8 east to the El Cajon Boulevard exit. Drive to the second light and turn right on Washington Street. Washington Street turns into Dehesa Road.

Contact: 3007 Dehesa Road, El Cajon, CA 92019, pro shop 619/442-3425, fax 619/444-5500, www.singinghills.com.

74 STEELE CANYON GOLF CLUB

Architect: Gary Player, 1991

27 holes   **Semiprivate**   **$79–99**

San Diego and Vicinity map, page 394

There are three nine-hole rotations: Canyon, Ranch, and Meadow. Each has distinct characteristics. The rugged Canyon nine provides dramatic shot-making challenges and significant elevation changes. The Ranch course winds through the picturesque fields of a working ranch, and the Meadow nine drifts along a pastoral valley enhanced with scenic woodlands, streams,

and native wildlife. Any combination provides a very pleasant round of golf. It demands good shots but plays well for all golfers. Women find the courses very playable. Steele Canyon received a four-star rating from *Golf Digest.*

Play Policy and Fees: Green fees are $79 Monday–Thursday and $99 Friday, weekends, and holidays. Twilight, super twilight, and junior rates are available.

Tees and Yardage: Canyon/Meadow—*Men:* Blue: yardage 6446, par 70, rating 72.0, slope 138; White: yardage 5943, par 70, rating 69.5, slope 133; Gold: yardage 5290, par 70, rating 66.9, slope 127; *Women:* Red: yardage 4440, par 70, rating 67.1, slope 116. Ranch/Canyon—*Men:* Blue: yardage 6718, par 71, rating 73.1, slope 139; White: yardage 6225, par 71, rating 70.5, slope 134; Gold: yardage 5515, par 71, rating 67.7, slope 123; *Women:* Red: yardage 4566, par 71, rating 66.8, slope 118. Ranch/Meadow—*Men:* Blue: yardage 6766, par 71, rating 73.4, slope 141; White: yardage 6218, par 71, rating 70.4, slope 133; Gold: yardage 5653, par 71, rating 68.0, slope 127; *Women:* Red: yardage 4818, par 71, rating 67.9, slope 124.

Tee Times: Reservations can be booked seven days in advance. For an additional $10 fee, reservations can be made up to 60 days in advance.

Dress Code: Appropriate golf attire and nonmetal spikes are mandatory.

Tournaments: A 20-player minimum is needed to book a tournament. Carts are required. Shotgun tournaments are available on weekdays only. Events should be booked nine months in advance. The banquet facility can accommodate up to 200 people.

Directions: From I-5 in San Diego, exit east onto I-94 (which turns into Highway 54). Proceed to Willow Glen Drive. Turn right and drive to Steele Canyon Drive. Turn right on Steele Canyon Drive to Jamul Drive (the first traffic light). Turn left and drive one mile to the club.

Contact: 3199 Stonefield Drive, Jamul, CA 91935, pro shop 619/441-6900, fax 619/441-6909, www.steelecanyon.com.

COLINA PARK GOLF COURSE

Architect: Course designed, 1954; renovated 2003

18 holes　　　　**Public**　　　　**$10–12**

San Diego and Vicinity map, page 394

This 18-hole, family-friendly par-3 course was renovated in 2003, when new greens and additional bunkers were crafted. It is carved into a neighborhood in the middle of the city. It has rolling fairways, undulating greens, and trees— lots of trees. Bring your straight game. Colina Park is a delightful little track for seniors and juniors. Colina Park is the home of the Pro Kids Golf Academy and Learning Center and the site of the San Diego Chapter PGA "Clubs for Kids" program. Funded through foundations and corporations, a two-story clubhouse facility is underway that will include a community room, golf library, classrooms, computer learning center, patios, barbecue area, and a toddler golf area.

Play Policy and Fees: The green fees are $10 weekdays, $12 weekends for 18 holes. Junior, senior, and replay discounts are offered.

Tees and Yardage: *Men and Women:* yardage 1500, par 54, rating n/a, slope n/a.

Tee Times: Reservations can be made at any time.

Dress Code: Shirts and shoes are necessary. Nonmetal spikes are required.

Tournaments: Please inquire.

Directions: Take I-805 to University Avenue and go east a few blocks. At 52nd Street, turn left to the course on the right.

Contact: 4085 52nd Street, San Diego, CA 92105, pro shop 619/582-4704, fax 619/582-9377.

76 BALBOA PARK GOLF CLUB

Architect: William P. Bell, 1915 and 1921

27 holes　　　**Public**　　　**$20–40**

San Diego and Vicinity map, page 394

There are two courses here, a regulation 18-hole course and a par-32 nine-hole course. Both are tight, old-style designs with small greens.

One regular golfer reports that, "Aggressive play will, sooner or later, lead to disastrous consequences. A good course for not-very-long and straight hitters, and patient players. A bad course for those who are wild off the tee and inaccurate iron players." Sam Snead holds the course record of 60, shot in 1943.

Play Policy and Fees: Green fees are $35 weekdays and $40 weekends, carts additional. Resident and twilight rates are available. Junior and senior monthly tickets are offered. Green fees on the nine-hole course are $20.

Tees and Yardage: *Men:* Blue: yardage 6288, par 72, rating 71.1, slope 127; White: yardage 5801, par 72, rating 68.9, slope 124; *Women:* Red: yardage 5389, par 72, rating 72.1, slope 120.

Tee Times: Reservations can be booked seven days in advance.

Dress Code: Appropriate attire and soft spikes are required.

Tournaments: A 16-player minimum is needed to book a tournament, and carts are required.

Directions: Take the Pershing Drive exit off I-5 and drive east to 26th Street. Turn right, drive to Golf Course Drive, and turn left. Continue to the club.

Contact: 2600 Golf Course Drive, San Diego, CA 92102, pro shop 619/239-1660, reservations 619/570-1234, www.balboaparkgolf.com.

77 SEA 'N AIR

Architect: Jack Daray and Stephen Halsey, 1981

18 holes　　　　**Military**

San Diego and Vicinity map, page 394

This flat course features a links-style feel, with three holes that run along the ocean. The course is directly below the North Island Naval Air Station's flight path.

Play Policy and Fees: Active or retired military personnel and guests only. Rates vary according to military rank and status.

Tees and Yardage: *Men:* Blue: yardage 6289, par 72, rating 70.4, slope 128; White: yardage 6086, par 72, rating 69.6, slope 126; *Women:* Red: yardage 5510, par 72, rating 72.9, slope 127.

Tee Times: Not applicable.

Dress Code: No tank tops or cutoffs are allowed.

Tournaments: This course is available for outside events as long as at least 51 percent of the players in the tournament are military personnel.

Directions: Take the Coronado exit off I-5 in San Diego and drive across the Coronado Bay Bridge through the toll gate. Continue on 3rd Avenue and turn left on Alameda Street. At 4th Avenue, turn right through the main gate, drive one-quarter mile to Rogers Road, and turn left to the club.

Contact: Building 800 NAS North Island, Coronado, CA 92178 (P.O. Box 357081, San Diego, CA 92135), pro shop 619/545-9659.

78 CORONADO GOLF COURSE

Architect: Jack Daray, 1957; Wllllam F. Bell, 1968

18 holes **Public** **$20**

San Diego and Vicinity map, page 394

Open fairways and large greens typify this course. It hosts a large number of rounds each year due to its wonderful setting and low rates, but prides itself on being in good condition for every visitor. Set beneath the Coronado Bay Bridge, it has some of the best views of San Diego and its harbor. Former president Bill Clinton has been known to frequent this course.

Play Policy and Fees: Green fees are $20, and carts are $15 per rider.

Tees and Yardage: *Men:* Blue: yardage 6590, par 72, rating 71.5, slope 120; White: yardage 6276, par 72, rating 70.0, slope 117; *Women:* Gold: yardage 5742, par 72, rating 73.0, slope 126.

Tee Times: Reservations may be booked two days in advance.

Dress Code: Shirts must have sleeves, and no cutoffs are permitted. Nonmetal spikes are preferred.

Tournaments: Tournaments should be booked at least a year in advance. The banquet facili ty can accommodate 200 people.

Directions: From I-5 in San Diego, take the

Coronado Bay Bridge west and turn left at the end of the bridge. Go left on 5th Street to Glorietta Boulevard and turn right to the club.

Contact: 2000 Visalia Row, Coronado, CA 92178 (P.O. Box 18190, Coronado, CA 92118), pro shop 619/435-3121.

79 NAVAL STATION SAN DIEGO GOLF COURSE

9 holes **Military** **$5-8**

San Diego and Vicinity map, page 394

This is a short course with open fairways and small greens. Holes vary between 110 and 175 yards. It's all tucked snugly into the 32nd Street Naval Station, just south of downtown San Diego.

Play Policy and Fees: Military personnel and guests only. Green fees vary according to military status.

Tees and Yardage: *Men and Women:* yardage 1250, par 27, rating n/a, slope n/a.

Tee Times: All play is on a first-come, first-served basis.

Dress Code: No cutoffs or tank tops are allowed on the course.

Tournaments: This course is not available for outside events.

Directions: Going south from San Diego on I-5, take the Main Street exit. Cross Main Street and drive directly to the gate.

Contact: MWR Code 10, NSGC, San Diego, CA 92136, pro shop 619/556-7502.

80 BONITA GOLF CLUB

Architect: William F. Bell, 1958

18 holes **Semiprivate** **$22-34**

San Diego and Vicinity map, page 394

This flat course in a river valley has a few doglegs. The friendly greens do not have any bunkers directly in front of them. There are two lakes on the course, and although the breeze tends to pick up in the afternoon, this is a user friendly layout.

Play Policy and Fees: Green fees are $22

weekdays and $34 weekends. Twilight, super twilight, and senior rates are offered. Carts are $12 per rider.

Tees and Yardage: *Men:* Blue: yardage 6287, par 71, rating 68.8, slope 117; White: yardage 5781, par 71, rating 67.3, slope 114; *Women:* Red: yardage 5442, par 71, rating 71.0, slope 119.

Tee Times: Reservations can be booked seven days in advance.

Dress Code: Collared shirts are required.

Tournaments: Shotgun tournaments are available weekdays only and require a 120-player minimum.

Directions: Drive on I-805 south from San Diego to Highway 54. Drive east on Highway 54 to Sweetwater Road, turn right, and drive three-fourths of a mile to the course.

Contact: 5540 Sweetwater Road (P.O. Box 455), Bonita, CA 91902, pro shop 619/267-1103, fax 619/267-1146, www.bonitagolfclub.com.

81 CHULA VISTA GOLF COURSE

Architect: Harry Rainville, 1961

18 holes   Public $21–41

🧍 📷 🍽 🏌 🚗 🏌

San Diego and Vicinity map, page 394

This is a walkable, level course with five par-5s. It has large greens and wide-open, rolling terrain. A creek meanders through most of the course, which adds to the test already presented by the prevailing afternoon breeze.

Play Policy and Fees: Green fees on weekdays are $21 to walk or $34 to ride. On weekends and holidays, fees are $28 to walk and $41 to ride. Twilight and super twilight rates are available, as are AGPA discounts.

Tees and Yardage: *Men:* Black: yardage 6759, par 73, rating 72.4, slope 130; Blue: yardage 6520, par 73, rating 71.3, slope 128; White: yardage 6186, par 73, rating 70.1, slope 121; *Women:* Red: yardage 5411, par 72, rating 70.8, slope 120.

Tee Times: Reservations can be booked seven days in advance.

Dress Code: No tank tops are allowed on the golf course.

Tournaments: A 16-player minimum is needed to book a tournament. A banquet facility is available that can accommodate up to 350 people.

Directions: From I-805 in Chula Vista, take the E Street exit and travel east two miles to the club.

Contact: 4475 Bonita Road, Bonita, CA 92002, pro shop 619/479-4141, fax 619/479-0438.

82 NATIONAL CITY GOLF COURSE

Architect: Harry Rainville, 1961; Richard Bermudas, 1985

9 holes   Public $10–14

🧍 📷 🍽 🏌 🚗 🏌

San Diego and Vicinity map, page 394

This course is extremely tight, with out-of-bounds markers on almost every hole. The 525-yard second hole is very narrow and needs pinpoint placement for success.

Play Policy and Fees: Green fees are $10 for nine holes weekdays and $14 weekends. Replay, senior, and twilight rates are available.

Tees and Yardage: *Men:* yardage 2220, par 34, rating n/a, slope n/a; *Women:* yardage 2000, par 34, rating n/a, slope n/a.

Tee Times: Reservations can be booked seven days in advance.

Dress Code: Golf attire is encouraged.

Tournaments: A 16-player minimum is needed to book a tournament. Events should be scheduled three months in advance.

Directions: Follow I-805 south from San Diego to Sweetwater Road. Turn west and drive to the course.

Contact: 1439 Sweetwater Road, National City, CA 91950, pro shop 619/474-1400, fax 619/474-8910.

83 SAN DIEGO COUNTRY CLUB

Architect: William P. Bell, 1921

18 holes   Private

🧍 📷 🍽 🏌 🚗 🏌

San Diego and Vicinity map, page 394

This course is the last golf stop before reaching the Mexican border. It was built in the

1920s, making it the oldest private course in San Diego County. Flat to gently rolling, it's a traditional layout with medium to large greens. This is the course on which the great PGA Tour player Billy Casper learned to play. It was the site of the 1993 U.S. Women's Amateur.

Play Policy and Fees: Members and guests only. The course is closed on Monday.

Tees and Yardage: *Men:* Black: yardage 6890, par 70, rating 73.6, slope 133; Blue: yardage 6635, par 70, rating 72.2, slope 130; White: yardage 6316, par 70, rating 70.7, slope 126; *Women:* Gold: yardage 5207, par 70, rating 71.2, slope 125.

Tee Times: Out-of-state private club members may have their home professional call to inquire.

Dress Code: Soft spikes are mandatory.

Tournaments: This course is not available for outside events.

Directions: From I-5, take the L Street exit and drive 1.5 miles east, or take the Telegraph Canyon/L Street exit off I-805 and drive one mile west.

Contact: 88 L Street, Chula Vista, CA 91911, pro shop 619/422-0108.

84 EASTLAKE COUNTRY CLUB
Architect: Ted Robinson Sr., 1991
18 holes   Public $52–72

San Diego and Vicinity map, page 394

This course winds through the Eastlake area of Chula Vista. It offers four sets of tees, undulating fairways, bent-grass greens, and six lakes. The putting surfaces are large but not multitiered. The course is forgiving, although afternoon winds can be tough. It's a good test for players of all abilities.

Play Policy and Fees: Green fees are $52 weekdays and $72 weekends, including cart. Early bird, twilight, super twilight, and San Diego County resident rates are available. Pull carts are allowed during twilight hours only. Monthly and annual memberships are available.

Tees and Yardage: *Men:* Championship: yardage 6606, par 72, rating 71.2, slope 132; Gold:

yardage 6224, par 72, rating 69.6, slope 129; Black: yardage 5834, par 72, rating 68.0, slope 124; *Women:* Forward: yardage 5118, par 72, rating 70.9, slope 120.

Tee Times: Reservations can be booked seven days in advance.

Dress Code: Collared shirts and nonmetal spikes are required.

Tournaments: This course is available for outside tournaments. Carts are required.

Directions: Take I-805 south to the Telegraph Canyon Road exit in Chula Vista. Drive east four miles to East Lake Greens Community/East Lake Parkway. Turn right and drive one-quarter mile to Clubhouse Drive. The course is on the left.

Contact: 2375 Clubhouse Drive, Chula Vista, CA 91915, pro shop 619/482-5757, fax 619/482-5700.

85 THE AULD COURSE
Architect: John Cook, Cary Bickler, 2001
18 holes   Public $45–95

San Diego and Vicinity map, page 394

Resting in the foothills of Mount Miguel, this traditional course includes 18 distinctive holes. It features panoramic ocean and mountain views, acres of natural wetlands, and no homes or roads. The hillsides influence most tee shots, so placement off the tee is important. It is a big course with no trees, which is significant because it tends to get windy in the afternoons. The greens are all open in front so players can roll the ball on. Management has placed a welcome emphasis on pace of play.

Play Policy and Fees: Green fees are $75 Monday–Thursday, $85 Friday, $95 Saturday and holidays, and $90 Sunday. San Diego County resident green fees are $45 Monday–Thursday, $55 Friday, $75 Saturday and holidays, and $70 Sunday. JC Card holder, twilight, and super twilight rates are offered.

Tees and Yardage: *Men:* Cook: yardage 6855, par 72, rating 73.4, slope 135; Gold: yardage 6514, par 72, rating 71.7, slope 131; Blue: yardage 6083, par 72, rating 70.0, slope 124; White: yardage 5505, par 72, rating 67.2, slope 116; *Women:* Copper: yardage 4814, par 72, rating 68.9, slope 121.

Tee Times: Reservations may be made up to one week in advance.

Dress Code: Men must wear collared shirts, and no denim is allowed. Nonmetal spikes are required.

Tournaments: Events are welcome and may be booked up to one year in advance.

Directions: Take I-805 south of San Diego to H Street East, which becomes Proctor Valley Road. Drive east 6.7 miles to Hunte Parkway and turn left. Hunte dead-ends into the golf course after roughly one-half mile.

Contact: 525 Hunte Parkway, Chula Vista, CA 91915, pro shop 619/482-4666, fax 619/656-6490, www.theauldcourse.com.

Chapter 15

LA QUINTA RESORT AND CLUB, MOUNTAIN COURSE © GEORGE FULLER

Palm Springs and the Deserts

Palm Springs
and the Deserts

With more than 100 courses in the region, the California desert boasts more golf facilities than many states. Private, public, resort, nine-hole, RV courses—you name it and you can find it here.

During the summer months, the desert is hot and dry. Still, one man's "hot and dry" is another man's paradise. So if the climate suits you (average temperature in Palm Springs in summer tops 100 degrees during the heat of the day), so will the green fees, which are excellent this time of year, often greatly reduced from other months. Of course, during winter, or "peak season," golfers flock to these warm climes for some of the most enjoyable golf there is.

If you have not played here before, the land itself might surprise you. If you imagine the desert to be flat, barren, and featureless, it's not. Instead, the greater Mojave Desert features the Santa Rosa Mountains backdropping the Palm Springs/La Quinta areas to the west, and several other smaller ranges dot the horizon. This makes for some scenic vistas as you play golf.

Also occupying part of this desert landscape is Joshua Tree National Park, an international destination where geologic marvels abound, and farther north, Death Valley National Park. Photographers have a field day, although there is but one golf course in park bounds, Death Valley's Furnace Creek. Plan extra time on your visit to the region to explore these treasured national parks.

The most populous cities are found around Palm Springs. Former presidents, movie stars, comedians, entertainers—the desert is teeming with celebrities of all kinds who have chosen to call the region home.

Most of them are clustered in the Rancho Mirage, La Quinta, Palm Springs, and Palm Desert areas, and many are members of exclusive private clubs, of which there are many excellent choices.

But it's important to remember that from one end of the Coachella Valley to the other, and out across the Mojave, there are many golf courses open for resort and public play. For example, among the most respected public facilities in the nation is PGA West in La Quinta. Here, you can tee it up at Pete Dye's famous Stadium Course, or at equally impressive and demanding designs by Jack Nicklaus and Greg Norman. Nearby, at luxurious La Quinta Resort & Club, two excellent Pete Dye courses await, including the Mountain Course, perennially near the top of everybody's list of "bests." And the list goes on and on with top-notch courses at your disposal.

Tournament golf is very popular in the desert. The PGA Tour comes through in January to contest the Bob Hope Classic at several courses, including PGA West, Indian Wells, La Quinta, and Bermuda Dunes. The LPGA visits Mission Hills Country Club for the Kraft Nabisco Championship in March.

There has been much growth in the desert region of California in recent years. From Hemet to Cathedral City, new designs are opening every year, and there are many more in various phases of planning or construction. La Quinta alone has seen the opening of 72 new holes at three new facilities in the past two years.

There are many courses to play in California's varied desert landscape, and a whole lot more on the way.

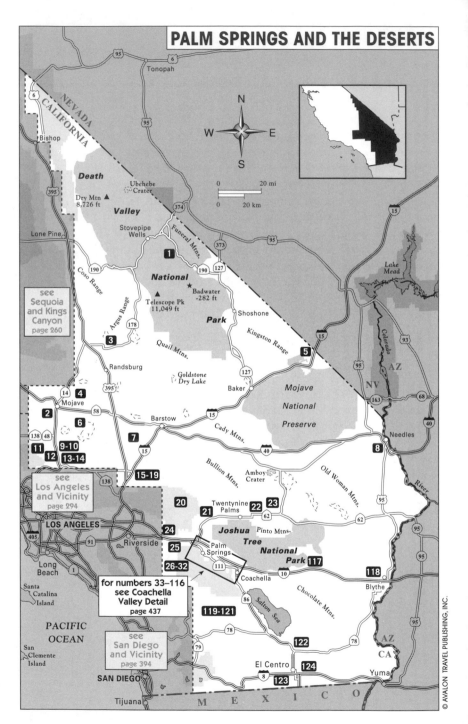

PALM SPRINGS AND THE DESERTS

see
Sequoia
and Kings
Canyon
page 260

see
Los Angeles
and Vicinity
page 294

for numbers 33–116
see Coachella
Valley Detail
page 437

see
San Diego
and Vicinity
page 394

NEVADA

CALIFORNIA

Tonopah

Bishop

Death

Dry Mtn ▲
8,726 ft

Ubehebe
Crater

Valley

Stovepipe
Wells

Lone Pine

Coso Range

National

Telescope Pk
11,049 ft ▲

★ Badwater
-282 ft

Funeral Mtns.

Park

Shoshone

Lake
Mead

Argus Range

Quail Mtns.

Kingston Range

Randsburg

Goldstone
Dry Lake

Baker

Mojave

National

Colorado

AZ

NV

Mojave

14

Barstow

Cady Mtns.

Preserve

Needles

58

Bullion Mtns.

Amboy
Crater

Old Woman Mtns.

River

Twentynine
Palms

Joshua

Pinto Mtns.

Tree

National

Park

LOS ANGELES

Riverside

Palm
Springs

Coachella

Chocolate Mtns.

Blythe

Long
Beach

Santa
Catalina
Island

Salton
Sea

PACIFIC

OCEAN

San
Clemente
Island

El Centro

AZ

CA

Yuma

SAN DIEGO

Tijuana

M E X I C O

1
3
5
2
4
6
7
8
9-10
11
12
13-14
15-19
20
21
22
23
24
25
26-32
117
118
119-121
122
124
123

© AVALON TRAVEL PUBLISHING, INC.

Coachella Valley Detail

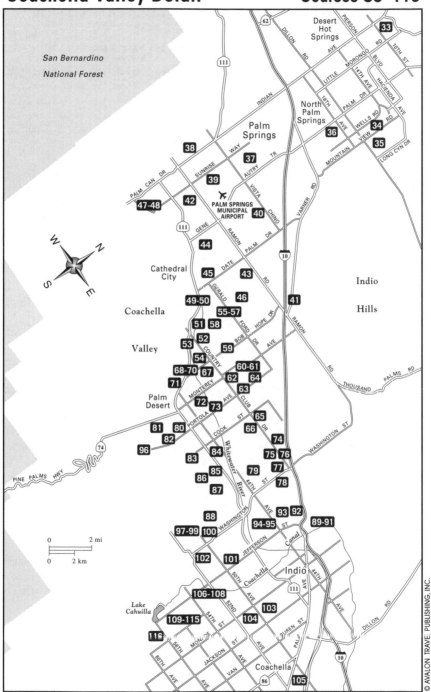

1 FURNACE CREEK GOLF COURSE

Architect: William P. Bell, 1931;
William F. Bell, 1969; Perry Dye, 1997

18 holes   Resort $35–55

🏌 📷 🍴 🛏 🏌 🛺 🍴

Palm Springs and the Deserts map, page 436

Perry Dye completed a redesign here in 1997. This is the world's lowest grass golf course at 214 feet below sea level. If that is not unique enough, golfers report having golf balls stolen by coyote pups and their concentration challenged by passing roadrunners. From the 12th hole, there is a spectacular view of the towering Panamint Mountains. During its early years, the course was closed and leased to a cattle rancher for the summer and the fairways were kept mowed by a small flock of sheep in winter. The most difficult hole at Furnace Creek is the sixth, a 440-yard par-4 that requires you carry over water off the tee to reach the fairway.

For reservations at the Furnace Creek Inn and Ranch Resort, call 760/786-2345.

Play Policy and Fees: Outside play is accepted. Green fees are $55 October–May, $35 June–September, and carts are $25.

Tees and Yardage: *Men:* Blue: yardage 6236, par 70, rating 69.7, slope 117; White: yardage 5873, par 70, rating 68.0, slope 117; Gold: yardage 5357, par 70, rating 66.5, slope 108; *Women:* Red: yardage 4724, par 70, rating 62.8, slope 99.

Tee Times: Reservations are not required, but they are recommended for tee times August–May.

Dress Code: Collared shirts are required. No sleeveless shirts or cutoff shorts are allowed.

Tournaments: Tournaments should be scheduled 90 days in advance. The banquet facility can accommodate up to 100 people.

Directions: This course is in Death Valley National Park on California State Highway 190.

Contact: Highway 190 (P.O. Box 187), Death Valley, CA 92328, pro shop 760/786-2301, fax 760/786-2762, www.furnacecreekresort.com.

2 CAMELOT GOLF COURSE

Architect: Course designed, 1969

9 holes   Public $8–15

🏌 📷 🍴 🏌 🛺 🍴

Palm Springs and the Deserts map, page 436

This course features tree-lined, narrow fairways. The greens, which are in excellent shape, are extremely difficult to read and putt. The par-3 fifth hole offers a tough and humbling green. The world's largest Joshua tree stands on the course.

Play Policy and Fees: Green fees are $8 for nine holes and $12 for 18 holes weekdays, $10 for nine holes and $15 for 18 holes weekends. Call for special rates. Carts are $16. Pull carts are $2 for nine holes and $3 for 18 holes.

Tees and Yardage: *Men (18 holes):* Yellow/White: yardage 6331, par 72, rating 70.2, slope 119; *Women (18 holes):* Red/Yellow: yardage 5796, par 72, rating 72.5, slope 125.

Tee Times: Reservations can be booked up to seven days in advance.

Dress Code: Nonmetal spikes are required, and golf attire is encouraged.

Tournaments: Saturday shotgun tournaments must start after noon. A 40-player minimum is needed to book an event. Tournaments should be scheduled two months in advance.

Directions: Drive one mile south of the town of Mojave on Highway 14. Turn west on Camelot Boulevard and drive two miles to the course.

Contact: 3430 Camelot Boulevard, Mojave, CA 93501, pro shop 661/824-4107.

3 CHINA LAKE GOLF COURSE

Architect: George Bell, 1957

18 holes   Military $10–27

🏌 📷 🍴 🏌 🛺 🍴

Palm Springs and the Deserts map, page 436

This is a flat desert course with lots of bunkers and trees. There are no water hazards. Beware of the 10th hole, a 548-yard par-5. It is an uphill, dogleg right with two fairway traps. China Lake hosts a men's and women's club championship each year. It gets real hot out here in summer, so play early. Winter provides perfect weather to play.

Play Policy and Fees: Outside play is accepted. Green fees are $18 for civilian guests, walking, and $27 riding in a cart. Fees for current and former enlisted personnel vary by rank and begin at $10.

Tees and Yardage: *Men:* Blue: yardage 6832, par 72, rating 72.6, slope 121; White: yardage 6499, par 72, rating 71.0, slope 121; Gold: yardage 5898, par 72, rating 68.2, slope 117; *Women:* Red: yardage 5519, par 72, rating 71.1, slope 123.

Tee Times: Weekend reservations can be made beginning on the preceding Wednesday. All other days are on a first-come, first-served basis.

Dress Code: Soft spike shoes and collared shirts are required.

Tournaments: This course is available for outside tournaments. Two weeks advance notice is required.

Directions: From the town of Mojave, travel north on Highway 14 for approximately 40 miles to Highway 178. Turn right and drive east for about 13 miles to the entrance of China Lake Naval Weapons Station. Obtain a pass at the gate and continue to the course on Midway Drive.

Contact: 411 Midway Drive (P.O. Box 507), Ridgecrest, CA 93555, pro shop 760/939-2990.

4 TIERRA DEL SOL GOLF CLUB

Architect: Bruce Devlin and Robert Von Hagge, 1977
18 holes   **Public**   **$15–20**

🏌️ 🏤 🍴 ⛳ 🛺 🧺

Palm Springs and the Deserts map, page 436

This course is level, long, and open. There is water on 12 holes, there are 146 bunkers, and most of the greens are elevated. All the bunkers were renovated several years ago with a new drainage system and sand. In 2004 the blue and white tees were extended on several holes, adding some length to the course. A new hotel, driving range, and clubhouse are planned.

Play Policy and Fees: Green fees are $15 weekdays and $20 weekends. Carts are $11 per rider.

Twilight, resident, military, junior, senior, and corporate rates are available.

Tees and Yardage: *Men:* Blue: yardage 6908, par 72, rating 74.1, slope 130; White: yardage 6310, par 72, rating 70.6, slope 121; *Women:* Red: yardage 5225, par 72, rating 68.6, slope 122; Yellow: yardage 5000, par 72, rating n/a, slope n/a.

Tee Times: Reservations can be booked 14 days in advance.

Dress Code: Appropriate golf attire is required. Soft spikes only.

Tournaments: This course is available for outside events. Carts are mandatory.

Directions: Drive north on Highway 14 from Lancaster to Mojave. Continue on Highway 14 five more miles to California City Boulevard and turn right. Drive 8.5 miles to North Loop, turn left, and continue two miles to the clubhouse.

Contact: 10300 North Loop Drive, California City, CA 93505, pro shop 760/373-2384, fax 760/373-3354.

5 PRIMM VALLEY GOLF CLUB

Architect: Tom Fazio, 1997
36 holes   **Resort**   **$55–175**

🏌️ 🏤 🍴 🛏️ 🛺 🧺

Palm Springs and the Deserts map, page 436

The Lakes Course and the Desert Course contrast in both design and playability. The Lakes Course is a traditional design, showcased by rolling fairways, waterfalls, streams, lakes, and a forest of trees. The Desert Course is landscaped to blend with the surrounding cacti, desert plants, and grasses, and it features plenty of sand, desert waste areas, and well-placed lakes. Although the Desert Course has a higher slope rating, the low handicapper may find the Lakes Course more difficult. The Lakes Course is far more demanding on and around the greens, while the biggest challenge on the Desert Course is getting to the green.

For reservations at Primadonna Resorts, call 800/386-7867.

Play Policy and Fees: Green fees for hotel

guests range $55–125. Green fees for nonguests range $75–175. There are special rates for Las Vegas residents. Special seasonal golf packages are available.

Tees and Yardage: Lakes Course—*Men:* Black: yardage 6945, par 71, rating 73.3, slope 135; Blue: yardage 6444, par 71, rating 71.2, slope 130; White: yardage 6008, par 71, rating 69.0, slope 125; *Women:* Green: yardage 4842, par 71, rating 68.5, slope 121. Desert Course—*Men:* Black: yardage 7131, par 72, rating 74.6, slope 138; Blue: yardage 6540, par 72, rating 71.7, slope 130; White: yardage 6085, par 72, rating 69.5, slope 124; *Women:* Green, yardage 5397, par 72, rating 71.6, slope 129.

Tee Times: Reservations can be made 60 days in advance for hotel guests and golf packages. Nonguest reservations can be made 21 days in advance.

Dress Code: Collared shirts and nonmetal spikes are required. No jeans are allowed on the course; shorts must be an appropriate length.

Tournaments: A 12-player minimum is needed to book an event. Tournaments with 12–48 players can be booked up to nine months in advance. Tournaments with 48 or more players can be booked up to one year in advance. Tournament packages can include scoring, box lunches, tee prizes, special events, and banquets.

Directions: On I-15 at the California-Nevada border, exit left on Yeates Well Road. Follow Yeates Well Road until it ends. Take a right to the golf course and another right to the front gate.

Contact: 1 Yeates Well Road, Primm, NV 89019, pro shop 702/679-5510, fax 702/679-5413, www.primadonna.com.

6 MUROC LAKE GOLF COURSE

18 holes   **Military**   **$6–16**

🚹 📷 🍽 🏌 🚙 🍺

Palm Springs and the Deserts map, page 436

This is the greenest place in this part of the Mojave Desert, and it's not because of all the military uniforms. The course is well main-tained and features a small lake and numerous mature trees lining the fairways. Tall trees, which offer a welcome relief from the afternoon sun, are spaced every 20 yards on both sides of the fairways. If you hit through the trees, you're at the mercy of the desert.

Play Policy and Fees: Military personnel and guests only. Reciprocal play is accepted with members of other air force bases. Green fees vary $6–16 depending on military status.

Tees and Yardage: *Men:* Blue: yardage 6915, par 72, rating 73.5, slope 129; White: yardage 6446, par 72, rating 71.3, slope 125; *Women:* Red: yardage 5561, par 72, rating 72.3, slope 125.

Tee Times: Reservations can be made seven days in advance.

Dress Code: Collared shirts are required.

Tournaments: Outside events must be sponsored by someone affiliated with the base.

Directions: Between the towns of Lancaster and Mojave on Highway 14, take the Rosamond exit and travel northeast for 15 miles to Lancaster Boulevard. Turn left and drive to Fitzgerald Boulevard. Turn left again and drive to Yucca Street and follow the signs.

Contact: P.O. Box 207, Edwards AFB, Edwards, CA 93523, pro shop 661/277-3469, clubhouse 661/277-3467.

7 SILVER LAKES COUNTRY CLUB

Architect: Ted Robinson, 1974

27 holes   **Private**   **$25–35**

🚹 📷 🍽 🏌 🚙 🍺

Palm Springs and the Deserts map, page 436

This private facility has 27 holes. All combinations are very distinctive. The South Course has lots of water. The East Course has one hole with water, and the North Course has two holes with water. All three courses have a good mix of long, tight, and challenging holes.

Play Policy and Fees: Reciprocal play is accepted with members of private clubs. Guests at the Inn at Silver Lakes are also welcome. Green fees are $25 weekdays and $35 weekends. Carts are $14.

Tees and Yardage: East/North—*Men:* Blue:

yardage 6697, par 72, rating 71.6, slope 131; White: yardage 6311, par 72, rating 69.9, slope 127; *Women:* Red: yardage 5467, par 72, rating 71.4, slope 119. East/South—*Men:* Blue: yardage 6768, par 72, rating 72.4, slope 131; White: yardage 6365, par 72, rating 70.7, slope 129; *Women:* Red: yardage 5635, par 72, rating 72.6, slope 123. North/South—*Men:* Blue: yardage 6851, par 72, rating 72.9, slope 133; White: yardage 6462, par 72, rating 71.2, slope 130; *Women:* Red: yardage 5564, par 72, rating 72.3, slope 122.

Tee Times: Have your pro call ahead to make reservations up to five days in advance.

Dress Code: Appropriate golf attire and nonmetal spikes are required.

Tournaments: This course is available for outside tournaments with board approval.

Directions: Take I-15 north from San Bernardino to the D Street/Apple Valley exit in Victorville. Turn left on Apple Valley/Highway 66 and continue for 14 miles to Vista Road. Turn left to the club.

Contact: 14814 Clubhouse Drive (P.O. Box 2130), Helendale, CA 92342, pro shop 760/245-7435.

8 NEEDLES GOLF COURSE
Architect: Harry Rainville and David Rainville, 1964
18 holes   Public $30–35

Palm Springs and the Deserts map, page 436

This well-maintained course has generous, fairly level fairways with mature trees. Lateral hazards are in play on five holes. The greens are overseeded with rye in the winter months and Bermuda in the summer months. This course is walkable and is a fair test for the average golfer.

Play Policy and Fees: Green fees are $30 April, May, November, and December. Carts are $10 per person. The senior rate is $25 during these months. January–March, rates are $35, plus $10 for carts. Reservations are recommended November–April. Reduced fees are offered during summer months. Twilight rates and annual passes are offered.

Tees and Yardage: *Men:* Blue: yardage 6506, par 71, rating 71.4, slope 117; White: yardage 6189, par 71, rating 70.1, slope 112; *Women:* Red: yardage 5595, par 71, rating 71.6, slope 121.

Tee Times: Reservations can be made seven days in advance.

Dress Code: Shirts must be worn. Soft spikes only.

Tournaments: This course is available for outside tournaments. Tournaments should be booked six months in advance.

Directions: From I-40 in Needles, take the West Broadway exit and drive one mile east on Needles Highway. Cross K Street and proceed to the course entrance on the left.

Contact: 144 Marina Drive, Needles, CA 92363, pro shop 760/326-3931, fax 760/326-6606, www.golfneedlesca.com.

9 RANCHO SIERRA GOLF CLUB
Architect: Jack Roesinger and Sam Fogo, 1963
9 holes   Public $11–19

Palm Springs and the Deserts map, page 436

This is a flat, interesting course with narrow fairways. It features four lakes, and water comes into play on all but three holes. Mature trees line the fairways, and the bunkers are all grass.

Play Policy and Fees: Green fees are $11 for nine holes and $17 for 18 holes weekdays, $12 for nine holes and $19 for 18 holes weekends. Power carts are $5 for nine holes and $8 for 18 holes weekdays, $7 for nine holes and $10 for 18 holes weekends. Pull carts are $2.50.

Tees and Yardage: *Men and Women (18 holes):* White: yardage 5200, par 70, rating 63.4 (M)/70.7 (W), slope 100 (M)/115 (W).

Tee Times: Reservations can be booked seven days in advance.

Dress Code: No tank tops are permitted on the course. Soft spikes only.

Tournaments: A 12-player minimum is needed to book a tournament.

Directions: Take the Avenue G exit off Highway 14 in the town of Lancaster and travel east

for about nine miles to 60th Street. Turn left and drive one-quarter mile to the course.
Contact: 47205 60th Street East, Lancaster, CA 93535, pro shop 661/946-1080.

10 LANCASTER GOLF CENTER

Architect: Course designed, 1997

9 holes **Public** **$6–14**

Palm Springs and the Deserts map, page 436

This pitch-and-putt golf course is good for juniors, seniors, and those who want to sharpen their short game. The longest hole is 112 yards, and players have the option of teeing off either mats or grass. Lancaster features a night-lit covered driving range.

Play Policy and Fees: Green fees are $6 for nine holes and $10 for 18 holes on weekdays, $8 for nine holes and $14 for 18 holes on weekends. Junior and senior rates are available.

Tees and Yardage: *Men and Women:* yardage 793, par 27, rating n/a, slope n/a.

Tee Times: Reservations are not taken.

Dress Code: No steel spikes are permitted.

Tournaments: Tournaments welcome.

Directions: From Los Angeles, drive north on I-5 and take Highway 14 north to Lancaster. Take the K Avenue exit. Take a right on K and then another right on 5th, heading east to the course.

Contact: 431 East Avenue K-4, Lancaster, CA 93535, pro shop 661/726-3131.

11 LAKE ELIZABETH GOLF & RANCH CLUB

Architect: Course designed, 1952

18 holes **Public** **$37–45**

Palm Springs and the Deserts map, page 436

This medium-length course is very challenging and fairly hilly with small greens. Seven lakes come into play. The par-4 fifth hole is 434 yards from the championship tees, which doesn't seem significant except for the fact that there is a 200-foot drop from tee to fairway. Many golfers have been fooled into thinking their tee shots traveled farther. In 2004,

new cart paths were added and a GPS system was installed. In addition, 100 new cabins, some RV hookups, and additional recreational facilities were added.

Play Policy and Fees: Standard green fees are $37 weekdays and $45 weekends, including carts. Senior, junior, all day, midday, and twilight rates are available.

Tees and Yardage: *Men:* Blue: yardage 6037, par 70, rating 68.9, slope 126; White: yardage 5658, par 70, rating 67.5, slope 122; *Women:* Red: yardage 5074, par 70, rating 72.9, slope 115.

Tee Times: Reservations can be made seven days in advance.

Dress Code: No cutoffs or short shorts are allowed. Nonmetal spikes are preferred.

Tournaments: This course is available for outside tournaments. Carts are required. A 24-player minimum is needed to book an event. The banquet facility can hold 200 people. Tournaments should be scheduled at least two months in advance.

Directions: From I-5 north of Los Angeles, take the Valencia Boulevard exit. Go east on Valencia Boulevard one mile to McBean Parkway. Turn left on McBean and drive four miles to San Francisquito. Turn left onto San Francisquito, go 19 miles to Elizabeth Lake Road, and drive one mile to Ranch Club Road. Turn left on Ranch Club Road and proceed one mile to the clubhouse.

Contact: 42505 Ranch Club Road, Lake Elizabeth, CA 93532, pro shop 661/724-1221.

12 RANCHO VISTA GOLF COURSE

Architect: Ted Robinson Sr., 2001

18 holes **Public** **$28–47**

Palm Springs and the Deserts map, page 436

This course is within a large master-planned community. Ten greenside lakes and plenty of sand give this moderate-length desert course its personality. It can get extremely hot at Rancho Vista in the summer months, so bring lots of drinking water and try to play early or late in the day.

Play Policy and Fees: Green fees are $28 walking, $40 riding on weekdays, and $47 on weekends with a mandatory cart. Twilight, junior, and senior rates are available.

Tees and Yardage: *Men:* Blue: yardage 6632, par 72, rating 71.9, slope 126; White: yardage 6250, par 72, rating 70.5, slope 122; *Women:* Red: yardage 5730, par 72, rating 73.5, slope 128; *Junior:* Gold: yardage 5262, par 72, rating 67.8, slope 115.

Tee Times: Reservations are accepted up to two weeks in advance.

Dress Code: Proper golf attire and soft spikes are required.

Tournaments: Events may be booked up to one year in advance.

Directions: Follow Highway 14 to Palmdale and exit at Rancho Vista Boulevard (Avenue P). Drive west on Rancho Vista Boulevard, then turn right on Town Center Drive. Take a left on Bolz Ranch Road and travel three-quarters of a mile to Club Rancho Drive.

Contact: 3905 Club Rancho Drive, Palmdale, CA 93551, pro shop 661/272-9903, fax 661/272-9854, www.ranchovista.com.

13 ANTELOPE VALLEY COUNTRY CLUB

Architect: William F. Bell, 1957
18 holes   **Private**   **$45–55**

🏃 📷 💰 🏌 🚗

Palm Springs and the Deserts map, page 436
Don't forget to bring a sand wedge to this course. It is well bunkered but level, with many trees lining the fairways. Water can be found on several holes of this challenging course. The lake has been enlarged on the par-3, 183-yard 11th. You must hit over the water to the large green. Wind makes every hole on this course play differently each day. The men's course record is 64, and the women's is 66.

Play Policy and Fees: Reciprocal play is accepted with members of other private clubs; otherwise, members and guests only. Reciprocators are $45 weekdays, $55 weekends and holidays. Carts are $12 per rider.

Tees and Yardage: *Men:* Blue: yardage 6740, par 72, rating 71.9, slope 126; White: yardage 6408, par 72, rating 70.2, slope 122; *Women:* Red: yardage 6157, par 74, rating 76.5, slope 129.

Tee Times: No tee times required.

Dress Code: Shorts must be mid-thigh in length, and shirts must be collared. Nonmetal spikes are required.

Tournaments: All outside events are scheduled for Monday and must be approved by the head professional and the board.

Directions: Take Avenue P east off Highway 14 in Palmdale and drive east for one block to Country Club Drive. Turn left and drive one-quarter mile to the club.

Contact: 39800 Country Club Drive, Palmdale, CA 93551, pro shop 661/947-3400.

14 DESERT AIRE GOLF COURSE

Architect: Ted Robinson Sr., 1960
9 holes   **Public**   **$11–14**

🏃 📷 💰 🏌 🚗 ⛳

Palm Springs and the Deserts map, page 436
This level desert course is nicely bunkered and has one lake. Mature trees line the fairways and offer welcome shade in the afternoon. The toughest hole is the 401-yard, par-4 eighth. It's straight and narrow, with out-of-bounds to the right. Accuracy on a windy day is a must on this hole.

Play Policy and Fees: Green fees for nine holes are $11 weekdays and $14 weekends and holidays. Replays are $6. Carts are $5.50 per person.

Tees and Yardage: *Men:* Blue: yardage 3178, par 36, rating n/a, slope n/a; White: yardage 3031, par 36, rating n/a, slope n/a; *Women:* Red: yardage 2775, par 35, rating n/a, slope n/a.

Tee Times: Can be made 3–4 days in advance.

Dress Code: Appropriate attire and soft spikes are required.

Tournaments: Events may be booked one month in advance.

Directions: Take Avenue P east off Highway 14 in Palmdale and drive four miles to the course.

Contact: 3620 East Avenue P, Palmdale, CA 93550, pro shop 661/538-0370.

15 GREENTREE GOLF COURSE

Architect: William F. Bell, 1962
18 holes   **Public**   **$19–35**

🏌️ 📷 🍺 🏌️ 🚗 🍽️

Palm Springs and the Deserts map, page 436

This is a mostly flat, traditional course lined by trees and out-of-bounds on both sides. It is also a user-friendly course noted for its well-maintained greens.

Play Policy and Fees: Green fees are $19 weekdays to walk, plus $12 to ride. Weekend rates are $35 to ride (mandatory) before noon. Midday, twilight, and other special rates are available.

Tees and Yardage: *Men:* Blue: yardage 6643, par 72, rating 71.3, slope 123; White: yardage 6332, par 72, rating 69.8, slope 120; *Women:* Red: yardage 5874, par 73, rating 73.7, slope 131.

Tee Times: Reservations can be booked 14 days in advance.

Dress Code: No cutoffs, short shorts, or tank tops are allowed. Soft spikes only.

Tournaments: Carts are required for tournament play on certain days. Call the pro shop for more details.

Directions: From San Bernardino, drive north on I-15 to Victorville. Exit at Palmdale Road and turn left to Greentree Boulevard; turn right. The course is 100 yards down the road.

Contact: 14144 Greentree Boulevard, Victorville, CA 92392, pro shop 760/245-4860, www.ci .victorville.ca.us/golf.

16 APPLE VALLEY COUNTRY CLUB

Architect: William F. Bell, 1949
18 holes   **Private**   **$36–47**

🏌️ 📷 🍺 🏌️ 🚗 🍽️

Palm Springs and the Deserts map, page 436

This is a fairly level course with wide fairways, mature trees, and some water. The greens can be hard and fast. The course plays much more difficult than it looks, especially when the wind is blowing.

Play Policy and Fees: Reciprocal play is accepted with members of other private clubs; otherwise, members and guests only. Green fees are $36 weekdays and $47 weekends, including cart.

Tees and Yardage: *Men:* Blue: yardage 6805, par 71, rating 72.3, slope 123; White: yardage 6477, par 71, rating 70.5, slope 119; *Women:* Red: yardage 5929, par 73, rating 74.5, slope 130.

Tee Times: Reciprocal players can make reservations seven days in advance.

Dress Code: Appropriate golf attire is enforced. No cutoffs, short shorts, or blue jeans are allowed on the course. Collared shirts and non-metal spikes are required.

Tournaments: A 72-player maximum is allowed for tournament play. Events should be scheduled 12 months in advance. The banquet facility can accommodate 180 people.

Directions: From San Bernardino, drive north on I-15 to the Apple Valley exit. Head east on Highway 18 to Rancherias Road and turn right. The course is on the right.

Contact: 15200 Rancherias Road, Apple Valley, CA 92507, pro shop 760/242-3125, clubhouse 760/242-3653, www.avcc.cc.

17 SPRING VALLEY LAKE COUNTRY CLUB

Architect: Robert Trent Jones Jr., 1970
18 holes   **Private**   **$60**

🏌️ 📷 🍺 🏌️ 🚗 🍽️

Palm Springs and the Deserts map, page 436

Traditionally in excellent condition, this course has plenty of water on the front nine and is relatively hilly on the back. It all toughens up when the winds blow, as they often will. Greens are medium-sized, fast, and true.

Play Policy and Fees: Reciprocal play is accepted with members of other private clubs; otherwise, members and guests only. Green fees for reciprocators are $60. Carts are included.

Tees and Yardage: *Men:* Blue: yardage 6535, par 72, rating 71.3, slope 130; White: yardage 6179, par 72, rating 69.7, slope 126; *Women:* Red: yardage 5680, par 72, rating 73.9, slope 133.

Tee Times: Reciprocators should have their club pro call to make arrangements.

Dress Code: Shorts must be Bermuda length, and no denim is allowed on the course. Soft spikes only.

Tournaments: On Monday a minimum of 50 players is needed to book a tournament. During the rest of the week, a tournament will consist of no more than 50 players. Events are allowed only in the afternoons.

Directions: From Victorville, take I-10 to I-15. Drive north on I-15 to the Lucerne Valley exit. Turn right and travel east for five miles on Bear Valley Road to Spring Valley Parkway. Turn left through the big archway to Spring Valley Lake and turn left on Country Club Drive.

Contact: 13229 Spring Valley Parkway, Victorville, CA 92392, pro shop 760/245-7921, clubhouse 760/245-5356.

18 JESS RANCH GOLF CLUB

Architect: David Rainville, 1993

18 holes   Public $18–33.50

Palm Springs and the Deserts map, page 436

This is a short links-style course in a residential development. It features very nice bent-grass greens. Water comes into play on seven holes. There are currently no par-5s but several long par-4s. The first hole is the number-one handicap hole, measuring 378 yards. Note: Expansion of the existing course to regulation length, plus the addition of nine new holes, is planned for a 2005 opening. More than 1400 new homes were built around the course in 2004.

Play Policy and Fees: On weekdays, green fees are $18 to walk and $28.50 to ride. On weekends, rates are $30 to walk and $33.50 to ride.

Tees and Yardage: *Men:* Blue: yardage 4873, par 65, rating 64.0, slope 110; White: yardage 4446, par 65, rating 62.7, slope 105; *Women:* Silver: yardage 3699, par 65, rating 63.7, slope 105.

Tee Times: Reservations are requested and may be booked seven days in advance.

Dress Code: Collared shirts are required and no cutoffs are allowed. Soft spikes only.

Tournaments: This course is available for

tournaments. Three weeks advance notice is requested.

Directions: Exit off I-15 on Bear Valley Road. Take Bear Valley Road east eight miles to Apple Valley Road and turn right. Follow Apple Valley Road until it ends. The course entrance is at the end of the road.

Contact: 10885 Apple Valley Road, Apple Valley, CA 92308, pro shop 760/240-1800, fax 760/240-1636.

19 HESPERIA GOLF & COUNTRY CLUB

Architect: William F. Bell, 1955

18 holes   Semiprivate $20–37

Palm Springs and the Deserts map, page 436

This former PGA Tour stop offers a championship layout. It was designed and built in 1957 and is still a tough test. The fairways are separated by mature trees. The course is well-bunkered and features three lakes and rolling terrain. The toughest hole is the 18th. Trees guard each side of the fairway. Rumor has it that pro Doug Sanders once took a 12 on this hole. In the mid-1950s and early 1960s, legends such as Arnold Palmer, Gary Player, Billy Casper, Gene Littler, Sam Snead, and Julius Boros played in the Hesperia Open Invitational.

Play Policy and Fees: Green fees are $20 to walk weekdays, $32 to ride, and $25 to walk on weekends and holidays, $37 to ride. Junior, senior, and nine-hole rates are available. Memberships are offered.

Tees and Yardage: *Men:* Blue: yardage 6996, par 72, rating 73.5, slope 131; White: yardage 6695, par 72, rating 61.9, slope 128; *Women:* Red: yardage 6136, par 72, rating 74.5, slope 128.

Tee Times: Reservations may be booked seven days in advance.

Dress Code: Golf attire and nonmetal spikes are encouraged.

Tournaments: This course is available for outside tournaments. Events may be booked up to a year in advance. The banquet facility can hold 145 people.

Directions: From Los Angeles, take I-10 to I-15 and travel 33 miles north on I-15 to the first Hesperia exit. Turn right on Main Street and travel 5.5 miles to I Avenue and turn right. Go 1.5 miles to Bangor Avenue and turn left. **Contact:** 17970 Bangor Avenue, Hesperia, CA 92345, pro shop 760/244-9301, fax 760/244-9238, www.hesperiagolf.com.

20 BEAR MOUNTAIN GOLF COURSE

Architect: Course designed, 1940
9 holes   **Public**   **$23-28**

Palm Springs and the Deserts map, page 436

The elevation here is 7200 feet, and the course closes when it snows. It offers long par-3s and gently rolling hills. A lake comes into play on several holes, and a river runs through most of the layout. This is a fun, relaxed mountain course.

Play Policy and Fees: Green fees are $23 Monday–Friday and $28 weekends and holidays. Carts are $14 on weekdays and $16 on the weekends. There is a $5 discount for juniors and seniors. The course is closed November–March depending on the weather. Twilight rates and season passes are offered.

Tees and Yardage: *Men (18 holes):* Blue: yardage 5460, par 70, rating 65.6, slope 108; White: yardage 5202, par 70, rating 64.3, slope 108; *Women (18 holes):* Red: yardage 4416, par 70, rating 65.2, slope 107.

Tee Times: Reservations are encouraged.

Dress Code: No tank tops or sandals are allowed. Tee shirts are acceptable, but golf attire is encouraged. Soft spikes are mandatory.

Tournaments: This course is available for tournaments and outside events.

Directions: In San Bernardino, take Highway 330 to Highway 18 and head east to Moonridge Road. Drive 1.25 miles to Club View Drive. Turn left on Goldmine Drive and left into the parking lot. It is about 40 miles from San Bernardino.

Contact: 43100 Goldmine Drive, Big Bear Lake, CA 92315, pro shop 909/585-8002, www.bearmtn.com.

21 BLUE SKIES COUNTRY CLUB

Architect: Roscoe Smith, 1958
18 holes   **Public**   **$15-25**

Palm Springs and the Deserts map, page 436

This upgraded course has tree-lined fairways and two lakes. The fairways are fairly open. The third is a scenic lake hole, par-3 and 164 yards from an elevated tee over a lake. The green is bunkered in the front, and the tee is situated in a chute of trees. And what trees—towering cottonwoods and Chinese elms line every fairway.

Play Policy and Fees: Green fees are $15 to walk, $25 to ride. Senior, junior, and twilight rates are available, as are memberships.

Tees and Yardage: *Men:* Blue: yardage 6400, par 71, rating 69.3, slope 120; White: yardage 6115, par 71, rating 68.0, slope 116; *Women:* Red: yardage 5757, par 73, rating 70.9, slope 123.

Tee Times: Reservations can be booked seven days in advance by calling 800/877-1412, ext. 1.

Dress Code: Shirts with sleeves are required. Soft spikes only.

Tournaments: This course is available for outside tournaments.

Directions: Take the Twentynine Palms/Yucca Valley exit off I-10 and drive about 18 miles north on Highway 62. Turn left at the Yucca Inn sign and continue to the club.

Contact: 55100 Martinez Trail, Yucca Valley, CA 92284, pro shop 760/365-0111.

22 ROADRUNNER DUNES RV RESORT

Architect: Lawrence Hughes, 1964
9 holes   **Public**   **$13-22**

Palm Springs and the Deserts map, page 436

This challenging, nine-hole course offers large greens with water coming into play on two holes.

Play Policy and Fees: Green fees are $13 to walk and $17 to ride for nine holes, $18 to walk and $22 to ride for 18 holes.

Tees and Yardage: *Men (18 holes):* White/Blue: yardage 6243, par 72, rating 69.8, slope 117;

Women (18 holes): Yellow/White: yardage 5623, par 72, rating 73.7, slope 123.

Tee Times: This course is in a motor home park, so reservations are a must in the winter months and can be made seven days in advance.

Dress Code: Nonmetal spikes are required.

Tournaments: A 16-player minimum is required to book an event. The banquet facility can accommodate 130 people.

Directions: Take the Twentynine Palms/Yucca Valley exit off I-10 and drive about 40 miles to the town of Twentynine Palms. Turn left on Adobe Road and drive two miles. Turn right on Amboy and then left on Desert Knoll Avenue.

Contact: 4733 Desert Knoll Avenue, Twentynine Palms, CA 92277, pro shop 760/367-5770.

23 DESERT WINDS GOLF COURSE

Architect: Course designed, 1965
18 holes   **Military**   **$20**

Palm Springs and the Deserts map, page 436

If you like toying with the elements, this course is for you. Built on the side of a hill in the middle of the desert, it is wide open but challenging, with out-of-bounds, desert-style rough, and seasonal winds. Five ponds come into play, but during the summer the water is a welcome sight. Approximately 20,000 rounds per year are played at Desert Winds.

Play Policy and Fees: Military personnel and guests only. Civilian guest fee is $20 for 18 holes plus $12 for a cart. Military personnel fees are based on rank.

Tees and Yardage: *Men:* Blue: yardage 6930, par 72, rating 72.9, slope 122; White: yardage 6335, par 72, rating 70.5, slope 117; *Women:* Yellow: yardage 5608, par 72, rating 67.1, slope 110.

Tee Times: Reservations are required up to a week in advance for weekends and holidays.

Dress Code: No tank tops or cutoffs are allowed on the course. Nonmetal spikes are required.

Tournaments: All outside events must have a military sponsor.

Directions: Take the Twentynine Palms/Yucca

Valley exit off I-10 and drive about 40 miles to the town of Twentynine Palms. Turn left at Adobe Road and drive five miles to the main gate at the Marine Combat Center. Continue through the main gate for three miles to the flashing light. Turn left and drive one-half mile to the first paved road, then right to the course.

Contact: MCAGCC Golf Course, Building 3812, Twentynine Palms, CA 92278, pro shop 760/830-6132.

24 HIGHLAND SPRINGS VILLAGE GOLF COURSE

Architect: Course designed, 1975
9 holes   **Private**

Palm Springs and the Deserts map, page 436

This short executive course is in a mobile home park and is open only to residents who live there. It wanders through olive trees, and two lakes keep things interesting. There are eight par-3s and one par-4 from the back tees, and seven par-3s and two par-4s from the forward tees.

Play Policy and Fees: Members and guests only. The course is closed on Monday.

Tees and Yardage: *Men and Women (18 holes):* yardage 3188, par 57, rating n/a, slope n/a.

Tee Times: Not applicable.

Dress Code: Golfers must wear collared shirts. No tank tops or short shorts are allowed. Nonmetal spikes are preferred.

Tournaments: This course is not available for outside events.

Directions: From Beaumont, take Highland Springs Boulevard three miles north to the course. The course is in Highland Springs Village.

Contact: 10370 ½ Chisholm Trail, Cherry Valley, CA 92223, pro shop 909/845-3060.

25 SUN LAKES COUNTRY CLUB

Architect: David Rainville, 1987
27 holes   **Private**

Palm Springs and the Deserts map, page 436

The championship layout is a long, traditional design set in an active adult living community.

Bring sand-moving equipment—there are 104 bunkers. There are also seven lakes and small-ish greens to make this challenging course even more difficult. The winds make this an interesting test, especially in winter, but the rough areas have been trimmed in recent years, making this a playable layout. A nine-hole, par-30 executive course opened here in 2002.

Play Policy and Fees: Members and guests only.

Tees and Yardage: *Men:* Gold: yardage 7102, par 72, rating 73.6, slope 129; Blue: yardage 6523, par 72, rating 71.0, slope 120; White: yardage 6111, par 72, rating 68.7, slope 116; *Women:* Red: yardage 5505, par 72, rating 71.4, slope 125.

Tee Times: Reservations can be booked four days in advance for public play.

Dress Code: Appropriate golf attire is required. Nonmetal spikes are encouraged.

Tournaments: Outside events are limited. Please inquire.

Directions: Take the Highlands Springs Avenue exit off I-10 in Banning (east of San Bernardino) and travel south to Sun Lakes Boulevard. Head east and turn on Country Club Drive south to the club.

Contact: 850 South Country Club Drive, Banning, CA 92220, pro shop 909/845-2135, www.sunlakescc.com.

26 GOLDEN ERA GOLF COURSE

Architect: Stephen Halsey, 1991
9 holes   **Public**   **$12–25**

Palm Springs and the Deserts map, page 436

This challenging, well-conditioned course has three lakes and an abundance of trees to keep golfers honest. The undulating greens are quick, so stay below the hole. The pride of the course is the 353-yard, par-4 sixth hole, a dogleg left around water. Beware of the oak tree guarding the left side of the green. Golden Era Golf Course is steeped in a rich golf history. A restoration of the best nine holes of the old Massacre Canyon course, Golden Era takes full advantage of its towering eucalyptus trees and serene lakes. This is a very nice golf experience.

Play Policy and Fees: Green fees are $12 to walk, $18 to ride nine holes; 18 holes cost $17 to walk, $20 to ride Monday–Thursday and $20 to walk, $25 to ride Friday, weekends, and holidays. Twilight rates are available.

Tees and Yardage: *Men:* Blue: yardage 6156, par 72, rating 69.5, slope 131; White: yardage 5860, par 72, rating 68.3, slope 126; *Women:* Red: yardage 5664, par 72, rating 72.1, slope 123.

Tee Times: Reservations may be booked seven days in advance.

Dress Code: Casual attire is accepted. Non-metal spikes are mandatory.

Tournaments: This course is available for outside tournaments.

Directions: From Highway 60 (Pomona Freeway) in Los Angeles, drive east to the Gilman Springs Road exit. Follow Gilman Springs Road east for 12 miles. The course is on the right.

Contact: 19871 Highway 79, Gilman Hot Springs, CA 92583, pro shop 909/654-0130, www.goldeneragolf.com.

27 SOBOBA SPRINGS ROYAL VISTA

Architect: Desmond Muirhead, 1967
18 holes   **Semiprivate**   **$35–55**

Palm Springs and the Deserts map, page 436

The course lies at the base of the San Jacinto Mountains. It has a traditional layout, with beautiful mature trees and 22 acres of lakes that come into play on nine of the 18 holes. This is a good test of golf for all skill levels.

Play Policy and Fees: Green fees are $35 weekdays and $55 weekends. Carts are included. Twilight and seasonal rates, as well as memberships, are available.

Tees and Yardage: *Men:* Blue: yardage 6888, par 72, rating 72.6, slope 130; White: yardage 6232, par 72, rating 70.3, slope 125; *Women:* Red: yardage 5673, par 72, rating 73.2, slope 126.

Tee Times: Reservations can be booked seven days in advance.

Dress Code: No tee shirts or tank tops are allowed, and nonmetal spikes are mandatory.

Tournaments: A 16-player minimum is needed to book a tournament. Carts are mandatory and included in price.

Directions: Travel east of San Bernardino on I-10 to the town of Beaumont. Drive south on Highway 79 and turn left on Romona Expressway. Drive to Lake Park, turn left, and turn left again on Soboba Road. Follow it to the course.

Contact: 1020 Soboba Road, San Jacinto, CA 92583, pro shop 909/654-9354, clubhouse 909/654-7111, fax 909/654-6068.

28 COLONIAL COUNTRY CLUB

Architect: Course designed, 1971
18 holes   **Private**

Palm Springs and the Deserts map, page 436

These are short executive courses called North and South. Combined, they make an 18-hole loop. One features a pair of par-4s. Both courses are reserved for residents and guests of the adjoining mobile home park.

Play Policy and Fees: Members and guests only.

Tees and Yardage: North/South—*Men and Women (18 holes):* yardage 4466, par 54, rating n/a, slope n/a.

Tee Times: Not applicable.

Dress Code: Appropriate golf attire is required. No tank tops or cutoffs are permitted.

Tournaments: This course is not available for outside events.

Directions: In Hemet, take Florida Avenue (Highway 74) to Warren Avenue. Turn left and continue three-quarters of a mile to Kirby Street and turn right. Follow Kirby to the course.

Contact: 25115 Kirby Street, Hemet, CA 92545, pro shop 909/925-2664.

29 LANDMARK AT HEMET GOLF CLUB

Architect: Schmidt Curley Golf Design, 2003
18 holes   **Public**   **$45–60**

Palm Springs and the Deserts map, page 436

This course features fairways meandering through the picturesque edges of the colorful foothills, revealing the natural beauty of the terrain and the spectacular snowcapped peaks of the San Jacinto Mountains. Wide fairways and bent-grass greens add to the pleasure of this well-maintained course.

Play Policy and Fees: Green fees are $45 Monday–Friday and $60 weekends and holidays. Carts and warm-up range balls are included. Resident, twilight, and senior rates are available.

Tees and Yardage: *Men:* Tournament: yardage 6590, par 71, rating 71.0, slope 120; Championship: yardage 6212, par 71, rating 69.0, slope 116; Regular: yardage 5777, par 71, rating 67.1, slope 110; *Women:* Forward: yardage 5260, par 71, rating 70.8, slope 122.

Tee Times: Reservations can be made 90 days in advance.

Dress Code: Appropriate golf attire is required. Soft spikes only.

Tournaments: Tournaments of all types are welcome.

Directions: From Los Angeles, take I-215, exit Highway 74. Travel east to California Street, turn left to Devonshire, then turn left and follow it to the club entrance.

Contact: 7575 World Cup, Hemet, CA 92545, 909/926-4653, fax 909/926-0599, www.hemet golfclub.com.

30 SEVEN HILLS GOLF CLUB

Architect: Harry Rainville, 1970
18 holes   **Public**   **$28–37**

Palm Springs and the Deserts map, page 436

This flat course is easy to walk. It is medium to short with trees, four water hazards, and a few bunkers. The greens are small, which can make approach shots demanding.

Play Policy and Fees: Green fees to walk are $28 weekdays and $37 weekends. Nine-hole, twilight, senior, and junior rates are available. Carts are $11 per rider.

Tees and Yardage: *Men:* Blue: yardage 6557, par 72, rating 70.2, slope 116; White: yardage 6312, par 72, rating 69.0, slope 113; *Women:* Red: yardage 5416, par 72, rating 72.0, slope 113.

Tee Times: Reservations can be booked seven days in advance.

Dress Code: Collared shirts are preferred, and nonmetal spikes are required.

Tournaments: This course is available for outside tournaments. A 24-player minimum is needed to book a tournament. Tournaments should be booked 12 months in advance. The banquet facility can accommodate up to 110 people.

Directions: Take the Highway 79 exit off I-10 east of San Bernardino and travel south to Highway 74 in Hemet. Turn left and drive to Lyon Avenue, then turn right to the club.

Contact: 1537 South Lyon Avenue, Hemet, CA 92545, pro shop 909/925-4815, clubhouse 909/925-5469, fax 909/766-1958.

31 ECHO HILLS GOLF CLUB

Architect: Ed Dover, 1958
9 holes   **Public**   **$12**

Palm Springs and the Deserts map, page 436

This course is short enough to walk, but long enough to provide a challenge. The course has narrow fairways and many mature trees. It is a good nine-hole track for beginners and serious golfers.

Play Policy and Fees: Green fees are $12 for nine holes any day. Carts are $9. Twilight and super twilight rates are offered.

Tees and Yardage: *Men (18 holes):* Back: yardage 4458, par 70, rating 58.4, slope 92; *Women (18 holes):* Forward: yardage 4216, par 70, rating 58.4, slope 92.

Tee Times: Reservations can be booked seven days in advance.

Dress Code: Shirts and shoes are necessary.

Tournaments: Shotgun tournaments are available weekdays only. A 36-player minimum is needed for a regular tournament. Events must be booked two months in advance.

Directions: From I-215, take the Highway 74 exit to the town of Hemet and drive through town. Turn right on Buena Vista Street and drive 1.5 miles to Thornton Avenue, then go left to the club.

Contact: 545 East Thornton Avenue, Hemet, CA 92543, pro shop 909/652-2203.

32 DIAMOND VALLEY GOLF CLUB

Architect: Art Magnuson, 1998; Bill Martin, 1998
18 holes   **Public**   **$37–52**

Palm Springs and the Deserts map, page 436

Diamond Valley Golf Club is a links-style public course with a country club feel. At 6720 yards from the back tees, it isn't long by new course standards, instead choosing to challenge players in a traditional manner by making them think. The key to scoring well here is keeping the ball in the fairway, even if you have to leave your driver in the bag.

Play Policy and Fees: Green fees are $37 weekdays and $52 weekends and holidays, including cart. Twilight, super twilight, nine-hole, resident, early bird, and senior green fees are available.

Tees and Yardage: *Men:* Black: yardage 6720, par 72, rating 73.0, slope 135; Blue: yardage 6452, par 72, rating 71.8, slope 131; White: yardage 6118, par 72, rating 70.2, slope 128; *Women:* Red: yardage 5634, par 72, rating 72.3, slope 128; Gold: yardage 5313, par 72, rating 70.5, slope 124.

Tee Times: Reservations can be made seven days in advance.

Dress Code: No jeans are allowed on the course. Collared shirts and nonmetal spikes are required.

Tournaments: A 24-player minimum is required to book an event. Tournaments should be booked at least 12 months in advance.

Directions: From Los Angeles, take I-10 east to Highway 79 south. Follow Highway 79 to the end. Take a left on Domenigoni Parkway,

then a right on State Street. State Street turns into Sage Road. The course is on the left.
Contact: 31220 Sage Road, Hemet, CA 92543, pro shop 909/767-0828, fax 909/767-2266, www.diamondvalleygolf.net.

33 MISSION LAKES COUNTRY CLUB
Architect: Ted Robinson Sr., 1971
18 holes   Semiprivate $25–75

Coachella Valley Detail map, page 437

This is a high-desert course, which means you can expect searing sun and wicked wind. Three holes climb into the mountains. Long par-3s also make this a demanding course; five of the six measure 200 yards or longer.
Play Policy and Fees: Green fees range $60–75 during high season, $25–40 during summer months.
Tees and Yardage: *Men:* Blue: yardage 6739, par 71, rating 72.1, slope 124; White: yardage 6404, par 71, rating 70.5, slope 121; Gold: yardage 5891, par 71, rating 67.9, slope 115; *Women:* Red: yardage 5505, par 72, rating 71.5, slope 121.
Tee Times: Reservations can be made seven days in advance.
Dress Code: Appropriate golf attire and non-metal spikes are required.
Tournaments: This course is available for outside events. Restrictions apply for weekend shotgun tournaments.
Directions: Take the Indian Avenue exit off I-10 at Palm Springs. Drive north to Mission Lakes Avenue east and turn north on Club-house Drive.
Contact: 8484 Clubhouse Drive, Desert Hot Springs, CA 92240, pro shop 760/329-8061, clubhouse 760/329-6481.

34 SANDS RV RESORT
Architect: Ron Garl, 1983
9 holes   Public $12

Coachella Valley Detail map, page 437

This is an executive course adjoining an RV park. It is short and wide open, with a few trees

and no bunkers. It's a beginner's paradise. A lake on the seventh offers some suspense.
Play Policy and Fees: Green fees are $12 for nine holes. Replays are $6. Pull carts $2. For disabled golfers, power carts are available with 24-hour advance request.
Tees and Yardage: *Men:* yardage 2127, par 32, rating n/a, slope n/a; *Women:* yardage 1832, par 32, rating n/a, slope n/a.
Tee Times: Reservations can be booked 24 hours in advance.
Dress Code: Appropriate attire and soft spikes are required.
Tournaments: This course is not available for outside events.
Directions: Take the Palm Drive exit north off I-10. Turn right on Dillon Road and drive three-quarters of a mile to Bubbling Wells Road. The entrance to the RV park and the course is on the corner.
Contact: 16400 Bubbling Wells Road, Desert Hot Springs, CA 92240, pro shop 760/251-1173.

35 DESERT CREST COUNTRY CLUB
Architect: Course designed, 1965
9 holes   Semiprivate $10–12

Coachella Valley Detail map, page 437

This well-maintained, level par-3 course has four lakes and lots of trees. Desert Crest is part of a mobile home community and is very popular among seniors.
Play Policy and Fees: The course is open to members only Tuesday, Wednesday, and Friday 7 A.M.–noon; otherwise, the public is welcome. Green fees are $10 for nine holes and $12 for 18 holes.
Tees and Yardage: *Men and Women:* yardage 999, par 27, rating n/a, slope n/a.
Tee Times: Reservations are not accepted.
Dress Code: Appropriate golf attire is required.
Tournaments: Events should be scheduled at least eight months in advance. The banquet facility can accommodate up to 190 people.
Directions: From Los Angeles on I-10, take

the Palm Drive exit and head north. Follow Palm Drive until you reach Dillon Road. Take a right on Dillon Road and head east three miles. Stay on Dillon one mile past Mountain View. The course is on the left.

Contact: 69400 South Country Club Drive, Desert Hot Springs, CA 92241, pro shop 760/329-8711, fax 760/329-0872.

36 DESERT DUNES GOLF CLUB
Architect: Robert Trent Jones Jr., 1988

18 holes	Public	$89–99

Coachella Valley Detail map, page 437

Highly rated by national golf publications, this course has a unique Scottish-links flavor. Natural sand dunes and mesquite brush line the fairways. There is an abundance of wildlife, including jackrabbits, roadrunners, and coyotes in the surrounding desert. The par-3 fifth hole requires a long tee shot over a desert setting to a severely undulating green with a mesquite backdrop. It's a terrific layout. In 1996 Desert Dunes hosted the second stage of PGA Tour Qualifying School, and in 1994 it hosted the first stage of U.S. Open qualifying.

Play Policy and Fees: Green fees are $89 Monday–Thursday and $99 Friday–Sunday and holidays during peak season, carts included. Call for special seasonal rates. Twilight rates are offered.

Tees and Yardage: *Men:* Black: yardage 6825, par 72, rating 73.8, slope 142; Gold: yardage 6595, par 72, rating 72.7, slope 134; White: yardage 6175, par 72, rating 70.2, slope 124; *Women:* Red: yardage 5395, par 72, rating 70.7, slope 116.

Tee Times: Reservations can be booked seven days in advance.

Dress Code: Collared shirts and nonmetal spikes are required. No blue jeans are allowed.

Tournaments: A 16-player minimum is needed to book a tournament. Carts are required.

Directions: From I-10 in Palm Springs, take Gene Autry Trail and cross over the freeway. When you cross the freeway, the street name

changes to Palm Drive. Continue on Palm Drive two miles to the course.

Contact: 19300 Palm Drive, Desert Hot Springs, CA 92240, pro shop 760/251-5368, fax 760/251-5371, www.desertdunesgolfclub.net.

37 PALM SPRINGS COUNTRY CLUB
Architect: Robert Bell, 1957

18 holes	Public	$35–45

Coachella Valley Detail map, page 437

This is a mature desert course with very narrow, tree-lined fairways that require shot accuracy. The well-conditioned greens are also well protected. Water comes into play on five holes.

Play Policy and Fees: Green fees are $35 Monday–Thursday and $45 Friday–Sunday and holidays. Carts are included but not mandatory. Junior rates are offered.

Tees and Yardage: *Men:* Blue: yardage 6201, par 72, rating 68.9, slope 115; White: yardage 5869, par 72, rating 66.6, slope 110; *Women:* Red: yardage 5129, par 72, rating 67.0, slope 109.

Tee Times: Reservations may be booked seven days in advance.

Dress Code: Collared shirts are required and nonmetal spikes are recommended. No cutoffs or blue jeans are permitted.

Tournaments: This course is available for tournaments.

Directions: Take the Palm Drive exit off I-10 and travel south half a mile to Vista Chino. Turn right and drive one-quarter mile to Whitewater Club Drive. Turn right and continue to the club.

Contact: 2500 Whitewater Club Drive, Palm Springs, CA 92262, pro shop 760/323-2626, fax 760/325-4917.

38 O'DONNELL GOLF CLUB
Architect: Johnny Dawson and T. O'Donnell, 1926

9 holes	Private	$26.50–53.75

Coachella Valley Detail map, page 437

This is a tranquil course in downtown Palm Springs, set against the base of the mountains.

It is a peaceful spot for some mellow golfing. This was the first course in the Springs and a mecca for the Hollywood set 80 years ago. Today, it's a sporty course with two par-5s and a 207-yard par-3. "We're in a time warp here," course officials say. "That's a good thing."

Play Policy and Fees: Members and guests only. Reciprocal play is accepted only during the off-season. Guest fees are $26.50 for nine holes and $53.75 for 18 holes, cart included.

Tees and Yardage: *Men and Women (18 holes):* White/Red: yardage 5310, par 70, rating 65.2 (M)/70.7 (W), slope 108 (M)/120 (W).

Tee Times: Reciprocators should have their club pro call to make arrangements.

Dress Code: Collared shirts and nonmetal spikes are required. Bermuda shorts are acceptable.

Tournaments: This course is not available for outside events.

Directions: From I-10, take Highway 111 east on Palm Canyon Drive into the town of Palm Springs. Turn west on Amado Road and drive one block to the club.

Contact: 301 North Belardo Road, Palm Springs, CA 92262, pro shop 760/325-2259, fax 760/325-8123.

39 CIMARRON GOLF RESORT
Architect: John Fought, 2000

| 36 holes | Public | $39–95 |

Coachella Valley Detail map, page 437

There are two 18-hole John Fought–designed courses here, one regulation length called Long Course (par 71), and a shorter course called Short Course (par 56). The Long Course, at 6858 yards, will test anybody's best game, while the Short Course is perfect for tuning up your short game, as well as for seniors, beginning players, and families. Cimarron combines traditional desert design with some interesting European-style design elements, such as stacked-sod bunkers filled with white crushed marble. The layout features some wonderful views of the surrounding mountains. It was voted in the top 100 women-friendly courses by *Golf for Women* magazine.

Play Policy and Fees: Green fees on the Long Course are $85 weekdays, $95 weekends and holidays. Green fees on the Short Course are $39 weekdays, $45 weekends and holidays. Frequent player, twilight, and junior rates are available. Discounts are also offered to anyone staying at the on-property time-share units.

Tees and Yardage: Long Course—*Men:* Cimarron: yardage 6858, par 71, rating 72.4, slope 123; Championship: yardage 6474, par 71, rating 70.7, slope 119; Middle: yardage 5879, par 71, rating 67.9, slope 114; *Women:* Forward: yardage 5127, par 71, rating 69.7, slope 117. Short Course—*Men:* Cimarron: yardage 3156, par 56, rating 54.1, slope 84; Championship: yardage 2872, par 56, rating n/a, slope n/a; *Women:* Forward: yardage 2313, par 56, rating n/a, slope n/a.

Tee Times: Reservations can be made 90 days in advance.

Dress Code: Appropriate golf attire is required. Soft spikes only.

Tournaments: Tournaments of all types are welcome.

Directions: From I-10, exit Date Palm south. Drive west on Vista Chino, south on Landau, then west on 30th to the clubhouse.

Contact: 67-603 30th Avenue, Cathedral City, CA 92234, tee times 760/770-6060, fax 760/770-2876, www.cimarrongolf.com.

40 DESERT PRINCESS COUNTRY CLUB
Architect: David Rainville, 1985

| 27 holes | Resort | $85–130 |

Coachella Valley Detail map, page 437

These courses are well maintained and mostly flat. Water comes into play on 17 holes. The Cielo Course is located in a wash and features six holes with a Scottish-links flair. The well-bunkered greens and bent grass make these courses a challenge.

There is a Doral hotel on property, plus roughly 700 condominiums, some of which are for lease. Call 760/322-7000 for information or reservations.

Play Policy and Fees: Green fees are seasonal. During peak season green fees for resort guests are $85 weekdays, $100 weekends. For nonresort guests, green fees in peak season are $100 weekdays, $130 weekends. Twilight rates offered. Call for off-season rates.

Tees and Yardage: Cielo/Vista—*Men:* Gold: yardage 6808, par 72, rating 72.9, slope 131; Blue: yardage 6366, par 72, rating 70.8, slope 126; White: yardage 5933, par 72, rating 68.9, slope 122; *Women:* Red: yardage 5373, par 72, rating 71.9, slope 124. Lagos/Cielo—*Men:* Gold: yardage 6596, par 72, rating 72.4, slope 126; Blue: yardage 6117, par 72, rating 70.1, slope 124; White: yardage 5662, par 72, rating 68.1, slope 120; *Women:* Red: yardage 5211, par 72, rating 70.8, slope 120. Vista/Lagos—*Men:* Gold: yardage 6692, par 72, rating 72.6, slope 127; Blue: yardage 6259, par 72, rating 70.5, slope 124; White: yardage 5823, par 72, rating 68.6, slope 118; *Women:* Red: yardage 5293, par 72, rating 71.1, slope 121.

Tee Times: Reservations can be booked two days in advance.

Dress Code: Appropriate golf attire and non-metal spikes are required.

Tournaments: A 72-player minimum is needed to book a tournament. Events should be scheduled 12 months in advance. The banquet facility can accommodate 200 people.

Directions: Take the Date Palm exit off I-10 southeast of Palm Springs. Turn right and drive to Vista Chino. Turn right and drive to Landau Boulevard. Go left to the club.

Contact: 28-555 Landau Boulevard, Cathedral City, CA 92234, pro shop 760/322-2280, clubhouse 760/322-1655, fax 760/322-2741.

41 IVEY RANCH COUNTRY CLUB

Architect: William F. Bell, 1985

9 holes   Semiprivate $15–35

Coachella Valley Detail map, page 437

This well-maintained course has bent-grass greens, strategically placed trees, and fairly narrow fairways. It's a regulation nine-hole course, with doglegs and out-of-bounds on several holes.

Play Policy and Fees: Green fees range $15–35 depending on the season. Discounts are available. Call for rates.

Tees and Yardage: *Men (18 holes):* Blue: yardage 5310, par 70, rating 65.8, slope 108; White: yardage 4984, par 70, rating 64.4, slope 103; *Women (18 holes):* Red: yardage 4644, par 70, rating 66.4, slope 107.

Tee Times: Reservations can be booked seven days in advance.

Dress Code: Appropriate golf attire is required.

Tournaments: This course is available for outside tournaments. A 15-player minimum is needed. Tournaments can be booked one month in advance. The banquet facility can accommodate 150 people.

Directions: Take the Monterey Avenue exit off I-10 near Thousand Palms and drive east to Varner Road. Turn north and take the frontage road 1.5 miles to the club.

Contact: 74-580 Varner Road, Thousand Palms, CA 92276, pro shop 760/343-2013, fax 760/343-0683.

42 MESQUITE GOLF & COUNTRY CLUB

Architect: Bert Stamps, 1984

18 holes   Semiprivate $65

Coachella Valley Detail map, page 437

This is a flat course with beautiful mountain scenery. It is well bunkered, with eight small lakes and many palm trees. The course plays over and along a streambed, so it's considerably tougher when the water flows. Mac O'Grady and Wayne Byrd share the course record of 62.

Play Policy and Fees: High season rates are $65 seven days, including cart. Twilight, midday, and junior (17 and under) rates are offered. Memberships are also available.

Tees and Yardage: *Men:* Back: yardage 6328, par 72, rating 69.8, slope 117; Middle: yardage

5944, par 72, rating 67.9, slope 111; *Women:* Forward: yardage 5281, par 72, rating 70.8, slope 120.

Tee Times: Reservations may be booked up to two weeks in advance.

Dress Code: Collared shirts are required, and no denim is allowed.

Tournaments: This course is available for tournaments. Call for more information.

Directions: Take the Palm Drive exit off I-10, drive south to Ramon Road, and turn west. At Farrell, turn south and drive to the course at Mesquite Avenue.

Contact: 2700 East Mesquite Avenue, Palm Springs, CA 92264, pro shop 760/323-9377.

43 OUTDOOR RESORT & COUNTRY CLUB

Architect: Kelly Johnson, 1986
27 holes   Private $9–18

Coachella Valley Detail map, page 437

There are two par-3 courses at this RV park, an 18-holer and a nine-hole pitch-and-putt. The greens are small and well protected. A skins game was once held on the 18-hole course with local pros, including Mac O'Grady and Mark Pfeil. The pitch-and-putt is 561 yards long, par 27.

Play Policy and Fees: Members and guests only. The guest fee is $9 for nine holes and $18 for 18 holes.

Tees and Yardage: *Men:* yardage 1833, par 56, rating n/a, slope n/a; *Women:* yardage 1785, par 56, rating n/a, slope n/a.

Tee Times: No outside play is accepted.

Dress Code: Collared shirts are required.

Tournaments: This course is not available for outside events.

Directions: Take I-10 to Date Palm Drive and go south to Ramon Road. Turn left and drive half a mile to the resort.

Contact: 69-411 Ramon Road, Cathedral City, CA 92234, pro shop 760/324-8638.

44 TOMMY JACOBS' BEL AIR GREENS

Architect: Len Girken, 1975
9 holes   Public $19–27

Coachella Valley Detail map, page 437

This is a well-maintained, nine-hole executive course with small, quick greens and narrow fairways. It is one of the most scenic courses in the desert, with mature trees and a lot of water. An 18-hole miniature golf course is part of the complex.

Play Policy and Fees: During high season, green fees are $19 for nine holes and $27 for 18 holes. Twilight and off-season rates are available.

Tees and Yardage: *Men:* Back: yardage 1768, par 32, rating n/a, slope n/a; Middle: yardage 1570, par 32, rating n/a, slope n/a; *Women:* Forward: yardage 1397, par 32, rating n/a, slope n/a.

Tee Times: Reservations are required during high season and may be booked 14 days in advance.

Dress Code: Shirts are required.

Tournaments: This course is available for tournaments.

Directions: In Palm Springs, take Highway 111 (East Palm Canyon Drive) to Escoba Drive. Follow Escoba one-third mile to El Cielo and turn left. Drive half a mile to the course, which is one-half mile south of the Palm Springs Airport.

Contact: 1001 South El Cielo Road, Palm Springs, CA 92264, pro shop 760/322-6062, fax 760/322-3162.

45 CATHEDRAL CANYON GOLF & TENNIS CLUB

Architect: David Rainville, 1975 and 1978
27 holes   Semiprivate $80

Coachella Valley Detail map, page 437

These scenic, tree-lined courses are fairly tight and require a variety of shot-making skills. Refreshing water comes into play on almost every hole. There are 20 lakes dotting the course and lots of mature trees. Golfers can glimpse the surrounding mountains from every hole. This facility has hosted several major California state tournaments.

Play Policy and Fees: Green fees are seasonal. During peak season fees are $80 seven days, but specials are often offered. Call for off-season rates. Carts are included. Memberships are available.

Tees and Yardage: Lake/Arroyo—*Men:* Blue: yardage 6366, par 72, rating 70.3, slope 125; White: yardage 6021, par 72, rating 68.8, slope 121; *Women:* Red: yardage 5183, par 72, rating 70.1, slope 124. Lake/Mountain—*Men:* Blue: yardage 6510, par 72, rating 71.1, slope 130; White: yardage 6177, par 72, rating 69.5, slope 128; *Women:* Red: yardage 5423, par 72, rating 71.6, slope 127. Mountain/Arroyo—*Men:* Blue: yardage 6482, par 72, rating 70.9, slope 126; White: yardage 6072, par 72, rating 69.0, slope 124; *Women:* Red: yardage 5182, par 72, rating 70.8, slope 124.

Tee Times: Reservations can be booked seven days in advance.

Dress Code: Appropriate golf attire is required. Soft spikes are preferred.

Tournaments: A 16-player minimum is required to book a regular tournament. Sixty players are required to book a shotgun tournament. Carts are required.

Directions: Take the Date Palm exit off I-10 near Palm Springs. Drive south to Dinah Shore Drive and turn right. Drive one mile to Cathedral Canyon Drive and turn left. Continue one mile to the club.

Contact: 68311 Paseo Real, Cathedral City, CA 92234, pro shop 760/328-6571, www.cathedral-canyon.com.

46 MISSION HILLS COUNTRY CLUB

Architect: Desmond Muirhead (Dinah Shore Tournament Course), 1970; Arnold Palmer and Ed Seay (Arnold Palmer Course), 1978; Pete Dye (Pete Dye Challenge Course), 1988

54 holes   **Private**   **$45–250**

Coachella Valley Detail map, page 437

You cannot go wrong on any of these three scenic courses. All three are very well maintained and sport lovely views of the surrounding mountains. The Arnold Palmer Course is a links-style layout. It is a relatively flat course, heavily bunkered, and features immaculate greens. The Pete Dye Challenge Course is a stadium-type layout with big rolling hills and deep bunkers. The greens on this course are small but undulating. The rough and surrounding area are natural desert. Some new lakes were added to the Pete Dye Challenge Course in 2003. The Dinah Shore Tournament Course has rolling terrain, mature trees, and undulating Bermuda greens. Mission Hills is the home of the LPGA Nabisco Dinah Shore Tournament and LPGA qualifying. This is one of the better clubs in California.

Privately owned condominiums around the course are leased through the club's leasing department. Please call 760/328-2200 for information.

Play Policy and Fees: Reciprocal play is accepted with members of other private clubs. Reciprocator fees range $90–250, depending on course and season. Carts and range balls are included. Renters of condominium units on the course have playing privileges on the Arnold Palmer and Pete Dye Challenge Courses for fees ranging $45–110, depending on season.

Tees and Yardage: Dinah Shore Tournament Course—*Men:* Tournament: yardage 7221, par 72, rating 74.8, slope 133; Championship: yardage 6906, par 72, rating 73.1, slope 127; Club: yardage 6286, par 72, rating 70.4, slope 121; *Women:* Forward: yardage 5684, par 72, rating 73.6, slope 132. Arnold Palmer Course—

Men: Championship: yardage 6743, par 72, rating 72.4, slope 119; Regular: yardage 6171, par 72, rating 69.5, slope 119; *Women:* Forward: yardage 5482, par 72, rating 72.3, slope 123. Pete Dye Challenge Course—*Men:* Tournament: yardage 6955, par 72, rating 73.9, slope 135; Championship: yardage 6568, par 72, rating 71.8, slope 129; Regular: yardage 6065, par 72, rating 69.2, slope 121; *Women:* Silver: yardage 5543, par 72, rating 72.3, slope 131; Forward: yardage 5079, par 72, rating 69.3, slope 125.

Tee Times: Reciprocators should have their club pro call to make arrangements.

Dress Code: Appropriate golf attire and nonmetal spikes are required.

Tournaments: The courses are available for outside tournaments. Carts are required.

Directions: Take the Date Palm Drive/Cathedral City exit south off I-10 and drive three miles to Dinah Shore Drive. Turn left and drive 1.5 miles to the club.

Contact: 34-600 Mission Hills Drive, Rancho Mirage, CA 92270, pro shop 760/324-7336, www.missionhills.com.

47 CANYON COUNTRY CLUB
Architect: William F. Bell, 1962
18 holes   Private

Coachella Valley Detail map, page 437

This mature, very private course is beautifully maintained. It's set among million-dollar homes, with out-of-bounds on all but one hole.

Play Policy and Fees: Members and guests only.

Tees and Yardage: *Men:* Blue: yardage 6909, par 72, rating 72.3, slope 125; White: yardage 6505, par 72, rating 70.6, slope 121; Gold: yardage 6041, par 72, rating 68.4, slope 116; *Women:* Red: yardage 5857, par 72, rating 73.7, slope 127.

Tee Times: Not applicable.

Dress Code: Appropriate golf attire and nonmetal spikes are required.

Tournaments: This course is not available for outside events.

Directions: Take the Indian Avenue exit off

I-10 near Palm Springs and drive south to Murray Canyon. Turn left and drive six blocks to the club.

Contact: 1100 Murray Canyon Drive, Palm Springs, CA 92264, pro shop 760/327-5831, clubhouse 760/327-1321.

48 INDIAN CANYONS GOLF COURSE
Architect: William F. Bell, 1962; redesign Casey O'Callaghan and Amy Alcott, 2004
18 holes   Public

Coachella Valley Detail map, page 437

It is hard to consider the work done on Indian Canyons (formerly Canyon South Golf Course) a remodel, since it created practically an entirely new course. Architect Casey O'Callaghan did the design, and LPGA professional Amy Alcott consulted on this course, which reopened in late 2004. The work done included rerouting the holes, creating five new lakes, and extensive earth moving and shaping to create mounding. The result is a fun, resort-style layout with many lovely mature palm trees that were saved from the previous course.

Play Policy and Fees: Not available at press time.

Tees and Yardage: Not available at press time.

Tee Times: Reservations can be booked seven days in advance.

Dress Code: Collared shirts are required. No denim is allowed on the course. Soft spikes are preferred.

Tournaments: This course is available for outside tournaments.

Directions: Take the Highway 111 exit off I-10 near Palm Springs and drive south on Palm Canyon Drive to Murray Canyon. Turn left and drive three blocks to the club.

Contact: 1097 Murray Canyon Drive, Palm Springs, CA 92264, pro shop 760/327-2019.

49 DATE PALM COUNTRY CLUB

Architect: Ted Robinson Sr., 1970

9 holes   Semiprivate

Coachella Valley Detail map, page 437

This course is in a retirement area.

Play Policy and Fees: Green fees are seasonal.

Tees and Yardage: *Men and Women:* yardage 3083, par 58, rating n/a, slope n/a.

Tee Times: Not applicable.

Dress Code: No tank tops are allowed on the course.

Tournaments: This course is available for outside events.

Directions: Take the Date Palm Drive exit off I-10 in Cathedral City and drive south for four miles to the club entrance on the left.

Contact: 36-200 Date Palm Drive, Cathedral City, CA 92234, pro shop 760/328-1315.

50 RANCHO MIRAGE COUNTRY CLUB

Architect: Harold Heers Jr., 1984

18 holes   Semiprivate $70

Coachella Valley Detail map, page 437

This gently rolling course has narrow fairways and small greens. Water comes into play on nine holes. Centrally located in the valley, the course offers views of the Santa Rosa and San Jacinto Mountains. It's a good test for both the advanced and beginning golfer.

Play Policy and Fees: Green fees during peak season are $70, cart included. Rates go down seasonally. Call for current rates. Twilight rates are offered. Memberships are available. The course is closed during October.

Tees and Yardage: *Men:* Blue: yardage 6111, par 70, rating 69.4, slope 122; White: yardage 5823, par 70, rating 68.0, slope 119; *Women:* Red: yardage 5386, par 70, rating 70.8, slope 118.

Tee Times: Reservations can be made three days in advance. Members can book tee times 14 days in advance.

Dress Code: Appropriate golf attire is required.

Tournaments: This course is available for outside tournaments.

Directions: Take the Bob Hope Drive/Ramon Road exit off I-10 southeast of Palm Springs. Head south on Bob Hope Drive and drive four miles to the club entrance on the left.

Contact: 38-500 Bob Hope Drive, Rancho Mirage, CA 92270, pro shop 760/324-4711, clubhouse 760/328-1444, www.ranchomiragegolf.com.

51 AVONDALE GOLF CLUB

Architect: Jimmy Hines, 1969

18 holes   Private $115

Coachella Valley Detail map, page 437

This is not a typical desert course. There are water hazards and lots of trees dispersed on rolling terrain.

Play Policy and Fees: Space-available reciprocal play is accepted with members of other private clubs at a peak-season rate of $115. Carts are included. Otherwise, members and guests only. The course is closed mid-September–early November.

Tees and Yardage: *Men:* Blue: yardage 6782, par 72, rating 72.4, slope 127; White: yardage 6400, par 72, rating 70.5, slope 122; *Women:* Red: yardage 5781, par 72, rating 74.6, slope 130.

Tee Times: Reciprocators should have their club pro call to make arrangements.

Dress Code: Collared shirts and nonmetal spikes are required.

Tournaments: Outside events must have board approval.

Directions: Take the Washington Street exit off I-10 southeast of Palm Springs and drive south. Turn right on Country Club Drive and travel 2.5 miles to El Dorado. Turn right to the course.

Contact: 75-800 Avondale Drive, Palm Desert, CA 92260, pro shop 760/345-3712, clubhouse 760/345-2727.

52 THE CLUB AT MORNINGSIDE

Architect: Jack Nicklaus, 1982

18 holes   **Private**   **$175**

🧍 📷 🍴 🚗 🍺 3

Coachella Valley Detail map, page 437

There is a championship 18-hole course here, plus a 1044-yard par-3 course that is sometimes open for play. Jack Nicklaus designed the championship course with a linkslike style. It's immaculate and scenic. Almost every hole provides an option to gamble or play it safe. Contoured fairways, deep bunkers, and water make this a challenge from start to finish. The nine-hole course was completed in 2000.

Play Policy and Fees: Reciprocal play is accepted with members of other private clubs at a rate of $175, including cart and range balls. Otherwise, members and guests only. The course is closed Monday and Tuesday July–October.

Tees and Yardage: *Men:* Black: yardage 6773, par 72, rating 72.7, slope 131; Blue: yardage 6404, par 72, rating 71.0, slope 127; White: yardage 6200, par 72, rating 70.1, slope 124; Gold: yardage 6618, par 72, rating 67.1, slope 117; *Women:* Red: yardage 5448, par 72, rating 71.6, slope 126.

Tee Times: Reservations can be booked seven days in advance.

Dress Code: Appropriate golf attire and nonmetal spikes are required.

Tournaments: This course is not available for outside events.

Directions: Take the Bob Hope Drive/Ramon Road exit off I-10 southeast of Palm Springs and drive south on Bob Hope Drive. Turn right on Frank Sinatra Drive and travel one-half mile to Morningside Drive. Turn left and travel one-quarter mile to the club entrance on the right.

Contact: Morningside Drive, Rancho Mirage, CA 92270, pro shop 760/321-1555.

53 THUNDERBIRD COUNTRY CLUB

Architect: Johnny Dawson, 1952; Ted Robinson Sr., 1982

18 holes   **Private**

🧍 📷 🍴 🛏 🚗

Coachella Valley Detail map, page 437

This is one of the very first and most exclusive courses in the area. Water, bunkers, and palm trees make this mostly flat, narrow course an interesting challenge.

Play Policy and Fees: Members and guests only. No reciprocal play is accepted. Guests must be accompanied by a member at time of play.

Tees and Yardage: *Men:* Blue: yardage 6460, par 71, rating 70.7, slope 129; White: yardage 6179, par 71, rating 69.4, slope 126; *Women:* Bronze: yardage 5814, par 72, rating 74.0, slope 133.

Tee Times: Not applicable.

Dress Code: Appropriate golf attire and nonmetal spikes are required.

Tournaments: This course is not available for outside events.

Directions: Take the Bob Hope Drive/Ramon Road exit off I-10 southeast of Palm Springs and drive south on Bob Hope Drive. Turn right on Country Club Drive and travel 1.5 miles to the club entrance on the left.

Contact: 70-612 Highway 111, Rancho Mirage, CA 92270, pro shop 760/328-2161.

54 SUNRISE COUNTRY CLUB

Architect: Ted Robinson Sr., 1971

18 holes   **Private**

🧍 📷 🍴 🚗 🍺

Coachella Valley Detail map, page 437

This is a mature, 18-hole executive course with water and lots of sand. It boasts 10 par-4s and eight par-3s. If you drive the ball 180–190 yards and want to use every club in your bag, this is the course for you.

Play Policy and Fees: Members and guests only. No reciprocal play is accepted.

Tees and Yardage: *Men and Women:* yardage 3837, par 64, rating 56.9 (M)/61.5 (W), slope 85 (M)/101 (W).

Tee Times: Not applicable.

Dress Code: Appropriate golf attire and non-metal spikes are required.

Tournaments: This course is not available for outside events.

Directions: Take the Bob Hope Drive/Ramon Road exit off I-10 southeast of Palm Springs and drive about six miles south on Bob Hope Drive. Turn right on Country Club Drive and travel several yards to the entrance on the left.

Contact: 71-601 Country Club Drive, Rancho Mirage, CA 92270, pro shop 760/328-1139, clubhouse 760/328-6549.

55 TAHQUITZ CREEK GOLF RESORT

Architect: William F. Bell, 1959; Ted Robinson Sr., 1995

36 holes   **Resort**   **$35-95**

🏃 📷 🍴 🛏 🚜 🍺

Coachella Valley Detail map, page 437

The Legend Course is a well-maintained, tree-lined course, providing some much-needed shade in the summer. Palmer Design renovated this design several years ago. Water comes into play on seven holes on the Resort Course, as it does on most all of Ted Robinson's designs. The seventh hole features an island fairway. If you miss the fairway right, left, short, or long, you will find yourself reaching in your bag for another ball. Both courses are a pleasure to play.

Play Policy and Fees: During high season, green fees are $69 on the Legend Course, $95 on the Resort Course, carts included, seven days. Green fees range from $35 on the Legends to $50 on the Resort during summer months. Call for seasonal rates.

Tees and Yardage: Legend—*Men:* Championship: yardage 6815, par 71, rating 72.3, slope 123; White: yardage 6504, par 71, rating 70.9, slope 121; Yellow: yardage 6161, par 71, rating 69.7, slope 117; *Women:* Red: yardage 5811, par 72, rating 72.3, slope 118. Resort—*Men:* Championship: yardage 6705, par 71, rating 71.8, slope 125; White: yardage 6256, par 71, rating 69.9, slope 123; Yellow: yardage 5825, par 71, rating 68.1, slope 119; *Women:* Red: yardage 5206, par 72, rating 70.0, slope 119.

Tee Times: Reservations can be booked 30 days in advance.

Dress Code: Collared shirts and golf shoes are required.

Tournaments: Tournaments welcome, with a 16-player minimum. A banquet facility can accommodate up to 100 people.

Directions: From I-10 near Palm Springs, take the Date Palm Drive exit and drive south 4.5 miles to Ramon Road and turn left. Drive one-half mile to Crossley Road, turn right, and drive one mile to the club.

Contact: 1885 Golf Club Drive, Palm Springs, CA 92264, pro shop 760/328-1005, fax 760/324-8122, www.tahquitzcreek.com.

56 WESTIN MISSION HILLS: GARY PLAYER COURSE

Architect: Gary Player, 1991

18 holes   **Resort**   **$70-145**

🏃 📷 🍴 🛏 🚜 🍺

Coachella Valley Detail map, page 437

Approximately one mile from the Westin Mission Hills Resort grounds, this course features nine lakes and four waterfalls. It is as challenging as the Pete Dye Course back at the resort, but more forgiving on the greens. There are some wonderful views of the surrounding mountains, and it is always in impeccable condition. Seasonally, Resort Golf holds schools here.

The Westin Mission Hills has 512 rooms. For reservations, call 760/328-3198.

Play Policy and Fees: Guests of the Westin Mission Hills Resort have priority on tee times. Public play is welcome at the course. Green fees are seasonal and range from $70 in summer to $145 in high season. Carts and range balls are included in the fee. Call for current rates.

Tees and Yardage: *Men:* Black: yardage 7062, par 72, rating 73.4, slope 131; Gold: yardage 6643, par 72, rating 71.3, slope 124; Silver: yardage 6044, par 72, rating 68.5, slope 115; *Women:* Jade: yardage 4907, par 72, rating 68.0, slope 118.

Tee Times: Hotel guests may book times 90

days in advance; public players may book 30 days in advance.

Dress Code: Appropriate golf attire is required. Soft spikes are recommended.

Tournaments: Events should be booked a year in advance. The banquet facility can accommodate 1000 people.

Directions: Southeast of Palm Springs, take the Bob Hope Drive/Ramon Road exit off I-10. Travel west on Ramon Road for one mile to the club.

Contact: 70-705 Dinah Shore Drive, Rancho Mirage, CA 92270, pro shop 760/770-2908, www.troongolf.com.

57 WESTIN MISSION HILLS: PETE DYE COURSE

Architect: Pete Dye, 1986

18 holes   **Resort**   **$70–145**

Coachella Valley Detail map, page 437

Adjacent to the Westin Mission Hills Resort, this course is a links-style layout with rolling fairways and large, undulating greens. There are also numerous pot bunkers and railroad ties. Though it is shorter than its sister Gary Player Course, it is perhaps more challenging, particularly on the greens. Go figure—it's a Pete Dye design. Again, delightful mountain views abound on this well-conditioned course. The Golf Digest Golf School is here.

The Westin Mission Hills has 512 rooms. For reservations, call 760/328-5955. Play-and-stay packages are available.

Play Policy and Fees: Guests of the Westin Mission Hills Resort have priority on tee times. Public play is welcome at the course. Green fees are seasonal and range from $70 in summer to $145 in high season. Carts and range balls are included in the fee. Call for current rates.

Tees and Yardage: *Men:* Black: yardage 6706, par 70, rating 72.2, slope 131; Gold: yardage 6158, par 70, rating 69.6, slope 126; Silver: yardage 5587, par 70, rating 66.7, slope 116; *Women:* Jade: yardage 4841, par 70, rating 67.6, slope 117.

Tee Times: Hotel guests may book times 90 days in advance; public players may book 30 days in advance.

Dress Code: Appropriate golf attire is required. Soft spikes are recommended.

Tournaments: Events should be booked a year in advance. The banquet facility can accommodate 1000 people.

Directions: Take the Bob Hope Drive/Ramon Road exit off I-10 southeast of Palm Springs and drive south on Bob Hope Drive to Dinah Shore Drive. Turn right and drive half a mile to the resort entrance.

Contact: 71-501 Dinah Shore Drive, Rancho Mirage, CA 92270, pro shop 760/328-3198, fax 760/770-4984, www.troongolf.com.

58 TAMARISK COUNTRY CLUB

Architect: William P. Bell, 1952

18 holes   **Private**

Coachella Valley Detail map, page 437

This classic design is one of the oldest and most exclusive in the desert. It's a very challenging, mature course with lots of trees. Part of the PGA Tour's Bob Hope Classic has been held here. The club's first golf pro was Ben Hogan. It is a very private club.

Play Policy and Fees: Members and guests only.

Tees and Yardage: *Men:* Gold: yardage 6811, par 72, rating 72.6, slope 123; Blue: yardage 6555, par 72, rating 70.9, slope 119; White: yardage 6219, par 72, rating 69.5, slope 115; *Women:* Red: yardage 5937, par 72, rating 74.5, slope 126.

Tee Times: Not applicable.

Dress Code: Appropriate golf attire is required.

Tournaments: This course is not available for outside events.

Directions: Take the Bob Hope Drive/Ramon Road exit off I-10 southeast of Palm Springs and drive south on Bob Hope Drive. Turn right on Frank Sinatra Drive and drive one mile to the club on the right.

Contact: 70-240 Frank Sinatra Drive, Rancho Mirage, CA 92270, pro shop 760/328-2141.

59 DESERT ISLAND GOLF & COUNTRY CLUB

Architect: Desmond Muirhead, 1972
18 holes **Private**

Coachella Valley Detail map, page 437

This well-maintained course is set around an enormous lake with an island in the middle—condominiums are on the island. It is challenging, with narrow fairways and numerous bunkers surrounding the greens. This course also offers panoramic views of the mountains.
Play Policy and Fees: Members and guests only. No reciprocal play is accepted.
Tees and Yardage: *Men:* Blue: yardage 6686, par 72, rating 71.6, slope 127; White: yardage 6310, par 72, rating 69.9, slope 122; Gold: yardage 5705, par 72, rating 66.8, slope 116; *Women:* Red: yardage 5604, par 72, rating 72.9, slope 123.
Tee Times: Members must call on behalf of their guests.
Dress Code: Standard private club attire, such as collared shirts, and nonmetal spikes are required. Long shorts are acceptable. Denim is not permitted.
Tournaments: This course is available for some outside events.
Directions: From I-10 southeast of Palm Springs, take the Bob Hope Drive/Ramon Road exit and drive south on Bob Hope Drive to Frank Sinatra Drive. Turn right and drive one block to the course entrance on the left.
Contact: 71-777 Frank Sinatra Drive, Rancho Mirage, CA 92270, pro shop 760/328-0841, clubhouse 760/328-2111, fax 760/321-8340.

60 DESERT WILLOW GOLF RESORT

Architect: Michael Hurdzan, Dana Fry, and John Cook, 1997
36 holes **Resort** **$55–165**

Coachella Valley Detail map, page 437

 Showcasing a painstaking commitment **BEST** to the preservation of the native desert surroundings, these beautiful courses reward those who can keep the ball in the fairway. If you miss the fairway, you're liable to find yourself in the most common obstacle found in the desert: sand. With five sets of tees, there is plenty of room for golfers of all levels. The two designs are similar in nature, with the Mountain View Course a little more women-friendly. Both are always in excellent shape and well managed. They are among the very best daily fee courses in the region.
Play Policy and Fees: Green fees are seasonal, ranging from $55 in summer months, to $130 April–May and October–December 24, to $165 December 25–March. Sunrise, midday, twilight, and sunset rates are also available. Carts are included.
Tees and Yardage: Firecliff—*Men:* Black: yardage 7056, par 72, rating 73.6, slope 138; Blue: yardage 6676, par 72, rating 71.7, slope 133; White: yardage 6173, par 72, rating 69.3, slope 124; Gold: yardage 5642, par 72, rating 67.2, slope 117; *Women:* Red: yardage 5079, par 72, rating 69.0, slope 120. Mountain View—*Men:* Black: yardage 6913, par 72, rating 73.4, slope 130; Blue: yardage 6507, par 72, rating 71.5, slope 128; White: yardage 6128, par 72, rating 69.8, slope 126; Gold: yardage 5573, par 72, rating 67.2, slope 121; *Women:* Red: yardage 4997, par 72, rating 68.9, slope 116.
Tee Times: Reservations can be made up to seven days in advance. For an additional $10 per player, reservations can be booked eight days and more in advance.
Dress Code: Appropriate golf attire is required.
Tournaments: A 12-player minimum is needed to book a tournament. Tournaments may be booked 12 months in advance. The resort can accommodate groups of up to 400 people.
Directions: From I-10 near Palm Desert, take the Monterey exit. Take a right on Monterey and continue to Frank Sinatra Drive. Turn left on Frank Sinatra Drive and then right on Portola Drive. The course is one-quarter mile along on the left.
Contact: 38-500 Portola Avenue, Palm Desert, CA 92260 (P.O. Box 14062, Palm Desert, CA 92255), pro shop 760/346-7060, fax 760/346-7444, www.desertwillow.com.

61 MARRIOTT'S SHADOW RIDGE RESORT GOLF CLUB

Architect: Nick Faldo, 2000

18 holes   **Resort**   **$50–130**

🏌 📷 🍴 🏨 🚗 🏌

Coachella Valley Detail map, page 437

Set against the backdrop of the Santa Rosa Mountains, Shadow Ridge clearly demonstrates Nick Faldo's passion for strategic design. This course was his first design in the United States, and it is typical of the sandbelt courses of Australia, with generous landing areas and bold bunkering. Fescue grasses adorn many holes.

Play Policy and Fees: During the regular season (January–April), green fees are $108 for resort guests, $130 nonguests. Carts and range balls included. Fees during off-peak seasons run $50–80. Twilight rates available.

Tees and Yardage: *Men:* Black: yardage 7006, par 71, rating 73.9, slope 134; Green: yardage 6621, par 71, rating 71.8, slope 130; Gold: yardage 6204, par 71, rating 69.6, slope 125; *Women:* White: yardage 5200, par 71, rating 69.6, slope 119.

Tee Times: Reservations may be made up to 90 days in advance for resort guests, 30 days for nonguests.

Dress Code: Men must wear collared shirts, and no denim is allowed.

Tournaments: Corporate outings and charity events are welcome. Reservations may be made up to one year in advance.

Directions: From either direction on I-10, exit at Monterey and turn south. The course is just past Gerald Ford Drive on Monterey Avenue, approximately one mile from the freeway.

Contact: 9002 Shadow Ridge Road, Palm Desert, CA 92211, pro shop 760/674-2700, fax 760/674-2710, www.marriottgolf.com.

62 SUNCREST COUNTRY CLUB

Architect: Richard Watson, 1980

9 holes   **Public**   **$20–30**

🏌 📷 🍴 🏌 🚗 🏌

Coachella Valley Detail map, page 437

Set in Suncrest Park, this nicely maintained course is flat, with trees and two lakes. The course is elevated and provides nice views.

Play Policy and Fees: Green fees are $20 for nine holes, $30 for 18 holes. Carts are $12 for nine holes and $20 for 18 holes. Reservations are recommended. The course is closed during September and October.

Tees and Yardage: *Men (18 holes):* Blue: yardage 4946, par 66, rating 62.3, slope 101; White: yardage 4500, par 66, rating 60.6, slope 95; *Women (18 holes):* Red: yardage 3896, par 66, rating 60.6, slope 96.

Tee Times: Reservations can be booked seven days in advance.

Dress Code: Proper golf attire is expected.

Tournaments: A 20-player minimum is required to book a tournament. Events should be scheduled one month in advance. The banquet facility can accommodate 140 people.

Directions: Take the Monterey Avenue exit off I-10 southeast of Palm Springs and drive south to Country Club Drive. Turn left and travel one-half mile to the club on the left.

Contact: 73-450 Country Club Drive, Palm Desert, CA 92260, pro shop 760/340-2467.

63 PALM DESERT GREENS COUNTRY CLUB

Architect: Ted Robinson Sr., 1971

18 holes   **Private**

📷 🍴 🏌 🚗 🏌

Coachella Valley Detail map, page 437

This 18-hole executive course is flat, with several lakes and mature trees. It has a fun layout and is usually in great shape.

Play Policy and Fees: Members and guests only. Guests must be accompanied by members at time of play. The course is closed in October. Carts are $16.

Tees and Yardage: *Men:* White: yardage 4079, par 63, rating 58.9, slope 93; *Women:* Red: yardage 3681, par 63, rating 59.6, slope 63.

Tee Times: Not applicable.

Dress Code: Golf attire and nonmetal spikes are mandatory.

Tournaments: This course is not available for outside events.

Directions: Take the Monterey Avenue exit off I-10 southeast of Palm Springs and drive south to Country Club Drive. Turn left to the club entrance.

Contact: 73-750 Country Club Drive, Palm Desert, CA 92260, pro shop 760/346-2941.

64 SANTA ROSA COUNTRY CLUB

Architect: Leonard Gerkin, 1978

18 holes   Private $65

🏌 📷 🍴 🛺 🍽

Coachella Valley Detail map, page 437

This desert course has tree-lined fairways and two large lakes. It's challenging and offers a view of the Santa Rosa Mountains. Adding new tees is the latest step in a program to upgrade the course. A rarity in the desert, this course consists of 80 acres of golf course and clubhouse—no homes are built on or around it.

Play Policy and Fees: Reciprocal play is accepted with members of other private clubs; otherwise, members and guests only. Reciprocal fees are $65 in high season. Carts are additional.

Tees and Yardage: *Men:* Back: yardage 5568, par 70, rating 67.0, slope 111; Middle: yardage 5247, par 70, rating 65.0, slope 108; *Women:* Forward: yardage 4761, par 70, rating 66.7, slope 113.

Tee Times: Guest reservations are recommended one day in advance.

Dress Code: Appropriate golf attire and non-metal spikes are required.

Tournaments: This course is available for outside events during the off-season, May–September. A 12-player minimum is required. Tournaments can be booked three months in advance. The banquet facility can hold 100 people.

Directions: Take the Monterey Avenue exit off I-10 southeast of Palm Springs and drive south to Gerald Ford Drive. Turn left on Portola and right on Frank Sinatra Drive. The course is on the right.

Contact: 38-105 Portola Avenue, Palm Desert, CA 92260, pro shop 760/568-5717.

65 DESERT FALLS COUNTRY CLUB

Architect: Ron Fream, 1984

18 holes   Semiprivate $35–165

🏌 📷 🍴 🛺 🍽

Coachella Valley Detail map, page 437

Lengthened to more than 7000 yards in 2003, this course will truly test your golf skills. It is generally kept in immaculate condition. The greens sport Tiff Dwarf Bermuda grass and are big enough to play football on. The 14th green is 18,000 square feet. It is one of the best tracks in the Coachella Valley. This course has served as a Stage I PGA Tour qualifying site.

Play Policy and Fees: Public play is welcome. Green fees are seasonal, ranging from $35 during the off-season (summer) to $165 during the high season (winter). Call for rates. Carts are included. Reservations are recommended. This course is closed in October.

Tees and Yardage: *Men:* Tournament: yardage 7084, par 72, rating 74.0, slope 133; Championship: yardage 6702, par 72, rating 72.2, slope 128; Regular: yardage 6230, par 72, rating 70.1, slope 123; Seniors: yardage 5792, par 72, rating 68.0, slope 118; *Women:* Red: yardage 5273, par 72, rating 72.1, slope 125.

Tee Times: Reservations can be booked 10 days in advance.

Dress Code: Collared shirts are required. No jeans are allowed on the course. Soft spikes only.

Tournaments: Carts are required. A 30-player minimum is required to book a tournament.

Directions: Take the Cook Street exit off I-10 southeast of Palm Springs and drive south to Country Club Drive. Turn left and travel one-half mile to the club.

Contact: 1111 Desert Falls Parkway, Palm Desert, CA 92211, pro shop 760/340-4653, clubhouse 760/340-5646, www.desert-falls.com.

66 THE LAKES COUNTRY CLUB

Architect: Ted Robinson Sr., 1982
27 holes   **Private**

Coachella Valley Detail map, page 437

These well-bunkered courses have lots of water and spectacular views of the Santa Rosa Mountains. Two of the nines are set among the condos. They are similar in terrain and shot value, and are typical of Ted Robinson design: very beautiful with many water features.

Play Policy and Fees: Members and guests only.

Tees and Yardage: East/South—*Men:* Black: yardage 6620, par 72, rating 71.7, slope 129; Gold: yardage 6215, par 72, rating 69.8, slope 126; Silver: yardage 5671, par 72, rating 67.3, slope 120; *Women:* Bronze: yardage 4984, par 72, rating 68.5, slope 120. North/East—*Men:* Black: yardage 6361, par 72, rating 70.5, slope 129; Gold: yardage 5972, par 72, rating 68.6, slope 125; Silver: yardage 5392, par 72, rating 66.2, slope 116; *Women:* Bronze: yardage 4711, par 72, rating 68.0, slope 119. South/North—*Men:* Black: yardage 6631, par 72, rating 72.1, slope 128; Gold: yardage 6223, par 72, rating 70.2, slope 124; Silver: yardage 5687, par 72, rating 67.5, slope 120; *Women:* Bronze: yardage 5043, par 72, rating 69.6, slope 117.

Tee Times: Members can make reservations seven days in advance, and members with guests can make reservations three days in advance.

Dress Code: Appropriate golf attire and nonmetal spikes are required. Men's and women's shorts must be no more than four inches above the knee.

Tournaments: This course is not available for outside events.

Directions: Take the Cook Street exit off I-10 southeast of Palm Springs and drive south to Country Club Drive. Turn left and drive one-half mile to the course.

Contact: 161 Old Ranch Road, Palm Desert, CA 92211, pro shop 760/568-4321.

67 THE SPRINGS CLUB

Architect: Desmond Muirhead, 1975
18 holes   **Private**

Coachella Valley Detail map, page 437

At this course amidst an upscale residential community, water comes into play on 11 holes. The greens are heavily bunkered and undulating, and the tree-lined fairways are always nicely maintained.

Play Policy and Fees: Members and guests only. No reciprocal play is accepted. Guests must be accompanied by a club member.

Tees and Yardage: *Men:* Gray: yardage 6637, par 72, rating 71.9, slope 128; Blue: yardage 6279, par 72, rating 70.1, slope 124; White: yardage 5889, par 72, rating 68.0, slope 119; *Women:* Red: yardage 5614, par 72, rating 72.6, slope 127.

Tee Times: Reservations may be booked two days in advance.

Dress Code: Collared shirts and nonmetal spikes are required. Short shorts are not allowed.

Tournaments: This course is not available for outside events.

Directions: Take the Bob Hope Drive/Ramon Road exit off I-10 southeast of Palm Springs and drive south on Bob Hope Drive four miles to the club entrance on the right.

Contact: 1 Duke Drive, Rancho Mirage, CA 92270, pro shop 760/328-0590, clubhouse 760/324-8292, www.thespringsclub.com.

68 BIGHORN GOLF CLUB

Architect: Arthur Hills, 1991 (Mountains Course); Tom Fazio, 1999 (Canyons Course)
36 holes   **Private**

Coachella Valley Detail map, page 437

These dramatic desert courses are part **BEST** of an upscale private residential community. Carved into the Santa Rosa Mountains, with elevation changes of up to 400 feet, the courses provide spectacular close-up views of the surrounding mountains and canyon walls into which they were built. One of the best and most respected clubs in the United States, Bighorn hosted the PGA Tour Skins Game from 1992 through 1995, and The Battle at Bighorn in 2001 and 2002, when Jack Nicklaus and Tiger Woods played against Lee Trevino and Sergio Garcia. They are both extremely scenic, with rock formations jutting into fairways, panoramic vistas, and gurgling streams.

Play Policy and Fees: Members and guests only. No reciprocal play is accepted.

Tees and Yardage: The Canyons—*Men:* Gold: yardage 7131, par 72, rating 74.8, slope 141; Silver: yardage 6737, par 72, rating 72.6, slope 137; Member: yardage 6504, par 72, rating 71.8, slope 131; Blue: yardage 6319, par 72, rating 70.8, slope 129; White: yardage 5877, par 72, rating 68.9, slope 124; *Women:* Yellow: yardage 5145, par 72, rating 69.8, slope 123. The Mountains—*Men:* Gold: yardage 6874, par 72, rating 73.6, slope 143; Silver: yardage 6521, par 72, rating 71.7, slope 138; Member: yardage 6303, par 72, rating 70.9, slope 139; Blue: yardage 6151, par 72, rating 70.1, slope 132; White: yardage 5714, par 72, rating 68.3, slope 128; *Women:* Yellow: yardage 4971, par 72, rating 70.0, slope 122.

Tee Times: Not applicable.

Dress Code: Appropriate golf attire and non-metal spikes are required.

Tournaments: This course is not available for outside events.

Directions: From I-10 near Palm Desert, exit on Monterey Avenue. Drive south on Monterey Avenue/Highway 74. The club is 3.5 miles south on Highway 74.

Contact: 255 Palowet Drive, Palm Desert, CA 92260, pro shop 760/773-2468, clubhouse 760/341-4653, fax 760/776-7125, www.bighorngolf.com.

69 MARRIOTT'S DESERT SPRINGS RESORT AND SPA

Architect: Ted Robinson Sr., 1987 and 1988

36 holes   Resort $120–150

Coachella Valley Detail map, page 437

Both the Palms and Valley Courses are well maintained and fairly level. Players have ample

room for error off the tee, so swinging away with the driver is okay. For those who stray too far outside the generous fairways, you can find bunkers, lakes, and palm trees. These fun courses can give you a challenge but will not overwhelm the average golfer. Marriott's Desert Springs also offers an 18-hole putting course.

For reservations at the resort, call 760/341-2211.

Play Policy and Fees: Green fees for resort guests during peak season range from $120 weekdays to $150 weekends. All green fees include range balls and a cart. Please call for off-season rates. Twilight rates are offered.

Tees and Yardage: Palms—*Men:* Black: yardage 6761, par 72, rating 72.1, slope 130; Blue: yardage 6381, par 72, rating 70.3, slope 126; White: yardage 6143, par 72, rating 69.2, slope 123; *Women:* Red: yardage 5492, par 72, rating 71.9, slope 125. Valley—*Men:* Black: yardage 6627, par 72, rating 71.5, slope 127; Blue: yardage 6323, par 72, rating 70.1, slope 125; White: yardage 6023, par 72, rating 68.7, slope 122; *Women:* Red: yardage 5262, par 72, rating 70.2, slope 118.

Tee Times: Reservations can be made up to 60 days in advance for hotel guests and three days in advance for nonguests.

Dress Code: Appropriate attire and soft spikes are required.

Tournaments: Tournaments are accepted. Please inquire.

Directions: Take I-10 to Palm Desert. Exit at Cook Street a go south to Country Club Drive. Turn right on Country Club Drive to the entrance.

Contact: 74-855 Country Club Drive, Palm Desert, CA 92260, pro shop 760/341-1756, fax 760/341-1828, www.marriott.com.

70 PORTOLA COUNTRY CLUB

18 holes   Private

Coachella Valley Detail map, page 437

Situated on 27 acres inside a mobile home park, this par-3 course is somewhat rolling, with many lakes and water hazards.

Play Policy and Fees: Members and guests only.

Tees and Yardage: *Men:* Back: yardage 2134, par 54, rating n/a, slope n/a; *Women:* Forward: yardage 1820, par 54, rating n/a, slope n/a.

Tee Times: Reservations are not accepted. All play is on a first-come, first-served basis.

Dress Code: Golf attire and nonmetal spikes are mandatory.

Tournaments: This course is not available for outside events.

Directions: From I-10 southeast of Palm Springs, take the Cook exit and turn right on Country Club. Drive to Portola Avenue. Go left on Portola and follow it about one mile to the club.

Contact: 42-500 Portola Avenue, Palm Desert, CA 92260, pro shop 760/568-1592, fax 760/779-1761.

71 MARRIOTT'S RANCHO LAS PALMAS RESORT & COUNTRY CLUB

Architect: Ted Robinson Sr., 1976

27 holes   Semiprivate $99–109

Coachella Valley Detail map, page 437

The North nine is the longest and has the most hills. The South nine is the narrowest and threads through condominiums. The West nine is the shortest and most scenic, and it also has the most water. Numerous palm trees are spread throughout this well-maintained course. All are lots of fun to play and always nicely maintained.

For hotel reservations, call 760/341-2211.

Play Policy and Fees: Rates are seasonal. During peak season, green fees are $99 during the week, $109 weekends, including carts. Call for off-peak season rates. Twilight and super twilight rates are available.

Tees and Yardage: North/South—*Men:* Blue: yardage 6025, par 71, rating 67.1, slope 117; White: yardage 5662, par 71, rating 65.8, slope 114; *Women:* Red: yardage 5420, par 71, rating 71.8, slope 125. West/North—*Men:* Blue: yardage 6113, par 71, rating 67.8, slope 116; White: yardage 5677, par 71, rating 66.3, slope 113; *Women:* Red: yardage 5387, par 71, rat-

ing 71.6, slope 125. South/West—*Men:* Blue: yardage 6128, par 70, rating 67.8, slope 115; White: yardage 5725, par 70, rating 66.3, slope 112; *Women:* Red: yardage 5289, par 70, rating 73.6, slope 126.

Tee Times: Reservations may be booked seven days in advance.

Dress Code: For men, collared shirts are required. For women, shorts must be thigh-length. Tank tops, bathing suits, and denim are not permitted.

Tournaments: Available for outside tournaments on a limited basis. Call for information.

Directions: Southeast of Palm Springs, take the Bob Hope/Ramon Road exit off I-10. Drive five miles south to the resort entrance on the left.

Contact: 42-000 Bob Hope Drive, Rancho Mirage, CA 92270, pro shop 760/862-4551, fax 760/862-4582.

72 MONTEREY COUNTRY CLUB

Architect: Ted Robinson Sr., 1978

27 holes   Private $80

Coachella Valley Detail map, page 437

This tight target course has strategically placed bunkers and lots of water. The fairways are lined with palm trees and feature nice views of the Santa Rosa Mountains. Condos line most fairways.

Play Policy and Fees: Reciprocal play is accepted with members of other private American Golf–managed clubs. Reciprocal fees are $80 per person. Carts and range balls are included. Reservations are required.

Tees and Yardage: East/South—*Men:* Black: yardage 6005, par 71, rating 68.8, slope 121; Silver: yardage 5698, par 71, rating 67.7, slope 117; *Women:* Red: yardage 5231, par 71, rating 71.6, slope 124. South/West—*Men:* Black: yardage 6185, par 72, rating 69.6, slope 126; Silver: yardage 5876, par 72, rating 68.3, slope 123; *Women:* Red: yardage 5417, par 72, rating 72.9, slope 132. West/East—*Men:* Black: yardage 6108, par 71, rating 69.3, slope 125;

Silver: yardage 5790, par 71, rating 67.9, slope 122; *Women:* Red: yardage 5264, par 71, rating 71.6, slope 124.

Tee Times: Have your home professional make the arrangements.

Dress Code: Appropriate golf attire and nonmetal spikes are required.

Tournaments: Please inquire.

Directions: Take the Monterey Avenue exit off I-10 near Palm Desert and drive south four miles to the club.

Contact: 41-500 Monterey Avenue, Palm Desert, CA 92260, pro shop 760/346-1115, clubhouse 760/568-9311, www.montereycc.com.

73 CHAPARRAL COUNTRY CLUB

Architect: Ted Robinson Sr., 1979
18 holes   Private

Coachella Valley Detail map, page 437

Known as the "Little Monster," this tough executive course is well bunkered, with water on 13 holes. It is a shot-maker's course.

Play Policy and Fees: No reciprocal play is accepted. Guests must be accompanied by a member.

Tees and Yardage: *Men:* Blue: yardage 3916, par 60, rating 58.8, slope 97; White: yardage 3664, par 60, rating 57.7, slope 95; *Women:* Red: yardage 3103, par 60, rating 57.6, slope 89.

Tee Times: Reservations may be booked one week in advance.

Dress Code: Appropriate golf attire is required. Jeans and tank tops are not permitted.

Tournaments: This course is not available for outside events.

Directions: Take the Monterey Drive exit off I-10 near Palm Desert, then drive south to Country Club Drive. Turn left and drive to Portola Road. Turn right and travel 1.5 miles to the club.

Contact: 100 Chaparral Drive, Palm Desert, CA 92260, pro shop 760/340-1501, clubhouse 760/340-1893, fax 760/773-4893.

74 PALM VALLEY COUNTRY CLUB

Architect: Ted Robinson Sr., 1984/1986
36 holes   Private $42

Coachella Valley Detail map, page 437

The Championship Course has surprising undulation for a desert course and offers beautiful panoramic views of the area. The Challenge Course is a difficult short course, with water hazards coming into play on 15 holes. It's a tough challenge for mid- to low-handicap players. Both of these are lovely courses with nice views.

Play Policy and Fees: Reciprocal play is accepted on the Challenge Course only, at a rate of $42 year-round. The Championship Course is for members and guests only. Carts are included.

Tees and Yardage: Challenge—*Men:* Blue: yardage 4439, par 63, rating 61.5, slope 107; White: yardage 4234, par 63, rating 60.7, slope 102; *Women:* Gold: yardage 3427, par 64, rating 60.7, slope 101. Championship—*Men:* Blue: yardage 6545, par 72, rating 72.2, slope 131; Players: yardage 6324, par 72, rating 71.1, slope 129, White: yardage 6191, par 72, rating 70.5, slope 128; Silver: yardage 5731, par 72, rating 68.4, slope 119; *Women:* Gold: yardage 5294, par 72, rating 71.8, slope 129.

Tee Times: Reciprocators should have their club pro call to make arrangements.

Dress Code: Appropriate golf attire and nonmetal spikes are required.

Tournaments: This course is available for outside tournaments on Monday November–May. Off-season outside tournaments can be booked Monday–Friday.

Directions: Take the Washington Street exit off I-10 southeast of Palm Springs and drive south to Country Club Drive. Turn right and travel one mile to the club on the right.

Contact: 76-200 Country Club Drive, Palm Desert, CA 92260, pro shop 760/345-2742.

75 PALM DESERT RESORT COUNTRY CLUB

Architect: Joe Molleneaux, 1980
18 holes   **Semiprivate**   **$30–69**

🏌 📷 🍽 🍺 🛏 🚗 🍴

Coachella Valley Detail map, page 437

This course has fairly wide fairways, bent-grass greens, and nine lakes that come into play. It's well bunkered and in excellent condition. It challenges good and average players alike.

Play Policy and Fees: Green fees are seasonal, with peak season rates being $69 seven days. Carts are included. Off-season rates start as low as $30. Early bird and twilight rates are offered. Memberships are available.

Tees and Yardage: *Men:* Blue: yardage 6616, par 72, rating 71.1, slope 122; White: yardage 6343, par 72, rating 70.4, slope 119; Gold: yardage 5978, par 72, rating 68.8, slope 114; *Women:* Red: yardage 5462, par 72, rating 71.0, slope 121.

Tee Times: Reservations can be booked five days in advance.

Dress Code: Golfers are not allowed to wear tank tops or cutoffs. Nonmetal spikes are recommended.

Tournaments: A 40-player minimum is needed to book an event. Weekend shotgun tournaments must be approved by the homeowners' association.

Directions: Take the Washington Street exit off I-10 and drive south to Country Club Drive. Turn right and travel three-quarters of a mile to the club on the left.

Contact: 77-333 Country Club Drive, Palm Desert, CA 92260, pro shop 760/345-2791, clubhouse 760/345-2781, www.theresorter.com.

76 INDIAN RIDGE COUNTRY CLUB

Architect: Arnold Palmer, 1992 and 1999
36 holes   **Private**

🏌 📷 🍽 🚗 🍴

Coachella Valley Detail map, page 437

These courses are both typical Palmer designs, with lots of undulations and an abundance of water that seldom comes into play. Wide fairways are receptive to all golfers, and the mountain views are very nice. The newer Arroyo Course is more of a desert-style design, and it's particularly nicely landscaped. Besides the golf courses, Indian Ridge Country Club offers clay tennis courts and croquet. The Grove Course hosted the Bob Hope Classic in 1995, 1996, and 1997.

Play Policy and Fees: Members and guests only.

Tees and Yardage: Arroyo Course—*Men:* Gold: yardage 6915, par 72, rating 73.4, slope 129; Black: yardage 6671, par 72, rating 72.2, slope 126; Blue: yardage 6289, par 72, rating 70.5, slope 123; White: yardage 5914, par 72, rating 68.6, slope 118; *Women:* Green: yardage 5453, par 72, rating 71.5, slope 130; Silver: yardage 5146, par 72, rating 69.6, slope 123. Grove Course—*Men:* Gold: yardage 7070, par 72, rating 73.4, slope 137; Black: yardage 6735, par 72, rating 72.5, slope 132; Blue: yardage 6410, par 72, rating 70.9, slope 128; White: yardage 5030, par 72, rating 68.8, slope 122; *Women:* Green: yardage 5485, par 72, rating 72.2, slope 132; Silver: yardage 4923, par 72, rating 68.8, slope 126.

Tee Times: Members can make reservations seven days in advance.

Dress Code: Appropriate golf attire and nonmetal spikes are required.

Tournaments: This course is not available for outside events.

Directions: From I-10 southeast of Palm Springs and near Palm Desert, take the Washington Street exit. Take a right on Washington, then another right on Country Club. The entrance is on the left.

Contact: 76-375 Country Club Drive, Palm Desert, CA 92211, pro shop 760/772-7272, fax 760/772-7902, www.indianridgecc.com.

77 WOODHAVEN COUNTRY CLUB

Architect: Harold Heers Jr., 1985
18 holes   **Semiprivate**   **$65**

🏌 📷 🍽 🚗 🍴

Coachella Valley Detail map, page 437

This is a short but challenging course that presents narrow fairways, lots of trees lining the fairways, bunkers, small greens, and some water. Always in good condition, it is set among numerous condominiums.

Play Policy and Fees: Fees during peak season are $65 seven days, carts and range balls included. Twilight rates available. Call for off-season rates. The course is closed in October.

Tees and Yardage: *Men:* Blue: yardage 5794, par 70, rating 67.1, slope 118; *Women:* Red: yardage 5240, par 70, rating 70.0, slope 118.

Tee Times: Reservations can be booked four days in advance.

Dress Code: Collared shirts are required. No denim shorts are allowed on course.

Tournaments: Tournaments welcome.

Directions: Take the Washington Street exit off I-10 near Palm Desert and drive south three-quarters of a mile to the club on the right.

Contact: 41-555 Woodhaven Drive East, Palm Desert, CA 92211, pro shop 760/345-7513.

78 MOUNTAIN VISTA AT SUN CITY PALM DESERT

Architect: Billy Casper and Greg Nash, 1992 (Santa Rosa) and 2000 (San Gorgonio)

36 holes   Semiprivate $35-98

🏌 📷 🍴 🛺 🍺

Coachella Valley Detail map, page 437

Set within a Sun City retirement village, these are both spacious courses with receptive greens and few elevation changes. Most holes are bordered by homes. Water comes into play frequently on both courses, including several waterfalls. Both designs feature lovely views of the surrounding Santa Rosa, San Jacinto, and San Gorgonio mountain ranges. They are nicely landscaped with colorful plantings and always kept in excellent condition.

Play Policy and Fees: Green fees are $98 seven days a week during peak season, November–March, and go as low as $35 during off-peak season.

Tees and Yardage: Santa Rosa—*Men:* Black: yardage 6720, par 72, rating 72.3, slope 125; Gold: yardage 6162, par 72, rating 69.5, slope 119; Blue: yardage 5693, par 72, rating 67.2, slope 114;

Women: Red: yardage 5305, par 72, rating 70.7, slope 116. San Gorgonio—*Men:* Black: yardage 6669, par 72, rating 72.0, slope 128; Gold: yardage 6202, par 72, rating 69.7, slope 123; Blue: yardage 5635, par 72, rating 66.9, slope 118; *Women:* Red: yardage 5035, par 72, rating 68.2, slope 111.

Tee Times: Call two days in advance Monday–Thursday for reservations and seven days in advance for Friday–Sunday.

Dress Code: No denim is allowed on the course, and collared shirts are required.

Tournaments: A 16-player minimum is needed for tournament play.

Directions: Take I-10 southeast of Palm Springs to the Washington Street exit. Drive one-half mile to the course.

Contact: 38180 Del Webb Boulevard, Bermuda Dunes, CA 92203, pro shop 760/200-2200.

79 PALM DESERT COUNTRY CLUB

Architect: William F. Bell, 1962

27 holes   Semiprivate $50

🏌 📷 🍴 🛺 🍺

Coachella Valley Detail map, page 437

There is an 18-hole championship course and a nine-hole executive course here. Both are mature layouts designed by the prolific William F. Bell. The wide, tree-lined fairways are laid out well and challenging. The executive nine, like the championship course, is bordered by homes. Bunkers, trees, and flower beds help beautify the layouts. The executive nine consists of eight par-3s and one par-4.

Play Policy and Fees: Green fees are seasonal. During peak season, rates on the championship course are $50 seven days, carts included. Memberships are available.

Tees and Yardage: Championship—*Men:* Blue: yardage 6643, par 72, rating 70.9, slope 116; White: yardage 6370, par 72, rating 69.3, slope 111; *Women:* Red: yardage 5909, par 72, rating 73.7, slope 123. Executive—*Men and Women:* yardage 1280, par 28, rating n/a, slope n/a.

Tee Times: Reservations can be booked seven days in advance. Soft spikes are preferred.

Dress Code: Collared shirts are required. No denim is allowed on the course.

Tournaments: This course is available for outside tournaments.

Directions: Take the Washington Street exit off I-10, turn right, and drive 1.5 miles to Avenue of the States. Turn right and merge into California Drive and continue one mile to the club entrance.

Contact: 77-200 California Drive, Palm Desert, CA 92211, pro shop 760/345-2525.

80 SHADOW MOUNTAIN GOLF CLUB

Architect: Gene Sarazen, 1959
18 holes   Private $71

Coachella Valley Detail map, page 437

This short course is well bunkered, with some water and lots of palm trees. It's a challenging course for the average player. The 17th hole, which winds slightly uphill through rock gardens, is the signature hole on this well-hidden gem. The course is lined with 700 50-foot-tall palm trees, but it's so protected that it's the last place the wind blows or the rain falls. The course is walkable.

Play Policy and Fees: Reciprocal play is accepted with members of other private clubs at a rate of $71 in season, including cart. Please inquire for off-season rates.

Tees and Yardage: *Men:* White: yardage 5388, par 70, rating 66.3, slope 114; *Women:* Red: yardage 5200, par 71, rating 65.4, slope 113.

Tee Times: Reciprocal players should have their home professional make the arrangements.

Dress Code: Appropriate golf attire and non-metal spikes are required.

Tournaments: This course is not available for outside events.

Directions: Take the Monterey Avenue exit off I-10 southeast of Palm Springs, drive south to Highway 111 in Palm Desert, and turn left. At San Luis Rey Avenue, turn right and drive to the end of the road. Turn left into the club.

Contact: 73-800 Ironwood Street, Palm Desert, CA 92260, pro shop 760/346-8242.

81 THE RESERVE

Architect: Jay Morrish and Tom Weiskopf, 1998
18 holes   Private

Coachella Valley Detail map, page 437

This course was built on one of the last pristine sites in the desert. Built up against the mountains, the course features elevation changes subtle to the eye but dramatic in the way you must play the course. The slight elevations to some of the greens will find newcomers underclubbing. The fairways, for the most part, allow you to take out the driver, but a few holes give you the chance to hone your nerves. Is the risk worth the reward? The Reserve has three practice holes.

Play Policy and Fees: Members and guests only. No reciprocal play is accepted.

Tees and Yardage: *Men:* Black: yardage 7034, par 72, rating 73.5, slope 139, Players: yardage 6798, par 72, rating 72.2, slope 134; Gold: yardage 6554, par 72, rating 70.9, slope 131; Green: yardage 5946, par 72, rating 68.2, slope 122; *Women:* Red: yardage 5243, par 72, rating 70.8, slope 117.

Tee Times: Not applicable.

Dress Code: Appropriate golf attire and non-metal spikes are required.

Tournaments: No outside events are allowed.

Directions: From I-10 southeast of Palm Springs, take Highway 111 east to Portola Avenue. Take Portola south. The golf course entrance will be on your left.

Contact: 74001 Reserve Drive, Indio, CA 92210, pro shop 760/674-2240.

82 MARRAKESH COUNTRY CLUB

Architect: Ted Robinson Sr., 1983
18 holes   Private

Coachella Valley Detail map, page 437

This hilly course, with excellent mountain views, is in a community of 364 homes. The longest of the six par-4s is 304 yards, and the par-3s range 126–198 yards. The course is well bunkered and has four lakes and many trees, so it's a test. It plays much tougher than it looks. Players need every club in the bag on this fine 18-hole executive course.

Play Policy and Fees: Members and guests only.

Tees and Yardage: *Men:* Blue: yardage 3750, par 60, rating 57.4, slope 87; White: yardage 3614, par 60, rating 56.8, slope 86; *Women:* Red: yardage 3220, par 60, rating 57.8, slope 95.

Tee Times: Call the pro shop for availability of tee times.

Dress Code: Collared shirts are required, and metal spikes are not allowed. Bermuda-length shorts are acceptable.

Tournaments: This course is not available for outside events.

Directions: From Palm Desert, take I-10 to the Monterey Avenue exit. Take Monterey Avenue south to Country Club Drive and turn left, then proceed to Portola Avenue. Turn right on Portola Avenue to the club.

Contact: 47-000 Marrakesh Drive, Palm Desert, CA 92260; 47001 Portola Avenue, Palm Desert, CA 92260, pro shop 760/568-2660.

83 THE VINTAGE CLUB

Architect: Tom Fazio, 1981 (Mountain Course) and 1984 (Desert Course)

36 holes   Private

🏌️ 📷 🍴 🚃 ⛳

Coachella Valley Detail map, page 437

There are two Tom Fazio–designed jewels here. **BEST** The Desert Course is short but deceptive, requiring precise shot-making to very small greens. It has a Scottish flavor, with deep pot bunkers, sand, and shrubbery. The Mountain Course is a wide-open, easy-driving course with a British accent. It features deep pot bunkers, sprawling fairways, natural rock formations, citrus groves, indigenous shrubs, colorful flowers, and waterfalls. The 387-yard, par-4 16th hole is flanked by three lakes and two greenside waterfalls, while the scenic 126-yard, par-3 17th is fronted by a lake and affords a panoramic view. This club was used for the Senior PGA Tour's Vintage Invitational from 1981 to 1992.

Play Policy and Fees: Members and guests only.

Tees and Yardage: Mountain—*Men:* Black: yardage 7066, par 72, rating 74.2, slope 135; Gold: yardage 6566, par 72, rating 72.3, slope 130; Blue: yardage 6423, par 72, rating 70.5, slope 126; *Women:* Green: yardage 5663, par 72, rating 72.8, slope 126; Red: yardage 5166, par 72, rating 69.7, slope 121; Desert—*Men:* Gold: yardage 6301, par 72, rating 70.5, slope 130; Blue: yardage 5892, par 72, rating 68.8, slope 124; *Women:* Green: yardage 5664, par 72, rating 74.3, slope 132; Red: yardage 4770, par 72, rating 68.7, slope 121.

Tee Times: Not applicable.

Dress Code: Appropriate golf attire and non-metal spikes are required.

Tournaments: This course is not available for outside events.

Directions: Take the Monterey Avenue exit off I-10. Drive south to Highway 111 in Palm Desert and turn left. At Cook Street, turn right and drive one-half mile to the club at the end of the road.

Contact: 75-001 Vintage Drive West, Indian Wells, CA 92210, pro shop 760/862-2076, clubhouse 760/340-0500.

84 DESERT HORIZONS COUNTRY CLUB

Architect: Ted Robinson Sr., 1979

18 holes   Private

🏌️ 📷 🍴 🚃 ⛳

Coachella Valley Detail map, page 437

This very private championship course within an upscale residential community features an abundance of palm trees, sand, and water. In other words, it is very challenging. Beware of the ninth hole. It's a long par-3 brute that demands a 180-yard carry over water to a three-tiered, hourglass green. The green is bunkered on the left, with water on the right. The facility also features an 18-hole putting course complete with water and bunkers.

Play Policy and Fees: Members and guests only. No reciprocal play is accepted.

Tees and Yardage: *Men:* Gold: yardage 6813,

par 72, rating 71.7, slope 124; Blue: yardage 6163, par 72, rating 70.1, slope 119; White: yardage 5792, par 72, rating 68.5, slope 116; *Women:* Red: yardage 5498, par 72, rating 71.8, slope 126.

Tee Times: Not applicable.

Dress Code: Appropriate golf attire and non-metal spikes are required.

Tournaments: This course is not available for outside events.

Directions: Travel one mile west of Indian Wells on Highway 111. At Desert Horizons Drive, turn north and drive to the club.

Contact: 44-900 Desert Horizons Drive, Indian Wells, CA 92210, pro shop 760/340-4651, www.deserthorizons.com.

85 THE GOLF RESORT AT INDIAN WELLS

Architect: Ted Robinson Sr., 1986

36 holes   Resort $120–130

Coachella Valley Detail map, page 437

Both 18-hole courses here were designed by Ted Robinson. They feature spacious greens, rolling fairways, and lush, parkland settings. There are many parallel fairways, but plenty of mounding separates them. Spread over 400 acres, these 36 holes provide a challenging yet fair test for golfers of all abilities. Beautiful plantings and water features beautify both layouts. During the 1990s, the Senior Tour played here twice, and the California State Open was held here three times. When in doubt, know that the greens break toward Indio, to the east. On distance sprinkler heads, lines like "Tiger who?" appear. These are two of the most enjoyable resort courses in the California desert.

The resort has golf packages with the Hyatt Grand Champions Resort & Spa (760/341-1000), Indian Wells Resort Hotel (760/345-6466), Miramonte Resort (800/237-2926), and Renaissance Esmeralda Resort & Spa (760/773-4444).

Play Policy and Fees: During peak season, green fees are $120 Monday–Thursday, $130

Friday–Sunday. Rates include cart and range balls. Other seasonal rates vary, please call for details. Twilight rates are available. Special rates are often posted online.

Tees and Yardage: East Course—*Men:* Championship: yardage 6631, par 72, rating 72.1, slope 133; Regular: yardage 6232, par 72, rating 70.1, slope 131; *Women:* Forward: yardage 5616, par 72, rating 71.0, slope 127. West Course—*Men:* Championship: yardage 6500, par 72, rating 71.6, slope 130; Regular: yardage 6157, par 72, rating 69.9, slope 128; *Women:* Forward: yardage 5408, par 72, rating 71.5, slope 118.

Tee Times: Reservations may be booked 14 days in advance.

Dress Code: Tee shirts, gym clothes, denim, and swimwear are not allowed. Soft spikes only.

Tournaments: This course is available for outside tournaments. At least 60 days advance notice is required.

Directions: From I-10 near Palm Springs, take the Cook Street exit three miles to Highway 111. Turn left on Highway 111 to Indian Wells Lane.

Contact: 44-500 Indian Wells Lane, Indian Wells, CA 92210, pro shop 760/346-4653, fax 760/340-1035, www.indianwells.org, www.golfresortatindianwells.com.

86 ELDORADO COUNTRY CLUB

Architect: Lawrence Hughes, 1957; redesign Tom Fazio, 2003

18 holes   Private

Coachella Valley Detail map, page 437

This course was dug up and completely remodeled by Tom Fazio in 2003. The routing stayed the same, but new grasses were laid throughout, including fairways, tees, and greens, giving new life to this layout that was first built in 1957 and was used in the Bob Hope Classic rotation for almost 30 years.

Play Policy and Fees: Members and guests only

Tees and Yardage: *Men:* Black: yardage 6739, par 72, rating 72.5, slope 131; Blue: yardage

6514, par 72, rating 71.5, slope 128; White: yardage 6206, par 72, rating 70.1, slope 125; Gold: yardage 5463, par 72, rating 66.7, slope 118; *Women:* Silver: yardage 5280, par 72, rating 71.7, slope 120.

Tee Times: Not applicable.

Dress Code: Proper golf attire and nonmetal spikes are mandatory. No short shorts are allowed on the course.

Tournaments: This course is not available for outside events.

Directions: Take the Monterey Avenue exit off I-10. Drive south to Highway 111 in Palm Desert and turn left. At Eldorado Drive, turn right and drive one-half mile to Fairway Drive. Turn right and drive half a block to the club on the left.

Contact: 46000 Fairway Drive, Indian Wells, CA 92210, pro shop 760/346-8081.

87 INDIAN WELLS COUNTRY CLUB

Architect: Harry Rainville, 1955; redesign Ted Robinson Sr., 1984

36 holes   **Private**   **$225**

Coachella Valley Detail map, page 437

The two courses here are distinctly different. The Classic 18 is the oldest and has tree-lined fairways. It is a course that requires solid decision-making and shot-making. The Cove is a newer design by Ted Robinson and is a bit more generous in the landing areas. Choose your poison—the courses are not overly long, by today's standards, but they demand accuracy and a deft short game. The Classic Course is part of the Bob Hope Classic rotation each year.

Play Policy and Fees: Reciprocal play is accepted with members of other ClubCorp facilities. Otherwise, members and guests only. During the season (November–May), reciprocal fees are $225. Inquire about off-season guest fees. Rates include cart and use of the range.

Tees and Yardage: Classic—*Men:* Black: yardage 6478, par 72, rating 71.0, slope 127; White: yardage 6095, par 72, rating 69.1, slope 124; *Women:* Red: yardage 5665, par 72, rating 73.5,

slope 133. Cove—*Men:* Black: yardage 6558, par 72, rating 71.5, slope 121; White: yardage 6229, par 72, rating 70.1, slope 117; *Women:* Red: yardage 5640, par 72, rating 72.6, slope 124.

Tee Times: Members can book tee times 48 hours in advance.

Dress Code: Bermuda shorts no higher than the knee, tucked-in collared shirts, and nonmetal spikes are required.

Tournaments: This course is available for tournaments on a limited basis in summer months.

Directions: From I-10, take the Washington Avenue exit. Go south to Highway 111, then west to Club Drive.

Contact: 46-000 Club Drive, Indian Wells, CA 92210, pro shop 760/345-2561, clubhouse 760/345-2561, fax 760/360-4856.

88 RANCHO LA QUINTA COUNTRY CLUB

Architect: Robert Trent Jones Jr., 1993; Jerry Pate, 2000

36 holes   **Private**

Coachella Valley Detail map, page 437

These two courses are very scenic and feature wide, rolling fairways, lots of water in play, ample sand, and some elevated greens that require precise approach shots. Both layouts boast great views of the Santa Rosa Mountains. Colorful plantings and water features are everywhere. The Jones Course hosted the PGA Tour Skins Game from 1996 to 1998. Winners included Fred Couples, Tom Lehman, and Mark O'Meara.

Play Policy and Fees: Members and guests only. Rare reciprocal play.

Tees and Yardage: Jones—*Men:* Gold: yardage 7063, par 72, rating 73.6, slope 134; Blue: yardage 6452, par 72, rating 71.2, slope 129; White: yardage 5986, par 72, rating 69.2, slope 124; *Women:* Red: yardage 5282, par 72, rating 71.5, slope 126. Pate—*Men:* Gold: yardage 6972, par 72, rating 74.0, slope 140; Blue: yardage 6476, par 72, rating 71.7, slope 135; White: yardage 5941, par 72, rating 69.2, slope 129; *Women:* Red: yardage 5224, par 72, rating 70.9, slope 126.

Tee Times: Not applicable.

Dress Code: Appropriate golf attire and non-metal spikes are required.

Tournaments: This course is not available for outside events.

Directions: From Highway 111 in La Quinta, drive one mile south on Washington Street to the course.

Contact: 79325 Cascades Circle, La Quinta, CA 92253, pro shop 760/777-7799, fax 760/777-7785, www.rancholaquinta.com.

89 EMERALD DESERT GOLF & RV RESORT

Architect: James Laier Jr., 1990

9 holes   **Public**   **$12–33**

Coachella Valley Detail map, page 437

This nine-hole executive course features six lakes, bent-grass greens protected by numerous sand traps, and narrow fairways. The par-4, 263-yard sixth hole demands good shot placement. The steeply elevated green is protected front and left by water. It's nicely landscaped and can offer a fun round with some nice mountain views.

Play Policy and Fees: For non-RV park play, November–April, green fees are $22 for nine holes and $33 for 18 holes. For golfers staying at the RV park, rates are $12 for nine holes, $18 for 18 holes weekdays, on weekends $17 for nine and $28 for 18 holes. Call for discounted off-season rates. Electric carts are $12/$18, and pull carts are $2.

Tees and Yardage: *Men:* yardage 1246, par 31, rating n/a, slope n/a; *Women:* yardage 960, par 32, rating n/a, slope n/a.

Tee Times: Reservations are not required, but they are recommended November–April. Tee times may be booked up to three days in advance.

Dress Code: Proper golf attire and nonmetal spikes are required.

Tournaments: This course is available for outside tournaments April–November only. Two weeks advance notice is required.

Directions: From I-10, take the Monterey Av-

enue exit near Palm Desert to Frank Sinatra Drive. Go east approximately four miles to the course.

Contact: 76-000 Frank Sinatra Drive, Palm Desert, CA 92260, pro shop 760/345-4770, fax 760/345-3471, www.emeralddesert.com.

90 INDIO GOLF COURSE

Architect: Lawrence Hughes, 1964

18 holes   **Public**   **$15**

Coachella Valley Detail map, page 437

This great little track is one of the better par-3 courses in the country. The holes range 120–230 yards, so bring all your irons. One lake intersects three or four holes, depending on your shot. With two holes over 200 yards, it's tougher than it looks. A fun round!

Play Policy and Fees: Green fees are $15 for 18 holes. Carts are available for $14. The course is fully lighted and open until 10 P.M. Monday–Friday.

Tees and Yardage: *Men:* White: yardage 3004, par 54, rating 54.1, slope 77; *Women:* Red: yardage 2662, par 54, rating 56.3, slope 80.

Tee Times: Reservations may be booked three days in advance.

Dress Code: No tank tops are allowed on the course.

Tournaments: This course is available for tournaments.

Directions: Take the Jackson Street exit off I-10 near Indio, drive north to Avenue 42, and turn right to the course.

Contact: 83-040 Avenue 42, Indio, CA 92202, pro shop 760/347-9156, fax 760/347-5282.

91 LANDMARK GOLF CLUB

Architect: Landmark Golf Company, Schmidt Curley Golf Design, 1999

36 holes   **Public**   **$55–145**

Coachella Valley Detail map, page 437

Landmark Golf Club is a 36-hole facility in the foothills of the Indio Hills. The designs feature constant elevation change, undulating greens, and views ranging from the San Gorgonios Mountain to the Chocolate Mountains. Both are heavily bunkered, so course management is a must. The bridges at Landmark are crafted from vintage railroad cars. Aside from the tournament tees, the two courses are very similar in length and character, with the North design being a bit easier on women. Landmark Golf Club has been host of the PGA Tour Skins Game. Winners have included Greg Norman, Colin Montgomerie, Mark O'Meara, and Fred Couples. These are two of the better public courses in the Coachella Valley.

Play Policy and Fees: Green fees vary seasonally, ranging from $55 on weekdays in July to $145 on weekends in January, February, and March. Call for more information about fees. This is a daily fee facility, and all rates include range balls and golf carts.

Tees and Yardage: Skins North—*Men:* Tournament: yardage 7060, par 72, rating 73.7, slope 137; Championship: yardage 6511, par 72, rating 71.4, slope 132; Regular: yardage 5870, par 72, rating 68.5, slope 125; *Women:* Forward: yardage 5067, par 72, rating 69.7, slope 124. Skins South—*Men:* Tournament: yardage 7229, par 72, rating 75.1, slope 140; Championship: yardage 6500, par 72, rating 71.6, slope 133; Regular: yardage 5905, par 72, rating 68.9, slope 126; *Women:* Forward: yardage 5097, par 72, rating 71.0, slope 129.

Tee Times: Reservations are accepted up to one month in advance.

Dress Code: Collared shirts, Bermuda-length shorts, and nonmetal spikes are required. No denim permitted.

Tournaments: An eight-player minimum is required to book an event. Tournaments should be booked eight months in advance. The banquet facility can accommodate up to 350 people.

Directions: From I-10 heading east to Indio, take the Golf Center Parkway exit and head north one mile. The course is on the right.

Contact: 84-000 Landmark Parkway, Indio, CA 92203, pro shop 760/775-2000, fax 760/775-1988, www.landmarkgc.com.

92 PALM ROYALE COUNTRY CLUB

Architect: Ted Robinson Sr., 1985
18 holes   **Public**   **$16–28**

Coachella Valley Detail map, page 437

This is a short par-3 course with water on nine holes. It's a scaled-down version of the Marriott Desert Springs courses, with palms backing the greens, loads of bunkers, grass moguls, and water hazards. The longest hole is 150 yards, the shortest 80 yards. Great practice course and fun for the family.

Play Policy and Fees: Green fees are $28 seven days in peak season and as low as $16 in the off-peak seasons. This course is closed the first two weeks of October.

Tees and Yardage: *Men:* Back: yardage 1992, par 54, rating n/a, slope n/a; *Women:* Forward: yardage 1689, par 54, rating n/a, slope n/a.

Tee Times: Reservations can be booked three days in advance in season and seven days in advance off-season.

Dress Code: No tank tops are allowed on the course. Soft spikes only.

Tournaments: This course is available for outside tournaments.

Directions: Take I-10 and exit at Washington Street near La Quinta. Follow Washington Street for about three-quarters of a mile to the club at the intersection of Washington and Fred Waring Road.

Contact: 78-259 Indigo Drive, La Quinta, CA 92253, pro shop 760/345-9701.

93 BERMUDA DUNES COUNTRY CLUB

Architect: William F. Bell, 1957
27 holes   **Private**

Coachella Valley Detail map, page 437

The Classic Course, which is the original 18-hole layout here, is one of the courses used in the Bob Hope Classic rotation. Since the course is private, watching the tournament is the only time many golfers have to see this club. These are not typical desert courses. They offer rolling hills with an abundance of palm trees dotting the fairways. There are also some lovely water features. Expect a lot of variation from hole to hole. Of the three loops, the Classic 18 is toughest, requiring more shot-making ability and sound decisions. They are all extremely well conditioned, particularly in peak season at tournament time.

Play Policy and Fees: Members and guests only. The course is closed in October.

Tees and Yardage: Classic 1/Lake—*Men:* Black: yardage 6716, par 72, rating 72.3, slope 127; Blue: yardage 6360, par 72, rating 70.6, slope 123; White: yardage 5844, par 72, rating 68.6, slope 120; *Women:* Gold: yardage 5416, par 72, rating 72.1, slope 121. Classic 2/Lake—*Men:* Black: yardage 6749, par 72, rating 72.7, slope 130; Blue: yardage 6434, par 72, rating 71.2, slope 128; White: yardage 5931, par 72, rating 69.5, slope 127; *Women:* Gold: yardage 5398, par 72, rating 72.1, slope 120. Classic—*Men:* Black: yardage 6907, par 72, rating 73.5, slope 129; Blue: yardage 6542, par 72, rating 71.6, slope 126; White: yardage 5997, par 72, rating 69.7, slope 123; *Women:* Gold: yardage 5448, par 72, rating 72.0, slope 122.

Tee Times: Not applicable.

Dress Code: Appropriate golf attire and non-metal spikes are required.

Tournaments: This course is not available for outside events.

Directions: Southeast of Palm Springs, take the Washington Street exit off I-10 and drive south to Avenue 42. Turn left and drive one mile to the club.

Contact: 42-360 Adams Street, Bermuda Dunes, CA 92201, pro shop 760/345-2771, fax 760/345-8697, www.bermudadunescc.org.

94 HERITAGE PALMS GOLF CLUB

Architect: Arthur Hills, 1996
18 holes   Semiprivate $95

Coachella Valley Detail map, page 437

Heritage Palms is a manicured golf course

with spectacular mountain views. The hardest hole is the fourth, a par-4 with a lake running down the left side. But don't miss right—the ball may find a trap, or worse yet, out-of-bounds. It is very women-friendly from the forward tees.

Play Policy and Fees: During peak season green fees are $95 seven days, cart and range balls included. Twilight and replay rates are available.

Tees and Yardage: *Men:* Championship: yardage 6727, par 72, rating 71.9, slope 124; Regular: yardage 6293, par 72, rating 69.9, slope 119; Middle: yardage 5577, par 72, rating 66.6, slope 111; *Women:* Forward: yardage 4784, par 72, rating 66.7, slope 108.

Tee Times: Reservations can be booked seven days in advance.

Dress Code: Collared shirts are a must. No denim is allowed on the course and shorts must be Bermuda-length. Soft spikes are preferred.

Tournaments: A 16-player minimum is needed to book a tournament. Carts are required. The banquet facility can accommodate 500 people.

Directions: From I-10, take the Jefferson Street exit and head south. Make a left on Fred Waring Drive; the course is on the right.

Contact: 44-291 Heritage Palms Drive, South Indio, CA 92201, pro shop 760/772-7334, fax 760/360-4124.

95 THE OASIS COUNTRY CLUB

Architect: David Rainville, 1984
18 holes   Semiprivate $25–50

Coachella Valley Detail map, page 437

This is a fun and challenging executive course with some of the finest greens to be found in the desert. There are 22 lakes guarding six par-4s and 12 par-3s.

Play Policy and Fees: Memberships are available, but public play is welcome. In-season green fees run $50, carts included. Twilight rates available. The course is closed in October. During the summer months green fees can run as low as $25.

Tees and Yardage: *Men:* Black: yardage 3489,

par 60, rating 56.2, slope 92; *Women:* White: yardage 3118, par 60, rating 56.9, slope 85.

Tee Times: Reservations can be booked three days in advance.

Dress Code: Appropriate golf attire and non-metal spikes are required.

Tournaments: This course is available for outside tournaments.

Directions: Take the Washington Street exit off I-10 and drive south to Avenue 42. Turn right and drive one mile to Casbah Way. Turn left to the club.

Contact: 42-330 Casbah Way, Palm Desert, CA 92211, pro shop 760/345-2715, clubhouse 760/345-5661.

96 IRONWOOD COUNTRY CLUB

Architect: Desmond Muirhead (South Course), 1973, Ted Robinson Sr. (North Course), 1975; redesign John Fought (both), 2002 and 2004

36 holes   **Private**

Coachella Valley Detail map, page 437

Situated above the desert floor, the South Course at Ironwood is very scenic. There are several tough holes from the back tees, hence its 74.8 rating. The North Course is also very scenic, with mountain and desert valley views. There are some water hazards and the fairways are lined with condos and homes, but it isn't as tough as the South Course, which has hosted qualifying rounds for the U.S. Open.

Play Policy and Fees: Members and guests only. No reciprocal play is accepted.

Tees and Yardage: North—*Men:* Championship: yardage 6065, par 70, rating 69.3, slope 127; Regular: yardage 5699, par 70, rating 67.6, slope 123; *Women:* Forward: yardage 5248, par 70, rating 71.3, slope 124. South—*Men:* Professional: yardage 7256, par 72, rating 74.8, slope 130; Championship: yardage 6902, par 72, rating 73.0, slope 127; Regular: yardage 6489, par 72, rating 71.5, slope 124; *Women:* Forward: yardage 5608, par 72, rating 74.2, slope 131.

Tee Times: Not applicable.

Dress Code: Appropriate golf attire and non-metal spikes are required.

Tournaments: This course is not available for outside events.

Directions: Take the Monterey Drive exit off I-10 southeast of Palm Springs and drive south to Highway 111. Turn left and drive to Portola Avenue. Turn right and drive about two miles to the club.

Contact: 73-735 Irontree Drive, Palm Desert, CA 92260, pro shop 760/346-0551, fax 760/773-4858, www.ironwoodcountryclub.com.

97 LA QUINTA RESORT & CLUB, DUNES COURSE

Architect: Pete Dye, 1981

18 holes   **Resort**   **$50–160**

Coachella Valley Detail map, page 437

This course is set in a dramatic landscape with wonderful views of the nearby mountains. It is one of the top resort designs in the country. The layout is heavily bunkered, with Dye's signature railroad ties used to shore up tee boxes and greens, and lots of water in play. Solid shot-making is essential to scoring, particularly approach shots to the well-guarded greens. The PGA Tour Qualifying School has been held on this course many times. But even though it is a test to the pros from the tournament tees, it is very playable from the resort tees, particularly for women.

For reservations at the award-winning La Quinta Resort, call 800/598-3828.

Play Policy and Fees: Fees vary seasonally $50–160. Golf and lodging packages and other discounts are available for hotel guests. Fees include cart and use of the driving range.

Tees and Yardage: *Men:* Tournament: yardage 6747, par 72, rating 73.1, slope 137; Championship: yardage 6230, par 72, rating 70.1, slope 124; Middle: yardage 5748, par 72, rating 67.1, slope 114; *Women:* Forward: yardage 4997, par 72, rating 68.9, slope 114.

Tee Times: Priority is given to guests staying

at La Quinta Resort & Club, who can book one year in advance. Nonguests may book three days in advance, and with an additional fee up to 30 days in advance.

Dress Code: Appropriate golf attire and non-metal spikes are required. Dress code is strictly enforced.

Tournaments: Tournaments are welcome. The tournament office can be reached at 760/564-7660.

Directions: Take the Washington Street exit off I-10 near La Quinta. Drive south past Highway 111 to Avenue 50 and turn right. Continue past Eisenhower Drive to the gate and follow the road to the club.

Contact: 50-200 Vista Bonita, La Quinta, CA 92253, pro shop 760/564-7686, clubhouse 760/564-7610, www.laquintaresort.com.

98 LA QUINTA RESORT & CLUB, MOUNTAIN COURSE

Architect: Pete Dye, 1980

18 holes   **Resort**   **$75–235**

Coachella Valley Detail map, page 437

We name this course among our top picks in the state, and deservedly so. One of the best courses in the desert, the Mountain Course is a challenging layout noted for pot bunkers, rock formations, sand, and water. The large, undulating greens are set naturally against the mountains. Accuracy is the key. Watch for the par-3 16th hole: The green is surrounded by mountain rocks. This course has been the venue for the World Cup, the PGA National Club Pro Championships, and the California State Open. Many golf pros rate it the top course in the desert. Fred Couples holds the course record with a 63. Like the Dunes Course, even though this design is a true test for the professionals, it is a fun layout for resort guests.

For reservations at the award-winning La Quinta Resort, call 800/598-3878

Play Policy and Fees: Fees vary seasonally $75–235. Golf and lodging packages and other discounts are available for hotel guests. Fees include cart and use of the driving range.

Tees and Yardage: *Men:* Tournament: yardage 6756, par 72, rating 74.1, slope 140; Championship: yardage 6320, par 72, rating 71.5, slope 130; Middle: yardage 5405, par 72, rating 67.0, slope 113; *Women:* Forward: yardage 5005, par 72, rating 71.0, slope 123.

Tee Times: Priority is given to guests staying at La Quinta Resort & Club, who can book one year in advance. Nonguests may book three days in advance, and with an additional fee up to 30 days in advance.

Dress Code: Appropriate golf attire and soft spikes required. Dress code is strictly enforced.

Tournaments: This course is available for outside tournaments.

Directions: Take the Washington Street exit off I-10 southeast of Palm Springs. Drive south past Highway 111 to Avenue 50 and turn right. Drive past Eisenhower Drive to the gate and follow the road to the club.

Contact: 50-200 Vista Bonita, La Quinta, CA 92253, pro shop 760/564-7686, clubhouse 760/564-7610, www.laquintaresort.com.

99 LA QUINTA RESORT & CLUB, CITRUS COURSE

Architect: Pete Dye, 1987

18 holes   **Private**

Coachella Valley Detail map, page 437

This is a level course carved out of a citrus orchard, and it is anything but a lemon. In fact, this is one of the more scenic courses in the area. A typically challenging Pete Dye design, the course features rolling contours, bent-grass greens, and scenic views of the Santa Rosa Mountains. This layout has plenty of character, with a mix of sand and water, but it's more forgiving than the neighboring Mountain and Dunes Courses. Lee Trevino holds the course record with a 64.

For reservations at the La Quinta Resort, call 800/598-3828.

Play Policy and Fees: Reciprocal play is accepted only if accompanied by a member at Citrus.

Tees and Yardage: *Men:* Black: yardage 7151, par 72, rating 74.1, slope 132; Blue: yardage 6811, par 72, rating 72.4, slope 128; White: yardage 6396, par 72, rating 70.3, slope 123; *Women:* Gold: yardage 5641, par 72, rating 72.8, slope 129; Red: yardage 5326, par 72, rating 70.9, slope 126.

Tee Times: Reciprocators should have their club pro call to make arrangements.

Dress Code: Appropriate golf attire and non-metal spikes are required.

Tournaments: This course is not available for outside events.

Directions: Take the Jefferson Street exit off I-10 and drive south for three miles to the course.

Contact: 50-503 Jefferson Street, La Quinta, CA 92253, pro shop 760/564-7620.

100 LA QUINTA COUNTRY CLUB

Architect: Lawrence Hughes, 1959;
redesign Billy Bell Jr., 2000

18 holes   **Private**   **$42.50**

Coachella Valley Detail map, page 437

This mature, immaculately maintained course has tree-lined fairways, lakes, bunkers, and undulating greens. The emphasis is on driving accuracy. La Quinta has been used in the Bob Hope Classic since 1964 and is one of the top courses in the desert. It is said that President Dwight D. Eisenhower first became devoted to golf on this course.

Play Policy and Fees: During peak season, members and guests only. After May, reciprocal play is accepted with members of other private clubs at a rate of $42.50 to walk. Carts are $20. The course is closed in October.

Tees and Yardage: *Men:* Classic: yardage 7060, par 72, rating 74.2, slope 136; Long: yardage 6554, par 72, rating 71.8, slope 131; Middle: yardage 5786, par 72, rating 67.8.3, slope 124;

Women: Forward: yardage 5338, par 72, rating 71.5, slope 124.

Tee Times: Reciprocal players should have their home professional call to make arrangements.

Dress Code: Appropriate golf attire and non-metal spikes are required.

Tournaments: This course is not available for outside events.

Directions: Take the Washington Street exit off I-10 near La Quinta. Drive south for six miles to Avenue 50 and turn right. Drive one mile to the club on the right.

Contact: 77-750 Avenue 50 (P.O. Box 99), La Quinta, CA 92253, pro shop 760/564-4151, fax 760/564-6396.

101 INDIAN SPRINGS GOLF AND COUNTRY CLUB

Architect: John Gurley and Hoagy Carmichael, 1960;
redesign David Ginkel, 2000

27 holes   **Semiprivate**   **$39–89**

Coachella Valley Detail map, page 437

This layout was completely remodeled in 2000, with extensive work done to tees, greens, and fairways. Plus, a new nine-hole par-3 course was added. Great mountain views, colorful flowers and plantings, and enough water in play to keep things interesting define the characteristics of this course. Everything is in front of you, and landing zones are generous. All you have to do is execute!

Play Policy and Fees: Rates are seasonal, so please check ahead. During peak season, green fees on the regulation course are $79 weekdays, $89 weekends. During off-peak seasons, fees range $39–79. Fees include a cart. Rates on the nine-hole par-3 course are $15. Twilight rates are offered, as are memberships.

Tees and Yardage: *Men:* Gold: yardage 6711, par 72, rating 72.1, slope 126; White: yardage 6052, par 72, rating 68.8, slope 121; *Women:* Burgundy: yardage 5601, par 72, rating 70.7, slope 120.

Tee Times: Reservations may be booked seven days in advance.

Dress Code: Golf shirts are required. Soft spikes only.

Tournaments: This course is available for outside tournaments.

Directions: Take the Jefferson Street exit off I-10 southeast of Palm Springs and drive south about 2.5 miles to the course.

Contact: 46080 Jefferson Street, La Quinta, CA 92253, pro shop 760/775-3360, www.indianspringsgc.com.

102 TRADITION GOLF CLUB

Architect: Arnold Palmer and Ed Seay, 1998

27 holes   **Private**

Coachella Valley Detail map, page 437

In an upscale residential community abutting the Santa Rosa Mountains, this layout is traditional, yet unusual in that is has five par-5s and five par-3s. The signature hole is the 17th, a short par-4 set 150 feet above the green. Looking down from the tee, players see a lake that guards the left side and the mountains that guard the right. An accurate drive is a must. In general, this course offers generous fairways but punishes those players who miss the greens. In addition to its 18-hole course, the Tradition Golf Club has a nine-hole practice course of all par-3s. To read about the rich history of this property and Hacienda del Gato, which dates back to 1902, visit the website.

Play Policy and Fees: Members and guests only. All guests must be accompanied by a member.

Tees and Yardage: *Men:* Palmer: yardage 6925, par 72, rating 72.8, slope 140; Tradition: yardage 6530, par 72, rating 71.0, slope 136; Deacon: yardage 6163, par 72, rating 69.4, slope 130; *Women:* Charger: yardage 5545, par 72, rating 72.3, slope 131.

Tee Times: Not applicable.

Dress Code: Appropriate golf attire and non-metal spikes are mandatory.

Tournaments: This course is not available for outside events.

Directions: Take I-10 to the Washington Street exit to La Quinta. Go south on Washington Street and follow it six miles to the course.

Contact: 78505 Old Avenue 52, La Quinta, CA 92253, pro shop 760/564-1067, www.traditiongolfclub.net.

103 INDIAN PALMS COUNTRY CLUB

Architect: J. Cochran and H. Detweiler, 1948; renovated 2002 (Indian Palms), 2003 (Mountain), and 2004 (Royal)

27 holes   **Semiprivate**   **$67**

Coachella Valley Detail map, page 437

This facility is the centerpiece of a residential community. The original nine-hole course, called Indian Palms, was built in 1948 by world-famous aviatrix Jackie Cochran, whose ranch served as a retreat for the rich and famous of the 1940s and '50s. The Mountain and the Royal nines were built around 1980. The Royal has eight holes where water comes into play. All the courses have mature trees and natural growth along gently rolling terrain, leading to elevated greens. Dwight D. Eisenhower stayed at Indian Palms to write his memoirs. All three nines have been renovated, including new tees, greens, sand, and water features. Note: Because of the renovations, the yardage and ratings are subject to change.

Play Policy and Fees: Green fees vary seasonally. During peak season, rates are $67, carts included. Call for off-season rates. Twilight and super twilight rates are offered. Memberships are available.

Tees and Yardage: Indian/Mountain—*Men:* Blue: yardage 6633, par 71, rating 72.7, slope 125; White: yardage 6199, par 71, rating 70.1, slope 122; *Women:* Red: yardage 5859, par 71, rating 74.1, slope 120. Mountain/Royal—*Men:* Blue: yardage 6566, par 71, rating 72.2, slope 129; White: yardage 6014, par 71, rating 69.1, slope 124; *Women:* Red: yardage 5622, par 71, rating 72.1, slope 122. Royal/Indian—*Men:* Blue: yardage 6771, par 71, rating 73.2, slope 123; White: yardage 6191, par 71, rating 70.4, slope

116; *Women:* Red: yardage 5547, par 71, rating 72.1, slope 119.

Tee Times: Reservations are recommended and may be booked seven days in advance. Hotel guests may book 60 days in advance.

Dress Code: Collared shirts and nonmetal spikes are required. No cutoffs, gym shorts, or tank tops are allowed.

Tournaments: Outside tournaments and events are welcome.

Directions: Take the Monroe Street/Central Indio exit off I-10 near Indio. Drive south on Monroe for 2.5 miles to the course.

Contact: 48630 Monroe Street, Indio, CA 92201, pro shop 760/347-2326, fax 760/775-4447, www.indianpalms.com.

104 THE PLANTATION GOLF CLUB

Architect: Brian Curley and Fred Couples, 1998
18 holes   Private

Coachella Valley Detail map, page 437

This Brian Curley–Fred Couples design is situated on the flat desert floor, but subtle creative mounding and bunkering make it a compelling test of golf, one of the very best in the area. Couples's influence on the design is reflected in his affection for Augusta National and Riviera. Date palms and citrus trees line the fairways of this former nursery, making it appear that the course has been around beyond its years.

Play Policy and Fees: Members and guests only. No reciprocal play is accepted.

Tees and Yardage: *Men:* Back: yardage 7042, par 72, rating 73.5, slope 135; Middle: yardage 6597, par 72, rating 71.6, slope 128; Front: yardage 6196, par 72, rating 69.7, slope 124.

Tee Times: Not applicable.

Dress Code: Appropriate golf attire is required.

Tournaments: No outside events are allowed.

Directions: From I-10 in Indio, take the Monroe exit and turn right on Monroe. The course is on the left-hand side just past 50th Avenue.

Contact: 50994 Monroe Street, Indio, CA 92201, pro shop 760/775-3688.

105 THE VINEYARDS GOLF CLUB

Architect: David Ginkel, 2003
9 holes   Semiprivate $35

Coachella Valley Detail map, page 437

Four lakes and many bunkers make this course, in a luxury motor coach country club, a test to play. It is a scenic course with mountain views from every hole. The community is unique in that every motor coach pad comes with a living space, called a casita, next to it. A clubhouse is available for community activities.

Play Policy and Fees: Limited outside play is accepted. Green fees are $35 for 18 holes, including cart. The nine-hole rate is $20. Junior rates available.

Tees and Yardage: *Men:* Gold: yardage 3137, par 36, rating n/a, slope n/a; Black: yardage 2872, par 36, rating n/a, slope n/a; Maroon: yardage 2655, par 36, rating n/a, slope n/a; *Women:* Green: yardage 2398, par 36, rating n/a, slope n/a.

Tee Times: Reservations can be made 30 days in advance.

Dress Code: Soft spikes only.

Tournaments: A limited number of tournaments welcome, particularly those catering to motor coach enthusiasts.

Directions: From I-10 east, exit at Dillon; the facility is one mile north.

Contact: 44790 Dillon Road, Coachella, CA 92236, golf shop 760/863-1936, www.vineyardsmotorcoachcc.com.

106 THE HIDEAWAY CLUB

Architect: Pete Dye, 2003; Clive Clark, 2004
36 holes   Private

Coachella Valley Detail map, page 437

These two ultraprivate courses are both delightful. The Pete Dye Course is typical Dye design: hard-fought par, railroad tees, strategy required. The two finishing holes are the highlight of this layout, with the 17th being a par-3 of 230 yards and the 18th being a medium-length par-5, both over water. The Clive Clark Course is an aesthetic wonder, with brightly colored flowers in abundance and waterfalls beautifying the landscape. Both boast excellent course conditioning and pleasing mountain views. Note: At press time, the Clive Clark Course had not yet been rated.

Play Policy and Fees: No outside play accepted. No reciprocal play is accepted. Guests must be accompanied by a member.

Tees and Yardage: Pete Dye—*Men:* Tee 1: yardage 7115, par 72, rating 75.7, slope 143; Tee 2: yardage 6630, par 72, rating 72.6, slope 137; Tee 3: yardage 6179, par 72, rating 69.9, slope 128; *Women:* Tee 4: yardage 5647, par 72, rating 73.4, slope 135; Tee 5: yardage 5133, par 72, rating 70.8, slope 125. Clive Clark—*Men:* Tee 1: yardage 6963, par 72, rating n/a, slope n/a; Tee 2: yardage 6462, par 72, rating n/a, slope n/a; Tee 3: yardage 5921, par 72, rating n/a, slope n/a; *Women:* Tee 4: yardage 5503, par 72, rating n/a, slope n/a; Tee 4/5 (combo): yardage 5201, par 72, rating n/a, slope n/a.

Tee Times: Members only.

Dress Code: Appropriate golf attire is required. Soft spikes only.

Tournaments: No outside tournaments.

Directions: From I-10 south of Palm Springs, take the Jefferson exit; drive south four miles to club entrance on the left between 52nd and 54th.

Contact: 52500 Village Club Drive, La Quinta, CA 92253, golf shop 760/777-7400.

107 MOUNTAIN VIEW COUNTRY CLUB AT LA QUINTA

Architect: Arnold Palmer, 2004

18 holes   **Private**   **$105**

Coachella Valley Detail map, page 437

On 365 acres within an upscale residential development, this private Palmer design runs a stout 7400 yards. The finishing trio here is very strong, with the 470-yard par-4 16th being a strategic hole with an arroyo carry off the tee. The 17th is a beauty of a par-3, playing 221

yards uphill to a narrow green with a huge bunker protecting front and left. And the 18th is a 570-yard par-5 that has a risk/reward element off the tee. As the name implies, there are some pleasing mountain views from every hole, plus lots of elevation change, unique for the desert. More than 20 acres of lakes add to the beauty of this design.

Play Policy and Fees: Reciprocal play is accepted with members of other clubs at a rate of $105; otherwise, members and guests only.

Tees and Yardage: *Men:* Palmer: yardage 7371, par 72, rating 75.3, slope 139; Black: yardage 7221, par 72, rating 74.4, slope 135; Blue: yardage 6834, par 72, rating 72.6, slope 130; White: yardage 6307, par 72, rating 70.1, slope 124; Green: yardage 5685, par 72, rating 67.2, slope 118; *Women:* Red: yardage 5297, par 72, rating 70.9, slope 125.

Tee Times: Reciprocal players should have their home professional call to make arrangements at least seven days in advance.

Dress Code: Appropriate golf attire is required. Soft spikes only.

Tournaments: Outside tournaments are not accepted.

Directions: From I-10 or Highway 111, exit at Jefferson Street (south) and proceed 4.8 miles. Pass Avenue 50 and turn left onto Pomelo, the entrance of Mountain View Country Club.

Contact: 50-400 Jefferson Street, La Quinta, CA 92253, phone 760/771-4311, fax 760/771-4280, www.mountainviewatlaquinta.com.

108 TRILOGY GOLF CLUB AT LA QUINTA

Architect: Gary Panks, 2003

18 holes   **Public**   **$60–119**

Coachella Valley Detail map, page 437

This course at the base of the Santa Rosa Mountains boasts wide-open fairways and big greens that place an emphasis on golfers having fun. Architect Panks crafted this course through a high-density, amenities-rich housing development. The pretty views are of the surrounding

Santa Rosa Mountains. Trilogy Golf Club at La Quinta will be hosting the 2005 PGA Skins Game the weekend after Thanksgiving.

Play Policy and Fees: Green fees vary from $60 off-season to $119 during peak season. Annual play, homeowner, twilight, and other rates are often available. Carts and range balls included.

Tees and Yardage: *Men:* Black: yardage 6883, par 72, rating 72.7, slope 127; Blue: yardage 6455, par 72, rating 70.8, slope 124; Gold: yardage 6004, par 72, rating 68.8, slope 118; *Women:* White: yardage 5542, par 72, rating 71.6, slope 120; Green: yardage 4998, par 72, rating 68.5, slope 116.

Tee Times: Reservations can be made seven days in advance.

Dress Code: Appropriate golf attire is required. Soft spikes only.

Tournaments: Tournaments welcomed.

Directions: From I-10, exit Jefferson south to 5th Street, go east on Madison Street, then south to Avenue 60; the entrance is on the right.

Contact: 60-151 Trilogy Parkway, La Quinta, CA 92253, pro shop 760/771-0707, fax 760/771-3355, www.intrawestgolf.com.

109 THE PALMS GOLF CLUB
Architect: Brian Curley and Fred Couples, 1999
18 holes   **Private**

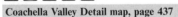

Coachella Valley Detail map, page 437

A solid players' layout, with close to 40 professional golfers and many low-handicap players in membership, The Palms is a core golf course in an upscale residential community with no homes on the interior. It is a traditional layout, with small greens and tree-lined fairways. In fact, the course features more than 2000 mature date palms and 1000 mesquite trees, which come into play if you are off the fairways. Wide-ranging views encompass the Santa Rosa Mountains, and several pretty creeks meander through five holes.

Play Policy and Fees: Members and guests only. No reciprocal play is accepted.

Tees and Yardage: *Men:* Black: yardage 7049,

par 70, rating 73.7, slope 137; Blue: yardage 6687, par 70, rating 71.8, slope 132; White: yardage 6244, par 70, rating 69.9, slope 127; *Women:* Gold: yardage 5600, par 72, rating 73.0, slope 130.

Tee Times: Not applicable.

Dress Code: Appropriate golf attire and non-metal spikes are required.

Tournaments: Outside events are not permitted.

Directions: From I-10, take the Monroe Street exit. Travel south to Airport Boulevard and turn right. The club is on the left.

Contact: 57000 Palms Drive (P.O. Box 29), La Quinta, CA 92253, pro shop 760/771-2606, fax 760/771-2693.

110 PGA WEST: ARNOLD PALMER COURSE
Architect: Arnold Palmer, 1986
18 holes   **Private**

Coachella Valley Detail map, page 437

This demanding course plays as long as any of the courses in the area, except perhaps the Stadium Course. Palmer sculpted five par-3s and five par-5s into the layout, creating many opportunities for heroics. The most challenging opportunity comes at the 532-yard, par-5 finishing hole, where the brave player can take a chance over the rock-lined lake, go for the green in two, and finish the round with a birdie. Bunkers distinguish the front nine, and hills mark the back nine. The last four holes are tight against the Santa Rosa Mountains. The tees are elevated above large greens, just the way Arnie likes them. Some greens are backed by massive boulders.

Play Policy and Fees: Members and guests only. Guests must be accompanied by members.

Tees and Yardage: *Men:* Black: yardage 6950, par 72, rating 74.0, slope 143; Blue: yardage 6462, par 72, rating 71.4, slope 133; White: yardage 5995, par 72, rating 69.3, slope 126; *Women:* Gold: yardage 5557, par 72, rating 73.0, slope 133; Red: yardage 5225, par 72, rating 70.0, slope 130.

Tee Times: Not applicable.

Dress Code: Appropriate golf attire and non-metal spikes are required.

Tournaments: This course is not available for outside events.

Directions: Take the Indio Boulevard/Jefferson Street exit off I-10 or Highway 111 and drive south to the end of Jefferson Street to PGA Boulevard.

Contact: 55-955 PGA Boulevard, La Quinta, CA 92253, pro shop 760/564-7100, www.pgawest.com.

111 PGA WEST: GREG NORMAN COURSE

Architect: Greg Norman, 1999

18 holes   Resort $50–190

Coachella Valley Detail map, page 437

Located 40 feet below sea level, this is the newest of six courses at PGA West. It is a true desert/target design, with only 62 acres grassed as landing areas. The fairways are tight and relatively narrow, with a number of ponds coming into play. Wildflowers and native grasses abound. Featuring multiple sets of tees, this challenging course is appropriate for players of all levels. Forecaddies are available with advance request.

For reservations at the award-winning La Quinta Resort, call 800/598-3828.

Play Policy and Fees: Green fees are seasonal and range from $50 in summer months to $190 (weekends) in peak season, including cart. Twilight and super twilight rates are available, as is a Winter Golf Pass ($299), which buys three rounds at any of the PGA West public courses or La Quinta Resort & Club courses. Call for details. Guests at La Quinta Resort & Club receive preferential tee times.

Tees and Yardage: *Men:* Tournament: yardage 7156, par 72, rating 75.1, slope 139; Championship: yardage 6671, par 72, rating 72.8, slope 133; Middle: yardage 6227, par 72, rating 70.6, slope 126; *Women:* Forward: yardage 5281, par 72, rating 71.0, slope 122.

Tee Times: Reservations can be booked three days in advance for outside play.

Dress Code: Appropriate golf attire and non-metal spikes are required.

Tournaments: A 12-player minimum is required to book an event. Events should be booked 3-6 months in advance.

Directions: From I-10, take the Indio Boulevard/Jefferson Street exit and drive south on Jefferson. Turn left on Avenue 54 and right on Madison Avenue to the course.

Contact: 56-150 PGA Boulevard, La Quinta, CA 92253, pro shop 760/564-4111, www.pgawest.com.

112 PGA WEST: JACK NICKLAUS PRIVATE COURSE

Architect: Jack Nicklaus, 1987

18 holes   Private

Coachella Valley Detail map, page 437

This is a unique course, with flowers, tall desert grasses, and water off the fairways. There are huge desert bunkers throughout the course. You may need a dune buggy to get in and out of these traps. Many fairways are defined by large mounds of grass.

Play Policy and Fees: Members and guests only. Guests must be accompanied by members at time of play.

Tees and Yardage: *Men:* Black: yardage 6951, par 72, rating 74.3, slope 146; Blue: yardage 6365, par 72, rating 71.4, slope 139; White: yardage 5658, par 72, rating 68.3, slope 129; *Women:* Gold: yardage 5272, par 72, rating 71.9, slope 133; Red: yardage 4822, par 72, rating 69.4, slope 126.

Tee Times: Not applicable.

Dress Code: Appropriate golf attire and non-metal spikes are required.

Tournaments: This course is not available for outside events.

Directions: Take the Indio Boulevard/Jefferson Street exit off I-10 or Highway 111 and drive south to the end of Jefferson Street and PGA Boulevard.

Contact: 55-955 PGA Boulevard, La Quinta,

CA 92253, pro shop 760/564-7100, clubhouse 760/564-7111, www.pgawest.com.

113 PGA WEST: NICKLAUS TOURNAMENT COURSE

Architect: Jack Nicklaus, 1987
18 holes   Resort $75–235

Coachella Valley Detail map, page 437

This course is a tamer version of the adjacent Stadium Course. There are Jack Nicklaus's trademark elevated tees and Pete Dye's trademark railroad ties, forced carries over water, and huge, multitiered greens. The course can be as difficult as you choose to make it, depending on what tees you use. The course has hosted the Bob Hope Classic and the PGA Tour Qualifying School.

For reservations at the award-winning La Quinta Resort, call 800/598-3828.

Play Policy and Fees: Fees vary seasonally $75–235. Fees include cart and use of the driving range. Twilight and super twilight rates are available, as is a Winter Golf Pass ($299), which buys three rounds at any of the PGA West public courses or La Quinta Resort & Club courses. Call for details. Guests at La Quinta Resort & Club receive preferential tee times.

Tees and Yardage: *Men:* Tournament: yardage 7204, par 72, rating 74.7, slope 139; Championship: yardage 6522, par 72, rating 71.9, slope 131; Middle: yardage 6061, par 72, rating 69.0, slope 124; *Women:* Forward: yardage 5023, par 72, rating 69.9, slope 121.

Tee Times: Reservations can be booked three days in advance for outside play.

Dress Code: Appropriate golf attire and non-metal spikes are required.

Tournaments: A 12-player minimum is required to book an event.

Directions: Take the Indio Boulevard/Jefferson Street exit off I-10 and drive south to the end of Jefferson Street.

Contact: 56-150 PGA Boulevard, La Quinta, CA 92253, pro shop 760/564-7170, fax 760/771-3109, www.pgawest.com.

114 PGA WEST: TOM WEISKOPF COURSE

Architect: Tom Weiskopf, 1996
18 holes   Private

Coachella Valley Detail map, page 437

The Weiskopf Course is a well-maintained, long, and challenging golf course, with plenty of desert areas to keep you on your toes. Although much of the challenge comes in the length of the course, the fairways are fairly wide open, giving players a chance to use their drivers. The large, rolling greens and liberal use of parallel waste areas gives this course a links-style feel. A unique feature is the special "Bye" hole, or 19th hole, that is used to decide the outcome of matches tied after 18. This short par-3 is over water the entire way and finishes with a diabolical donut-shaped green that surrounds a yawning pot bunker right in the middle!

Play Policy and Fees: Members and guests only. Guests must be accompanied by members at time of play.

Tees and Yardage: *Men:* Black: yardage 7164, par 72, rating 74.2, slope 130; Blue: yardage 6654, par 72, rating 71.6, slope 123; White: yardage 6129, par 72, rating 69.3, slope 117; *Women:* Red: yardage 5536, par 72, rating 72.2, slope 122.

Tee Times: Not applicable.

Dress Code: Appropriate golf attire and non-metal spikes are required.

Tournaments: This course is not available for outside events.

Directions: Take the Indio Boulevard/Jefferson Street exit off I-10 or Highway 111 and drive south to the end of Jefferson Street to PGA Boulevard.

Contact: 55-955 PGA Boulevard, La Quinta, CA 92253, pro shop 760/564-7100, www .pgawest.com.

115 PGA WEST: STADIUM COURSE

Architect: Pete Dye, 1986

18 holes   **Resort**   **$75–235**

Coachella Valley Detail map, page 437

This course opened in 1986 and immediately secured a place in golf lore. Pete Dye earned his "Marquis de Sod" moniker here. It is packed with pot bunkers, sand, water, and sidehill lies. Large, undulating greens with several tiers make putting a chore. Among the course highlights is an 18-foot-deep, greenside bunker that flanks the par-5 16th hole. The course is difficult, time-consuming in the busy season, deathly hot in off-season, and one of the top-10 "must-play" courses in the country. Many professional tournaments have been held here, including the PGA Tour Skins Game and the PGA Grand Slam of Golf. The Bob Hope Classic has also used this course in its rotation.

For reservations at the award-winning La Quinta Resort, call 800/598-3828.

Play Policy and Fees: Fees vary seasonally $75–235. Fees include cart and use of the driving range. Twilight and super twilight rates are available, as is a Winter Golf Pass ($299), which buys three rounds at any of the PGA West public courses or La Quinta Resort & Club courses. Call for details. Guests at La Quinta Resort & Club receive preferential tee times.

Tees and Yardage: *Men:* Tournament: yardage 7266, par 72, rating 75.9, slope 150; Championship: yardage 6739, par 72, rating 73.0, slope 142; Middle: yardage 6166, par 72, rating 69.9, slope 132; *Women:* Forward: yardage 5092, par 72, rating 70.0, slope 124.

Tee Times: Reservations can be booked three days in advance for outside play.

Dress Code: Collared shirts and nonmetal spikes are required. No blue jeans are allowed.

Tournaments: A 12-player minimum is needed to book a tournament.

Directions: Take the Indio Boulevard/Jefferson Street exit off I-10 or Highway 111 and drive south to the end of Jefferson Street to PGA Boulevard. Follow PGA Boulevard to the Resort Golf House.

Contact: 56-150 PGA Boulevard, La Quinta, CA 92253, pro shop 760/564-7170, www.pgawest.com.

116 THE QUARRY AT LA QUINTA

Architect: Tom Fazio, 1994

28 holes   **Private**

Coachella Valley Detail map, page 437

Nestled in the foothills, this Tom Fazio design is routed through an abandoned rock quarry and covers 375 acres. The entire course was sodded. A 70-foot waterfall serves as a backdrop for the 10th and 17th holes. The par-5 10th hole is considered the signature hole. A river and stream run through the course, a typical Fazio creation with subtle mounding and small, traditional greens. John Daly holds the course record here with a 62. A new 10-hole Fazio-designed short course opened in 2004.

The Quarry offers course-side cottages. Call the pro shop for information.

Play Policy and Fees: Members and guests only. Guests must be accompanied by a member.

Tees and Yardage: *Men:* Black: yardage 7083, par 72, rating 73.7, slope 135; Blue: yardage 6334, par 72, rating 71.3, slope 128; White: yardage 6248, par 72, rating 69.3, slope 124; *Women:* Rose: yardage 5226, par 72, rating 69.9, slope 123.

Tee Times: No outside play is accepted.

Dress Code: Appropriate golf attire and nonmetal spikes are required.

Tournaments: This course is not available for outside events.

Directions: From La Quinta, take the Jefferson Street exit south to 54th Avenue. Turn left on 54th Avenue and follow it to Madison. Turn right on Madison and continue to 58th Avenue. Turn right on 58th Avenue and drive 1.5 miles to the course.

Contact: 1 Quarry Lane, La Quinta, CA 92253, pro shop 760/777-1100, fax 760/777-1107, www.quarryinfo.com.

117 LAKE TAMARISK GOLF CLUB

Architect: T. A. Preston, 1967
9 holes   **Public**   **$16**

Palm Springs and the Deserts map, page 436

This is literally an oasis in the middle of the desert. Nineteen acres of refreshing lakes line the course, and palm trees and oleanders flank the fairways. The course is fairly level, but the tees and greens are elevated. If "warm" weather doesn't bother you, head for Lake Tamarisk and play unlimited golf for $6 per day in June, July, and August. An RV park is adjacent.

Play Policy and Fees: Green fees are $16 for 18 holes. Carts are $10 for nine holes and $12 for 18 holes. Reservations are recommended January–April. Nine-hole rates offered.

Tees and Yardage: *Men (18 holes):* Back: yardage 5952, par 70, rating 66.9, slope 100; *Women (18 holes):* Forward: yardage 5590, par 70, rating 69.9, slope 104.

Tee Times: Reservations can be booked 24 hours in advance.

Dress Code: Shirts must be worn.

Tournaments: Shotgun tournaments are available weekdays only.

Directions: Travel east from Indio on I-10 for about 50 miles and take the Desert Center Road exit north. Bear left onto Kaiser Road and drive 1.5 miles to the entrance.

Contact: 26-251 Parkview Drive (P.O. Box 316), Desert Center, CA 92239, pro shop 760/227-3203.

118 BLYTHE MUNICIPAL GOLF COURSE

Architect: William F. Bell, 1969
18 holes   **Public**   **$13–25**

Palm Springs and the Deserts map, page 436

This nicely maintained course sits on top of a mesa overlooking the Palo Verde Valley. Eucalyptus and pine trees line the fairways that go up and down the mesa. The 220-yard second hole drops 150 feet to a tiered green. The 395-yard seventh hole has a blind second shot, usually calling for two strong irons.

Play Policy and Fees: Green fees are $13 for nine holes and $25 for 18 holes. Carts are $19 for nine holes and $37 for 18 holes. Please inquire about seasonal rates.

Tees and Yardage: *Men:* Back: yardage 6866, par 73, rating 72.4, slope 121; *Women:* Forward: yardage 5684, par 73, rating 72.6, slope 117.

Tee Times: Reservations may be booked one day in advance in January, February, and March.

Dress Code: Shirts and shoes are required.

Tournaments: This course is available for outside tournaments. Call the pro shop for booking information.

Directions: From I-10, travel east of Palm Springs and take the Lovekin Boulevard exit north. Travel three miles to 6th Avenue and turn left. At Wells Road, turn right to the course.

Contact: 4708 Wells Road, Blythe, CA 92225, pro shop 760/922-7272.

119 DE ANZA COUNTRY CLUB

Architect: Lawrence Hughes, 1956
18 holes   **Private**

Palm Springs and the Deserts map, page 436

This flat course has plenty of mature trees and two lakes. It's surrounded by homes. One of the toughest challenges is the third hole, a 211-yard par-3. Players must hit over a lake and bunker to reach the green. The course is closed during the month of October.

Play Policy and Fees: Members and guests only.

Tees and Yardage: *Men:* Blue: yardage 6778, par 72, rating 72.1, slope 123; White: yardage 6373, par 72, rating 69.8, slope 117; Gold: yardage 5959, par 72, rating 67.6, slope 112; *Women:* Red: yardage 5557, par 72, rating 71.4, slope 118.

Tee Times: Not applicable.

Dress Code: No blue jeans or short shorts are allowed. Nonmetal spikes are required.

Tournaments: This course is not available for outside events.

Directions: From Palm Canyon Drive in Borrego Springs, turn north on Ocotillo Circle and drive one-half mile to Lazy S Drive. Turn right and travel 1.5 miles to Pointing Rock Drive and turn right.

Contact: 509 Catarina Drive (P.O. Box 120), Borrego Springs, CA 92004, pro shop 760/767-5577, www.deanzacc.com.

120 BORREGO SPRINGS RESORT & COUNTRY CLUB

Architect: Cary Bickler, 1997 and 2002
27 holes   Resort $54–64

Palm Springs and the Deserts map, page 436

A desert resort course with 27 holes, Borrego Springs features quite a few bunkers, and water comes into play on many holes. A new nine was added here in 2002, so there is always available play. No matter what time of year, Borrego Springs rounds average less than four hours.

For reservations at the hotel, call 760/767-5700 or 888/826-7734.

Play Policy and Fees: Green fees are $54 Monday–Thursday and $64 Friday–Sunday and holidays. In summer fees drop by roughly half. All prices include a cart.

Tees and Yardage: Desertwillow—*Men:* Blue: yardage 3332, par 36, rating n/a, slope n/a; White: yardage 3050, par 36, rating n/a, slope n/a; *Women:* Red: yardage 2833, par 36, rating n/a, slope n/a. Mesquite—*Men:* Blue: yardage 3237, par 35, rating n/a, slope n/a; White: yardage 3002, par 35, rating n/a, slope n/a; *Women:* Red: yardage 2756, par 35, rating n/a, slope n/a. Palms—*Men:* Blue: yardage 3288, par 36, rating n/a, slope n/a; White: yardage 3081, par 36, rating n/a, slope n/a; *Women:* Red: yardage 2588, par 36, rating n/a, slope n/a.

Tee Times: Reservations are suggested, and they can be made 14 days in advance.

Dress Code: Appropriate golf attire is required. Soft spikes only.

Tournaments: Outside events are welcome and can be booked 90 days in advance. A 16-player minimum is needed to book a tournament. A banquet facility holds 300 people.

Directions: Take I-10 from Palm Springs south to Highway 86. Follow Highway 86 south to County Road S-22 west. Take S-22 to Borrego Valley Road. Turn left, and the course is one mile along on the right.

Contact: 1112 Tilting T Drive (P.O. Box 981), Borrego Springs, CA 92004, pro shop 760/767-3330, fax 760/767-5710, www.borregosprings resort.com.

121 RAMS HILL COUNTRY CLUB

Architect: Ted Robinson Sr., 1983
18 holes   Semiprivate $85–95

Palm Springs and the Deserts map, page 436

Located on a 3200-acre oasis within the nation's largest state park, the Anza Borrego Desert State Park, Rams Hill is a residential/resort community with a long, well-maintained golf course. The layout is characterized by sloping, palm-lined fairways and seven scenic water holes complete with lakes and waterfalls. It features bent-grass greens, thousands of trees, and panoramic views of the surrounding mountains. Rams Hill closes in October for fairway reseeding. This course annually hosts U.S. Open qualifying tournaments.

Accommodations are in privately owned homes that offer daily, weekly, and monthly rates, as well as golf package discounts. For information, call 800/292-2944.

Play Policy and Fees: Green fees are $85 during the week and $95 on weekends. Fee includes cart. Discounts are offered to guests staying on the property. Twilight rates are available.

Tees and Yardage: *Men:* Black: yardage 6866, par 72, rating 72.9, slope 130; Gold: yardage 6328, par 72, rating 70.1, slope 123; *Women:* Silver: yardage 5694, par 72, rating 73.4, slope 128.

Tee Times: Reservations are not required, but they are recommended for desired tee times.

Dress Code: Appropriate golf attire is required.

Tournaments: Events should be scheduled at least 30 days in advance to ensure availability and desired time.

Directions: Travel on I-10 or Highway 111 to

Indio. Turn on Highway 86 to Salton City. Turn right on County Road S-22 to Borrego Valley Road. Take a left and drive six miles to the club.

Contact: 1881 Rams Hills Road (P.O. Box 2190), Borrego Springs, CA 92004, pro shop 760/767-5124, ext. 25, fax 760/767-5023, www.ramshillcc.us.

 DEL RIO COUNTRY CLUB

Architect: William P. Bell, 1926

18 holes   Semiprivate $26–39

Palm Springs and the Deserts map, page 436

This course is short and tight, demanding strategic shot placement. It has fairly level terrain, tree-lined fairways, many doglegs, and small greens. Del Rio hosts approximately 25,000 rounds annually.

Play Policy and Fees: Green fees during peak season are $36 weekdays, $39 weekends, carts included. During the summer, fees drop to $26 every day. Twilight green fees are offered.

Tees and Yardage: *Men:* Back: yardage 6001, par 70, rating 67.6, slope 115; *Women:* Forward: yardage 5738, par 73, rating 73.2, slope 120.

Tee Times: Reservations can be booked seven days in advance.

Dress Code: No tank tops or short shorts are allowed.

Tournaments: A 50-player minimum is needed to book a tournament. Carts are mandatory. A banquet facility holds 330 people.

Directions: Travel east on I-10 to the town of Indio and take Highway 86 south to Brawley. Take Highway 111 north and drive two miles to the course.

Contact: 102 East Del Rio Road (P.O. Box 38), Brawley, CA 92227, pro shop 760/344-0085, fax 760/344-9446.

123 LAKE VIEW GOLF COURSE AT RIO BEND

Architect: Course designed, 1990

9 holes   Public $12–18

Palm Springs and the Deserts map, page 436

Set within an RV park popular with snow-birds escaping winter, this unique course plays around little Drew Lake. It features lots of undulation and elevation changes. The pride of the course is the sixth hole, a 183-yard par-3 over water. Rabbits, skunks, and ground squirrels are regulars.

Play Policy and Fees: Green fees are $12 for nine holes and $18 for 18 holes. Carts are $8 for nine holes and $11 for 18 holes. Please call for summer rates.

Tees and Yardage: *Men:* White: yardage 2176, par 33, rating n/a, slope n/a; *Women:* Red: yardage 1889, par 33, rating n/a, slope n/a.

Tee Times: Reservations can be booked 3–4 days in advance.

Dress Code: Shirts and shoes are necessary.

Tournaments: This course is available for outside tournaments.

Directions: From El Centro, drive eight miles west to the Drew Road exit. Drive south on Drew Road for one mile to the course. Note: For RV information, call 760/352-7061.

Contact: 1589 Drew Road, El Centro, CA 92243, pro shop 760/352-6638, fax 760/356-2043.

124 BARBARA WORTH RESORT

Architect: Lawrence Hughes, 1928

18 holes   Resort $28–48

Palm Springs and the Deserts map, page 436

This older desert course has a rich history, which can be read on the resort's website. The course has tree-lined fairways, good greens, and several ponds. Have your bets won by the time you reach the par-3 17th—it's 150 yards over water. And the 18th hole covers 430 yards uphill to a small, well-bunkered green. Tony Lema is said to have won his first professional event here. It is level and therefore walkable, but judge the heat of the day before deciding.

Barbara Worth has a motel with more than 104 rooms, three apartments, and four executive suites. For reservations, call 760/356-2806.

Play Policy and Fees: Green fees during peak season are $43 to ride weekdays, $28 to walk; on weekends carts are mandatory for non-members, and the fee (including cart) is $48. Nine-hole, senior, and twilight rates are available. Call for seasonal rates. Guests staying at the Barbara Worth Resort can book discounted stay-and-play packages.

Tees and Yardage: *Men:* White: yardage 6302, par 71, rating 70.1, slope 119; *Women:* Red: yardage 5827, par 73, rating 72.9, slope 125.

Tee Times: Reservations can be booked seven days in advance.

Dress Code: Golf attire is encouraged, and nonmetal spikes are required.

Tournaments: This course is available for tournaments. Carts are required for weekend tournaments. Events should be booked six months in advance. The banquet facility can accommodate 800 people.

Directions: From I-8 in San Diego, travel east about 125 miles to Bowker Road and turn left. At S-80, turn right and drive to the club.

Contact: 2050 Country Club Drive, Holtville, CA 92250, pro shop 760/356-5842, clubhouse 760/356-2806, www.bwresort.com.

THE TOURNAMENT PLAYERS CLUB (TPC) AT VALENCIA © GEORGE FULLER

Resources

Golf Organizations

American Junior Golf Association
1980 Sports Club Drive
Braselton, GA 30517
877/373-2542
www.ajga.org

American Society of Golf Course Architects
221 North LaSalle Street
Chicago, IL 60601
312/372-7090
www.asgca.com

Ladies Professional Golf Association
100 International Golf Drive
Daytona Beach, FL 32124
904/274-6200
www.lpga.com

National Golf Foundation
1150 South U.S. Highway 1, Suite 401
Jupiter, FL 33477
561/744-6006
www.ngf.org

Northern California Golf Association
P.O. Box NCGA or 3200 Lopez Road
Pebble Beach, CA 93953
831/625-4653
www.ncga.org

PGA of America
100 Avenue of the Champions
Palm Beach Gardens, FL 33418
561/624-8400
www.pga.com

PGA Tour
112 PGA Tour Boulevard
Ponte Vedra Beach, FL 32082
904/285-3700
www.pgatour.com

Southern California Golf Association
3740 Cahuenga Boulevard
North Hollywood, CA 91604
818/980-3630
www.scga.org

The United States Golf Association
P.O. Box 708
Far Hills, NJ 07931
908/234-2300
www.usga.com

Women's Southern California Golf Association
402 Arrow Highway, Suite 10
San Dimas, CA 91733
909/592-1281
www.womensgolf.org

Index

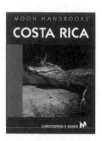

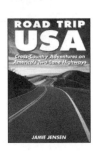